1995 LECTURES
and
MEMOIRS

Published for THE BRITISH ACADEMY
by OXFORD UNIVERSITY PRESS

Oxford University Press, Walton Street, Oxford OX2 6DP

Oxford New York
Athens Auckland Bangkok Bombay
Calcutta Cape Town Dar es Salaam Delhi
Florence Hong Kong Istanbul Karachi
Kuala Lumpur Madras Madrid Melbourne
Mexico City Nairobi Paris Singapore
Taipei Tokyo Toronto

and associated companies in
Berlin Ibadan

British Library Cataloguing in Publication Data
Data available

ISBN 0–19–726169–8
ISSN 0068–1202

Typeset by J&L Composition Ltd, Filey, North Yorkshire
Printed in Great Britain
on acid-free paper by
Bookcraft (Bath) Ltd
Midsomer Norton, Avon

All the papers in this volume have been refereed

The Academy is grateful to Dr Marjorie Chibnall, FBA
for her editorial work on this volume

Contents

List of Plates

Marcel Duchamp and the Paradox of Modernity

Proceedings of the British Academy, **90**, 1–28

SIR JOHN RHŶS MEMORIAL LECTURE

Wales's Second Grammarian: Dafydd Ddu of Hiraddug

R. GERAINT GRUFFYDD

University of Wales
Fellow of the Academy

IT IS OF COURSE a great honour to be invited to deliver a Sir John Rhŷs Memorial Lecture of the British Academy, and I am very conscious of that honour and very grateful to the Academy for inviting me, however unworthy of the occasion I might feel. I live about thirteen miles from John Rhŷs's birthplace, and when Celtic scholars from overseas come to visit Aberystwyth I try to take them to see the place. I never make the journey to that tiny ruined cottage in the fastnesses of Pumlumon without reflecting on the strength of that Nonconformist culture which provided Rhŷs with the motivation and opportunity to take his first steps up the educational ladder, although it must also be remembered that the Established Church later played a crucial part in furthering his career. Rhŷs was for several years a pupil teacher at Pen-llwyn British School — Pen-llwyn is a village some five miles from Aberystwyth — and a fellow pupil-teacher was John Cynddylan Jones, who later became a renowned preacher and theologian. (Of him the great London preacher Charles Haddon Spurgeon is reputed to have remarked, 'I don't know who this Mr Kindlin' Jones is, but he certainly kindles me!'). Cynddylan Jones once said about the time he and John Rhŷs spent together at Pen-llwyn: 'Rhŷs loved roots [referring to his early passion for comparative philology], I loved fruits [referring presumably to the fruits of the Holy Spirit as listed in the fifth chapter of St

Read at the Academy 8 November 1995. © The British Academy 1996.

Paul's Epistle to the Galatians]'. Even if we agree, as I do, with the system of values implicit in that statement, we can hardly deny that Rhŷs's preoccupation with roots was later to prove immensely fruitful.

There have already been two lectures in this series that have dealt with what may be called Celtic vernacular grammar. In 1937 the great Osborn Bergin took as his theme 'The Native Irish Grammarian' and gave a lecture which summarised the results of many years of work on his part, work which was later refined and extended by such scholars as Father Lambert McKenna SJ, Professor Brian Ó Cuív and, most recently, Professor Anders Ahlqvist.[1] In 1961 my old teacher Sir Thomas Parry gave a Rhŷs lecture entitled 'The Welsh Metrical Treatise Attributed to Einion Offeiriad' and this too has been followed by a number of important studies during the last thirty years or so. Sir Thomas himself, as his title suggests, concentrated on the metrical aspects of Einion Offeiriad's grammar, and so definitive was his treatment that this aspect has attracted very little attention since then. However, Professor J. Beverley Smith has shed new light on Einion Offeiriad's life; Saunders Lewis on the possible philosophical implications of his work; Dr Rachel Bromwich on the use he makes of snatches of verse as examples of metres or metrical faults; Professor Ceri Lewis on his treatment of syllables and diphthongs (and much else); Professor Anne Matonis on virtually all aspects of his work; Dr Iestyn Daniel on the problem of authorship; and Professor Erich Poppe on Einion Offeiriad's use of rhetorical and grammatical categories: the wide scope of Professor Matonis's four contributions must particularly be stressed.[2]

---

[1] O. Bergin, 'The Native Irish Grammarian', *Proceedings of the British Academy*, xxiv (1938), pp. 205–35; idem, 'Irish Grammatical Tracts', published as supplements (pp. i–iv, 1–293) to *Ériu*, viii (1916), ibid. ix (1921–3), ibid. x (1926–8), ibid. xiv (1946), ibid. xvii (1955). L. McKenna SJ, *Bardic syntactical tracts* (Dublin, 1944). B. Ó Cuív, 'Linguistic Terminology in the Medieval Bardic Tracts', *Transactions of the Philological Society* (1965), pp. 141–64; idem, 'The Linguistic Training of the Medieval Irish Poet', *Celtica*, x (1973), 114–40. A. Ahlqvist(ed.), *The Early Irish Linguist* (Helsinki, 1983). Cf. also G. B. Adams, 'Grammatical Analysis and Terminology in the Irish Bardic Schools', *Folia linguistica*, iv (1970), 157–66, and various contributors to *Metrik und Medienwechsel*, ed. Hildegard L. C. Tristram (Tübingen, 1991).

[2] T. Parry, 'The Welsh Metrical Treatise Attributed to Einion Offeiriad', *Proceedings of the British Academy*, xlvii (1961), 177–95. J. Beverley Smith, 'Einion Offeiriad', *Bulletin of the Board of Celtic Studies* [hereafter cited as *BBCS*], xx (1962–4), 339–47. S. Lewis, *Gramadegau'r Penceirddiaid* (Caerdydd, 1967). R. Bromwich, 'Gwaith Einion Offeiriad a Barddoniaeth Dafydd ap Gwilym', *Ysgrifau beirniadol* [hereafter cited as *YB*], x (1977), 157–80. C. W. Lewis, 'Einion Offeiriad and the Bardic Grammar' and 'The Content of Poetry and the Crisis in the Bardic Tradition' in *A Guide to Welsh Literature*, ed. A. O. H. Jarman and G. R. Hughes, ii (Swansea, 1979), pp. 58–87, 88–111. A. T. E. Matonis, 'The Welsh Bardic

All in all it has been a rich harvest, and we are certainly better placed today to appreciate the significance of Einion Offeiriad's contribution than we were when Sir Thomas Parry read his lecture to the Academy in 1961. We still lack a general comparative account of grammatical studies in the four Western European vernacular languages where they took root — in Irish from perhaps the seventh century, in Old Norse from the twelfth, in Provençal from the thirteenth and in Welsh from the early fourteenth century — although Professor Pierre-Yves Lambert has begun to make good this deficiency in a valuable symposium edited by Professor Ahlqvist.[3] It is noteworthy that in all the countries where these studies flourished there existed at the relevant time a strong tradition of professional or semi-professional court poetry.

But to turn at last to the theme of tonight's lecture, 'Wales's second grammarian'. Before we fix our attention on him, however, we shall have to linger a little longer in the company of Wales's first grammarian, namely (as I believe) that Einion Offeiriad, 'Einion the Priest', about whose metrical treatise, as he called it, Sir Thomas Parry gave his lecture. We know a certain amount about the life of Einion Offeiriad, thanks primarily to the researches of Professor Beverley Smith.[4] He appears in records relating to southern Cardiganshire and northern Carmarthenshire between 1344 and 1354, and what seems to be a notice of his death is contained in a document emanating from northern Caenarfonshire — a document in which he is described as parson of Llanrug in the commot of Is Gwyrfai — in the year 1349: the likelihood

---

Grammars and the Western Grammatical Tradition', *Modern Philology*, lxxix (1981), 121–45; idem, 'The Concept of Poetry in the Middle Ages: The Welsh Evidence from the Bardic Grammars', *BBCS* xxxvi (1989), 1–12; idem, 'Problems Relating to the Composition of the Welsh Bardic Grammars' in *Celtic Language, Celtic Culture. A Festschrift for Eric P. Hamp*, ed. A. T. E. Matonis and D. F. Melia (Van Nuys, CA, 1990), pp. 273–9; idem, 'Literary Taxonomies and Genre in the Welsh Bardic Grammar', *Zeitschrift für celtische Philologie*, xlvii (1995), 211–34. I. Daniel, 'Awduriaeth y Gramadeg a Briodolir i Einion Offeiriad a Dafydd Ddu Hiraddug', *YB* xiii (1985), 178–209. E. Poppe, 'The Figures of Speech in *Gramadegau'r Penceirddiaid*', *BBCS* xxxviii (1991), 102–4; idem, 'Latin Grammatical Categories in the Vernacular: The Case of Declension in Welsh', *Historiographia linguistica*, xiii (1991), 269–80; idem, 'Tense and Mood in Welsh Grammars, *c.*1400 to 1621', *National Library of Wales Journal* [hereafter cited as *NLWJ*], xxix (1995–6), 17–38.
[3] P.-Y. Lambert, 'Les premières grammaires celtiques', *Histoire épistémologie langage*, ix. 1 (1987), 13–45. On Old Norse see *First Grammatical Treatise*, ed. E. Haugen (2nd ed.; London, 1972); on Provençal see *The Donatz Proensals of Uc Faidit*, ed. J. H. Marshall (London, 1969) and *The Razos de trobar of Ramon Vidal and associated texts*, ed. J. H. Marshall (London, 1972).
[4] See the article by Professor Smith cited in n. 2, above.

is that he died during the first visitation of the Black Death. His grammar — if I may here anticipate my own conclusions — is contained in three medieval manuscripts and a mid-sixteenth-century copy of a fourth medieval manuscript.[5] These are: Jesus College Oxford MS 111 'The Red Book of Hergest' of around 1400; the National Library of Wales Aberystwyth MS Llanstephan 3 of around 1425; the University of Wales Bangor MS 1 of around 1450; and Balliol College Oxford MS 353, which was carefully copied around 1550 from an exemplar which is to be dated to around 1400. There are also several copies of the grammar in manuscripts dating from the late sixteenth century onwards, all of which are interesting but none of which is without its problems. In none of the four early versions is it stated that Einion Offeiriad was the author of the grammar, but in the two earliest — Jesus College 111 and Llanstephan 3 — it is said that it was he who devised three new metres, the *hir-a-thoddaid*, the *cyrch-a-chwta* and the *tawddgyrch cadwynog* (I tried to translate these technical terms into English, but despaired!). One of the late sixteenth-century copies, however, that made by the humanist scholar Thomas Wiliems of Trefriw in Caernarfonshire and preserved in the National Library of Wales MS Mostyn 110, states in its colophon 'Ac felly y terfyna y Llyfr Cerddwriaeth a wnaeth Einion Offeiriad o Wynedd i Syr Rhys ap Gruffudd ap Hywel ab Ednyfed Fychan er anrhydedd a moliant iddo ef' ('And thus ends the Book of Versecraft which Einion Offeiriad of Gwynedd made for Sir Rhys ap Gruffudd ap Hywel ap Gruffudd ab Ednyfed Fychan in his honour and in praise of him'). Thomas Wiliems claims that his exemplar dated from *c.*1475, and we may suppose that it included the colophon. There seems no good reason to reject the information contained in the colophon, which at once tells us a great deal about Einion Offeiriad and his grammar. One might add that the information is confirmed, apparently independently, by another north Welsh humanist, Robert ab Ifan of Brynsiencyn in Anglesey, in a manuscript which he wrote in 1587. Moreover, the connection between Einion Offeiriad and Rhys ap Gruffudd is conclusively demonstrated by the existence, in nine manuscript copies, of an *awdl*, a panegyric ode, by Einion in praise of Rhys.[6]

---

[5] Details of all the manuscripts mentioned will be found in the work cited in n. 10, below. I wish to thank Mr Graham C. G. Thomas of the Department of Manuscripts and Records, the National Library of Wales, Aberystwyth for generously sharing his knowledge of the manuscript tradition with me.

[6] I. Williams, 'Awdl i Rys ap Gruffudd gan Einion Offeiriad', *Y Cymmrodor*, xxvi (1916), 115–46; particulars of further manuscript sources will be found in *Gwaith Einion Offeiriad a Dafydd Ddu o Hiraddug*, ed. R. G. Gruffydd and Rh. Ifans (Aberystwyth, forthcoming).

Professor R. R. Davies has memorably described Sir Rhys ap Gruffudd as the 'virtual governor of south-west Wales in the first half of the fourteenth century',[7] although he was of course of north Welsh origin, as his pedigree indicates. Ednyfed Fychan, his great-great-grandfather, was the powerful steward of prince Llywelyn ab Iorwerth of Gwynedd, and his descendants continued to serve the princes of Gwynedd loyally, until Edward I's show of strength in 1277, foreshadowing the final conquest in 1282–3, persuaded some of them, Rhys ap Gruffudd's grandfather included, to change their allegiance.[8] We can think of Einion Offeiriad as a native of Gwynedd — witness his rectorship of Llanrug — who became a clerical henchman of Sir Rhys ap Gruffudd's in south-west Wales and who was granted lands by him in that area. It is entirely credible — for reasons that we shall have to explore briefly later — that Sir Rhys ap Gruffudd should have asked Einion Offeiriad to compose a handbook of instruction for the professional poets of his day, and that he should have done so drawing freely on the material available to him in his south Cardiganshire home, as Professor Beverley Smith has convincingly shown. Professor Smith has also supplied us with a *terminus post quem* for the composition of the grammar.[9] Einion Offeiriad's example of the *toddaid* metre is taken from an *awdl* composed by the court poet Gwilym Ddu of Arfon for Sir Gruffudd Llwyd of Tregarnedd in Anglesey and Dinorwig in Caernarfonshire when Sir Gruffudd was imprisoned in Rhuddlan Castle between December 1316 and April 1317, after which time he was removed to the Tower of London. In spite of this imprisonment, the circumstances of which remain obscure, Sir Gruffudd Llwyd was in fact a loyal servant of the Crown, playing a similar role in north-west Wales to that which his nephew-once-removed, Sir Rhys ap Gruffudd, played in south-west Wales. The grammar cannot therefore be earlier than 1317 and it cannot be later than *c.*1330 when, as we shall see, a second recension was promulgated. The best guess at present is that it was written perhaps fairly early in the 1320s.

---

[7] R. R. Davies, *Conquest, Coexistence and Change: Wales 1063–1415* (Oxford and Cardiff, 1987), p. 415.

[8] J. Beverley Smith, *LLywelyn ap Gruffudd: Tywysog Cymru* (Caerdydd, 1986), pp. 301–8, 372.

[9] Idem, 'Gruffydd Llwyd and the Celtic Alliance', *BBCS* xxvi (1974–6), 463–78, especially 467. See now *Gwaith Gruffudd ap Dafydd ap Tudur, Gwilym Ddu o Arfon, Trahaearn Brydydd Mawr ac Iorwerth Beli*, ed. N. G. Costigan (Bosco) *et al.* (Aberystwyth, 1995), pp. 51–6, 67–72.

What in fact was the nature of this grammar or handbook which
Einion Offeiriad composed for Sir Rhys ap Gruffudd *c.*1325? This
question can be answered with considerable confidence because all
the important manuscripts, with the exception of Balliol 353, were
edited in exemplary fashion by Griffith John Williams, with the help
of Evan John Jones, in 1934 — a landmark of twentieth-century Welsh
scholarship.[10] (Incidentally, Balliol 353 was not included because the
editors only became aware of it when the book was already at press.) In
the Williams-Jones edition the texts from Jesus 111 and Llanstephan 3
take up about 18 pages each: rather less than 10,000 words. Griffith
John Williams himself divides the text into six sections, but I prefer,
with Mr Eurys Rowlands,[11] to split up his last section into three, thus
giving us eight sections. These are discussions of:

1   the letters used in writing Welsh;
2   the syllables and diphthongs;
3   the parts of speech, syntax and figures of speech;
4   the traditional Welsh metres;
5   metrical faults to be avoided;
6   how everything is to be praised;
7   the duties of a professional poet;
8   triads relating to versecraft.

Such a scheme, combining instruction in grammar and in poetry,
will not seem strange to those familiar with the Latin grammatical
tradition of Western Europe or with the vernacular grammars we
have briefly touched upon. On the other hand, of course, in its precise
combination of elements it is presumably unique. Of the first three
sections, the first and third — those on the letters and on the parts of
speech, syntax and figures of speech — are heavily dependent on the
handbooks of Latin grammar associated with the names of Aelius
Donatus (a fourth-century Roman) and Priscianus (a sixth-century
citizen of Constantinople) and the derivatives of those handbooks.
Much work needs to be done to try to establish as far as possible the
precise affiliations of the Welsh text, and a promising start has been
made by Professors Matonis and Poppe; incidentally, Professor Matonis
is surely right to argue, chiefly against Saunders Lewis, that there is no
hint of the influence of the speculative grammarians or *modistae* on the

---

[10] *Gramadegau'r penceirddiaid*, ed. G. J. Williams and E. J. Jones (Caerdydd, 1934)
[hereafter cited as *GP*].
[11] E. I. Rowlands, 'Bardic Lore and Education', *BBCS* xxxii (1985), 143–55.

Welsh material.[12] The second section of Einion Offeiriad's handbook is concerned, it will be remembered, with the syllables and diphthongs of Welsh, and this section is almost wholly based on the oral instruction imparted by the master-poets to their pupils during the course of their apprenticeship. If we look at the last five sections of the grammar as we have looked at the first three, we can say that the fourth, sixth and seventh sections — those describing the traditional metres, how everything is to be praised and the duties of a professional poet — are almost certainly the work of Einion Offeiriad himself, although it is naturally based on what he regarded as good practice among the professional poets of his day. On the other hand, the fifth and eighth sections — those listing metrical faults and the triads relating to versecraft — are again a distillation of the teaching of the master-poets to their apprentices, although the triads, in particular, give the impression of having been quite heavily edited by Einion. One not unexpected, but still striking, feature of Einion Offeiriad's work is the use he makes of examples drawn from earlier and contemporary verse to illustrate the metres which he describes and the faults to which the users of these metres were prone. Einion has thirty-nine of these examples, most (although not all) of them four-line stanzas, and they form a body of evidence the significance of which Dr Rachel Bromwich has done more than anyone to elucidate. Of the thirty-nine, no more than twelve can be assigned to known poets, most of them seemingly contemporary with Einion, although a few are earlier. We shall have to return briefly to the import of this body of verse later on.

So much then for Wales's first grammarian, Einion Offeiriad of Gwynedd. We now turn squarely to consider the true subject of this lecture (although some of you may have begun to despair of our ever reaching him), Wales's second grammarian, Dafydd Ddu of Hiraddug. Dafydd Ddu, of course, means black or swarthy David. Hiraddug is, strictly speaking, the name of a township in the parish of Cwm in western Flintshire — the township may in fact have been split between Cwm and the adjoining parish of Diserth — but it also seems to have been used to denote the whole commot of which Cwm was a part, that is the commot of Rhuddlan.[13] The commot of Rhuddlan, together with those of Prestatyn and Coleshill, formed the *cantref* or hundred of

---

[12] A. T. E. Matonis, 'The Concept of Poetry . . .', 2.
[13] M. Richards, *Welsh Administrative and Territorial Units* (Cardiff, 1969), p. 91.

Tegeingl or Englefield (the two names are interchangeable in four-teenth-century documents).[14] In various Renaissance manuscripts which purport to be copies of Dafydd Ddu's work (possibly all deriving from the same source) he is called 'Dafydd Ddu Athro o Degeingl a Hiraddug',[15] which can plausibly be rendered 'Magister David Black (or David the Black) from Englefield and Hiraddug'. Unfortunately we have virtually no episcopal records from the diocese of St Asaph in the fourteenth century. Between February and November 1357, however, the see was vacant through the death of bishop John Trefor I and was administered during the vacancy, according to custom, by Simon Islip, the Archbishop of Canterbury. In Simon Islip's register in Lambeth Palace Library there are during that period eight references to a certain Magister David de Englefield, a canon of St Asaph, who was appointed by Archbishop Islip to be Vicar-General of the diocese and guardian of the spiritualities while the see remained vacant.[16] I think it likely that this Magister David de Englefield is indeed our Dafydd Ddu Athro o Degeingl a Hiraddug who is thus revealed — if I am right — as an important dignitary in the diocese of St Asaph during the middle years of the fourteenth century. The historian of the diocese, Archdeacon D. R. Thomas, made Dafydd Ddu chancellor, but I do not know on what evidence, although (as we shall see) he may have been right.[17] No other likely record reference to Dafydd Ddu has yet come to light. In 1318 a certain Dafydd de Rhuddallt was provided (that is, appointed by the pope) to a canonry with the expectation of a prebend in the diocese of Bangor, and indeed in 1328 he reappears as a prebendary; there is a village named Rhuallt (from Rhuddallt) in the parish of Tremeirchion in the commot of Rhuddlan, otherwise known, as we have seen, as the commot of Hiraddug, so that in Dafydd de Rhuddallt we may be looking at Dafydd Ddu climbing the first rungs of the ladder of

---

[14] Ibid. p. 202; an instance of the interchangeability of the two terms is at University of Wales Bangor Mostyn MSS 2801 (dated 1315/16) and 2803 (dated 1327).

[15] The evidence is at GP p. xiv. All quotations from Welsh are given in normalised spelling.

[16] London, Lambeth Palace Library, Register of Archbishop Simon Islip, ff. 218^r–219^r, 220^v, 279^{r-v}, 342^v. I am most grateful to Miss Melanie Barber, Deputy Librarian and Archivist at Lambeth Palace Library, for directing my attention to A. C. Ducarel's index to the register and for verifying that the references in the index are correct. Evidence of princely interference with David de Englefield at this time will be found in *Register of Edward the Black Prince* (4 vols., Stationery Office, London, 1930–3), iii, p. 280.

[17] D. R. Thomas, *The History of the Diocese of St Asaph* (2nd ed., 3 vols., Oswestry, 1909–13), i, p. 253 (cf. ibid., p. 62). Thomas here follows E. Edwards, *Willis' Survey of St. Asaph, considerably enlarged* (2 vols., Wrexham, 1801), i, p. 247. Thomas, op. cit. iii, p. 327 was the first to suggest that David de Englefield may have been the same as Dafydd Ddu o Hiraddug.

ecclesiastical preferment in the diocese of Bangor, presumably before transferring later to his home diocese of St Asaph.[18] Various shadowy canons of St Asaph flit in and out of the estate records of the period: in the massive Bangor Mostyn collection, for example, we have a Dafydd ap Hywel ap Goronwy and a Dafydd ab Ithel, but neither of these is styled *magister*.[19] Perhaps more promising than all of these, however, is a reference by the great Renaissance scholar Dr John Davies of Mallwyd in Merionethshire to Dafydd Ddu of Hiraddug as archdeacon of Diserth; Davies also assigns to Dafydd Ddu the date 1340.[20] By the archdeaconry of Diserth Davies meant the archdeaconry of St Asaph itself, since the church of Diserth formed part of the endowment of the archdeaconry.[21] By the end of the sixteenth century the bishop of St Asaph was permitted to hold the archdeaconry *in commendam*, and when Davies accompanied Bishop William Morgan on his translation from Llandaff to St Asaph in 1601, it was to the archdeacon's house in Diserth that they went to live.[22] Davies was therefore exceptionally well placed to consult any surviving records (if there were any) relating to the archdeaconry, and to receive any surviving oral traditions about former occupants of that dignity. It is pertinent to add that the vacancy of the see of St Asaph in 1357, over which Magister David de Englefield presided, came to an end when the then archdeacon, Llywelyn ap Madog ab Elis, was provided to the bishopric,[23] and it is by no means impossible that Magister David de Englefield succeeded him as

[18] *Calendar of Entries in the Papal Registers relating to Great Britain and Ireland. Papal Letters Vol. II A.D. 1305–1342*, ed. W. H. Bliss (London, 1895), p. 176; John Le Neve, *Fasti Ecclesiae Anglicanae 1300–1541. XI The Welsh Dioceses*, ed. B. Jones (London, 1965), p. 12 (Dr M. Bateson of the Canterbury Cathedral Archives kindly informs me that the form of the name in Dean and Chapter of Canterbury Register Q, fo. 17. 1ᵛ is in fact 'M David de Rudallt'). Intriguingly, a boy named 'David Duy' was a member of the household of Bishop Llywelyn ab Ynyr in 1311: see O. E. Jones, 'Llyfr Coch Asaph: A Textual and Historical Study' (University of Wales M.A. thesis, 1968), i, 13.

[19] University of Wales Bangor Mostyn MSS 3242 (Dafydd ap Hywel ap Goronwy, 1337/8), 2491 (Dafydd ab Ithel, 1341). On the collection see the typescript description at Bangor University Library by E. Gwynne Jones and A. Giles Jones, 'A Catalogue of the (Bangor) Mostyn collection' (six volumes, 1967).

[20] *Peniarth 49*, ed. T. Parry (Caerdydd, 1929), p. 208; J. Davies, *Antiquae Linguae Britannicae . . . et Linguae Latinae, Dictionarium Duplex* (London, 1632), sig. 315ᵛ.

[21] John Le Neve, op. cit. above, n. 18, p. 43n2.

[22] D. R. Thomas, op. cit. above, n. 17, i, pp. 97–100, 245, 400; Rh. F. Roberts, 'Dr John Davies o Fallwyd', *Llên Cymru*, ii (1952–3), 19–35, 97–110; R. G. Gruffydd, 'Y Beibl a droes i'w bobl draw' (Llundain, 1988), pp. 65–7, 72–5, 76–9, 80–3.

[23] John Le Neve, op. cit. above, n. 18, p. 37.

archdeacon. Archdeacon Thomas states that William de Spridlington, a
servant of the Black Prince, was made archdeacon at this time, but he
gives no authority for this statement, and since de Spridlington eventually became dean — and, indeed, bishop — it is perhaps unlikely that
he ever took what was technically the lesser office.[24] By 1371 the
archdeaconry was held by Ithel ap Robert, a notable patron of the
important professional poet Iolo Goch, and the likelihood is that David
de Englefield, if he ever held the post, was dead by then.[25] It might be
added that the canons of St Asaph at this time were a pugnacious lot,
who in 1344 informed the pope that the 'people of Wales, inhabiting as
they do wild places, are themselves untamed and fierce, so that they will
hardly receive discipline from those expert in their own tongue, and . . .
if they had a prelate ignorant of it they would be the more disobedient
and rebellious': this, of course, was an argument for a bishop of their
own choosing![26] Regarding Dafydd Ddu's final resting place, the
antiquary Edward Lhuyd recorded in 1696 in the parish of Cwm a
tradition, 'Mae bedd Dafydd Ddu dan sylfaen, dan y ffenestr briodas
yn eglwys y Ddiserth' ('the grave of Dafydd Ddu is under the foundation, under the marriage window in Diserth church').[27] For what it is
worth this tends to confirm the statement of Dr John Davies that Dafydd
Ddu once resided in Diserth as archdeacon.

Before I move on to discuss Dafydd Ddu's work as grammarian,
there are two problems relating to his life which I should address
briefly. Some years ago Professor R. R. Davies was good enough to
mention to me that he had seen in the fourteenth-century court rolls of
the Lordship of Dyffryn Clwyd references to someone who could be
Dafydd Ddu of Hiraddug, and Dr Oliver Padel, when he was working on
the court rolls, kindly supplied me with transcripts of the references.[28]
They concern a certain David Duy de Hirrathok (or alternatively
Hyr(r)aythok) who was accused in 1358 of attacking a certain Dafydd
ab Iorwerth ap Cadwgan in his own house; David Duy failed to appear

[24] D. R. Thomas, op. cit. above, n. 17, i, p. 246; John Le Neve, op. cit. above, n. 18, pp. 37,
40.
[25] Ibid. p. 43; cf. ibid. pp. 3, 12. *Gwaith Iolo Goch*, ed. D. R. Johnston (Caerdydd, 1988), pp.
55–74.
[26] *Calendar of Entries in the Papal Registers relating to Great Britain and Ireland.
Petitions to the Pope. Vol. I A.D. 1342–1419*, ed. W. H. Bliss (London, 1896), p. 48.
[27] *Parochialia . . . by Edward Llwyd*, ed. R. H. Morris (supplement to *Archaeologia
Cambrensis*; 3 vols., London, 1909–11), i, p. 64.
[28] London, Public Record Office: SC 2/218/6, m. 28; SC 2/218/6, m. 24d; SC 2/218/7, m. 24.
I am most grateful to Professor Davies and Dr Padel for their kind assistance.

six times in succession, was found to be without property and was declared an outlaw. It is not so much the circumstances of the case that I find perplexing — although if the defendant were Dafydd Ddu it would seem that his fortunes had suffered a sea-change in a very few months — but the fact that the name of his home as spelt in the documents could be interpreted not only as Hiraddug but also as Hiraethog, and that the subsidiary court in which the case was tried was that of Clocaenog and Trefor, which was situated in the shadow of the uplands of Hiraethog. On balance, at present, I tend regretfully to the conclusion that the Dafydd Ddu of the court case was not our Dafydd Ddu, but I may of course be wrong.

The second problem relating to the life of Dafydd Ddu is both more complicated and more vexing. As Mr Julian Roberts has amply shown,[29] in 1574 that wayward genius John Dee undertook an antiquarian tour of his Welsh homeland and during the course of that tour he appears to have heard stories about Dafydd Ddu which convinced him that Dafydd was none other than Roger Bacon, the thirteenth-century Franciscan polymath who achieved posthumous fame as a magician: the fact that the two lived in different centuries appears not to have worried Dee overmuch. Since Dee also thought that he and Dafydd Ddu were related to each other, his discovery meant that he could now claim kinship with Roger Bacon, which pleased him greatly, since he regarded Bacon as his mentor.[30] Dee appears to have convinced at least some members of the circle of Welsh humanists with whom he was in contact — that circle which had as its focus Richard Vaughan, later Bishop of Bangor, Chester and London in quick succession — since Henry Salesbury in his *Grammatica Britannica* of 1594 refers to Dafydd Ddu as '*insignis mathematicus*' (a famous mathematician), which was certainly true of Bacon.[31] On the other hand, another member of the circle, Maurice Kyffin, in his translation of Bishop John Jewel's *Apologia Ecclesiae Anglicanae* the following year,

[29] R. J. Roberts, 'John Dee and the Matter of Britain', *Transactions of the Honourable Society of Cymmrodorion*, 1991, pp. 129–43. I wish to thank Mr Roberts for his expert help with matters relating to Dee.

[30] N. H. Clulee, *John Dee's Natural Philosophy* (London and New York, 1988), p. 190. Cf. J. H. Bridges, *The Life and Work of Roger Bacon* (London, 1914), p. 37, quoting Corpus Christi Oxford MS 254, f. 159[r] (I am very grateful to Ms Christine Butler, Assistant Archivist of the College, for ascertaining the precise reference on my behalf).

[31] H. Salesbury, *Grammatica Britannica* (London, 1593 [*recte* 1594]), sig. 2*2[r]. On Richard Vaughan's circle see R. G. Gruffydd, 'Thomas Salisbury o Lundain a Chlocaenog: ysgolhaig-argraffydd y Dadeni Cymreig', *NLWJ* xxvii (1991–2), 1–19.

expresses caution about the equation: referring to Bacon he says 'hwn a eilw *rhai* ymhlith y Cymry, Dafydd Ddu o Hiraddug' ('this is he whom *some* among the Welsh call Dafydd Ddu of Hiraddug'):[32] but Kyffin, it should be added, was not only a very able but also an exceptionally level-headed person. By the eighteenth and nineteenth centuries stories about Dafydd Ddu's activities as a magician had proliferated, as Lewis Morris bears trenchant witness in 1757.[33] He, and the stories about him, had also become associated with a fine late fourteenth-century canopied tomb in Tremeirchion parish church, a tomb with an effigy of a priest and bearing the inscription 'HIC IACET DAVID FILIVS HOVEL FILIVS MADOC' ('here lies David son of Hywel son of Madog').[34] Thomas Pennant in 1781, Edward Jones 'Bardd y Brenin' (king's harpist) in 1808, and Father C. A. Newdigate SJ in 1897 all testify to the fact that oral tradition was firmly of the opinion that this was Dafydd Ddu of Hiraddug's tomb, and that Dafydd Ddu was a notable magician.[35] According to Father Newdigate the tomb was opened sometime during the 1830s and the remains left in the church porch overnight, 'in mortal dread lest Satan should come and claim his property', before they were reinterred the following day.[36] It may be added that even in this century Jonathan Ceredig Davies and Evan Isaac were able to collect stories about Dafydd Ddu, although the stories they tell do not connect him with the tomb at Tremeirchion.[37] Returning to that tomb, and in spite of the high authority of the late Colin Gresham,[38] I have to say that I think the identification of its occupier with Dafydd Ddu of Hiraddug is extremely dubious. First, there is no Dafydd ap Hywel ap Madog in the relevant genealogical collections, heroically assembled by Dr Peter

---

[32] *Deffynniad Ffydd Eglwys Loegr a gyfieithiwyd i'r Gymraeg . . . gan Maurice Kyffin*, ed. W. Prichard Williams (Bangor, 1908), p. [103].

[33] C. A. Gresham, *Medieval Stone Carving in North Wales* (Cardiff, 1968), pp. 224–7; E. Hubbard, *The Buildings of Wales: Clwyd* (Harmondsworth and Cardiff, 1986), p. 449.

[34] *Celtic Remains by Lewis Morris*, ed. D. Silvan Evans (supplement to *Archaeologia Cambrensis*; London, 1878), pp. 122, 244; I wish to thank Professor Geraint H. Jenkins for kindly drawing my attention to Lewis Morris's important evidence.

[35] T. Pennant, *The Journey to Snowdon* (London, 1781), p. 24; E. Jones, *Musical and Poetical Relicks of the Welsh Bards* (3rd ed., London, 1808), p. 16; C. A. Newdigate SJ, 'Carved and Incised Stones at Tremeirchion, Flints', *Archaeologia Cambrensis*, 5th ser., xiv (1897), 108–24.

[36] Ibid. 114.

[37] J. C. Davies, *Folk-lore of West and Mid-Wales* (Aberystwyth, 1911), p. 250; E. Isaac, *Coelion Cymru* (Aberystwyth, 1938), p. 111. Davies's account may be compared with Lewis Morris's (above, n. 34) and Isaac's with Edward Lhuyd's (above, n. 27).

[38] C. A. Gresham, op. cit. above, n. 33, p. 227.

Bartrum, who can plausibly be equated with Dafydd Ddu.[39] Secondly, and much more important, in the Pennant of Downing collection of deeds and documents in the Clwyd Record Office at Hawarden there is a notable series of deeds which show a certain Madog Rwth ap Robert, together with his children and grandchildren, busily buying up small parcels of land in Tremeirchion and the vicinity, so as to form in the end, we may assume, a sizeable estate. One of Madog Rwth's grand-children was Dafydd ap Hywel ap Madog,[40] and I strongly suspect that it is he who lies in that stately tomb in Tremeirchion parish church. There is, incidentally, another tomb in the church, supposedly that of Sir Robert Pounderling, keeper of Diserth Castle in the thirteenth century, and he would have been Dafydd ap Hywel ap Madog's great-great-great-great-grandfather.[41] The parishioners of Tremeirchion will not thank me for depriving them of their most famous vicar (although John Roberts, vicar between 1807 and 1829, was also a man of considerable distinction), and if I am proved wrong about Dafydd ap Hywel ap Madog I shall not be sorry. Two arguments might help the case against me.

1 The effigy on the tomb is that of a man dressed in a priest's vestments, and there is no hint in the Pennant of Downing deeds that Dafydd ap Hywel ap Madog was a priest (although I suppose he could have been ordained late in life).

2 None of the armorial crests on the tomb matches that ascribed to Madog Rwth by the greatest authority in the field of Welsh heraldry, Dr Michael Siddons.[42]

Whatever the outcome of that debate, the existence of stories about Dafydd Ddu's magical exploits is undeniable, and those stories may in fact tell us something about him as he was in real life. I am not

---

[39] P. C. Bartrum, *Welsh Genealogies A.D. 300–1400* (8 vols; Cardiff, 1974): see the 'Index of persons born c.1215–1350' in vol. v.

[40] Hawarden, Clwyd Record Office, Pennant of Downing deeds and papers 226–9, 231–2, 475–8 (dates between 1340 and 1352), referring to Dafydd ap Hywel ap Madog; other members of the family occur *passim* in the collection; see the typescript schedule at the Record Office, 'Report on deeds and papers of the Pennant family of Downing, Flintshire, 1299–1929' (1981). I am extremely grateful to Dr A. D. Carr of the University of Wales Bangor for directing my attention to this collection, among others.

[41] C. A. Gresham, op. cit. above, n. 33, pp. 174–5; E. Hubbard, op. cit. above, n. 33, p. 449; P. C. Bartrum, op. cit. above, n. 39, [iv], pp. 739–40 ('Pounderling 1–2'). Dafydd ap Hywel ap Madog does not appear in the pedigree, which may be a marginal argument in favour of his having been a celibate.

[42] M. P. Siddons, *The Development of Welsh Heraldry* (3 vols., Aberystwyth, 1991–3), ii, p. 103 (Dafydd ap Hywel ap Madog), p. 358 (Madog Rwth).

suggesting that he was a magician, but he may well during his lifetime
have made an impression on his contemporaries as a learned and book-
ish man, and such a man may then, as later, have attracted stories about
mastery of the black arts, congress with demons and so forth. The title
magister ascribed to David de Englefield in Archbishop Simon Islip's
register does suggest the possession of a university degree of some kind,
or at least a period of residence at a university: the title *athro* ascribed
to Dafydd Ddu of Hiraddug may point in the same direction. In Dafydd
Ddu's case the university in question would almost certainly have been
Oxford, and if he did graduate *magister* there, it would have involved at
least seven years' intensive study, concentrating at that time on logic
and physics, although other branches of the *trivium* and *quadrivium*,
and of the philosophies, would not have been wholly neglected.[43] To his
unlettered contemporaries, such a man would indeed have seemed a
paragon of learning, and it would have been natural for stories of
supernatural attainments to have become attached to him. That is, after
all, exactly what happened to Dafydd Ddu's *alter ego* (as John Dee
thought), Roger Bacon.[44]

    We now turn from Dafydd Ddu the man, as it were, to his work as
grammarian. That work is contained in a single medieval manuscript,
National Library of Wales MS Peniarth 20, which has been dated by Mr
Daniel Huws (whose authority in the field is unrivalled) to *c*.1330, a
date confirmed by Dr and Mrs Thomas Charles-Edwards in a recent
valuable study.[45] The manuscript was produced in the scriptorium of
the Cistercian abbey of Glynegwestl, Valle Crucis, near Llangollen in
Denbighshire, which is about twenty-five miles from St Asaph, a day's
journey in the fourteenth century. The text of the grammar in Peniarth
20 was included by Williams and Jones in their edition of 1936, so that
it is as easily accessible as the two oldest texts of Einion Offeiriad's
grammar. Like them Peniarth 20 contains no ascription of authorship
within the text itself, as in an incipit or colophon, but again like them it
states that the three new metres, *cyrch-a-chwta*, *hir-a-thoddaid* and

---

[43] J. M. Fletcher, 'The Faculty of Arts', in *The History of the University of Oxford . . . I The
Early Oxford Schools*, ed. J. I. Catto with R. Evans (Oxford, 1984), pp. 369–99, especially
pp. 393–4; for the intellectual history of the period the volume as a whole is indispensable.
[44] A. G. Holland, 'Roger Bacon as Magician', *Traditio*, xxx (1974), 445–60.
[45] D. Huws, 'Llyfrau Cymraeg 1250–1400', *NLWJ* xxviii (1993–4), 1–21, especially pp. 8,
20; G. and T. M. Charles-Edwards, 'The Continuation of *Brut y Tywysogion* in Peniarth MS
20' in *Ysgrifau a cherddi cyflwynedig i Daniel Huws/Essays and poems presented to Daniel
Huws*, ed. E. B. Fryde and T. Jones (Aberystwyth, 1994), pp. 293–305.

tawddgyrch cadwynog, were devised, not by Einion Offeiriad this time, but by 'Dafydd Ddu Athro'. It is again National Library of Wales MS Mostyn 110 which includes a copy of the grammar with a colophon which states: 'Ac felly y terfyna llyfr celfyddyd y gerddwriaeth o awdurdod Dafydd Ddu Athro o Degeingl a Hiraddug. Allan o hen decst ar femrwn' ('And thus ends the book on the art of versecraft authorised by *Magister* Dafydd Ddu of Englefield and Hiraddug. Out of an old text on vellum'). As it happens, that particular copy is of Einion Offeiriad's original grammar and not of Dafydd Ddu's revision of it, which means that the textual tradition had become hopelessly confused during the two and a half centuries which separate Peniarth 20 and Mostyn 110, but that need not vitiate the colophon's witness to an early belief that Dafydd as well as Einion had compiled a grammar-book. I think we may confidently accept the Peniarth 20 text as a very early copy of Dafydd Ddu's recension. It is in fact a much earlier and rather better text than any that have survived of Einion Offeiriad's original grammar, but that should not blind us to its essentially derivative nature.

How then did Dafydd Ddu set about revising Einion Offeiriad's work? To answer that question in detail would require much more time than I have at my disposal and would also, I fear, try your patience sorely. Ideally, too, it would require the use of a definitive edition of Einion Offeiriad's grammar, which is an urgent desideratum: it is good to know that Professor Matonis has such an edition in contemplation. The first point to make is that Dafydd Ddu's work is firmly based on Einion's: he follows the same general arrangement, uses many of the same definitions, is content to cite many of the same metrical examples. But, secondly, he also feels free to amend Einion's treatment at virtually every point: within sections the order of material is rearranged, the wording of definitions is changed, some examples of metres and metrical faults are dropped and new ones introduced, a certain amount of fresh material is added and a rather smaller amount of material included by Einion is omitted. To take an extreme example, at the end of Einion's third section there is a short disquisition on figures of speech of which the third and last is *ymoralw*, possibly corresponding to the Latin *evocatio*. This is supposed to excuse the fault known as *gŵydd ac absen* ('presence and absence'). Einion defines this fault only in terms of non-agreement of the subject and finite verb, but Dafydd Ddu adds a second category in which two different tenses of the verb occur in the same sentence. This enables him to cite as the second metrical example in his recension an *englyn* which Einion cites last but two, as an example of the metrical fault *carnymorddiwes* ('hoof-clash'), in which the last two lines of an *englyn* are both accented on the penultimate syllable rather than alternately on the penultimate and ultima.[46] The *englyn* in question was composed by the court poet Gwilym Rhyfel towards the middle of the twelfth century:

> Pei prynwn seithbwn sathrgrug — i'th oddau,
> Pedolau pwyll gaddug
> Mangre grawnfaeth, saeth seithug,
> Main a'u nadd yn Hiraddug!

> If I were to buy seven sackfuls cast into a heap for you,
> Sackfuls of horseshoes meant to cover
> The hooves of a stud fed on grain, that would be a vain thing to attempt,
> Stones will wear them down in Hiraddug![47]

One cannot resist the suspicion that Dafydd Ddu saw in this *englyn* a chance early on in his work to make honourable mention of his own home ground and that he rearranged his material accordingly.

Many more examples could be cited of Dafydd Ddu's free and easy way with Einion Offeiriad's material, and I must here be selective (although, it must be stressed, not particularly systematic). A clearer instance of relocation than the one above has to do with Einion's rule on how to identify the quality of a syllable by putting the word in which it occurs into the plural, a rule which is found in his fifth section: Dafydd moves it to his second section and amplifies it somewhat.[48] Dafydd sometimes not only amplifies but also adds: Einion has nothing to correspond to Dafydd's innovative discussion of the two values of the vowel *y* in the first section, nor to his rather acerbic comment on the *englyn cyrch* metre:

> A'r modd hwnnw ar englyn ni pherthyn ar brydydd ei ganu namyn ar deuluwr diwladaidd, rhag ei hawsed a'i fyrred.

> And it is not appropriate for a master-poet to compose that kind of *englyn* but only for a cultivated apprentice-poet, because it is so easy and short.[49]

On the other hand, possibly because he thought such matters relatively unimportant, Dafydd omits Einion's interesting directive on how to interpret ambiguous material (the more favourable sense is always to

---

[46] *GP* pp. 25, 45–6.

[47] *Gwaith Llywelyn Fardd I ac eraill o feirdd y ddeuddegfed ganrif*, ed. K. A. Bramley *et al.* (Caerdydd, 1994), pp. 515–21 (an edition by J. E. Caerwyn Williams).

[48] *GP* pp. 32, 41–2.

[49] *GP* pp. 39, 48.

be preferred), and his stern demand that professional poets should observe the strictest moral standards.[50] In the section on metres, Dafydd does not follow precisely the order adopted by Einion in describing the various metrical forms, nor (as I have already mentioned) does he always use the same examples. His treatment is also rather more expansive. Compared with Einion's thirty-nine examples of metres and metrical faults, Dafydd has forty-seven, of which eleven are new, more than balancing the six examples used by Einion which Dafydd omits. Finally the section 'How everything is to be praised' is much more elaborate in Dafydd Ddu's version than it is in Einion Offeiriad's. Dafydd has twenty categories of people worthy of praise compared to Einion's eight (although it should be noted that there are interesting variations in this section between the various texts of Einion's grammar itself). Since Dafydd refers to himself as '*athro*' within the text of the grammar itself, it is interesting to compare his and Einion's treatment of that term. Einion defines '*athro*' as one of the lower clergy and describes him thus (I follow the Llanstephan 3 and Balliol 353 versions):

> Athrawon a folir o ddoethineb a chymhendod a haelioni a thegwch a defodau da a dyfnder deall ac athrylith a goruchelder celfyddydau a synhwyrau, a buddugoliaethau yn ymrysonau a phethau eraill ardderchogion.

> Teachers are praised for wisdom and talent and generosity and beauty and laudable customs and depth of understanding and innate ability and high mastery of arts and experiments, and victories in disputations and other exalted things.[51]

Dafydd Ddu's version is longer and, I think, displays a greater awareness of the university curriculum of the day. He defines '*athro*' as 'a secular scholar' who is not, however, a layman: perhaps he thought of him as someone in minor orders.

> Athrawon a folir og eu celfyddydau a'u gwybodau ac uchelder natur, a chyfreithiau, a blaenwydd canon, a buddugoliaethau yn ymrysonau, a doethi-neb ar ofynnau a gollyngau drwy athrylith a chelfyddydau a dosbarth.

> Teachers are praised for their arts and sciences and their mastery of nature and laws [presumably civil law] and supremacy in canon law, and victories in disputations and wisdom when dealing with questions and conclusions by means of innate ability and arts and discernment.[52]

[50] *GP* pp. 33–4, 35.
[51] *GP* p. 34.
[52] *GP* p. 56.

Incidentally Dafydd, unlike Einion, also has a section on how '*disgy-blion*' (pupils) are to be praised, and this may be worth quoting for the light it may throw on Dafydd's own activities at the time when his revision of the grammar was written:

> Disgyblion a folir og eu dysg a'u hathrylith a'u gwybodau a'u haddfwynder ac o'u bod yn ddefnyddiau gwyrda.

> Pupils are praised for their learning, and innate ability, and knowledge, and docility and because they are potential gentlemen.[53]

That last point suggests strongly that Dafydd Ddu may have taught lay children as well as those who aspired to holy orders, and it may confirm Archdeacon D. R. Thomas's suggestion that Dafydd may, as chancellor, have been responsible for the cathedral school of the diocese. That laymen as well as clergy attended such schools is proved by a well-known passage in an amusing poem by Iolo Goch to Ithel ap Robert, whose aspirations to become a bishop were never realised and who had finally to be content, as we have seen, with the archdeaconry of St Asaph. Ithel ap Robert was a BCL, presumably of Oxford, but he seems to have received his basic education in Latin grammar and liturgical singing within the diocese of St Asaph, possibly at the cathedral school:

> Cydwersog, cof diweirsalm,
> Fûm ag ef yn dolef dalm
> Gyda'r un athro, clo clod,
> A'n henfeistr . . .

> Singing together the same verses, memorising the chaste psalm [i.e.
>   Psalm 51],
> Was I with him chanting awhile
> Under the same teacher, most deserving of praise,
> And our old instructor . . . [54]

It would be pleasing to think that the 'old instructor' was in fact Dafydd Ddu himself, but I am afraid chronological considerations make that unlikely (although not impossible).

It may be profitable to linger for another few minutes over the question of whether there is anything further his grammar can tell us about Dafydd Ddu. There are intriguing hints here and there, especially in the examples Dafydd gives to illustrate points of grammar. Sometimes he gives examples when Einion Offeiriad has none, and some-

---

[53] Ibid.
[54] *Gwaith Iolo Goch*, p. 56.

times Dafydd's examples differ from Einion's. For instance, Einion has nothing to correspond to Dafydd's mention of Gwrecsam, then as now an important town in the diocese of St Asaph, nor to his plain statement, of the kind one meets constantly in medieval grammar-books, 'Mi yw Dafydd' ('I am Dafydd').[55] On the other hand we find Dafydd replacing Einion's 'Mynnwn fy mod yn gyfoethog' ('I would like to be rich') by 'Mynnwn fy mod yn esgob' ('I would like to be a bishop').[56] Einion's 'Ieuan a gâr Gwenllïan' ('Ieuan loves Gwenllian) becomes in Dafydd's hands 'Mi a garaf Gweirful' ('I love Gweirful'); and, most daring of all, Einion's conventional 'gwraig wen ei dwylo' ('a woman with white hands') is transformed by Dafydd into 'gwraig wen ei hesgeiriau' ('a woman with white legs').[57] In view of this, it is perhaps not surprising to find that Dafydd has substituted for Einion's example of the *gwawdodyn* metre (whatever that example may have been: the texts differ on the point) four lines from a delightful love poem by Iorwerth Fychan ab Iorwerth ap Rhotbert of which the last line of the four is 'Mor wen ei hesgair uwch ei hesgid' ('How white is her leg above her shoe').[58] Nor is it surprising to find that one of the examples of the *englyn proest* cited by both Einion and Dafydd is a snatch of love-lyric composed by Dafydd himself:

> Llawen dan glaerwen len laes,
> Lleddf olwg gloyw amlwg glwys;
> Llathrlun manol a folais,
> Llariaidd foneddigaidd foes.

> Joyful under a glowing-white long robe,
> With downcast, shining, clear and comely eyes;
> A lovely bright form that I have praised,
> Of generous and courteous custom.[59]

---

[55] *GP* pp. 39, 45; it may be worth noting that the Rectory of Wrexham belonged to Valle Crucis Abbey: see D. R. Thomas, op. cit. above, n. 17, iii, pp. 293–6.

[56] *GP* pp. 23, 43.

[57] *GP* pp. 24, 45; ibid. pp. 25, 45. The conventional nature of 'gwraig wen ei dwylo' was pointed out to me by Miss Morfydd E. Owen.

[58] *GP* pp. 9, 28; ibid. p. 49. In her edition of Iorwerth Fychan's poem, Dr Christine James argues that the two amendments by Dafydd cited in the preceding note are also evidence of Iorwerth's influence on him (Gweirfyl is the name of the girl celebrated in the poem): see *Gwaith Bleddyn Fardd a beirdd eraill ail hanner y drydedd ganrif ar ddeg*, ed. Rh. M. Andrews *et al.* (Cardiff, 1996), p. 311. Since Iorwerth in another poem (ibid. pp. 320–30) mentions the obscure river Ffyddion, which joins the Clwyd near Rhuddlan, it is tempting to relocate him in this area, although it is unlikely on chronological grounds that he is to be connected with the family to which Ithel ap Robert belonged: see P. C. Bartrum, op. cit. above, n. 39, [ii], p. 263 ('Ednywain Bendew 2').

[59] *GP* pp. 27, 48.

That last example raises a more general point. If a stanza by Dafydd
Ddu was included in Einion Offeiriad's original grammar, Einion must
at least have known of Dafydd's work. More than that, they may have
been known to each other, the one presumably a middle-aged cleric
with his base in the diocese of St David's but with connections with the
diocese of Bangor, the other a rising young scholar also with possible
connections during the 1320s with the diocese of Bangor before
transferring to St Asaph. It is not impossible that the grammar may
have been to some extent a work of collaboration from the beginning,
which could explain the fact that the invention of the three new
metres is ascribed to Einion Offeiriad in one group of texts and to
Dafydd Ddu in another text. At least this theory would enable us to
avoid having to charge Dafydd Ddu with plagiarism, if that concept
had any meaning then. Were the theory to be accepted, it would mean
that the Peniarth 20 text represents a later revision by Dafydd Ddu of
the original grammar compiled by both Einion Offeiriad and Dafydd
Ddu together: it is, if you like, a second revised edition undertaken by
one only of the two original authors. But clearly this argument cannot
be pressed too far.

Finally, we might ask the question 'What is it all about?' Why did
Sir Rhys ap Gruffudd, possibly with the knowledge and support of Sir
Gruffudd Llwyd,[60] encourage Einion Offeiriad, possibly with Dafydd
Ddu as collaborator, to undertake the compilation of the grammar at
all? I think there may be a threefold answer to that question. First,
there was certainly a pedagogic motive, an attempt to supply the
professional poets with a manual of useful knowledge, which at least
bowed in the direction of the dominant educational tradition of the
day, that of Latin grammar, although of course the manual could not
hope and did not aim to include all the information necessary to
enable a professional poet to practise his art — the most obvious
example of omission is of course the lack of any discussion of
cynghanedd or metrical ornament. Secondly, there was probably an
attempt in the manual to redefine the function of Welsh panegyric
poetry after the catastrophe of the Conquest, and also to set it on an
overtly Christian basis: if there were no longer royal courts to welcome professional poets and royal law to guarantee their status, the
new Welsh élite in both church and secular society would make them

---

[60] It may be worth noting that Sir Gruffudd Llwyd's court at Dinorwig was no more than a
mile and a half away from Einion Offeiriad's church of Llanrug.

welcome in their halls and provide them with a livelihood; the career of Iolo Goch, with his judicious mixture of secular and ecclesiastical patrons — something of the ratio of eight to five — exemplifies this point.[61] Thirdly, the manual may be seen as an attempt by the Welsh secular and clerical élite to regulate the practices of the Welsh professional poets. If we take sections 6 and 7 of the classification suggested above together (those are the sections on 'How everything is to be praised' and 'The duties of a professional poet') it is clear that the poets were forbidden to compose:

1   satire;

2   love-poetry to married women;

3   anything smacking of their primitive mantic function, particularly (it may be assumed) vaticination.

With regard to the second prohibition, forbidding the composition of love-poetry to married women, it is noteworthy that love-poetry to young unmarried women was allowed, especially by young poets, and was indeed tacitly encouraged by the high proportion of fragments of love-lyric quoted as examples of metres and metrical faults. Taken together, these three prohibitions appear to reflect fairly accurately the situation obtaining during the time of the court poets of the Welsh princes in the twelfth and thirteenth centuries, whose complete works the Centre which I had the honour to direct has just finished editing;[62] but they do not seem to reflect what was happening during the Conquest and in the ensuing turbulent period when satire, in particular, flourished mightily. The publication of the poets' manual has been plausibly seen as an attempt to get a grip on this situation.[63] To what extent it succeeded may partly be obscured by the towering figure of Dafydd ap Gwilym, whose work consists largely of what purport to be love-poems to married women. (I choose my words carefully because Dafydd ap Gwilym is an extraordinarily complex figure.) But if we look past him, we see that the more typical professional poets largely conform to the prescriptions of the manual. Praise of God and man, and of young women, was their stock-in-trade, although they never entirely renounced satire, and when occasion demanded, as during the War of

---

[61] *Gwaith Iolo Goch, passim.*

[62] The seventh and last volume of 'Cyfres Beirdd y Tywysogion' (the Poets of the Princes Series) was published by the University of Wales Press in Cardiff in March, 1996.

[63] See, in particular, Saunders Lewis, 'Dafydd ap Gwilym', *Blackfriars*, March 1953, pp. 131–5; reprinted in *Presenting Saunders Lewis*, ed. A. R. Jones and G. Thomas (Cardiff, 1973), pp. 159–63.

Independence of Owain Glyndŵr and the Wars of the Roses, their old
facility for vaticination was again found useful.[64]

Before we bid farewell to Dafydd Ddu of Hiraddug, I would like to
consider very briefly two further aspects of his work. In the first place
he was not only a grammarian but also a considerable religious poet in
his own right. Three poems by him have been preserved, all of them in
manuscripts typically dating from the later sixteenth and earlier seventeenth centuries. The first of them, a long *cywydd* outlining the History
of Redemption from the Creation of Christ, was apparently immensely
popular, since it is still extant in more than seventy manuscript copies.[65]
After stating what happened on each of the six days of Creation, the
poet describes Adam's fall (at Eve's instigation), his exile to the Valley
of Hebron, his death and committal to Hell for 4,604 years, and then the
coming of Christ to redeem him. The poem ends by reminding the
reader (or hearer) that there is only one sacrifice for sin:

> Ac nid oes, gwedi'i foes Fo,
> Mab Brenin mwy a'i pryno.

> And there will not be, after what He has achieved,
> Any other King's Son that will once more redeem him.

The second poem is again a *cywydd*, rather shorter than the first and
extant in far fewer manuscript copies — some twenty-one have come to
light to date.[66] It is a metrical recital of the Ten Commandments, except
that the order of the commandments and to some extent their content is
curiously different from the normal medieval version (which corresponds to the Hebrew version in the Book of Exodus except that it
omits the second commandment (against graven images), and splits the
tenth (against coveting a neighbour's property) into two). The reason
for this discrepancy is that Dafydd Ddu attempts to combine the
Dominical precepts about loving God and one's neighbour with the
Ten Commandments, and I would be glad to know to what extent this
happens elsewhere. The poem ends with an appeal to the pupil to learn
and heed every word of the commandments, which shows clearly its
educational intent:

---

[64] See, most recently, M. B. Jenkins, 'Aspects of the Welsh prophetic verse tradition in the
Middle Ages' (University of Cambridge Ph.D. thesis, 1990).

[65] e.g. Cardiff, South Glamorganshire Libraries MS 5.167, ff. 7ʳ–8ʳ; see further the second
work referred to in n. 6 above.

[66] e.g. Aberystwyth, National Library of Wales MS Brogyntyn I.2, ff. 337ᵛ–338ᵛ; see further
the second work referred to in n. 6 above.

Disgyblaeth, fab, arfaeth fu,
Disgybl a gâr eu dysgu;
Diangall ydyw'r Dengair:
Dysgwn ac eurwn bob gair!

To be a pupil, my son, was foreordained,
A pupil will love to learn these;
Full of wisdom are the Ten Precepts:
Let us learn and honour every word!

Dafydd Ddu's third and last poem is an *awdl* and it occurs in a mere seven manuscripts: it is, however, better known than the two *cywyddau* because it was printed in the *Myvyrian Archaiology of Wales* in 1801.[67] It is a prolonged and moving meditation on the fate awaiting a man or woman's body in the grave, no matter what his or her rank or pretensions might be, concluding with an appeal to God, the Virgin Mary and the saints for clemency and succour on the Day of Judgement:

Yno y diolchir
Ymadrodd cywir;
Yno y dielir
    Pob anwiredd.

There each just utterance
Will be rewarded;
There each act of wrongdoing
    Will be punished.

This is of course a common theme of late medieval religious verse, but Dafydd Ddu handles it with skill and conviction, foreshadowing to some extent the powerful macabre poetry of Siôn Cent a generation or two later. One wonders whether Dafydd Ddu's sombre view of the human condition may not have been coloured somewhat by his experience of the Black Death, the first onslaught of which he apparently survived. His religious poetry, as both Dr Brynley F. Roberts and Sir Glanmor Williams have emphasised, is essentially didactic in character and forms part of that considerable body of prose and verse which was intended to instruct and enlighten the Welsh clergy and laity, the origin of which must at least partly be sought in Archbishop John Peckham's Constitutions of 1281 and, ultimately, in the decrees of the Fourth Lateran Council of 1215.[68]

---

[67] *The Myvyrian Archaiology of Wales*, ed. O. Jones *et al.* (3 vols., London, 1801–7), i, pp. 536–7; see further the second work referred to in n. 6 above.
[68] *Gwasanaeth Mair*, ed. Brynley F. Roberts (Cardiff, 1961), pp. lxxix–lxxx; G. Williams, *The Welsh Church from Conquest to Reformation* (Cardiff, 1962), pp. 81–113, esp. 109, 112–13.

There is one other point about Dafydd Ddu that I want to mention before I finish. In about ten manuscripts, the earliest of which dates from around 1400, there is extant a Welsh version of the text known in Latin as *Officium Parvum Beatae Mariae Virginis*, 'the Little Office of the Blessed Virgin Mary', otherwise known as 'The Hours of the Virgin'; the Welsh title is 'Gwasanaeth Mair' ('The Office (or Service) of Mary'). As its Latin title implies, the text is modelled on the Divine Office contained in the Breviary, but is much shorter and simpler: it includes brief services for the seven canonical hours and consists of psalms, hymns, lessons and prayers. The Little Office originated in the religious orders but was soon adopted by the secular clergy and spread from them to the laity. The Welsh version was impeccably edited by Dr Brynley F. Roberts in 1961.[69] It is a metrical version: the twenty-eight psalms and four canticles are rendered, with one exception, into a flexible 'free' metre consisting basically of a ten-syllable line bearing four accents and rhyming in couplets (although there is wide variation); whereas the hymns, four of which are Marian and the fifth the 'Te Deum', are given a more formal garb of 'strict' metres, in which the line-length is quite firmly regulated and a measure of ornamentation obligatory — the metres used are the *toddaid*, the *cyhydedd hir*, the *rhupunt*, the *rhupunt hir* and the *hir-a-thoddaid*. Considering the difficulty of the task which the translator set himself, it seems to me that he succeeded admirably. Our greatest authority on Welsh Biblical translation, the Revd Dr Isaac Thomas, has remarked on how well the author of 'Gwasanaeth Mair' conveys the spirit, if not the exact wording, of the Vulgate Psalter.[70] These are the first four lines of his rendering of Psalm 129 (130), which correspond to the following two verses of the Authorised Version:

> 'Out of the depths have I cried unto thee, Lord.
> Lord, hear my voice: let thine ear by attentive to the voice of my
>   supplication.'

> *De profundis clamavi ad te Domine*
> *Domine exaudi vocem meam: fiant aures tuae*
> *intendentes in vocem deprecationis meae.*

> O'r eigion y llefais arnat, Arglwydd.
> Arglwydd, gwarando fy ngweddi yn rhwydd.

---

[69] See Brynley F. Roberts, op. cit. above, n. 68.

[70] I. Thomas, 'Cyfieithu'r Hen Destament i'r Gymraeg. Cyn y Diwygiad Protestannaidd', *NLWJ* xxi (1979–80), 317.

Bŷnt dy glustiau yn ystyredigion
Wrth lef fy ngweddi a gwawdd fy nghalon.[71]

In the translator's renderings of the hymns in 'strict' metres, it is clear from the outset that he could not hope to reproduce the succinctness of the original Latin, but he substitutes for that a certain majestic sonorousness. The third stanza of one of the Marian hymns, 'Ave maris stella', might be translated roughly as follows:

'Loose the chains of prisoners.
Give light to the blind;
Repel our evil deeds,
Ask [on our behalf] for all good things.'

Solve vincla reis,
profer lumen cecis;
mala nostra pelle,
bona cuncta posce.

In Welsh those four lines become:

Gollwng rwym echwng achwyn llu bedydd,
Gwrthladd, Fair, o'n gradd greddfawl aflonydd;
Cynnull olau dull y deillion efrydd,
Cynnal i'th ardal eurdeml gyfluydd;
Cannerth didrafferth drwy ffydd — a geisiwn,
Credwn y caffwn coffa cerennydd.[72]

But why am I talking about 'Gwasanaeth Mair' in a lecture about Dafydd Ddu of Hiraddug? In a copy of the text made in 1631, but transcribed from a manuscript dated 1537, Dr John Davies of Mallwyd, whom we have already met, says that the translation was done 'I gan Ddafydd Ddu o Hiraddug hyd y mae pawb yn tybiaid' ('by Dafydd Ddu of Hiraddug, as everyone supposes'), and he repeats the statement the following year in a printed book which includes the 'Gwasanaeth Mair' text of the 'Te Deum' 'a gyfieithwyd yn Gymraeg i gan Dafydd Ddu o Hiraddug fel yr ydys yn tybiaid' ('translated into Welsh by Dafydd Ddu of Hiraddug as is supposed').[73] You will have noticed that there is a hint of reservation about those two statements, and Dr Brynley F. Roberts in his edition is very properly cautious

---

[71] *Gwasanaeth Mair*, 30.

[72] Ibid. 34.

[73] Aberystwyth, National Library of Wales MS 4973B, fo. 377[r]; Robert Persons SJ (trs. J. Davies), *Llyfr y resolusion* (Llundain, 1632), p. [523].

about the ascription to Dafydd Ddu. On the other hand there are two considerations that I think may just tilt the balance in favour of Dafydd's authorship.

1   First, he makes use, as we have seen, of the *hir-a-thoddaid* metre. This, as you will recall, is one of the metres devised by Einion Offeiriad according to Einion's grammar and by Dafydd Ddu according to Dafydd's. As far as I have been able to discover, the only examples of the *hir-a-thoddaid* metre from the whole of the fourteenth century are in the texts of the grammar, in Einion Offeiriad's panegyric ode for Rhys ap Gruffudd, and in 'Gwasanaeth Mair'. Although we cannot be fully certain about this matter until the Centre where I work completes — in a year or two's time, it is hoped — its edition of the whole corpus of extant fourteenth-century Welsh verse,[74] I think that even now we may feel reasonably certain about it. That fact — the strictly limited occurrence of the *hir-a-thoddaid* metre — seems to me a powerful argument for accepting John Davies's tentative ascription of 'Gwasanaeth Mair' to Dafydd Ddu.

2   Secondly, Dr Roberts has discovered that the liturgical use most nearly reflected in 'Gwasanaeth Mair' is that of the Order of Friars Preachers, the Dominicans. While there is no good evidence that Dafydd Ddu was a Dominican, in spite of his epithet, there was a flourishing Dominican friary in Rhuddlan, a bare two miles from Diserth, where we may assume Dafydd Ddu resided.[75] If he had been so minded he could easily have acquired a copy of the Dominican Use of the *Officium Parvuum Beatae Mariae Virginis* from the friary at Rhuddlan.

I have no wish to appear greedy on behalf of the subject of my lecture this evening, but I think I have to point out before finishing that in 1596 Thomas Wiliems of Trefriw came to the tentative conclusion that Dafydd Ddu of Hiraddug was also the author (or rather, as he thought, the translator) of the notable Middle Welsh mystical treatise 'Ymborth yr Enaid' ('Food for the Soul'). He arrived at this conclusion on the slender basis that a fragment of the treatise in the same hand as a copy of Dafydd Ddu's grammar (as he thought) had

---

[74] In the series known as 'Cyfres Beirdd yr Uchelwyr' (the Poets of the Nobility Series) published by the University of Wales Centre for Advanced Welsh and Celtic Studies at Aberystwyth; five volumes have so far appeared.

[75] D. Knowles and R. N. Hadcock, *Medieval Religious Houses: England and Wales* (2nd ed., London, 1971), pp. 214, 218; cf. also E. Hubbard, op. cit. above, n. 33, p. 427.

come into his possession, and he may even have thought, as did later the humanist John Jones of Gellilyfdy in Flintshire, that the hand was that of Dafydd Ddu himself.[76] However, 'Ymborth yr Enaid' has recently been very carefully edited by Dr Iestyn Daniel, and he argues strongly that the treatise — and indeed the grammar and 'Gwasanaeth Mair' as well — are all to be ascribed to a thirteenth-century Dominican author, possibly a poet named Cnepyn Gwerthrynion.[77] While accepting the force of Dr Daniel's arguments, I feel at present that his conclusions have to be regarded with a measure of reserve, as you will perhaps have gathered. Another possibility that presents itself is that a text in the same manuscript as Dafydd Ddu's recension of the grammar, Peniarth 20, a text known as 'Y Beibl yng Nghymraeg' ('The Bible in Welsh'), which is essentially a translation of *Promptuarium Bibliae* by Petrus Pictaviensis, may also be the work of Dafydd Ddu, and may have reached Valle Crucis abbey at the same time as the grammar.[78] But there is no external evidence to support this possibility, and it can only be tested, if at all, by minute linguistic analysis.

I hope that as a result of this lecture the figure of Dafydd Ddu of Hiraddug emerges from the mists of the fourteenth century with rather more solid lineaments than he possessed before. He was, it seems, an important dignitary of the cathedral church of St Asaph during the middle years of the century, possibly as chancellor and then as archdeacon. Before *c.*1330 he completed a revision of the poets' grammar or manual of versecraft which had been compiled by Einion Offeiriad a few years previously, and he may even have had a hand in its original compilation. He was a good poet in his own right, devoting his talent to the edification of his fellow clergy and of those members of the laity who were able to appreciate Welsh versecraft, of which there must have been many. It is, I think, not unlikely that he translated the Little Office of the Blessed Virgin Mary into Welsh metre, with notable success. We need not press his claim to have written 'Ymborth yr Enaid' and 'Y Beibl yng Nghymraeg' as well. But even without them I think he has done enough to secure for himself an honoured place in the literary history of Wales during the crucial first half of the fourteenth century.

---

[76] I. Daniel, art. cit. above, n. 2, pp. 182–4.

[77] *Ymborth yr Enaid*, ed. R. I. Daniel (Caerdydd, 1995), pp. 1–1v.

[78] *Y Bibyl Ynghymraec, sef cyfieithiad Cymraeg Canol o'r "Promptuarium Bibliae"*, ed. T. Jones (Caerdydd, 1940).

Perhaps he may even have done enough to claim a modest mention in the *New Dictionary of National Biography*!

Note.   I wish to thank Professors Emeriti R. M. Jones and J. E. Caerwyn Williams for their perceptive comments.

Proceedings of the British Academy, **90**, 29–64

Shakespeare's Renaissance Realism

ALASTAIR FOWLER

University of Edinburgh and University of Virginia
Fellow of the Academy

I

AFTER DECADES OF EXPERIMENTAL THEATRE, no one now supposes that the realism of fifty years ago is the only realistic mode.[1] Several realisms are recognised, each with its own conventions; although realism can sometimes be thoughtlessly contrasted with 'convention'. But mind-sets change slowly, so that the realism of William Archer is still taken as normative for Elizabethan drama, much as single-point perspective is, for Renaissance art. Undeniable 'exceptions'—like Holbein's *The Ambassadors* with its anamorphic skull, or the *Unton Memorial* with its differently-scaled spatio-temporal insets—are commonly treated as oddities. Yet the possibility of multiple perspective and temporal viewpoints continued, well into the seventeenth century.[2] And Elizabethan

---

Read at the Academy 26 April 1995. © The British Academy 1996.

[1] There is a large literature on mimesis and on realism in its various senses; see, e.g., Auerbach (1953); Stern (1973); Lyons and Nichols (1982), especially Beaujour; Nuttall (1983) 56–7 etc. Ermarth (1983) valuably traces the development of realism away from the spatial and temporal discontinuities of medieval art; relating this to the introduction of single-point perspective (albeit with some confusion between viewpoints and vanishing points). Hagen (1986) is useful on different perspective systems. And, for those who speak the language of poststructuralism, there is an interesting theory of meta-representational discourse in Weimann (1985).

[2] For Unton, see Llewellyn (1991) Figure 28; for Rubens, Vergara (1982) 48. Many Elizabethan portraits contain additional scenes or *parergies*, often removed in place or time: see, e.g., Strong (1987). Study of Renaissance perspective needs to begin with White (1987); Kemp (1990); Elkins (1994). See also Alpers (1983), e.g., 64–9; Bunim (1970); Lindberg (1976).

drama was similarly free to move among spatial discontinuities on the
'imagined wing' of its 'swift scene'.[3] Time and place could be left
unspecified, or have mainly symbolic import.[4] Indeed, scenery came to
the British stage only during the 1630s;[5] and, even in Italy, architectural
stages might exhibit incompatible perspectival recessions.[6] Despite this,
a continuous, single-point perspective—what I shall call 'spectator
realism'—tends to be read back into drama innocent of its assumptions.
Traditional and postmodern critics alike assume that by Shakespeare's
time discontinuous, allegorical representation was more or less replaced
by modern realism, with its post-Cartesian continuum of cause-effect
sequences, inviting speculative extrapolation to supply missing details.[7]
But there is a distinct Renaissance realism, an intermediate mode
between medieval and modern. Locally, this may imitate reality natur-
alistically; but in its larger coherence it adopts multiple perspective
viewpoints that are often related morally or psychologically rather than
causally.

Shakespeare's comedies even combine allegory with illusionistic
representation. Instead of forcing them into a teleologically naturalistic
strait-jacket, we should accept their own terms of realism. It is futile,
for example, to demand a unified plot. Despite classicising theorists,
Renaissance drama at its best often implies a romance poetic of interlace, separate viewpoints and multiple plots.[8] Some of the more honest
cinquecento theorists even doubted whether a single plot could hold an
audience.[9] Yet nowadays directors mostly rationalise Shakespeare's
interwoven structures to a single sequence, or at least to a 'main plot'
and 'sub-plot'. Elizabethan comedy was structured by scenes, not acts,

---

[3] *Henry V*, III Chorus.

[4] Dessen (1984); Kernodle (1944).

[5] In a production of William Strode's *The Floating Island* (1638). Self-referring dialogue in
J. Shirley, *The Triumph of Peace* (1633) 295–315, seems to imply the novelty of scenery; but
this may need to be qualified for private theatres and great house venues, if the speculations
in Mowl (1993) 150 are right.

[6] e.g. G. B. Albanese's drawing of the proscenium of Palladio's Teatro Olympico, Vicenza:
Puppi (1989) 281.

[7] Auerbach (1953) and Ermarth (1983) contrast the two mimetic methods.

[8] See, e.g., Pettet (1949). On *entrelacement*, see Vinaver (1971); Bloomfield (1986). Illustration of *Orlando Furioso* is an obvious instance of the interaction of polyphonic romance
and compressed-narrative, multi-perspective picturing; see Falaschi (1975).

[9] Also, whether the 'other perfection' of romance was not preferable. See, e.g., Bernardo
Tasso: Weinberg (1961) 1010; cf. Camillo Pellegrino, and especially Giuseppe Malatesta:
ibid. 1020, 1061.

however: by ideas, as much as plots.[10] Suspend belief in plot unity, and Shakespeare's comedies turn out to have plot multiplicity.

Twelfth Night has something like eight stories.[11] Yet we conspire to discuss a main plot, with Orsino, Viola and Olivia as 'protagonists'— the solecistic plural gives all away—and a subplot, with Sir Toby, Feste and the rest. Malvolio's confinement in 'hideous darkness' (IV. ii. 30), when Sir Topas catechises him in Pythagorean doctrine, is treated as peripheral 'fooling'. Yet the play's occasion was Epiphany, and the Lesson for Epiphany concerned the palpable Egyptian darkness of sin. The Magi seeking the light were interpreted as the *praeparatio evangelii* of pagan wisdom, specifically including Pythagoras's.[12] Malvolio's instruction in ancient theology is thus anything but peripheral.

The Merchant of Venice, too, has many independent (although allegorically connnected) plot strands. Among these is Shylock's plot of revenge on Antonio, which has proved hard to motivate without resorting to the soft focus of Heinrich Heine and Graham Midgeley, or (like Lancelot Gobbo and Barbara Lewalski[13]) identifying him with the devil. As recipient of the ring of Leah (allegorised by St Paul himself as the Law[14]), Shylock symbolises legalistic belief in the Old Covenant, or its Christian equivalent, justification by works. He may be related to the intense seventeenth-century interest in the relation of Law and Gospel.[15] Yet of course no allegorical interpretation can adequately address the play's complex treatment of the ethics of lending, venture capital, and contracts. Its profusion of stories, vignettes, cases enacted and cases alluded to constitutes a realism as multifarious as that of, say, Dos Passos' *USA*. It may include, for example, the unanticipated moral circumstance that in standing surety for Bassanio, Antonio was culpable.[16] Again, Shylock perhaps calls Antonio a 'fawning publican'

[10] Forgotten until recently. See Jewkes (1958); Jones (1971).

[11] e.g. Orsino's, Cesario's, Andrew's and Malvolio's suits to Olivia; Viola's love for Orsino; the intrigue of Maria's riddle; Antonio's love and imprisonment; Cesario's and Andrew's duel. Draper (1950); Hollander (1961).

[12] Gash (1988); Lewalski (1965); Fowler (1995) 120–6.

[13] Lewalski (1962) 339.

[14] Gal. 4: 22, a key passage in this context.

[15] As witness, e.g., Rembrandt's Hebraism, and Milton's: see, e.g., Schwartz (1993). Portia's important speech on 'the quality of mercy' is based on Isa. 55, then commonly interpreted as an invitation to the New Covenant.

[16] Nelson (1969) 153 cites Luther's condemnation of suretyship as un-Christian. The economic history is complex. Luther at first condemned usury, but later altered his position. Shakespeare's choice of *mise en scène* is pertinent: Venetian fraternities made free lending a condition of membership, only introducing usury (at low interest) in the sixteenth century. See Bossy (1985) 61, 77 ff; Ferber (1990) 461, 459–62; Braudel (1982) 438.

because he is like those Biblical publicans (Matthew 5: 47) who salute
only their own friends.[17] Shylock is usually discussed in relation to
Antonio's sacrifice. But Shylock has a sacrifice, and a plot, of his own.
He could be seen as a sharp business man enforcing a bond that,
allowing for metaphor, is only a little more rigorous than some Elizabethans would have approved.[18] His revenge gets as far as it does
because the authorities worry about Venice's credit, if the bond is not
honoured. They can find no way of saving Antonio, since in effect
Shylock's law is theirs too.[19] He comes close to being a revenge
hero. He might have exposed the horrors of the new business world
of unregulated contracts[20] more heroically, however, if he had kept his
'oath in heaven' (IV. i. 228). What if he had taken, as we say, his pound
of flesh? In a good production, much will hang in the balance as
Shylock hesitates—'Why doth the Jew pause?' But in the event he
breaks his oath. Unable to cut Antonio's flesh without spilling blood
and so incurring the death penalty, he shrinks from performance of his
covenant, which is impossible without self-sacrifice.[21] W. H. Auden, in
what A. D. Nuttall calls 'one of the most brilliant critical remarks of the
century', gets it exactly wrong when he writes that Shylock 'did, in fact,
hazard all for the sake of destroying the enemy he hated'.[22] Shylock is
not prepared to sacrifice his life, as Antonio is.

Michael Ferber is right, then, to reject Terry Eagleton's idea of a
Shylock with more respect for the law than Portia, and impelled to
expose Venetian law as a sham.[23] But it will not do to rule out Eagleton's
view on the ground that it does not fit with the overall meaning of the
play's unified plot—its 'sequence of virtual actions unfolding in time
before a real audience'.[24] Elizabethans were used to multiple plots with
multiple meanings, and would have been quite prepared to consider
Shylock's perspective. It may well have had for them, however, a

[17] Lewalski (1962) 330–1.
[18] On possible English referents for Shylock, see Ferber (1990), esp. 444–5.
[19] *Pace* Eagleton (1986) 37, Venice to preserve its credit is quite prepared to sacrifice
Antonio.
[20] Ferber (1990) 457–8.
[21] Leviticus 17: 10–16 requires separation of flesh and blood in sacrifice: Ferber (1990) 463.
[22] Auden (1963) 235; Nuttall (1983) 127: 'W. H. Auden in one of the most brilliant critical
remarks of the century observed that this requirement [to give and hazard all] is met by two
people in the play, neither of whom is Bassanio'. In fact only Antonio hazards his life.
[23] Ferber (1990) 461. On Marxist interpretations by Nerlich, Eagleton, Greenblatt and
others, see ibid. 457 ff.
[24] Ferber (1990) 462.

more religious point: namely, the impossibility of satisfying the law, and the need for grace. 'Is this the law?' exclaims Shylock. When the Duke forces Shylock to give away all he has (in literal enactment of Luke 18: 22), he makes the Jew a fuller practitioner of the New Covenant than the Venetian Christians themselves—a characteristically Shakespearean outcome, barbed and thought-provoking.

In such ways, Shakespearean comedy is a mosaic of parts, realistic or romantic, which may have tenuous motivational or causal connection at a narrative level. The overall coherence lies in a pattern of ideas, rather than in naturalistic realism.

II

Perhaps true of the comedies, it may be argued; but some of the major tragedies are more naturalistic. In *Macbeth*, or *Othello*, all plots are tributaries of the main stream; 'causes are all contained';[25] and the protagonist's motivation is continuous and detailed. Already in the cinquecento, theorists focused on tragedy their calls for unified mimesis. Even in England, continuity was obligatory by the end of the seventeenth century, just as artists (in Shaftesbury's view) were 'debarred the taking advantage from any other action than what is immediately present'.[26] From chronological continuity, it is a short journey to novelistic motivation—which more distinctly originates in the tragic art of Richardson than in the comic art of Fielding. The route is a familiar one: from Romantic subjectifying of *Hamlet* (in 1713 William Guthrie thought Hamlet spoke the language 'of the human heart'[27]), to A. C. Bradley's separation of character from plot, to Freud and Ernest Jones. Hamlet's delays must have psychological causes, discoverable through sufficiently minute analysis.[28] This is far from ridiculous. Hamlet displays simulated or actual symptoms of melancholy, or depression, as identified by Renaissance authorities. His vituperation, his histrionism, his seeing of ghosts: all these were melancholy symptoms.[29] He displays enough symptoms, indeed, to suggest

---

[25] Kastan (1982) 26.

[26] Cooper (1713): reprinted Holt (1958) 2. 246.

[27] e.g. Wiggins (1994) 209.

[28] ibid. 213.

[29] Colie (1974) 211. For ghosts as a melancholic symptom, see R. Burton, *Anatomy of Melancholy* I. ii. 1. ii, cit. Dodsworth (1985) 50; Aubrey (1898) ii. 266; (1972) 460.

'anatomy', or epitome, rather than case study: some of his complexity comes from Shakespeare's amalgamating distinct melancholic types (or else from Hamlet's indiscriminate drawing on his reading of psychology).[30] And it is true that motivation abounds in *Hamlet*. That is not quite the same, though, as continuous motivation throughout the play. The Renaissance theatre had no continuity girl. Psychological motivation was less relentlessly expected, when actions could be moral or spiritual.

Romantic focus on expressive language was succeeded by two centuries of criticism devoted to construing psychological motives, sometimes for moral actions that had none. Well may Howard Felperin say 'we half-perceive and half-create Falstaff'.[31] For we invent streams of consciousness like our own—or like those in novels. So Felperin, Graham Bradshaw, and others have done a service by showing that Shakespeare constructs characters on archaic armatures, or as types, and afterwards plasters them with complications and deviations—as if Hamlet were not so much like a real-life revenger as unlike the revenger of the ur-*Hamlet*.[32] Neverthless A. D. Nuttall's view, or Arthur Kirsch's, seems preferable: that Hamlet is drawn from life. Only, to appreciate Shakespeare's realism, one needs perpetually to adjust to his assumptive world (to use the psychologists' convenient term). Modern assumptions are so strong as to be easily confused with nature herself. And when that happens, any departure from the uniformity of 'nature' (like the double time-scheme in *Othello*) is so disconcerting that it calls all in doubt.[33]

Yet such anomalies are the rule, not the exception. *Hamlet*, too, has multiple time-schemes, as one can find by asking, with Barbara Everett, how young the young prince is. Hamlet changes, without corresponding lapse of fictive time, from the undergraduate age (somewhere between sixteen and twenty-three) to the politically dangerous near-maturity of thirty. (The gravedigger entered his trade 'that very day that young Hamlet was born . . . thirty years'.)[34] Hamlet's age is not ambiguous;

---

[30] As Colie (1974) 210 suggests.

[31] Felperin (1977) 66.

[32] See Felperin (1977) *passim*; Empson (1986) 86 etc.

[33] On this so-called double time-scheme, see Ridley (1958) lxvii–lxx.

[34] V. i. 143, 157. Throughout, *Hamlet* references are to the text in Jenkins (1982). Questions of textual revision are largely passed over, since they do not alter the fact that multiple perspectives were allowed to remain in late versions of the play. See Everett (1989) 19–20. For documentation, see Jenkins's Long Note to V. i. 139–57. Jones (1971) 80 ff proposes a two-part structure, corresponding to the two temporal phases.

rather does he age during his sea voyage in a quantum leap—'jumping o'er times'[35] or stages of life. The representation comprises two 'takes', from distinct chronological viewpoints, which are juxtaposed without any attempt to reconcile them within a single temporal frame. (One might compare the compressed narrative of many Renaissance pictures.) We are given two perspectives of Hamlet, or two Hamlets, one young and another mature. In the second perspective, the Ghost—already silenced by the oaths of Act I—has disappeared altogether as a public, debatable phenomenon. Deutero-Hamlet may be said to have introjected the Ghost, abandoning scepticism and suspicion.[36] He is now hardened to honourable revenge, unlike the hesitant, perplexed young Hamlet.[37] Such multiple perspectives must surely figure in a critical account, even if they usually pass unnoticed in the theatre.

It seems appropriate to broach the subject of mimesis on this occasion, since Shakespearean tragedy early achieved great triumphs of realism. In *Hamlet*, as early critics observed, we seem to see nature herself.[38] The speeches, movingly natural, appear to voice a human consciousness directly. And Hamlet's censorious advice to the players—surely it is a manifesto of naturalism, the basis of Shakespeare's own art?—except that that would put it under the head of art rather than nature. 'Hold, as 'twere the mirror up to nature': surely the actors are to make themselves virtual images of life? But the Elizabethans had no large mirrors like ours; and Hamlet tells the actors to hold the mirror, not appear in it.[39] He means, in short, a moral mirror, in which audiences may see themselves—a mirror 'To show Virtue her feature, Scorn her own image'. This verse, by the way, invites a *distinctio*.[40] Virtue and Scorn are now rightly regarded as opposites; but the aristocratic Hamlet (though not Shakespeare) may well mean them as synonyms. Virtue may be *virtus*, valour or the inward aspect of honour; Scorn may be *sdegno*, noble disdain for everything base.

[35] Shakespeare, *Henry V*, Prol. 29.

[36] Cf. Alexander (1971) 50.

[37] See Dodsworth (1985) 236, 252, 264 against the notion that the deutero-Hamlet is regenerate or superior.

[38] Although there would soon be more methodically uniform examples in Beaumont and Fletcher; cf. Felperin (1977) 60. On eighteenth-century appreciation of the natural in Shakespeare, see Nuttall (1983) 99–100.

[39] Frye (1984) 5. On the implications of the mirror, see Grabes (1982) 102–3. Felperin (1977) 45–6 transfers the demand for 'lifelike illusion' to the passage following ('the very age and body of the time his form and pressure'), which however will not bear that sense.

[40] On this strategic figure, see Skinner (1994).

Hamlet clearly conceives honour as requiring disdain. He scorns his servants ('I am most dreadfully attended': II. ii. 369); he scorns the courtier Osric ('’Tis a chuff [churl]': V. ii. 88–9); he scorns Polonius; he scorns Rosencrantz and Guildenstern ('baser natures': V. ii. 60); he scorns the players; and he scorns Ophelia, Gertrude, and women generally. He even scorns those who write legibly (another 'baseness': V. ii. 34).[41]

If the speeches in *Hamlet* are natural, the soliloquies are positive touchstones of the natural, direct expressions of Hamlet's thoughts. Of the fourth soliloquy ('To be or not to be': III. i. 56–88) Harry Levin writes 'we are permitted to share the stream of [Hamlet's] consciousness'.[42] Yet, marvellously eloquent as the speech is, it lacks immediate motivation. The audience last saw Hamlet eagerly planning to put on *The Murder of Gonzago*, the mousetrap to catch Claudius's soul; they have no reason to expect thoughts of suicide.[43] Among attempts to supply motives, Levin, working on old Freudian assumptions, diagnoses a 'death-wish'; Philip Edwards finds a pessimistic sense of the impossibility of reform; Harold Jenkins, a vision of total depravity; Kay Stanton, improbably, a 'performance' by Hamlet (to divert the eavesdroppers' attention from his *Gonzago* plan).[44] Others cut the Gordian knot by moving the soliloquy elsewhere.[45] It is not felt to belong to the same cause-effect sequence with the scene before and after.[46]

Many feel it as direct address (a more common form of dramatic discourse before proscenium arches framed off the fictive world[47]): a *parodos* speech in the dramatist's own person: an archaic convention: an example of what Levin Schücking called 'primitive devices'.[48] For it

---

[41] *Scorn* can be taken as 'objects of scorn': Jenkins (1982). For disdain as a basis for moral action, cf. Bruno's *Degli Eroici Furori* (1570), cit. Alexander (1971) 65, and see Fowler (1964) 108, 110, 112–13. On Hamlet's standing on rank, dispensing with degree only when it suits, see Dodsworth (1985) 105–6, 154, *et passim*. For a good guide on the honour code, see Dodsworth (1985), esp. ch. 1, with refs.; also Empson (1986) 118 ff; Quint (1992*b*).

[42] Levin (1959) 68.

[43] Clemen (1987) 133 has to admit that here 'the dovetailing with the dramatic action is less apparent'.

[44] Levin (1959) 70; Jenkins (1982) 152; Stanton (1994) 175.

[45] Edwards (1985) 25–7. On the placing of the speech, see Dodsworth (1985) 109.

[46] Dodsworth (1985) 94 strains to find a single sequence.

[47] Bradbrook (1952) 111.

[48] Cit. Clemen (1964) 26 n. 9. Nuttall (1983) 145 discusses the German tradition Levin Schücking represents. On the actor as rhetorician, cf. Burns (1990) 10. Rose (1985) 111–12 needlessly invokes Freud's idea of plays depending on 'the neurotic in the spectator' and 'crossing over the boundaries between onstage and offstage'.

is a general meditation, only broadly appropriate to the immediate circumstances. 'The insolence of office' is hardly a scorn Hamlet has to bear; far from suffering 'pangs of disprised love', he is about to inflict them on Ophelia; and not all the 'thousand natural shocks/ That flesh is heir to' have shocked *him*. The perspective is as general as that of the Gravedigger's cogitation (which similarly extends to a whole community of sinners—lords, lawyers, tanners, ladies, jesters). It is as Everyman, elsewhere, that Hamlet admits to being an arrant knave (although he is complacent in the knowledge of being 'indifferent honest'); it is as Everyman that he shares the universal melancholy anatomised by Burton.[49]

This is not to say, with Edward Burns, that Hamlet's 'To be or not to be' speech is *un*motivated,[50] a *declamatio* or essay like Seneca's, say, or St Augustine's, ordered rhetorically rather than psychologically.[51] Indeed, Hamlet might say with Montaigne 'I only speak others in order better to speak myself'.[52] For one thing, the speech follows a specific, dichotomising method: 'To die—to sleep/ No more [sc. no more than a sleep]'; and later 'To die, to sleep;/ To sleep, perchance to dream.' Levin shrewdly identifies this method as Ramist; one may add that Ramist rhetoric was in England a mark of militant Protestantism.[53] The monologue is apt, then, to a student from Wittenberg, the home of scepticism, reform, Lutheran Protestantism in religion and 'mixed Ramism' in rhetoric.[54] In its highly theoretic generalising about human-kind, the speech suits Hamlet's youth and his evasion of simple duty.[55] Its extremity may suggest the 'beleaguered sanity' characteristic of

---

[49] III. i. 122–30; cf. Alexander (1971) 27, 60. Hamlet may however *think* of himself as suffering all this by a sort of legal fiction: cf. Dodsworth (1985) 158.

[50] Burns (1990) 147.

[51] Clemen (1964) 23 remarks its unusual reflectiveness; cf. Edwards (1985) ('extraordinary'). The soliloquy, and much else in *Hamlet*, owes a debt to St Augustine's study of the infirm will in *Confessions* VIII. ix–x. There may also be an echo of Petrarch's assurance that the 'arrows of fortune' cannot touch the citadel of mind, unless will opens the gates: *Fam. Epist.* XVIII. xv.

[52] Montaigne, *Essays* I. xxvi.

[53] Levin (1959) 69. See Miller (1939); Seaton (1950) xi; Ong (1958); Shuger (1988) Index s.v. Ramism, Puritan, esp. 96; and the Ramist analysis of Sir Philip Sidney's *Apology* by his secretary William Temple: Webster (1984).

[54] Wittenberg was associated with both Martin Luther and Philip Melanchthon. For mixed or Philippo-Ramism, Melanchthon's systematic version of Ramism, see Ong (1958) 298–9; Howell (1956). Jenkins (1982) 436 and Brandes (1902) 358 take the reference as local colour: it was common for Danes to go for education to Wittenberg.

[55] Everett (1989) 22.

stoicism's contained passions.[56] And it is thematically apt, in that it sets out the play's central issue—in the central of seven soliloquies—the choice between responsibility and evasion, between being and not being, between aggressive action and passive submission. (Alternatives developed separately in the perspectives of Laertes and Ophelia, according to the convention of genealogical allegory whereby siblings stand for complementary or contrasting effects.)[57] The malcontent diatribe is also apt, in that it amounts to a *contemptus mundi* removing any justification for ever avoiding a duty, no matter how dangerous. The monologue is on a different scale, however, from the rest of the scene. It dramatises the *longue durée*, as it were, of Hamlet's consciousness of evasion. Its perspective is more distant, if not exactly detached.[58] Yet, like Pyrrhus's speech, it is indispensable. No less indispensable than, say, Bellini's landscape parergon in the throne of his Pesaro *Coronation of the Virgin*, or insets in the picture-within-a-picture genre, or the play within the play.[59] Nigel Alexander has shown how closely relevant such elements as Pyrrhus's speech are. My aim is to generalise this, arguing that such apparently artificial digressions come within the orbit of Renaissance realism.

Others of Shakespeare's soliloquies similarly disappoint modern expectations of a continuously maintained viewpoint.[60] 'Oh what a rogue and peasant slave am I' (II. ii. 575–673) follows closely enough after the weeping Player's compassion for Hecuba—a compassion Hamlet himself lacks. But then (again convincingly) Hamlet thinks of a plan—'I'll have these players/ Play something like the murder of my father' (590–1)—which is the very plan he put into effect forty lines earlier (at 531–6). The soliloquy thus resembles his stream of consciousness, but not consciousness of the same time when it is voiced. Here Muriel Bradbrook and Wolfgang Clemen fall back on the non-explanation of a special archaic convention, retrospectively explanatory direct address.[61] And there is talk of textual inconsistency. Already in

---

[56] Cf. Nuttall (1983) 103, 107.

[57] Cf. Alexander (1971) 75, 121; Backman (1991).

[58] For arguments against detachment here, see Dodsworth (1985) 108; elsewhere, however, Hamlet often affects a spurious aristocratic detachment; see ibid. 263.

[59] 'Repetition, discontinuity and excess . . . run right through the fabric of the play': Rose (1985) 117. Cf. Burns (1990) 145–6 on the difficulty of putting Ophelia's report of Hamlet's 'down-gyved' state into a cause-effect sequence.

[60] Similarly the second soliloquy compresses several states of consciousness: Fowler (1987) 79.

[61] Clemen (1964) 14.

1935, however, J. Dover Wilson suggested that the soliloquy recapitulates Hamlet's earlier emotions, and is 'a dramatic reflection of what has already taken place'.[62] This gives us our clue. The earlier, external representation shows the putting of the plan in motion; the later voices the vague internal planning that achieved specificity in enactment. Again, two distinct versions of the same action. Such redundancy is sometimes put down to incomplete revision. But this explanation (or explaining away) may often be unnecessary. Multiple, paratactic representations of the same action are normal in Elizabethan drama, as in Renaissance picturing.[63]

III

Questions about mimesis have often centred on Hamlet's problematic character. From the time of William Richardson (1743–1814), those identifying with Hamlet—and who has not done that?—have had difficulties with his cruelty, aggression, and especially his wish to kill Claudius in a state of mortal sin (Dr Johnson called this 'too horrible to be read or to be uttered'). Hazlitt, Levin, George Hunter, Nuttall and others have followed Richardson in supposing, subtly, that Hamlet's holding back in the prayer scene results from 'amiable sensibility'.[64] The malicious reason he expresses for delay must be rationalisation, since 'nothing in the whole character . . . justifies such savage enormity'. Hamlet deceives himself, since he is ashamed of his moral scruples (his true reason, or excuse, for inaction).[65] Without disagreeing with Hunter that Hamlet's sympathetically hesitating nature is 'fully human',[66] one is struck by how often such rescuing of Hamlet's amiability generates increasingly speculative interiorisation.[67] Yet all these idealising efforts have scarcely irradiated Hamlet's obscure irresolution. (Martin Dodsworth seems nearer the mark in detecting culpable evasion of responsibility.) And psychoanalytic criticism, while admittedly raising more

---

[62] Wilson (1935) 142n.

[63] Cf. Dodsworth (1985) 163–6 on double representation in the dumb show and the Gonzago play.

[64] Richardson: Vickers (1974–81) 5. 159; Hazlitt (1902) 234; Levin (1959) 34; Nuttall (1983) 107. On eighteenth-century censure of Hamlet, see also Prosser (1967) 244 ff.

[65] These 'would expose him . . . to censure': Richardson, reprinted in Vickers (1974–81) 6. 365–8.

[66] Hunter (1963) 98.

[67] Cf. de Grazia (1991) Afterword, esp. 223 ff.

metaphysical questions, has supplied so many answers to them that one concludes they are not answerable. Is Hamlet an Oedipal father-hater perplexed to find his new rival a fellow-father-killer? Does Hamlet's femininity identify passively with Gertrude's?[68] (One suspects that family relations may have been a good deal different in an age when well-born infants seldom saw their mothers.) So many psychological inferences have been invented that fainthearted poststructuralists despair of a coherent protagonist; announcing that there is no reality, no 'essential Hamlet', behind his show.[69] But this capitulation hardly satisfies.[70] Constructive inference needs to be sustained; although hopefully with more thought for relevance to pre-novelistic conditions.

The old question why Hamlet delays is not exclusively one of character; at times, indeed, delay seems a device to allow prolonged analysis of honourable duty.[71] The duty to revenge is seldom questioned very deeply in revenge tragedy; and some critics accept it as par for the Jacobean course.[72] Yet revenge is anything but Christian.[73] And Shakespeare's profound realism examines the call to requite wrong more searchingly than to accept repetition of the wrong as a duty. In particular, a distinction between private revenge and civil retribution emerges as crucial.[74] Not least for a prince, honour itself—the displaced chivalric ethic of an outworn ancestral order—had grown problematic.[75] Hamlet is torn between disagreeable alternatives: on one hand public confrontation, challenge and perhaps insurrection; on the other, individual heroic agency. Significantly, the Ghost has for Horatio a political explanation, whereas Hamlet avoids any political role.[76] After the inset play (which might have been an opportunity for public initiatives), deutero-Hamlet's thoughts of revenge take on an increasingly private, malicious character.[77] The change is emblemised by the Ghost's third appearance, to Hamlet alone, in a private closet. He

---

[68] Jones (1955) 88, 106, cit. Rose (1985) 113.

[69] e.g. de Grazia (1991) 224–5; Belsey (1985) 50.

[70] Cf. Nuttall (1988) 59.

[71] As Alexander (1971) 10. On the ambiguity of the Ghost's 'call to honour', and Hamlet's unpreparedness for it, see Dodsworth (1985) *passim*.

[72] Levin (1959) 35; Cruttwell (1963) 118 ff.; Alexander (1971) 189–90.

[73] As Alexander (1971) rightly stresses. Cf. Montaigne, *Essays* II. xi, 'Of Cruelty'.

[74] Cf. Kirsch (1993) 113–14.

[75] As Mousley (1994) 79 suggests, overstressing Hamlet's conscious scepticism. For the broad sense revenge might have in the sixteenth century, see Dodsworth (1985) 63.

[76] e.g. I. i. 83–4; cf. Robson (1975) 20; Dodsworth (1985) 49; Battenhouse (1969) 246. On Hamlet's eventual choice of private revenge, see Bowers (1989) 96; Nuttall (1988) 61.

[77] *Pace* Bowers (1989); cf. Prosser (1967) 199.

appears 'in his nightgown', lacking the moral armour of the public appearances on the Platform, when he was visible to Horatio and the others.[78]

Much turns on the Ghost's authority. The challenge of the dead is that of honour, of duty to an inherited, ancestral ethic. But is the voice of honour to be obeyed without question? Is there a divine commission to revenge—an appointment, even, as 'scourge and minister'? All this is left realistically uncertain. And when Hamlet ceases to question it, when he becomes a 'true believer', a certain moral coarsening sets in. Nevertheless, Shakespeare does so much to make the Ghost's visitations portentous, that they acquire an authoritative significance, perilous to ignore. Honour must be satisfied. The generalising application seems inescapably universal: everyone is given, like Hamlet, an absolute obligation to reform the world ('born to set it right'). In this very broad sense, Hamlet's delaying needs no explanation. He delays as culpably as everyone else, leaving undone those things which he ought to have done. (In 1713, interestingly, Guthrie could still perceive Hamlet as an Everyman, speaking 'the real language of mankind, of its highest to its lowest order'.)

Hamlet's delay is sometimes attributed to mental disturbance. But, as Arthur Kirsch reminds us, 'Hamlet is always conscious of the manic roles he plays and is always lucid with Horatio'.[79] If Hamlet is continuously rational, though, his apologies to Laertes for the distraction with which he is 'punished' invite unpleasant inferences. Assuming he was only ever 'mad in craft' (III. iv. 187), with north-north-west madness, his apologies must be similarly Machiavellian. Patrick Cruttwell shrewdly remarks that Hamlet's madness is most emphasised by those who wish to avoid confessing his faults.[80] Perhaps his protean madness may partly be explicable in terms of multiple perspectives corresponding with different irrational responses to the rational madness of society. His irrationality can be youth's subversive wildness,[81] careful evasiveness ('crafty madness keeps aloof', III. i. 8), licence for aggressive truth-telling (as in Marston's satiric malcontents and the Amleth of Saxo's *Danish History*), or simply a refuge in which to

---

[78] For the doffing of armour as implying a dangerous moral fluidity, cf. Spenser, *The Faerie Queene*, I. vii. 2 (also VI. iii. 7 etc.), discussed in Leslie (1983) 126.
[79] Cf. Kirsch (1990) 33.
[80] Cruttwell (1963) 114; cf. Alexander (1971) 27, 'What alienates Hamlet from us is his inhumanity.'
[81] Cf. Everett (1989) 22.

hide from responsibility.[82] And, of course, with continued pressure, there is also the threat of really insane sanity like that of Kohlhaas in Kleist's powerful story. To Polonius, Hamlet is insolent in a way once taboo with seniors, even if socially inferior. To Rosencrantz and Guildenstern he is as deviously manipulative, taking advantage of inconsequentiality, perhaps, to turn a casual question about recorder-playing into sudden accusation. Hamlet is a chameleon. Or, as W. S. Gilbert puts it in his *Rosencrantz and Guildenstern* libretto,

> Some men hold
> That he's the sanest, far, of all sane men —
> Some that he's really sane, but shamming mad —
> Some that he's really mad, but shamming sane —
> Some that he will be mad, some that he *was* —
> Some that he couldn't be. But on the whole
> (As far as I can make out what they mean)
> The favourite theory's somewhat like this:
> Hamlet is idiotically sane
> With lucid intervals of lunacy.[83]

Undoubtedly 'one man in his time plays many parts'. Nevertheless to regard Hamlet as a walking contradiction would be simplistic. Allowing for subclinical instability and occasional losses of control ('passions'),[84] his moods vary intelligibly enough with his interlocutors.

IV

Consider the nunnery scene, Hamlet and Ophelia's first meeting on stage. The dutiful daughter, who is being used to test Hamlet's disposition, returns his love tokens. But Hamlet says — with the thoughtlessness of recently acquired honesty — 'I never gave you aught' (III. i. 96). After a few clever, sharp words, he makes inadequate amends: 'I did love you once' (III. i. 115); yet within four lines he takes even that away: Ophelia should never have believed his vows — 'I loved you not'. And he launches defensively into misogynistic diatribe.[85] Faced with these baffling vacillations, some follow Dover Wilson in supposing

---

[82] Cf. Dodsworth (1985) 86.

[83] Gilbert (1982) 176.

[84] On the extent of Hamlet's madness, see Dodsworth (1985), e.g. 156.

[85] This aggressiveness continues, as V. i. 190 ff. shows.

Hamlet aware of eavesdroppers.[86] Many invent previous erotic passages. Salvador de Madariaga, like some earlier German critics, thought Ophelia was Hamlet's mistress; Kay Stanton imagines Hamlet's visit to Ophelia's closet as a scene of rape—his doublet was not unbraced for nothing; and even Eleanor Prosser visualises the leave-taking of a lover too sensitive to be a trifler.[87] Harold Goddard, in a way more sceptical, takes the entire visit to be Ophelia's invention; perhaps he remembers Goethe's percipient remark that Hamlet's feeling is 'without conspicuous passion'.[88] Others invent various acceptable emotions explaining Hamlet's cruelty in the nunnery scene. He is ending a relationship that must now lead to suffering.[89] Or, he is voicing disgust at Gertrude: 'I loved you not' means 'there is no such thing as pure love'.[90] Or, Ophelia has taken his love too seriously; he realises he has never been in love as she is. Faced by honest love, he is guiltily incoherent: his vacillation expresses faltering commitment.[91] Or (a plea of self-defence), he would rather reject than be rejected. Or (applying Felperin's genetic theory), Hamlet falls short of the revenger's role, and turns to the reformer's—to *sermo*, to the satiric, misogynistic discourse of Wittenberg.[92] But it is useless. We are like eavesdroppers ourselves, unable to make sense of what we hear. Even Bradley, who carried motive-hunting as far as anyone, confesses its futility here: 'What is pretence, and what sincerity, appears to me an insoluble problem'.[93]

Instead of immediately construing motives that exculpate Hamlet, one might consider what other perspectives Shakespeare has given of Hamlet's love. Ophelia, reporting his visit to her closet, describes him as mad with love (II. i. 85–6). But her wishful view is surely undercut by dramatic irony. The audience recognises Hamlet's 'wildness' as simulated, his disordered dress as antic costume; being prompted to

[86] The text counts against this speculation, as the best recent editors, Harold Jenkins and Philip Edwards, agree.

[87] Madariaga (1948) 64; Stanton (1994) 168; Prosser (1967) 130, 146. Everett (1989) 31 more subtly suggests that Ophelia's madness takes the form of *believing* she has been 'brutally seduced'; but see Empson (1986) 108.

[88] Goddard (1946) 462–74; Gervinus (1883) 579.

[89] Hazlitt (1902) 236 obscurely argues that Hamlet could not 'wound her mind by explaining the cause of his alienation'.

[90] Cf. Burns (1990) 145: the diatribe has little to do with Ophelia herself.

[91] Cf. Alexander (1971) 112.

[92] On the composition of role from fictional ingredients, see Felperin (1977) 55–61, Dodsworth (1985) 252.

[93] Bradley (1920) 157–8. The insolubility has continued to influence acting: Ian McKellen's style consistently seeks to validate indeterminacy: cf. Hodgdon (1994) 263, 270.

this recognition by an introjected memory of the Ghost in Hamlet's look—Ophelia describes him looking 'As if he had been loosed out of hell/ To speak of horrors'.[94] He is not thinking of her.

Then, there is the love-letter, which to Polonius proves Hamlet to be in love. This letter carries the weight (considerable in that age) of documentary evidence:

> Doubt thou the stars are fire,
> Doubt that the sun doth move,
> Doubt truth to be a liar,
> But never doubt I love. (II. ii. 115–18)

Jenkins is alert to a danger here of insincerity: 'Since each of the poem's first two lines assumes the certainty of what had now begun to be doubted, there is an irony of which Shakespeare (though not, I take it, Hamlet) must have been aware.' But Hamlet must have meant the irony. He cannot for a moment have been unaware of the controversies besetting the sun's motion, for his university was famously in the forefront of astronomical thought. The junior mathematical professor at Wittenberg was George Joachim Rheticus himself; while the senior professor was none other than Erasmus Rheinhold, foremost astronomer of the century after Copernicus.[95] In short, Hamlet's love letter is malapert, as flip as its facile parody of poetic conventions might suggest.[96] Beneath its frivolity there is a disagreeable suggestion of evasiveness, of casual, patronising over-confidence. Its only sign of grace is the compunction of its breaking off—unless that, too, is a trick of languid offhandedness. Hamlet and Ophelia, in fact, have very different conceptions of the love that divides them—hers the true nobility of generous, virtuous love, his the lordliness that does honour by loving.[97] Ophelia, we recall, admits Hamlet never promised marriage, but only gave 'countenance' to his love speeches 'With *almost* all the holy vows of heaven'.[98]

---

[94] II. i. 83. Cf. Alexander (1971) 129.

[95] Rheticus, an enthusiastic disciple of Copernicus, did much to assist the publication of the Copernican hypothesis by his *Narratio Prima* (1540); and Rheinhold compiled the first Copernican tables. Rheticus's edition of Sacrobosco was printed at Wittenberg, as was one of Copernicus's mathematical works. Other scientific luminaries there included Johannes Fleischer (optics and astronomy); and Michael Neander (medicine and astronomy).

[96] Cf. Dodsworth (1985) 155: 'innocently ludicrous sophistication'. Polonius's introduction of his reading ('I will be faithful': II. ii. 114) already introduces the notion of trust.

[97] On the distinction between *vera nobilitas* and merely ancestral nobility, a favourite theme in Jonson, see McCanles (1992).

[98] I. iii. 114 (my italics).

There is an additional viewpoint in the nunnery scene itself. Words are heard as well as spoken; and Ophelia *hears* Hamlet say 'I did love you . . . I loved you not'. What he means by this *correctio* or reformulation is reserved to his private consciousness (in which, possibly, he never gives Ophelia much thought).[99] What stands out for the audience is the words' painful impact on Ophelia. They are as relevant to her consciousness as to his; conveying, as they do, the contradictory feelings of rejected, 'disprised love'. Poor Ophelia has herself become uncertain about the mutual love her little intrigue was to prove (III. i. 39). The words mime *her* uncertainty, although Hamlet speaks them.

This reflexiveness appears in other ways too. Hamlet and Ophelia are both excessively attached to a parent; and each suffers 'distraction'. It is not exactly that Ophelia's 'real madness punishes the feigned insanity of Hamlet, which gave the first shock to her mind'.[100] In her image, rather, we see the morbid potential of Hamlet's irrationality. Their resemblances have been attributed to a 'multiple focus casting attention on Ophelia' and other characters 'as well as the protagonist'.[101] But the reverse seems nearer the truth: the multiple foci are all on aspects of the protagonist. What they all reflect is Hamlet's experience, and, through his, Everyman's and Everywoman's.[102]

V

The mirroring extends to details. Both Hamlet and Ophelia are given to carrying books, as critics have noticed. Attention to such material viewpoints has led to considerable advances in Shakespeare criticism.[103] Previously, exclusive concentration on verbal mimesis induced neglect of indirect, dispersed characterisation such as Warren Ginsberg has traced in ancient literature.[104] For one has to imagine, before our spectator realism, a realism more participatory, engaging the emotions

---

[99] On Hamlet's total silence about Ophelia to others, not to be explained in theatrical terms as concentration of focus, see Bradley (1920) 154, 158; he is not prepared, however, to think of the prince as having taken advantage of his rank.

[100] Gervinus (1883) 581.

[101] French (1992) 109.

[102] But see Showalter (1985) 113, where she objects to Lacan's treating Ophelia as an aspect of Hamlet.

[103] e.g. Alexander (1971), Doebler (1974), Dessen (1984), Manning (1994).

[104] Ginsberg (1983); cf. Dessen (1984).

in a world less externalised. When Hamlet enters 'reading on a book',[105] the book is not only an appropriate accessory for a scholar: it characterises him. And when he swears that the Ghost's 'command-ment all alone shall live/ Within the book and volume of my brain' (I. v. 102–3), one may guess that the actor carried Hamlet's figurative tablets literally, thus supporting Alexander's connection of Hamlet's 'word' (or motto) with the art of memory.[106] For, as Cesare Ripa explains, a book is Memory's attribute—her memory-prompt.[107] Frances Yates's white magic has rather obscured the fact that artificial memory was a religious discipline, designed to form the soul through meditation.[108] Hamlet's word 'adieu, adieu, remember me', besides referring to the sacred obligation imposed by the Ghost, echoes the Eucharist's memor-ial, 'do this in remembrance of me'. Yet in the same breath Hamlet speaks of forgetting:

> Remember thee?
> Yea, from the table of my memory
> I'll wipe away all trivial fond [foolish] records,
> All saws of books, all forms, all pressures past
> [impressions on his memory]
> That youth and observation copied there (I. v. 97–101)

This must have been deeply shocking to a generation for whom the book was a symbol of devout Protestantism, appearing as such in countless sepulchral monuments.[109] In effect Hamlet's soon-broken promise is to forget all religion and tradition: to remember only revenge.[110] He claims to prefer the sword of violence to the political, persuasive book.[111] And the passage may seem still more insistently

---

[105] II. ii. 167 Folio s. d.

[106] Dessen (1984) 67–8, 171n. 15; Alexander (1971) 47.

[107] Ripa (1976) 335–6. When Polonius accosts Hamlet when reading (II. ii. 168–71), another book emblem may be evoked: Whitney (1586) 171 ('study is useless without practice').

[108] See, e.g. Carruthers (1990).

[109] See Mowl (1993) 31.

[110] Hamlet is not unaware, then, that memory's recollection counts against revenge, as Alexander (1971) 117 asserts. Mousley (1994) 71 sees an act of simplifying; Cruttwell (1963) 118 an act of forgetting.

[111] Since Hamlet's sword is probably unsheathed continuously from I. iv. 85 to I. v. 154, Shakespeare may also allude to a familiar emblem picturing a king (or Hercules his type) with book and sword, to signify that 'the ideal king masters both skill in arms and knowledge of liberal arts' (Wither (1635) I. xxxii), or that 'eloquence is better than strength' (le Fèvre (1536) 93: Alciati (1985) clxxxi).

overdetermined, still sharper in ironic challenges, if one recalls the VINDICTA DIVINA book emblem.[112] 'Vengeance is mine, saith the Lord.'

In the nunnery scene, Ophelia's book is similarly eloquent. She carries it to 'colour' her 'loneliness . . . with devotion's visage' (III. i. 45–6): to suggest 'orisons'. Hamlet, perhaps deceived, begs 'in thy orisons/ Be all my sins remembered' (III. i. 89–90). But, beneath its false appearance, Ophelia's book is a book of memory, too — memory of their mutual vows of love. Silently, it puts Hamlet's subsequent moralising in a bad light.[113]

In such ways, any material object or action may have an aspect to add to the total representation. The most profound example, perhaps, is that of the inset play, brilliantly interpreted by Anne Barton and Nigel Alexander. Hamlet may claim to 'know not "seems"', and have 'that within which passes show'.[114] But as the plot unfolds, he is increasingly involved with show. He puts on an 'antic disposition'; he dresses for the part of prisoner of love (or of Denmark), with stockings 'down-gyved';[115] he recites a dramatic speech; and he organises the performance of a show-within-a-show-within-a-show. All these counter-shows have the implicit effect of suggesting that Hamlet knows (or comes to know) 'seems' only too well.[116] Illusion and false appearance are universal in the fallen world. Thus, the broken oaths in *The Murder of Gonzago* are Hamlet's too, to the extent that he spends time on theatricals — only tangentially relevant to his mission — instead of revenging. In the denouement, similarly, the ceremonious duel with its salutes of ordonnance completes the picture of Hamlet's ensnarement within the shows and customs of honour, the repetitive pattern of conflict that makes up fallen history.[117]

[112] See, e.g., Peacham (1612) 140: the divine wings of the emblem are appropriated at I. v. 29.

[113] On the book as Ophelia's devotion, see Lyons (1977) 61. Alexander (1971) 131 supposes a book of contemplation; but the text's insistence is on memory: the love tokens are 'remembrances' (III. i. 93).

[114] I. i. 76, 85. Often misinterpreted: e.g. Mousley (1994) 70 following Belsey; Potter (1991) 121; Burns (1990) 141, 154. 'That within' has little to do with 'essential subjectivity': Hamlet means he has real grief, not just its show — so Wiggins (1994) 215–16.

[115] Dessen (1984) 37.

[116] Cf. Weimann (1985) 288 ('Hamlet is both a product and, as it were, a producer of mimesis, a character performed in a role and one who himself performs and commissions a performance') and Wiggins (1994) 221 ('Hamlet must maintain an exterior persona that is wholly discontinuous with his inner self'). In *Doctor Faustus*, similarly, the middle scenes mime Faustus's frivolity: all he can think of to do with his powers is tricks.

[117] Hunter (1963) 107.

These are large perspectives; but lesser details may have their own aspects. When Hamlet stabs Polonius, the arras functions of course as a necessary hiding-place (although not an inevitable one: in Saxo the eavesdropper is under the rushes). And it is a deliberately superfluous detail serving the rhetoric of realism: Hans Knieper's tapestry workshop at Elsinore was famous.[118] Dessen suggests that symbolically the arras is 'a surface that prevents one from seeing the truth, . . . that epitomises the seeming world of Denmark' (tapestry was often symbolic, from its presenting figures and texts[119]); his Hamlet seeks truth under surface appearances. But a more relevant clue may be found in R. B. Graves's reminder that 'the overall illumination' of the Elizabethan stage encouraged 'a sense of continuity between . . . the actors and their background'.[120] Perhaps, then, the closet tapestry is to be interiorised. We recall how Spenser's Britomart gazes a long day at Busirane's erotic tapestries, while she orders her own chaste thoughts about love. And Francis Bacon quotes the observation 'that speech was like cloth of Arras, opened, and put abroad; whereby the imagery doth appear in figure; whereas in thoughts, they lie but as in packs'.[121] If tapestries were associated with words and thoughts, Hamlet's killing through one may suggest that his thoughts have indeed become bloody, his words aggressive to a fatal degree. This resonates with his resolution to 'speak daggers' (III. ii. 387) and Gertrude's cry 'these words like daggers enter in my ears' (III. iv. 95); strengthening the idea of a matricidal impulse.[122] Hamlet's emblematic insertion into his self-righteous text is intemperate violence—now the revenger's, now the reformer's, now the satirist's.[123] The incident, however indirect its mimesis may now seem, is plausibly realistic. Recognising such dispersed aspects of character, far from disintegrating Hamlet as an individual, helps to resynthesise his Renaissance subjectivity.

---

[118] See Heiberg (1988) 115.

[119] Dessen (1984) 151. Cf. *As You Like It*, III. ii. 273.

[120] cit. Dessen (1984) 77.

[121] Bacon (1985) 84, developing Plutarch, *Lives*, 'Themistocles': 'men's words did properly resemble the stories and imagery in a piece of arras: for both in the one and in the other, the goodly images of either of them are seen, when they are unfolded and laid open. Contrariwise they appear not, but are lost, when they are shut up, and close folded.'

[122] Mooted in French (1992) 104.

[123] On emblematic insertions in *Hamlet*, see Manning (1994). Cf. Mousley (1994) 73; and Prosser (1967) 199, on Hamlet's self-righteousness in the closet scene.

VI

Most often character was dispersed among personal surrogates. In *Hamlet*, these may be mythological, like the moral Hercules; historical, like the ruler-hero Julius Caesar;[124] or else contemporary, fictional people of Elsinore with characters of their own. Much as real princes were supposed to be mirrored in their courts,[125] Claudius's half-remorseful Machiavellianism is half-reflected in his unwitting *ficelles* Rosencrantz and Guildenstern. And, when Laertes' machismo is perverted by Claudius, his devious plot against Hamlet is a distorted reflection of the devious plots of his politique father. (Polonius makes deviousness so much a principle as to defend the family name by having his son accused of whoring—a tactic effectively revealing honour's double standard.) As for Hamlet himself, he is mirrored in Horatio his mentor, Laertes and Fortinbras his rivals for honour, the Ghost his chivalric self, and the First Player his compassionate self.[126] (Hamlet's compassion, being fictitious, is displaced onto an actor.) The First Player weeps for Hecuba as Hamlet cannot: a 'monstrous' disparity at which Hamlet exclaims, 'Had he the motive and the cue for passion/ That I have' (II. ii. 555–6). The occasion of the Player's tears is the important point in his speech when even Pyrrhus stops killing, arrested by Hecuba's piteousness; when an alternative to endless revenge is momentarily suggested.[127]

Hamlet's personal mirrors, although usually treated as thematic parallels, are more integral than that—surrogates, rather; 'parts' he plays; sides of his nature; exemplars or descriptions;[128] selfs or potential selfs of social existence. (Hotspur and Falstaff are comparably selfs of Prince Hal and his father.) One is reminded that St Augustine's analysis of irresolution posits that 'there are as many contrary natures as there are wills in someone beset by indecision'.[129] Moreover, Hamlet's character-mirrors add independent views of him to the main representation, additional perspectives. Mirrors, we recall, were closely

---

[124] On these character-mirrors see Colie (1974) 231–2.

[125] For court as the king's mirror, see Grabes (1982) 79.

[126] Alexander (1971) 97; Colie (1974) 223–4.

[127] Hamlet (or Shakespeare) may allude to Plutarch, *Moralia* 334B, where the tyrant Alexander of Pherae was ashamed to weep for Hecuba in Euripides' *Troades*, when he himself had killed far more people, without emotion. See Jenkins (1982) 481.

[128] Cf. Hunter (1963) 94: 'figures whose meaning depends on their relationship inside the observing and discriminating mind of Hamlet himself'; Jenkins (1974) 98.

[129] *Confessions*, VIII. x. 23 (transl. H. Chadwick).

associated with perspective construction, from its origin in Brunelleschi's Florentine Baptistery demonstration, through its application
in catoptric or reflected anamorphism, to its apotheosis in Vermeer's
use of the camera obscura.[130] Shakespeare's mirroring can generally be
naturalised into modern realism by treating the virtual images as completely separate individuals. But not always. In the closet scene, when
Hamlet sees the Ghost, Gertrude sees 'nothing but ourselves' (III. iv.
134 f). To resolve this contradiction, some accept Hamlet's version of
reality—confirmed, after all, by the Ghost's presence on stage[131]—and
reject Gertrude's version. Perhaps Gertrude (innocent of considerations
of honour) somehow cannot retrieve Hamlet senior's memory enough to
shape the Ghost in her imagination; or perhaps she cannot remember
what it was like to be honourable.[132] Alternatively, Gertrude and her
corrupt world may be sane, and the Ghost Hamlet's hallucination—
'alas! he's mad' (III. iv. 106). But on the basis of continuous spectator
realism, neither resolution will work. The Ghost's earlier appearances
were seen by all.[133] Here, at least, the alterity of Shakespeare's realism
must be admitted. In its own terms, the action of the closet scene is not
contradictory.

Without inconsistency, the scene dramatises defective moral vision
twice over, in two character-mirrors.[134] Thus, Hamlet sets a glass for
Gertrude; but she is also a glass for him, as frequent verbal repetitions
underline.[135] He makes her look at his father's portrait, the 'counterfeit

---

[130] See Kemp (1990), s.v. *Camera*; *Mirrors*; and especially 189, on use of the camera
obscura in the sixteenth century. On distorted cylindrical mirroring, and anamorphic images
generally, see Baltrušaitis (1977). Shakespeare had opportunities to see the anamorphic
portrait of Edward VI in Whitehall Palace (a *memento mori* double image): see ibid. 18–
19. Shakespeare several times uses 'perspective' in the sense of an anamorphic double view:
see *Henry V*, V. ii. 338 'you see them perspectively, the cities turned into a maid'; *Richard
II*, II. ii. 16–20 'sorrow's eye, glazed with blinding tears,/ Divides one thing entire to many
objects,/ Like perspectives, which, rightly gazed upon,/ Show nothing but confusion; eyed
awry,/ Distinguish form.' For 'mirror' = true description, see *OED* s.v. *Mirror* 4; for 'mirror'
= play, work of art, cf. Alexander (1971) 20–21.
[131] Authorised by the important Q1 s. d., 'enter the ghost in his night gown'. See Potter (1991).
[132] Cf. Dessen (1984) 141, 153.
[133] The same objection counts against Dodsworth (1985) 50, naturalising the Ghost as a
manifestation of Hamlet's own nature. The Ghost is intelligible only as a separate, indirect
perspective on Hamlet and other honourable men.
[134] See Dessen (1984) esp. 153 ff.
[135] e.g. III. iv. 8–9: 'Hamlet, thou hast thy father much offended./ Mother, you have my
father much offended'—discussed from a different viewpoint in Dodsworth (1985) 130,
185–6, 191, 212. On the Gertrude mirror generally, see ibid. 200 'In attacking his mother,
Hamlet attacks the weak and "feminine" part of himself.'

presentment' of honour, to bring home to her the state of her 'inmost part' (III. iv. 19), her sinful soul. He repeatedly directs her to watch the Ghost—'look you, there, look' (III. iv. 136). But all the time Hamlet himself fails to see Polonius's body, to feel remorse for his death, to look into his own soul.[136] (I would have Gertrude, meanwhile, keep looking horrified at the corpse.) It is like the parable of the mote and the beam:[137] Hamlet is oblivious to the dead man he killed, yet impatient with Gertrude's obliviousness to a dead man's ghost, of whose death she is innocent. Similarly, Hamlet calls Polonius 'rash, intruding fool', having just himself committed a 'rash and bloody deed', as Gertrude rightly calls it.[138] He has broken his own vows, yet blames Gertrude for breaking hers. And he says heaven is 'thought-sick' at her act (III. iv. 50), without thinking to repent his own. Dessen treats Gertrude's blindness to the Ghost as a conventional device, adducing many comparable metaphorical failures of vision in contemporary plays. (In *Hamlet* itself, Claudius fails at first to see the dumb show.[139]) But 'convention' hardly seems to fit the immediacy—psychological illusionism, even—of such discrepant perceptions. They are more like the discrepant viewpoints that form much of our experience of moral reality. In Shakespeare's world, Hamlet's and Gertrude's experiences both reflect the same moral failure. T. S. Eliot complains that Gertrude 'is not an adequate equivalent' for Hamlet's disgust; failing to see how adequately she mirrors Hamlet's lack of self-awareness.[140] She constitutes a powerfully diffuse metaphor of his moral insensitivity. For Hamlet the moral accuser displays a positively Pharisaic self-righteousness. Far from being exceptional, the closet scene typifies Shakespeare's realism. Dissatisfied with simple, direct representation of experience, he also represents it indirectly through mirroring characters, so adding subliminal complications.

As Gertrude offers a perspective of Hamlet's deficient self-aware-

---

[136] 'The pivotal not-seer is . . . Hamlet': Dessen (1984) 153. On Hamlet's lack of remorse for killing Polonius, cf. Dodsworth (1985) 253.

[137] Matthew 7: 3 f.

[138] Cf. Dodsworth (1985) 259–61.

[139] Prosser (1967); Robson (1975); Hawkes (1985) 325. Wilson (1935) naturalises Claudius's neglect of the dumb show, against W. W. Greg; so does Robson, more plausibly suggesting a gradual comprehension, reconcileable with the failure-to-see convention.

[140] Eliot (1945) 101, to which Rose (1985) 96 concedes too much. Hypocrisy is already a topic in Saxo: Amleth says to his mother 'thou shouldst weep for the blemish in thine own mind, not for that in another's': Bullough (1973) 66.

ness, so Claudius mirrors his heartlessness.[141] Claudius's ruthlessness reflects Hamlet's own potential for Machiavellianism, as his mission degenerates into criminal counter-intrigue. Eventually the 'mighty opposites', never very mighty, are not opposites either. Hamlet, who once shared a compassionate speech with the First Player, now shares with Claudius the responsibility for a death-warrant. The murders of Rosencrantz and Guildenstern have been justified by Hamlet's admirers as self-defence.[142] But they were unnecessary—and not even poetic justice, if, as seems likely, Hamlet's travelling companions were ignorant of the contents of their sealed commission.[143] Would Hamlet senior, whose ring reseals the commission, have judged the forgery honourable? The everlasting 'fixed/ His canon' against slaughtering others; only Hamlet's arrogant divinising of his rank allows him to eliminate 'baser nature' at will. Whatever else the doctrine of the Unjust Magistrate might legitimise, it hardly extended to murdering fellow students.[144] Significantly, this crime puts Hamlet in the same boat, or rather ship, with pirates, a type of lawless inhumanity.

VII

That Laertes is another character-mirror, Hamlet himself tells us, in curiously recursive, not to say reflexive, syntax: 'by the image of my cause I see/ The portraiture of his [Laertes']' (V. ii. 77–8); and again (addressing Osric): Laertes' 'semblable is his mirror, and who else would trace him, his umbrage [shadow], nothing more' (V. ii. 118–20). To translate this camped-up, ironically encomiastic court-speak: Hamlet cannot emulate Laertes except by becoming Laertes himself. The comparison with painting, implied in 'portraiture', signals a fresh perspective on Hamlet, in which he becomes, or assimilates, Laertes the new man of correct honour.[145] Contrasts between Laertes and Hamlet

---

[141] And much else; cf. e.g. Dodsworth (1985) 93.

[142] On the speculation that Hamlet found evidence incriminating them as accomplices: Bowers (1989); Cruttwell (1963).

[143] Cf. Prosser (1967) 203–4; Dodsworth (1985) 180.

[144] On resistance theory, see Frye (1984) 41 ff. Although Calvin himself argued for obedience even to tyrannical magistrates, *Institutes* IV. ii was used to justify ecclesiastical and political disobedience. Belsey (1985) 114–16 imagines that 'orthodoxy' permitted passive disobedience only. Whose orthodoxy?

[145] Cf. Alexander (1971) 120. On shadow ('umbrage') as a painter's term of art (sometimes used for the painting itself), see Gent (1981) and Dundas (1993) Index s.v. *Shadow*.

are regularly remarked;[146] but the resemblances that emphasise these, and the strikingly similar circumstances, are more numerous. Each loses a father; each loves Ophelia; each gives her moral advice; each is a gambler and a duellist; each, out of filial piety, is bent on revenge. Each is the 'calendar of gentry', 'the glass of fashion and the mould of form'—the latter Ophelia's description of Hamlet, not Osric's of Laertes. Each, moreover, is represented in two phases. As there is a young as well as a mature Hamlet, so there is a callow embarrassed stuffed-shirt Laertes who goes off to Paris to learn French fashions and earn a reputation, to sow wild oats and imitate Lamord; and there is a tougher Laertes who returns, in whom we see 'immaturity harden into forms positively evil'.[147] The young Laertes can set nature above—or at least alongside—honour; the elder reverses this hierarchy. Laertes the honour machine is of course very different from Hamlet the humanly perplexed, hesitating Prince. But in his stereotypical behaviour Laertes reveals the pressure of the time—of the honour code—under which Hamlet also acts, albeit more consciously and reluctantly. The virtual image brings out how Hamlet, confronted by a similar challenge, chose not to respond.[148] For, if the rabble call Laertes lord, Hamlet too is 'loved of the distracted multitude'.[149] Laertes' insurrection shows how Hamlet might have used his own much greater eloquence to enforce retribution publicly.[150] Hamlet's sympathy with Laertes' cause is thus insightful. But it is also inculpatory, since Laertes represents the questionable aspects of honour Hamlet has been drawn to imitate. He is much given to measuring himself against the field of honour—against Laertes, against Fortinbras.

When Hamlet wrestles with Laertes in Ophelia's grave, he thus wrestles with his own image—with the Antaeus of his own 'towering passion', his competitive vying ('emulate pride'). Descending to Laertes' level as a man of earth and invoker of rebellious Titan myths ('o'ertop old Pelion': V. i. 246), Hamlet lowers himself to competitive boasting. He is more bereaved; his honour is more injured. Although he thinks he is like 'Hercules himself' (V. i. 286), Hamlet loses this wrestling: to engage in it at all shows that status matters more to him

---

[146] e.g. Jenkins (1982) on IV. v. 132–5.

[147] Dodsworth (1985) 28.

[148] Cf. Jenkins (1974) 103.

[149] IV. iii. 4; cf. IV. vii. 18. Not merely Claudius' improvisation: Laertes finds the excuse plausible.

[150] Cf. Jenkins (1974) 103. But see Hunter (1963) 97–8; Frye (1984) 132–5.

than anything. He is more passionately resentful of the 'bravery' or magnificence of [Laertes'] grief than passionate with grief himself, or even respectful of poor Ophelia's grave. It hardly seems apropos to speculate whether Hamlet belatedly falls in love.[151] Both wrestlers think they love; but both, thinking they love honour more, trample the loved body. Some say the Folio and Q1 stage direction here must be corrupt: no sensitive person like Hamlet would ever jump into a grave. But even above ground, wrestling at a funeral is not a very convincing sign of sensitivity. In fact, the struggle shows how brutalising a single-minded pursuit of honour has been to Hamlet.[152] There is little to choose, at this stage, between his histrionics and Laertes'. The episode is not exactly a psychomachia—allegorising, say, a struggle against false honour. ('Shakespeare never sacrifices naturalism to symbolism'.[153]) But neither does the doubled image dramatise external behaviour of a brother and a lover, merely for the sake of sociological comparison. The complementary perspectives of bereavement emphasise by repetition how the emulousness of competitive honour is able to displace the natural passion of grief.

Making a triptych with the perspectives of Laertes and Hamlet, there is a third character-mirror, Fortinbras. That 'delicate and tender prince . . . with divine ambition puffed' (IV. iv. 48–9) is the subject of Hamlet's seventh and last soliloquy, full of admiration of his rival's honourable achievements:

> Rightly to be great
> Is not to stir without great argument,
> But greatly to find quarrel in a straw
> When honour's at the stake. (IV. iv. 53–6)

There is no ironic censure in Hamlet's wonder-struck admiration of this prince's readiness to send 20,000 men to their deaths 'for a fantasy and trick of fame'. Like Hamlet's, Fortinbras' portraiture comes in two perspectives, two very different temporal views. The earlier Fortinbras is an adventurer of 'unimproved mettle, hot and full', who has 'sharked up a list of lawless resolutes'. But the later is a 'tender prince', the ego-ideal of Hamlet's mirror-gazing, who leads a regular, well-disciplined

---

[151] As Alexander (1971) 127, 131, 149, 159.

[152] Cf. Dessen (1984) 21. Edwards (1985) 27 and Nuttall (1988) 58 reject the leap, the latter describing Hamlet's demeanour as courteous. Empson (1986) 100 is good on this issue.

[153] Colie (1974) 236. Ophelia's 'maimed rites' (V. i. 212) might hint at the Reformation's disfigurement of traditional ceremonies; but only as an enhancing suggestion.

army. The contrast is so extreme that to Jenkins it suggests revision.[154] But it may be that here again we have to do with the before-and-after vignettes of Renaissance compressed narrative.

Fortinbras, unlike Laertes and Hamlet, seems not to suffer moral deterioration. He submits to the King of Norway, and promises not to proceed revengefully against Denmark. He pursues, in fact, a legal course of action, however displeasingly martial this may seem to modern critics. Similarly, he is prepared to submit his 'rights of memory' in Denmark to due election by 'the noblest'; thus again taking an honourable course.[155] Is then Fortinbras' honour superior to Hamlet's, as Hamlet himself thinks? Certainly war was an appropriate context for chivalric honour—was, indeed, its ultimate validation. The symmetry of the triptych implies a formal distribution of matter between the private honour of Laertes and the monarchic or martial honour of Fortinbras. Hamlet himself is irresolute, divided between ideals of revenge (passionate Laertes) and of public redress (disciplined Fortinbras). The highest honour must, it seems, be Fortinbras'. But Shakespeare with his usual realism complicates this scheme to the point of enigma. For Fortinbras' incessant martial enterprises have an alarmingly Tamburlainian or Cromwellian aspect. Is Fortinbras' efficiency altogether preferable to Hamlet's hesitations and botched attempts? Would the world not be better off without an honour that kills so many thousands? Honour has been one of the cultural forms bringing mankind from the law of the jungle to the order of civil society. And indeed elements of the code continue still to be valuable. Yet, as ever, Shakespeare challenges still more discrimination, more charity.

From the mirror of Hamlet's confidant Horatio (to whom he mostly presents his agreeable side), one might expect a more flattering image. And indeed, in the final scene Horatio projects his own resignation, so that many suppose Hamlet dies well, justifiably comparing himself to the Morality Everyman—'this fell sergeant, Death,/ Is strict in his arrest'.[156] Taking his cue from this, the scholarly Horatio alludes to

---

[154] Jenkins (1974) 101–6.

[155] In contrast to Claudius, who 'popped in' (V. ii. 65).

[156] Jenkins (1982) V. ii. 341 Long Note; Felperin (1977) 64. Cf. *Pilgrimage of the Soul* (*OED* s.v. *Sergeant* 4b) ('death's sergeant, malady'); Tourneur, *The Transformed Metamorphosis* xli ('sergeant death'); John Knox, *The History of the Reformation in Scotland* IV (*OED* s.v. *Sergeant*, 1563) (Death 'laid on his areist'); Sylvester, *Divine Weeks*, I. iv. 818 ('Serjeant Death's sad warrant').

the Everyman morality in his prayer 'flights of angels sing thee to thy rest'.[157] But, if Hamlet is Everyman, what of Everyman's companion, Good Deeds? Fredson Bowers thinks Hamlet guiltless of murder: his death expiates all.[158] And Roland Mushat Frye, with able special pleading, finds triple 'endorsements' of Hamlet, by his friend, his adversary, and his rival for royal honour.[159] But Laertes' forgiveness of Hamlet ('my father's death come not upon thee': V. ii. 335) partly depends on his believing Hamlet's dubious excuse ('what I have done ... was madness': V. ii. 226–8).[160] And Fortinbras' endorsement proceeds from ignorance; he accords Hamlet the 'rite of war' with no more to go on than an impressive head-count ('This quarry cries on havoc': 'what a king is this!'), and, of course, reputation.[161] Hamlet's mission of retribution has come down to messy slaughter: his 'most royal' martial honour is achieved largely by accident.[162]

But what of the third endorsement, Horatio's? Hamlet's better part can hardly endorse private vengeance. Promising to tell 'How these things came about', Horatio specifies 'casual [chance] slaughters', which must include Polonius's killing, and 'deaths put on by cunning and forced [contrived] cause', which presumably includes Rosencrantz and Guildenstern's. Hamlet may think himself a divine minister (V. II. 48), but Horatio says nothing about that. There remains only his prayer that Hamlet may be sung to rest by angels, which is surely well short of an endorsement. Meanwhile, Hamlet has something other than angels in mind: namely fame's afterlife of honourable remembrance. He forbids

---

[157] Cf. Felperin (1977) 64. With Horatio's prayer cf. *Everyman* 891–3, where an angel sings 'come excellent elect spouse'. The detail of the singing angel indicates allusion, as against the commonplace envisaged in Frye (1984) 270–1.

[158] 'There can be no question of Hamlet's death in continuing sin or crime': Bowers (1989) 135. Cf. Everett (1989) 27 on the 'accidental killing of Polonius'; Alexander (1971) 182 (Polonius was killed in self-defence); Cruttwell (1963) 119 on the 'wild justice' of killing Rosencrantz and Guildenstern.

[159] Frye (1984) 135, 256, 259–62.

[160] V. ii. 226–8. Nuttall (1983) 164 compares Agamemnon's excuse in Homer, *Iliad* xix. Another pertinent source is St Augustine's analysis of the infirm will in *Confessions* VIII. ix. 21, asking whether it has an explanation in *latebrae poenarum hominum et tenebrosissimae contritiones filiorum Adam* ('the hidden punishments and secret despondences that befall the sons of Adam').

[161] V. ii. 404. Hawkes (1985) 331 improbably proposes that Fortinbras orders the rite for Claudius.

[162] Kastan (1982) 27 argues that Fortinbras' command to bear Hamlet 'like a soldier' symbolises the displacement of humane by martial values. Perhaps, rather, displacement of Christian values by honour.

his friend's suicide because he wants his own reputation cleared.[163]
Felperin connects the 'multiplicity of responses' to Hamlet's guilt with
Shakespeare's repudiating the older 'drama of salvation and damna-
tion'.[164] But, even on the newest Renaissance assumptions, the dying
perspective reveals desperate obduracy. There cannot have been many
different responses to Hamlet's total lack of remorse, let alone contri-
tion, at this solemn juncture.[165] Claudius voices remorse in the prayer
scene; Laertes voices remorse in his dying speech; Hamlet, never.
Rosencrantz and Guildenstern are 'not near [his] conscience'.[166] Do
we honestly suppose that Hamlet—a man who destroys the entire
Polonius family and who murders two former friends—do we suppose
that such a man can make a good end without repentance? Yet, if any
perspective is privileged in Renaissance tragedy, it is that of the dying
scene.

VIII

All the character-mirrors and multiple representations—whether models, foils, contrasts, *repoussoirs*, 'sides' of Hamlet, analogous narra-
tions, or relational images—together compose an astonishingly
complex representation. The individual identity, the self, was formed
and apprehended—then as now—through relations with others.
(Shakespeare anticipated the psychologies of Jung and Fairbairn, quite
as much as that of Freud.) I am not suggesting that Shakespeare's magic
can be explained as all done by mirrors. But, by assembling the
relational images of Hamlet, one can in principle arrive at a full
estimate of his character (one not without its vacuities). Defective
motives have been taken to betray the absence of inner subjectivity.
But often the gaps are defects only on the assumption of continuous
spectator realism. In Shakespeare's Renaissance realism, what may
seem gaps are really transitions between perspectives. And the separate

---

[163] Kastan (1982) 90 finds this quite fitting.

[164] Felperin (1977) 64–5.

[165] For all Hamlet's talk about Gertrude's repentance, his own remorse for Polonius's death
is limited to the perfunctory 'For this same lord/ I do repent'—followed by self-exoneration,
blaming heaven. Cf. Prosser (1967) 199, 202n. on Gertrude's invention of his weeping;
Battenhouse (1969) 251.

[166] V. ii. 58; cf. V. ii. 67. Cf. Prosser (1967) 202 and Dodsworth (1985) 180 on Hamlet's
malice towards Rosencrantz and Guildenstern.

psychological perspectives can be synthesised, much as a multi-per-spectival illusion is formed by a stereoscopic viewer. Whatever it is that Catherine Belsey calls 'essential subjectivity'[167] may not yet have developed; but that does not mean there was no realism, no dramatic illusion. Still less, that 'emergent illusionism' was in 'collision' with an emblematic mode. Realism through relational mirror images seems to have been quite accessible to Renaissance audiences. Direct and indir-ect mimesis were not conflicting opposites but complementary, mutually supportive perspectives. Shakespearean mimesis could 'suit the action to the words', combining indirect with direct representation, 'external' metaphors with subjective introspection.[168]

Shakespeare's psychological realism may be compared with that of *The Faerie Queene*.[169] In Spenser, he found not only precedents for mixing allegory with direct mimesis, but also examples of multiple character-mirrors. Spenser tells us he represents Queen Elizabeth in Gloriana, 'and yet in some places else' (that is, in Belphoebe and Britomart) 'I do otherwise shadow her'.[170] Perhaps because few Shakespeareans have been avid readers of Spenser, the extent of emblem and allegory in his tragedies—like the frequency of multiple perspectives—is insufficiently recognised. What I have tried to describe is no mere 'residue' of untransmuted archaism 'left behind by the ever-encroaching tide of naturalism',[171] but rather a distinct mode of realism, corresponding to a changed experience of the world itself. Although Shakespeare, like Spenser, was to be a pivotal figure in the development of naturalistic realism, he did not practise it as auto-matically as we have come to suppose. Indeed, it was a conspicuous mark of his dramatic style to enliven traditional genres, supplementing the new with the old, direct with indirect mimesis.[172] He may have sensed that indirect implication was more richly communicative.

What, then, do the separate perspectives in *Hamlet* combine to represent? Most generally, our inheritance of depravity, the 'vicious

---

[167] Belsey (1985) 26.
[168] III. ii. 17–18, related in Weimann (1985) to the discursive/non-discursive polarity.
[169] See Potts (1958); Watkins (1950); Hamilton (1990).
[170] Letter to Raleigh.
[171] Felperin (1977) 58–60.
[172] Cf. Felperin (1977) 58. In the inset play, similarly, 'we watch Shakespeare's play approach and embrace, as it were, its own archaic prototype, only to turn and flee it in an almost choreographic pattern of meeting and parting'.

mole of nature'[173] in a world like 'an unweeded garden/ That grows to seed', 'rank and gross' (I. ii. 135–6), where the legacy from father to son, from Achilles to Pyrrhus, Polonius to Laertes, Hamlet to Hamlet, is evil and the duty to reform it, 'to set it right' (I. v. 197). More particularly, the tragedy of chivalric honour's displacement by unheroic, politique forms of ambition.[174] The change and decay of honour is, indeed, a frequent subject in Shakespeare: one thinks of *Henry IV, Henry V, Troilus and Cressida*. From *Romeo and Juliet* to *As You Like It*, duelling especially is attacked—a practice to which the militant Protestant nobility (Leicester, Sidney, Essex, Raleigh) were prone. And in *Hamlet*, the new honour, although not a central subject, is a principal assumption.[175] Hamlet never swerves from commitment to princely honour: his doubt is only whether it is *nobler* in the mind to suffer or take arms. But he shrinks from the duties of honourable action, and, at least at first, hesitates before the homicidal implications of the honour code. More particularly still, *Hamlet* is the tragedy of an attractive but unstable, idealistic but weak young prince, yearning for true nobility, faced with a moral challenge too formidable for him: the tragedy of the ruin of his better features by the logic of honour. As he matures and his hesitancy disappears, his noble honour hardens into egomaniac self-justification.

The problem of *Hamlet* criticism is not Hamlet's delay, but the delay of the critics. Eleanor Prosser made a case against him already in 1967, and Martin Dodsworth's decisive examination should have clinched the matter in 1985. Yet the enigma of Hamlet is still defended against all their arguments. There is a natural reluctance to admit how unpleasant the Everyman in Hamlet is. Just as Hamlet satirises many sorts and conditions of people who have motes blinding them, so he himself has many planks; and we, identifying with him, share this denial. But there is also an aesthetic reason for our delay: namely, the difficulty of appreciating Renaissance realism.

The play's hermeneutic task is to discern the corruption of Hamlet's honesty, in face of an eloquence that gilds his words seductively—the seductive charm honour really had for many Elizabethans. After all, 'the right use' of Renaissance tragedy was to show forth 'ulcers that are

---

[173] I. iv. 17–38. The theme is already present in Saxo, whose Amleth mysteriously discerns the inheritance of death in things: e.g. Bullough (1973) 68.

[174] Cf. Cruttwell (1963) 121–2 on the muddle of contradictory moralities; Mousley (1994) 72–3, 79.

[175] See Dodworth (1985) *passim*, esp. ch. 1.

covered with tissue' and the 'weak foundations gilden roofs are builded' upon[176]—as Hamlet himself is clearly aware when he plans to 'tent [probe] Claudius to the quick' (II. ii. 593) with *The Murder of Gonzago*, or when he warns Gertrude not to ignore his censure, since that 'will but skin and film the ulcerous place'.[177] But in his righteousness he is oblivious of the tragedy designed to tent his own, and our, ulcers. Dr Shakespeare comes with his lancet, and we say, 'No need to operate, doctor! The patient has an amiable sensibility'.

Note. This is a version of a lecture delivered on 26 April 1995. I should like to acknowledge the help of David Howarth and Paul Barolsky on particular points. The general approach owes much to A. D. Nuttall's; on *Hamlet* itself I am indebted to the work of Nigel Alexander, Harold Jenkins and Martin Dodsworth, as well as to memorable conversations with the late Wallace Robson.

References

Alciati, A. 1985. *Emblems in Translation*, ed. P. M. Daly (Toronto).

Alexander, N. 1971. *Poison, Play and Duel* (London).

Alpers, S. 1983. *The Art of Describing: Dutch Art in the Seventeenth Century* (London).

Aubrey, J. 1898. *Brief Lives* . . . , ed. A. Clark, 2 vols. (Oxford).

——— 1972. *Brief Lives* . . . , ed. O. L. Dick (Harmondsworth).

Auden, W. H. 1963. *The Dyer's Hand* (London).

Auerbach, E. 1953. *Mimesis: The Representation of Reality in Western Literature*, transl. W. R. Trask (Princeton, NJ).

Backman, G. 1991. *Meaning by Metaphor* (Stockholm).

Bacon, Sir F. (1985) *The Essays or Counsels, Civil and Moral*, ed. M. Kiernan (Oxford).

Baltrušaitis, J. 1976. *Anamorphic Art*, transl. W. J. Strachan (Cambridge).

Battenhouse, R. W. 1969. *Shakespearean Tragedy: Its Art and Its Christian Premises* (Bloomington, IN, and London).

Beaujour, M. 1982. 'Speculum, Method, and Self Portrayal: Some Epistemological Problems', in Lyons and Nichols (1982), 188–96.

Belsey, C. 1985. *The Subject of Tragedy* (London and New York).

Biggs, M., et al. (eds.)1991. *The Arts of Performance in Elizabethan and Early Stuart Drama: Essays for George Hunter* (Edinburgh).

Bloomfield, M. W. 1986. '"Interlace" as a Medieval Narrative Technique with

---

[176] Sidney (1973) 96.

[177] III. iv. 149; cf. IV. iv. 27–8: 'th'impostume of much wealth and peace,/ That inward breaks, and shows no cause without/ Why the man dies.'

Special Reference to "Beowulf"', in *Magister Regis Studies in Honor of Robert Earl Kaske* (New York), 49–59.

Bossy, J. 1985. *Christianity in the West 1400–1700* (Oxford).

Bowers, F. 1989. *Hamlet as Minister and Scourge and Other Studies in Shakespeare and Milton* (Charlottesville, VA).

Bradbrook, M. C. 1952. *Themes and Conventions of Elizabethan Tragedy* (Cambridge).

Bradley, A. C. 1920. *Shakespearean Tragedy* (rev. ed.: London).

Bradshaw, G. 1987. *Shakespeare's Scepticism* (Brighton).

Brandes, G. 1902. *William Shakespeare* (London).

Braudel, F. 1982. *The Wheels of Commerce*, transl. Siân Reynolds (New York).

Brown, J. R., and Harris, B. 1963, (eds.). *Hamlet* (Stratford-upon-Avon Studies: London).

Bullough, G. 1973. *Narrative and Dramatic Sources of Shakespeare*, vii (London).

Bunim, M. S. 1970. *Space in Medieval Painting and the Forerunners of Perspective* (rpt: New York).

Burnett, M. T., and Manning, J. 1994. *New Essays on Hamlet* (New York).

Burns, E. 1990. *Character: Acting and Being on the Pre-Modern Stage* (London).

Carruthers, M. 1990. *The Book of Memory: A Study of Memory in Medieval Culture* (Cambridge).

Chaudhuri, S. 1995. *Renaissance Essays for Kitty Scoular Datta* (Calcutta).

Clemen, W. 1964. *Shakespeare's Soliloquies* (Cambridge).

———— 1987. *Shakespeare's Soliloquies* (London and New York).

Colie, R. L. 1974. *Shakespeare's Living Art* (Princeton, NJ).

Cooper, A. A., Earl of Shaftesbury 1713. *An Essay on Painting . . .* (London).

Coyle, M. 1992. *Hamlet* (London).

Cruttwell, P. 1963. 'The Morality of Hamlet—"Sweet Prince" or "Arrant Knave"?', in Brown and Harris (1963).

de Grazia, M. 1991. *Shakespeare Verbatim* (Oxford).

de Madariaga, S. 1948. *On Hamlet* (London).

Dessen, A. C. 1984. *Elizabethan Stage Conventions and Modern Interpreters* (Cambridge).

Dodsworth, M. 1985. *Hamlet Closely Observed* (London).

Doebler, J. 1974. *Shakespeare's Speaking Pictures: Studies in Iconic Imagery* (Albuquerque, NM).

Donawerth, J. 1984. *Shakespeare and the Sixteenth-Century Study of Language* (Urbana, IL, and Chicago, OH).

Drakakis, J. (1985)(ed.), *Alternative Shakespeares* (London and New York).

Draper, J. W. 1950. *The 'Twelfth Night' of Shakespeare's Audience* (Stanford, CA).

Dundas, J. 1993. *Pencils Rhetorique: Renaissance Poets and the Art of Painting* (Newark, DE, and London).

Eagleton, T. (1986) *William Shakespeare* (Oxford).

Edwards, P. (ed.) (1985), *Hamlet, Prince of Denmark* (Cambridge).

Eliot, T. S. 1945. *The Sacred Wood: Essays on Poetry and Criticism* (rpt: London).

Elkins, J. 1994. *The Poetics of Perspective* (Ithaca, NY, and London).

Empson, Sir W. 1986. *Essays on Shakespeare* (Cambridge).

Ermarth, E. D. 1983. *Realism and Consensus in the English Novel* (Princeton, NJ).

Everett, B. 1989. *Young Hamlet: Essays on Shakespeare's Tragedies* (Oxford).

Falaschi, E. T. 1975. 'Valvassori's 1553 Illustrations of *Orlando Furioso*: the Development of Multi-Narrative Technique in Venice and its Links with Cartography', *La Bibliofilia*, 77: 227–51.

Felperin, H. 1977. *Shakespearean Representation: Mimesis and Modernity in Elizabethan Tragedy* (Princeton, NJ).

Ferber, M. 1990. 'The Ideology of *The Merchant of Venice*', *ELR*, 20: 431–64.

Fowler, A. 1964. *Spenser and the Numbers of Time* (London).

—— 1987. *A History of English Literature* (Cambridge, MA, and Oxford).

—— 1994. 'Two Notes on *Hamlet*', in Burnett and Manning (1994), 3–10.

—— 1995. '*Twelfth Night* and Epiphany', in Chaudhuri (1995), 116–31.

French, M. 1992. 'Chaste Constancy in *Hamlet*', in Coyle (1992), 96–112.

Frye, R. M. 1984. *The Renaissance Hamlet: Issues and Responses in 1600* (Princeton, NJ).

Gash, A. 1988. 'Shakespeare's Comedies of Shadow and Substance', *Word and Image*, 4: 626–62.

Gent, L. 1981. *Picture and Poetry 1560–1620* (Leamington Spa).

Gervinus, G. G. 1883. *Shakespeare Commentaries*, transl. E. E. Bunnètt (London).

Gilbert, W. S. 1982. *Plays*, ed. G. Rowell (Cambridge).

Ginsberg, W. 1983. *The Cast of Character: The Representation of Personality in Ancient and Medieval Literature* (Toronto, Buffalo, and London).

Goddard, H. 1946. 'In Ophelia's Closet', *The Yale Review*, 35: 462–74.

Grabes, H. 1982. *The Mutable Glass: Mirror-Imagery in Titles and Texts of the Middle Ages and the English Renaissance*, transl. G. Collier (Cambridge).

Hagen, M. A. 1986. *Varieties of Realism: Geometries of Representational Art* (Cambridge and New York).

Hamilton, A. C. (gen. ed.) 1990. *The Spenser Encyclopedia* (Toronto and London).

Hawkes, T. 1985. '*Telmah*', in Parker and Hartman 1985. 310–32.

Hazlitt, W. 1902. *The Collected Works*, ed. A. R. Waller and A. Glover, Vol. 1 (London and New York).

Heiberg, S. (ed.) 1988. *Christian IV and Europe*, Council of Europe Exhibition Catalogue (Herning).

Hodgdon, B. 1994. 'The Critic, the Poor Player, Prince Hamlet, and the Lady in the Dark', in McDonald (1994).

Hollander, J. 1961. *The Untuning of the Sky: Ideas of Music in English Poetry 1500–1700* (Princeton, NJ).

Holt, E. G. 1947, 1958. *A Documentary History of Art*, 2 vols. (Garden City, NY).

Howell, W. S. 1956. *Logic and Rhetoric in England 1500–1700* (Princeton, NJ).

Hunter, G. K. 1963. 'The Heroism of Hamlet', in Brown and Harris (1963), 90–109.

Jenkins, H. 1963. 'Hamlet and Ophelia', *Proceedings of the British Academy*, 49: 135–51.

—— (ed.) 1982. *Hamlet* (London and New York).

Jewkes, W. T. 1958. *Act Division in Elizabethan and Jacobean Plays 1583–1616* (Hamden, CT).

Jones, Emrys 1971. *Scenic Form in Shakespeare* (Oxford).

Jones, Ernest 1955. *Hamlet and Oedipus* (Garden City, NY).

Kastan, D. S. 1982. *Shakespeare and the Shapes of Time* (London).

Kemp, M. 1990. *The Science of Art: Optical Themes in Western Art from Brunelleschi to Seurat* (New Haven, CT, and London).

Kernodle, G. R. 1944. *From Art to Theatre: Form and Convention in the Renaissance* (Chicago, IL, and London).

Kirsch, A. 1990. *The Passions of Shakespeare's Tragic Heroes* (Charlottesville, VA, and London).

Kirsch, A. 1993. 'Montaigne and *The Tempest*', in Sorelius and Srigley (1993), 111–21.

le Fèvre, J. (1536), *Livret des Emblèmes de . . . Alciat . . .* (Paris).

Leslie, M. 1983. *Spenser's 'Fierce Warres and Faithfull Loves'* (Woodbridge and Totowa, NJ).

Levin, H. 1959. *The Question of Hamlet* (New York).

Lewalski, B. K. 1962. 'Biblical Allusion and Allegory in *The Merchant of Venice*, *Shakespeare Quarterly*, 13: 327–343.

———— B. K. 1965. 'Thematic Patterns in *Twelfth Night*', *Shakespeare Studies*, 1: 168–81.

Lindberg, D. C. 1976. *Theories of Vision from al-Kindi to Kepler* (Chicago).

Llewellyn, N. 1991. *The Art of Death: English Culture in the English Death Ritual c.1500–c.1800* (London).

Lyons, B. G. 1977. 'The Iconography of Ophelia', *English Literary History*, 44: 60–74.

Lyons, J. D., and Nichols, S. G. (eds.) 1982. *Mimesis: From Mirror to Method, Augustine to Descartes* (Hanover, NH, and London).

Manning, J. 1994. '*Symbola* and *Emblemata* in *Hamlet*', in Burnett and Manning (1994), 11–20.

McCanles, M. 1992. *Jonsonian Discriminations: The Humanist Poet and the Praise of True Nobility* (Toronto).

McDonald, R. 1994. *Shakespeare Reread: The Texts in New Contexts* (Ithaca, NY, and London).

Miller, P. 1939. *The New England Mind* (New York).

Mousley, A. 1994. 'Hamlet and the Politics of Individualism', in Burnett and Manning (1994), 67–82.

Mowl, T. 1993. *Elizabethan and Jacobean Style* (London).

Nelson, B. 1969. *The Idea of Usury* (rev. ed.: Chicago and London).

Nuttall, A. D. 1983. *A New Mimesis: Shakespeare and the Representation of Reality* (London and New York).

———— 1988. 'Hamlet: Conversations with the Dead', *Proceedings of the British Academy*, 74: 53–70.

Ong, W. J., SJ 1958. *Ramus: Method, and the Decay of Dialogue*, (Cambridge, MA).

Parker, P., and Hartman, G. 1985. *Shakespeare and the Question of Theory* (New York and London).

Peacham, H. 1612. *Minerva Britanna . . .* (London).

Pettet, E. C. 1949. *Shakespeare and the Romance Tradition* (London).

Potter, L. 1991. 'Seeing and Believing', in Biggs *et al.* (1991) 113–23.

Potts, A. F. 1958. *Shakespeare and 'The Faerie Queene'* (Ithaca, NY).

Prosser, E. 1967. *Hamlet and Revenge* (Stanford, CA, and London).

Puppi, L. 1989. *Andrea Palladio: The Complete Works* (New York).

Quint, D. (ed.) 1992a. *Creative Imitation: New Essays on Renaissance Literature in Honor of Thomas M. Greene* (Binghamton, NY).

——— 1992b. 'Bragging Rights: Honor and Courtesy in Shakespeare and Spenser', in Quint (1992a), 391–430.

Ridley, M. R. (ed.) 1958. *Othello* (London).

Ripa, C. 1976. *Iconologia (Padua 1611)* (New York and London).

Robson, W. W. 1975. *Did the King See the Dumb-Show?* (Edinburgh).

Rose, J. 1985. 'Sexuality in the Reading of Shakespeare: *Hamlet* and *Measure for Measure*', in Drakakis (1985), 95–118.

Schwartz, R. M. 1993. *Remembering and Repeating* (Chicago and London).

Seaton (ed.) 1950. *The Arcadian Rhetorike by Abraham Fraunce* (Oxford).

Showalter, E. 1985. 'Representing Ophelia: Women, Madness, and the Responsibilities of Feminist Criticism', in Parker and Hartman (1985), 77–94.

Shuger, D. K. 1988. *Sacred Rhetoric: The Christian Grand Style in the English Renaissance* (Princeton, NJ).

Sidney, Sir P. 1973. *Miscellaneous Prose*, ed. K. Duncan-Jones and J. van Dorsten (Oxford).

Skinner, Q. 1994. 'Moral Ambiguity and the Renaissance Art of Eloquence', *E in C*, 44: 267–92.

Sorelius, G., and Srigley, M. (eds.) 1993. *Cultural Exchange between European Nations during the Renaissance* (Uppsala).

Stanton, K. 1994. '*Hamlet*'s Whores', in Burnett and Manning (1994), 167–88.

Stern, J. P. 1973. *On Realism* (London and Boston, MA).

Strong, R. 1987. *Gloriana: The Portraits of Queen Elizabeth I* (London).

Vergara, L. 1982. *Rubens and the Poetics of Landscape* (New Haven, CT, and London).

Vickers, B. (ed.) 1974–81. *Shakespeare: The Critical Heritage*, 6 vols. (London).

Vinaver, E. 1971. *The Rise of Romance* (Oxford).

Watkins, W. B. C. 1950. *Shakespeare and Spenser* (Princeton, NJ).

Webster, J. (ed.) 1984. *William Temple's Analysis of Sidney's Defence of Poetry* (New York).

Weimann, R. 1985. 'Mimesis in *Hamlet*', in Parker and Hartman (1985), 275–91.

Weinberg, B. 1961. *A History of Literary Criticism in the Italian Renaissance*, 2 vols. (Chicago).

White, J. 1987. *The Birth and Rebirth of Pictorial Space* (rev. ed.: London).

Whitney, G. 1586. *A Choice of Emblems* (Leyden).

Wiggins, M. 1994. '*Hamlet* within the Prince', in Burnett and Manning (1994), 209–26.

Wilson, J. D. 1935. *What Happens in 'Hamlet'* (Cambridge).

Wither, G. 1635. *A Collection of Emblems* . . . (London).

Proceedings of the British Academy, **90**, 65–93

CHATTERTON LECTURE ON POETRY

'Servant, but not Slave': Ben Jonson at the Jacobean Court

MARTIN BUTLER

University of Leeds

IT SEEMS APPROPRIATE on this occasion to begin by evoking the moment in 1621 when Ben Jonson nearly became a Fellow of the British Academy. Of course in 1621 the Academy as we know it did not yet exist, but towards the end of James I's reign the historian Edmund Bolton presented a series of proposals to the Crown for the establishment of an 'Academ Royal', which is today understood as part of the present institution's pre-history. As reported to the 1621 parliament, this Academy would have been a showcase for the cultural accomplishments of James's Britain—as James himself described it, 'an Academy for bettering the breeding of the youth of our dominions, and also to encourage diverse men of arts, for the honour and profit of us and our kingdom'—and among the eighty-four antiquaries, authors and scientists whose inclusion was subsequently mooted was Ben Jonson. Given the gap between James's ambitions and his finances, it is perhaps unsurprising that Bolton's scheme never secured the necessary funding, but it is pleasant to suppose that, had this Jacobean Academy materialised, Jonson might have been one of its founding members.[1]

Read at the Academy 12 December 1995. © The British Academy 1996.

[1] Bolton's proposals were first described by Ethel M. Portal in 'The Academ Roial of King James I', *Proceedings of the British Academy*, 1915–16, pp. 189–208. There is an authoritative analysis by R. W. Caudill, 'Some Literary Evidence of the Development of the English Virtuoso in the Seventeenth Century', D.Phil. dissertation (Oxford, 1975), pp. 279–86, 397–8; and a recent account of Bolton by D. R. Woolf, *The Idea of History in Early Stuart England* (Toronto, 1990), pp. 190–99. The full Academy list, with Jonson's name included, actually

Jonson's inclusion in Bolton's proposals testifies to his success at this stage of his career in establishing a position for himself at the heart of Jacobean élite culture. 1621 was a good year for him: Buckingham gave him £100 for writing *The Gipsies Metamorphosed*, he gained the reversion of the office of Master of the Revels, and gossips rumoured that he had narrowly missed being knighted.[2] But the proposals remind us that Jonson's profile was by no means solely that of courtier, place-seeker and parvenu. Beside him in the scheme were friends like Robert Cotton and John Selden, men who stood amongst the foremost scholars of the day, and Jonson too may have been listed as much for his intellectual as his poetic achievements. Although he was still writing the annual masques, he had severed his connections with the stage, and was increasingly living the life of a scholar. When in 1623 his library was burned, the lost works listed in his 'Execration upon Vulcan' included translations of Aristotle and Horace, an English grammar, notes on literature and theology, and a history of Henry V based on documents loaned by Selden, Cotton and Carew. It is sometimes forgotten that, as well as pursuing a career at court, Jonson had a material claim to belong to the international world of scholarship, and registered as a presence in what was gradually emerging as the republic of letters.

Now, the ideological co-ordinates of Bolton's Academy were not at all republican. On the contrary, Bolton would have appropriated his fellows' talents emphatically in the service of Jacobean kingship. He suggested that they should study not only 'antiquity' but 'honour', censor translations of foreign books, compile an expurgatory index of English books, and write an authorised British history to 'repress the ignorance and insolencies of Italian Polidores, Hollandish Meterans, [and] rhapsodical Gallo-Belgias'.[3] Such a yoking of intellectual radic-alism and political conservatism is perhaps to be expected from a historian who was closely attached to Buckingham, but it does bear on Jonson also, since a comparable ideological mix has come of late to seem distinctive and problematic about much of his poetry. A genera-tion ago Jonson was safely regarded as a crusty moralist, and his poems were respected, if not exactly loved, for their apparently detached

---

dates from 1626; James's remarks are in a letter recommending an earlier version of the scheme to Prince Charles in June 1622 (cited by Caudill from Public Record Office [here-after PRO] SP14/131/70).

[2] See D. Riggs, *Ben Jonson: A Life* (Cambridge, Mass., 1989), p. 271.

[3] Portal, 'The Academ Roial of King James I', p. 196.

reflections on the good life. But in recent years a series of seismic critical shifts has effectively foregrounded agendas in the poems that seem less moral than social.[4] In literary studies, the so-called New Historicism has collapsed the gap between poet and society, denying Jonson the luxury of aesthetic distance. At the same time, a new historiography has redrawn our picture of early modern Whitehall, replacing that old decadent court, ripe for the cropping, with a more historically-informed account of the systems of favour and reward by which a kingly state conducted its business. In these frameworks, Jonson figures not so much as a detached observer of the social process as one aspirant among many competing for access to power, whose poems were strategic interventions in the ubiquitous and ongoing struggle for patronage.

Consequently, much recent criticism has become preoccupied with Jonson the place-seeker, and the pragmatic requirements of self-promotion which could be seen as driving his poetry. As Michael McCanles with some justice complains, Jonson is in danger of being turned into 'just the sort of figure he most abhorred, an envious and resentful syco-phant'.[5] One recent study, by Bruce Thomas Boehrer, has called him just that, James's 'chief metrical sycophant', a cravenly subservient absolutist who was 'dazzled by the magnificence of the big bourgeoisie' (meaning the Jacobean aristocracy).[6] This view is self-evidently one-sided, but it echoes at a distance the far more subtle account by Jonathan Goldberg, for whom Jonson's poems align themselves so instinctively with the court that he should be taken as quite literally

---

[4] These new perspectives on Jonson effectively begin with D. E. Wayne's essay 'Poetry and Power in Ben Jonson's *Epigrammes*: The Naming of "Facts" or the Figuring of Social Relations?', *Renaissance and Modern Studies*, 23 (1979), pp. 79–103, an account developed in Wayne's book, *Penshurst: The Semiotics of Place and the Poetics of History* (London, 1984). Other important contributions have been R. Helgerson, *Self-Crowned Laureates: Spenser, Jonson, Milton and the Literary System* (Berkeley, 1983); J. Goldberg, *James I and the Politics of Literature* (Baltimore, 1983); S. Fish, 'Authors-readers: Jonson's Community of the Same' *Representations*, 7 (1984), pp. 26–58; D. Riggs, *Ben Jonson: a Life*; and R. C. Evans, *Ben Jonson and the Poetics of Patronage* (Lewisburg, 1989). I do not mean to imply that these promote an identical view of Jonson, only that they have all underlined the social politics latent in his poetry. The most distinguished extension of the earlier 'Old Historicist' view is perhaps E. Partridge, 'Jonson's *Epigrammes*: The Named and the Name-less', *Studies in the Literary Imagination*, 6 (1973), pp. 153–98.

[5] M. McCanles, *Jonsonian Discriminations: The Humanist Poet and the Praise of True Nobility* (Toronto, 1992), p. vii.

[6] B. T. Boehrer, 'Renaissance Overeating: The Sad Case of Ben Jonson', *Proceedings of the Modern Languages Association* [hereafter *PMLA*], 105 (1990), pp. 1076, 1078, 1081. There is a critique by G. Schmidgall in *PMLA*, 106 (1991), pp. 317–8.

the 'representative voice' of Jacobean absolutism.[7] Goldberg emphasises the tensions that score Jonson's writing, but, in a crucial move, he
argues that such tensions were produced by James's culture of absolutism, rather than being signs of any conflict with it. Jonson's obsessive
oscillation between self-assertion and self-abasement was, he argues, a
strategy required by the Machiavellian discourse of Jacobean power,
which presented itself as relentlessly absorbing contradiction and containing subversion. And in Stanley Fish's meticulous and compelling
analysis of the poems, Jonson's verse is seen as frankly psychological
compensation for the rigours of place-seeking, the creation of an
imaginary circle centred on the poet which betrays his actual anxiety
about being excluded from power. Jonson writes as if he were self-
authorising, transcending social obligations, but, says Fish, he proclaims that freedom 'in the very posture of supplication and dependence'.[8]

   I shall not argue that Jonson's politics were anything other than
monarchical: from any angle he was a devoted supporter of the Crown.
But it seems to me that these now prevailing views are in danger of
simply collapsing Jonson's politics into the systems of Jacobean patronage, and of overestimating the completeness with which those systems
were integrated. These readings tend to assume that the seventeenth-
century state was an unchanging monolith, and to deny the possibility
of unresolved ideological conflicts amongst Jonson's patrons. With
Whitehall presented as a closed and enveloping economy, all dissent
from Jacobean norms is folded back within the structures of power, and
all resistance always-already contained. But if some literary critics have
denied that the court had any margin for dissent, political historians
have often emphasised that Stuart England was only an imperfect
absolutism, and that the early modern state was relatively heterogeneous.[9] English monarchs always lacked money and bureaucracy, and
governed through the co-operation of unsalaried officials, many of whom
held their own views about the obligations of kingship. James's court may
have seemed to resemble its continental counterparts, but he was
obliged to rule by comparatively consensual methods, and make concessions to the fiction that sovereignty lay with the king-in-parliament:

---

[7] Goldberg, *James I and the Politics of Literature*, p. 230 (and see generally pp. 219–20).
[8] Fish, 'Authors-readers: Jonson's Community of the Same', pp. 56–7.
[9] This case can be traced in much historiography, but has been argued most recently by D. L.
Smith in *Constitutional Royalism and the Search for Settlement, c.1640–1649* (Cambridge,
1994).

his speeches oscillated between divine right conceptions of monarchy and reassurances that his discretion would always be exercised according to law. In this differently inflected court context, I want to suggest that Jonson's poetry did not merely recirculate a totalising absolutism but sought to manage and shape the heterogeneous forms of Jacobean power. In identifying itself with James's monarchy his verse had also to negotiate the potential faultlines of Stuart kingship, the structural tensions by which the supposedly unified Jacobean state was in fact vexed.

The ideological premise of all Jonson's poetry is the centrality of the monarch to the state: his remarks in the notebook *Discoveries* consistently describe government in autocratic terms. In his most famous formulation (borrowed from the Spanish humanist Juan Luis Vives), Jonson represents the prince as ideally counselled by a few men of proven intellectual worth: 'Learning needs rest: sovereignty gives it. Sovereignty needs counsel: learning affords it. There is such a consociation of offices, between the prince, and whom his favour breeds, that they may help to sustain his power, as he their knowledge'.[10] This mutually supportive symbiosis between knowledge and power, learning and sovereignty envisages a special place at the prince's side for men like Jonson's friends Selden and Cotton, and allows correspondingly small place for wider consultation: *Discoveries* is very negative about popular assemblies, saying that they give monarchs unreliable advice, for parliamentary suffrages go by number rather than by weight.[11] The problem with this system is the absence of restraints on monarchs who won't take advice, and *Discoveries* dwells on the circumspection needful in addressing princes, the 'modesty' and 'respect' counsellors have to use. Since princes will not 'suffer themselves to be taught, or reprehended', Jonson writes, it is best not to address them insolently,

[10] *Ben Jonson* (eds C. H. Herford, P. Simpson and E. Simpson, 11 vols, Oxford, 1925–52), 8, p. 565. All subsequent quotations from Jonson refer to this edition. However, I have modernised the spelling, and in punctuating the poems I have followed Ian Donaldson's excellent Oxford Standard Authors edition (1975).

[11] *Ben Jonson*, 8, p. 579 (ll.508–12). Jonson's source for this sentiment is Pliny. It might be added that Jonson's only poem addressed to a parliament (Epigram 24) implies a strictly top-down view of its responsibility: parliament's duty is to make good laws by which men's vile manners can be restrained. Compare also *The Underwood* 64, which reflects on the 1629 Parliament.

but as if they 'were already furnished with the parts [they] should have'.[12] Clearly, this is a recipe for evasion — by sugar-coating advice with praise it could all too easily become subservience — and Jonson returns to the problem in his poems 'To John Selden' (*Underwood* 14) and 'To my Muse' (Epigram 65), arguing that when he lavished praise on unworthy objects ''twas with purpose to have made them such'.[13] Although this acknowledges the problem, it is hard to feel that it really solves it. Still, if Jonson's alternative to princely rule is an anarchy of democratic individualism, pragmatism is his price worth paying, and he does represent the monarch as ethically bound, required to be a father rather than a tyrant. As *Discoveries* notes, 'A good king is a public servant'.[14]

Jonson was not enthusiastic about all monarchs alike, and his image of a strong sovereign listening attentively to respectful but responsible intellectuals did not readily translate into the terms of Elizabethan courtiership. He failed to achieve much laureate status in Elizabeth's reign, and his difficulties in finding an appropriate formula for addressing the Queen can be seen in the lyric that represents his only significant poetic contribution to the cult of her sovereignty, the celebrated hymn 'Queen and Huntress' from *Cynthia's Revels* (1600–1):[15]

> Queen and huntress, chaste and fair,
> Now the sun is laid to sleep,
> Seated in thy silver chair,
> State in wonted manner keep:
>   Hesperus entreats thy light,
>   Goddess excellently bright.
>
> Earth, let not thy envious shade
> Dare itself to interpose;
> Cynthia's shining orb was made
> Heaven to clear, when day did close:
>   Bless us then with wished sight,
>   Goddess excellently bright.
>
> Lay thy bow of pearl apart,
> And thy crystal-shining quiver;
> Give unto the flying hart
> Space to breathe, how short soever:

---

[12] *Ben Jonson*, 8, p. 566.
[13] 'An Epistle to Master John Selden' (*The Underwood*, 14), l.22 (*Ben Jonson*, 8, p. 159); and compare Epigram 65 (*Ben Jonson*, 8, p. 48).
[14] *Ben Jonson*, 8, p. 601.
[15] *Ben Jonson*, 4, p. 161.

Thou that mak'st a day of night,
Goddess excellently bright.

This hymn is often read as if it were the culminating instance of late-Elizabethan poetic compliment, and it does indeed represent Cynthia as a transcendent deity, serenely transmitting her visionary light to a benighted lower world. Yet while being a panegyrical culmination, the poem manipulates the image of the goddess in directions which are significantly more this-worldly. Unlike other versions of the Elizabethan cult in which Elizabeth is depicted as unapproachable and aloof — for example, *A Midsummer Night's Dream*, which alludes to her as a remote and inscrutable vestal, or Chapman's hymns, which make Cynthia into an esoteric and occult deity[16] — 'Queen and Huntress' invests Jonson's goddess with more actively political expectations. His Cynthia is luminous, but her light is expected to purge and clarify, and as a huntress she is contingently engaged in that pursuit of vice towards which the hymn delicately marshals her.[17]

The tensions underlying Jonson's lyric may be registered by considering its structural function in *Cynthia's Revels* as a whole. In the play, 'Queen and Huntress' is sung at the beginning of Act V, and signals the moment of transition between brazen world and golden. Acts I to IV exhibit Cynthia's courtiers in various postures of extravagantly self-regarding folly, but with the goddess's arrival they are exposed, censured and punished, a purgation achieved by the goddess and her wise poet, Criticus, working hand in hand.[18] The hymn therefore not only welcomes Cynthia but predicts the reformation of courtly folly which she will undertake, and ties the discovery of her excellence to the irresistible cleansing which that disclosure brings about. Shifting the play into a higher aesthetic and political gear, it harks forward to the

---

[16] There is a recent taxonomy of lunar imagery as applied to Queen Elizabeth in H. Hackett, *Virgin Mother, Maiden Queen: Elizabeth I and the Cult of the Virgin Mary* (Houndmills, 1995), pp. 174–97.

[17] There is a direct link with the end of *Time Vindicated* (1623), which praises James's hunting in similar emblematic terms: 'Man should not hunt Mankind to death, / But strike the enemies of man; / Kill vices if you can, / They are your wildest beasts. / And when they thickest fall, you make the gods true feasts' (*Ben Jonson*, 7, p. 673).

[18] For a rather different reading, arguing for a more sceptical attitude to Criticus's authority, see J. Loewenstein, *Responsive Readings: Versions of Echo in Pastoral, Epic, and the Jonsonian Masque* (New Haven, 1984), pp. 87–8. I should add that in using the name Criticus, and in describing the positioning of the hymn, I am following the 1601 Quarto which (contrary to the views of E. K. Chambers and the Oxford editors) I believe represents the play as it was performed in 1600/01.

Jacobean masques, with their parallel moments of moral and political epiphany. Nonetheless, since the hymn both announces Cynthia and partially prescribes the reformation which is expected of her, it is positioned uneasily somewhere between an invocation and an admonition; and elsewhere in the play Criticus is presented as vulnerable to the scorn of her ignorant but conceited attendants, and badly in need of her protection. Subsequently Jonson never returned to any comparable adulation of Elizabeth, and the attitude that by 1603 he had towards the counsels prevailing at Whitehall may be gauged from the *Particular Entertainment . . . at Althorpe*, the show he wrote to welcome Queen Anne to England. In this, the Fairy Queen, with her charming but rather trivial elves, greets Anne and symbolically abdicates to her, while a satyr pokes fun at the fairies and warns that today's courtiers are going to need more than dancing skills to earn their promotion. James's attendants, says the satyr,

> can neither bribe a grace,
> Nor encounter my lord's face
> With a pliant smile, and flatter,
> Though this lately were some matter
> To the making of a courtier.[19]

Evidently Jonson expected James to be much less susceptible than Elizabeth had been to the blandishments of charming young men.

At the Jacobean court, Jonson achieved a much securer place. For all James's lack of charisma, his paternalism, pacificism and serious intellectual pretensions made him just the kind of monarch to appeal to Jonson, and Jonson's subsequent poetry is, I believe, entirely without nostalgia for Elizabeth. In a magisterial study, Anne Barton has argued that Jonson's career developed into a gradual 'harking-back to Elizabeth', in which the literary legacy of the previous reign became increasingly important to the work of the Stuart poet.[20] My feeling, though, is that however sympathetically Jonson reassessed Elizabethan literature, his recollection of Elizabeth's politics was altogether more disenchanted, and that his contributions to James's political culture took a quite radical attitude to the new monarchy. Unlike other poets who responded to the accession by seeking out continuities with the past, Jonson always represented James's arrival as a total break, an upheaval which freed the future from the dead hand of recent history. In the

[19] *Ben Jonson*, 7, p. 126–7.
[20] A. Barton, *Ben Jonson, Dramatist* (Cambridge, 1984).

speeches which he wrote in 1604 for James's formal entry into London, he hailed him as an Augustus bringing a Golden Age to a State weary of war, injustice and female government, whose inauguration was legitimated not by lines of dynastic continuity but by his miraculous re-embodiment of a lost imperial ideal. No less radical were the court festivals which Jonson wrote over the next twenty years. His masques repeatedly situated James as a strong, peaceful and masculine ruler, who instantaneously brought order out of disorder and changed darkness into light, and their eulogies were reinforced by constant reference to the change of old England into new Britain. Unlike many contemporaries, for whom the new name was a source of anxiety, Jonson made it a symbolic centrepiece, the most visible sign of the transformed, king-centred State.[21] His panegyric identified itself wholeheartedly with the Stuart revolution, presenting James as a strong but moderate and responsible ruler who would ensure peace and stability, and protect the State against fanaticism and anarchy.

The affinity between poet and king is well seen in what is perhaps Jonson's most considerable political poem, the 'Panegyre' of 1604.[22] Written for the opening of James's first Parliament, it describes the monarch's passage to Westminster Hall and the acclamations that he receives from the people as he passes through the city:

> Upon his face all threw their covetous eyes,
> As on a wonder: some amazed stood,
> As if they felt, but had not known their good;
> Others would fain have shown it in their words,
> But when their speech so poor a help affords
> Unto their zeal's expression, they are mute
> And only with red silence him salute.
> Some cry from tops of houses, thinking noise
> The fittest herald to proclaim true joys;
> Others on ground run gazing by his side,
> All as unwearied as unsatisfied;
> And every window grieved it could not move
> Along with him, and the same trouble prove. (ll.34–46)

[21] I argue this case fully in the essay 'The Stuart Masque and the Invention of Britain', in *The Stuart Court and Europe*, ed. R. Malcolm Smuts (Cambridge, 1996), pp. 65–85.

[22] *Ben Jonson*, 7, pp. 113–7. Surprisingly, given its importance, the 'Panegyre' has been very little discussed. There are useful accounts by Goldberg, *James I and the Politics of Literature*, pp. 120–3, and Jean Le Drew Metcalfe, 'Subjecting the King: Ben Jonson's praise of James I', *English Studies in Canada*, 17 (1991), 135–49.

But while shouts fill the streets, the real action in the poem is going on elsewhere, since James is represented as communing privately with Themis, the Homeric goddess of Divine Law, who whispers into his ear all the 'knowing arts' (1.128) he needs for kingship. By emphasising the gap between the people's disorderly enthusiasm and James's secret inner calm, the 'Panegyre' shifts attention away from the public event that it is commemorating, and for all that it celebrates James's first parliamentary consultation it projects a scepticism about popular politics which is very reminiscent of that in *Discoveries*. The people are depicted as grateful but undisciplined, and with Themis at his side James seems not so much advised as inspired. The poem's material politics happen neither in the assembly towards which the monarch travels, nor in the ceremonial's 'vain stirs' (1.75) which Themis tells him to ignore, but in the conversation taking place privately inside the royal breast.

A world of difference separates Jonson's 'Panegyre' from similar poems written for James around this time, such as Samuel Daniel's 'Panegyric Congratulatory' on the accession, presented to him the previous spring during his journey south. Daniel's panegyric welcomes James warmly, but it takes the poet's obligation to counsel the monarch with tedious literalness, and subjects him to a laborious lecture on the Daniellian vision of government. By contrast, Jonson's 'Panegyre' represents James as needing no such warnings, since he has already effortlessly internalised the necessary statecraft. Particularly, Themis's words instruct him in the needful distinctions between good laws and bad, telling him which of his predecessors' statutes he should awaken or let sleep:

> She showed him who made wise, who honest acts,
> Who both, who neither: all the cunning tracts
> And thriving statutes she could promptly note;
> The bloody, base, and barbarous she did quote;
> Where laws were made to serve the tyran' will,
> Where sleeping they could save, and waking kill . . . (ll.95–100)

Themis thereby foregrounds the statutory basis of Jacobean absolutism, but also identifies James as the law's interpreter, the voice of equity: the safeguards of good government are presented as lying not in the checks and balances of imperfect representative institutions but in the monarch's self-regulation and prior assurance as to what justice is. And the poem creates a special place in James's counsels for Jonson himself, since he has privileged access to the royal mind and only he and James can hear Themis's voice. The point is driven home in the epigraph, '*Solus rex et poeta non quotannis nascitur*', a favourite quotation from the Roman historian Florus: '[new consuls are made annually,] only kings and poets are not born every year'.[23] This maxim places poets and kings into their own special category, set politically apart by virtue of an authority that is never dependent on re-election. With poetry empowering monarchy and empowered by it, with kings and poets ranged together against vulgar democracy, the 'Panegyre' promotes a very close alignment between Jonson and James, if not a virtual identity.

Against this framework, we can begin to explore the politics of the better-known collections of poems published in 1616 as *The Epigrams* and *The Forest*. These have sometimes been read as anti-court gatherings. With their depiction of the good as a tiny élite almost overwhelmed by a tide of vice, their praise of withdrawal to the country, and their insistence that goodness and greatness rarely co-ordinate with one another, they seem far removed from the celebratory attitudes of Jonson's more public panegyric. Indeed, in his epistle to Lady Aubigny, Jonson warns 'I am at feud / With sin and vice, though with a throne endued' (*The Forest* 13.9–10).[24] Yet by and large these poems hold back from finding much vice in James's throne. *The Epigrams* situate James as the one figure in the collection who is entirely exempt from criticism — the poem 'To the Ghost of Martial' declares that whereas Martial flattered his prince, Jonson's 'cannot flattered be' (Epigram 36.4)[25] — and they underline his centrality by excluding any poems to his wife or children, thereby situating him squarely above the collection as a whole.[26] While James cannot make his people be good, the *Epigrams* need his presence in order to offset potential disturbers of the peace. His implied antagonists are the conspiracy theorists of 'The New Cry' (Epigram 92), who discuss state-affairs in ignorance of their real

---

[23] This maxim is also quoted or alluded to in Epigrams 4.1, and 79.1; *Every Man in his Humour*, V. v. 38–9; *The New Inn*, epilogue 23–4; and *Discoveries*, 2432–4.

[24] *Ben Jonson*, 8, p. 116.

[25] *Ben Jonson*, 8, p. 38.

[26] It is worth noticing that this remark holds good for the organisation of the Folio as a whole, even in respect of the masques which the Folio headings and title pages acknowledge were written for other members of the royal family. For example, although the *Masque of Queens* carried a dedication to Prince Henry in the quarto and to Queen Anne in the holograph, both of these were omitted when it was reprinted in 1616.

meaning, and the pompous Captain Hungry (Epigram 107), whose table-talk is a farrago of nonsensical foreign news: careless opinion-formers who in James's absence would destabilise society. As the collection unfolds, so other figures who are freighted with moral authority are drawn in, but Jonson assumes a stable and centralised kingly authority as his point of political departure and he implicitly parallels James's political supremacy with the author's poetic supremacy in his own literary community. When in Epigram 4, Jonson describes his Muse as flying 'to the best / Of Kings for grace, of poets for my test',[27] he imagines James stamping his verses as current, much as in the 'Tribe of Ben' epistle he sets his own seal on members of his poetic circle.

But if Jonson elevates the throne, by doing so he clears a space for significant political contrasts lower down. Stanley Fish points out that Jonson's good men all end up sounding alike, and certainly there's a considerable similarity about them,[28] but if we analyse who the people were that Jonson foregrounds, it is striking how much his élite is calibrated so as to avoid seeming directly to reproduce Whitehall's hierarchies. Noticeably, there are no epigrams to the favourites, Montgomery, Hay, and Somerset, and of James's closest advisors, only one poem goes to Suffolk and none at all to Northampton.[29] The chief minister, Salisbury, has three epigrams, but these are followed by the poem complaining that a lord whom Jonson had praised turned out to be worthless, the juxtaposition strongly insinuating that the understanding reader should not take Salisbury's portrayal simply at face value.[30] By contrast, poems bulk large to men whose relationship with the centre

---

[27] Epigram 4.9–10 (*Ben Jonson*, 8, p. 28).

[28] Fish, 'Authors-readers: Jonson's Community of the Same', pp. 38–9, 45–8.

[29] According to Drummond, Northampton was responsible for Jonson's prosecution over *Sejanus* and Jonson regarded him as an enemy (*Ben Jonson*, 1, p. 141). Jonson did write one poem to Somerset (*Ungathered Verse*, 18), but suppressed it after the 1615 scandal. Jonson was to write an entertainment for Lord Hay in 1617 (*Lovers Made Men*), but he was responsible neither for the masque for Hay's wedding (1607) nor for Hay's Essex House masque of January 1621 (recently rediscovered by Tim Raylor and forthcoming in *English Manuscript Studies*).

[30] On this evident structural irony, se R. Wiltenburg, ' "What need hast thou of me? or of my Muse?": Jonson and Cecil, Politican and Poet', in *"The Muses Common-Weale": Poetry and Politics in the Seventeenth Century*, eds C. J. Summers and T.-L. Pebworth (Columbia, Mo., 1988), pp. 34–47. Jonson expressed a very negative view of Salisbury in his conversations with Drummond (*Ben Jonson*, 1, p. 141). On the general circulation of hostile representations of Salisbury, see P. Croft, 'The Reputation of Robert Cecil: Libels, Political Opinion and Popular Awareness in the Early Seventeenth Century', *Transactions of the Royal Historical Society*, 6th ser., 1 (1991), 43–69.

was conflicted, or who, when the *Epigrams* were collected (probably in 1612),[31] stood only at the edges of power.[32] Quite a few epigrams are addressed to survivors of the circle of the disgraced Earl of Essex. Although restored to favour by James, the Essexians lacked real influence, and while not sharing their forward politics, Jonson did appreciate their Tacitean view of the state. One of these men, Sir Henry Neville (Epigram 109), led the attempt to manage the 1614 Parliament.[33] Another ambitious place-seeker was Sir Thomas Overbury (Epigram 113), his name made prominent in the Folio after his murder by Frances Howard.[34] The poem to the Earl of Pembroke (Epigram 102) has a conspicuous place, and he was a more entrenched figure, who was in James's favour from the outset. Still, he did not reach the Privy Council until 1611, and he was from early on perceived as no ready ally to the conservative ruling group, his dealings with the Howards being distinctly antagonistic.[35] And in both *The Epigrams* and *The Forest* special

[31] The question of the date at which Jonson made the collections is discussed in the appendix to this lecture.

[32] My argument here runs close to that of B. Worden's essay 'Ben Jonson Among the Historians', in *Culture and Politics in Early Stuart England*, eds K. Sharpe and P. Lake (Houndmills, 1994), p. 87.

[33] On Neville, see P. W. Hasler, *The House of Commons 1558–1603* (3 vols, London, 1981), 3, pp. 122–3; C. Roberts, *Schemes and Undertakings* (Columbus, Oh., 1985); and A. Patterson, *Reading Between the Lines* (New Haven, 1993), pp. 182, 199–200. Other former Essexians in *The Epigrams* and *The Forest* include Sir Robert Sidney and (via three poems addressed to his wife) the Earl of Rutland; Lord Monteagle (who had been imprisoned and fined in 1601, but had come into high favour through his discovery of the Gunpowder Plot); the friends 'Shelton' and 'Heydon' who are named in 'The Famous Voyage' (Epigram 133; discussed in my as yet unpublished essay 'Jonson's Brave Wights'); and some of the military men such as Sir John Roe, Sir John Radcliffe, Sir Henry Goodyere and Sir Henry Cary, who also emanated from the Essex network (though Roe was not in fact one of Essex's knights, and Goodyere was from 1603 a Gentleman of the Privy Chamber). Sir Henry Savile (Epigram 95) had also found himself under question after the Essex affair. As the references to Essex in *Cynthia's Revels* suggest, Jonson's attitude to the Essex group was far from simple. For some general commentary, see *Poetaster*, ed. T. G. S. Cain (Manchester, 1995), pp. 40–7; and J. H. M. Salmon, 'Seneca and Tacitus in Jacobean England', in *The Mental World of the Jacobean Court*, ed. L. L. Peck (Cambridge, 1991), pp. 169–88. For James's treatment of the Essexians, see N. Cuddy, 'The Revival of the Entourage: the Bedchamber of James I, 1603–1625', in *The English Court: From the Wars of the Roses to the English Civil War*, ed. D. Starkey (London, 1987), pp. 173–225, and 'Anglo-Scottish Union and the Court of James I, 1603–1625', *Transactions of the Royal Historical Society*, 5th ser., 39 (1989), 107–24.

[34] The most illuminating discussion of the Overbury affair is D. Lindley, *The Trials of Frances Howard* (London, 1994).

[35] Pembroke quarrelled with Somerset over the Mastership of the Horse in 1612, was reconciled by Neville, then decisively fell out again in 1614; he was a leader of the anti-

place is given to the Sidneys, a dynasty eclipsed at court by the Howard revival. Although Sir Robert Sidney was Anne's chamberlain and spent lavishly at Whitehall, he too had been involved with Essex, and access to the higher offices he wanted was blocked by Northampton. His notebooks, with their sombre thoughts on liberty and sovereignty, suggest that his views were coloured by aristocratic anxieties inherited from his dead brother Philip. His career passed off quietly, but the family legacy was played out in later generations. In the 1640s his son withdrew from public life rather than choose between parliament and king, and two of his grandsons sat on Cromwell's Council of State. One of these, Algernon, was executed in 1683 for republican conspiracy.[36]

By the time the Folio reached print, the scandals which brought down Somerset had drastically altered the face of the court, and in dedicating the *Epigrams* and *Catiline* to Pembroke Jonson proudly drew attention to his new appointment as Chamberlain (which almost certainly happened while the volume was in the press).[37] But the Folio's ideological alignment with Whitehall might have seemed more indirect had its publication not been overtaken by these events. For example, the 1611 quarto of *Catiline* had coupled Pembroke's dedication with an address to 'the reader extraordinary', describing such a reader as 'the better man, though places in court go otherwise': in 1616 this was tactfully dropped.[38] Of course, praise and blame for individual courtiers did not in itself call the system into question, and Jonson's favoured

---

Somerset cabal promoting the new favourite Villiers in 1614–15. See PRO SP14/70, fo. 46; T. Birch, *The Court and Times of James I* (2 vols, London, 1849), 2: 210; Historical Manuscripts Commission *Report* 45 (Buccleuch MSS), 1: 131; 60 (Mar and Kellie), supplement, p. 51; and Brian O'Farrell, Politican, Patron, Poet: William Herbert, Third Earl of Pembroke 1580–1630, Ph.D. thesis (UCLA 1966). Another Pembroke connection in the *Epigrams* is his close parliamentary ally Sir Benjamin Rudyerd (Epigram 121).

[36] There are full accounts by B. Worden, 'Classical Republicanism and the Puritan Revolution', in *History and Imagination*, eds H. Lloyd-Jones, V. Pearl and B. Worden (London, 1981), pp. 185–7; M. V. Hay, *The Life of Robert Sidney, Earl of Leicester (1563–1626)* (Washington, D.C., 1984); and J. Scott, *Algernon Sidney and the English Republic, 1623–1677* (Cambridge, 1988), pp. 55–8. Northampton's enmity to Robert Sidney continued beyond the grave, since at his death (in 1614) he commanded that none of the offices which he left behind should be allowed to fall into Sidney's hands. I should like to acknowledge how much conversations with the late Margot Heinemann have shaped my thinking about Jonson and the Sidneys.

[37] See M. Butler, 'Jonson's Folio and the Politics of Patronage', *Criticism*, 35 (1993), 379–81.

[38] *Ben Jonson*, 5, p. 432.

friends were not at all a courtly 'opposition' but men who participated fully in court life and were eager for office.[39] Although Jonson praises Pembroke for keeping 'one true posture, though beseiged with ill / Of what ambition, faction, pride can raise' (Epigram 102.14–15),[40] Pembroke was actually far more involved in the pursuit of power than the poem about him acknowledged. Equally, the satirical epigrams on bad courtiers such as Court-Worm and My Lord Ignorant do not signal an attack on Whitehall as such but are a device brought into being by Jonson's strategies of conditional praise. Reproducing a manoeuvre made familiar in the masques, in which heroes are legitimated through the delegitimation of opposing figures in the antimasques, the Epigrams display their bad examples in order that the excellence of good courtiers like Pembroke can be established. Not so much satirising the court as recalling it to a standard of value to which it ought constantly to aspire, they imagine a world of 'strife'[41] and incorrigibly vicious courtiers so that the better few, when in the Epigrams they eventually arrive, may be marked out as different.

Nonetheless, by embodying this value in 'outs' as well as 'ins', Jonson imagines a code of obligation which cuts against the unregulated pursuit of courtly reward, and implies an ideal economy in which aristocrats ought to act as responsible servants to the Crown's political needs. If the main political danger in the Epigrams is excessive democracy, the second is excessive aristocratic self-will, and the anti-social attitudes which that creates. The embodiment of this tendency is Don Surly, in Epigram 28:[42]

> Don Surly, to aspire the glorious name
>   Of a great man, and to be thought the same,
> Makes serious use of all great trade he knows.
>   He speaks to men with a rhinocerote's nose,
> Which he thinks great; and so reads verses, too;
>   And that is done as he saw great men do.
> He has tympanies of business in his face,
>   And can forget men's names with a great grace.
> He will both argue and discourse in oaths,

---

[39] This point is strongly made by D. Norbrook in *Poetry and Politics in the English Renaissance* (London, 1984), pp. 184–5. Although I am trying to effect some modifications to Norbrook's case, it will be readily seen that the whole of this lecture is immensely indebted to his brilliant discussion.

[40] *Ben Jonson*, 8, p. 66.

[41] Epigram 102, 1.5 (*Ben Jonson*, 8, p. 66).

[42] *Ben Jonson*, 8, p. 35–6.

Both which are great; and laugh at ill-made clothes —
    That's greater yet — to cry his own up neat.
He doth, at meals, alone, his pheasant eat,
    Which is main greatness. And at his still board
He drinks to no man; that's too, like a lord.
    He keeps another's wife, which is a spice
Of solemn greatness. And he dares at dice
    Blaspheme God, greatly; or some poor hind beat
That breathes in his dog's way; and this is great.
    Nay more, for greatness' sake, he will be one
May hear my epigrams, but like of none.
    Surly, use other arts; these only can
Style thee a most great fool, but no great man.

It's not entirely clear whether Surly is a bad aristocrat or a would-be
aristocrat emulating what he thinks is proper carriage. Either way, he
reduces greatness to merely externalised markers, a puppet-like beha-
viourism of manners and dress. Jonson's special scorn is reserved for
Surly's pompousness and the contempt with which he treats others.
Mistakenly supposing that isolation sets off greatness, Surly lives a life
that is profoundly solipsistic, and he is condemned by this most convivial of poets to the ultimate Jonsonian hell, dining on his own. By
contrast, Epigram 101, 'Inviting a Friend to Supper', promises a feast
the collegiality of which overrides barriers of social distinction. The
opening lines of Jonson's invitation draw attention to the difference in
'gravity' between host and guest — 'Tonight, grave sir, both my poor
house and I / Do equally desire your company' (ll.1–2)[43] — but by the
end every mark of social difference has been left behind in the 'liberty'
(1.42) which all Jonson's worthy friends will enjoy alike. Inevitably this
liberty is not open to all, as is shown by the further contrast with
Captain Hungry in Epigram 107. Jonson feeds Hungry but refuses
him any social condescension, and evidently he would not have been
welcome at the other supper. Still, if plebeian trouble-makers are denied
admission, so too are self-aggrandising figures like Don Surly. Jonson
expects that good aristocrats will be properly communicative to deserving men such as himself.

The poem which most elaborately develops this ideal political
economy is 'To Penshurst' (*The Forest* 2), with its exemplary images

---

[43] *Ben Jonson*, 8, p. 64. The Oxford editors interpreted this epigram's implied addressee to
be some such 'grave sir' as Camden (*Ben Jonson*, 11, p. 20), but the poem is eloquently
interpreted as an argument about social difference by T. M. Greene in *The Light in Troy:
Imitation and Discovery in Renaissance Poetry* (1982), pp. 278–82.

of the King favouring the Sidney family, and the Sidneys fulfilling their social function as bridges between the monarch and the wider community. This poem is sometimes read as implicit advice to the Sidneys to keep a low profile and avoid excess spending, as at the time of writing the family finances were indeed being badly eroded by the need to follow the court.[44] But this interpretation somewhat misses the mark, since although 'To Penshurst' praises the country life, it is not exactly against the court, nor even is it against spending as such. Rather, it praises the generous hospitality maintained by the Sidneys at Penshurst and associates it with qualities of sociability and altruism, whereas the blame for bad spending is laid at the door of aristocrats whose consumption lacks equivalent social motive. Although Jonson's language avoids scoring specific points, it must have been hard for contemporaries not to make some passing connections between his poem's dispraise of selfish aristocatic display and the reputation that had come to be attached to the Earl of Salisbury. If, as seems likely, the poem was written in the summer of 1612,[45] it came immediately in the wake of Salisbury's death, and it contains at least one submerged allusion to him: its remark that at Penshurst guests eat the same food as their host, unlike tables where the guests sit with the lord 'yet dine away' (1.66), echoes a complaint which Jonson later (and of course privately) made to William Drummond about his own experience of Salisbury's defective hospitality.[46] Further, the mention of Penshurst's household gods (1.79) harks back to the show that Jonson had written when Salisbury's palace at Theobalds was given to the King, the scene for which depicted the household gods at Theobalds.[47] Although the architectural contrast between Penshurst and other estates 'built to envious show' (1.1) fitted any number of Jacobean prodigy houses, Salisbury had more than any other official invested his gains in astonishing mansions, what Lawrence Stone has called a 'fantastic orgy of building' in London and the provinces, culminating in the £40,000 he lavished on Hatfield House before his death.[48] As Treasurer, Master of the Court of Wards and

---

[44] The seminal account is J. Rathmell's essay 'Jonson, Lord Lisle, and Penshurst', *English Literary Renaissance*, 1 (1971), 250–60.

[45] The reference to Prince Henry in 1.77 puts the poem before November 1612 (when Henry died), and John Rathmell suggests that the 'walls . . . of the country stone' (1.45) allude to the estate building being undertaken from May 1612. Salisbury died on 12 May 1612.

[46] *Ben Jonson*, 1, p. 141.

[47] *Ben Jonson*, 7, p. 155.

[48] L. Stone, *Family and Fortune: Studies in Aristocratic Finance in the Sixteenth and Seventeenth Centuries* (Oxford, 1973), p. 32; and see, generally, pp. 31–2, 62–113.

Secretary of State, he had been in a position to exploit three offices that offered unrivalled opportunities for profit, and lived in a style that manifested it. Against such prodigious spending-power, the Sidneys were small beer indeed.

The project of 'To Penshurst' is to find values in the Sidney lifestyle which offer a more productive model than this for the relationship between aristocrats, the monarch and the realm. The Sidneys are presented as stewards of their domain, landlords whose ownership is justified by the life of exemplary discipline which they lead. They are neither self-aggrandising courtiers nor an oppositional 'country' party, but channels of influence between centre and periphery, who instil into their locality attitudes of obligation which render it tractable to Stuart power. A great deal of ink has been spilled accusing Jonson of mystifying social relations at Penshurst, as if the poem somehow sought to conceal the structures of power which, notwithstanding, it quite conspicuously describes.[49] But on the contrary, 'To Penshurst' overtly represents the estate as existing for the Sidneys' benevolent exploitation — its produce is shown as being cultivated in order that it may be eaten — and the structure of its second half pointedly underlines the importance of hierarchy in Sidney affairs. The visitors who are described as coming to the Penshurst estate pass through the poem in order of rank, from the local farmers, then guests from further afield, then the King himself, while the poet is welcomed like a veritable monarch, who eats Penshurst's food 'As if thou then wert mine, or I reigned here' (1.74). Penshurst is neither a status-free Utopia nor an oppositional counter-community set against the court, but a perfect court in the country, a reproduction in little of what the good state ought to be.

In Jonson's depiction, then, the Sidneys appear admirable because of the absorption of their aristocratic individualism into the corporate structures of a smoothly-functioning estate. At Penshurst, everything has purpose within the controlling hierarchies — even the walks are 'for health as well as sport' (1.9) — and the estate is bound into a corporate deference fostered by the family's aristocratic bearing, the 'mysteries of manners, arms and arts' (1.98) which they embody. Down in the pastures the lower land 'bends' (1.22) deferentially to the centre, while

---

[49] On this topic, see the important series of discussions by A. Fowler: *Conceitful Thought* (Edinburgh, 1975); 'Country House Poems: The Politics of a Genre', *The Seventeenth Century*, 1 (1986), pp. 1–14; *The Country House Poem* (Edinburgh, 1994).

at table the waiter serves without anxiety, knowing the reserves of food that lie below (ll.67–70). The passage depicting the estate's creatures offering themselves as produce is a playful exaggeration of just such service:

> The painted partridge lies in every field,
>> And for thy mess is willing to be killed.
> And if the high-swoll'n Medway fail thy dish,
>> Thou hast thy ponds that pay thee tribute fish:
> Fat, aged carps, that run into thy net;
>> And pikes, now weary their own kind to eat,
> As loath the second draught or cast to stay,
>> Officiously, at first, themselves betray;
> Bright eels, that emulate them, and leap on land
>> Before the fisher, or into his hand. (ll.29–38)

The creatures are presented as not only sacrificing themselves but doing so eagerly, competing for the honour of being the lord's most devoted servant. Jonson's hyperbole suggests that there are circumstances in which such subordination is not entirely admirable: his politicised language — 'tribute', 'officiously', 'emulate' — implies a reflection on power relations beyond Penshurst, the competitiveness and self-promoting servility that service is seen to be under less altruistic masters. By comparison, relations with the tenants are dignified and reciprocal. Unlike the clientage system at Whitehall, where gifts are the currency of favour and business only gets done through bribes, the tenants at Penshurst bring offerings to their landlords even when 'they have no suit' (1.50). And by addressing the poem directly to Penshurst, and only indirectly to its owner, Jonson makes it sound as though everything is done for a corporate ethos, the pronouns implying that the estate itself is the object of all this goodwill. The Sidneys seem less owners than deputies, servants to the royal master who arrives at the poem's culmination, their good stewardship channelling his authority outwards to the realm at large. Whereas grand palaces (like Hatfield?) make power 'grudged at', Penshurst exemplifies a harmony of purpose between monarch, deputy and realm, and consequently is 'reverenced the while' (1.6).

When in the 1616 Folio Jonson reprinted *Cynthia's Revels*, with its satire on late-Elizabethan Whitehall, he substantially revised it so as to underline the now-closer relationship between poet and monarch, and added a dedication to the court under James, contrasting the present courtiers with those of the last reign, and warning them that they had to be a mirror for the whole kingdom: to this he signed himself off, politely but provocatively, as 'thy servant, but not slave'.[50] I am suggesting that the political relationships between king, poet and court implied in the 1616 dedication for *Cynthia's Revels* were being worked out across *The Epigrams* and *The Forest* as a whole. On one side, Jonson seems to assume the need for a strong and centralised monarchy: he presents James's rule as autocratic yet just, imperious yet still responsible. On the other side, James's aristocracy is praised insofar as it fulfils this king-centred ideal, and dispraised for failures of pride, selfish ostentation and vain pursuit of title: while the Sidneys' relations with the centre may have been more vexed than the poems addressed to them admit, Jonson fashions the family into idealised public servants who are both instrumental and exemplary to the Jacobean state. And although the King is only passingly invoked in the two collections themselves, the positioning of the poems within the whole Folio volume reinforces their mediatory function in Jonson's encompassing poetic kingdom. The Folio situates the poems as a bridge between the satirical drama written for the stage and the political ceremonials staged for Jacobean Christmas festivities, so that they act as preludes to Jonson's public and more elaborately ritualised representations of James as the founder of a new British monarchy. Not only do the masques enunciate the themes of union, peace and stability which as political context the poems require, they give consolidated expression to an aesthetic economy built on a sustained and reciprocal alliance between poetry and power.

In 1616 Jonson's public poetry might have been seen as closely aligned with the ideological co-ordinates of Jacobean monarchy, and serviceable to its political needs. Yet during the two remaining decades of the poet's life, the political economy of Stuart Britain was to come under intense pressure, with significant consequences for the practice of Jonsonian panegyric. James's rule was premised on the maintenance of a broad ideological consensus and on the overriding value of peace, but after 1620 the crisis which rapidly developed on the Continent threatened to overwhelm his eirenic commitments, and he kept out of the escalating European war only at the cost of polarising opinion at home. In 1625, Charles did take England into war, but the administrative

---

[50] *Ben Jonson*, 4, p. 33.

traumas which resulted nearly wrecked his rule at the outset, and the decade ended with deadlock between Crown and Parliament and a legacy of anxiety about the arbitrary tendencies of Caroline kingship. The consequences for Jonson can be simply described. He continued to act as court panegyrist, writing masques which propounded the desirability of peace and vigorously praised the wisdom of James's cautious diplomacy and far-seeing sovereign authority. Yet during the 1620s a series of his friends and associates appeared on the opposite side of the emerging rift with the Crown. Pembroke functioned increasingly as Buckingham's main political rival from within Whitehall; Selden was twice imprisoned following his repeated participation in parliamentary attacks on royal policy; in 1626 Sir Francis Stewart, the dedicatee of *Epicoene*, helped the Commons' attempt to impeach the Duke;[51] in 1628 another friend, Zouch Townley, fled the country when his verses praising Buckingham's assassin were found at Cotton's library;[52] and the library itself was closed after the 1629 Parliament on suspicion that it had become a source for the dissemination of dangerous literature and seditious ideas.

In the Folio's arrangement of *The Epigrams*, Jonson's virtuous men occupy a space that seems outside politics and free from ideological contention. Like the performers in the court masques, they are a band of brothers between whom no disagreements appear to exist, since potential antagonisms in the horizontal plane have all been absorbed by their common commitment to vertical loyalties. But such images were harder to sustain in the more polarised circumstances of Jonson's later life, and the sense of lost bearings which has been found in some of the later verse may be traced not so much to his supposed poetic dotage, as to a climate of dissolving consensus in the nation at large which profoundly impacted on the established co-ordinates of his early Jacobean poetry. If 'Inviting a Friend to Supper' had envisaged sociable meetings at which aristocrats and intellectuals talked innocently about Virgil and Tacitus, by 1630 that imagined space had become badly eroded. Tacitus alone gave off dangerous signals: indeed, both in parliamentary debates and in libels circulating beyond Westminister, Buckingham had been lampooned as a Sejanus.[53] At the same time, it was becoming harder for

---

[51] See M. Butler, 'Sir Francis Stewart: Jonson's Overlooked Patron', *Ben Jonson Journal*, 2 (1996) (forthcoming).

[52] *Ben Jonson*, 1, p. 242–4.

[53] See the examples quoted by J. Forster, *Sir John Eliot: A Biography*, 2 vols (London, 1864), 1, pp. 548, 552, and by R. Cust, 'News and Politics in Early Seventeenth Century England', *Past and Present*, 111 (1986), pp. 65–6.

court panegyric to make the disposings of the royal will seem indisputably authoritative, and in Jonson's later masques James had repeatedly to be depicted as vindicating his sovereign power in the face of challenges presented to it by newsmongers, political meddlers, and rebelliously disruptive plebeians. The masques may still have represented James as triumphantly schooling his people for opinions that were foolishly seditious and warmongering, but their cost was the damage which such representations did to assumptions about his kingly transcendence. Effectively, the fables mounted by these masques conceded that Jacobean rule was no longer seen as being simply beyond contest.

The poem which most fully registers the erosion of past certainties is the 'Epistle Answering unto One that Asked to be Sealed of the Tribe of Ben' (*Underwood* 47).[54] This was written in the autumn of 1623 while Prince Charles was still on his way home from Madrid after his ill-starred mission to bring back a Spanish bride. Jonson had not been invited to help prepare the welcome that had been planned for the Infanta, and the poem voices a personalised complaint about his neglect, so that here, for once, the contrast between the poet's circle of a few select friends and a public world where relationships are sordid and mercenary seems genuinely motivated by resentment. Contemptuously describing the dancers in even his own masques as 'Christmas clay / And animated porcelain' (ll.52–3), Jonson consoles himself with a fantasy of superiority which is easily understood in Stanley Fish's terms, as private compensation for having been excluded. But unexpectedly, the poem's central section presents a review of current politics and, particularly, of the possibility that England might now side with France in a war against Spain, which connects Jonson's personal discomfiture with misgivings of a more political kind:

> What is't to me whether the French design
>   Be, or be not, to get the Valtelline?
> Or the States' ships sent forth belike to meet
>   Some hopes of Spain in their West Indian fleet?
> Whether the dispensation yet be sent,
>   Or that the match from Spain was ever meant?
> I wish all well, and pray high heaven conspire
>   My prince's safety and my king's desire;
> But if, for honour, we must draw the sword,
>   And force back that which will not be restored,

---

[54] *Ben Jonson*, 8, pp. 218–20.

> I have a body yet that spirit draws
> To live, or fall a carcass in the cause. (ll.31–42)

This is often read as Jonson's statement of indifference towards politics ('What is't to me . . . ?'), or as covert criticism of James's long appeasement of Spain by a poet willing to embrace more resolute action.[55] In fact, the policy considerations which Jonson so loftily disregards — control of the strategically-important Valtelline pass, speculation that Spain's treasure fleet might be captured, and suspicions that the Spanish marriage proposals had all along been just a diversionary tactic — were those dear to the hearts of the war party, whose aim was always to foment a general European combination against Spain.[56] But a land campaign for the recovery of the Palatinate (that territory which, with the collapse of the marriage, 'will not be restored' through diplomacy), was a war for an altogether narrower objective. If Jonson's lines picture him drawing his sword, it was because this specific and rather more limited aim had now become the will of Prince Charles, who was returning brideless from Madrid, disenchanted with the negotiations and convinced that his 'honour' had been impugned.[57]

This passage, then, seems unhappily caught between Jonson's investment in James's old peace policy, which was now self-evidently faltering, and the need to find ways of accommodating the war towards which Charles seemed likely to move without appearing simply to capitulate to the general European bloodbath that Jacobean diplomacy had always sought to avert. But the importance of these lines lies less in the minutiae of the specific strategies to which they allude, significant though they are, than in their admission that the singularity of royal power had been called into question, and that in this crisis it was no longer clear that James's will would prevail. With James's peace stalled, and a rift opening with Prince Charles, it must have seemed as though the political certainties which underpinned the earlier poetry were under severe pressure, if not on the verge of collapse. So while the

---

[55] For the indifference interpretation, see Riggs, *Ben Jonson: A Life*, p. 286; for covert criticism, see R. C. Evans, ' "Men that are Safe and Sure": Jonson's "Tribe of Ben" Epistle in its patronage context', *Renaissance and Reformation*, 21 (1985), 235–54.

[56] The relationship of this passage to the rapidly shifting politics of 1623 is discussed in much greater detail in M. Butler, 'The Dates of Three Poems by Ben Jonson', *Huntington Library Quarterly*, 55 (1992), 284–7.

[57] The best narrative of the domestic response to the collapse of James's foreign policy is T. Cogswell's *The Blessed Revolution: English Politics and the Coming of War, 1621–1624* (Cambridge, 1989).

poem as a whole voices Jonson's response to fears of being margin-
alised, it also lacks that countervailing public reassurance, so central to
the earlier verse, that his poetic authority was ultimately guaranteed by
a framework of stable royal power. On the contrary, the wits from
whom, in the first part of the 'Epistle', the threat to the poet seems to
come are not only shallow and immoral jeerers whose views are
beneath contempt, but political meddlers reminiscent of Captain Hungry and the pocket statesmen of 'The New Cry', dangerous and opinio-
nated voices of a kind that were increasingly clamorous in the 1620s. If
in those earlier texts, such noise-makers were overtly or implicitly
contained by the stabilities of a world at peace, in this poem peace
appears to be in the balance and 'wild anarchy' (1.10) to have invaded
all but that privileged space with which Jonson tries to associate
himself. What seems most conspicuously absent from the 'Epistle' is
any conviction that the Crown would rise confidently and serenely
above the current crisis. On the contrary, the poem's disconcerting
perception that the monarchy's political voice had suddenly become
divided leaves Jonson's affirmations sounding fragile and disoriented.
The poem that most anxiously asserts the pre-eminence of Jonson's
private space does so at the precise historical moment at which James's
public authority seemed itself to be coming into question.

In his last years, Jonson lived a shadowy half-life near the Caroline
court and only fitfully experienced reliable patronage from the Crown.[58]
He seems to have enjoyed a number of links to the circle of Edward
Hyde and Lucius Cary, men who though strong supporters of monarchy
were critics of Charles's arbitrary exactions and were deeply attached to
a vision of Church and State governed according to stable principles of
law. In the early months of the Long Parliament they would emerge as
the leading moderate reformers, and were eventually to compose the
nucleus of the constitutional royalists. He also had good patrons in two
men who were more closely tied to the Crown. One recipient of a series
of poems was Charles's Treasurer, Richard Weston, who was well
known for his advocacy of peace, fiscal retrenchment and prerogative
finance. After Buckingham's death, it was Weston on whom the leaders
of the 1629 Parliament turned their fire and, not surprisingly, he was
thereafter one of the firmest proponents of Charles's personal rule.

[58] In this paragraph I am summarising the more detailed account given in M. Butler, 'Late
Jonson', in *The Politics of Tragicomedy: Shakespeare and After*, eds G. McMullan and J.
Hope (London, 1992), pp. 168–71.

Jonson's other major patron was the Earl of Newcastle, who gave the ageing poet support of both a material and aesthetic kind. One of Charles's most cultured but also most conservative aristocrats, Newcastle was out of step with fashionable Whitehall, but he believed fervently in the values of order, ceremony and title and was eventually to general the royal army: he is perhaps one model for Lovel, the idealised Caroline aristocrat, in *The New Inn*.[59] In the context of these friendships, Jonson preserved that image of himself as the favoured laureate poet whose masques should have been celebrations of Stuart power. In practice, though, his pension was often in arrears and the alignment of political and poetic authority which his verse assumed was no longer so confident.

When in 1629 *The New Inn* had a disastrous public reception at the Blackfriars, Jonson's response, as ventriloquised in the 'Ode to Himself', was to spurn his critics as an unworthy jury and turn for his justification to a better, more royal audience. From now on, the ode claimed, the Jonsonian lyre would only 'sing / The glories of [my] king', 'tuning forth the acts of his sweet reign, / And raising Charles his chariot 'bove his wain'.[60] But in the event Jonson had few opportunities of tuning forth the acts of Charles's sweet reign, since he wrote only one more pair of masques before his catastrophic quarrel with Inigo Jones, and thereafter the commissions went to other poets, denying him his usual forum for sustained public performances. As a consequence, for all the ode's political resolve, Jonson's work for Charles beyond the two masques lacks the prestigious invocations of Stuart monarchy which are so crucial a component of his Jacobean career, and is confined to frequent but fugitive congratulatory verses on royal births and anniversaries. These short poems seem dutiful rather than distinguished, and despite their praise of the dynasty, they are remarkable for the difficulty they have in finding ways of making Charles's power sound persuasive. They insist on the King's piety and glory, and his status as an example to his people, but they are equally preoccupied with the inner political divisions which persist, in spite of the outward peace:[61]

---

[59] There are recent treatments of Jonson's relations with Newcastle in R. C. Evans, *Jonson and the Contexts of his Time* (Lewisburg, 1994), pp. 35–44, and N. Rowe, ' "My Best Patron": William Cavendish and Jonson's Caroline Drama', *The Seventeenth Century*, 9 (1994), 197–212.

[60] *Ben Jonson*, 6, p. 494.

[61] *Ben Jonson*, 8, pp. 236–7.

> How happy were the subject, if he knew,
>   Most pious king, but his own good in you!
> How many times, "Live long, Charles!" would he say,
>   If he but weighed the blessings of this day.

These lines, from the epigram on the fourth anniversary of the accession, make Charles sound not so much imperious as beleaguered, and they admit almost inadvertently that Stuart majesty had been diminished. The only solution is for the poet to instil respect for the monarch into his subjects, but as the poem goes on perplexedly to admit, if the people refuse to see the efficacy of Charles's rule there is nothing more poets can do to inculcate it:

> O times! O manners! sufeit bred of ease,
>   The truly epidemical disease!
> 'Tis not alone the merchant, but the clown
>   Is bankrupt turned; the cassock, cloak and gown
> Are lost upon account! and none will know
>   How much to heaven for thee, great Charles, they owe!

Not surprisingly, the more strongly Jonson needs to protest that the goodness of Caroline government is self-evident, the more unconvincing these protests sound: the claim to royal legitimation which the poem makes is belied by the fact that, if it was felt to be incontestable, the poem would not have to be written. This is a contradiction which continues to reverberate through all the public poems written after 1628 and which severely damages Jonson's ability to project images of a transcendent royal authority. It is symptomatic of how far the ideological co-ordinates of his Jacobean poetry were being undermined by the more polarised politics of the later reign.

In one of the last of his panegyrics, the 1633 epigram on the christening of the royal infant James, Jonson once again urged Charles's people to recognise 'how much they are beloved of God in thee', but by going on to add 'Would they would understand it!' he seemed to acknowledge the unlikelihood of this kind of rhetoric taking hold any longer. Instead, this epigram pointedly harked back to less divided times, to the reign of the new prince's namesake and to the British certainties which it had been one project of Jonson's earlier verse to associate with him:[62]

> Grow up, sweet babe, as blessed in thy name,
>   As in renewing thy good grandsire's fame;

[62] ibid. p. 268.

> Methought Great Britain in her sea before
>   Sat safe enough, but now secured more.
> At land she triumphs in the triple shade
>   Her rose and lily, intertwined, have made.

It's tempting to speculate that from the vantage point of a monarchy that was less receptive to humanistic ideas of poetic counsel and that could no longer be represented as automatically validated by its kingly transcendence, Jonson may have looked back with some nostalgia to James's reign, and to the relatively confident belief which he had then enjoyed, and sought to project, in a productive symbiosis between king and poet. There is relatively little evidence from Jonson's Caroline writings for a conscious reassessment of the age of James, but perhaps he was indeed seeking to reinvoke the assurances of earlier times when he reserved for the title-page of his finest play, *Bartholomew Fair* — written in 1614 but not printed until 1631 — the brief but resonant dedication: 'to King JAMES, of most blessed memory, by the author, Ben Jonson'.[63]

Appendix: The Dating of the *Epigrams*

Although as a group the Epigrams first appeared in print in the 1616 Folio, there is evidence which suggests that Jonson had plans to publish them separately rather earlier. On 15 May 1612 the printer John Stepneth made an entry in the Stationers' Register for 'A Booke called, Ben Johnson his Epigrams', and this seems strongly to indicate that by this date Jonson may already have assembled his collection. In the event, Stepneth died shortly afterwards and the volume probably did not appear, though in one of William Drummond's manuscript notes 'Ben Jhonsons epigrams' are listed amongst the 'bookes red be me anno 1612'.[64] This may be evidence that the book actually was published and Drummond did possess a copy of it. Alternatively, he might have had access to the Epigrams in a manuscript collection: certainly if the book was printed, no copies have as yet been found. Strikingly, when the Epigrams appeared in the Folio, they bore the title-page designation 'EPIGRAMMES. I. BOOKE', which suggests that Jonson kept in mind the possibility of collecting a second volume of epigrams for separate

[63] *Ben Jonson*, 6, p. 9.
[64] *Ben Jonson*, 8, p. 16.

publication later. Two further points in favour of the hypothesis of 1612 collection are the facts that the potentially satirical treatment of Salisbury's epigrams (discussed above) would have been very indelicate before the Treasurer's death, and that by far the bulk of the Epigrams that can be dated seem to have been written by 1612.

The two obstacles to this deduction are Epigrams 67 ('To Thomas, Earl of Suffolk') and 133 ('On the Famous Voyage'), both of which, it can be argued, possibly allude to events of *c*.1613–14. However the evidence, which has recently been fully reviewed by Ian Donaldson,[65] is by no means straightforward.

Epigram 67

Ian Donaldson notes the suggestion in Peter Whalley's 1756 edition that the concluding lines of Suffolk's epigram might refer to his appointment in 1614 as Lord Treasurer. Yet the lines, describing Suffolk as 'confirmed [in] thy king's choice' (l.11), are not at all specific, and could without difficulty have been applied to him at any time from 1603 onwards, when he was appointed Lord Chamberlain. In favour of a date considerably before 1614 is the fact that Jonson's relationship with Suffolk seems to have been at its strongest early in the reign. Suffolk was one of the noblemen to whom Jonson appealed for help when he was imprisoned in 1605 over *Eastward Ho!*, and shortly afterwards he received the prestigious commission for the masque to mark the wedding between Suffolk's daughter, Frances Howard, and the Earl of Essex (*Hymenaei*, danced in January 1606). As a frequent author of court masques, Jonson would have had to negotiate directly with Suffolk during James's first decade, since as Lord Chamberlain he had overall responsibility for the running of these occasions. Arguably, Suffolk's 1614 appointment as Treasurer would actually have reduced Jonson's opportunities for contact with him.

Epigram 133

The Oxford editors dated 'The Famous Voyage' *c*.1610, but Ian Donaldson notes a suggestion that the penultimate couplet alludes to building works at Clerkenwell (to the north-east of the city) connected

---

[65] See Ian Donaldson's edition of the Oxford Authors *Ben Jonson* (Oxford, 1985), p. 646.

with Sir Hugh Myddleton's New River scheme, which opened in 1613:[66]

> In memory of which most liquid deed,
> The city hath since raised a pyramid.

This suggestion is very plausible, as the New River was one of Jacobean London's most important engineering projects, the creation of a new freshwater supply attracting considerable notice as a 'liquid deed'. Yet the very specificity of a 'pyramid' works against the identification, since as the surviving contemporary picture of the Clerkenwell water-house demonstrates, the building itself did not correspond with Jonson's lines, being square-set and not at all pyramidical.[67] In all other respects the internal evidence suggests a date around 1610. The epigram cannot have been written before 1607, as it mentions the parliamentary fart which occurred in that year's session (1.108). An upward date of 1610 is made likely by Jonson's only other mention of this incident, his allusion in *The Alchemist* (II. ii. 63) to Sir John Hoskyns's widely-circulated satirical verses upon it.[68] A 1610 date would also fit with the epigram's repeated allusions to the plague, since in that year the plague visitation was unusually severe. On balance, then it seems safest to reaffirm the date of *c*.1610, which is not significantly undermined by the 'pyramid'.

Note. I am very grateful to Ian Donaldson for a precise and thorough commentary on the penultimate version of this lecture; and to my colleagues David Fairer and David Lindley, and to my wife Jane, for their real material help during its long gestation.

---

[66] *Ben Jonson*, 8, p. 89.

[67] See J. W. Gough, *Sir Hugh Myddleton, Entrepreneur and Engineer* (Oxford, 1964), illustration facing p. 58.

[68] Hoskyns's verses were unprinted in Jonson's lifetime but circulated in manuscript, and were added to as subsequent parliaments came along. The fart itself seems to have happened on 11 March 1607, and most of the MPs mentioned in the best text of the satire sat in the 1607 Parliament. See B. W. Whitlock, *John Hoskyns, Serjeant-at-Law* (Washington, D.C. 1982), pp. 283–8.

Proceedings of the British Academy, **90**, 95–127

Edward Thomas, Robert Frost and the Uses of Negation

GERALD HAMMOND
University of Manchester

Edward Thomas and Negation

EDWARD THOMAS'S 'RAIN' ends on a line which tries to stare death full in the face. Lying awake, listening to the rain, hoping that none whom once he loved 'Is dying tonight or lying still awake/Solitary, listening to the rain', he focuses upon his own state of lovelessness, as one who has 'no love which this wild rain/Has not dissolved', this double negative giving way, in the poem's penultimate line, to a conditional positive, 'except the love of death,/If love it be towards what is perfect and'.[1] He ends the line on 'and,' an unusual thing for a poet to do, even in blank verse. Then the poem's final line delivers one more double negative: 'and/Cannot, the tempest tells me, disappoint', the doubling of the negative all the more emphatic because of the clause about the tempest being inserted between the auxiliary and the verb.

'Disappoint' is a negative because of its negating prefix, but it is one of those negatives which has got away. While 'disobey' means only not to obey, and 'distrust' means not to trust, 'disappoint' has long since unhitched itself from its positive. If death cannot disappoint, this means, in some remote etymological sense, that it can appoint. We can make good poetic sense of this. After all, each of us knows that we have an

---

Read at the Academy 9 November 1995. © The British Academy 1996.
[1] All references to Thomas's poems are from R. G. Thomas (ed), *The Collected Poems of Edward Thomas* (Oxford, 1981).

appointed time to meet our maker; but Thomas's poem is doing more
than asking us to think more precisely about the word 'appoint'. Its
double negatives, 'no love which this wild rain/Has not dissolved' and
'cannot, the tempest tells me, disappoint', embody a power and control
comparable with the rain's, whose saturation of everything generates
this unflinching stare into death. Only by negation is it possible for
Thomas to do this, to utter his own 'Nocturnal Upon St Lucy's Day'.

'Negation in judgment,' writes Julia Kristeva, 'like strictly linguistic
(morphological or lexical) negation, puts the subject in a position of
mastery over the statement as a structured whole, and in a position to
generate language, which in turn implies . . . competence in selection
and an ability to grasp infinity through a recursive movement. Negation
is a symptom of syntactic capacity.'[2] And she goes on to revise
Mallarmé's statement that 'a guarantee is needed: syntax' to read 'a
guarantee is needed: negation'. The two are parallelled because, she
says, 'Negation serves, along with syntax, as the strongest breakwater
for protecting the unity of the subject and offers the most tenacious
resistance to the shattering of the verbal function in the psychotic
process.'

Edward Thomas repeatedly finds the kind of mastery which Kristeva
identifies in order to enter and control the unknown and unfathomable.
The forest in 'Lights Out', towering 'shelf above shelf' and completely
'silent,' he steels himself to enter through a stanza of negatives:

> There is not any book
> Or face of dearest look
> That I would not turn from now
> To go into the unknown
> I must enter, and leave, alone,
> I know not how.

No psychotic, but a poet, Thomas exemplifies the parallel between the
two which Kristeva describes as being bound up with 'the process of
rejection which pulsates through the drives in a body that is caught
within the network of nature and society.' The model is Freud's. In his
paper on negation, *Die Verneinung*, written in 1925, Freud identified the
centrality of rejection and expulsion to the emergence of identity:

> Judging is a continuation, along lines of expediency, of the original process
> by which the ego took things into itself or expelled them from itself,

---

[2] J. Kristeva, *Revolution in Poetic Language*, trans. Margaret Waller (New York, 1984), pp. 124–5.

according to the pleasure principle . . . . But the performance of the function of judgment is not made possible until the creation of the symbol of negation has endowed thinking with a first measure of freedom from the consequences of repression and, with it, from the compulsion of the pleasure principle.[3]

In Thomas's poetry striking examples of negatives clustering in rejection occur in poems addressed to his father and to his son. The poem to his father, [P.H.T.], is short, just seventy-four words, and seven of these are negatives (italics added):

> I may come near loving you
> When you are dead
> And there is *nothing* to do
> And much to be said.
>
> To repent that day will be
> *Impossible*
> For you, and vain for me
> The truth to tell.
>
> I shall be sorry for
> Your *impotence*:
> You can do and *undo no more*
> When you go hence,
>
> *Cannot* even forgive
> The funeral.
> But *not* so long as you live
> Can I love you at all.

Thomas's editor notes of this poem that it presents a bleaker view of the father-son relationship than the facts merit, calling for support on the direct evidence that many of the father's grandchildren 'and one grand-nephew have told me that they regard this picture as a partial and incomplete one'.[4] To which one can only say that it is necessary for sons to regard fathers in a partial and incomplete way: which is how Edward Thomas sees his own son's angry relationship with him in the poem 'Parting'. The poem's occasion is the departure for the United States of Thomas's son Merfyn with the Frost family in February 1915. Thomas begins by defining the past as a landscape of negation:

> The Past is a strange land, most strange.
> Wind blows not there, nor does rain fall:

[3] S. Freud, *On Metapsychology: The Theory of Psychoanalysis*, transl. James Strachey, Pelican Freud Library, vol. II (Harmondsworth, 1984), p. 441.
[4] *Collected Poems*, p. 160.

If they do, they cannot hurt at all.
Men of all kinds as equals range

The soundless fields and streets of it.
Pleasure and pain there have no sting,
The perished self not suffering
That lacks all blood and nerve and wit,

And is in shadow land a shade . . .

This vision is what we instinctively think of as deepest negation, the
absence of all distinction and distinctiveness. At the moment of parting
from his son, Thomas finds himself racked by a double pain. The first
'because it was parting', the second derived from the history of trouble
between the two which is already, and will be ever more, part of that
landscape of the past which has neither wind nor rain, and to describe
which the negatives cluster:

First because it was parting; next
Because the ill it ended vexed
And mocked me from the Past again,

Not as what had been remedied
Had I gone on — not that, oh no!
But as itself no longer woe;
Sighs, angry word and look and deed

Being faded: rather a kind of bliss,
For there spiritualized it lay
In the perpetual yesterday
That naught can stir or stain, like this.

Thomas's editor is as interesting here as he is dull about the poem to his
father, commenting that the last phrase 'like this' refers to the poem:
'Stir or stain' may refer to the actual manuscript (as well as the act of
memory): the page in *BM* is blotted in a few places'.[5] When a poet blots
out a word in his manuscript he rejects it, an even stronger act of
negation than the syntactic or affixal ones bound up in 'no' and 'not'
and 'un-' and '-less'.

   Although both are expressions of negation we ought to distinguish
between the two. Negation by blotting out is different from negating by
grammar or syntax. Blotting out is annihilating rather than distinguishing between things. It was an inability to make such a distinction, the
consequence of a bad dream, which led Andrei Bumblowski ('formerly

---

[5] *Collected Poems*, p. 139.

professor of philosophy in a now extinct university of Central Europe'),
to develop a peculiar personal trait, described by Bertrand Russell in his
Nightmares of Eminent Persons.[6] Bumblowski dreamt one night of
Hell, presided over by a Satan who was *der Geist der stets verneint*,
'the Spirit of Negation', and who enlarges himself and his empire every
time there is a rejection, a denial, or a prohibition.

> He is surrounded by a chorus of sycophantic philosophers who have sub-
> stituted pandiabolism for pantheism. These men maintain that existence is
> only apparent; non-existence is the only true reality. They hope in time to
> make the non-existence of appearance appear, for in that moment what we
> now take to be existence will be seen to be in truth only an outlying portion
> of the diabolic essence.

Awoken from his nightmare, Bumblowski realises that all Satan really
is is 'a bad linguistic habit'. All one has to do is 'avoid the word "not"
and His empire is at an end.' And he proceeds to put this realisation into
action by avoiding all negation in his speech:

> He would not say 'this egg is not fresh,' but 'chemical changes have
> occurred in this egg since it was laid.' He would not say 'I cannot find
> that book,' but 'the books I have found are other than that book.' He would
> not say 'thou shalt not kill,' but 'thou shalt cherish life.'

It may be possible to describe the world without negation but it is a
primitive thing to attempt, and ultimately laughable, as the fate of the
noble professor demonstrates. That negation is actually the most powerful tool which we possess was argued first by Francis Bacon, in his
Novum Organum. Only God and his angels, wrote Bacon, are able 'at
once to recognise forms affirmatively from the first glance of contemplation'. Man, in contrast, 'is unable to do so, and is only allowed to
proceed first by negatives, and then to conclude with affirmatives, after
every species of exclusion'.[7] Here Bacon is describing the process of
reasoning whereby the road to yes runs through many nos. Milton's
dictum that 'reason is but choosing' means, in Baconian terms at least,
that Reason is choosing to reject and deny, knowledge being derived
from a series of negations rather than affirmations. While George

---

[6] B. Russell, 'The Metaphysician's Nightmare', in *Nightmares of Eminent Persons* (Harmondsworth, 1954), pp. 38–43.
[7] *Francis Bacon: Works*, ed. James Spedding, *et al.* vol. 4, (London, 1853), p. 474. Cp. also
Bacon's argument that 'the induction which is to be available for the discovery and
demonstration of sciences and arts must analyse nature by proper rejections and exclusions;
and then after a sufficient number of negatives, come to a conclusion on the affirmative
instances' (p. 98).

Herbert praised the English language for its homophones *sun* and *son*, we, less pious, and more attracted by the dialectic process, might praise it more for its homophones *know* and *no*, a pair which poets have long played on, from Milton's 'know to know no more,' to, say, Robert Frost, in 'The Times Table', who clusters negatives together round the verb:

> Nor I, nor nobody else may say,
> Unless our purpose is doing harm,
> And then I know of no better way . . . [8]

Negation and Knowledge

To identify negation with knowledge is instinctively difficult for us to do, for negation, defined either as rejection or denial, seems to imply a kind of inferiority or posteriority. First comes the positive, 'to be happy', and then follows the negation, 'to be unhappy'. To be unhappy is a lesser state than being happy, perhaps even a later state: first we are happy, then we are 'unned' from this state. But whereas being unhappy depends upon the possibility of being happy, being happy does not depend upon the possibility of being unhappy. As linguistics scholars have long pointed out, negating affixes attach themselves only to affirmative, or positive, words, not to negative words. You can only describe yourself as 'unsad' if you are a poet. If you are sane you can go insane, but if you are mad you can not, except from a psychotic's point of view, go unmad. However, the matter is not so simple for, as 'unhappy' or 'disappoint' indicate, the negation of a word reveals not the bleak and blank universe of indistinction which Professor Bumblowski's Satan embodies, but a universe of many more distinctions and complexities than the simple affirmative from which it derives. Here Tolstoy's epigram is useful. All happy marriages are essentially the same as each other; all unhappy marriages are different. Happy is a monolith, unhappy a range of possibilities.

When a negation moves from the level of word to sentence, the complexities multiply. 'I am happy' is a simple, single statement, essentially conclusive. 'I am not happy' has a boundless set of possibilities inherent in it, not merely from 'I am not happy, I am sad', to 'I

---

[8] All references to Frost's poems are from Richard Poirier and Mark Richardson, eds, *Robert Frost: Collected Poems, Prose, and Plays* (New York, 1995).

am not happy, I am ecstatic', but also 'I am not happy, I support Arsenal' or 'I am not happy, I am dopey.' Take a sentence much used in linguistics: 'Maxwell killed the judge with a silver hammer'. This is a monolith, a statement of total, detailed certainty which allows no rejection or denial of any of its elements: Maxwell did it; the deed was killing; the judge was the victim; he did it with a hammer; the hammer was a silver one. Now negate the sentence and enter the world of complex experience: 'Maxwell did not kill the judge with a silver hammer'. In speech, or in a written form which allows the use of italics, the negation opens up all kinds of possibilities: it was not Maxwell, it was someone else; he did not kill him, he only injured him; it was not the judge he killed, but the judge's wife; it was not a hammer but a gavel; it was not silver but stainless steel. Strangely enough, the one thing which the negation will not easily allow is the negation of the whole sentence. To utter it without any stress, or stresses, would be near nonsense; and if it were a line in a poem we would have to decide how to stress it to give it meaning — just as in the opening line of Robert Frost's poem 'The Self-Seeker', 'Willis, I didn't want you here today,' we need to think about the stresses: *I* didn't; I didn't want *you*; I didn't want you *here*; I didn't want you here *today*.[9] True, if the line were affirmative, 'Willis, I wanted you here today', it would still be possible to stress it in various ways, but in the opening line of a poem we would be unlikely to do this, accepting rather the affirmation as a totality. Syntactic negation worries us into trying to work out which elements are being negated, as in the second stanza of Edward Thomas's poem 'The Wasp Trap,' which uses negation to puzzle and confuse. The first stanza we can all accept, in its pure affirmation of the moonlight's effect:

> This moonlight makes
> The lovely lovelier
> Than ever before lakes
> And meadows were.

Then Thomas moves into a negating syntax and the vision becomes a perplexing one:

> And yet they are not,
> Though this their hour is, more

---

[9] Katherine Kearns discusses the problems inherent in the speaking of Frost's poems, in relation to his theory of 'sentence sounds,' in *Robert Frost and a Poetics of Appetite* (Cambridge, 1994), pp. 68–9.

Lovely than things that were not
Lovely before.

This means, I think, that moonlight transforms everything, negating all distinction, making the lovely and unlovely equally radiant, but the double negative makes the brain reel, trying to comprehend the complexity of the vision.

These are, then, two uses of negation which makes it attractive for poets. It gives them mastery and it gives their visions complexity. In these ways, at least, negation is superior to affirmation; not, as we might assume without thinking much about the matter, inferior and dependent. The assumption that negation is inferior, or secondary, is described by linguistic philosophers as the asymmetricalist position. Whereas 'I am happy'/'I am sad' are symmetrical constructions, along the lines of 'I am black'/'I am white', neither 'I am happy'/'I am not happy' nor 'I am happy'/'I am unhappy' are symmetrical. Laurence Horn lists the theses which underpin the asymmetricalist position:

a Affirmation is logically prior, negation secondary.
b Affirmation is ontologically prior, negation secondary.
c Affirmation is epistemologically prior, negation secondary.
d Affirmation is psychologically prior, negation secondary.
e Affirmation is basic and simplex, negation complex.
f Affirmation is essential, negation eliminable.
g Affirmation is objective, negation subjective.
h The affirmative sentence describes a fact about the world, the negative sentence a fact about the affirmative.
i In terms of information, the affirmative sentence is worth more, the negative less (if not worthless).[10]

Horn's book, *A Natural History of Negation*, offers a constantly enchanting survey of attitudes to negation from Aristotle and the early Indian philosophers to the present day and is, in part, an attempt to mediate between the two camps, taking in, on the way, such extremists of the asymmetricalist position as the philosopher Bergson, who argues that negation 'is only an attitude taken by the mind toward an eventual affirmation' or those other philosophers, Arlen and Mercer, whose call was for us to 'Accentuate the positive,/Eliminate the negative,/Latch on to the affirmative,/Don't mess with Mr. In-Between'.[11] In the symmetricalist camp there are fewer forces. One might seem to be Bacon, with

---

[10] L. R. Horn, *A Natural History of Negation* (Chicago, 1989), pp. 45–6.
[11] Horn, pp. 62 and 45.

his call to proceed through negatives, but this, of course, is a procession towards the superior affirmation known only to God and His angels. More actually a symmetricalist is Austin, who argues that 'Affirmation and negation are exactly on a level, in this sense, that no language can exist which does not contain conventions for both and that both refer to the world equally directly, not to statements about the world.'[12] Freud incidentally, belongs to the asymmetricalists. His assertion, repeated over and over again in her various books by Kristeva, 'that in analysis we never discover a "no" in the unconscious', points obviously to negation's secondary nature.[13] The extreme asymmetricalist view, shared by Professor Bumblowski and the unconscious of all of us, according to Freud, is that it is possible to describe the world without negation — that it is just a bad linguistic trick.

The practice of many poets reveals them to be instinctively symmetricalists, at least in the sense that they believe in negation's claim to have an absolutely equal status with affirmation. Indeed, some go further and are even asymmetricalists on the other side, as it were, their poetry seeming to embody a position in which the negation is primary and superior. It is not difficult to see how this philosophy should attract anyone who thinks about words for negation, as denial, is implicit in many of the words we use. This is obviously so in words with negative affixes; and almost as obvious in the case of those words, described by Gunnel Tottie as 'fuzzy negatives', in which we feel, as we use them, a sense of absence, loss, limitation, or decline.[14] Those very words, *absence* and *loss*, have such a connotation, as do such words as *short*, *bad*, and *sad*. It is arguable too that all words have comparable connotations. *Short* carries a negative loading because we think of it as meaning not tall or not long. So, most words have their meanings defined through their not meaning something else. *Long*, which is not a

---

[12] Horn, p. 58.

[13] *On Metapsychology*, p. 442; repeated by Kristeva, pp. 163–4. Freud's statement, coming at the end of his essay on negation is, in some ways, a logical consequence of his statement, in the essay's opening, about psychoanalytic practice, in which negation is absolutely ignored: 'The manner in which our patients bring forward their associations during the work of analysis gives us an opportunity for making some interesting observations, "Now you think I mean to say something insulting, but really I've no such intention." We realize that this is a repudiation, by projection, of an idea that has just come up. Or: "You ask who this person in the dream can be. It's *not* my mother." We emend this to: "So it *is* his mother." In our interpretation, we take the liberty of disregarding the negation and of picking out the subject-matter alone of the association' (p. 437).

[14] G. Tottie, 'Fuzzy Negation in English and Swedish', *Stockholm Studies in English*, 39, 1977.

fuzzy negative, is still a negative insofar as it means not short. Sometimes the negation is a simple binary one, as in *alive*, which means not
dead; but often the negation is of many other possibilities. *It is raining*
means it is not sunny, not hailing, not foggy, and so on. For certain
poets the instinct is to distrust the affirmation as something too simple
and to prefer to describe through negation. Edward Thomas's poem
'For These' is a fine model for such poetry. Begun the day he was
passed medically fit for enlistment and finished the next day, he
originally started it with a negation:

> I don't wish for an acre of land
> But for content and something to be contented with . . . [15]

In its final version, however, it opens with three stanzas of affirmation,
seemingly describing the heart's desire, or at least the heart's desire of a
true Briton:

> An acre of land between the shore and the hills,
> Upon a ledge that shows my kingdoms three,
> The lovely visible earth and sky and sea,
> Where what the curlew needs not, the farmer tills:
>
> A house that shall love me as I love it,
> Well-hedged, and honoured by a few ash-trees
> That linnets, greenfinches, and goldfinches
> Shall often visit and make love in and flit:
>
> A garden I need never go beyond,
> Broken but neat, whose sunflowers every one
> Are fit to be the sign of the Rising Sun:
> A spring, a brook's head, or at least a pond:

Then, in the final stanza, undercutting all of this, comes the true desire,
now expressed through negation:

> For these I ask not, but, neither too late
> Nor yet too early, for what men call content,
> And also that something may be sent
> To be contented with, I ask of fate.

'Old Man', although early, is one of Thomas's deepest explorations
of negation's superiority. This herb of paradoxical names, 'Old Man or
Lad's love', has a meaning which other, more apparently fragrant herbs
do not, but the meaning is only reachable through negations which
promise to stretch into infinity (infinity, too, is a negation):

---

[15] For the earlier draft, see *Collected Poems*, p. 152.

> I cannot like the scent,
> Yet I would rather give up others more sweet,
> With no meaning, than this bitter one
>
> I have mislaid the key. I sniff the spray
> And think of nothing; I see and I hear nothing;
> Yet seem, too, to be listening, lying in wait
> For what I should, yet never can, remember:
> No garden appears, no path, no hoar-green bush
> Of Lad's-love, or Old Man, no child beside,
> Neither father nor mother, nor any playmate:
> Only an avenue, dark, nameless, without end.

Negation and Repetition

According to some, Edward Thomas's negations actually reveal him to be an asymmetricalist along Baconian lines. He is, after all, an affirmer, one who uses 'litotes . . . words beginning un-, im-, or dis-' as part of a 'battery of understatement . . . by which he establishes a kind of affirmation'. He has the 'ability to affirm by means of negatives'.[16] These are Andrew Motion's words, but I could equally well be quoting a variety of commentators on Thomas's poetry. I quote Motion, however, because it seems clear to me that one major purpose of his book on Thomas is to disentangle him from Robert Frost: not that Frost is not also a denier who affirms. We have the word of one of Frost's best critics, Richard Poirier, for that: he identifies in Frost's poetry the use of negatives in order to affirm by an 'act of denial'.[17] But, Motion argues, the two poets achieve their denial-affirmations through different means. Edward Thomas 'whispers' while Robert Frost 'speaks aloud', to paraphrase Motion's discussion of 'Aspens', the poem of Thomas's which Frost prized above all others. While Frost 'habitually rationalises his experience in order to extract a moral from it', he writes, 'Thomas prefers to suggest and qualify, avoiding round conclusions'; but the multiple qualifications add up to 'completeness'.[18] 'Aspens' seems to present a fine example of this. It proceeds by negations, qualifying the sound of the aspens, which 'is not drowned . . . not ceasing . . . nor fails . . . And it would be the same were no house near'. Aspens cannot help but make the sound they do, 'and men may hear/But need not

[16] A. Motion, *The Poetry of Edward Thomas* (London, 1980), p. 78.
[17] R. Poirier, *Robert Frost: The Work of Knowing* (New York, 1977), p. 84.
[18] Motion, pp. 73–4.

listen, more than to my rhymes'. All of these negatives lead into a final stanza in which Thomas pushes home the equation of his poetry to the aspen's leaves:

> Whatever wind blows, while they and I have leaves
> We cannot other than an aspen be
> That ceaselessly, unreasonably grieves,
> Or so men think who like a different tree.

'Ceaselessly' and 'unreasonably' are two more negations which help make the kind of complete statement which Motion praises in Thomas's poetry, a completeness which seems to be supported by the final stoical shrug of a line, in which all who have no taste for aspens are, if not dismissed, then put in their marginal place.[19] But the verb is 'grieves', a fuzzy negative if ever there was one, so if there is a completeness of statement here, it is a completely negative one. To gloss the poem as Motion does, as Thomas's affirmation of the Keatsian idea that poetry comes as naturally to Thomas as do leaves to a tree is to miss the point of that fuzzily negative verb. It is grieving which comes as naturally to Thomas as the losing of its leaves does to the aspen. Like many of his poems, and Frost's as well, the aim is towards silence. Just as the opening stanza looks forward to the last leaves dropping, so the body of the poem itself looks forward to the inevitable silencing of the smithy and the inn. At their height they could not, with their 'ringing/Of hammer, shoe, and anvil' and 'The clink, the hum, the roar, the random singing', drown out the 'whisper of the aspens', any more than Thomas's noise can drown out the whisper of a ceaseless, unreasonable grieving.

Freud's brief, powerful essay on negation, emerging from his exploration of the pleasure principle, picks up one element in particular which marks obsessive neurotic behaviour, but which is sublimated in 'normal' behaviour, namely the 'compulsion to repeat.'[20] Expelling objects, the origin of rejection and denial, introduces reality testing, whose aim is 'not to *find* an object in real perception which corresponds to the one presented, but to *refind* such an object, to convince oneself

---

[19] 'Stoical shrug' is close to a phrase used by Ian Hamilton about Frost's poetry, quoted by Motion (p. 74).

[20] In 'Beyond the Pleasure Principle', Freud writes of the neurotic patient as one who 'is obliged to *repeat* the repressed material as a contemporary experience instead of, as the physician would prefer to see, *remembering* it as something belonging to the past' (*On Metapsychology*, p. 288). This is the ' "compulsion to repeat", which emerges during the psychoanalytic treatment of neurotics' (p. 289), which he develops in the essay on negation

that it is still there.'[21] Refinding is bound up with repetition, the compulsion to reassure oneself that one is real by locating 'once more' the world outside oneself.[22] When repetition is involuntary, out of one's control, then the effect is disturbing, to be described by a negative in another of Freud's essays, the *unheimlich*, or 'uncanny'.[23] In his discussion of this phenomenon, incidentally, Freud makes the significant observation that 'the prefix "un" is the token of repression'.[24] This integral connection between negation and repetition is a feature of Edward Thomas's poem 'The Long Small Room', one of the many of his poems which explore an idea bordering on the uncanny. In this case it is the memory of something apparently disturbing which he was fascinated by, the shape of a room with a window at one end and a fireplace at the other, described in the first two stanzas:

> The long small room that showed willows to the west
> Narrowed up to the end the fireplace filled,
> Although not wide. I liked it. No one guessed
> What need or accident made them so build.
>
> Only the moon, the mouse and sparrow peeped
> In from the ivy round the casement thick.
> Of all they saw and heard there they shall keep
> The tale for the old ivy and older brick.

The last two stanzas set up an absolute negative, 'never', against an apparent affirmation, that 'one thing' is constant:

> When I look back I am like moon, sparrow and mouse
> That witnessed what they could never understand
> Or alter or prevent in the dark house.
> One thing remains the same — this my right hand

---

in describing the function of judgment as one 'not made possible until the creation of the symbol of negation has endowed thinking with a first measure of freedom from the consequences of repression and, with it, from the compulsion of the pleasure principle' (p. 441).

[21] *On Metapsychology*, p. 440.

[22] 'The antithesis between subjective and objective does not exist from the first. It only comes into being from the fact that thinking possesses the capacity to bring before the mind once more something that has once been perceived, by reproducing it as a presentation without the external object having still to be there' (*On Metapsychology*, p. 440).

[23] See S. Freud, *Art and Literature*, transl. James Strachey, Pelican Freud Library, 14 (Harmondsworth, 1985), pp. 335–76; especially the comment (p. 361) that 'whatever reminds us of this inner "compulsion to repeat" is perceived as uncanny'.

[24] *Art and Literature*, p. 368.

> Crawling crab-like over the clean white page,
> Resting awhile each morning on the pillow,
> Then once more starting to crawl on towards age.
> The hundred last leaves stream upon the willow.

Again the negation is primary, the affirmation secondary. Never being able to understand, alter, or prevent is the one thing which the right hand can affirm, hence the peculiar final line which only avoids the narrowing down to the fireplace by looking plainly at the hundred last leaves streaming from the willow. Thomas himself recognised the oddness of the line, wondering, in a letter to Eleanor Farjeon, whether it had too much of a 'japanesy suddenness of ending'. But he kept it in partly because, as he boldly states, 'it is true'.[25] The real, if denied, focus of the poem is not the window or the tree, but the fireplace towards which the room narrows. The house is a dark house, so the memory is not of a roaring fire, but of a dark grate.

Thomas's impulse towards negation points to a profound entanglement with Frost's poetry, and a nearly equivalent entanglement of Frost's with Thomas's. I can understand why critics of these two should want to detach them from each other, arguing in various ways for the superior toughness of the one or the other, and there are many ways in which they are quite distinct.[26] My argument, however, is that this overriding force of negation pulls them more closely together than any of the finer distinctions which may separate them. What they share, through negation, is a modern grasp of the process of repetition. Kristeva, glossing Freud's account of negation, explains it this way: 'Rejection rejects origin since it is always already the repetition of an impulse that is itself a rejection. Its law is one of returning, as opposed to one of becoming; it returns only to separate again immediately and thus appear as an impossible forward movement.'[27] Something like this impossible forward movement occurs in the Thomas poem which I have just examined, 'The Long Small Room', in the crab-like act of writing. Thomas presents the clean white page as the equivalent of a life, with one line written a day, then a rest, then 'once more' the 'crawl on towards age'. There is a progress down the page, just as there is progress towards age, but the movement is neither forward nor back but sideways across the page. 'Once more' in this poem links the

---

[25] *Collected Poems*, p. 170.
[26] See, for example, J. C. Squire's early contrast of Thomas's 'Celtic melancholy' with Frost's 'harder and soberer' nature; quoted by Motion, p. 76.
[27] Kristeva, p. 147.

movement of writing to the movement of ploughing in 'As the Team's Head Brass', in which Thomas watches the team plough and talks to the ploughman one minute in every ten as they reach the end of the furrow:

> Every time the horses turned
> Instead of treading me down, the ploughman leaned
> Upon the handles to say or ask a word,
> About the weather, next about the war.
> Scraping the share he faced towards the wood,
> And screwed along the furrow till the brass flashed
> Once more.

But ploughing is not exactly analogous, for its sideways movements are more easily interpreted as a form of progress, from left to right, right to left, left to right. A better parallel would be the one drawn by Robert Frost with hoeing, in his dialogue poem 'From Plane to Plane', where Pike, the man who has 'hoed and mowed for fifty years' asserts his absolute refusal to hoe from left to right and right to left: 'I wouldn't hoe both ways for anybody!' and gets this reply from Dick, the college boy:

> 'And right you are. You do the way we do
> In reading, don't you, Bill? — at every line end
> Pick up our eyes and carry them back idle
> Across the page to where we started from.
> The other way of reading back and forth,
> Known as boustrophedon, was found too awkward.'

Robert Frost and Negation

Reading *North of Boston*, the volume of Frost's which he so admired, and *Mountain Interval*, issued in 1916, Thomas is likely to have been impressed most of all by the dialogue poems, and, more narrowly, by how much of these dialogues is underpinned by negation. There is something of this in the first volume's opening poem, 'Mending Wall', where the dialogue is ostensibly between the superior, if only because more articulate and thinking, view of the poet and the inferior, because of its smug traditionalism, view of his neighbour. The situation is a repeated one: 'on a day we meet to walk the line/And set the wall between us once again'. The neighbour is an affirmer, who gets to repeat his affirmation 'good fences make good neighbors'. Frost's counter view is an affirmation of a negation, 'Something there is that doesn't love a wall', also repeated in the poem; and although the neighbour gets the last word in the last line, Frost gets the first in the first line. And the more intimate dialogue, the one with himself which runs through the poem, uses negation both for repetitive purposes and to give the poem the skewed, awkward syntax which negation frequently accompanies. In Kristeva's words, rejection is 'inscribed in an abundance of negative statements . . . or in syntactic distortions'.[28] So, the awkwardness of the poem's opening negative, 'Something there is that doesn't love a wall', is picked up again, in 'The gaps I mean,/No one has seen them made or heard them made' (ll. 9–11); 'There where it is we do not need the wall' (l. 23); 'Isn't it/Where there are cows? But here there are no cows' (ll. 30–1); and in the nearly clear vision which he gets of his neighbour's essential ignorance, 'He moves in darkness as it seems to me,/Not of woods only and the shade of trees' (ll. 41–2).

In Frost's purer dialogues, especially those between married couples, negation is seen to operate at the heart of human relationships. This is equally the case in happy and unhappy marriages. In the terrible doomed dialogue around the dead and buried child in 'Home Burial', we see first the husband moving awkwardly in syntax and sentiment until he says the wrong thing. The whole journey is one of negatives:

> 'My words are nearly always an offense.
> I don't know how to speak of anything
> So as to please you. But I might be taught
> I should suppose. I can't say I see how.
> A man must partly give up being a man
> With women-folk. We could have some arrangement
> By which I'd bind myself to keep hands off
> Anything special you're a-mind to name.
> Though I don't like such things 'twixt those that love.
> Two that don't love can't live together without them.
> But two that do can't live together with them.'
> She moved the latch a little. 'Don't — don't go.
> Don't carry it to someone else this time.
> Tell me about it if it's something human.
> Let me into your grief. I'm not so much
> Unlike other folks as your standing there
> Apart would make me out. Give me my chance.
> I do think, though, you overdo it a little.
> What was it brought you up to think it the thing
> To take your mother-loss of a first child
> So inconsolably — in the face of love.
> You'd think his memory might be satisfied — '

[28] Kristeva, p. 126.

When his wife Amy protests that this is a sneer, he argues back that 'it's come to this,/A man can't speak of his own child that's dead', only to be answered by her double negative: 'you can't because you don't know how to speak'. The hollowest thing in the whole dialogue is the husband's final affirmation of the action he will take:

'Where do you mean to go? First tell me that.
I'll follow and bring you back by force. I *will!* — '

In complete contrast with this couple are the husband and wife, long married, who have just moved house, in 'In The Home Stretch'. Yet, at their most intimate, summarising years of shared experience, they too exchange negations with each other:

'It's all so much what I have always wanted,
I can't believe it's what you wanted, too.'
'Shouldn't you like to know?'
                                    'I'd like to know
If it is what you wanted, then how much
You wanted it for me.'
                                    'A troubled conscience!
You don't want me to tell if *I* don't know.'
'I don't want to find out what can't be known.
But who first said the word to come?'
                                    'My dear,
It's who first thought the thought. You're searching, Joe,
For things that don't exist; I mean beginnings.
Ends and beginnings — there are no such things.
There are only middles.'
                                    'What is this?'
                                    'This life?
Our sitting here by lantern-light together
Amid the wreckage of a former home?
You won't deny the lantern isn't new.
The stove is not, and you are not to me,
Nor I to you.'
                                    'Perhaps you never were?'
'It would take me forever to recite
All that's not new in where we find ourselves . . . '

These two poems show that conversation is less movement forward than it is movement sideways, repetition rather than development, negation rather than affirmation. Gunnel Tottie, in her study of the variety of syntactic forms which negation attracts, makes the basis of her study the observation that negation is twice as common in spoken English as it is in the written form. Her frequency count is 27.6 items of negation per thousand words in spoken texts against 12.8 per thousand in written texts. Fortunately for her figures she does not consider poems, otherwise her sample would have been alarmingly disturbed.[29] To take extreme, but not untypical examples, Frost's poem 'The Census Taker', which has *c*.550 words, has twenty-five negations; and Thomas's poem to his mother matches the one to his father with its frequency count: twelve negations in 173 words.

Frost wrote 'The Census Taker' after Thomas's death, but it merely continues and intensifies the use of negation which he developed in his first three volumes. The third poem in *New Hampshire*, it follows the title poem, whose best known line is 'Nothing not built with hands of course is sacred' and 'A Star in the Stone Boat', whose opening line is 'Never tell me that not one star of all'. That second poem demonstrates how repetitive negation can become. It is not enough to negate once, but the poet keeps negating: 'He noticed nothing . . . He was not used . . . He did not recognize . . . He did not see . . . Nor know . . .' . So, 'The Census Taker's' twenty-five negations are no surprise. Frank Lentricchia calls the poem 'as explicit a confrontation with nothingness as anything in modern American poetry', and he includes 'The Waste Land' in that category.[30] Set against the nothingness is the lone individual, the 'I' of the poem, its other great repetition. 'I' occurs fifteen times in the poem to set itself repeatedly against the negatives:

> I came as census-taker to the waste
> To count the people in it and found none,
> None in the hundred miles, none in the house,
> Where I came last with some hope, but not much,
> After hours' overlooking from the cliffs
> An emptiness flayed to the very stone.
> I found no people that dared show themselves,
> None not in hiding from the outward eye.

There is a similar pattern in the coda to a poem which occurs a little later in this volume, 'Wild Grapes', in which the speaker is a girl, out playing with her older, heavier brother. She comes near death when the birch tree which he bends right down so that she may pick its fruit suddenly swings upright carrying her with it. Her brother saves her by

---

[29] G. Tottie, *Negation in English Speech and Writing: A Study in Variation* (San Diego, 1991), p. 17.

[30] F. Lentricchia, *Robert Frost: Modern Poetics and the Landscapes of Self* (Durham, 1975), p. 80.

bending the tree back down, and when she is saved he admonishes her for her insubstantiality:

> My brother said: 'Don't you weigh anything?
> Try to weigh something next time, so you won't
> Be run off with by birch trees into space.'

To which the girl responds in the final lines, thinking back on the experience many years later:

> It wasn't my not weighing anything
> So much as my not knowing anything —
> My brother had been nearer right before.
> I had not taken the first step in knowledge;
> I had not learned to let go with the hands,
> As still I have not learned to with the heart,
> And have no wish to with the heart — nor need,
> That I can see. The mind — is not the heart.
> I may yet live, as I know others live,
> To wish in vain to let go with the mind —
> Of cares, at night, to sleep; but nothing tells me
> That I need learn to let go with the heart.

Between the 'I's', seven of them in eleven lines, and the negations, ten of them, there are three other *nos*, all spelt with a *k*: the old homophone of *no* and *know* doing its work to remind us that learning is a process of negation. Knowledge is denial and rejection — or, more precisely, a repeated denial or rejection. In a letter to John Cournos in July 1914 Frost drew attention to the repeated negations in 'Home Burial'. They come at the point where her husband tells Amy that he knows what it is that she sees through the window:

> 'But I understand: it is not the stones,
> But the child's mound —'
>   'Don't, don't, don't, don't,' she cried.

As Frost wrote, 'I also think well of those four "don'ts" in Home Burial. They would be good in prose and they gain something from the way they are placed in the verse'.[31] In total the poem has sixteen *don'ts* in it, as well as three *didn'ts*, five *won'ts*, a *couldn't* and a *haven't*. As Frost puts it in that letter, all of the poems in *North of Boston* 'talk', with the exception of 'Apple Picking', the one poem which 'intones', and, as Tottie's research shows, such repetitive negation is an elemental feature of talking.

[31] L. Thompson ed., *Selected Letters of Robert Frost* (New York, 1964), p. 130.

Frost and Thomas

North of Boston was the volume of Frost's which impressed Thomas so
keenly. In their walking and talking together the very sound of each
other's sentences was mutually registered — indeed, it is worth reminding ourselves that Frost was in the process of developing his theory of
the sound of the sentence during this period. The key letter in which he
identifies himself as the one poet, 'alone of English writers' who has
'consciously set myself to make music out of what I may call the sound
of sense', was written to John Bartlett in July 1913; and Thomas, we
know, was intent upon writing the work of literary criticism which
would justify Frost's theory.[32]

The Frost voice was one particularly characterised by negation, not
least because it gave him, in his talk as much as in his poetry, the
possibility of achieving that ironic distance which critic after critic of
his work has, at one point or other, come to focus on. Frank Lentricchia,
early in one of his studies, identifies the 'characteristic movement of the
imaginative man in Frost's poetry' as one of 'advance and retreat', a
dialectic which bespeaks 'implicitly of an ironic consciousness', and
Margaret Kearns, recuperating Frost for a feminist criticism, sees not so
much the imaginative man as the imaginative being whose irony lies in
the sense that 'what is most important must remain unsaid'.[33] One can
hear just that leaving unsaid in Frost's letters, as when he writes to his
son Carol a letter of ironic puzzlement at the ease with which the Carol
Frost family can drive across the United States, transforming distance
into miles easily clocked up on the speedometer, making America itself
one continuous experience: 'It was melancholy to see you start rolling
down the hill, but there is an excitement in all this travel in the family
that I can't say it is in my nature to dislike'.[34] And this is Frost some
years earlier, writing to Louis Untermeyer a letter pledging and defining
friendship, in September 1915, shortly after his return to America from
England. After a paragraph asking for a relationship which is built on
'emotional terms where there is no more controversy neither is there
any danger of crediting one or the other with more or less than we

---

[32] *Selected Letters*, p. 79. Frost refers to Thomas's wish 'to write a book on what my
definition of a sentence means to literary criticism' in a letter to Sidney Cox in December
1914 (*Selected Letters*, p. 140).
[33] Lentricchia, pp. 24–5; Kearns, pp. 35–6.
[34] *Selected Letters*, p. 397.

mean', Frost suddenly becomes ironic, distancing himself slightly from the potential embarrassment of writing to a man so intimately: 'Even here I am only fooling my way along as I was in the poems in the Atlantic (particularly in The Road Not Taken) . . . I trust my meaning is not too hidden in any of these places. I can't help my way of coming at things'.[35] Frost's way of coming at things, certainly from *North of Boston* onwards, was characteristically through the methods of negation.

'The Road Not Taken', the poem he ironically distances himself from in that phrase 'fooling my way along', is probably the one which troubled him most of all, hence his frequent warning to audiences at his readings to guard themselves against any interpretation of it — 'You have to be careful of that one; it's a tricky poem — very tricky'.[36] It certainly worries American critics, who either savage it, as Yvor Winters notoriously did, or praise it excessively, as 'the wolf in sheep's clothing', and who know, and keep telling us that it is the outstanding example of Frost's irony, the one poem above all where he speaks in someone else's voice, and not really his own.[37] The someone else is Edward Thomas, the poem being built around Thomas's frequently expressed regret, when out walking with Frost, for the road which they did not take over the one which they did:

> Two roads diverged in a yellow wood,
> And sorry I could not travel both
> And be one traveler, long I stood
> And looked down one as far as I could
> To where it bent in the undergrowth;

---

[35] *Selected Letters*, p. 189.

[36] *Selected Letters*, p. 44.

[37] 'Wolf in sheep's clothing' is Frank Lentricchia's phrase, in 'Lyric in the Culture of Capitalism,' *American Literary History*, 1 (1989), p. 84. Yvor Winters included this poem in his general attack on Frost, in 'Robert Frost: or, the Spiritual Drifter as Poet', in *The Function of Criticism* (1957), reprinted in J. M. Cox, *Robert Frost: A Collection of Critical Essays* (Englewood Cliffs, 1962) pp. 58–82. Katherine Kearns is one example of an American critic who senses that this poem's ironies are neither simple nor easily stated: 'It might be argued that in becoming Thomas in 'The Road Not Taken', Frost momentarily loses his defensive preoccupation with disguising lyric involvement to the extent that ironic weapons fail him. A rare instance in Frost's poetry in which there is a loved and reciprocal figure, the poem is divested of the need to keep the intended reader at bay . . . 'The Road Not Taken', far from being merely a failure of poetic intent, may be seen as a touchstone for the complexities of analyzing Frost's ironic voices' (pp. 73–4).

Then took the other, as just as fair,
And having perhaps the better claim,
Because it was grassy and wanted wear;
Though as for that, the passing there
Had worn them really about the same,

And both that morning equally lay
In leaves no step had trodden black.
Oh, I kept the first for another day!
Yet knowing how way leads on to way,
I doubted if I should ever come back.

I shall be telling this with a sigh
Somewhere ages and ages hence:
Two roads diverged in a wood, and I—
I took the one less traveled by,
And that has made all the difference.

Lawrance Thompson puts the American case emphatically:

> More than once . . . the New Englander had teased his Welsh-English friend
> for those wasted regrets. Disciplined by the austere biblical notion that a
> man, having put his hand to the plow, should not look back, Frost found
> something quaintly romantic in sighing over what might have been. Such a
> course of action was a road never taken by Frost, a road he had been taught to
> avoid. In a reminiscent mood, not very long after his return to America as a
> successful, newly discovered poet, Frost pretended to 'carry himself' in the
> manner of Edward Thomas just long enough to write 'The Road Not Taken.'
> Immediately, he sent a manuscript copy of the poem to Thomas, without
> comment, and yet with the expectation that his friend would notice how the
> poem pivots ironically on the un-Frostian phrase, 'I shall be telling this with
> a sigh.' As it turned out Frost's expectations were disappointed. Thomas
> missed the gentle jest because the irony had been handled too slyly, too
> subtly.[38]

I suppose it is unfair to quote a letter which a man wrote nearly twenty-
five years later as evidence of how to read his poem, but I do so mainly
to argue that irony is always a dangerous assumption, especially when it
is the poet himself who argues for it. This is Frost, writing to Untermeyer in October 1940, shortly after the news of Carol's suicide:

> Dear Louis:
>   I took the wrong way with him. I tried many ways and every single one of
> them was wrong. Something in me is still asking for the chance to try one
> more. That's where the greatest pain is located. . . . [39]

[38] *Selected Letters*, pp. xiv–xv.
[39] *Selected Letters*, p. 491.

It may be that Winters is more right than the other American critics, including Frost himself, in his dogged refusal to read this poem ironically. It is not that the negation of the title, the road not taken, is an ironic means of describing the road which Frost has taken, or, more simply, that the very negation itself is a form of syntactic affectation, typical of the effete British consciousness of an Edward Thomas, which Frost is merely mimicking; but that Thomas's negation is also Frost's. Both men take the road not taken by others and describe it to the rest of us who take the other one.

This is not to say that Frost's negation is not an ironic one, only that it goes deeper than we suspect and, more to the point, it is one which he intimately shares with Thomas. Certainly, both poets delight in double and multiple negations, and particularly in the odd, slightly distorted syntax which such constructions generate. This is Edward Thomas, in his poem 'The Mountain Chapel', telling us of poets' attempts to describe and define what they have only glimpsed and not seen clearly:

> And yet somewhere
> Near or far off there's some man could
> Live happy here,
> Or one of the gods perhaps, were they
> Not of inhuman stature dire
> As poets say
> Who have not seen thee clearly, if
> At sound of any wind of the world
> In grass-blades stiff
> They would not startle and shudder cold
> Under the sun.

And this is Thomas remembering the mystery of 'The Unknown Bird', unknown to naturalists and never properly seen by Thomas, but whose notes he keenly recalls:

> But I cannot tell
> If truly never anything but fair
> The days were when he sang, as now they seem.

At the heart of such syntactic knots is the most canny of rhetorical forms, that of litotes, 'in which a thing is affirmed by stating the negation of its opposite', a trope defined by the Elizabethan theorists as 'the moderator' because it gives a paradoxical emphasis to a statement 'by seeming to understate, moderate, or diminish its case by negating its contrary'.[40] Frost, as good a rhetorician as any Elizabethan poet, uses this weapon frequently, as in 'The Fear of Man', which ends in the litotic request to his readers, 'May I in my brief bolt across the scene/Not be misunderstood in what I mean', or, to return to the *North of Boston* volume, in the husband's protest to his wife in 'Home Burial', that 'I'm not so much/Unlike other folks as your standing there/Apart would make me out', or in the slightly sinister room-mate's description of his job to his nervous companion in 'A Hundred Collars', 'It's business, but I can't say it's not fun'.

This form of negation always allows in irony. Elizabeth McCutcheon gives a nice example in her paper on litotes in More's *Utopia*: a *New Yorker* cartoon which shows a couple at a front door, whose mat reads 'Not Unwelcome', eliciting the comment from the wife, 'See what I mean? You're never sure just where you stand with them'.[41] From litotes to double and multiple negation is a short step, if, indeed, one can trace a line between them at all, at least insofar as the giving of emphasis is concerned. Early in this century, around the time Frost was compiling *North of Boston*, Otto Jespersen speculated that double and multiple negation occurs because 'under the influence of a strong feeling the two tendencies . . . to attract the negative to the verb as a nexal negative and the other to prefix it to some other word capable of receiving this element, may both be gratified in the same sentence'.[42] And a later linguist, Labov, offers an example from a modern American source, 'it ain't no cat can't get in no coop'.[43] Frost, again, is repeatedly in touch with such conversational emphases, as in the grandmother's quoted words in 'The Generations of Men', 'There ain't no names quite like the old ones, though,/Nor never will be to my way of thinking'; or, the crucial articulation of the code which governs behaviour between men and their employers in 'The Code', 'Never you say a thing like that to a man,/Not if he values what he is', or, moving from *North of Boston* to *Mountain Interval*, in the exchange between husband and wife in 'In The Home Stretch', 'You don't want me to tell if *I* don't know./I don't want to find out what can't be known'.

Something very like such double negation occurs in a poem in the

---

[40] E. McCutcheon, 'Denying the Contrary: More's Use of Litotes in the *Utopia*', *Moreana*, nos 31–2 (1971), 107–21. I am indebted to Ward Allen for reference to this essay.
[41] McCutcheon, p. 118.
[42] O. Jespersen, *Negation in English and Other Languages* (Copenhagen, 1917), p. 71.
[43] Quoted by Tottie, *Negation in English Speech and Writing*, p. 5. Labov's paper is 'Negative Attraction and Negative Command', *Language*, 48 (1972), 773–818.

volume *New Hampshire*, another dialogue, except that here there is only one speaker, for the other one is dead: 'I meant, you meant, that nothing should remain/Unsaid between us, brother . . .'. It must be this poem which Margaret Kearns is thinking of when she says of Frost's irony, that what is most important must remain unsaid. Here Frost laments 'the chance I missed in life'. His 'Lycidas', the poem 'To E.T.', is a memorial to what he and Thomas did and a lament for what they would have done had Thomas survived the war:

> I slumbered with your poems on my breast,
> Spread open as I dropped them half-read through
> Like dove wings on a figure on a tomb,
> To see if in a dream they brought of you
>
> I might not have the chance I missed in life
> Through some delay, and call you to your face
> First soldier, and then poet, and then both,
> Who died a soldier-poet of your race.
>
> I meant, you meant, that nothing should remain
> Unsaid between us, brother, and this remained —
> And one thing more that was not then to say:
> The Victory for what it lost and gained.
>
> You went to meet the shell's embrace of fire
> On Vimy Ridge; and when you fell that day
> The war seemed over more for you than me,
> But now for me than you — the other way.
>
> How over, though, for even me who knew
> The foe thrust back unsafe beyond the Rhine,
> If I was not to speak of it to you
> And see you pleased once more with words of mine?

'One thing more' and 'see you pleased once more' articulates Frost's desire to see Edward Thomas one more time, as he expressed it in his letter to Helen Thomas on news of her husband's death:

> Of the three ways out of here, by death where there is no choice, by death where there is a noble choice, and by death where there is a choice not so noble, he found the greatest way. There is no regret — nothing that I will call regret. Only I can't help wishing he could have saved his life without so wholly losing it and come back from France not too much hurt to enjoy our pride in him. I want to see him to tell him something. I want to tell him, what I think he liked to hear from me, that he was a poet. I want to tell him that I love those he loved and hate those he hated . . . I had meant to talk endlessly with him still, either here in our moutains as we had said or, as I

found my longing was more and more, there at Leddington where we first
talked of war.[44]

Here are three ways rather than the two of 'The Road Not Taken',
and, as we have seen in the letter on his son's suicide, three ways
could be multiplied to many, but the idea is the same, that the
positive, affirmative paths leave a landscape of negatives to become
overgrown and abandoned. It was all there in 'The Road Not Taken',
the realisation that for all of our intentions to explore what we leave
behind, the choice never will be repeated: 'Yet knowing how way
leads on to way,/I doubted if I should ever come back'. There is no
'one more' and no 'once more', only the most uncanny of English
negations, *no more*.

No More

My own road not taken in this paper was to explore the phrase *no more*
in English poetry. I gave it up very early when I realised that to do so
would involve the whole of English poetry, from Chaucer and Wyatt
onwards, good and bad poets alike. William Shenstone, the very minor
eighteenth-century poet, is a good example of a bad poet who uses the
phrase virtually *ad infinitum*, as in:

> No more, ye warbling birds, rejoice
>   Of all that cheer'd the plain,
> Echo alone preserves her voice,
>   And she — repeats my pain.

Or,

> Come then, DIONE, let us range the grove,
>   The science of the feather'd choirs explore;
> Hear linnets argue, larks descant of love,
>   And blame the gloom of solitude no more.[45]

For all of his pallid verse, however, Shenstone was the man who
identified and described the peculiar force of the phrase, in his *Essays
on Men, Manners and Things*: 'The words "no more" have a singular
pathos; reminding us at once of past pleasure, and the future exclusion
of it'.[46] F. W. Bateson first noted Shenstone's analysis, followed by

---

[44] *Selected Letters*, p. 216.
[45] W. Shenstone, *Works in Verse and Prose*, vol. 1 (London, 1764), pp. 166; 25.
[46] *Works*, vol. 2, p. 187.

Christopher Ricks, in a discussion of Housman's poetry.[47] Shenstone clearly picked up its pathos from 'Lycidas', whose opening 'Once more' is eventually modulated into 'Weep no more', although he might have picked up its sternness too from *Paradise Lost*'s admonition 'know to know no more', or the combination of the two in the stern, sad opening of Book IX of *Paradise Lost*:

> No more of talk where God or angel guest
> With man, as with his friend, familiar used
> To sit indulgent . . .
>   . . . I now must change
> Those notes to tragic.

Behind Milton is Shakespeare, who uses the phrase in nearly all of the major tragic soliloquies: Lear's five *nevers*, the outstanding example of repeated negation, are there to comprehend the horror of 'Thou'lt come no more' — almost as terrible as Othello's 'no more breathing'.

My untaken road would wind forward through every poet's work, especially the unacknowledged ones like the writer of 'The Wild Rover', right through to today, when poets still obey its seduction. This form of negation which, in Shenstone's words, reminds us 'at once of past pleasure and the future exclusion of it', comes to us very early and stays very late. For evidence, consider the very young Eric and the very old Sigmund. Eric is not his real name, for he was one of the three children studied by Lois Bloom in her groundbreaking account of language acquisition in children.[48] Negation forms an area of special interest in language acquisition, and while all three children mastered negation fairly early on, it seems to have been Eric who encouraged Lois Bloom to extend the categories of negation from denial and rejection to a third category, non-existence.[49] Eric, at twenty months, could express rejection, 'I don't want baby', but could also

---

[47] From 'The Nature of Housman's Poetry', in C. Ricks (ed), *A. E. Housman: A Collection of Critical Essays* (Englewood Cliffs, 1968), pp. 115–16; this essay was first published in *Essays in Criticism*, 14, 1964.

[48] L. Bloom, *Language Development: Form and Function in Emerging Grammars* (Cambridge, Mass., 1970).

[49] 'When Eric said "no more noise," the noise had stopped; when he said "no more cleaner," the cleaner was gone; when he said "no more juice," he had finished his juice. Thus, the linguistic and contextual features shared by these utterances . . . were the expression of a negative element ("no more") and the *nonexistence* of the referent' (Bloom, p. 172). Tottie discusses Bloom's third category of non-existence (after denial and rejection) in *Negation*, pp. 20–1.

express non-existence, 'no more noise', 'no more light', 'no more juice'.[50] What is striking about Eric is that he fell completely in love with *no more*. At twenty-two months, out of thirty-five negative sentences which he uttered, thirty of them expressed non-existence, the great majority with the phrase *no more*. At twenty-three months *no more* had taken over completely, to express non-existence and rejection; but by twenty-six months it had retreated to occasional usage.[51] Lois Bloom quotes, at this age, under the category of rejection, the sad sentence, 'I think no more'.[52] As for Sigmund, he is a case of special pleading on my part because he spoke and wrote in German: but his English translator ends that remarkable, haunting, near final essay of his, 'A Disturbance of Memory on the Acropolis', when his whole family life seems to get replayed in relation to his and his brother's visit to Athens a generation earlier, with the sentence: 'And now you will no longer wonder that the recollection of this incident on the Acropolis should have troubled me so often since I myself have grown old and stand in need of forbearance and can travel no more'.[53]

That Robert Frost was open to the attractions of this form of ultimate negation is borne out by the poem 'Out, Out —', in the volume *Mountain Interval*. Here the brief candle is the boy who dies the night his hand is taken off by the buzz-saw, Macbeth's final soliloquy, with its poor player who is heard no more being echoed in the final lines:

> No one believed. They listened at his heart.
> Little — less — nothing! — and that ended it.
> No more to build on there. And they, since they
> Were not the one dead, turned to their affairs.

As for Edward Thomas, *no more* comes to dominate his poetry from the time that he begins to be a soldier. 'October', written after his first week's training with the Artists' Rifles at High Beech, is ostensibly a

---

[50] Bloom, p. 178; compare Kristeva's comment (p. 154), 'The oral cavity is the first organ of perception to develop and maintains the nursing infant's first contact with the outside but also with the *other*. His initial "burrowing" movement, which is meant to establish contact — indeed biologically indispensable fusion — with the mother's body, takes on a *negative* value by the age of six months. The rotating movement of the head at that age indicates refusal even before the "semantic" abstract word "no" appears at fifteen months'.
[51] Bloom, p. 202.
[52] Bloom, p. 207.
[53] *On Metapsychology*, p. 456. Freud wrote the essay in 1936.

poem about autumn, although he clearly wanted it to relate to his own situation, commenting in a letter to Eleanor Farjeon, 'I suppose the influence of High Beech and the Artists ought to be clearer.'[54] The poem embraces negations in its second (and last) stanza, as Thomas wishes to be 'as happy . . . as earth is beautiful,/Were I some other or with earth could turn', in alternation with seasonal flowers and 'gorse that has no time not to be gay'. This double negative sets the context for the final reflection on his state of mind:

> But if this be not happiness, who knows?
> Some day I shall think this a happy day,
> And this mood by name of melancholy
> Shall no more blackened and obscured be.

His next poem, 'There's Nothing Like the Sun', develops its strange adaptation of Shakespeare's words, pushing them firmly into a new, entirely negative context in its last two lines:

> 'There's nothing like the sun that shines today.'
> There's nothing like the sun till we are dead.

Then 'The Thrush', still in November 1915, plays off November against April, in stanzas three and four, 'know' and 'more' in stanza three becoming 'no more' in stanza four:

> Is it more that you know
> Than that, even as in April,
> So in November,
> Winter is gone that must go?
>
> Or is all your lore
> Not to call November November,
> And April April,
> And Winter Winter — no more?

And so the phrase runs like a refrain through succeeding poems. 'This is No Case of Petty Right or Wrong' has:

> Dinned
> With war and argument I read no more
> Than in the storm smoking along the wind
> Athwart the wood.

The poem to his father has 'You can do and undo no more/When you go hence'. The poem to his mother has:

---

[54] *Collected Poems*, p. 193.

> Till sometimes it did seem
> Better it were
> Never to see you more
> Than linger here

which modulates in the next poem, 'The Unknown', to *no more* in its opening stanza:

> She is most fair,
> And when they see her pass
> The poets' ladies
> Look no more in the glass
> But after her.

'Celandine', which follows, has this in its final stanza:

> But this was a dream: the flowers were not true,
> Until I stooped to pluck from the grass there
> One of five petals and I melt the juice
> Which made me sigh, remembering she was no more,
> Gone like a never perfectly recalled air.

Then comes 'Home', very much a war poem, which ends like this:

> Never a word was spoken, not a thought
> Was thought, of what the look meant with the word
> 'Home' as we walked and watched the sunset blurred.
> And then to me the word, only the word,
> 'Homesick,' as if it were playfully occurred:
> No more. If I should ever more admit
> Than the mere word I could not endure it
> For a day longer: this captivity
> Must somehow come to an end, else I should be
> Another man, as often now I seem,
> Or this life be only an evil dream.

And there are further *no mores*: two in the poem to Merfyn, his son who had gone to America with the Frosts, and one in the poem to his daughter Myfanwy.

Of course, I do all of these poems an injustice simply to plunder them for a phrase; but I sacrifice them to my main point, to describe the compulsive repetition of negation, the force through which, according to Kristeva, in the form of denial or rejection, or even, to take Lois Bloom's category of assertion of non-existence, we find 'the very mechanism of reactivation, tension, life; aiming towards the equalization of tension, toward a state of inertia and death, it *perpetuates* tension and life.'[55] *No more*, as Lear's desperate repetition of 'never' embodies,

---

[55] Kristeva, p. 150.

refuses to deliver its promised silence, requiring us, instead, to keep on talking and writing. In some poems we can see Thomas playing on the very edge of the phrase, repeatedly swerving round it — lightly, in 'Bugle Call', in the lines

> Only the bugles *know*
> What the bugles say in the *mor*ning

And sombrely, in 'As the Team's Head Brass', which has 'once more', 'a minute more' and 'nothing more' neatly spaced into it. And on the last page of his diary, one of the four single lines written probably as material for future poems is 'And no more singing for the bird.'[56] Enlisting because he wanted, like Eric, to think no more, Thomas found himself repeating and repeating the phrase, just like Ivor Gurney in 'The Not Returning' — 'No more they come. No more' — or as Ford Madox Ford does in *Parade's End* to epitomise the yearning of the whole British nation in the First World War — 'No more Hope, no more Glory, no more parades for you and me any more. Nor for the country . . . nor for the world, I dare say . . . None . . . Gone . . . Na poo, finny! No . . . more . . . parades!'[57]

That Robert Frost became so enamoured of *no more* is not something I can necessarily pin to his close reading of Thomas. As 'Out, Out — ' demonstrates, he used it lovingly before he knew Thomas's verse well and, anyway, any reader of Shakespeare or Milton, leave alone Tennyson or Longfellow, is likely to have fallen for the phrase's seduction.[58] What I would emphasise, however, is how creatively American is Frost's use of it, leaping one step further than even Thomas did, making this ultimate poignant negation the very conscious means of creation. Out of many which could be cited, I shall finish with two quite distinct examples. One is the four-line poem 'Immigrants', possibly the most condensed of all of the articulations of the American dream. This is Thomas's English dream of oblivion transformed into an American vision of constant battling against the odds to create something:

---

[56] *Collected Poems*, p. 194.
[57] I. Gurney, *Selected Poems* (Oxford, 1990), p. 87; Ford Madox Ford, *Parade's End* (Harmondsworth, 1982), p. 307 (the elision marks are in the original). The title of the second novel in Ford's tetralogy, from which this quotation is taken, is *No More Parades*.
[58] Added to that list should, of course, be Poe, who uses the phrase repeatedly, and its intensification, *nevermore*, he identifies as the key element in his composition of 'The Raven'. Slighly elongated, as *Never More*, the phrase became the motto of all who mourned the dead of the First World War.

> No ship of all that under sail or steam
> Have gathered people to us more and more
> But Pilgrim-manned the *Mayflower* in a dream
> Has been her anxious convoy in to shore.

No and *more* are split by the clause which contains all of the successive waves of immigration; and the old 'Lycidas' rhyme of *no more* and *shore* is used to convey the same idea of a presiding genius, safe-guarding and piloting to safety.

My second example is more substantial, the Frost poem which makes his American critics feel that here they are in touch with absolute American greatness, whether Randall Jarrell, in the 1950s, simply celebrating Frost's qualities, or Frank Lentricchia, in the 1970s, making a case for Frost's modernism. The poem is 'Directive', from the 1947 volume *Steeple Bush*. Jarrell says of 'Directive' that it is 'one of the strangest and most characteristic, most dismaying and most gratifying, poems any poet has ever written . . . the coalescence of three of Frost's obsessive themes . . . isolation . . . extinction, and . . . the final limitations of man . . . Frost's last word about all three', and Lentricchia calls it 'probably his greatest poem . . . Frost's *summa*, his most compelling and encompassing meditation on the possibilities of redemption through the imagination, the one poem that a critic of Frost must sooner or later confront if he hopes to grasp the poet's commitment to his art as a way of saving himself.'[59] The poem opens like this:

> Back out of all this now too much for us,
> Back in a time made simple by the loss
> Of detail, burned, dissolved, and broken off
> Like graveyard sculpture in the weather,
> There is a house that is no more a house
> Upon a farm that is no more a farm
> And in a town that is no more a town

The repeated *no mores* take us back through time to our childhood and ultimately to the future, possible redemption of 'Lycidas', when Frost leads us to discover the children's broken playhouse:

> Weep for what little things could make them glad.
> Then for the house that is no more a house.

The poem ends with some kind of consolation for our growing up and growing old. Like Freud at the Acropolis, we may discover, if we

---

[59] From R. Jarrell, 'To the Laodiceans', in Cox, p. 91; Lentricchia, *Robert Frost*, pp. 112 and 184.

follow Frost through his *no mores*, what Edward Thomas finds in his narrow room and in the rain, and what one critic who enjoys such journeys has called the genesis of secrecy, hidden in the negations of the poem's ending:

> I have kept hidden in the instep arch
> Of an old cedar at the waterside
> A broken drinking goblet like the Grail
> Under a spell so the wrong ones can't find it,
> So can't get saved, as Saint Mark says they mustn't.
> (I stole the goblet from the children's playhouse.)
> Here are your waters and your watering place.
> Drink and be whole again beyond confusion.[60]

---

[60] Frank Kermode uses these lines to introduce *The Genesis of Secrecy: On The Interpretation of Narratives* (Cambridge, Mass, 1980).

Proceedings of the British Academy, **90**, 129–145

Marcel Duchamp and the Paradox of Modernity

DAWN ADES

University of Essex

Fellow of the Academy

THE PARADOXICAL NOTION of a modern tradition seems valid to describe Duchamp's long impact on twentieth-century artistic practices. One thing that has made him irresistible to generations of artists is his probing of modernism (taking modernism in its narrow sense of an increasingly autonomous and medium-specific art), a questioning or even a kind of resistance to modernism that was generated by his responses to the paradoxes of modernity.[1] The areas of modernist anxiety Duchamp touched upon included the relation of art to new and outmoded technologies, of mass culture to the individual, mechanical perfectibility and human frailty, the superstition of the new, the promises and failures of progress.

Duchamp's influence is now so endemic that much twentieth-century art seems like a footnote to him.[2] His name is invoked across not just diverse but theoretically and artistically opposite practices: although this does not necessarily tell us much about his work, it does condition the ways in which it is seen and the selectivity with which it is treated. Jasper Johns, Andy Warhol, Joseph Beuys and Jeff Koons, for instance, have claimed to inherit his legacy, as have many other minimalist and conceptual artists; recently, artists working with

---

Read at the Academy 1 November 1995. © The British Academy 1996.

[1] See A. Compagnon, *Les cinq paradoxes de la modernité* (Paris, 1990).

[2] D. Hopkins, unpublished chapter, from Ades, Cox and Hopkins, *Marcel Duchamp*, forthcoming.

moulds, casts, and the human body, and other ready-found materials (such as Rachel Whiteread, Robert Gober, Mark Quinn, Damien Hirst) have brought back into focus other aspects of his work.

On the other hand, he is also seen as embodying the 'negative cast of modernism' or as presaging post-modernity. This has demonised him for modernist critics like Michael Fried as being responsible for what Fried called the incurable theatricality of literalist art, resulting in a disastrous confusion of the arts and, in Thomas Hess's view, of art with life. Hess also called him a failed modernist.[3] Some regard him as the greatest villain of modern art, a kind of serial pied piper who has led three generations of artists up a cul de sac.

There is, in fact, not so much of his work, given his antipathy, having abandoned painting round about 1914, to repeating himself.[4] It is quite slight, as Lyotard said, and lightly armed.[5] Four aspects of it could be singled out as having imposed especially on his reputation: his use of what Rodin called 'low forms of realism': moulds, casts and photography, as opposed to the high realism of bronze or stone; the invention of the ready-made; his rejection of the retinal and sanction of the conceptual (this, with clear roots as early as 1914, was increasingly urgently reiterated in the 1950s and 1960s as idea-free retinal art in the form of Abstract Expressionism, triumphed); and finally, his apparent retirement as an artist. For this he was chided by André Breton, the surrealist leader, in the *Second Surrealist Manifesto* of 1929. Breton, for whom Duchamp had always been the one to arrive most swiftly at the critical point of ideas, reproached him for giving up the game.

I would like to pause on this last point for a moment, not so much because it turned out to be quite untrue, once the work on which he had been secretly engaged for twenty years, *Etant donné*, was finally revealed to the public after his death in 1968, but because this view of him overlooked or undervalued his known, consistent and prolonged engagement with what were seen as simply technical matters.

In 1935, a few months after publishing *La mariée mise à nu par ses célibataires, même*, a facsimile edition of 70 odd notes and drawings for the eponymous work known familiarly as 'The Large Glass', Duchamp wrote to Katherine Dreier that he was considering making 'an album of

---

[3] See A. Jones, *Postmodernism and the Engendering of Marcel Duchamp* (MIT, 1995).
[4] The last painting on canvas Duchamp executed was *Tu m'* (1918).
[5] J.-F. Lyotard, *Duchamp's TRANS/formers* (Venice, 1990), p. 11.

approximately all the things I produced'.[6] He immediately began the time-consuming job of gathering photographs of the works he intended to include in what was initially conceived as a book, but quickly assumed a unique format. The *Boîte-en-valise* (literally box in a suitcase, sometimes translated as Travelling Box, rendered by Ecke Bonk as Portable Museum), as it became, allowed for three- as well as two-dimensional facsimiles, and as a consequence raised new problems of reproduction. The *Boîte-en-valise* combined the practice of publishing facsimiles of his notes loose in boxes (which had begun with the *Box of 1914*, a tiny edition with notes and a drawing reproduced scrupulously from templates of the original paper scraps, housed in a Kodak box for photographic paper), with three-dimensional arrangements related to ideas of storage and display. The works could be packed away in portable form, then, like a travelling salesman's wares, unpacked, revealing the ingenious partly mobile display frames fitted inside. (Plate 1.)

In spite of the fact that he worked on this project off and on over three decades, it was for a long while virtually invisible, or at least ineffectual in the face of Duchamp's reputation for having withdrawn his activity as an artist. Tinkering with the Box was regarded as a kind of mechanical activity with less status than the enigmatic objects and fragments that also occasionally appeared in that long lull following the abandonment of 'The Large Glass' in 1923. However, the nature of the mechanical reproductions he was devising was intimately bound up with his conception of the artist and modernity. If they are technical exercises, they are such in the light of a meditation on the historical relations of art and technology, and on industrial and pre-industrial modes of production, in the context especially of photographic and pictorial illusionism.

Take, for instance, the process he chose for the reproduction of those paintings to be included in the *Boîte-en-valise*. First he collected black and white photographic reproductions of the works, and then hand-coloured them or recorded their colours in detailed notes. From these, monochrome collotypes were made, the first proofs of which Duchamp hand-coloured himself (the *coloriages originaux*, one copy of which he placed in each of the twenty de luxe editions of the box). The sequence of colours was then established through a series of watercolours made by *pochoir* specialists, and hand-cut stencils were prepared, for each colour, which was applied individually with a special brush. This

---

[6] E. Bonk, *Marcel Duchamp: The Portable Museum* (London, 1989), p. 147. The following account of the *Boîte* is indebted to Bonk's detailed study.

process is highly skilled and time-consuming, and 'cannot be used for projects of a commercial nature'.[7] The miniature replicas of the ready-mades raised another interesting problem: the irony of needing to hand-craft a mould for what was originally a mass-produced object, in order then to mass-produce it again. The original of *Fountain* (Plate 2a) — itself a cast — having been lost, Duchamp made in 1938 a tiny papier-mâché model of the urinal (Plate 2b), which was the basis for an 'inter-positive' copy made to scale, commissioned from a potter, and from which a mould was taken to produce the cast multiples. Slowly Duchamp received the miniatures, the first batch made using an elaborate white porcelain glaze, later changed to a cheaper matt glaze. By 1940, he had about 270 units, but it was not until the 1950s that he completed the run of 300 needed for the full edition. Duchamp had, in other words, deliberately eschewed the banal modes of mechanical reproduction represented by the book for forms of reproduction which are part-manual and part-mechanical — which resisted commodification while being amenable to production in multiples. In pursuing this idea, he seems to be pinpointing a moment in modernity in which the artist is not cut off from the craftsman/technician through the processes of indus-trialisation and mass production.

The first point I want to draw from this can perhaps best be high-lighted through Walter Benjamin's ideas about aura and its loss in such texts as 'The Work of Art in the Age of Mechanical Reproduction' (written in 1936, the year Duchamp started work on the *Boîte-en-valise*) or 'A Small History of Photography' (1931). In the latter, Benjamin isolates a moment at the beginning of the new technology of photo-graphy, before its first full industrial exploitation with the visiting card pictures, when the portrait miniaturist painters became professional photographers, bringing with them a craft training which contributed to the exceptionally high standard of these early photographs. Once industrialised, Benjamin argues, a sharp decline in quality set in. He traces in these early instances the presence of an 'aura', due to the continuum of illumination from brightness to the dark, a consequence of such technical facts as the long exposure time. But the crucial point is that at this moment the painter had not parted company with the technician, in the new science — or art — of photography:

> . . . in that early period subject and technique were as exactly congruent as they became incongruent in the period of decline that immediately followed. For soon advances in optics made instruments available that put darkness to

[7] ibid. p. 153.

flight and recorded appearances as faithfully as any mirror. After 1880, though, photographers made it their business to simulate . . . the aura which had been banished from the picture with the rout of darkness through faster lenses, exactly as it was banished from reality by the deepening degeneration of the imperialist bourgeoisie.

Duchamp's dissatisfaction with contemporary notions of art were sometimes expressed as regret for a lost unity of artist and technician; his absorption in technical issues was not regressive or nostalgic, although he referred sometimes to outmoded or archaic machines (the chocolate grinder, for instance). It was rather an open questioning of a misunderstood gap. The question of 'art' or 'anti-art' did not enter into it: Duchamp was all too aware of the kind of bourgeois attack on photography which initiated a hundred years of inappropriate agonising over whether or not photography was an art: 'The very wish [to capture fleeting mirror images] is blasphemous. Man is made in the image of God, and God's image cannot be captured by any machine of human devising. The utmost the artist may venture, borne on the wings of divine inspiration, is to reproduce man's God-given features without the help of any machine, in the moment of highest dedication, at the higher bidding of his genius'. 'Here', Benjamin comments, 'we have the philistine notion of *art* in all its overweening obtuseness, a stranger to all technical considerations, which feels that its end is nigh with the alarming appearance of the new technology.'[8]

Duchamp did not pretend that art had not lost its grander functions in terms of simple, communicable and repeatable meanings. His famous comment to Cabanne that 'Formerly, painting had other functions, it could be religious, philosophical, moral'[9] can be read as regretful and nostalgic, or as simply stating a fact. Upon this, in a sense, hinges the cast of the work that followed his withdrawal from the avant-garde, the character of its irony. Perhaps it is what he imagined figured in one of his notes: *'allégorie d'oubli'*. *'Oubli'* can be used in the sense of oblivion as well as forgetfulness, and Duchamp seems to be taking allegory in its classical sense here, of figuring an abstract concept. However, how can allegory figure absence? The irony here does inform his 'Large Glass', but not in purely negative terms.

There is a possibly apocryphal story of Duchamp visiting the Salon

[8] W. Benjamin, 'A Small History of Photography', in *One-Way Street* (1931), p. 241. Duchamp's experiments with film and with optical machines during the 1920s could be discussed in this context.
[9] P. Cabanne, *Entretiens avec Marcel Duchamp* (Paris, 1967), p. 74.

de la Locomotion Aérienne at the Grand Palais in Paris in 1912 (26
October–10 November), with Léger and Brancusi.[10] According to
Léger, Duchamp 'walked among the motors and propellers without
saying a word. Then he suddenly turned to Brancusi: "Painting is
finished. Who can do better than that propeller. Tell me, can you do
that?" He was very taken with these precise things.' It is significant
that it was Léger, not Duchamp, who remembered this, for Léger
expressed very similar sentiments in those pre-war years, and was to
remain an optimistic adherent to a machine aesthetic rooted in a belief
in the demotic. Apollinaire too embraced modernity: 'I think the modern style exists, but what characterises today's style is less noticeable in
the façades of houses than in the iron constructions, machines, cars,
bicycles, aeroplanes.'[11] Of Duchamp, however, Apollinaire noted on
the one hand an outmoded attachment to the nude, and on the other
suggested that 'perhaps it will be the task of an artist as detached from
aesthetic preoccupations and as intent on the energetic as Marcel
Duchamp, to reconcile art and the people.' (A comment Duchamp
dismissed, but now seems more than half prophetic.[12])

Duchamp himself, however, even before the First World War
altered perceptions of technology and the machine, from beneficent
aids to human progress and welfare, to destructive and dehumanising
forces, mocked the metaphorical use of man/machine imagery: 'Against
compulsory military service: a "deferment" of each limb, of the heart
and the other anatomical parts; each soldier being already unable to put
his uniform on again, his heart feeding telephonically, a deferred arm,
etc.'[13]

However, if there is one constant theme to whose service the
absorbing investigation of technological and material potentialities is
put in Duchamp's work, it is, not the nude, but sexuality as a fundamental aspect of human identity. 'I believe in eroticism a lot, because
it's truly a rather widespread thing throughout the world, a thing that
everyone understands. It replaces, if you wish, what other literary

[10] D. Vallier interview with F. Léger, 'La vie fait l'oeuvre de Fernand Léger' in *Cahiers
d'Art* 29, no. 3 (Paris, 1954), p. 140. Transl. in W. Camfield *Marcel Duchamp's Fountain*
(Houston, 1989), p. 44.
[11] G. Apollinaire, 'La Renaissance des arts décoratifs', *L'Intransigeant*, 6 June 1912.
[12] G. Appollinaire, 'Aesthetic Meditations' (Transl. H. B. Chipp) *Theories of Modern Art*
(London, 1968), p. 246.
[13] Marcel Duchamp, 'The Box of 1914', in ed. Michel Sanouillet and Elmer Peterson, *The
Writings of Marcel Duchamp* (New York, 1973), p. 23.

schools called Symbolism, Romanticism. It could be another ''ism'' so to speak.'[14]

The Bride Stripped Bare by Her Bachelors, Even, or 'The Large Glass', (Plate 3), was constructed in New York between 1915 and 1923, when it was abandoned 'definitively unfinished'. It was a technically elaborate transcription via various traditional or wholly unexpected mediums, from notes, sketches and finished paintings of the period between 1912 and 1914, made in Paris, with additional planned intrusions of chance. Later, Duchamp indicated that it was more a mass of ideas than a picture, but among these ideas were ones very materially to do with the physical substance of the object. It was a 'delay in glass, as one might say a poem in prose or a spittoon in silver'.[15] This fragment comes from another collection of his notes, published in a limited edition of loose sheets in the *Green Box* in 1934, with the same title as the glass: *The Bride Stripped Bare by Her Bachelors, Even*. The collections of notes were meant to be read together with the 'Glass', as a catalogue 'genre Armes de St Etienne', to 'go with the ''Glass'', and it could be consulted in order to see the ''Glass'', because in my view it should not be looked at in the aesthetic sense of the word. It was necessary to consult the book and to see them together. The conjunction of the two things removed the retinal side that I don't like. It was very logical.'[16] Their publication prompted the very first attempt to provide a coherent account of the 'Glass's' imagery: André Breton's 'Lighthouse of the Bride', published in the surrealist journal *Minotaure* in 1934.

Simply to be able to name the parts of the 'Glass' at this stage was a major advance, but Breton went further. For him, the work stood alone among all the other art and artists he championed — surrealist, cubist, primitive — as a hieroglyph of modernity and its failures. 'This ''delay'' will continue to be a yardstick by which one may measure everything that artistic routine may still attempt fraudulently to register as an advance. It is wonderful to see how perfectly the Large Glass keeps intact its powers of anticipation. It is imperative that it should be kept luminously erect, its light there to guide the ships of the future through the reefs of a dying civilisation.'[17] The negative dialectic here

[14] A. d'Harnoncourt and K. McShine, *Marcel Duchamp* (The Museum of Modern Art and Philadelphia Museum of Art, 1973), p. 309.

[15] *The Bride Stripped Bare by Her Bachelors, Even*, typographic version of *The Green Box* by Richard Hamilton, transl. by George Heard Hamilton (1960), n.p.

[16] P. Cabanne, *Entretiens avec Marcel Duchamp* (Paris, 1967), p. 73.

[17] A. Breton, 'Phare de la mariée', *Minotaure*, 6, Winter 1935, p. 49.

seems unusual in that Breton normally stressed the positive reconciliation of Surrealism's poles of dream and reality, waking and sleeping. But it should be remembered that the first *Surrealist Manifesto* (1924) had attacked the proscription by civilisation (progress and rationality) of all those things that it rightly or wrongly condemned as superstition, or irrationality. Here, with his depiction of man reduced to the immediate needs of self-preservation, shorn through estrangement from the rights to his own imagination, Breton anticipated Adorno and Horkheimer's *Dialectic of Enlightenment*.

With the 'Glass', Breton writes, 'we are in the presence of a mechanistic, cynical interpretation of the phenomenon of love: the passage of woman from the state of virginity to the state of non-virginity adopted as the theme of a basically non-sentimental speculation which would almost seem to have been engaged in by a visitor from outer space making a conscientious effort to visualise this kind of operation.'[18] The cold speculation of the mechanised erotic hints at Leonardo, whose diagram-drawing of copulation prompted Duchamp's *Virgin 1* (Plate 4) — a disquieting drawing, Apollinaire said.

Many readings of the 'Glass' have followed Breton's, relating it to alchemy, to catholicism and other myths such as Hindu and Greek, to psychoanalysis, to the Cabbala, to the dialectic between nature and science; it is packed with references to laws of physics, mathematics, and so on.[19] It has been seen as a giant photographic analogue, and as a polemic against the idea of the autonomous art work. All are in a sense possible, but for the moment I just want to stress the structure of the 'Glass': two identically sized panes, whose respective imagery is of a visual disunity striking even for the twentieth century.

The lower part of the glass notably rehabilitates perspective; the radical or reactionary character of this might be understood in the context of cubism. The cubists had, it was generally agreed, recently finally eliminated this cornerstone of the mechanics of Western illusionism. The pictorial images in this part of the glass, notably the chocolate grinder, were based on the paintings that marked Duchamp's adoption of a dry machine style, following his abandonment of experiments in the fragmentation of space and objects and in movement.

---

[18] ibid. p. 41.

[19] See for instance O. Paz, *Marcel Duchamp or The Castle of Purity* (London, 1970), and '*Water writes in always in* plural', *Marcel Duchamp*, 1973; A. Schwarz, *The Complete Works of Marcel Duchamp* (1970); L. Dalrymple Henderson, *The Fourth Dimension and Non-Euclidean Geometry in Modern Art* (Princeton, 1983).

Was this move simply Duchamp's reaction against the cubism that had forced him to withdraw his *Nude Descending a Staircase* from the cubists' room at the 1912 Salon des Indépendents? This had certainly profoundly shaken his faith in the freedom of the avant-garde. But more seems to be at stake than this institutional disappointment. If it concerns a larger loss of conviction in either cubism or futurism, what caused this? Or does it relate to his reaction, not just to the organised Puteaux group of cubists to which he belonged, but to the infinitely more original, troubling and restless cubism of Picasso and Braque?

Duchamp was certainly familiar with the claims to a new language that his circle especially among the groups of modern artists was promoting; in 1911 the Société Normande de Peinture Moderne, to whose exhibition Duchamp contributed a *Portrait* of his father, *Chess Game* and a *Nude*, blandly stated that 'each generation contributes a new form of thought expressed in a new language.'[20] But what would this 'new language' look like, which was to do away with the old forms of pictorial illusionism, among them perspective? Jacques Rivière, writing in 1912, described the ideal plenitude that should result from the dismissal of one-point perspective, which was accidental (indicating the position of the spectator) and hypocritical, because it denied the painting's flatness.

> This to and fro, this coming and going, by making hollows and saliences, will end up giving the picture as a whole a certain volume, more or less independent of perspective. The whole scene, like the individual object, will be endowed with a geometrical firmness; it will show itself in its true solidity, which is altogether different from the dry and fictive depth of a stage setting. We shall have before our eyes no longer the fragile and artificial vision of an instant, but an image as dense and full as reality.[21]

However, Rivière himself had misgivings about the results of cubist experiments, which he couched in the form of a lecture to the cubists on their mistakes. The efforts to give depth, which had replaced perspective, should only mark the independence of objects in the third dimension; if the artist gives to objects and to what separates them the same appearance they are confused and welded into an inexplicable continuum; if nothing is sacrificed as secondary there is no selection and

---

[20] Jennifer Gough-Cooper and Jacques Caumont, 'Ephemerides on and about Marcel Duchamp and Rrose Sélavy', 6 May 1911, *Marcel Duchamp* (Venice, 1993), n. p.

[21] J. Rivière, 'Sur les tendances actuelles de la peinture', *Revue d'Europe et d'Amerique*, March 1912, quoted in T. J. Clark, 'Cubism and Collectivity', unpublished chapter from forthcoming book, p. 41.

pictures collapse into anarchy; if space is made solid the intervals themselves become in the end entirely imaginary objects.

T. J. Clark has recently argued that the changes in Picasso's cubist paintings between 1910 and 1912 reveal a failure to find a sustainable alternative to the old practices of illusionism that had long sustained and challenged painting. It was still the old signs that do 'the main work of describing' in paintings like *The Poet* (Plate 5), but they pretend, in a sense, not to. They are facile and extrinsic, the snatches of the external world, the pipe and jaunty moustache, suggesting by their very banality that the true job of revealing something particular about the objects depicted by the painter, the metaphorical dimension, must be happening elsewhere, in the vaunted new idiom. But, in converting materialisation into mapping, the solid body with shaded sides into a diagram and the reversible cube into a grid 'the alternative models that had seemed so promising had ended by swallowing the techniques of illusionism, or standing in ironic relation to them.'[22] Clark suggests that the contrast to these facile signs, remnants of the old language, is not a new but a 'counterfeit' new language.

Perhaps, then, the sense that cubism was in a magnificent end-game that he couldn't follow contributed to the moves Duchamp began to make away from painting in 1913–14. His own cubist experiments had already included a formal and literal comment on pictorial metaphor; in 1911 he painted a chess game with the sides of the canvas painted out to the dimensions of a board, as if the picture were the chess grid itself, while the chess pieces scattered in the heads of the players as well as on the board offer a temporal dimension (Plate 6). He described this later as 'indefinite space',[23] though he may also have been aware of Jouffret's notion that the operation of the chess player's mind resembles a visualisation of the fourth dimension.[24] In 1913, in response both to Picasso's cubist Constructions which used 'real' materials, and to futurism, he placed a bicycle wheel on a stool, and in 1914 chose his first ready-made, the *Bottlerack*. At the same time, he abandoned the 'new language' of cubism for a dry, machine style in which, as in the first version of the chocolate grinder, he returns to the full panoply of

[22] ibid.

[23] M. Duchamp, Lecture, 1964.

[24] See L. Dalrymple Henderson, *The Fourth Dimension and Non-Euclidean Geometry in Modern Art* (Princeton, 1983).

PLATE 1

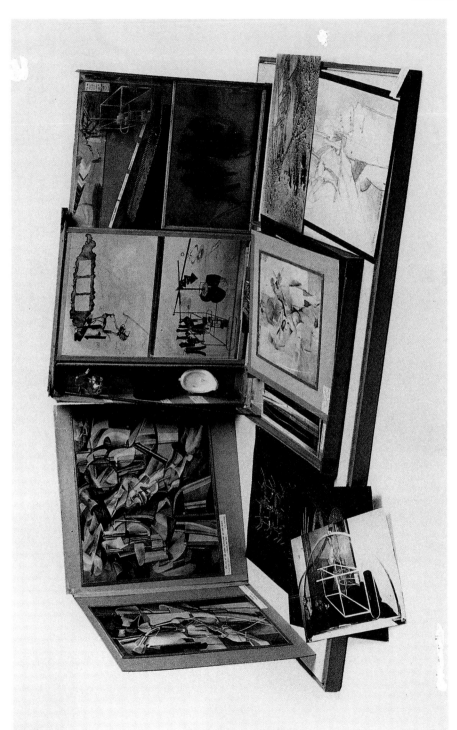

Marcel Duchamp, *Boîte-en-valise*, 1936–41, Totyama, Museum of Modern Art. © ADAGP, Paris and DACS, London 1996

PLATE 2

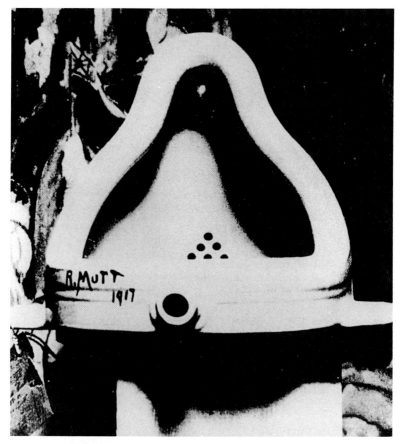

a. Marcel Duchamp, *Fountain*, 1917, porcelain urinal. Original lost (photograph by
Alfred Stieglitz 1917). © ADAGP, Paris and DACS, London 1996

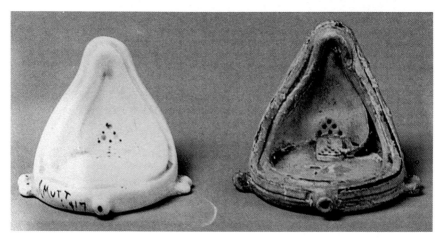

b. Marcel Duchamp, 1st miniature version of *Fountain* for *Boîte-en-valise*, glazed ceramic,
4.5 × 6 × 8 cm, with papier mâché model. © ADAGP, Paris and DACS, London 1996

PLATE 3

Marcel Duchamp, *The Bride Stripped Bare by Her Bachelors, Even*, 1915–23, New York, oil, varnish, lead foil, lead wire and dust on two glass panels, each mounted between two glass panels, w. wood and steel frame, 227.5 × 175.8 cm. The Philadelphia Museum of Art: Bequest of Katherine S. Dreier. Photo by Graydon Wood, 1992.

PLATE 4

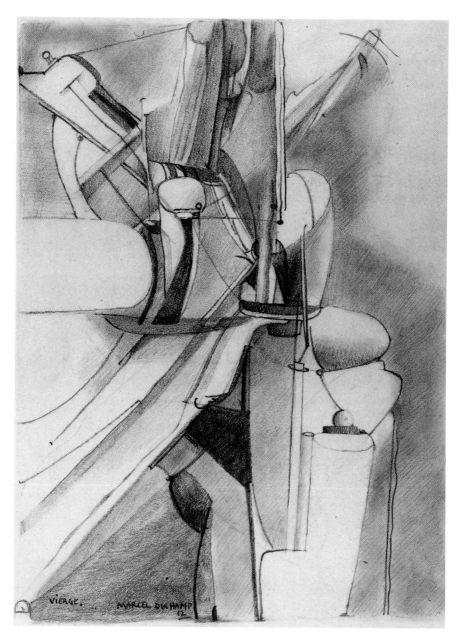

Marcel Duchamp, *Virgin [No.1]*, July 1912, pencil on paper, 428 × 220 mm.
The Philadelphia Museum of Art: A. E. Gallatin Collection. Photo by Lynn Rosenthal, 1994.

PLATE 5

Pablo Picasso, *The Poet*, 1911, oil on canvas, 131.7 × 89.7 cm.
Photograph © 1995 The Solomon R. Guggenheim Foundation.
© Succession Picasso/DACS 1996

PLATE 6

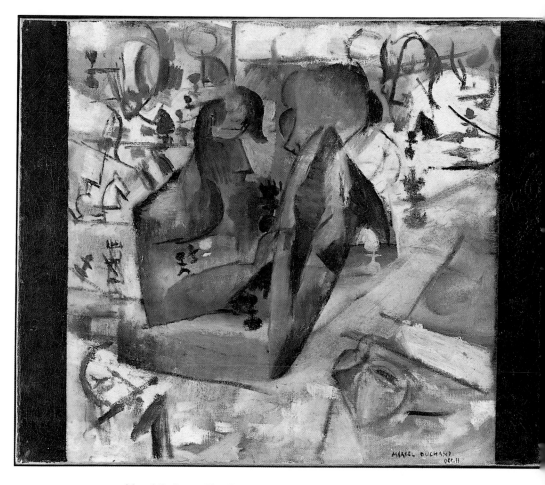

Marcel Duchamp, *The Chess Players*, 1911, oil on canvas, 50 × 61 cm.
Paris, Musée National d'Art Moderne, Centre Georges Pompidou.
© ADAGP, Paris and DACS, London 1996

PLATE 7

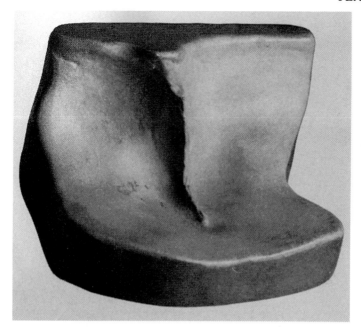

a. Marcel Duchamp, *Female Fig Leaf*, 1950, galvanised plaster, 9 × 14 × 12.5 cm.
Private Collection. © ADAGP, Paris and DACS, London 1996

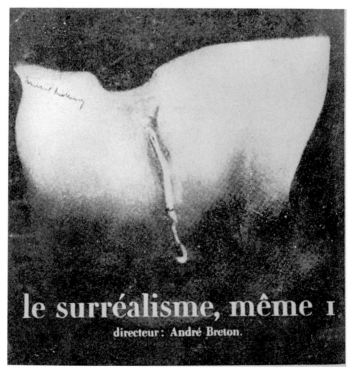

b. Cover of *le surréalisme, même*, No. 1, October 1956
(with photograph of *Female Fig Leaf*)

PLATE 8

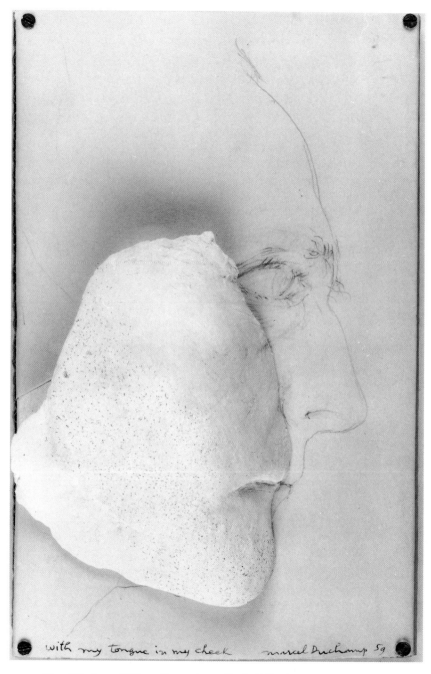

Marcel Duchamp, *With my Tongue in my Cheek*, 1959, plaster mounted on wood,
pencil and paper, 25 × 15 × 5.1 cm. Paris, Musée National d'Art Moderne,
Centre Georges Pompidou. © ADAGP, Paris and DACS, London 1996

the old methods of illusionistic depiction including perspective and shadows.

To what purpose then, does he systematically set about examining the old techniques, both pictorial and scuptural, such as perspective? Whether ironically or not, he ponders them in the context of different materials and technologies — such as glass. 'Perspective was very important. The Large Glass constitutes a rehabilitation of perspective which was completely ignored, disparaged. For me, perspective became absolutely scientific . . . based on calculations and dimensions.'[25]

In the lower half of *The Bride Stripped Bare by Her Bachelors, Even*, the bachelors' domain, the various forms which pertain to the bachelors (nine malic moulds on the left, watermill, glider, sieves, chocolate grinder and at the right the three oculist witnesses), are tightly drawn and apparently disposed according to the rules of scientific perspective. Their forms are 'imperfect and mensurable'.[26]

The 'Glass' as a whole, its two identical panes of glass one above the other, resembles whole page diagrams in such classic treatises on perspective as Abraham Bosse or Dubreuil. In these, normally, one section refers to the geometrical plan, the other to a perspective view (the surface seen in a single glance) of the same figure. Jean Clair lists numerous parallels in the catalogue to the Duchamp retrospective which inaugurated the Pompidou Centre in 1977.[27] But in the lower half of the 'Glass' there is no domain as such, no circumambient to complete the perspectival illusion. 'All that background on the canvas that had to be thought about, tactile space like wallpaper, all that garbage . . . I wanted to sweep it away. With the glass, you can concentrate on the figure if you want, and you can change the background if you want by moving the glass. The transparency of the glass plays for you'.[28]

The elimination of the background in the medium of glass has another effect, however. When the 'Glass' can be viewed with sufficient space behind it, the bachelor machines appear firmly situated on the ground, in the space of the real objects of which they are the perspectival projections. There is an uncanny doubling, as they are both on the

---

[25] Cabanne op. cit. p. 65.

[26] *The Writings of Marcel Duchamp*, p. 44.

[27] J. Clair, 'Perspective: Marcel Duchamp et la tradition des perspecteurs', *Marcel Duchamp*, 3, 'abécédaire' (Paris, 1977).

[28] Interview with Marcel Duchamp by F. Roberts, 'I propose to strain the laws of physics', 1963, *Art News*, December 1968, p. 46.

surface and beyond it, entering our space backwards, as it were, as figures already perspectivally distorted.

The sieves, on the other hand, borrowed straight from de Bosse, fan flatly across the surface, while the oculist witnesses, are drawn as ellipses, in depth, but without recession. The nine malic moulds conform precisely to the schema in that those in the foreground are largest. Their metal outlines or casings are curved to indicate volume but there is no shading. They are positioned, however, according to a special unit of measurement: Duchamp's *Standard Stoppages*, the three threads each one metre long dropped from a height of one metre to give a new unit of measurement produced by chance — canned chance.

This is not a scene constructed according to the laws of perspective, but a series of demonstrations of the uses of perspective in the male domain to map and control objects. In the upper part of the glass, the bride's domain, the apparent lack of perspective is equally significant. Its absence is compensated by copious notes in which Duchamp's interest in n-dimensional geometries and the fourth dimension is playfully displayed. 'By a simple intellectual analogy I considered that the fourth dimension cd. project a 3-dimensional object — in other words, that every 3-dimensional object that we coldly see is a projection of a thing with 4 dimensions, that we don't know. It's a bit of a sophism, but after all, it's possible.'[29]

Thus Duchamp purports to render the pseudo-metaphysical language of the fourth dimension as a 'higher' dimension, relating to a 'higher' reality, as the cohort of Puteaux cubists had it; however, a note from the *Green Box*, which eschews any mention of the fourth dimension, offers an explanation of the absence of perspective in terms of perspective as an ontological system.

> The Pendu femelle
> is the form in ordinary perspective
> of a Pendu femelle for which one could perhaps
> try to discover
> the true form
>
> —
>
> This comes from the
> fact that any
> form is the perspective
> of another form

[29] ibid. p. 68.

according to a certain vanishing point
and a certain distance.[30]

Thus the unknown female form could be known according to the rules
of the masculine masters of perspective — the oculist witnesses, say —
below, but only in terms of an impossible condition.

The idea that it should be possible to know the true, the real form of
the bride through an apparently scientific method echoes the notion of
the gendered character of scientific enquiry. Woman is unknown, and
the unknown is also woman. This, as David Hopkins has argued,
gathered pace with the Enlightenment, so that the traditionally allegorised female figure of Natura/mother goddess becomes the object of
technological research, her mysterious processes stripped to the scientific gaze.[31] This image of knowledge as stripping was common also to
the related pseudo-science of alchemy, and of course crops up in
another pseudo-science, psychoanalysis. Witness Freud's notorious
aside in the 'Three Essays on Sexuality': 'The erotic life of
women — partly owing to the stunting effects of civilised condition,
and partly owing to their conventional secretiveness and insincerity —
is still veiled in impenetrable obscurity.'[32] Duchamp, however, is closer
to a dialectic of knowledge and being, which exposes the pretension of
science: 'there is no form of being in the world that science could not
penetrate, but what can be penetrated by science is not being.'[33]

The bride is, unlike Natura as earth, placed in the upper regions. She
is the bride of Christ as well as the bride of man, and, as John Golding
has pointed out, the vertical disposition recalls the traditional Christian
imagery of assumptions and transfigurations.[34] The symbolic structures
Duchamp sets in play have their significance always as possibles, in
which the very overlappings and transformations — from male to
female, up to down, machine to flesh, science to myth — call into
question the very idea of any one authoritative paradigm.

For there are often dislocations and reversals, for instance with the
'stripped bare' of the title. 'The life of eroticism . . . is completely close

[30] *The Green Box*, op. cit. above, n. 15 n.p.
[31] D. Hopkins, Hermeticism, Catholicism and Gender as Structure in the work of Marcel
Duchamp and Max Ernst, unpublished Ph.D. dissertation (University of Essex, 1989).
[32] S. Freud, 'Three Essays on Sexuality', Pelican Freud Library, 7, *On Sexuality* (London,
1977), p. 63.
[33] T. Adorno and M. Horkheimer, *Dialectic of Enlightenment* (London), p. 26.
[34] J. Golding, *Duchamp: The Bride Stripped Bare by Her Bachelors, Even* (London, 1973),
reprinted in J. Golding, *Visions of the Modern* (London, 1994), p. 265.

to life in general . . . more than philosophy or anything like that . . . it's
there stripped bare . . . it's a form of fantasy . . . it's a little to do also
. . . stripped bare, probably had even a "naughty" connotation with
Christ . . . you know Christ was stripped bare and it was a naughty form
of introducing eroticism and religion . . . I'm ashamed of what I'm
saying.'[35]

The *Green Box* Notes reveal a whole gamut of forms of propulsion
and movement, visible and invisible sources of energy in 'The Large
Glass'. The Bachelor machine passes from steam to internal combustion
engine; it includes a water fall, glider and a hook made of a substance of
oscillating density (extendible rubber). The bride is/runs on love-gaso-
line; her stripping produces sparks, she is a one-stroke engine, desire
magneto, the second stroke controls the clockwork machinery like 'the
throbbing jerk of the minute hand.'

There are no prime movers in this mechanistic universe on glass: the
Handler of Gravity and the Inspector of Space mentioned in the Notes
were not represented. It alternates between activity and stasis, energy
and dissolution. Among the notes listing forms of energy, is the single
word *Repos*, rest. And in spite of the vivid expressions of generative
power, the machine is running down. It gathers dust, and rusts, as
though Duchamp were pondering the Second Law of Thermodynamics
in relation to the loss of desire.

The glass is a pictured algebraic equation: a over b, 'a is to b as . . .',
a formula Duchamp particularly relished, insofar as it left all sorts of
possible substitutes for the term of the equation. For Duchamp, one of
the coefficients was usually art.[36] In the *Box of 1914*, he noted that
'arrhe is to art as merdre is to merde, and that the arrhe of painting was
feminine in gender'.

Michel Sanouillet compared this Jarryesque equation to the special
law of relativity, but surely it is not a law of the same kind. It postulates
a set of relatives apparently analogical in character; but the analogies
are only not tautological insofar as each side of the double equation
diverges, ludicrously or irrationally or like a linguistic pun, from itself.

---

[35] Marcel Duchamp, radio interview with Richard Hamilton and George Heard Hamilton,
BBC London 1966.
[36] Alfred Jarry once reviewed a book by Gaston Danville, *La Psychologie de l'Amour*,
which tried to express the variation in the relation between the affective and mental states of
a subject, in response to their sexual desire for another person, in terms of an algebraic
equation ($\frac{A}{S} =$); A. Jarry, *La Revue Blanche* 1er Mars 1903, in Jarry, *La Chandelle Verte*
(Paris, 1969), p. 665.

Scientific rules, Duchamp held, are tautologies that lead straight back to myths. 'Take the notion of cause: cause and effect, different and opposite. It's quite indefensible. It's a myth from which the idea of God has been drawn, considered as a model for all cause. If one doesn't believe in God, the idea of cause has no meaning.'[37]

One of the last of Duchamp's secrets, which came to light more or less posthumously, like *Given*, is the infrathin (*inframince*). It was an idea, however, that Duchamp had pondered since at least 1937. Duchamp usually spoke of the infrathin through examples: ('When the tobacco smoke smells also of the / mouth which exhales it, the 2 odors / marry by infrathin (olfactory/infrathin').[38] It is the minimal change needed to pass from one dimension to another: from two to three dimensions, for instance, in the lifting of a flat cloth in a breeze; reflections in mirrors, creases in clothes; it is the difference between two mass-produced objects from the same mould, twins, or peas in a pod; allegory, Duchamp said, was 'in general an application of the infrathin'.

The ready-mades are shadowcasters, and as such 'work in the infrathin'. Shadows, which normally give depth, indicate inclination of a surface with respect to a light source or the position of a body. The urinal *Fountain* was famously photographed to produce the outline of the Virgin within its Buddha frame; shadows of other ready-mades reveal their linear bodiless character, spidery and formless as in *Tu m'* (Plate 7a). The *Female Fig Leaf* (Plate 7b) was lit and photographed so as to appear through a shifting of shadows from concave to convex.

The sporadic appearance of cast or partly cast objects after the War related to the posthumously revealed *Etant Donné, Given (1) The Waterfall, (2) The Illuminating Gas* (1946–66). Some were studies, others actual fragments from the casting of the nude figure which lies at the heart of this work. A large wooden door is pierced by two small holes, which give onto a dark passage, ending in a jagged hole through a brick wall, revealing a brightly lit landscape, with mist, cypress trees and a sparkling stream, with a mass of twigs and leaves in the foreground on which reclines a nude woman holding a gas lamp aloft, but with her face veiled in hair. Her legs are shockingly splayed towards the spectator as in Courbet's *L'Origine du monde*, but otherwise the scene sums up all the idyllic settings of the classical nude. The illusion is

[37] 'Ephemerides', 2nd August 1945, *Marcel Duchamp* (Venice, 1993), n.p.
[38] 'Infrathin', *Marcel Duchamp Notes* (ed. and transl. P. Matisse) (Boston, 1983).

brilliant and proclaims its artificiality even as we become aware that the elements of which it is constructed are 'real'.

The single most important fact about *Etant Donné, Given (1) The Waterfall, (2) The Illuminating Gas*, is that it physically demands the presence of the unique spectator. It cannot, quite literally, be photographed because the physical presence of the door/barrier remains as part of the experience even when the spectator's binocular sight has pierced it through the fixed eye-holes. The spectator must be present and must be barred, the position in relation to the object of his gaze fixed like that of the artist and his model in classical perspective. The vanishing point is a hole seen through a hole. Moulded from plaster covered with pigskin, the nude appears to belong to the Ovidian world of Diana at rest or Venus asleep, emblem of the anatomy of desire.

Benjamin's notion of 'aura' had reference to a special quality linked to uniqueness and a kind of distance in the work of art that was lost in forms of mechanical reproduction like photography and film. It is a notoriously ambiguous concept in that some have taken its absence from modern reproductive techniques as a regrettable loss of authenticity and uniqueness, while others have welcomed it as freeing the work of art from its 'parasitical dependence upon ritual' (in modern times the secular ritual of the exhibition), and introducing a modern form of perception suitable for mass consumption. For unlike film, 'Painting', Benjamin writes, 'simply is in no position to present an object for simultaneous collective experience.'[39]

In *Given*, another 'scene' of stripping bare like 'The Large Glass', everything is concentrated into the act of looking, and only one person at a time can ever see in. The aura of the work of art is also the aura of desire.

> What is aura, actually? A strange weave of space and time: the unique appearance of semblance of distance, no matter how close the object may be. While resting on a summer's noon, to trace a range of mountains on the horizon, or a branch that throws its shadow on the observer, until the moment or the hour become part of their appearance — that is what it means to breathe the aura of those mountains, that branch. Now, to bring things *closer* to us, or rather to the masses, is just as passionate an inclination in our day as the overcoming of whatever is unique in every situation by means of its reproduction. Every day the need to possess the object in close-up in the form of a picture, or rather a copy, becomes more imperative. And the

[39] W. Benjamin, 'The Work of Art in the Age of Mechanical Reproduction', *Illuminations* (London, 1977), p. 236.

difference between the copy, which illustrated papers and newsreels keep in readiness, and the picture is unmistakeable. Uniqueness and duration are as intimately conjoined in the latter as are transience and reproducibility in the former. The stripping bare of the object, the destruction of the aura, is the mark of a perception whose sense of the sameness of things has grown to the point where even the singular, the unique, is divested of its uniqueness — by means of its reproduction.[40]

The experience of looking at *Given* purports to be a to and fro between exposure and concealment, proximity and distance, realisation and desire, a wholly palpable work which one is barred from touching, objects in real space which we can only — one by one — gaze at. But Duchamp was perfectly aware that you cannot 'manufacture' aura, any more than you can force paintings to bear the didactic or moral messages they once confidently conveyed. The 'aura' here is so exaggerated that it becomes counterfeit; you can't go back to that tradition, and you can't deny its allure. Duchamp approaches the whole idea with irony, just as he did the symbolic structures in 'The Large Glass'. His genius is that it ends by being an affirmative irony (Plate 8).

[40] W. Benjamin, 'A Small History of Photography', p. 250.

Proceedings of the British Academy, **90**, 147–164

The Quest for a Systematic Civil Law

PETER STEIN
University of Cambridge
Fellow of the Academy

WE TAKE IT FOR GRANTED that law, whatever its tradition, forms some kind of system. When the research funding mechanisms of this Academy were reorganised recently, law was located by the Humanities Research Board, without any apparent dissent, in a category labelled 'systems of thought and belief'. All modern laws are systems in the sense that they form bodies of norms, with certain features and with recognised ways of making them and changing them.[1]

My concern today is not with whether law is a system but with how far it has been expected also to be systematic. Whether or not we think that our law should be both a system and also systematic depends to some extent on how we conceive of law in general. If law is seen as essentially the product of legislation, express statutory provisions, they will have to be placed in some kind of order. Putting statutory provisions in order does not necessarily lead to a systematic structure but, if there is an order, it will be subjected to criticism and reform and improvement, and sooner or later it is likely to move towards systematisation. If, on the other hand, law is not put into authoritative texts, it is much more difficult to systematise it, if only because it is less clear what has to be the subject of the systematisation.

One of the obvious characteristics which distinguish the English

---

Read at the Academy 28 November 1995. © The British Academy 1996.

[1] H. L. A. Hart, *The Concept of Law* (Oxford, 1961), pp. 90 ff., holds that the unofficial rules of a small community 'will not form a system', until they are supplemented by other rules of recognition, change and adjudication; it is the combination of the primary rules of obligation with these secondary rules which creates a system.

common law, on the one hand, from the continental civil law, on the other, is that the civil law is systematic and codified, whereas the common law is not. I propose to consider how the modern civil law acquired this feature. It is sometimes suggested that it derived its highly systematic form from the Roman law, which was the source of much of its substance. We tend to associate systematic order with codes and modern codes are associated with systematic order. In one of his famous, slightly inaccurate, aphorisms, Sir Henry Maine said that Roman law in antiquity 'begins, as it ends, with a Code'.[2] Maine was referring to the Twelve Tables in the fifth century BC and the compilation of Emperor Justinian in the sixth century AD. So my first question is, Did the Roman law of antiquity have some inbuilt tendency to be systematic?

I

The unwritten customary law existing at the time of the foundation of the Roman Republic was subjected to an authoritative written statement in the Twelve Tables. We know a great deal about the contents of the Twelve Tables from later quotations, but we do not know the precise order in which they were arranged.[3] The order in which the surviving fragments are printed in modern collections is a nineteenth-century creation, mainly of German scholars. They could not believe that topics which, from their perspective, were clearly related to each other, were not treated together by the compilers of the Twelve Tables. Their order is certainly far from the original order. We do know that the collection began with the procedural rules for beginning a legal action by summoning one's opponent before the magistrate and ended with personal execution of the judgment at the end of a trial. In between these procedural poles there seems to have been a jumble of rules relating to private law, public law and sacral law. As Maine correctly observed, the importance of the Twelve Tables was that they gave publicity to the law. 'Their value did not consist in any approach to symmetrical classifications, or to terseness and clearness of expression, but in their

---

[2] *Ancient Law*, ch. 1 (Everyman's Library, London, 1972), p. 1.
[3] A. A. Schiller, *Roman Law: Mechanisms of Development* (1978), p. 148, following M. Lauria, *Ius romanum*, I.1 (Naples, 1963), pp. 21 ff. See now M. H. Crawford, *Roman Statutes* (London, 1996), II. pp. 564 ff.

publicity, and in the knowledge which they furnished to everybody, as to what he was to do and what not to do'.[4]

It is likely that the order laid down in the Twelve Tables was that used later in the praetor's edict, the statement of the various remedies available to Roman litigants, and it is still discernible in Justinian's Digest, nearly a millenium after it appeared. It was essentially problematic in the sense that it brought together a series of problems of recurring practical importance and new solutions were just inserted where they were most convenient and accessible. Thus a traditional order, in which substantive rules of conduct were sandwiched between procedural rules, persisted throughout Roman law in antiquity.

In the period at the end of the Republic and the early empire, however, steps were taken to prepare the categories of legal phenomena, without which no move towards possible systematisation was possible. By this time professional jurists had appeared, who specialised in the technicalities of the law. Under the influence of Greek thought, these jurists began cautiously to organise their material into categories. The ambit of law, which constituted the area of concern for these jurists, was greatly reduced from the wide range of matters covered by the Twelve Tables. Now it was confined to the civil law, and the civil law, law for citizens, was essentially private law, the law governing the relations between one citizen and another. Sacral law, constitutional law and to a large extent criminal law had been 'factored out' of the jurists' concern. These latter topics were inevitably affected by political considerations but the jurists were able to establish the convention that the civil law that concerned private citizens was exclusively their concern and that politicians, including the emperors, had nothing to gain by interfering with it.

So the jurists began cautiously to classify the private law material into categories. At the beginning of the first century BC, Quintus Mucius Scaevola wrote a treatise on the civil law, which did not seek to impose an external logical order on the material but rather to bring out the categories which were immanent in the law.[5] He began with wills, legacies and intestate succession, which formed about one quarter of the whole work. Succession on death was the area of private law in which most disputes arose. It was central to the traditional social order,

---

[4] *Ancient Law*, p. 9.
[5] P. Stein, 'The Development of the Institutional System', in *Studies in Justinian's Institutes in memory of J. A. C. Thomas*, ed. P. G. Stein and A. D. E. Lewis (London, 1983), p. 152.

based on the family, and, through the institution of heirs, ensured the survival of the family from one generation to another. So inheritance was given pride of place. Various aspects of property, ownership, possession and acquiring ownership through long possession, were also treated together. But, apart from inheritance and property, Mucius seems to have arranged other topics loosely in the order of the Twelve Tables.

Mucius's arrangement was criticised by Cicero who considered it half-baked and insufficiently scientific.[6] Cicero pointed out that music, geometry, astronomy and grammar had also once consisted of disparate elements; but they had been classified systematically and consequently had attained the status of a science. Cicero took it for granted that civil law too was a complete and coherent body of principles and rules, which were waiting to be identified, if only a jurist with the requisite training in dialectic would tackle the task. Such a jurist should divide the whole civil law into a few general classes and clarify the particular scope of each category. According to Aulus Gellius,[7] Cicero wrote a treatise on how to turn the civil law into a science but it could hardly have been regarded by the jurists as valuable, since no trace of it has survived. Cicero had only a superficial knowledge of the law and he did not grasp that the civil law was not a finite set of data awaiting systematic treatment but an ever-expanding network of solutions to actual problems, and that as long as it was still developing, there was merit in leaving it open-ended.

By the mid first century AD, there are clear signs that the basic categories of the civil law were becoming recognised. For example, in Mucius's scheme, the various civil wrongs, such as theft of property and damage to property, were treated separately but now they are brought together.[8] This indicated the recognition of a category of delict, or tort. About the same time, also, it was noticed that various forms of personal obligation, by which a debtor voluntarily bound himself to a creditor, all had a similar source. The obligatory bond between debtor and creditor was created in different ways, according to the type of transaction, but they were all voluntary and all derived ultimately from an agreement between the parties.[9] So the category of contract emerged.

---

[6] *De Oratore*, I.42.190.

[7] *Noctes Atticae*, I.22.7.

[8] In the scheme of Masurius Sabinus, Stein, op. cit., above, n.5, p. 153.

[9] Sextus Pedius, cited by Ulpian, D.2.14.1.3.

By the beginning of the second century AD, most of the standard categories of the civil law, property, inheritance, contract and delict had come into being.

The stage was now set for a systematic arrangement of these categories. Legal practitioners, however, felt no need for such an arrangement. In the second century AD, the heyday of the classical period of Roman law, the professional literature of the civil law consisted mainly of commentaries on the praetor's edict or commentaries on the familiar treatises, such as that of Mucius. They were works whose order was familiar to all practitioners and enabled them to find what they were looking for with ease. Why alter it? It was left to an obscure academic lawyer of the late second century AD, called Gaius, to introduce a systematic order in his Institutes.[10] His aim was not to help practitioners but to make the subject more intelligible to his students.

Being a good teacher, Gaius followed the best educational precepts, which held that, in view of the difficulty of maintaining the attention of students, every subject should be divided into not more than three parts. So Gaius announced that all law was divided into three categories, persons, things and actions. These categories were for the most part descriptive. The first, that of persons, covered the different types of person of whom the law takes account and their various capacities, such as slaves and freemen, citizen and non-citizen. The third category, that of actions, was an innovation; it did not deal with the procedure but with different types of legal action and their respective characteristics. Previously actions had been discussed in relation to their subject matter, property actions with physical things, contractual actions with the various contracts. Now actions as a whole were seen to have certain defining features.

It was the second category, things, which had to bear the weight of Gaius's system. At this point Gaius was at his most original. Hitherto a thing was considered to be something physical, but Gaius extended the category by recognising incorporeal things, as well as physical things. This allowed him to classify inheritances, which were collectivities of things, and obligations as incorporeal things. They were things because they had a quantifiable money value. An obligation was an asset in the hands of a creditor, who could sue the debtor and force him to pay him money. So it was a thing, like a horse or land.

---

[10] Stein, op. cit., above, n.5, pp. 154 ff.

Finally Gaius held that there were two sources of obligations — not only the traditional contractual obligations but also those based on wrongdoing, delictual obligations. He saw that a theft of your property or damage to your property put you in a position *vis-à-vis* the delinquent that was essentially similar to that of a creditor against his debtor in contract.

Gaius's institutional system was destined in the distant future to have enormous influence, but for well over a millenium it was relatively ignored. It was followed in Roman academic circles but not by the legal profession. In Rome, as later in England, academic lawyers did not enjoy the prestige accorded to their practising colleagues. The professional jurists would have ageed with George Bernard Shaw's dictum: 'he who can, does; he who cannot, teaches'.[11]

In the sixth century, the Emperor Justinian ordered the compilation of his *Corpus iuris civilis*. He gave detailed instructions to the compilers about what they should include but he failed to prescribe the order in which they were to present it. The largest part is the Digest, an anthology of fragments from the works of the classical jurists and consisting mainly of discussions of cases. Essentially the order of the Digest is the traditional order of the Twelve Tables and the praetorian edict, beginning with legal actions. The second part of the compilation, the Code, consists of extracts from imperial legislation. The topics are arranged in the order of earlier collections of such material, which is itself a variant of the order of the praetor's edict. The Digest and Code were very bulky; sixty-two books in all. It was only because he had pity on students, who could hardly be offered all this material without help, that Justinian also included in his compilation an edited version of Gaius's Institutes, in four books, alongside the Digest and Code.

In Justinian's Institutes the treatment of obligations is different from that in Gaius's Institutes.[12] He widened the scope of the category by including various personal duties, which derived neither from voluntary agreement (contracts) nor from wrongdoing (delicts). Thus the mutual duties of co-owners of property, which had previously been part of the law of physical things, were now held to be obligations. So was the duty

[11] *Sub nom.* John Tanner, *Maxims for Revolutionists*, in the 'Revolutionist's Handbook and Pocket Companion', appended to *Man and Superman* (1903), cited from Limited Editions, New York, 1962, where it is a separate pamphlet, p. 50.

[12] Stein, op. cit., above, n.5, pp. 159 ff.

of the heir of a testator to pay legacies, which had been part of the law of inheritance. They were personal duties, owed by one person to another, and whatever their source, they were now transferred to obligations. They loosely resembled contracts but were not based on an agreement between the parties, so they were put in a new sub-category, called quasi-contracts. In order to maintain symmetry, a fourth sub-category of obligations, namely quasi-delicts, was then added, to balance quasi-contracts.

Obligations in this enlarged category could no longer be viewed primarily as the creditor's assets, items of property, as Gaius had seen them. An obligation now seemed to be more the cause of a personal action by one person against another. So Justinian effectively transferred obligations from the law of things to the law of actions. Both the Digest and the Code contained titles treating obligations and actions together.

When he presented his compilation to his subjects, Justinian assured them that it contained all that was necessary for solving any legal problem. The bulk of the material was contained in the Digest and Code and neither was marked by any attempt at a systematic presentation in Cicero's sense. Students might need to use the brief systematic version of the Institutes. Once they had grown up as lawyers, however, Justinian clearly expected them to discard it and see the law in all its magnificent complexity. The conclusion must therefore be that, although the Roman academic jurists worked out the categories which were necessary for a systematic presentation of the civil law, at no period did its principal exponents consider such a presentation to be important.

II

When the study of the Roman civil law was revived in the twelfth century, the medieval civil lawyers had such a reverence for the word of Justinian that they never ventured to criticise the lack of order in the various parts of the *Corpus iuris*. They made heroic efforts to show rational connections between one text and another and to identify principles and concepts which could be regarded as latent in the texts, but Justinian's order remained sacred. It was not until the humanist movement in sixteenth-century France that serious efforts were made to find a rational order for the civil law.[13] For the first time the content of Justinian's law was separated from its form, for the humanist system-atisers combined enormous respect for the substance of Roman law, with complete disregard for the way it was presented. There were some who used Justinian's texts to show that law was incapable of being presented as a science but most legal humanists were confident that they could at last implement Cicero's ideal of a 'civil law reduced to a science.'

These humanists were almost all Huguenots and there is a parallel between their attempt to strip Christian doctrine of its accretion of commentary and return to the basics of holy scripture and their efforts to recover the fundamental elements of Roman law, which had been submerged by the commentaries of the medieval glossators and com-mentators. They were seen as trampling on the works of the medieval commentators, who obscured those elements. Once the fundamentals had been identified, one should be able to use logic to deduce particular conclusions from them.

The manifesto of the humanist legal systematisers was Duarenus's *Epistula de ratione docendi discendi iuris*, published in 1544. Duarenus castigated the tedious methods of instruction that were traditional in faculties of law and argued that one should begin with what is universal and more familiar to us and proceed down to what is particular. What then is the basic purpose of all law? A Digest text (D.1.1.10) states that the end of law is 'to live honestly, avoid harm to others' and '*ius suum cuique tribuere*,' to render to each person his own *ius*. In Latin and all major European languages, except English, the same word *ius*, *droit*, *diritto*, *Recht*, is used to describe both the objective law, for example the law of obligations, and also a right appertaining to an individual, for example a creditor's right against his debtor. It is only in English that one has to choose which word, law or right, is more appropriate in a particular context. The humanists fulfilled a tendency, which can be observed already in medieval law, to understand the word *ius* as

---

[13] P. Stein, 'Legal Humanism and Legal Science, *Tijdschrift v. Rechtsgeschiedenis* 54 (1986), 297 ff. (= Stein, *The Character and Influence of the Roman Civil Law: Historical Essays* (London, 1988), pp. 91 ff.); A. London Fell, *Origins of Legislative Sovereignty and the Legislative State*, I and II (Königstein, 1983), on J. Corasius, *De iure civili in artem redigendo*, and his use of the Aristotelian four causes; V. Piano Mortari, 'Dialettica e Giurisprudenza: studio sui trattati di dialettica legale del sec. XVI', *Annali di Storia del diritto*, I (1957), 293 ff and 'Considerazioni sugli scritti programmatici dei giuristi del secolo XVI', *Studia et Documenta Historiae et Iuris*, 21 (1955), 276 ff. (= Piano Mortari, *Diritto Logica Metodo nel secolo XVI* (Naples, 1978), pp. 115 ff. and 267 ff).

subjective right rather than objective law.[14] So they understood Justinian's text to say that the end of all law was to render to each his rights. So if civil law was a science, it should take the form of a systematic presentation of the private rights of citizens.

Among the jurists who actually sought to arrange the whole contents of Justinian's law in a rational order, the most influential were Franciscus Connanus and Hugo Donellus. Both started from the Institutional system, which, 1300 years after Gaius devised it, at last came into its own. Their model was not, however, Gaius's original Institutes, the text of which was discovered only in 1816, but Justinian's Institutes. After all Justinian himself had described his Institutes as containing the first elements of the whole science of law (*totius legitimae scientiae prima elementa*, Inst. pref.).

Connanus began with the institutional division of persons, things and actions.[15] This arrangement is rational, he thought, insofar as it deals with the different capacities of persons and different types of things, for example movable and immovable, but it ceases to be rational when it deals with actions. He noted that, under the head of actions, Justinian did not treat of legal procedure but did include his broadened category of obligations. He inferred that the category of actions should not be confined to legal proceedings but should include all human actions that might have legal consequences. So actions should logically include marriages, which had traditionally been dealt with under persons, and also inheritances, which had previously been categorised under things. This accords with what Connanus insisted was a legal logic based on the natural order of things. Actions are what people do.

Connanus's ideas were developed by the seventeenth century German scholar Johannes Althusius.[16] Law is concerned with all kinds of dealing between parties, which he called *negotia*, transactions. One must distinguish the persons involved in such dealings and their subject matter (things) and then the main types of transaction, such as voluntary and involuntary transactions. Then one descends to a lower level of

---

[14] H. Coing, *Zur Geschichte des Privatrechtsystems* (Frankfurt, 1962), pp. 42 ff.

[15] V. Piano Mortari, 'La sistematica come ideale umanistico nell'opera di Francesco Connano', *La Storia del diritto nel quadro delle discipline storiche: Atti I Cong. int. Soci. ital. per la Storia del diritto* (1966), pp. 521 ff. (= *Diritto Logica Metodo* cit, above, n.13, pp. 303 ff.); C. Bergfeld, *F. Connan: ein Systematiker des römischen Rechts* (Cologne/Graz, 1968).

[16] *Dicaeologicae libri tres, totum et universum ius quo utimur methodice complectantes* (Frankfurt, 1617); M. Villey, *La formation de la pensée juridique moderne* (Paris, 1968), pp. 588 ff.

abstraction, in which one meets the legal institutions that regulate voluntary transactions intended to have legal consequences, such as the various forms of ownership and the various forms of obligation. Althusius's notion of *negotium* was the ancestor of one of the civil law concepts most baffling to common lawyers, namely the *Rechtsgeschäft* or *acte juridique*, which includes every transaction that has legal consequences, from a marriage to a will.

Less radical than that of Connanus was the scheme of Donellus.[17] He applied himself to identifying the rational structure underlying Justinian's law, which he assumed to be logical, even if it did not appear so on the surface. When the Romans spoke of civil law, he pointed out, they meant private law, the subject of the institutional scheme, and the aim of private law was to render to each what is his right.

In analysing the institutional scheme, Donellus concentrated first on the meaning of actions. He rejected Connanus's interpretation and observed that, if one looked at all the texts dispassionately, it was clear that for the Roman jurists, action meant essentially a legal proceeding. To bracket actions with obligations, as Justinian appeared to do, was wrong. If the introductory part of actions were really obligations, then every legal action would have to derive from an obligation and there would be no room for actions asserting ownership in property, to which Justinian gave particular prominence. The true reason that obligations come before actions is quite simply that one must know what one is claiming before one can bring an action. So civil law consists in identifying first, what right belongs to each individual, and secondly, the procedural means of obtaining that right.

Donellus insisted that any rational treatment of civil law must reflect this distinction between the substantive law of rights and the law of civil procedure. It is therefore illogical to begin the treatment of the civil law, as the compilers of Justinian's Digest did, with an account of courts and actions. The individual's rights properly include both rights which we enjoy as freemen, such as life and liberty, and our property rights over external things. There are also rights based on what another person is bound to do for us, that is, obligations. Although these are not truly and properly ours in the sense that our good name or our house is ours, yet they are still rights belonging to us. Donellus set out the whole

---

[17] P. Stein, 'Donellus and the origins of the modern civil law', *Mélanges Félix Wubbe* (Fribourg, 1993), pp. 439 ff.

civil law in twenty-eight books of Commentaries, of which he devotes the first sixteen to substantive law and the remaining twelve to civil procedure, which now became a subject quite distinct from the civil law.

Donellus's separation of substantive law and procedure meant that there was now no place for actions in the tripartite institutional system. Law was concerned with rights, not with remedies. The seventeenth-century writers on natural law, in stressing the axiomatic and universal character of natural law rules, popularised the idea that natural law was similar to mathematics. As he contemplated law, said the Dutch writer Hugo Grotius, he had sought to 'abstract his mind from every particular fact, in the way that mathematicians consider their figures abstracted from bodies'.[18] In searching for rules that had the certainty of a mathematical proposition, Grotius looked for rules of natural law which were recognised by all civilised peoples. When he set them out, however, they looked very like the familiar rules of Roman law, purged of their antiquarian features. In his treatise on the law of Holland, he followed the institutional arrangement of the civil law, but without the category of actions. In order to maintain the division into three categories, he divided the law into persons, things and obligations, which now became a category of its own.

With the growth of absolutism on the Continent, the medieval doctrine that much of the law in practice was essentially custom gave way to the idea that all law was essentially legislation. Benevolent despots could by comprehensive statute law instruct their subjects how to behave, with a view to providing them with a programme for the good life. As a result, the emphasis of legal analysis switched from legal rights to legal duties. The classical model was now Cicero's treatise *De officiis* ('On Duties'), which had been a popular handbook since the spread of printing in the late fifteenth century. The seventeenth-century equivalent of Cicero's work on duties was Samuel Pufendorf's 'On the duty of man and of the citizen according to natural law';[19] it was equally popular.

Pufendorf retained the Roman civil law categories but abandoned the Institutional arrangement in favour of a system based on Christian

---

[18] *De iure Belli ac Pacis* (Paris, 1625), proleg., sec.58.

[19] *De officio hominis et civis iuxta legem naturalem lib. II* (Lund, 1673); P. Stein, 'From Pufendorf to Adam Smith: The Natural Law Tradition in Scotland', *Europäisches Rechtsdenken in Geschichte und Gegenwart: Festschrift H. Coing* (Munich, 1982), I, pp. 667 ff. (= Stein, *Character and Influence*, cit., above n.13, pp. 381 ff.).

first principles. Dealing first with man's duties as a man, Pufendorf held that by creating man a social and rational being, God made a natural law for him. This law was expressed in the Gospel injunctions to love God and to love one's neighbour as oneself. Man, as a man, has therefore three kinds of duties: those owed to God, those owed to himself and those owed to others. From the time of St Augustine, Christian theologians had developed the doctrine of ordered love, according to which to love one's neighbour as oneself implied that one had a duty to oneself, which was as strong as one's duty to one's neighbour. Before we can be in a position to help others, we must see that our own essential interests are safeguarded. This is the cardinal virtue of prudence, expressed in the popular maxim, 'charity begins at home'.

These three basic duties form the first principles from which all specific duties of man must logically follow. Law is not concerned with one's duties to God or to oneself but with duties owed to others. The first of these is the obligation that arises when a man gives his word to another. Giving one's word provides the binding force for all voluntary transactions. Then comes the duty to respect property and the contracts which concern property, such as sale. When he turns to man as a citizen, Pufendorf deals with the various associations to which man belongs, ranging from his membership of the family-household, at one extreme, to the State, at the other. The relationships deriving from the family are those of husband and wife, parent and child, and master and servant. In a pre-industrial society, servants were considered more as family than as subjects of a contract of employment.

Pufendorf's scheme was merely a sketch but it set a trend. A feature of the geometrical order, based on duties rather than rights, was that the category of obligations now moved forward in the order and came immediately after persons. Obligations have been the joker in the pack of civil law categories.[20] Gaius originally placed them in the category of things, then Justinian tied them to actions, then, with the expulsion of actions from the system, obligations became an independent category and now, with the stress on duties, they became attached to persons.

The most important follower of the geometrical natural order was Jean Domat in his book *Les lois civiles dans leur ordre naturel.*[21]

---

[20] P. Stein, 'The Changing Place of Obligations in the Private Law System', *La sistematica giuridica: storia, teoria e problemi attuali* (Rome, 1991), pp. 141 ff.

[21] Vol. 1, Paris, 1689.

Domat insisted that law must follow mathematics in moving from what is obvious and familiar to what is less obvious. In regard to relationships outside the family, he began with the principles that Roman law considered axiomatic, such as that one should live honestly, avoid harm to others and render to each his rights. They were general rules applicable throughout the law. He then dealt with different kinds of persons and different kinds of things and came to duties. They are grouped into two great categories, which he calls 'engagements' and 'successions'. The first protects society in its present condition and the second safeguards society in the future. Domat's engagements is an expanded category of obligations. Indeed it includes not only contracts and delicts but all kinds of transactions, such as those which Althusius called *negotia*, with the exception of inheritance transactions. Thus a modification of the ownership of property, by the creation of a life interest (usufruct) or a right of way (servitude), was traditionally part of the law of things, but Domat treated it under the head of engagements. The category also covered security and prescription. When the English translation of Domat's book was published in 1722, the translator explained that it contained 'all the fundamental maxims of law and equity, which must be the same in all countries'.[22]

In the eighteenth century, attention turned from the arrangement of the system as a whole to the internal arrangement of the main categories. The rational method of the natural lawyers was still applied, whereby the general principles applicable to that branch of law were set out first, particular rules followed and cases showing their application in practice were included as illustrations of the working of the principles. The *Treatise on Obligations* of Robert Joseph Pothier of Orleans, which appeared in 1761, became the model for legal treatises in all western languages. It was largely concerned with contracts, whose principles were set out so persuasively that Sir William Jones in England wrote that 'the greatest portion of [them] is law at Westminster as well as Orleans'.[23]

Until the eighteenth century, argument about systematisation of the civil law was confined to the writings of scholars. Now it became a matter of high politics. The dominant view, at least on the continent, was that the duty of the sovereign law-maker was to provide his subjects with the best kind of law in the best possible form, and that

---

[22] W. Strahan, *The Civil Laws in their Natural Order* (London, 1722), p. vi.
[23] *Essay on Bailments* (London, 1781), p. 29.

form was an enacted code, organised according to the best principles. Indeed in the eighteenth century, it was widely believed that one might identify a 'right' order. In the forty-fourth chapter of the *Decline and Fall*, Edward Gibbon describes Justinian's compilation and observes that the Institutes, Digest and Code are each based on a different plan. 'Among the various combinations of ideas, it is difficult to assign any reasonable preference; but as the order of Justinian is different in his three works, it is possible that all may be wrong; and it is certain that two cannot be right'.[24]

The two codes of civil law which have stood the test of time are the French *Code civil* of 1804 and the German *Bürgerliches Gesetzbuch* of 1900. The French code is loosely based on the Institutional system, while the German code is organised on the geometrical natural system. The *Code civil* is divided into three books of very uneven size, the first covering persons and the second things. The third book, which is twice the size of the other two put together, ostensibly deals with methods of acquiring things, and largely reproduces Domat's category of engagements, since it covers both obligations and modifications of ownership. The compilers of the French code seem to have paid more attention to the internal arrangement of the individual sections than to the system as a whole, and much of the part dealing with obligations was lifted directly from Pothier.

The German *BGB*, a century later, is more elaborate, and reflects the intense discussions of nineteenth-century German Pandect science. It is divided into five books. The first is the General Part, which deals with general rules concerning persons and things and the rules common to all kinds of legal transactions. It places great emphasis on the notion of *Rechtsgeschäft*, the *negotium* of Althusius. Book 2 is concerned with obligations, Book 3 with physical things, Book 4 with family law (now quite separate from persons) and Book 5 with inheritances.

In nineteenth-century England the movement for the codification of English private law, urged by Jeremy Bentham, had little success, but during the course of the century, the continental ideals of systematisation were adopted by English treatise writers.[25] Traditionally English doctrinal writers who wanted to set out the common law systematically, from Bracton in the thirteenth century to Blackstone in the eighteenth,

---

[24] Edinburgh, 1811 ed., VIII, p. 39.
[25] A. W. B. Simpson, 'The Rise and Fall of the Legal Treatise: Legal Principles and the Form of Legal Literature, *University of Chicago Law Review* 48 (1981), 632 ff.

had borrowed not only the institutional categories but also a version of the institutional order. Now they concentrated on particular sections of private law, such as contracts or torts, or particular contracts, such as sale or partnership. Their original model was Pothier, but later in the century they copied the publicists of German Pandect science and adopted the characteristic features of their models. The nineteenth-century English treatises set out the common law in a deductive framework, with the implication that in the beginning there were basic principles, which might be latent and unexpressed. These principles were developed and applied in the decisions of the courts. The law did not appear to be derived from these decisions, for they were presented as illustrations of pre-existing principles, and as such were frequently relegated from the text to the notes.

Some of these nineteenth-century treatises originated in the need to expound English law in an intelligible way to law students in India[26] and there was an obvious attraction in showing the students of the subcontinent that, despite their bizarre appearance, the common law rules were really the particular expressions of universally recognised principles. The works of Frederick Pollock or Mackenzie Chalmers sought to expound the principles, and the rules derived from them, in the coherent manner appropriate to a science, and it seemed obvious that they should turn to the leaders of legal science in Germany for guidance. In some cases, such as partnership and sale of goods, the treatises led to the production of little systematic codes, which were enacted by Parliament.

The legislation resulting from the nineteenth-century English treatise movement did not significantly affect the traditional common law approach to legal development. Some of these treatise writers enjoyed high esteem, but unlike those of their continental counterparts, their doctrines had no formal authority in the courts. The rules of the English common law cannot be stated authoritatively in doctrinal juristic treatises. The common law does not have jurists; it only has academic lawyers. Common law rules are open-ended in that new extensions to them can be recognised at any time, but only by the courts. It has no existence as a body of material distinct from what the courts have decided. The common law judges are the oracles of the law and must take responsibility for their decisions. Formally all the academic lawyer

---

[26] C. H. S. Fifoot, *Judge and Jurist in the Reign of Victoria* (London, 1959), pp. 114 ff.

can do is to wait for a judicial decision or press for legislation to put his ideas in statutory form.

III

I conclude with a glance at the situation today. The drive for a systematic civil law impressed a particular type of reasoning on the continental civil law. Since the general acceptance of the systematic model through codification, civil law reasoning has been, at least in theory, deductive. The relevant article of the code, expressed in general terms, constitutes the major premiss of a syllogism, the facts of the particular case to be decided are the minor premiss and the conclusion is the application of the code article to the facts. This form of reasoning leads the civil lawyer to imagine that there can be only one right answer to any legal problem. Disagreement on the application of the code to the facts of the case must be the result of faulty logic by somebody. Civil law judges do not generally give dissenting opinions and every judgment is the judgment of the whole court rather than of the individual members.

A problem for the continental civil law, as systematised in codes, is that its scope is fixed and cannot be extended except with great difficulty. In effect the ambit of the civil law has been confined to the categories stated by Gaius in the second century AD. Although these categories have been constantly rearranged in an attempt to make the civil law more scientific, new categories have not been incorporated into the system. This is partly because from the time of the *Code civil*, commercial law was treated separately in a code of its own. The traditional categories of the civil law system have increasingly become less important than they used to be to the man in the street. His contact with the law is often most likely to be in consumer affairs, or labour law, which are outwith the scope of the civil law.

In the second half of the twentieth century the codes in some civil law countries have been seen as straight-jackets and there have been moves for what is called 'decodification'. This is not an expression of the abandonment of codes but an admission that the law should deal less in the abstract categories of the traditional schemes and more with topics familiar to ordinary people. Much greater emphasis has been put on case-law and as a result the continental civil law has lost some of its vaunted clarity and simplicity. But the systematic ideal, embodied in the codes, is planted too deep to be shifted.

Meanwhile, in England, lawyers have become increasingly preoccupied with the complexity and formlessness of the law. One of the declared aims of establishing the Law Commission thirty years ago was to reduce the complexity of the common law by making it more systematic. English law deals with the various branches of private law in discrete boxes, family law, land law, contracts, torts, succession, with little or no indication of how the boxes fit together into a coherent whole. In general the common lawyers have followed the Roman lawyers in leaving it to academic lawyers to counteract these centrifugal tendencies, for example, by making tentative use of the notion of obligation to show the connection between contracts and torts.

There is general agreement with the Law Commission's aim to make English law more accessible and more intelligible. The recent experience of civil law countries seeking to modernise their codes has not encouraged a demand for the preparation of a single code of English private law. But much attention has been focused on systematising particular areas of law rather in the style of the nineteenth-century treatise writers. Such an effort is in fact necessary, if only to deal with the possibility of the harmonisation of private law within the European Community. For any such harmonisation is bound to be in the civil law form of law applicable in the majority of Member States, whatever its substance.

Already in 1989 the European Parliament resolved to move towards the harmonisation of the private laws of the Member States. In particular a single contract law for all Member States is seen as essential for the effective working of the internal market, and that has been the first target.[27] The European Parliament has recognised with approval the work of the so-called Lando Commission,[28] which consists of academic lawyers from all the Member States, and enjoys financial support from the Community. In May, 1995 the Lando Commission produced the first part of the 'The Principles of European Contract Law'. The Unidroit Institute in Rome published its own 'Principles of International Commercial Contracts' in 1994 and at least one other group is also working on an alternative European contract code. Inevitably the arrangement

[27] R. Zimmermann, 'Die "Principles of European Contract Law"', Teil I', *Zeitschrift für Europäisches Privatrecht* (1995), p. 731.
[28] Resolution of 6 May 1994.

adopted in these projects is influenced by the systematic civil law model. It is important that English lawyers continue to participate fully in this work. I suggest that it is only if we understand some of the historical background of systematisation, which I have tried to sketch, that we shall be able to meet this challenge.

Proceedings of the British Academy, **90**, 165–221

The Economics of the Environment

PARTHA DASGUPTA

University of Cambridge, and
Beijer International Institute of Ecological Economics, Sweden
Fellow of the Academy

1. The Resource Basis of Human Activity

ALL OUR ACTIVITIES are dependent ultimately on resources found in
Nature. Whether it is consumption or production, or whether it is
exchange, the commodities and services that are involved can be traced
to constituents provided by Nature. Thus, the ingredients of a typical
manufactured product are other manufactured products, labour time and
skills, and resources found in Nature. Each of the constituent manufactured products is in turn a complex of yet other manufactured
products, labour time and skills, and resources found in Nature. And
so on. This means that the manufactured product with which we began
is ultimately a combination of labour time and skills, and resources
found in Nature.

But labour, too, is a produced good. Even raw labour is an output,
manufactured by those resources that sustain life; resources such as the
multitude of nutrients we consume, the air we breathe, and the water we
drink. It follows that *all* commodities are traceable to natural
resources.[1]

In many instances, natural resources are of direct value to us as

Read at the Academy 26 October 1995. © The British Academy 1996.

[1] This etymology of produced goods and services does not yield a 'resource theory of value'.
Like Marx's labour theory of value, any such theory would run aground. One reason is that
there are many natural resources, not one; and this alone would make the putative theory
incoherent. Koopmans (1957) contains a simple proof of why.

needs or as consumption goods (e.g. breathable air, drinkable water, and fisheries); in others, they are of indirect value (e.g. plankton, which serves as food for fish, which we, in turn, consume); sometimes they are both (e.g. drinking and irrigation water). The 'value' I am alluding to may be utilitarian (e.g. the resource may be a source of food, or a keystone species in an ecosystem), it may be aesthetic (e.g. a landscape), or it may be intrinsic (e.g. it could be a living animal); indeed, it may be all these things at once. Resource stocks are measured in different ways, depending on their character: in mass units (e.g. biomass units for forests, cow dung, and crop residues), in numbers (e.g. size of an animal herd), in indices of 'quality' (e.g. water- and air-quality indicators), in volume units (e.g. acre-feet for aquifers), and so forth.

There is a small tribe of economists, known as resource economists (I happen to belong to this tribe), who tend to view the natural environment through the lens of population ecology. The focus in population ecology is the dynamics of interacting populations of different species. So, it is customary there to take the background environmental processes as given, that is, they are not subject to analysis. The best known illustration of this viewpoint is the use of the logistic function to chart the time-path of the biomass of a single species of fish enjoying a constant flow of food. Predator-prey models (e.g. that of Volterra) provide another class of examples; as do the May–MacArthur models[2] of competition among an arbitrary number of species.

Depending on the context, the flow of value we derive from a resource stock could be dependent on the rate at which it is harvested, or on the size of the stock; in many cases, it would be dependent on both. For example, annual commercial profits from a fishery depend not only on the rate at which it is harvested, but also on the stock of the fishery, because unit harvesting costs are typically low when stocks are large and high when stocks are low. The valuation of resources and the rates at which populations are harvested in different institutional settings are among the resource economist's objects of enquiry (Clark, 1976; Dasgupta and Heal, 1979; Dasgupta, 1982).[3]

---

[2] See May (1972) and May and MacArthur (1972).

[3] Resource economists are interested in minerals, ores, and fossil fuels as well. As the natural regenerative rate of such resources is zero, they can be regarded as a limiting case of renewable natural resources. For this reason they are called exhaustible resources. For reasons of space, I will ignore them in this lecture. For an account of what economics looks like when we include exhaustible resources in the production process, see Dasgupta and Heal (1979), Hartwick and Olewiler (1986), and Tietenberg (1988).

There is another small tribe of economists, known as environmental economists (I happen to belong to this tribe as well), who, in seeming contrast to resource economists, base their studies on systems ecology.[4] There, the focus is on such objects as energy at different trophic levels and its rate of flow among them; and the distribution and flows of biochemical substances in soils and bodies of water, and of particulates in the atmosphere. The motivation is to study the biotic and abiotic processes underlying the services ecosystems provide for us. As is now well known, these services are generated by interactions among organisms, populations of organisms, communities of populations, and the physical and chemical environment in which they reside. Ecosystems are the sources of water, of animal and plant food, and of other renewable resources. In this way, ecosystems maintain a genetic library, sustain the processes that preserve and regenerate soil, recycle nutrients, control floods, filter pollutants, assimilate waste, pollinate crops, operate the hydrological cycle, and maintain the gaseous composition of the atmosphere.[5] The totality of all the ecosystems of the world represents a large part of our natural capital stock, which, for vividness, I will refer to as our environmental resource-base.[6] Environmental problems are thus almost always associated with resources that are regenerative, but are in danger of exhaustion from excessive use. It makes sense then to identify environmental resources with renewable natural resources. The valuation of ecological services and the patterns in which they are available under different institutional settings are among the environmental economist's objects of enquiry. Economic studies of global warming, eutrophication of lakes, the management of rangelands, and the pollution of estuaries are examples of such endeavour (Costanza, 1991; Mäler et al., 1992; Walker, 1993; Nordhaus, 1994).

In a formal sense, population and systems ecology differ only by way of the variables ('state variables', as they are called) that are taken to characterise complex systems. In the former, the typical variables are population sizes (or, alternatively, tonnage) of different species; in the latter, they are indices of various services. As noted above, it is often

[4] The contrast is illusory, as will become apparent below, which is why one can belong to both tribes with ease.

[5] Ehrlich, Ehrlich and Holdren (1977) remains the outstanding treatise on both population and systems ecology.

[6] As mentioned earlier, our natural capital stock includes, in addition, minerals, ores, and fossil fuels.

possible to summarise the latter in terms of indices of 'quality', such as those for air, soil, or water. Each such index should be taken to be a summary statistic (reflecting a particular form of aggregation) that enables the analyst to study complex systems by means of a few strategically chosen variables.

The viewpoint just offered, that of distinguishing population and systems ecology in terms of the state variables that summarise complex systems, allows us to integrate problems of resource management with problems of environmental pollution and degradation.[7] It reminds us that resource economics and environmental economics are the same subject. It also suggests that the environmental resource-base should be seen as a gigantic capital stock. Animal, bird, and fish populations (including the vast array of micro-organisms), water, soil, forest cover, and the atmosphere are among the components of this stock. Since it would be convenient to refer to resource and environmental economics by an overarching name, I will do so in this lecture by the term 'ecological economics'.[8]

2. The Neglect of Ecological Economics

Given the importance of the environmental resource-base in our lives, you would think that ecological matters must be a commonplace furniture of economic thinking. But you would be wrong. Not only are environmental resources only perfunctorily referred to in economics textbooks, they are also cheerfully ignored in economists' public pronouncements. Indeed, as a profession, it has been normal practice for economists to regard the environmental resource-base as an *indefinitely* large and adaptable capital stock. This has enabled them to offer macro-economic advice to political leaders, and encourage the lay public to aspire to levels of consumption that are consistent only with unlimited growth possibilities in material output. Macro-economic models involving long run production and consumption possibilities typically make no mention of the environmental resource-base; the implicit assumption being that natural resources aren't scarce now, and won't be scarce in the future. It is small wonder that ecological economics remains a fringe

[7] For a formal demonstration of this, see Dasgupta (1982).

[8] I am able to usurp the term from the literature, for the reason that it appears to have no fixed meaning: 'ecological economics' seems to mean different things to different people.

activity of what one could call 'official' economics. It is an unfortunate state of affairs.[9]

The lacuna has not been restricted to the study of economics in advanced industrial countries: more than forty years of development thinking in poor countries has also neglected environmental matters. A prime reason, often aired, is that, in earlier days, environmentalists in western industrial countries tended to focus on such problems as local air pollution (e.g. sulphur emissions) and deterioration of amenities (e.g. national parks, beaches and coastlines). To the development economist, environmental matters, therefore, appeared a trifle precious, not wholly relevant to the urgencies of poor societies. On innumerable occasions I have had this explanation offered to me by social scientists in developing countries. I wouldn't wish to doubt their claim, but the explanation doesn't tell us why, when they studied development problems, these same social scientists ignored their *own* environmental resource-base, nor why government planning models in poor countries so often have regarded this base to be of infinite size.

The neglect of the environment in development economics is ironic, because people in poor countries are in great part agrarian and pastoral. Rural people account for about 65 per cent of the population of what the World Bank classifies as low-income countries. The proportion of total labour force in agriculture is slightly in excess of this. The share of agriculture in gross domestic product in these countries is 30 per cent. These figures should be contrasted with those from industrial market economies, which are 6 per cent and 2 per cent, respectively, for the latter two indices. Poor countries are in large measure biomass-based subsistence economies, in that the rural poor eke out a living from products obtained directly from their *local* environment. For example, in their informative study of life in a micro-watershed of the Alaknanda river in the central Himalayas in India, the (Indian) Centre for Science and Environment (CSE 1990) reports that, of the total number of hours worked by the villagers sampled, 30 per cent was devoted to cultivation,

---

[9] Barro and Sala-i-Martin (1995) and Romer (1996) are treatises on macro-economic growth. The environmental resource-base does not appear in either exposition. By the same token, it has proved all too congenial for ecologists to regard the human presence as an inessential component of the ecological landscape. This has enabled them to ignore the character of human decisions and, so, of economics. Thus, ecologists in great part continue to think that environmental degradation resulting from increased human encroachment on ecosystems can be stemmed effectively by centralised command-and-control modes of operation (see below in the text). For further discussion of the interface of economic and ecological concerns, see Dasgupta and Ehrlich (1996).

20 per cent to fodder collection, and about 25 per cent was spread evenly between fuel collection, animal care, and grazing. Some 20 per cent of time was spent on household chores, of which cooking took up the greatest portion, and the remaining 5 per cent was involved in other activities, such as going to market. In their work on Central and West Africa, Falconer and Arnold (1989) and Falconer (1990) have shown how vital are forest products to the lives of rural people. Poor countries, especially those in the Indian sub-continent and sub-Saharan Africa, can be expected to remain largely rural economies for some while yet. The categories of natural resources that are of fundamental importance in advanced industrial countries no doubt differ from those in poor, agrarian societies; but nowhere is the environmental resource-base in unlimited supply. To treat the base as a free good is to practise bad economics.

Here is an example of how economic *analysis* can go awry when it neglects the environment. Barring sub-Saharan Africa over the past twenty-five years or so, gross income per head has grown in nearly all poor regions since the end of the Second World War. In addition, growth in world food production since 1960 has exceeded the world's population growth; by an annual rate of, approximately, 0.6 per cent. This has been accompanied by improvements in a number of indicators of human well-being, such as the under-five survival rate, life expectancy at birth, and literacy. In poor regions, all this has occurred in a regime of population growth rates substantially higher than in the past. These observations have led many economists to argue that the high rates of growth of population that have been experienced in recent years aren't a hindrance to economic betterment, but, rather, that economic development itself can be relied upon to bring down population growth rates.

But there is a problem with this argument. Statistics on past movements of gross world income and agricultural production say nothing about the environmental resource-base. They don't say if, for example, increases in gross national product (GNP) per head are not being realised by means of a depletion of natural capital; in particular, if increases in agricultural production are not being achieved by 'mining' the soil. Thus, it is today customary for international organisations to estimate social well-being by means of indices that capture only the current standard of living (e.g. GNP per head, life expectancy at birth, and the infant survival rate; see UNDP, 1993). But such measures bypass the concerns that ecologists have repeatedly expressed about the links that exist between continual population growth, increased material output, and the state of the environment. This is a serious limitation. In section 11 I will suggest an aggregate measure of social well-being that captures not only the current standard of living, but also the effect of changes in the composition of a country's natural capital on her *future* standard of living. This measure is called *net* national product (NNP).

Now the interesting point is this: it is possible for measures of current well-being, such as the under-five survival rate and GNP per head, to increase over an extended period of time even while NNP per head is declining. We should be in a position to say if this has been happening in poor countries. But we aren't, and this is a reflection of the neglect of ecological matters in economic modelling.[10]

Despite this neglect, ecological economics has developed considerably over the years, almost by stealth. So far in this lecture I have sketched the terrain of the subject. In what follows, I will try to give you a feel for what the subject amounts to and what insights it has to offer. Over many years now, I have tried to develop ecological economics in a way that speaks to the problems of economic development in poor countries (Dasgupta, 1982, 1990, 1993, 1995a, b; Dasgupta and Mäler, 1991, 1995); so my treatment will be coloured by my own research interests. I don't think there is any harm in this. Even though many of the problems I will discuss here arise from a study of rural poverty in poor countries, their structure is generic, and I think this fact will be transparent to you.

The plan of the rest of this lecture is as follows: In section 3 I will classify the reasons we face environmental problems, and in sections 4–9 I will elaborate them. Sections 10–11 will explore prescriptions. In large part the discussion there will be confined to local environmental problems. In section 12 I will extend the discussion to global environmental problems. One overall conclusion we will arrive at is that it won't do to rely entirely on a decentralised economic environment for avoiding environmental problems: collective action at different levels is necessary. So in section 13 I will speculate on the various pathways that could sustain agreements among peoples and nations. Even though I will present a number of hard results that have been obtained in ecological economics, I won't attempt a summary at the end. My intention here is to

---

[10] Attempts at estimating NNP, thus defined, are currently underway at the World Bank and the United Nations Statistical Office.

get you to peer at the environment through the economist's lens. Providing conclusions at the end would detract from this.

3. Poverty and Institutional Failure as Causes of Environmental Degradation

The early literature on ecological economics identified market failure as the underlying cause of environmental problems (Pigou, 1920; Lindahl, 1958; Arrow, 1971; Meade, 1973; Mäler, 1974; Baumol and Oates, 1975; Dasgupta and Heal, 1979). Indeed, the phenomenon of externalities looms large in what has traditionally been called environmental economics.

By 'markets' I mean institutions that make available to interested parties the opportunity to negotiate mutually advantageous courses of action. However, in order for someone to be able to negotiate, they need to know the extent to which they are empowered to negotiate, the extent to which the other parties are empowered to negotiate, and so on. In other words, for you to be able to negotiate, you need to know what you can negotiate with, what the other parties can negotiate with, and so forth. So it should come as no surprise that the functioning of markets is linked closely to the structure of property rights. This observation (Coase, 1960) was the starting point of modern ecological economics.

Thus, it was noted by authors that for many environmental resources markets simply don't exist. In some cases they don't exist because the costs of negotiation are too high. (The overarching term 'transactions cost' is often used these days to refer to a common or garden variety of costs that prevent markets from operating well.) One class of examples is provided by economic activities that are affected by ecological interactions involving long geographical distances (e.g. the effects of deforestation in the uplands on downstream activities hundreds of miles away: see section 4); another, by large temporal distances (e.g. the effect of carbon emissions on climate in the distant future, in a world where forward markets are non-existent because future generations aren't present today to negotiate with us).[11] Then there are cases (e.g.

---

[11] Problems arising from an absence of forward markets for the distant future are no doubt ameliorated by the fact that we care about our children's well-being and know that they in turn will care for theirs, and so on, down the generations. This means, by recursion, that even if we don't care directly for the well-being of our distant descendants, we do care for them indirectly. Arrow *et al.* (1995a) contains a succinct account of these considerations.

the atmosphere and the open seas) where the nature of the physical situation (namely the migratory nature of the resource) makes private property rights impractical and so keeps markets from existing; while in others (e.g. bio-diversity: see Perrings *et al.*, 1994), ill-specified or unprotected property rights prevent their existence, or make them function wrongly even when they do exist.

In each of these cases, the market prices of goods and services fail to reflect their social scarcities; that is, their accounting (or shadow) prices. For example, the market price of a number of environmental resources, *in situ*, is zero, even though, being in limited supply, their accounting prices are positive. Generally speaking, *laissez-faire* economies are not much good at producing publicly observable signals that would reflect environmental scarcities. Externalities do not create market distortions; they *are* a form of market distortion.[12]

One way to improve matters is to impose regulations on resource users; for example, restrictions on effluent discharges and quotas on fish harvests. Another is to introduce a system of taxes, often called Pigovian taxes; for example, pollution charges and stumpage fees. Each scheme has its advantages and disadvantages over the other (Weitzman, 1974a; Dasgupta, 1982; section 12, below). We cannot enter into details here, but it bears emphasis that environmental taxes, when properly designed, remove market distortions. In addition, there is a presumption that tax revenues, thus collected, would enable the government to reduce pre-existing distortionary taxes (e.g. taxes on earned income). There is, thus, a presumption that Pigovian taxes yield a 'double dividend', a rhetorical device that has been much used in recent years to persuade governments to impose 'green' taxes. Matters of public finance have been a recurrent theme in ecological economics (see, especially, Baumol and Oates, 1975; Bovenberg and van der Ploeg, 1994).

Thus far, market failure. Recently, however, certain patterns of environmental deterioration have been traced to government failure. For example, Binswanger (1991) has argued that, in Brazil, the exemption from taxation of virtually all agricultural income (allied to the fact

---

[12] The accounting price of a resource (whether or not it is an environmental resource) is the increase in the maximum value of social well-being if a unit more of the resource were made available costlessly. Formally, it is a Lagrange multiplier. The accounting price of a commodity is, thereby, the difference between its market price and the tax (or subsidy) that ought to be imposed on it. Dasgupta, Marglin and Sen (1972) and Little and Mirrlees (1974) offer procedures for estimating accounting prices. Neither book, however, has anything to say about environmental resources.

that logging is regarded as proof of land occupancy) has provided
strong incentives to the rich to acquire forest lands and to then deforest
them. He has argued that the subsidy the government has thereby
provided to the private sector has been so large, that a reduction in
deforestation is in Brazil's interests, and not merely in the interest of the
rest of the world. This has implications for international negotiations.
The current consensus appears to be that, as a country, Brazil has much
to lose from reducing the rate of deforestation she is engaged in. If this
were true, there would be a case for the rest of the world to subsidise
her, as compensation for losses she would sustain if she were to restrain
herself. But, as Binswanger's account suggests, it isn't at all clear if the
consensus is correct.[13]

This said, it is important to note that the causes of environmental
problems are not limited to market and government failure; they also
arise because such micro-institutions as the household can function
badly. In poor communities, for example, men typically have the bulk
of the political voice. We should then expect public investment in, say,
environmental regeneration to be guided by male preferences, not
female needs. On matters of afforestation in the drylands, for instance,
we should expect women to favour planting for fuelwood and men for
fruit trees, because it is the women and children who collect fuelwood,
while men control cash income (and fruit can be sold in the market).
This explains why, even as the sources of fuelwood continue to recede,
fruit trees are often planted.

That political instability (at the extreme, civil war) is a direct cause
of environmental degradation is obvious. What isn't obvious is that it is a
hidden cause as well. Political instability creates uncertainty in property
rights. In its presence, people are reluctant to make the investments that
are necessary for environmental protection and improvement: the
expected returns on such forms of investment are low. In a study
comprising 120 countries, Deacon (1994) has offered statistical evidence of a positive link between political instability and forest depletion.

Taken together, these examples reflect the environmental consequences of institutional failure. They have a wide reach, and in recent
years they have often been discussed within the context of the thesis
that environmental degradation, such as eroding soil, receding forests,
and vanishing water supplies, is a *cause* of accentuated poverty among

---

[13] Heath and Binswanger (1996) provide an illustration of government failure causing
environmental deterioration in Columbia.

the rural poor in poor countries. There is truth in this. But there is also much accumulated evidence that poverty itself can be a cause of environmental degradation (Dasgupta, 1993; Dasgupta and Mäler, 1995; Ehrlich, Ehrlich, and Daily, 1995). This reverse causality arises because some environmental resources (e.g. ponds and rivers) are essential for survival in normal times, while others (e.g. forest products) are a source of supplementary income in times of acute economic stress. This mutual influence can offer a pathway along which poverty, environmental degradation, and even high fertility, feed upon one another in a synergistic manner over time (Dasgupta, 1993, 1995a, b). The recent experience of sub-Saharan Africa would seem to be an illustration of this (Cleaver and Schreiber, 1994). Indeed, an erosion of the environmental resource-base can make certain categories of people destitute even while the economy's gross national product (GNP) increases.

These two causes of environmental degradation (namely, institutional failure and poverty), pull in different directions and are together not unrelated to an intellectual tension between the concerns people share about an increased greenhouse effect and acid rains, that sweep across regions, nations and continents; and about those matters (such as, for example, the decline in firewood or water sources) that are specific to the needs and concerns of the poor in as small a group as a village community. Environmental problems present themselves differently to different people. In part, it is a reflection of the tension I have just noted and is a source of misunderstanding of people's attitudes. Some people, for example, identify environmental problems with population growth, while others identify them with wrong sorts of economic growth (see sections 7 and 11). Then there are others who view them through the spectacle of poverty. Each of these visions is correct. There is no single environmental problem; rather, there is a large collection of them (Dasgupta and Mäler, 1995; Reardon and Vosti, 1995). Thus, growth in industrial wastes has been allied to increased economic activity; and in industrialised countries (especially those in the former Socialist block), neither preventive nor curative measures have kept pace with their production. Moreover, the scale of the human enterprise, both by virtue of unprecedented increases in the size of the world's population and the extent of economic activity, has so stretched the capabilities of ecosystems, that humankind can today rightly be characterised as the earth's dominant species. These observations loom large not only in ecological economics, but also in the more general writings of environmentalists and in the professional writings of ecologists in the West.

For example, Vitousek *et al.* (1986) have estimated that forty per cent of the net energy created by terrestrial photosynthesis (i.e. net primary production of the biosphere) is currently being appropriated for human use. To be sure, this is a rough estimate. Moreover, net terrestrial primary production isn't exogenously given and fixed; it depends in part on human activity. Nevertheless, the figure does put the scale of the human presence on the planet in perspective.

On the other hand, economic growth itself has brought with it improvements in the quality of a number of environmental resources. The large-scale availability of potable water, and the increased protection of human populations against both water- and air-borne diseases in industrial countries, have in great measure come in the wake of growth in national income these countries have enjoyed over the past 200 years or so. Moreover, the physical environment inside the home has improved beyond measure with economic growth. For example, cooking in South Asia continues to be a central route to respiratory illnesses among women. Such positive links between economic growth and environmental quality often go unnoted by environmentalists in the West. I would guess that this lacuna is yet another reflection of the fact that it is all too easy to overlook the enormous heterogeneity of the earth's environmental resource-base, ranging as it does from the atmosphere, oceans, and landscapes to water-holes, grazing fields, and sources of fuelwood. This heterogeneity needs constantly to be kept in mind.

4. Markets and their Failure: Unidirectional Interactions

Since we economists understand market competition better than political competition, we understand market failure better than government failure. In fact, ecological economics has provided us with much insight into the nature of those allocation failures that arise from malfunctioning markets. In this and sections 5 and 7, we will study this.

Market failure is prominent in those hidden interactions that are unidirectional; for example deforestation in the uplands, which can inflict damages on the lowlands in watersheds. It pays first to concentrate on the assignment of property rights before seeking remedies. The common law in many poor countries, if we are permitted to use this expression in a universal context, *de facto* recognises polluters' rights, not those of the pollutees. So, then, let us consider first the case where the law recognises polluters' rights. Translated into our present example, this means that the timber merchant who has obtained a concession in the upland forest is under no obligation to compensate farmers in the lowlands. If the farmers wish to reduce the risk of heightened floods, they will have to compensate the timber merchant for reducing the rate of deforestation. Stated this way, the matter does look morally bizarre, but that is how things would be with polluters' rights. Had property rights been the other way round, that is, one of pollutees' rights, the boots would have been on the other set of feet, and it would have been the timber merchant who would have had to pay compensation to the farmers for the right to inflict the damages that go with deforestation. However, even if the law were to see the matter in this light, there would be enforcement problems. When the cause of damages is hundreds of miles away, when the timber concession has been awarded to public land by the government, and when the victims are thousands of impoverished farmers, the issue of a negotiated outcome doesn't usually arise. The private cost of logging being lower than its social cost, we would expect excessive deforestation.

But when the market prices of environmental resources are lower than their accounting prices, resource-based goods can be presumed to be underpriced in the market.[14] Naturally, the less roundabout, or less 'distant', is the production of the final good from its resource base, the greater is this underpricing, in percentage terms. Put another way, the lower is the value added to the resource, the larger is the extent of underpricing of the final product. But this in turn means that if the country were to export primary products, there would be an implicit subsidy on these exports, possibly on a massive scale. Moreover, the subsidy would be paid not by the general public via taxation, but by some of the most disadvantaged members of society: the sharecropper, the small landholder or tenant farmer, the forest-dweller, the fisherman, and so on. The subsidy would be hidden from public scrutiny; nobody would talk of it. But it would be there; it would be real. We should have estimates of such subsidies in poor countries. As of now, we have no estimate.[15] An

---

[14] This example is taken from Dasgupta (1990). Chichilnisky (1994) provides an extended discussion of it.

[15] But see Hodgson and Dixon (1992) for an attempt at such an estimation for the Bacuit Bay and the El Nido watershed on Palawan, in the Philippines. The cause of damages (to tourism and fisheries) was logging in the uplands. In short, there is an effective subsidy on logging in the upper watershed. The authors' computations were incomplete, but such as they were, the analysis did suggest that the rate of logging ought to be lower; indeed, it is possible that logging ought not to occur there at all.

appropriate form of public policy would be a tax per unit of logging. This would be a Pigovian tax and, at an optimum, it would equal the damages that would be experienced downstream if logging were to increase by a marginal amount.

In some parts of the world, community leaders, non-government organisations, and a free press (where they exist) have been known to galvanise activity on behalf of the relatively powerless 'pollutees'. In recent years this has happened on a number of occasions in different contexts. One of the most publicised was the Chipko Movement in India, which involved the threatened disenfranchisement of historical users of forest resources. This was occasioned by the government claiming its rights over what was stated to be 'public property' and then embarking on a logging operation. Democratic protest was followed by a reversal of government action. The reversal came about because citizens could exercise their right to protest. This, and other, examples suggest that the connection betwen environmental protection and civil and political liberties is a close one. They indicate that such liberties are not only valuable in themselves, they also help realise other collective goals (Dasgupta, 1993). I will return to this most important matter in section 7, when we come to study the breakdown of communitarian forms of management of local commons.

5. Markets and their Failure: Reciprocal Interactions and the Problem of the Commons

Matters can be quite different for interactions that are reciprocal. Here, each party's actions affect all. Interactions of this sort are the hallmark of common-property resources, such as grazing lands, forests, fisheries, the atmosphere, aquifers, village tanks, ponds, lakes, and the oceans. They are often common property because private property rights are for a number of reasons difficult to define (e.g. in the case of mobile resources, such as air). Even when definable, they are on occasion difficult to enforce (e.g. in the case of forest resources in mountainous terrains). However, unlike public goods, consumption of common property resources is rivalrous: it is possible for at least one party to increase its consumption at the expense of others' consumption of them.

Resources such as local forests, grazing lands, village ponds, and rivulets, are often common property because that is how they have been since time immemorial. Moreover, in poor countries they have remained common property for long because they are basic needs and are at the same time geographically contained. Rivers may be long, but they don't flow through everyone's land. In any case, upstream farmers would have untold advantages over downstream ones if they were in a position to turn off the 'tap'. Exclusive private territoriality over them would leave non-owners at the mercy of the owners at the bargaining table.[16] Societies typically don't risk the institution of private-property rights over such resources.[17] However, unless there is collective action at some level, the private cost of using the resource falls short of its social cost; and, so, the common property is over-exploited. This was the point of a pioneering article by Gordon (1954).

In a famous essay that popularised Gordon's analysis, the biologist, Garrett Hardin wrote:

> Picture a pasture open to all. It is to be expected that each herdsman will try to keep as many cattle as possible on the commons . . . . As a rational being, each herdsman seeks to maximize his gain. Explicitly or implicitly, more or less consciously, he asks, 'What is the utility to me of adding one more animal to my herd?' . . . Adding together the component partial utilities, the rational herdsman concludes that the only sensible course for him to pursue is to add another animal to his herd. And another; and another . . . . But this is the conclusion reached by each and every rational herdsman sharing a commons. Therein is the tragedy. Each man is locked in a system that compels him to increase his herd without limit — in a world that is limited. Ruin is the destination toward which all men rush, each pursuing his own best interest in a society that believes in the freedom of the commons. Freedom in the commons brings ruin to all. (Hardin, 1968, p. 1244.)

The parable is compelling: it offers an example of the famous 'prisoners' dilemma' in a striking way. But is it trustworthy? The answer depends on how contained the commons happen to be geographically. Hardin's parable is apt for resources such as the atmosphere, the open seas, and urban pollution; but, as we will see in the next section, it is misleading for local common-property resources, such as ponds, streams, local forests, threshing grounds and, ironically, grazing fields. The theory of games teaches us that the local commons can in principle be managed efficiently by the users themselves, that there is

[16] And they are so left under the hundred-year-old water laws in South Africa, where small groups of upstream farmers enjoy ownership rights over the water that flows through their lands. See Koch (1996).

[17] Rulers had control over such resources in many early societies. But that was not the same as private property rights. Rulers were obliged to make them available to the ruled. Indeed, one of the assumed duties of rulers was to expand such resource bases.

no obvious need for some agency external to the community of users
(e.g. government) to assume a regulatory role. (See Dasgupta and Heal,
1979, chap. 3.) A large body of evidence that has recently been
collected confirms the theory's prediction: members of local communities have often cooperated in protecting their commons from excessive use.[18] I will elaborate this in section 6.

This said, the problem of the commons can rear its head through all
sorts of unsuspected sources. The introduction of cotton as an export
crop in Tanzania was successful in increasing farmers' incomes. But
other than cattle, there were few alternative forms of saving available to
farmers. So the quantity of livestock increased significantly, placing
communal grazing lands under stress — to the extent that herds declined
because of an increase in their mortality rate. And there have been many
cases throughout the world where, for disparate reasons, neither centralised nor communitarian solutions could take hold, so that the commons degraded over time (Ostrom, 1990; Baland and Platteau, 1996).
There have also been cases where control mechanisms once existed, but
broke down under the pressure of changing economic circumstances.
We will come to these matters in section 7.

Public concern about environmental degradation is often prompted
by disasters, such as nuclear leakage or floods. The environmental
impact of large undertakings (e.g. dams and irrigation systems, such
as the Narmada Project in India) also catches the public eye. This is not
surprising. Large-scale effects caused by single happenings are, often
enough, easy to detect. So they invite debate. In contrast, environmental
interactions that result in an overuse of common-property resources are
not so easy to detect, at least, not unless some threshold is reached and
catastrophies occur. The commons often involve large numbers of
users, each inflicting only a tiny damage on each of the others, which,
however, sum to a substantial amount; usually, over an extended period
of time. There is now evidence that environmental degradation in poor
countries is in large measure caused by those institutional failures
whose deleterious effects accumulate slowly over time; it is caused
less by large public projects (Repetto, 1988).

---

[18] See, e.g. Howe (1986); Wade (1988); Chopra, Kadekodi and Murty (1990); Feeny *et al.*
(1990); Ostrom (1990); Stevenson (1991); and Baland and Platteau (1996). Seabright (1993),
Young (1994), and Ostrom (1996) contain good theoretical discussions of modelling problems in this field of enquiry.

6. Local Commons and Communitarian Solutions

As noted earlier, there is a difference between global and local commons. The open seas are common-property resources, as are usually village ponds; but, what is a problem for the former isn't necessarily a problem for the latter.

Why? One reason is that individual use is more easily observable by others when the resource isn't spatially spread out; which means that it is easier to prevent individuals from 'free-riding' on the use of local commons. (Contrast the use of a village tube-well with the littering of streets in a metropolis; or cattle-grazing in the village commons with fuelwood collection in the mountains.) However, bargaining, enforcement, and information costs also play a role in the relative efficacy of the various rules that can in principle be invoked for sharing the benefits and burdens that are associated with an efficient use of common-property resources. Thus, it matters whether the users know one another (contrast a village grazing ground with oceanic fisheries: see section 13); it matters whether increased mobility makes future encounters among group members more uncertain (see section 13); and it matters whether population pressure leads bargaining costs to exceed the benefits of co-operation. The confirmation of theory by current evidence on the fate of different categories of common-property resources has been one of the most pleasing features of modern economic analysis.[19]

Typically, local commons are not open for use to all in a society: they are not 'open access' resources. In most cases they are open only to those having historical rights, through kinship ties, community membership, and so forth. 'Social capital', viewed as a complex of interpersonal networks (Putnam, 1993), is telling in this context: it hints at the basis upon which co-operation has traditionally been built.

It is as well to note though that the theory of bargaining is still so rudimentary that it offers little guidance to the analyst on how the benefits and burdens of co-operation would be shared if there were no impediments of the kind that are associated with bargaining, monitoring, enforcement, and information costs. Figure 1 demonstrates the case of two parties. The point labelled A denotes the levels of well-being the parties would attain, respectively, if they were not to co-

---

[19] There is now an enormous empirical literature recording both the successes and failures of common-property resource management. For an excellent discussion of what it has to tell us, see Baland and Platteau (1996, chaps. 10–13).

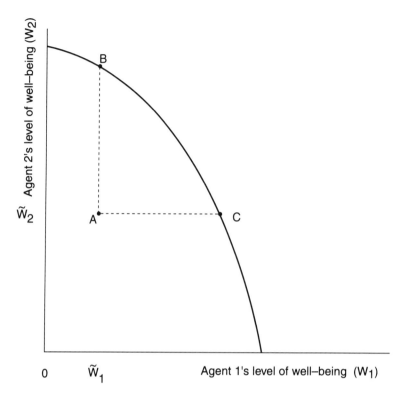

Figure 1. The Two-Person Bargaining Problem

operate in their use of the commons. Points to the north-east of A denote levels of well-being the pair would attain under various forms of co-operation. The frontier, BC, of this region represents the set of all efficient allocations of well-being. Even if we were to assume that the process of bargaining would lead the parties to agree on an efficient allocation (and there is no obvious reason why we should assume this), upon which point on BC would the bargainers converge?

The plain truth is, we don't know. It is, of course, tempting to appeal to that old war-horse of co-operative game theory, the Nash bargaining solution.[20] But, except for one (Chopra, Kadekodi and Murty, 1990), I don't know of any study that has used it to interpret observed sharing

[20] Denote by W_1 and W_2 the well-beings of persons 1 and 2, respectively. Suppose $\tilde{W}_1$ and $\tilde{W}_2$ are their values at the non-cooperative point, A. The Nash bargaining solution is that point on BC at which the function $(W_1 - \tilde{W}_1)(W_2 - \tilde{W}_2)$ is maximised. For accounts of the Nash bargaining solution, see Binmore and Dasgupta (1988) and Fudenberg and Tirole (1991).

arrangements of common-property resources. The Nash bargaining solution (like others, such as, the Kalai-Smorodinsky solution; see, e.g. Dasgupta, 1993) is independent of the context in which negotiation is assumed to take place. Nash (1950) regarded this as a virtue and was explicit on the point. But this feature of the solution makes it all the more likely that it doesn't often find application.[21]

If the number of parties were to exceed two, matters would be even more problematic: every bilateral negotiation would now have to be sensitive to others in the community. In addition to the Nash bargaining solution, there are other solution concepts in co-operative game theory, such as the core, the nucleolus, and the Shapley value.[22] I have not seen any of them being used in applied studies on the local commons.

In the absence of firm guidance from game theory, speculation has been rife in the theoretical literature on the commons; some, empirically dubious. For example, it has been suggested that heterogeneity of preferences amounts to transaction costs and, thereby, it impedes co-operation; or, in other words, that co-operation requires shared values. This sounds plausible, but is questionable. Every day, hundreds of thousands of people reach bilateral agreements in bazaars. How should we interpret this?

The applied literature, however, has been most illuminating. Not only has it confirmed that resource users in many instances co-operate, it has also explained observed asymmetries in the distribution of benefits and burdens of co-operation in terms of underlying differences in the circumstances of the various parties. For example, in her study of collectively-managed irrigation systems in Nepal, Ostrom (1996) has provided an explanation of observed differences in benefits and burdens among users (e.g. who gets how much water from the canal system and who is responsible for which maintenance task) in terms of such facts as that some farmers are head-enders, while others are tail-enders.

Wade (1988) has also conducted an empirical investigation of community-based allocation rules over water and the use of grazing land. Forty-one South Indian villages were studied, and it was found, for example, that downstream villages had an elaborate set of rules, enforced by fines, for regulating the use of water from irrigation canals. Most villages had similar arrangements for the use of grazing land. In

---

[21] Over the past several millenia, a wide variety of contextual solutions have been proposed for the problem of dividing an 'object' among claimants. See Young (1994) for an account.
[22] For a review of these concepts, see Aumann (1987).

an earlier work on the Kuna tribe in the Panama, Howe (1986) described the intricate set of social sanctions that are imposed upon those who violate norms of behaviour designed to protect their source of fresh water. Even the iniquitous caste system of India has been found to provide an institutional means of checks and balances by which communal environmental resources have been protected (Gadgil and Malhotra, 1983).

This said, it is important to caution against romanticising communitarian arrangements over the use of the local commons. Beteille (1983), for example, contains examples of how access is often restricted to the privileged (e.g. caste Hindus). Rampant inequities exist in rural community practices. I am laying stress upon the fact that the local commons are often not unmanaged; I am not claiming that they are invariably managed efficiently, nor that they are inevitably managed in ways that involve an equitable distribution of benefits and burdens. Good management of the commons requires more than mere local participation; it requires enlightened government engagement as well.

The extent of common-property resources as a proportion of total assets in a community varies considerably across ecological zones. In India they appear to be most prominent in arid regions, mountain regions, and unirrigated areas. They are least prominent in humid regions and river valleys (Agarwal and Narain, 1989; Chopra, Kadekodi and Murty, 1990). There is, of course, an economic rationale for this, based on the common human desire to pool risks. An almost immediate empirical corollary is that income inequalities are less where common-property resources are more prominent. However, aggregate income is a different matter, and it is the arid and mountain regions and unirrigated areas that are the poorest. This needs to be borne in mind when policy is devised. As may be expected, even within dry regions, dependence on common-property resources declines with increasing wealth across households. The links between undernourishment, destitution, and an erosion of the rural common-property resource base are close. They have been explored analytically in Dasgupta (1993, 1996).

In an important and interesting article, Jodha (1986) used data from over eighty villages in twenty-one dry districts from six dry tropical states in India to estimate that, among poor families, the proportion of income based directly on the local commons is for the most part in the range 15–25 per cent (see also Jodha, 1995). This is a substantial proportion. Moreover, as sources of income, they are often complementary to private-property resources, which are in the main labour, milch and draft animals, cultivation land and crops, agricultural tools (e.g. ploughs, harrows, levellers, and hoes), fodder-cutting and rope-making machines, and seeds. Common-property resources also provide the rural poor with partial protection in times of unusual economic stress. For landless people they may be the only non-human asset at their disposal. A number of resources (such as fuelwood and water for home use, berries and nuts, medicinal herbs, resin and gum) are the responsibility of women and children.[23]

A similar picture emerges from Hecht, Anderson and May (1988), who describe in rich detail the importance of the extraction of babassu products among the landless in the Brazilian state of Maranhão. The support such extraction activity offers the poorest of the poor, most especially the women among them, is striking. These extractive products are an important source of cash income in the period between agricultural-crop harvests (see also Murphy and Murphy, 1985; and for a similar picture in the West African forest zone, see Falconer, 1990).

7. Why do Communitarian Solutions Break Down?

It isn't difficult to see why the local commons matter greatly to the poorest of the rural poor, or to understand the mechanisms by which such people may well get disenfranchised from the economy even while in the aggregate the society of which they are members enjoys economic growth. If you are steeped in social norms of behaviour and understand community obligations, you don't calculate every five minutes how you should behave. You follow the norms. This saves on costs all round, not only for you as an 'actor', but also for you as 'policeman' and 'judge'.[24] It is also the natural thing for you to do if you have internalised the norms. But this is sustainable so long as the background environment remains, approximately, constant. It will not be sustainable if the social environment changes suddenly and trust is broken.

[23] The most complete account I have read of the centrality of local forest products in the lives of the rural poor is Falconer and Arnold (1989) and Falconer (1990) on Central and West Africa. The importance of common-property resources for women's well-being in historical times has been stressed by Humphries (1990) in her work on eighteenth-century rural England. The parallels with modern-day poor societies are remarkable.

[24] Provided people are sufficiently far-sighted, norms of behaviour that sustain co-operation can be shown to be self-enforcing in stationary environments. See section 13 for further discussion.

You may even be destroyed. It is this heightened vulnerability, often more real than perceived, which is the cause of some of the greatest tragedies in contemporary society. They descend upon people who are, in the best of circumstances, acutely vulnerable.[25]

Sources that trigger destitution by this means vary. Erosion of the local commons can come about in the wake of shifting populations (accompanying the growth process itself), rising populations and the consequent pressure on these resources, technological progress, unreflective public policies, predatory governments, and thieving aristocracies. There is now an accumulation of evidence on this range of causes, and in what follows I will present an outline of the findings in three sets of studies, covering three continents.

1 In his work on the drylands of India, Jodha (1986) noted a decline in the geographical area covering common-property resources ranging from twenty-six to sixty-three per cent over a twenty-year period. This was in part due to the privatisation of land, a good deal of which in his sample had been awarded to the rural non-poor. He also noted a decline in the productivity of common-property resources on account of population growth among the community. In an earlier work, Jodha (1980) identified an increase in subsistence requirements of the farming community and a rise in the profitability of land from cropping and grazing as a central reason for increased desertification in the state of Rajasthan. Jodha argued that, ironically, it was government land reform programmes in this area, unaccompanied by investment in improving the productive base, that had triggered the process.

2 Ensminger's (1990) study of the privatisation of common grazing lands among the Orma in north-eastern Kenya indicates that the transformation took place with the consent of the elders of the tribe. She attributes this willingness to changing transaction costs brought about by cheaper transportation and widening markets. The elders were, quite naturally, from the stronger families, and it does not go unnoted by Ensminger that privatisation has accentuated inequalities.

3 In an earlier, much-neglected work on the Amazon basin, Feder (1977, 1979) described how massive private investment in the expansion of beef-cattle production in fragile ecological conditions has been supported by domestic governments in the form of tax concessions and provision of infrastructure, and loans from international agencies, such

---

[25] In Dasgupta (1988) I have tried to develop some of the micro-economics of 'trust'. But we still have little understanding of the social pathways through which trust is created.

as the World Bank. The degradation of vast tracts of valuable environmental resources was accompanied by the disenfranchisement of large
numbers of small farmers and agricultural labourers from the economy.
At best it made destitutes of traditional forest-dwellers; at worst it
simply eliminated them (see also Barraclough, 1977; Hecht, 1985).
The evidence suggests that during the decades of the 1960s and
1970s protein intake by the rural poor declined even while the production of beef increased dramatically. Much of the beef was destined for
exports, for use by fast-food chains.

The sources that were identified in these studies as having transformed common-property resources into private resources differed considerably. Therefore, the pathways by which the transformation affected
those with historical rights were different. But each narrative is believ-
able. Since the impact of these forms of privatisation on the poorest of
the poor is confirmed by economic theory (Weitzman, 1974b; Dasgupta and Heal, 1979), the findings of these case-studies are almost
certainly not unrepresentative. They suggest that privatisation of village
commons and forest lands, while hallowed at the altar of economic
efficiency, can have disastrous distributional consequences, disenfran-
chising entire classes of people from economic citizenship. The point is
a simple one: unless an appropriate fraction of the rents that are earned
from the resource base subsequent to privatisation are given to the
historical users, they become worse off.[26] Ironically, case-studies also
show that public ownership of such resources as forest lands is by no
means necessarily a good basis for a resource allocation mechanism.
Decision-makers are in these cases usually far removed from site (living
as they do in imperial capitals), they have little knowledge of the
ecology of such matters, their time-horizons are often short, and they
are in many instances overly influenced by interest-groups far removed
from the resource in question.

All this is not at all to suggest that rural development is to be
avoided. It is to say that resource allocation mechanisms that do not
take advantage of dispersed information, that are insensitive to hidden
(and often not-so-hidden) economic and ecological interactions, that do
not take the long-term view, and that do not give sufficient weight to the
claims of the poorest within rural populations (particularly the women
and children in these populations) are going to prove environmentally

---

[26] Weitzman (1974b) proves this for the case where an open-access resource is privatised.
Dasgupta and Heal (1979, chap. 3) prove it for the local commons.

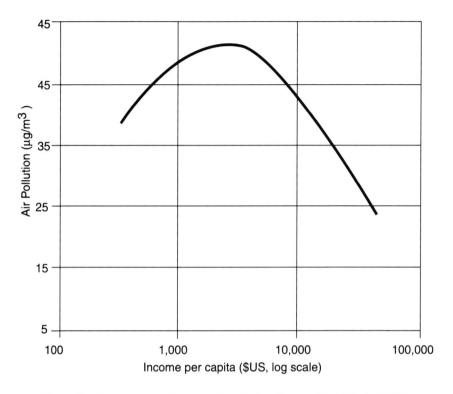

Figure 2. Income per capita versus air pollution. Source: World Bank (1992).

disastrous. It appears that, during the process of economic development there is a close link between environmental protection and the well-being of the poor, most especially the most vulnerable among the poor. Elaboration of this link has been one of the most compelling achievements at the interface of anthropology, economics, and nutrition science.

8. Economic Growth and the Environment[27]

Since economists have neglected the environment, it shouldn't come as a surprise that national economic policies have also neglected it. Interestingly, the idea that economic growth is perhaps even good for the environment has recently been given credence by the finding that, for a

---

[27] This section is taken from Arrow *et al.* (1995*b*), which was republished, with comments by a number of experts, in *Environment and Development Economics* (1996), vol. 1.

number of pollutants, there appears to be an empirical relationship between income per head and environmental quality: as income per head increases, environmental quality deteriorates up to a point, beyond which environmental quality improves (World Bank, 1992). In short, the relationship has a bell shape. Figure 2 provides an example.

It should be emphasised that Figure 2 is based on cross-section data, not time series. Nevertheless, this is how one is tempted to explain the finding; indeed, economists have been known to so explain it: People in poor countries can't afford placing weight on amenities over material well-being. Therefore, in the early stages of economic development, increases in pollution are regarded as an acceptable side-effect of economic growth. However, when a country has attained a sufficiently high standard of living, people care more about amenities. This leads them to pass environmental legislation, create new institutions for the protection of the environment, and so forth.

The argument has been invoked in the main for amenities. Even within this set, the bell-shaped curve has been uncovered for a few pollutants only. But as it is consistent with the notion that, as their incomes rise, people spend proportionately more on environmental quality, economists have conjectured that the curve applies to environmental quality, more generally.[28] It is as well to be clear, though, about the kinds of conclusion one can draw from these empirical findings. While the findings do indicate that economic growth can be associated with improvements in some environmental indicators, they imply neither that economic growth is sufficient to induce environmental improvement in general, nor that the environmental effects of growth may safely be ignored; nor, indeed, that the earth's resource base is capable of supporting indefinite economic growth. On the contrary, if the resource base were irreversibly degraded, economic growth itself could be at risk.

There are other reasons for caution in interpreting such bell-shaped curves. First, the relationship has been shown to be valid for pollutants involving local short-term costs (e.g. sulphur, particulates, fecal

---

[28] Whether the proportion of expenditure devoted to environmental amenities increases with rising income is an empirical matter, and little is known. The one study I have seen on this question, namely Kriström and Riera (1996), suggests otherwise: the proportion of expenditure devoted to amenities *decreases* with rising income! The authors correctly observe that the bell-shaped curve in Figure 2 is a 'reduced form', combining as it does technology, preferences, and other such primitives. From such curves we ought not to infer anything more than that the income elasticity of environmental improvements is positive.

coliforms), not for the accumulation of stocks of waste, nor for pollutants involving long-term and more dispersed costs, such as carbon dioxide, which typically increase with income (World Bank, 1992).

Secondly, the bell-shaped curves have been uncovered for emissions of pollutants, not generally for resource stocks. The relationship is less likely to hold wherever the feedback effects of resource stocks are significant, such as that which occurs in the case of mangroves.

Thirdly, the bell-shaped curves, as they have been estimated, say nothing about the system-wide consequences of reductions in emission. (For example, reductions in one pollutant in one country may involve increase in other pollutants in the same country or transfers of pollutants to other countries.) And fourthly, in most cases where emissions have declined with rising income, the reductions have been due to local institutional reforms, such as environmental legislation and market-based incentives to reduce environmental impacts. But such reforms often ignore international and inter-generational consequences. Where the environmental costs of economic activity are borne by the poor, by future generations, or by other countries, the incentives to correct the problem are likely to be weak. The environmental consequences of rising economic activity may, accordingly, be very mixed. Figure 2 is something of a mirage.

The solution to environmental degradation lies in such institutional reforms as would compel private users of resources to take account of the social costs of their actions. The bell-shaped relation is a suggestion that this can happen in some cases. It doesn't constitute evidence that it will happen in all cases, nor that it will happen in time to avert the irreversible consequences of growth. I will discuss these matters further in section 11, where we will see that growth in gross national product is a wrong objective. I will then ask what sort of economic growth we ought to be seeking, if indeed it is economic growth of some kind we ought to seek. In short, we will try to identify an operationally useful index of social well-being.

9. Trade and the Environment

Thus far national economic policy. But even in areas where the environment is beginning to impinge on international economic policy, as in GATT and NAFTA,[29] it has remained a tangential concern, and the presumption has often been that the liberalisation of international trade is, in some sense, good for the environment. Thus, policy reforms designed to promote trade liberalisation have been encouraged with little regard to their environmental consequences; presumably, on grounds that these consequences would either take care of themselves or could be dealt with separately.[30]

As a reaction to this, I would imagine, it has not been uncommon to view international trade liberalisation as a harbinger of a deteriorating environment (e.g. Daly, 1994). When stated so baldly, the view is false: it doesn't recognise the heterogeneity of environmental problems (as an extreme thought-experiment, imagine the extent to which forests, land, and water resources would be degraded if countries were to become autarkic); it doesn't distinguish between the volume and consumption effects of a growth in trade on the world's production of goods and services; it doesn't say if the growth is allied to international agreements on transfrontier pollution and a reduction in domestic market failure; and it is silent on whether the growth is brought about by a removal of government-induced distortions. To be sure, increased world trade is often associated with a relocation of production units in accordance with relative international labour, capital, and resource costs. One would expect free trade to shift polluting industries to poor countries (Copeland and Taylor, 1994), but insofar as the resultant pollution is local, this is a matter of national sovereignty. The argument that lobbies would succeed in lowering environmental standards in countries that have high standards, in order to meet competition from countries with low standards, is not dissimilar to the concern people have that trade with low-wage countries would eventually lower wages in high-wage countries. However, it is possible to design tax-subsidy schemes to offset the additional cost of higher standards, while retaining some of

---

[29] The General Agreement on Tariffs and Trade, and the North American Free Trade Agreement, respectively.

[30] Unless it is accompanied by judicious environmental policy, expansion of international trade should be expected to result in an increased stress on the global commons. Copeland and Taylor (1995) provide a formal analysis of the pathway through which this occurs.

the gains from trade.[31] Above all, the argument for trade protection arising from the thought that countries with lower environmental standards will become sinks for other countries' pollutants is to be resisted because of the kinds of considerations that were outlined earlier in this lecture.

A variant of these economic considerations formed the intellectual background of an argument in a widely-publicised memorandum issued in 1991 by the Chief Economist of the World Bank to his staff for discussion. It suggested that trade in pollutants should be encouraged between rich and poor nations because of at least two reasons: (i) poor countries (e.g. sub-Saharan Africa) suffer from lower industrial pollution than those in the West; and (ii) being poor, they could be expected to value environmental quality less at the margin.

The memorandum was much criticised in the international press, mostly along the lines that it read altogether too much like saying, 'let the poor eat pollution'. The arguments I have offered in this lecture imply that this is misplaced criticism. On the other hand, there are two reasons why we should be wary of the suggestion. First, it is based implicitly on the thought that there are no significant threshold effects associated with environmental pollution. If thresholds were important, it would not make sense to spread pollution evenly across geographical locations. Within municipalities, for example, household and industrial waste are typically deposited in rubbish dumps. This is a social response to the presence of environmental thresholds. We may now enlarge on this observation: assuming that it is true that poor countries currently enjoy a better environment as regards industrial waste, it could well be that global well-being would be enhanced if their environment were protected and promoted, and if selected sites in rich countries were used as global centres of deposits for industrial effluents.

The second reason one should be circumspect about the suggestion is that it doesn't note that the poor in poor countries are not the same as poor countries. There are both rich and poor people in poor countries. Typically, the rich in these countries don't absorb anything like the environmental risks the poor are forced to accept (e.g. health risks at work). In addition, the rich enjoy political advantages. Furthermore, there is nothing resembling a free press, nor open debate, in a majority of poor countries. It is then all too possible to imagine that if trade in industrial pollutants were to be encouraged, the poor in poor countries

---

[31] Low (1992) contains discussions of these matters.

would be made to absorb the health risks (industrial pollutants are usually spatially localised), and the rich in poor countries would grasp the income accruing from the trade (a private benefit). This should make for a difference in our attitude towards the proposal. As elsewhere in economics, the issue of governance lies somewhere at the heart of the matter.

10. Valuing Environmental Resources

As noted earlier, much ecological economics begins with the observation that prices in a decentralised economic environment often do not reflect social scarcities of goods and services. If they did, the criterion of private profitability would suffice, and there would be no need to pay special attention to the environmental resource-base. As they don't, a project's private profitability can't be regarded as an adequate indicator of its social worthiness.

So then, what criterion should we use for selecting among public policies? One idea, much pursued in recent years, is to estimate accounting prices and choose policies on the basis of their accounting profits.

How we should estimate accounting prices is a complex matter, but it isn't uniformly complex. There are now standard techniques for commodities like irrigation water, fisheries, timber, and agricultural soil.[32] The same techniques can be used for estimating losses associated with water-logging and overgrazing.

For commodities such as firewood and drinking and cooking water, the matter is more complex: they are inputs in household production. This means that we need estimates of the way households convert inputs into outputs; that is, we need to estimate household production functions. As an example, transportation costs (in particular energy costs, as measured in calories) for women and children would be less if the sources of fuelwood and water were not far away and receding. As a (very) first approximation, the value of water or fuelwood for household production can be estimated from these energy needs. In some

---

[32] See, for example, Brown and McGuire (1967) for irrigation water; Cooper (1977) for fisheries; Magrath and Arens (1989) and Repetto et al. (1989) for soil fertility; Anderson (1987) and Newcombe (1987) for forestry; and Solorzano et al. (1991) for the latter three. Dixon and Hufschmidt (1986) and Dixon et al. (1988) are excellent sets of case-studies on these matters.

situations (as on occasion with fuelwood), the resource is a substitute for a tradable input (e.g. paraffin or kerosene); in others (as with cooking water) it is a complement to tradable inputs (for example, food grain). Such facts enable one to estimate accounting prices of non-marketed goods in terms of the accounting prices of marketed goods (Mäler, 1974).[33]

The approach outlined above allows us to capture only the direct use-value of a resource. As it happens, its accounting price may well exceed this. Why? The reason is that there may be additional values 'embodied' in a resource. One additional value, mentioned in section 1, is applicable to living resources: it is their intrinsic worth as living resources. It is absurd to suppose that the value of a blue whale is embodied entirely in its flesh and oil, or that the value of the game in Kenyan safari parks is simply the present-discounted value of tourists' willingness-to-pay. The idea of 'intrinsic worth' of living things is inherent not only within traditional religious systems of ethics, but also in modern utilitarianism. The question is not so much whether living things possess intrinsic worth, but rather, about ways of assessing this worth. As it is almost impossible to get a quantitative handle on intrinsic worth, the correct thing to do is to take note of it, keep an eye on it, and call attention to it in public debate if the resource is threatened with extinction.

What is the point of basing accounting prices solely on use-value when we know that resources often possess intrinsic value as well? The answer is that it provides us with biased estimates of accounting prices, and this can be useful information. For example, in a beautiful paper on the optimal rate of harvest of blue whales, Spence (1974) took the accounting price of these creatures to be the market value of their flesh, a seemingly absurd and repugnant move. But he showed that under a wide range of plausible parametric conditions, it would be most profitable commercially for the international whaling industry to agree to a moratorium until the desired long-run population size were reached,

---

[33] A second approach to the estimation of accounting prices of environmental resources is based on contingent valuation methods (CVMs). They involve asking concerned individuals to reveal their valuation of hypothetical changes in the flow of environmental services. CVMs are useful in the case of amenities, and their applications have so far been confined to advanced industrial countries. As I am not focusing on amenities in this lecture, there is no point in developing the idea underlying CVMs any further here. The most complete account to date on CVMs is Mitchell and Carson (1989). See also the report on the NOAA Panel on Contingent Valuation (co-chaired by K. J. Arrow and R. M. Solow) in the *Federal Register*, 58 (10), 15 January 1993.

and for the industry to subsequently harvest the creatures at a rate equal to the population's (optimal) sustainable yield.[34] In other words, in Spence's analysis, preservation was recommended solely on commercial grounds. But if preservation is justified when the accounting price of blue whales is estimated from their market price, the recommendation would, obviously, be reinforced if their intrinsic worth were to be added. This was the point of Spence's exercise.

Environmental resources often possess another kind of value, one which is more amenable to quantification. It arises from a combination of two things: uncertainty in their future use-values, and irreversibility in their use. Genetic material in tropical forests provides a prime example. The twin presence of uncertainty and irreversibility implies that preservation of its stock has an additional value — the value of extending society's set of future options. Future options have an additional worth because, with the passage of time, more information is expected to be forthcoming about the resource's use-value. This additional worth is often called an option value. The accounting price of a resource is, at the very least, the sum of its use-value and its option value.[35]

11. Net National Product as an Index of Social Well-Being

Ideally, institutions should be in place that make it possible for market prices and accounting prices to coincide. In practice, they don't coincide. Private agencies choose their actions on the basis of market prices, not accounting prices; but it is public agencies with which I am concerned here.

The argument that the right criterion for choosing among alternative policies is their accounting profitability is closely related to the suggestion that in measuring changes in social well-being, we should estimate changes in net national product (NNP); that is, gross national product (GNP) corrected for the value of changes in the country's entire capital base, including its environmental resource-base. This suggestion is based on a well-known theorem in modern economics. The theorem states that, provided certain technical restrictions are met (on which, see

---

[34] During the moratorium the whale population grows at the fastest possible rate. In his numerical computations, the commercially most-profitable duration of the moratorium was found to be some ten to fifteen years.

[35] The pioneering works on option values are Arrow and Fisher (1974) and Henry (1974).

below in the text), for any conception of social well-being, and for any set of technological, transaction, and ecological constraints, there exists a set of accounting prices of goods and services that can be used in constructing a linear index of social well-being. The sense in which it can serve as an index of social well-being is this: small policy changes, including small investment projects, that are recorded as an improvement (deterioration) by the index are at once those that result in an increase (decrease) in social well-being.[36] This index is popularly known as 'green NNP'.

I cannot enter into details here, but (green) NNP, in a closed economy, reads as:

> NNP = Consumption + value of net investment in physical capital + value of the net change in human capital + value of the net change in the stock of natural capital − value of current environmental damages.[37]

Current estimates of NNP are biased because depreciation of environmental resources is not deducted from GNP. To put it another way, estimates of NNP are biased because a biased set of prices is in use: prices imputed to environmental resources on site are usually zero, and this amounts to regarding the depreciation of environmental capital as

---

[36] Dasgupta and Heal (1979), Dasgupta and Mäler (1991, 1995), Mäler (1991), and Dasgupta, Kriström and Mäler (1996) prove this in models of increasing generality. Lutz (1993) contains a collection of articles that explore the practicality of moving to a system of national accounts that includes the environmental resource-base.

[37] All values are assumed to be measured in terms of consumption. This involves no loss of generality, since all remaining objects that help realise social well-being (including distributional considerations) can in turn be valued in terms of consumption (Dasgupta, 1993). Note also that, in an open economy, the value of net exports ought to be deducted from the expression for NNP in the text (Sefton and Weale, 1996). Furthermore, the expression is correct only if labour is supplied inelastically (in this case it is a matter of indifference whether or not we include the wage bill). However, if the supply of labour is responsive to wages, the wage bill should be deducted from the expression (Nordhaus and Tobin, 1972).

By the value of net 'investment' in the expression in the text, I mean the value of net changes in capital assets, not changes in the value of these assets. This means that anticipated capital gains (or losses) should not be included in NNP. As an example, the value of the net decrease in the stock of oil and natural gas (net of new discoveries, that is) ought to be deducted from GNP when NNP is estimated.

Finally, it has been argued by Putnam (1993) that, in addition to manufactured, environmental, and human capital, 'social' capital (involving, among other things, trust and interpersonal networks) matters in the production of goods and services. Assuming that a suitable index of social capital were in hand, the expression for NNP in the text would include net investment in social capital. The answer to the question how we should estimate NNP should not be a matter of opinion today; it is a matter of fact. The problem is not that we do not know what items NNP should ideally contain, rather it is that we don't have adequate estimates of various accounting prices.

zero. But this in turn means that profits attributed to projects that degrade the environment are higher than their social profits. A consequence is that wrong sets of projects get selected, in both the private and public sectors.

The extent of the bias will obviously vary from project to project, and from country to country. But it can be substantial. In their work on the depreciation of natural resources in Costa Rica, Solorzano *et al.* (1991) have estimated that, in 1989, the depreciation of three resources — forests, soil, and fisheries — amounted to about ten per cent of gross domestic product and over one third of gross capital accumulation. Since, under current practice, environmental resources are often unpriced, resource-intensive projects look better than they actually are. In consequence, installed technologies are often unfriendly towards the environment.

One can go further: the bias extends to the prior stage of research and development. When environmental resources are underpriced, there is little incentive on anyone's part to develop technologies that economise on their use. The extent of the distortion created by this underpricing will vary from country to country. Poor countries inevitably have to rely on the flow of new knowledge produced in advanced industrial economies. Nevertheless, poor countries need to have the capability for basic research. The structure of accounting prices there is likely to be different from those in advanced industrial countries, most especially for non-traded goods and services. Even when it is publicly available, basic knowledge is not necessarily usable by scientists and technologists, unless they themselves have a feel for basic research. Often enough, ideas developed in foreign lands are merely transplanted to the local economy; whereas, they ought instead to be modified to suit local ecological conditions before being adopted. This is where the use of accounting prices is of help. It creates the right set of incentives, among both developers and users of technologies. Adaptation is itself a creative exercise. Unhappily, as matters stand, it is often bypassed. There is loss in this.

There is further loss associated with a different kind of bias, something we noted earlier: that arising from biased demand. For example, wherever household demands for goods and services in the market reflect in the main male (or for that matter, female) concerns, the direction of technological change would be expected to follow suit. Among poor countries, we would expect technological inventions in farm equipment and techniques of production to be forthcoming in regions where cultivation is a male activity (there would be a demand for them); we would not observe much in the way of process innovations in threshing, winnowing, the grinding of grain in the home, and in the preparation of food. Entrepreneurs have little incentive to bring about such technological innovations. Household demand for them would be expected to be low.

Such biases in NNP as I have identified here occur in advanced industrial countries as well. So then why do I stress their importance in the context of poor countries? The reason is that poor people in poor countries cannot cope with the same margin of error as people living in rich countries can: a 10 per cent drop in the standard of living imposes greater hardship on a poor household than a rich one. Recall too that the rural poor are especially dependent upon their local environmental resource-base. Losses in well-being due to an underpricing of this base are absorbed by them disproportionately. The estimation of accounting prices of environmental resources should now be high on the agenda of research in the economics of poor countries.

There is an important qualification to all this. The principles underlying the construction of (green) NNP assume, among other things, that ecological processes do not display threshold effects.[38] If threshold effects were important, a purely decentralised economic environment wouldn't do: accounting prices would need to be augmented by quantity controls on the use of a number of environmental resources. This would be a way of ensuring that the magnitude of economic activity does not reach a level that places undue stress on key ecosystems.

I conclude that economic liberalisation and other policies that promote growth in gross national product are not substitutes for environmental policy. On the contrary, it may well be desirable that they be accompanied by stricter policy reforms. Of particular importance is the need for reforms that would lead to an improvement in the quality of the signals on the basis of which resource users reach decisions. They include an array of prices, allied to more direct types of information concerning resource stocks. Environmental damage, including the loss of resilience of ecosystems, often occurs abruptly and is often not reversible. But abrupt changes can seldom be anticipated from signals

---

[38] The existence of thresholds means that an ecosystem can flip to a quite different state in a short space of time when subjected to stress. Formally, and more generally, an exclusive reliance on accounting prices is justified only if production technologies are convex. Threshold effects are a prime example of non-convexities. Key articles on this matter are Baumol and Bradford (1972) and Starrett (1972).

that are characteristically received by decision-makers in the world. Furthermore, the signals that are generated are often not observed, or are wrongly interpreted, or are not part of the incentive structure of societies. This is due to ignorance about the dynamic effects of changes in the variables that characterise ecosystems (e.g. thresholds, buffering capacity, and loss of resilience). It is also due to the presence of institutional impediments, such as a lack of well-defined property rights. The development of appropriate institutions depends, among other things, on understanding ecosystem-dynamics. Above all, given that we are vastly ignorant about the extent to which ecosystems are resilient, we should act in a precautionary way so as to maintain their diversity.

Economic growth is not a panacea for environmental quality; indeed, it is not even the main issue. What matters is not economic growth *per se*, but the content (i.e. the composition of inputs and outputs) of growth. The content is determined by, among other things, the economic institutions within which human activities are conducted. Such measures will not only promote greater efficiency in the allocation of environmental resources at all income levels, but would also assure a sustainable scale of economic activity within the ecological life-support system. Protecting the capacity of ecosystems to sustain human well-being is of as much importance to poor countries as it is to those that are rich.

12. International Governance and the Global Commons

Unlike the local commons, open access to the global commons is more the rule than the exception. This makes Hardin's parable apt. Moreover, the option of 'voting with one's feet' as a way of avoiding global environmental problems is unavailable. This gives added bite to the political economy of global common-property resources.[39]

Space forbids that I go into global issues in any detail here. So I will sketch a few mechanisms that have been suggested for dealing with them. It will prove convenient to do this in the context of two global commons: the atmosphere as a sink for gaseous emissions and international fisheries. I will take them up sequentially.

---

[39] See Barrett (1990), Mäler (1990) and Hoel (1992) for a more detailed discussion of these issues.

Global warming and ozone depletion

Emission of carbon dioxide (CO_2) at rates in excess of the capacity of the oceans and forests to 'absorb' it is a cause of global warming. This has been known for about a century. So too are chlorofluorocarbons (CFCs), a 'greenhouse' gas, (and there are others still). However, a little over two decades ago, the CFCs were found to have a more immediate and dramatic effect: they deplete the ozone shield that protects us from excessive ultra-violet radiation from the sun. For this reason, today the CFCs are discussed almost exclusively in the context of their effect on the ozone layer.

Even though the externalities that nations inflict upon one another when emitting, say, CO_2 are reciprocal, they are not symmetric: the costs and benefits of reducing emission rates differ greatly across nations. This means that, if agreements on major reductions are to be reached, financial transfers would be necessary (Carraro and Siniscalco, 1993; Heal, 1994). Several alternatives have been suggested, debt relief for developing countries being one. This isn't to say that agreements can't be reached in the absence of side-payments; it is only to say that they would tend to be less efficient (Carraro and Siniscalco, 1993). Barrett (1990) has argued, for example, that, while one would have expected a number of countries to sign the Montreal Protocol on CFCs, one shouldn't expect all countries to sign it. The reason is that if only a few countries were to sign the Protocol, national benefits from further reduction in CFC emission would be high. This would induce more countries to sign. However, if many countries were to sign the Protocol, national benefits from further reduction would be small, and it wouldn't then be worth a country's while to sign.

Nevertheless, international negotiations over the protection of the ozone layer have been remarkably successful. Nearly all countries have co-operated in creating a regime in which the emission of CFCs will soon be reduced to nil. In contrast, little has been achieved in the case of CO_2 emission. Why?

Barrett (1996) has pointed to a number of salient differences between the two cases. Ozone depletion increases the risk of skin cancer, and so kills people; in contrast, the economic consequences of an increase in the atmosphere's average temperature, though most likely to be very large, will be diffuse across the globe in unpredictable ways. The aggregate cost of reducing the consumption of fossil fuels in any significant amount would be gigantic; in contrast, the costs of moving away from CFCs to their substitutes are small. And so forth. Whatever the reasons, the public perception is that the ratio of benefits to costs of a ban on CFCs is large, whereas, for significant reductions in the use of fossil fuels, it is small. This interpretation of the public's perception must be right; otherwise, it is hard to see why the Montreal Protocol (in which the signatories agreed to ban the use of CFCs and to ban trade with non-signatories in goods involving CFCs) has been so effective, whereas the Framework Convention on Climate Change (which merely urges countries to stabilise their CO_2 emissions at 1990 levels by the year 2000, but does not require them to do so) resembles a toothless kitten. Unless an agreement is so designed that the parties have an incentive to comply, it amounts to little.[40]

What mechanisms, other than quantity restrictions and Pigovian taxes, are there for implementing international agreements, if agreement can be reached?[41] One broad category, well worth exploring, involves making the global commons quasi-private. The basic idea, which originated in Dales (1968), is similar to the principle currently being experimented with in the USA. The idea, if extended to the international sphere, would have the community of nations set an upper bound on the total use of a global commons, such as the atmosphere; have it allocate transferable national rights (which add up to the global upper bound); and allow the final allocation among different users to be determined by a market in these rights.

To give an example, consider the emission of CO_2. Suppose it is desired by the community of nations that the global emission rate should be reduced to some prescribed level. Countries would receive an assignment of permits which add up to the global bound and would be allowed to buy and sell permits. It transpires that under a wide range of circumstances, this scheme has informational advantages over both taxes and quantity controls. Furthermore, if the permits were to refer to *net* emissions (i.e. net of absorption of CO_2 by green plants), the scheme would provide an incentive for countries with fast-growing tropical rain forests to earn export revenue, by encouraging forest growth and then selling permits to other countries. The scheme also has the advantage that the necessary side-payments required to induce all (or most) coun-

---

[40] French (1994) argues that such incentives are lacking in most of the 170 or so environmental treaties that have been drafted in recent years.

[41] Admittedly, the one is not independent of the other; but for expositional ease, I will suppose they are.

tries to participate in the agreement could be made through the initial distribution of emission permits. Countries that do not expect severe damage from global warming would also wish to participate, if only they were to be provided initially with a sufficient number of permits.

The sticking point would clearly be in reaching an agreement on the initial distribution of permits among nations.[42] However, if the bound established on annual aggregate emission were approximately optimal, it would be possible, in principle, to distribute the initial set of permits in such a way that all countries have an incentive to join the scheme (Mäler and Uzawa, 1995). Having said this, it is important to note that in practice it is difficult to devise a rule for the distribution of initial rights that would satisfy all countries (recall the bargaining problem in Figure 1). So progress in this sphere of international co-operation can be expected to be slow. Nevertheless, one cannot over-emphasise the fact that there are large potential gains to be enjoyed from international cooperation. A scheme involving the issue of marketable permits in principle offers a pathway by which all nations can enjoy such gains. The argument that national sovereignty would be endangered is no argument: the point about the global commons is precisely that they are beyond the realm of national sovereignty.

International fisheries

If biodiversity and the emission of greenhouse gases dominate the literature on the global commons today, it isn't because international fisheries pose no problems; rather, it is because global food production hasn't been on the agenda of international concerns in recent years. But disputes in the Atlantic and the Pacific reflect unresolved conflicts of interest among contending parties. At the widest international level, the United Nations Law of the Sea Conferences were initiated several decades ago because of a clear recognition that the open seas pose a serious resource allocation problem.

The maximum potential harvest of ocean fisheries is estimated to be in the range 60 to 90 million metric tons.[43] There is evidence that,

---

[42] How a national government would allocate the nation's rights among agencies within the country is a different matter.

[43] Maximal potential harvest is not the same as maximum sustainable yield. This is because a good fraction of a fishery's production has to be left unharvested on ecological grounds. World Resources Institute (1994) and Safina (1995) offer succinct accounts of the problem of marine fisheries.

globally, stocks have declined in recent years through overfishing: worldwide, the extraction rate of wild fish reached a peak of 82 million metric tons in 1989. It is not only increases in world population and incomes that have caused this; fishing technology has become awesome, having both lowered the unit cost of large-scale fishing considerably and increased the rate of what is euphemistically called 'bycatch'.[44] Allied to this is the enormous subsidy a number of the most prominent national fishing industries receive from their governments. Recently, the cost of catching $US 70 billion worth of fish amounted to $US 124 billion. The deficit was largely covered by subsidies (Safina, 1995).

Cooper (1977) estimated that the annual revenue that could be generated from international marine fisheries by a Pigovian tax on harvests is of the order of $US 2.5 billion. He suggested that the tax could be administered by the United Nations, possibly as a contribution to its Development Fund. This is another illustration of the possibility of a 'double dividend', mentioned in section 3. But we are nowhere near such a form of international co-operation.

13. Collective Agreements and the Structure of Authority

A striking difference between local and global environmental problems is this: unlike agreements on the use of, say, local commons, there is no obvious central authority that can enforce agreements among nations over the use of transnational commons. To be sure, there are international authorities that have the mandate to act as overseers. But they don't, at least in principle, possess the coercive powers that national governments ideally enjoy. This has implications for the extent to which international authorities are able to enforce agreements.

Insights into the range of options open in the international sphere can be obtained by asking a prior question: How are agreements implemented in the case of local environmental problems? Notice that, while related, this is different from asking what agreement would be expected to be reached if the parties were to bargain. In section 6 we noted that the theory of games offers little guidance on the latter question. But it has things to say about the former.

---

[44] Bycatch refers to inadvertent harvest. Roughly, one of every four animals harvested from the open seas is unwanted.

Broadly speaking, there would appear to be three mechanisms by which an agreement can be implemented. (Of course, none may work in a particular context, in which case people will find themselves in a hole they can't easily get out of, and what could have been mutually beneficial agreements won't take place.)

In the first mechanism the agreement is translated into a contract, and is enforced by an established structure of power and authority. As noted in section 6, this may be the national government, but it need not be. In rural communities, for example, the structure of power and authority are in some cases vested in tribal elders (as within nomadic tribes in sub-Saharan Africa), in others in dominant landowners (such as the zamindars of eastern India), feudal lords (as in the state of Rajasthan in India), chieftains, and priests. On occasions there are even attempts at making rural communities mini-republics. Village panchayats in India try to assume such a form. The idea there is to elect offices, the officials being entrusted with the power to settle disputes, enforce contracts (whether explicit or only tacit), communicate with higher levels of State authority, and so forth. Wade's account (1988) of the collective management of common-property resources in South India describes such a mechanism of enforcement in detail.[45]

The question why such a structure of authority as may exist is accepted by people is a higher-order one, akin to the question why people accept the authority of government. The answer is that general acceptance itself is a self-enforcing behaviour: when all others accept the structure of authority, each has an incentive to accept it (or, in short, general acceptance is a Nash equilibrium). Contrariwise, when a sufficiently large number don't accept it, individual incentives to accept it weaken, and the system unravels rapidly. General acceptance of the structure of authority is held together by its own bootstraps, so to speak.

The second mechanism consists in the development of a disposition to abide by agreements, a disposition that is formed through the process of communal living, role modelling, education, and the experiencing of rewards and punishments. This process begins at the earliest stages of our lives. We internalise social norms, such as that of paying our dues, keeping agreements, returning a favour; and higher-order norms, as for example frowning on people who break social norms (even shunning them), and so forth. By internalising such norms as keeping agreements,

---

[45] See also Gadgil and Guha (1992) for a narrative on India's ecological history as seen from this perspective.

a person makes the springs of his actions contain the norm. The person therefore feels shame or guilt in violating a norm, and this prevents him from doing so, or, at the very least, it puts a break on his violating it unless other considerations are found by him to be overriding. In short, his upbringing ensures that he has a disposition to obey the norm. When he does violate it, neither guilt nor shame is typically absent, but the act will have been rationalised by him. A general disposition to abide by agreements, to be truthful, to trust one another, and to act with justice is an essential lubricant of societies. Communities where the disposition is pervasive save enormously on transaction costs. There lies its instrumental virtue. In the world as we know it, such a disposition is present in varying degrees. When we refrain from breaking the law, it isn't always because of a fear of being caught. On the other hand, if relative to the gravity of the misdemeanour the private benefit from malfeasance were high, some transgressions could be expected to take place. Punishment assumes its role as a deterrence because of the latter fact.

However, where people repeatedly encounter one another in similar situations, agreements could be reached and kept even if people were not trustworthy; and even if a higher authority were not there to enforce the agreements. This is a third kind of mechanism.

How does it work? A simple set of contexts in which it works is one where far-sighted people know both one another and the environment, where they expect to interact repeatedly under the same circumstances, and where all this is commonly known.[46] By a far-sighted person I mean someone who applies a low discount rate to the future costs and benefits associated with alternative courses of action. This means in particular that people in the community are not separately mobile; otherwise the chance of future encounters with others in the community would be low, and people would discount heavily the future benefits of co-operation.

The basic idea is this: if people are far-sighted, a credible threat by others that they would impose sanctions on anyone who broke the agreement would deter everyone from breaking it. Let us see how this works.

For expositional ease, consider those circumstances where actions are publicly observable, and where everyone has perfect memory of

[46] These are not necessary conditions, they are sufficient. For a good account of what is known in this line of inquiry, see Fudenberg and Tirole (1991).

how all others have behaved in the past.[47] Imagine, then, a group of
people who have agreed upon a joint course of action (e.g. in the case of
two people, a point on BC in Figure 1). The agreement could, for
example, be over the sharing of the benefits and burdens associated
with the construction and maintenance of an irrigation system. We may
suppose that the co-operative arrangement that has been agreed upon
assigns various responsibilities to the parties on a period-by-period
basis (e.g. maintaining a canal system annually, diverting to one's
own fields only the quantity of water that is one's due, and so forth).
How is this agreement to be kept in the absence of an external enforcement authority?

One might think that a social norm, requiring people to keep their
agreements, has a role here. But this merely begs the question: we
would want to know why the norm is accepted by all; that is, what
incentives people have for not violating the norm. Since by a social
norm we mean a rule of behaviour that is commonly obeyed by all, we
would need to show that it is in the interest of each party to obey the
norm if all others were to obey it.[48] For simplicity of exposition,
consider the case where the private gain to someone from breaking
the agreement unilaterally for a period is less than the discounted value
of the loss he would suffer if all others were to refrain from co-
operating with him in the following period. Call a person deserving if
and only if he co-operates with all who are deserving. This sounds
circular, but isn't; because we now assume that the norm requires all
parties to start the process of repeated interactions by keeping their
agreement (namely, maintaining the canal system, diverting to one's
own fields only the quantity of water that is one's due, and so forth). It
is then easy to confirm that, by recursion, it is possible for any party in
any period to determine who is deserving and who is not. If someone's
actions in any period made him non-deserving, the norm would enjoin
each of the other parties to impose a sanction on him (i.e. not co-operate
with him) in the following period (e.g. deny him the water he needs).
The norm therefore requires that sanctions be imposed upon those in
violation of an agreement; upon those who fail to impose sanctions
upon those in violation of the agreement; upon those who fail to impose

---

[47] Each of these qualifications can be relaxed. See Radner (1981) for weakening the first
qualification, and Sabourian (1988) for relaxing the second.

[48] In technical parlance, for a rule of behaviour to be a social norm, it must be a subgame-
perfect Nash equilibrium. Fudenberg and Tirole (1991) offer an account of this.

sanctions upon those who fail to impose sanctions upon those in violation of the agreement; and so on, indefinitely. This indefinite chain of what amounts to higher and higher order norms makes the threat of sanctions against deviant behaviour credible; because, if all others were to obey the norm, it would not be worth anyone's while to disobey the norm. In short, keeping one's agreement would be self-enforcing.[49]

This argument generalises to other situations. Provided people are sufficiently far-sighted, a social norm which instructs one to co-operate with, and only with, deserving parties, can lift communities out of a number of potentially troublesome social situations, including the repeated 'prisoners' dilemma' game. The reason each party would conform to the norm if a sufficient number of others were to conform is pure and simple self-interest: if someone were not to conform (i.e. were not to abide by the norm), they would suffer from sanctions from others for a sufficiently long period of time, long enough to make non-conformism 'unprofitable'.[50]

This sort of argument, which has been established in a general setting only recently, has been put to effective use in explaining the emergence of a number of institutions which facilitated the growth of trade in medieval Europe. Greif (1993), for example, has shown how the Maghribi traders during the eleventh century in Fustat and across the Mediterranean acted as a collective to impose sanctions on agents who violated their commercial codes. Greif, Milgrom and Weingast (1994) have offered an account of the rise of merchant guilds in late medieval Europe. These guilds afforded protection to members against unjustified seizure of their property by city-states. Guilds decided if and when a trade embargo was warranted against the city. In a related work, Milgrom, North and Weingast (1990) have analysed the role of merchant courts in the Champagne fairs. These courts facilitated members in imposing sanctions on transgressors of agreements.

A somewhat reverse set of actions also occurred in medieval Europe, where transgressions by a party were sometimes met by the rest of society imposing sanctions on the entire kinship of the party, or on the guild to which the transgressor belonged. The norm provided collec-

---

[49] Notice though that, as co-operation is self-enforcing, there would be no deviance along the path of co-operation; so, no sanctions would be observed. The higher-order norms pertain to behaviour off the path of co-operation.

[50] Of course, the non-co-operative outcome (e.g. the point A in Figure 1) is also self-enforcing; that is, it is also a subgame-perfect Nash equilibrium. Repeated games, such as the one I am studying here, have many equilibria.

tives with a natural incentive to monitor their own members' behaviour. (For a different instance of this, the context being the use of local common-property resources, see Howe, 1986.)

As matters stand, international agreements on environmental matters could be expected to be sustained by the latter two mechanisms in the list I have just discussed, not by the first. Ultimately, however, it is the second route that offers the strongest hopes for the emergence of collective responsibility over transnational commons. The problem is that institutional changes are easier to bring about than changes in personal and collective attitudes; or so it would seem. Economists generally take 'preferences' and 'demands' as given and try to devise policies that would be expected to improve matters collectively. This is the spirit in which ecological economics has developed, and there is an enormous amount to be said for it. But in the process of following this research strategy, we shouldn't play down the strictures of those social thinkers who have urged the rich to curb their material demands, to alter their preferences in such ways as to better husband the earth's limited resources. If such strictures seem quaint in today's world, it may be because we are psychologically uncomfortable with this kind of vocabulary. But that isn't an argument for not taking them seriously.

Note. I am grateful to Kenneth Arrow, Edward Barbier, Scott Barrett, John Dixon, Paul Ehrlich, Carl Folke, Frank Hahn, Geoffrey Heal, C. S. Holling, Bengt-Owe Jansson, Bengt Kriström, Simon Levin, Mohan Munasinghe, Charles Perrings, Jonathan Roughgarden, Ismail Serageldin, Robert Solow, David Starrett, Andrew Steer and, in particular, Karl-Göran Mäler, discussions with whom over the past many years have improved my understanding of the subject matter of the lecture.

Discussion

Christopher Bliss, *Nuffield College, Oxford; Fellow of the Academy*

Professor Dasgupta's lecture succeeded in enlivening a topic which can prove to be deadly dry. Following a wide-ranging lecture on a hugely diverse field, it is impossible for a discussant to do more than to pick up a few topics which may merit further discussion. I have chosen to offer brief comments on just three topics:

1   the idea of 'Greening' net national product;
2   planning with environmental risk; and
3   induced technical change and the environment.

Greening NNP

There can be no question that it is possible to define a measure of 'Green NNP' and to compute estimates of it. Such an exercise can be useful and enlightening. Indeed I favour a multiplicity of concepts and methods, on the grounds that the contrasts thus provided can only enrich. However, I confess that the prospect of national accounting being substantially re-defined to make it 'environmentally correct' causes me to feel considerable apprehension.

It is a merit of established NNP aggregates that they are familiar and routine, and we know what kind of things they measure. Broadly speaking, NNP measures the scale of national value-added activity roughly corrected for capital depreciation. Economists know that such a measure is non-ideal in all kinds of ways. NNP plunges when millions of rich men marry the old-time housekeepers who become old-time stay-at-home wives. Yet the measure is useful, to track national economic activity over trade cycles, and for admittedly rough-and-ready international comparisons of economic prosperity, particularly when corrected for differences in purchasing power.

If 'green corrections' were as clear and boring as the standard measures, they could be accepted as welcome refinements. But they are not, and there is a danger that their introduction would politicise NNP estimates without making them genuinely more useful. Take as a case in point the popular notion that over-inflated NNP estimates would be reduced were an allowance for using up exhaustible fossil fuels to be deducted. If all fossil fuel reserves were to be known and proven that would indeed be the case. In the real world, however, NNP estimates would at times leap up by very substantial fractions of the total following new discoveries. And if logic is to be respected, why should not NNP measures be augmented following technical innovations? How are pen-pushing census of production statisticians to estimate such corrections?

Risk and planning

The problem of how to compute the value of innovations arises because the future is dreadfully uncertain. There at least we have the option to walk away from the problem by leaving our NNP estimates alone, while recognising that they are most imperfect. That option does not exist where the possibility of catastrophic outcomes exists. How should we react to uncertainty, especially when catastrophic possibilities are involved? Standard economic theory of rational choice under uncertainty teaches that low probability disaster outcomes should carry high weights in our calculations because extreme utility weights multiply the low probabilities concerned. It also teaches that positive (possibly large) values attach to open options, so that at the margin doing nothing is preferable to jumping in and causing irreversible effects to the environment.

Such arguments work well in the classroom but run the danger in the cut and thrust of debate on real environmental issues of allowing the argument to be hijacked by the imagination of someone who can dream up a nightmare possibility, however improbable, which can certainly be avoided by doing nothing. The hypothetical example cheats by introducing an unnaturally sharp discontinuity between the safe and the risky.

In reality downside risks attach even to environmental correctness. What exactly will happen should a fear of global warming induce a drastic curtailment of carbon dioxide emissions is uncertain. Serious harm to human populations caused by energy shortage is a real possibility but complex to predict and analyse in detail. The probable good outcome is outweighed by the improbable catastrophic outcome because of the extremely different weights which multiply the widely differing probabilities. Nuclear engineering is rightly all about planning for highly improbable events and paying high costs to cope with them. In much of life, however, the not wildly improbable poor outcome stands beside the dreadful outcome on more equal terms.

Induced technical change and the environment

Economists' attempts to forecast the future to allow for environmental crisis, from Malthus, through Jevons to Forrester, were wrecked on the rocks of technical change. Innovation is the new goddess of Fortune, rewarding hugely but never promising or submitting to manipulation. The pattern is often that innovation tends to bypass shortage and to exploit abundance. Yet what that implies for the huge (although shrinking, as a proportion of total numbers), numbers of poor rural labourers of the world, and particularly for the women and children among them, is far from clear.

Should population pressure and mass urbanisation bring it about that the country can no longer feed the cities with existing foodgrain cultivation methods, however far the recombinant DNA scientists may take that technology, the next step may bypass the rural cultivators and their possibly degraded land rather than heaping rents upon them. Fermentation of biomass, for instance, could produce protein-rich nutrients for animal feed or for poor humans, out of capital intensive urban factories which are unlikely to favour women and children in employment.

The happy outcome that the solutions to environmental problems and the solutions to problems of inequality and human exploitation will all point in the same direction is something to pray for, not an economic theorem.

Scott Barrett, *London Business School*

I can't think of a social problem more momentous than the subject of Professor Dasgupta's lecture: that of how to improve the lot of the worst-off people living in the worst-off countries.

That economics not only could be used to address this problem but *should* be is a lesson I learned from Partha Dasgupta ten years ago when I came to study under him at the LSE. At our first meeting, Professor Dasgupta asked me what I intended to write my Ph.D. on. I had given this a lot of thought, and proceeded to tell him my ideas. He listened attentively and when I finished he said, 'Very interesting . . . but have you thought of the desertification problem?' Now I needn't tell you what my idea for a thesis was except to say it had absolutely nothing to do with the desertification problem. It couldn't have, because at the time I didn't even know there was such a problem. Suffice it to say that three years later I submitted a thesis that I wouldn't have written had I not understood the message that Partha Dasgupta was conveying to me. And though I have since turned to work on different subjects, even today, if you were to hold any of my work up to the light I think you'd find the Dasgupta watermark.

For my discussion, I would like to demonstrate this by applying the apparatus Professor Dasgupta has sketched in his lecture to a different class of problem: global, rather than local, environmental degradation. This would seem appropriate, not least because global environmental degradation also affects the lives of the poor. Let me, however, qualify the analysis which follows by saying that it is deliberately rough. To do a proper job of the subject would require more space than I am permitted.

A tale of two global environmental problems

Consider two, superficially similar, examples of global environmental degradation: stratospheric ozone depletion and global climate change. Both of these problems affect every country; and in both cases, effective management of the environment requires co-operation by at least a very large number of countries. There the similarities end, for the outcomes as regards these two problems couldn't be more different. Global co-operation in protecting the ozone layer has been miraculous: almost every country in the world has co-operated in a regime to protect the ozone layer, and in a very short time virtually all the important substances which deplete the ozone layer—I'll call them CFCs— either have been or soon will be eliminated. By contrast, next to nothing has been done to address the problem of global climate change. This is a puzzle: Why should the outcomes for such similar problems be so different?

A brief history of the science

It would be natural to suppose that the answer might relate to the science of these problems, but this turns out not to be the case. That CFCs could deplete ozone was not even contemplated until 1974 when it was first posited as a hypothesis. By contrast, the theory of global climate change, resulting from the burning of fossil fuels, goes back to the last century. In fact, in 1895 a Swedish chemist, using the back of an envelope, predicted that a doubling in carbon dioxide concentrations would increase global mean temperature by about 5°C. Today's climatologists, using the most advanced supercomputers, predict that the increase will be smaller—about 1°–3.5°C by the end of the next century. What the Swedish chemist didn't take account of were important feedbacks. Still, it is remarkable how little the estimates for climate change have shifted, despite a century's advancement in atmospheric science. So, while we have known that carbon dioxide emissions alter the climate for much longer than we have known that CFCs destroy ozone, we have done much more to address the latter problem than the former.

The nature of the environmental damage

If the science can't explain the different outcomes, what can? At least an important part of the answer can be found in the economics.

Ozone depletion would increase the incidence of skin cancer. Put bluntly, it would kill people. People in rich countries are willing to pay a lot to avoid this, and so the benefit to them of reducing ozone depletion is high. The cost to them of doing so, it turns out, is very low. In one economic study by the US government, the benefit to the US of signing the international treaty controlling CFCs exceeded the cost by about 170 times. There are not many public choices that have such a favourable benefit–cost ratio.

With global climate change, most of the available economic studies show that only modest reductions in carbon dioxide emissions would be warranted. Climate change damages are expected to be small, partly because climate change hasn't been shown to kill large numbers of people, but also because of certain offsets and behavioural responses. Consider what appears to be the most vulnerable economic sector: agriculture. If a warmer temperature reduced agricultural output in already warm regions, it would probably increase output in colder ones. Added to this, farmers could change the crops they planted and their use of inputs like water. Finally, the new biotechnology could develop seed varieties better suited to the changed climate. Further-more, the costs of abating carbon dioxide emissions are expected to be large in proportion to the benefits: to reduce carbon dioxide emissions substantially would require reducing fossil fuel consumption, and our economies depend on them.

I have some doubts about the analyses which show that the damages from climate change would be low. They have been based largely on the assumptions that the damage is a function of *average* temperature change, and that damage estimates for the US can simply be prorated across the rest of the globe. Professor Dasgupta's attention to ecology and the nature of environmental damage should make us wary of these assumptions.

The average temperature change may in itself matter very little. Much more important may be the changes triggered by the average temperature change, such as a flip in the Gulf Stream. And, as regards prorating US damage across the globe, consider the effect of increasing temperature in malaria-prone regions. Already, malaria strikes at 100 million people in the poor countries each year, killing 1–2 million of them. Even ignoring such scenarios, as Partha Dasgupta would be the first to observe, a $100 drop in the standard of living of a poor household would impose much greater hardship than would an equivalent reduction for a rich one. This last observation does not by itself mean that emissions should be reduced substantially, but it does mean that poor countries will potentially be harmed more severely than rich countries in well-being terms.

Abatement costs and incentives to innovate

Unfortunately, merely acknowledging that expected damage is high won't necessarily commend substantial abatement of greenhouse gases, for we still have the problem that the costs of abatement are large. To affect the outcome significantly would require substantial abatement. This essentially means finding a substitute for fossil fuels. What we require are incentives for innovation.

In the case of ozone depletion, the Montreal Protocol didn't just ban CFCs. For in doing this it created a market for CFC-substitutes, and thus provided incentives for innovation. By contrast, the Framework Convention on Climate change does not require that greenhouse gas emissions be cut, and for this reason the incentives to develop carbon-saving technologies are weak at present. These incentives will remain weak until business comes to believe that governments will be able to establish an international regulatory regime for the climate like the Montreal Protocol which is capable of imposing stiff abatement requirements. Perhaps the biggest challenge for climate change policy is to make the threat to impose such requirements credible.

Free riding and trade leakage

One reason the Framework Convention does not demand a sharp reduction in emissions is that the high expected costs of abatement make the temptation to free-ride hard to resist. The result is that each country abates its emissions very little. Furthermore, this would be true even if all countries believed that they would be better off if they all abated their emissions substantially. Again, much of Partha Dasgupta's work has been concerned with situations of this type, facing households or rural communities: situations in which, even if all parties make the decisions that are good for themselves, the result is bad for everyone.

In the case of global environmental problems, these 'free-rider' incentives are exacerbated by trade. If a country increases its abatement, its production costs rise, with the consequence that comparative advantage in the pollution-intensive good is shifted abroad: foreign output rises; and so do foreign emissions. Hence, as a direct result of reducing emissions at home, foreign emissions rise.

'Sticks'

This problem of 'leakage' was eliminated in the Montreal Protocol by the use of trade sanctions. Parties agreed not to trade with non-parties in CFCs, products containing CFCs, and products made using CFCs. The trade sanctions fundamentally altered the incentives to free-ride. Once enough countries were parties to the agreement, there was a huge loss in the gains from trade to non-signatories. This was the stick that made participation attractive to so many countries. Trade sanctions in the case of carbon dioxide would, however, probably not be as attractive. Greenhouse gases are emitted in the process of making every good or service. A comprehensive trade ban between signatories and non-signatories may not be credible, while a partial trade ban may in this case threaten the existing multilateral trading regime.

'Carrots'

Just as the Montreal Protocol needed to include all the major countries in the world, so any agreement to limit greenhouse gas emissions must include a large number of poor as well as rich countries. The UK emits no more today than it did twenty to twenty-five years ago. In China, emissions are rising about 7 per cent a year. This implies a doubling in emissions every ten years. There is not much point in negotiating an agreement to limit greenhouse gas emissions which doesn't include China and certain other poor countries. China and the other poor countries have other priorities, however. Sure, they would be harmed by climate change; but if they reduce their emissions they will receive only a fraction of the expected global benefit, and even this won't be realised for decades. At least as regards a significant abatement programme, the return on investment will be higher for them in other areas.

So the rich countries will have to pay poor countries to reduce their emissions. The Montreal Protocol again succeeded in this. You might recall the concern expressed a few years ago of the implications if every Chinese household owned a refrigerator. This is no longer a worry because under the Montreal Protocol China and other poor countries will be compensated for the higher cost of using CFC substitutes. It turns out that the cost of this substitution is small: in the order of a few hundred million pounds. By contrast, the cost of effecting a substantial shift away from fossil fuel burning will be more than all the rich countries currently spend on overseas development.

Concluding remark

I don't have time to go into any more detail. Professor Dasgupta's lecture has taught us that economics provides the means for understanding why the rural poor are in the terrible straits they are in, and what can be done to improve their condition. My goal was to reinforce this message, by showing how the same theoretical apparatus could be employed on the global scale.

References

Agarwal, A. and Narain, S. 1989. *Towards Green Villages: A Strategy for Environmentally Sound and Participatory Rural Development*. New Delhi.

Anderson, D. 1987. *The Economics of Afforestation*. Baltimore.

Arrow, K. J. 1971. 'Political and Economic Evaluation of Social Effects of Externalities', in Intriligator (1971).

——and Fisher, A. 1974. 'Preservation, Uncertainty and Irreversibility'. *Quarterly Journal of Economics*, 88.

——*et al.* 1995*a*. 'Intertemporal Equity, Discounting and Economic Efficiency', in Munasinghe, (1995).

—— 1995*b*. 'Economic Growth, Carrying Capacity, and the Environment'. *Science*, 268 (5210). (Reprinted in *Environment and Development Economics*, 1996 1(1).)

Aumann, R. 1987. 'Game Theory', in Eatwell, Milgate and Newman (1987).

Baland, J.-M. and Platteau, J.-P. 1996. *Halting Degradation of Natural Resources: Is There a Role for Rural Communities?*. Oxford.

Barraclough, S. 1977. 'Agricultural Production Prospects in Latin America'. *World Development*, 5.

Barrett, S. 1990. 'The Problem of Global Environmental Protection'. *Oxford Review of Economic Policy*, 6.

—— 1996. 'Comments on the 1995 Keynes Lecture'. *Proceedings of the British Academy*, 89. London.

Barro, R. and Sala-i-Martin, X. 1995. *Economic Growth*. New York.

Baumol, W. M. and Bradford, D. 1972. 'Detrimental Externalities and Non-Convexity of the Production Set'. *Economica*, 39.

Baumol, W. M. and Oates, W. 1975. *The Theory of Environmental Policy*. Engle-wood Cliffs, N.J.

Behrman, J. and Srinivasan, T. N. (eds.) 1995. *Handbook of Development Economics*, iiia Amsterdam.

Beteille, A. (ed.) 1983. *Equality and Inequality: Theory and Practice*. Delhi.

Binmore, K. and Dasgupta, P. (eds.) 1987. *The Economics of Bargaining*. Oxford.

Binswanger, H. 1991. 'Brazilian Policies that Encourage Deforestation in the Amazon'. *World Development*, 19.

Bovenberg, A. L. and van der Ploeg, F. 1994. 'Environmental Policy, Public Finance, and the Labour Market in a Second-Best World'. *Journal of Public Economics*, 55.

Brown, G. and McGuire, C. B. 1967. 'A Socially Optimal Pricing Policy for a Public Water Agency'. *Water Resources Research*, 3.

Carraro, C. (ed.), 1994. *Trade Innovation Environment*. Dordrecht.

———— and Siniscalco, D. 1993. 'Strategies for the International Protection of the Environment'. *Journal of Public Economics*, 52.

Chichilnisky, G. 1994. 'North-South Trade and the Global Environment'. *American Economic Review*, 84.

Chopra, K., Kadekodi, G. K. and Murty, M. N. 1990. *Participatory Development: People and Common Property Resources*. New Delhi.

Clark, C. W. 1976. *Mathematical Bioeconomics: The Optimal Management of Renewable Resources*. New York.

Cleaver, K. M. and Schreiber, G. A. 1994. *Reversing the Spiral: The Population, Agriculture, and Environment Nexus in sub-Saharan Africa*. Washington, D.C.

Coase, R. 1960. 'The Problem of Social Cost'. *Journal of Law and Economics*, 3.

Cooper, R. 1977. 'An Economist's View of the Oceans'. *Journal of World Trade Law*, 9.

Copeland, B. R. and Taylor, M. S. 1994. 'North-South Trade and the Environment'. *Quarterly Journal of Economics*, 109.

———— 1995. 'Trade and Transboundary Pollution'. *American Economic Review*, 85.

Costanza, R. (ed.) 1991. *Ecological Economics: The Science and Management of Sustainability*. New York.

CSE 1990. *Human-Nature Interactions in a Central Himalayan Village: A Case Study of Village Bembru*. New Delhi.

Dales, J. H. 1968. *Pollution, Property and Prices*. Toronto.

Daly, H. E. 1994. 'The Perils of Free Trade'. *Scientific American*, 270(2).

Dasgupta, P. 1982. *The Control of Resources*. Oxford.

Dasgupta, P. 1988. 'Trust as a Commodity', in Gambetta (1988).

———— 1990. 'The Environment as a Commodity'. *Oxford Review of Economic Policy*, 6.

———— 1993. *An Inquiry into Well-Being and Destitution*. Oxford.

———— 1995a. 'Population, Poverty, and the Local Environment'. *Scientific American*, 272(2).

———— 1995b. 'The Population Problem: Theory and Evidence. *Journal of Economic Literature*, 33.

———— 1996. 'Poverty Traps', in Kreps and Wallis (1996).

———— and Ehrlich, P. H. 1996. 'Nature's Housekeeping and Human House-keeping'. Discussion Paper. Stockholm.

Dasgupta, P. and Heal, G. M. 1979. *Economic Theory and Exhaustible Resources*. Cambridge.

Dasgupta, P., Kriström, B. and Mäler, K.-G. 1996. 'Net National Product as a Measure of Social Well-Being'. Discussion Paper. Stockholm.

Dasgupta, P. and Mäler, K.-G. 1991. 'The Environment and Emerging Development Issues'. *Proceedings of the Annual World Bank Conference on Development Economics, 1990*. Supplement to the *World Bank Economic Review* and the *World Bank Research Observer*.

———— 1995. 'Poverty, Institutions, and the Environmental Resource-Base', in Behrman and Srinivasan (1995).

Dasgupta, P., Marglin, S. and Sen, A. 1972. *Guidelines for Project Evaluation*. New York.

Deacon, R. T. 1994. 'Deforestation and the Rule of Law in a Cross Section of Countries'. *Land Economics*, 70.

Dixon, J. A. and Hufschmid, M. M. (eds.) 1986. *Economic Valuation Techniques for the Environment*. Baltimore.

Dixon, J. A. *et al.* 1988. *Economic Analysis of Environmental Impacts*. London.

Eatwell, J., Milgate, M. and Newman, P. (eds.) 1987. *The New Palgrave*. London.

Ehrlich, P. R., Ehrlich, A. H. and Daily, G. 1995. *The Stork and the Plow: The Equity Answer to the Human Dilemma*. New York.

Ehrlich, P. R., Ehrlich, A. H. and Holdren, J. P. 1977. *EcoScience: Population, Resources, Environment*. San Francisco, CA.

Ensminger, J. 1990. 'Co-opting the Elders: The Political Economy of State Incorporation in Africa'. *American Anthropologist*, 92.

Falconer, J. 1990. *The Major Significance of 'Minor' Forest Products*. Rome.

———— and Arnold, J. E. M. 1989. *Household Food Security and Forestry: An Analysis of Socio-Economic Issues*. Rome.

Feder, E. 1977. 'Agribusiness and the Elimination of Latin America's Rural Proletariat'. *World Development*, 5.

———— 1979. 'Agricultural Resources in Underdeveloped Countries: Competition between Man and Animal'. *Economic and Political Weekly*, 14.

Feeny, D. *et al.* 1990. 'The Tragedy of the Commons: Twenty-two Years Later'. *Human Ecology*, 18.

French, H. F. 1994. 'Making Environmental Treaties Work'. *Scientific American*, 272(6).

Fudenberg, D. and Tirole, J. 1991. *Game Theory*. Cambridge, MA.

Gadgil, M. and Guha, R. 1992. *This Fissured Land: An Ecological History of India*. Delhi.

Gadgil, M. and Malhotra, K. C. 1983. 'Adaptive Significance of the Indian Caste System: An Ecological Perspective'. *Annals of Human Biology*, 10.

Gambetta, D. (ed.), 1988. *Trust: Making and Breaking Co-operative Relations*. Oxford.

Gordon, H. Scott 1954. 'The Economic Theory of Common-Property Resources'. *Journal of Political Economy*, 62.

Greif, A. 1993. 'Contract Enforceability and Economic Institutions in Early Trade: The Maghribi Traders' Coalition'. *American Economic Review*, 83.

————, Milgrom, P. and Weingast, B. 1994. 'Co-ordination, Commitment, and Enforcement: The Case of the Merchant Guild'. *Journal of Political Economy*, 102.

Hahn, F. H. (ed.), 1988. *The Economic Theory of Missing Markets, Information and Games*. Oxford.

Hardin, G. 1968. 'The Tragedy of the Commons'. *Science*, 162.

Hartwick, J. and Olewiler, N. 1986. *The Economics of Natural Resource Use*. New York.

Heal, G. M. 1994. 'Formation of International Environmental Agreements', in Carraro (1994).

Heath, J. and Binswanger, H. 1996. 'Natural Resource Degradation Effects of Poverty and Population Growth are Largely Policy Induced: The Case of Columbia'. *Environment and Development Economics*, 1.

Hecht, S. 1985. 'Environment, Development and Politics: Capital Accumulation and the Livestock Sector in Eastern Amazonia'. *World Development*, 13.

————, Anderson, A. B. and May, P. 1988. 'The Subsidy from Nature: Shifting Cultivation, Successional Palm Forests and Rural Development'. *Human Organization*, 47.

Henry, C. 1974. 'Investment Decisions under Uncertainty: The Irreversibility Effect'. *American Economic Review*, 64.

Hodgson, G. and Dixon, J. 1992. 'Sedimentation Damage to Marine Resources: Environmental and Economic Analysis', in Marsh (1992).

Hoel, M. 1992. 'International Environmental Conventions: The Case of Uniform Reductions of Emissions'. *Environmental and Resource Economics*, 2.

Howe, J. 1986. *The Kuna Gathering*. Austin, Tex.

Humphries, J. 1990. 'Enclosures, Common Rights, and Women: The Proletarianization of Families in the Late Eighteenth and Early Nineteenth Centuries'. *Journal of Economic History*, 50.

Intriligator, M. (ed.), 1971. *Frontiers of Quantitative Economics*, i. Amsterdam.

Jodha, N. S. 1980. 'The Process of Desertification and the Choice of Interventions'. *Economic and Political Weekly*, 15.

———— 1986. 'Common Property Resources and the Rural Poor'. *Economic and Political Weekly*, 21.

———— 1995. 'Common Property Resources and the Environmental Context: Role of Biophysical versus Social Stress'. *Economic and Political Weekly*, 30.

Koch, E. 1996. 'A Watershed for Apartheid'. *New Scientist*. 12 April 2025.

Koopmans, T. C. 1957. 'The Price System and the Allocation of Resources', in Koopmans, T. C. *Three Essays on the State of Economic Science*. New York.

Kreps, D. and Wallis, K. (eds.), 1996. *Advances in Economic Theory*. i. 'Seventh World Congress of the Econometric Society'. Cambridge.

Kriström, B. and Riera, P. 1996. 'Is the Income Elasticity of Environmental Improvements Less than One?'. *Environmental and Resource Economics*, 7.

Lindahl, E. R. 1958. 'Some Controversial Questions in the Theory of Taxation', in Musgrave and Peacock.

Little, I. M. D. and Mirrlees, J. A. 1974. *Project Appraisal and Planning for Developing Countries*. London.

Low, P. (ed.) 1992. *International Trade and the Environment*. World Bank Discussion Papers 159. Washington, D.C.

Lutz, E. (ed.) 1993. *Toward Improved Accounting for the Environment*. Washington, D.C.

Magrath, W. and Arens, P. 1989. 'The Costs of Soil Erosion in Java: A Natural Resource Accounting Approach'. World Bank Environmental Department Working Paper No. 18.

Mäler, K.-G. 1974. *Environmental Economics: A Theoretical Enquiry*. Baltimore.

———— 1990. 'International Environmental Problems'. *Oxford Review of Economic Policy*, 6.

———— 1991. 'National Accounting and Environmental Resources'. *Environmental and Resource Economics*, 1.

———— *et al.* 1992. 'The Baltic Drainage-Basin Programme', mimeograph. Beijer Institute, Stockholm.

Mäler, K.-G. and Uzawa, H. 1995. 'Tradeable Emission Permits and the Stability of Lindahl Equilibrium'. Discussion Paper. Tokyo.

Marsh, J. B. (ed.), 1992. *Resources and Environment in Asia's Marine Sector*. London.

May, R. M. 1972. 'Will a Large Complex System be Stable?'. *Nature*, 238.

———— and MacArthur, R. H. 1972. 'Niche Overlap as a Function of Environmental Variability'. *Proceedings of the National Academy of Sciences of the U.S.*, 69.

Meade, J. E. 1973. *The Theory of Externalities*. Geneva.

Milgrom, P., North, D. and Weingast, B. 1990. 'The Role of Institutions in the Revival of Trade: The Law Merchant, Private Judges, and the Champagne Fairs'. *Economics and Politics*, 2.

Mitchell, R. C. and Carson, R. T. 1989. *Using Surveys to Value Public Goods: The Contingent Valuation Method*. Washington, D.C.

Munasinghe, M. (ed.), 1995. *Global Climate Change: Economic and Policy Issues*. World Bank Environmental Paper No. 2. Washington, D.C.

Murphy, Y. and Murphy, R. 1985. *Women of the Forest*. New York.

Musgrave, R. A. and Peacock, A. T. (ed.), 1958. *Classics in the Theory of Finance*. London.

Nash, J. 1950. 'The Bargaining Problem'. *Econometrica*, 18.

Newcombe, K. 1987. 'An Economic Justification of Rural Afforestation: The Case of Ethiopia'. *Annals of Regional Science*, 21.

Nordhaus, W. D. 1994. *Managing the Global Commons: The Economics of Climate Change*. Cambridge, Mass.

———— and Tobin, J. 1972. 'Is Economic Growth Obsolete?', in *Economic Growth*. 5th Anniversary Colloquium of the NBER. New York.

Ostrom, E. 1990. *Governing the Commons: The Evolution of Institutions for Collective Action*. Cambridge.

———— 1996. 'Incentives, Rules of the Game, and Development'. *Proceedings of the Annual World Bank Conference on Development Economics, 1995*.

Supplement to the *World Bank Economic Review* and the *World Bank Research Observer*.

Perrings, C. *et al.* 1994. *Biodiversity Loss: Ecologial and Economic Perspectives.* Cambridge.

Pigou, A. C. 1920. *The Economics of Welfare.* London.

Putnam, R. D., with Leonardi, R. and Nanetti, R. Y. 1993. *Making Democracy Work: Civic Traditions in Modern Italy.* Princeton, N.J.

Radner, R. 1981. 'Monitoring Cooperative Agreements in a Repeated Principle-Agent Relationship'. *Econometrica*, 49.

Reardon, T. and Vosti, S. A. 1995. 'Links Between Rural Poverty and the Environment in Developing Countries: Asset Categories and Investment Poverty'. *World Development*, 23.

Repetto, R. 1988. 'Economic Policy Reform for National Resource Conservation'. World Bank Environment Department Working Paper No. 4.

———— *et al.* 1989. *Wasting Assets: Natural Resources and the National Income Accounts.* Washington, D.C.

Romer, D. 1996. *Advanced Macroeconomics.* New York.

Sabourian, H. 1988. 'Repeated Games: A Survey', in Hahn (1988).

Safina, C. 1995. 'The World's Imperiled Fish'. *Scientific American*, 273(5).

Seabright, P. 1993. 'Managing Local Commons: Theoretical Issues in Incentive Design'. *Journal of Economic Perspectives*, 7.

Sefton, J. and Weale, M. 1995. 'The Net National Product and Exhaustible Resources: the Effects of Foreign Trade'. *Journal of Public Economics* (forthcoming).

Solorzano, R. *et al.* 1991. *Accounts Overdue: Natural Resource Depreciation in Costa Rica.* Washington, D.C.

Spence, A. M. 1974. 'Blue Whales and Optimal Control Theory', in Göttinger, H. ed., *Systems Approaches and Environmental Problems.* Göttingen.

Starrett, D. A. 1972. 'Fundamental Non-Convexities in the Theory of Externalities'. *Journal of Economics Theory*, 4.

Stevenson, G. G. 1991. *Common Property Resources: A General Theory and Land Use Applications.* Cambridge.

Tietenberg, T. 1988. *Environmental and Natural Resource Economics*, 2nd ed. Glenview, Ill.

UNDP 1993. *Human Development Report, 1993.* New York.

Vitousek, P. *et al.* 1986. 'Human Appropriation of the Product of Photosynthesis'. *BioScience*, 36.

Wade, R. 1988. *Village Republics: Economic Conditions for Collective Action in South India.* Cambridge.

Walker, B. H. 1993. 'Rangeland Ecology: Understanding and Managing Change'. *Ambio*, 22.

Weitzman, M. L. 1974*a*. 'Taxes vs. Quantities'. *Review of Economic Studies*, 41.

———— 1974*b*. 'Free Access vs. Private Ownership as Alternative Systems for Managing Common Property'. *Journal of Economic Theory*, 8.

World Bank 1992. *World Development Report.* New York.

World Resources Institute 1994. *World Resources 1994–1995.* New York.

Young, H. Peyton 1994. *Equity: in Theory and Practice.* Princeton, N.J.

Proceedings of the British Academy, **90**, 223–235

Prosperity, Civility and Liberty: Can We Square the Circle?

RALF DAHRENDORF

University of Oxford
Fellow of the Academy

THE JEWISH REFUGEES whose generous thank-offering to Britain led along with a research fellowship to this series of lectures, knew what they were grateful for. It was their survival, of course, but it was more, a new life in a free and civil country. Britain did not have 'the best constitution ever written' (as that of Weimar Germany has been described, which Hitler tore up in one short session of the Reichstag on 23 March 1933); Britain did — and does — not have a written constitution at all; yet no one who came to this country as a refugee from persecution in the 1930s ever doubted that he or she was safe from arbitrary rule and protected by institutions as well as deeply engrained habits which an unbroken tradition had made more reliable than any basic law or constitutional court can guarantee.

I came to this country not as a refugee but as one who wanted to make this his home, and thus I have, in a different way, every reason to be grateful to those who received me with such generosity. What is it that attracted a German who had spent more than half of his adult life outside Germany when he came in 1974 but had also been deeply involved in German academic and public affairs? Liberty certainly had something to do with it. There is a quality of freedom which is more than elections and parliamentary debates and incorruptible judges and the chance to write a letter to an editor or even to stand on a crate at

Read at the Academy 12 March 1996. © The British Academy 1996.

Speakers' Corner and harangue the bystanders. I suppose it has something to do with the absence of the ominous black cloud of doubt, even fear, which overshadows so much of life in other countries because it reminds them of violent storms of the past. It is the track record of the country and notably the sense that whatever illiberal sentiments creep into debate and behaviour, at the end of the day people will not allow the destruction of the liberal order to happen.

Then there is something else. Even the title of this lecture — to say nothing of my other publications — betrays my penchant for the family of words, indeed of ideas and institutions, associated with the city: citizenship, civilisation, civic sense and civic virtues, civil society, civility. Curiously, these words are not often used in British parlance. I remember a party leader saying to me: 'Unlike President Mitterrand I cannot go on television and start by addressing my audience as "Citizens and . . . and what, anyway?" ' (I later discovered in the *Oxford English Dictionary* that there is actually an obsolete word, 'citizette.') Civil society is a concept more often used in the post-communist countries of East Central Europe than here. Perhaps awareness for the values of civilised living in civic communities has grown in recent years; there is now a Citizenship Trust; civic sense is mobilised for initiatives notably at the local level; civil society may yet come to compete with the stakeholder society for the hearts and minds of voters. Could it be that the words become more current as the values behind them seem to retreat? Is the discovery of citizenship, of civil society, of civic sense and civil behaviour a response to the experience of disintegration, to widespread anti-social behaviour and to the crude competition between individuals embodied in the 'philosophy' of *enrichissez-vous, messieurs*?

You will notice that I have not yet mentioned prosperity; yet in some ways it is at the heart of my argument. To be sure, many recent refugees have come to Britain for its relative prosperity as much as its liberty and civility. But while wealth-creation has preoccupied businessmen and politicians in this country for over a century now — ever since those obsessed with league tables observed that Britain was about to be overtaken by others — somehow not much was done about it. Beveridge, even Keynes, were the heroes and both were as concerned about social cohesion as about wealth creation. Britain may have started it all, with the industrial revolution, but having done so it soon indulged in the dream of an 'English Culture' that can survive the 'decline of the industrial spirit' and in this way even represents a 'future that works' (to allude to the titles of two then much-quoted books of the 1970s by Martin Wiener and by Robert Nossiter).

The last fifteen years have swept such nostalgia away. Two great changes happened, not out of the blue, nor only through the deliberate action of governments, yet surprisingly, and certainly reinforced by political leaders. One is a great leap into modernity at the expense of all remaining traditional institutions; the other is a profound change of language, and more, from that of public-spirited, and often public-sector institutions, to that of business. Suddenly, the much-maligned and arguably least successful profession in the country, that of business-men and managers, was given prime position and direct responsibility even for public institutions, hospitals and prisons, schools and research councils. In fact, both transformations, that of modernity and that of economism can be seen as the late, the very late, triumph of the middle classes in a country which was dominated by upper-class and working-class values longer than any comparable society.

The implications of this change are vast, though I cannot dwell on them in the present context. When I wrote my little popular tract *On Britain* fifteen years ago, I pointed to the ambivalence of social values and structures. Strengths in one respect are weaknesses in another, and vice versa. Britain's civility may not have been good for business, but the exclusive emphasis on prosperity has dented a great tradition of civility. Do we have to make a choice? Insofar as lectures have a purpose beyond edification and entertainment, this one is intended to explore ways of having the best of all worlds, of squaring the circle of prosperity, civility and liberty.

This is not a British problem alone, though here it arises from a peculiar angle. The problem is as world-wide as the process of economic internationalisation which has followed the information revolution and the globalisation of financial markets. When I first wrote about it, the resulting paper was presented to a fringe meeting of the Copenhagen Summit on Social Development. A translated version of that paper has been in the top six of the Italian bestseller list — non-fiction, I should add — for more than six months. At the same time the founder of the American Communitarian movement, Amitai Etzioni, gave it prominence in his journal *The Responsive Community*. The thesis also formed the background of the work of the Commission on Wealth Creation and Social Cohesion which I had the pleasure to chair. Its Report was recently debated in the House of Lords, and I have spoken about it on more than one occasion.

The core thesis is simple. Internationalised modern economies pose a social and political dilemma. In free societies, the search for competitiveness seems to damage social cohesion. If, on the other hand, such free societies choose to give social cohesion a higher priority, their competitiveness and with it their prosperity are at risk. Some countries, or at least their leaders, insist on competitiveness but do not want to sacrifice social cohesion and seem to achieve this by restricting political freedom. More and more people think that you can have two but not all three: prosperity and cohesion without freedom; prosperity and freedom without civility; civility and freedom without prosperity. What would need to be done to square the circle?

The thesis sounds abstract but is in fact very close to the experience of many. In fact, the rest of my lecture is the tale of three cities, in different parts of the world, admittedly unequal in size but each in its way a part of the story that needs to be told. To the three I shall then add a sketch of a fourth, not exactly a city on the hill, but one that approximates the unachievable and nearly squares the circle of prosperity, civility and liberty.

The first city is a small town in the Middle West of the United States of America. Twenty years ago, the engine manufacturer was at the heart of the lives of its 40,000 or so inhabitants. Most of them were directly or indirectly employed by the company. The local hospital thrived on company-supported health schemes. The local college benefited from direct donations and of course the ability of well-paid parents to pay fees for their children's studies. Famous architects were invited by the company to design public buildings. Sports teams and amateur orchestras, school trips and retirement parties and much else, including a well-known French chef to please the palates of visitors, all owed their wherewithal to the company.

Then the winds of internationalisation hit the happy township with gale force. In two waves, several thousand employees were made redundant. Many of them found other jobs — we are, one must remember, in America — but these were, and are jobs at half the previous income and without any of the old perks. The hospital closed most of its specialist departments; the college lost its standing with its distinguished teachers; what is left of fun and games is no longer public and communal but has withdrawn to the virtual reality of television. The company is still competitive and successful, but the town is a sad shadow of its former self.

The example may sound a little too neat to be true; my friend, the chairman and chief executive of the company, would probably say that I overstated the change; moreover, the example is that of a one-factory town, and such towns have always been vulnerable. Also, American examples are unique in that they are set in a cultural environment unlike others, unlike in particular that of Britain. The capacity for job creation is but one relevant difference; the strength of civil society, and corresponding weakness of central government, is another. Yet when all is said and done, the city tells the Anglo-American story of the last fifteen years.

Turning to Britain, the emphasis of public policy was on creating conditions of competitive growth and encouraging entrepreneurs from both home and abroad to make use of this environment. The contribution of public policy to this end followed almost IMF style recipes (or were these recipes borrowed from the American experience in the first place?): (relatively) low direct taxation, (relatively) low non-wage labour cost, greater labour market flexibility, low entry cost for new companies, de-regulation, privatisation of state enterprises, in a word, the withdrawal of the State from the economic playing field. This environment allowed companies to become leaner and perhaps fitter; it opened the door to experimentation with allegedly optimal company sizes; it encouraged inward investment. Compared with those who took another route, the performance of the British economy in these fifteen years may not have been astounding; there certainly was no economic miracle; but Britain did better than was to be expected on past performance.

All this, moreover, was achieved under the auspices of elected governments and with the support of Parliament. Whatever the constitutional issues which have become a part of public debate may be, and however much Charter 88 and others may worry about civil liberties and democratic institutions, there can be little doubt that the constitution of liberty is basically alive and well in Britain.

If there is another side to this picture, it is social, and this is serious. Its most telling expression is the fact that in the mid-1990s, GNP growth is no longer an indicator of people's well-being. While governments still triumphantly produce macro-economic statistics, voters feel that something has gone wrong, or at least not gone right. The very concept of wealth has become an issue. (It has been that in the United States for some time, at least since Robert Reich, President Clinton's Labour Secretary, put it into the stark words that for the first time in American history parents have to tell their children that they will not be as well off as they, the parents, are). Wealth, in the full sense of Adam Smith's use of the word, or better still, well-being is obviously not a direct result of competitiveness.

The reasons for this disjunction are many. One is that the class which expected to be the harbinger of a better future, the middle class, is the main victim of the new competitiveness thrust. From (very) early retirement, if not outright redundancy, to a flagging housing market, middle class disenchantment has many causes and facets. They even include the reduced services of the Welfare State which paradoxically — some would say, perversely — always benefited the middle classes as much as the poor. Another reason why competitiveness does not produce happiness is the weakening of stakeholder relationships in favour of the cruder cash nexus of shareholders who can buy and sell their interest all too easily. The diminishing role of local communities tells the story most dramatically.

Looking at the wider society, the most serious effect of a leaner and fitter economy is the new exclusion of large social groups. This takes a number of forms. One is, lateral exclusion, or with a more drastic word, xenophobia. Frightened citizens do not like strangers. Another form of exclusion is the new poverty. It is now widely recognised that flexibility, especially labour market flexibility, has side-effects. It may well be that the most flexible economies create more jobs than the rigid ones, but a significant number of these jobs are so low-paid that they leave their holders unable to sustain a decent standard of living. The figures produced by the Rowntree Trust about growing inequalities are most significant with respect to the absolute position of poverty among the lowest paid twenty per cent. Then there is the underclass of those who have lost all hope of being a part of the labour market, the political community, civil society. Some say that as many as ten per cent have dropped to this status. The figure of twenty plus ten would tally with the 40:30:30 society described by Will Hutton in his book, *The State We're In*: 40 per cent fairly secure middle class, 30 per cent in a precarious and shifting condition, 30 per cent excluded in one way or another.

The precise figures are important but not the main point of the argument. Nor is the threat of revolution the point. The excluded will not start a new revolutionary movement. The problem is, in the most serious sense of the word, moral. A society which claims to be civil but tolerates the exclusion of significant numbers from its opportunities, has betrayed the values on which it is based. The citizens of such a society cannot be surprised if its values are flouted not just by the excluded themselves but by anyone who sees what is going on, and notably by the young. This is where the link between social exclusion and threats to law and order becomes apparent. It is not that the long-term unemployed let alone the single mothers of the underclass are the main perpetrators of crime (their main offence is for the most part to defraud an ineffectual social security system); the point is that the existence of such groups encourages others to ignore and then violate the civic values which are apparently no longer taken seriously.

The combination of greedy individualism and new exclusion is a high price to pay for macro-economic success in a free society. Our major partners in Continental Europe are as yet not ready to pay the price. They cling to what is variously called, *économie sociale* or *soziale Marktwirtschaft*, to a social market economy. In France or Germany or Italy, as in Britain, the constitution of liberty is an accepted framework. Democracy and the rule of law may not be as firmly anchored as in the Anglo-Saxon world, and may even have another meaning for many, but they are by and large beyond dispute. The difference is in the relative weight given to economic and social factors of well-being.

Another city comes to mind, somewhat larger than the one-factory town which I described earlier, and in Italy. While not a one-factory town, the beautiful place is basically a one-industry town. One way or another, everyone is connected with food-processing, including the production of machines for the purpose. The town is closely linked to its surrounding countryside where much of the food for processing is produced. It is justly proud of the quality of its products. But more, its economic community is as close-knit as its social and political texture. If any one of the dozens of small and medium-sized companies is in trouble, the others will help. Enthusiasm for the local football club is general, especially since it has become a contender for the national championship. The local radio and television station, as well as the leading newspaper, are owned by the industrialists' association. The companies also sustain a theatre and a gallery. People naturally like good eating for which the city is famous. It is indeed the envy of many.

And competitiveness? Global markets? Just recently, a trace of fear has crept into the European city. At first, confident producers would not believe that cheaper 'imitation' products could sweep the market; but when the first supermarket began to sell them outside the city boundaries, they began to wonder. Of course they believe that their tomato concentrate is better than tomato ketchup (of which there may soon be a synthetic variety); but young people will insist on covering everything they eat in cheap ketchup and will not ever buy what our civic entrepreneurs regard as the real thing. Moreover, contrary to their peers in the French province of Champagne, they failed to patent the name of the city as a brand name; suddenly, 'their' products appear from all over the European Union and beyond. Even the largest of the many companies begins to worry. And so this apparently healthy and happy town runs into the problems which we can now observe all over the European continent.

The profound differences in economic culture between Britain and its European partners are often underrated. Despite the fact that the winds of globalisation are common to all, these differences are unlikely to go away. Companies on the continent are for the most part not simply profit machines for shareholders; even in published statistics, turnover is regarded as more significant than profit or market capitalisation. Companies are even ranked by the number of people they employ, the implication being that high employment marks a positive contribution to the social economy. As a result — or as a part of the same syndrome — people saw no particular problem in high taxes, high non-wage labour cost, a well-financed Welfare State, low labour mobility. For many, a pay-as-you-go pension system, or as Germans prefer to call it, a 'contract between generations' is maintained by which today's workers pay for yesterday's and pensions are therefore not funded. This may well be the key difference between economic cultures, and also the one which raises the largest questions at a time at which the working population is shrinking and the retired population is growing apace.

For not only is the second city of my tale beginning to worry, the entire social market economy of Continental Europe is under strain. Sweden's transformation in recent years has been commented on by many. A country which used to have no unemployment and a cradle-to-grave Welfare State (as well as prohibitive taxes which drove many of the most successful abroad) has undergone a dramatic transformation. In fact, this was, and is, traumatic as much as dramatic, for it touches the core of Sweden's self-image and national pride. Many think that Germany will have to go down the same road. There are certainly indications: large-scale redundancies in major companies; a serious debate about the attractiveness, or otherwise, of Germany for business; massive cuts in public expenditure; increasing individual contributions to Welfare State services. The list is long, and familiar, and the issues dominate public and political debate.

However, there is little reason for *Schadenfreude* on the part of those who have been through the purgatory of competitiveness already. The main themes of socio-economic policy-making are very different in Britain and in, say, Germany. (It must be noted in passing that this does not exactly help European integration.) But it would be wrong to assume that as each country tackles its own perils, we are all eventually moving to the same destination. Economic cultures run as deep as the cultures of language and literature, or of governance. There may be a certain degree of convergence but despite exposure to the same winds of internationalisation, pension systems, levels of taxation, welfare arrangements, the role of stakeholders, of local communities, and even the structure of firms will remain very different in the English-speaking countries from those who speak French or German or Italian or Spanish. It may be that the new democracies of East Central Europe will find that their dream of emulating the social market economies cannot be realised for lack of resources, and that they will have to move therefore in the Anglo-Saxon direction. One country, the Czech Republic, has already done so. In any case, a true convergence of economic culture in Europe is very unlikely for a long time to come.

East Central Europe of course is not just faced with the alternative of individualistic Anglo-Saxon competitiveness and the social market economy. There is a third mode of combining economic, social and political factors, a third city as it were. It is beyond doubt competitive, indeed it is often held up as a model for economic success in internationalising markets. But competitiveness and increasing prosperity is not all. The third city — larger than the other two, and in Asia — also places great emphasis on social cohesion. It actually has public policies explicitly designed 'to promote social cohesiveness'. One central element of these policies is a gigantic organisation which provides people with housing. More than eighty per cent of the population come under its control. People have to buy their apartments and cannot sell them without permission. Moreover, the housing agency places them in estates in which the various ethnic groups of the city are represented in proportion to their strength. Once resident in their housing estate people assume a number of obligations to look after others, and they are looked after themselves in case of need.

The organisation of housing is only a part of a comprehensive system of state-backed social control. Young people are guided through the educational system in accordance with their assessed abilities. If they make it to a university degree they are even likely to be sent out to sea for cruises on 'marriage ships' with graduates of the opposite sex, in the expectation that they will breed a new generation of graduates. (Echoes of the eugenics debate among Fabians and other early social engineers a century ago?) The State determines not only in general terms but often in detail how people are to behave. They must not chew gum or throw away cigarette ends for example. Such laws are enforced rigorously. Even minor trespasses are punished by caning or prison sentences.

And of course this paradise without crime or unemployment, without eccentrics or dissidents is also a place in which political life is strictly regulated. The local papers report much about the evils of the rest of the world but only government pronouncements from home. Foreign papers are allowed in as long as they are compliant; if not, they are banned or sued. Those locals who tried to stand for opposition parties — and in two or three cases were actually elected to parliament — soon found their activities severely curtailed, if not cut short by trumped-up charges which ended them in prison.

This is the 'Asia that can say no' (to quote the prime minister of a State neighbouring on my third city). It is competitive and cohesive but certainly not free. It is, in the terms of political science, authoritarian. Authoritarian does not mean totalitarian; as long as people do their own thing, abide by the laws and abstain from meddling in public affairs, they are left unmolested. The temptation of such authoritarianism is not confined to Asia. I mentioned East Central Europe. The return of former communists to political power is at least in part due to the nostalgia of elderly voters for the orderly world of late communism with its full employment, institutionalised child care, secure if modest housing at low rents, complete welfare services, and the famous 'niches' of privacy in which people were allowed to enjoy their 'inner freedom' as long as they did not produce *samizdat* papers or support priests who refused to become poodles of the *nomenklatura*.

What is more, the temptation of authoritarianism is now widespread in the West. I have a growing file of utterances by Western businessmen and politicians, intellectuals and newspaper tycoons, which sound for example like this:

> Singapore is not liberal but clean and free of drug addicts. Not so long ago it was an impoverished, exploited colony with hunger, disease and other problems. Now people find themselves in three-bedroom apartments, with jobs and well-cleaned streets. Countries like Singapore take the right way forward.

Those who offered their thanks to Britain when it gave them shelter will remember similar descriptions of Nazi Germany at the time of the 1936 Olympics, and of course Mussolini's promise to make Italian trains run on time. This is not to say that authoritarianism is bound to lead to totalitarianism. On the contrary, while totalitarianism is inherently catastrophic and therefore unstable, authoritarian government can last for a long time. A new authoritarianism may indeed be the main challenge to liberal democracy in the decades to come. If we are prosperous and secure, why worry about liberty?

The answer is that liberty is untidy and complex, it is full of disunity and conflict, it demands activity rather than allowing passive withdrawal, but it is the only condition which enables us to be our best selves and enhance the life chances of all. Karl Popper has put this well in his peroration on the open society: 'If we wish to remain human,' he said, 'we must go on into the unknown, the uncertain and insecure, using what reason we may have to plan for both security *and* freedom.' Long before Popper, Immanuel Kant in his 'Idea for a Universal History with Cosmopolitan Intent' had mocked man's dream of an Arcadia in which 'people, good-natured like the sheep in their pastures, would give their existence no greater value than their animal flocks have.' Fortunately (thus Kant) 'nature' has endowed humans with contradictions, and notably with that of 'unsocial sociability'. Humans want peace and quiet but nature knows better what is good for them: it wants conflict and change. This is what liberty means. How do we bring it about? By creating, says Kant, a 'civil society within the rule of law.'

This is a British Academy lecture, not a parliamentary speech or even an address to a fringe meeting of the United Nations. I feel free, therefore, to end with principles rather than policy prescriptions. Not that it would be difficult to present such prescriptions. They would range from incentives for long-term investment to reforms of the Welfare State, from a new approach to education based on individual learning accounts to an improvement of economic reporting by a wealth audit. However, behind such specific policy proposals there is the search for an application of Kant's vision and Popper's moral imperative to contemporary Europe, and to Britain within it.

The key to squaring the circle is strengthening, and in part rebuilding civil society. This is notably the task in Britain where much has been done to enhance economic competitiveness, and democratic institutions are still strong. By civil society I mean that texture of our lives with others which does not need governments to sustain it because it is created by grass-root initiatives. Tocqueville called it democracy, though the institutional connotation is misleading. James Madison at the time of the foundation of democracy in America praised civil society as a guarantee of liberty because by being 'broken into so many parts, interests and classes of citizens', it curbs even majority rule. No word describes better the 'parts, interests and classes of citizens' which civil society is about than *association*. The creative chaos of associations coalesces as if guided by an invisible hand into the setting in which the greatest number find the greatest life chances. In economic terms, the market describes that setting; in political terms, it is the public. Nowadays, both are mediated in numerous ways; the days of simple markets, or indeed of the public assembling outside the town hall for debate and decision, are almost gone. But the principles of both are still valid. The market and the public are where the associations of civil society interact.

In other words, there is such a thing as society. What is more, there has to be if we do not want to end up in a state of anomy. The word 'association' also indicates the necessary element of cohesion in civil society. Apart from the indispensable framework of the rule of law, the associations of civil society represent values of trust and co-operation, and of inclusion. A civil society is a society of citizens who have rights and accept obligations, and who behave in a civil and civilised manner towards each other. It is a society which tries to make sure that no one is excluded, and which offers its members a sense of belonging as well as a constitution of liberty.

This is no Utopia. For a century after the Civil War the United States of America was certainly driven by the aspiration to be such a civil society. The same can be said for the United Kingdom during the larger part of the twentieth century. In Canada and Australia, but also in Sweden and Switzerland, other versions of achieving the same aspirations could be found. For a while after the Second World War, the entire First World was in these terms quite a good place to live in. The trouble is that so many of these statements now have to be made in the past tense. Somehow or other, either prosperity or civility or liberty (if not two of these or even all three) have taken a knock almost everywhere. That is why rebuilding civil society under new conditions is so important.

What then of the fourth city in my tale? First of all, it has to be a city. Whether it numbers 40,000, 180,000 or 2.5 million inhabitants, it must be an identifiable community with a strong sense of local commitment and institutions to match it. The city itself is an element of civil society. In economic terms, a variety of companies of different sizes and branches of business is obviously desirable. More important, indeed essential for economic well-being is, however, a combination of competitiveness and stakeholder involvement. If one wants to avoid fashionable language one could say that companies need to seek arrangements which assure as far as possible their long-term success and engender relations of trust and commitment with all who are involved in their fortunes. This is actually what many companies are groping for today, and the best provide benchmarks for the rest. Individuals have to respond to the analogous dual challenge of flexibility and security. People's lives will look different than they did in the days of old-style careers in an expectation of full employment. Security is no longer built into the world of work, or of education for that matter; people have to carry it with and within them, which means that their entitlements have to be transportable, and their strength lies in their skills including the ability to go on adjusting and enhancing them. There are signs that women find it easier to cope with the new balance of flexibility and security than men; perhaps they had to do so earlier. In institutional as well as personal terms, associations in the narrow and the organised sense will play a major part. The tradition of voluntarism, of volunteering as well as charitable giving, will see a new flowering. The result will be untidy and imperfect, it will not do away with pain and fear, or with conflict, but it may point the way to a prosperous, civil and liberal world.

My first city was in North America, the second in Continental Europe, the third in South East Asia — it would be fitting if the fourth emerged in the country to which this thank-offering is given, Britain.

DAVID ABERCROMBIE

Proceedings of the British Academy, **90**, 239–248

David Abercrombie
1909–1992

DAVID ABERCROMBIE was *the* British phonetician following Daniel Jones in the second half of the twentieth century. He redefined the subject, creating general phonetics as a university discipline that had not previously existed. But by the time of his death on 4 July 1992, new technology and a world with different needs had led to yet another change in the nature of the field.

Abercrombie was born on 19 December 1909 into an idyllic Edwardian world. His father was the poet Lascelles Abercrombie, who came from a large, prosperous Manchester family. For most of his first five years David Abercrombie lived in Ryton, a tiny hamlet in Gloucestershire. The American poet Robert Frost shared the house for part of that time, and the well known war poet Rupert Brooke was a visitor. Abercrombie particularly liked Brooke because he treated him like an adult.

When the First World War came, the family moved to Liverpool, where Lascelles Abercrombie, who was unfit for military service, became an inspector of munitions. They stayed in Liverpool until 1922, as after the war Lascelles Abercrombie became a Lecturer in Poetry at Liverpool University. David Abercrombie was sent to school at Liverpool College, suffering from the bullies of the time. When his father was appointed Professor of English Literature at the University of Leeds he was transferred to Leeds Grammar School. He went on to the university and received a Third Class Honours BA in English from Leeds in 1930. That was the highest formal academic level he ever achieved, perhaps explaining why he, an interesting, innovative, meticulous scholar of the highest level in his own right, never set much store on academic credentials.

He originally intended to continue his studies by taking an MA in English Language, writing a thesis on i-mutation, but a meeting with the dominant phonetician of the time, Professor Daniel Jones of University College, London, led to a change of plans. Jones cast his spell and Abercrombie became a student in his department. In order to understand Abercrombie's later contribution to the field of phonetics, it is necessary to understand the status of phonetics in 1930. Daniel Jones was at the height of his power. Over the preceding quarter of a century he had built up a remarkable department, instilling in his junior colleagues great ability in the production and perception of a wide range of sounds. They were skilled teachers of the pronunciation of many of the world's major languages. But the emphasis was on the individual languages and their sounds, and not on the nature of spoken language as a whole.

Abercrombie's colleagues at University College included J. R. Firth (who went on to become Britain's first Professor of General Linguistics), Ida Ward (who became Professor of West African Languages), Hélène Coustenoble (a notable French scholar who helped Abercrombie acquire his impeccable French pronunciation), and Stephen Jones, who was in charge of the UC phonetics laboratory and showed him the value of instrumental records of speech. All these and others, such as Bronislaw Malinowski, the anthropologist at the London School of Economics (where Abercrombie taught English as a Second Language and French from 1934 to 1938), and C. K. Ogden, the philosopher and inventor of Basic English, had a great influence on him. But none of these scholars, including Daniel Jones, shared his vision of phonetics as a basic university subject.

During World War II Abercrombie developed his view of the nature of phonetics. In 1939 when war broke out he had been teaching for a year at the British Council Institute at Athens. Others on the staff there included the phoneticians Ian Catford and Elizabeth Uldall, and the novelist Lawrence Durrell, whom Abercrombie recruited to teach Basic English. The German invasion of Greece in 1940 pushed the British first into Cyprus, and then into Egypt, where Abercrombie was employed in various government activities, as well as being a lecturer at the University of Cairo. He met Mary Marble, an American journalist who was working for the Office of Strategic Services, the forerunner of the Central Intelligence Agency, in 1943. Through his own official duties he had access to the British dossier on her, which must have been to his satisfaction, as they were married in 1944. At the end of the war, worrying, as he told his new wife, that he had no market value, he returned to England. Fortunately he found that he was able to take up his former position at the London School of Economics.

In 1947 Abercrombie was appointed as a Lecturer in Phonetics in the Department of English (his and his father's old department) at the University of Leeds. This took him closer to the ambition he had been nurturing to teach phonetics as a general university subject, but it was still not what he had planned. In 1948, when Edinburgh University invited him to start a Phonetics Department, he jumped at the chance. The following year saw the first year-long course in phonetics, attended by his wife and members of staff. The only regular student was his step-daughter, who was just beginning her first year at university.

From then on phonetics flourished at Edinburgh. Elizabeth Uldall had already joined the staff as a lecturer in 1949, and others soon followed. (The present writer was an Assistant Lecturer, later Lecturer, from 1953 to 1961.) By 1965, at its peak, the department had a staff of twelve, including three who went on to become well known professors (Gillian Brown first at Essex, now at Cambridge, Klaus Kohler at Kiel, and John Laver, who now holds a personal Chair at Edinburgh), as well as Walter Lawrence, the retired designer of the first parametric speech synthesizer, PAT. In 1964 Abercrombie was appointed to a personal Chair in Phonetics; this became an established Chair in 1967, just before the Department of Phonetics was amalgamated with the Department of General Linguistics, and then the School of Applied Linguistics, to form the Department of Linguistics. He retired in 1980, but continued to be active in the field. He was elected to the British Academy in 1991.

What was Abercrombie's view of phonetics as embodied in his Ordinary Course (the Edinburgh term for a year-long general introductory course in a subject)? It began, not surprisingly, with an account of the speech production mechanism. But it was a much more complete account of human phonetic capabilities than had been heretofore available for beginning students. Early on, students were introduced to the possibilities of different airstream mechanisms, as Abercrombie was well aware of the interest stimulated by discussions of clicks and ejectives. At the same time as this account of the set of possible speech sounds was being developed, students were introduced to phonetic transcription, gradually becoming experts in transcribing their own and others' speech. Abercrombie was the first person to make clear that there were many factors underlying the distinction between a broad and a narrow transcription. He pointed out that one transcription could be narrower than another because it used more specific symbols, such as **ɹ** instead of **r**, or symbols with diacritics such as **ḍ** instead of **d**. Alternatively it could be narrower in quite a different way, namely in that it used a greater number of symbols, distinguishing allophones such as English initial **t**[h] and final **ˀt**.

Abercrombie's Ordinary Course introduced students to the sounds of a wide range of languages and many different accents of English, with Scottish English and Scots dialects being given a prominent place. Abercrombie was far from an advocate of his own upper-class English accent, received pronunciation (RP), as the most important form of English pronunciation. His egalitarian views on accents of English were no doubt shaped by teaching in Scotland, having an American wife and step-children, and his own non-élitist politics.

The Ordinary Course also included lectures on instrumental phonetic techniques and acoustic phonetics, usually given by other members of his staff. Abercrombie saw the necessity for students to have some laboratory experience to round out their phonetic studies. He also stressed the importance of students becoming practically adept phoneticians, and not just experts in the theory of phonetic description. Ear training and performance exercises were an important part of the courses that he taught, often occupying forty per cent of the teaching time (two out of the five teaching hours a week).

Abercrombie never wrote a book corresponding to the full Ordinary Course. His introductory book, *Elements of General Phonetics* should perhaps have been titled 'Topics in General Phonetics', as it leaves out much that he considered to be at the core of the subject. The book begins with one of his major contributions to linguistic thought, the clear distinction between a language and the medium for expressing that language. A language is a system of rules for organising abstract lexical items into sentences. The medium, which can take several different forms, is the method for conveying messages in that system. The medium may be the physical sounds that phonetics describes, or the letters and devices used in written communications, or the bumps of Braille, or the waving of semaphore flags. Abercrombie points out that the medium, be it sounds or written letters or anything else, is an artefact created by humans. As such, as well as conveying linguistic information, it conveys something about whoever produced it. It does this by what Abercrombie (following the philosopher Charles S. Peirce) calls indexical features. Thus speech provides an index of the group to which the speaker belongs, a mark of the personal characteristics of the individual, and information on the speaker's physical or mental states such as excitement or drunkenness. The medium also has aesthetic properties which come to the fore in poetry (a natural interest of Abercrombie's), advertising slogans, and songs.

The main part of the book following this introductory material is an account of the mechanisms involved in the production of speech. What Abercrombie has to say on this topic is now commonplace, but when it appeared it incorporated many points, such as the nature of stress and an account of the possible airstream mechanisms, which had previously been available only in technical publications. There are also good accounts of basic topics such as the structure of syllables, phoneme theory and assimilation. It does all this in the most clear and simple way possible. Abercrombie took immense pains with his writing. He made sure that each thought followed logically, and was clearly expressed. Irrelevant points were cut out and difficult expressions simplified. As he once said to me, 'It is often difficult to get each sentence exactly right, but it is worth spending hours trying to do so.'

Some of the limitations of *Elements of General Phonetics* are due to its incomplete coverage of the field, but others can be ascribed to Abercrombie's aesthetic susceptibilities. In the Foreword he wrote: 'I hope that I have been able to show that it is possible to present the subject, or at least its elements, without disfiguring the text with the somewhat repulsive diagrams of the vocal organs and the exotic phonetic symbols which, for the general reader, are apt to make it seem unattractive.'

It is probably not feasible to do this. Not only are diagrams essential to show movements of the vocal organs that would need a thousand words to describe, but also phonetic symbols, some of them somewhat exotic, are at the heart of work in the field, and the text would have been more helpful in leading students on to further study if it had included more phonetic transcription.

Abercrombie's views on proper publication also had unfortunate results on another occasion. He was delighted when he heard from a friend of his on the editorial board that his book, *English Phonetic Texts* (1964) had been accepted for publication by Faber and Faber, notable publishers of poets such as T. S. Eliot. But as a result an important book never became widely available to the phonetic community. Faber and

Faber published an edition of only 1,000 copies, and had no real interest in promoting a book so different from the stock-in-trade of their regular list. So the careful exegesis and exemplification of different types of transcription, a subject on which Abercrombie was probably the world's leading authority, has taken much longer to have its full impact.

In addition to his wide knowledge of the theory and practice of different styles of phonetic transcription, Abercrombie was the foremost authority on the history of phonetics. One could ask him about almost any technical term in phonetics and he could tell you when it was first used and what its original meaning was. His paper on Isaac Pitman (1937) and his communication to the Philological Society on 'Forgotten Phoneticians' (1949) were early work in this area. Throughout his career he taught courses discussing the works of the nineteenth-century phoneticians, Bell, Ellis, and Sweet. At the time of his death he was still working on his study of the English phonetician William Holder, whose *Elements of Speech* was published in 1669. (This study has now been put into publishable form by his former student and colleague, Alan Kemp.)

The other main area of Abercrombie's research was the study of prosody and rhythm. Sometimes he was able to combine this with his historical interests, as in his paper on 'Steele, Monboddo and Garrick', in which he describes Garrick's performance of the soliloquy 'To be or not to be' in an eighteenth-century production of *Hamlet*, based on an early publication by Joshua Steele. At other times his work in this area reflected his long-standing interest in poetry, as in his 'A Phonetician's View of Verse Structure' (1967), or his concern with the contribution of phonetics to the teaching of English as a foreign language, as in his paper on 'Syllable Quantity and Enclitics' (1964). He was not a believer in the strict isochronicity of stressed syllables in English as might be evidenced (but is not) in laboratory records; but he showed very nicely how 'silent stresses', which he wrote with a stress mark in parentheses ('), might occur to maintain the rhythm, as at the ends of the first, second and last lines in a limerick:

> An 'elderly 'lady from 'Ryde (')
> Ate 'too many 'apples and 'died. (')
> The 'apples fer'mented
> In'side the la'mented
> Making 'cider in'side her in'side. (')

Abercrombie did not do much work in the phonetics laboratory himself, although he was always very encouraging of the endeavours

of others, even being a subject in a number of experiments. He wrote a
paper on palatography (1957), and another on speech synthesis in
parametric terms (1969). These and other valuable contributions are
included in his two collections of papers, *Studies in Phonetics and
Linguistics* (1965) and *Fifty Years in Phonetics* (1991). The latter
book includes an essay with the same title as the book, which is in
itself an excellent appraisal of his work.

Abercrombie had an extraordinarily wide range of interests, encompassing virtually anything related to speech and much related to the
other principal medium of language, writing. He never lost his interest
in Basic English, welcoming its approval by the War Cabinet in 1943.
He also conducted a lengthy correspondence with Sir James Pitman
concerning the parliamentary debates on Simplified Spelling. His interests in these topics were, however, more those of a scholar rather than
an advocate.

His outside interests included wine, malt whisky and cricket. His
students became educated in many of the different tastes of France and
Scotland, as well as in phonetics. He kept a diary for part of his life, but
seldom recorded much beyond appointments and incidental facts such
as 'Cricket vs. Streatham. Took 4 wickets' (31 May 1937), and 'played
cricket against Cyprus garrison' (11 May 1940).

Abercrombie retired in 1980, and, after an abortive attempt to fill his
Chair, two of the three subject heads in the Department of Linguistics
decided that filling the established Chair in Phonetics was not a departmental priority. Although this was probably not in their minds, in doing
so they were reflecting the fact that Abercrombie's definition of the field
of phonetics was becoming less appropriate. The reasons for studying
speech differ from generation to generation. In Abercrombie's hey-day
phonetics was important in a variety of ways. Abercrombie saw speech
as the primary means of conveying linguistic information ('the medium
of spoken language' as he would say), and also as a source of socio-
linguistic information ('indexical behaviour' in his terminology) and
personal data ('idiosyncratic information'). He was also concerned with
the relation between speech and poetry, speech and writing, and speech
as a window into the mind. In his view, phonetics should be of interest
to anyone with a natural curiosity about life.

Times have now changed, and although many of these aspects of
speech are still of concern, our motives for studying them are somewhat
different. Since the advent of Chomsky, who is clearly one of the most
powerful thinkers of the second half of this century, it is language, not

speech, that is the most fashionable object of study, and syntax, rather than phonology, is generally seen as the central core of language. The grammar of a language includes its phonology and how the sounds are related to phonetic substance, as well as its semantics and how utterances are related to observable meanings, but the study of language has at its heart the morphology of words and the syntax of sentences. Phonetics is thus now seen by linguists as on the periphery of general linguistics.

We must also note that the kind of phonetics that Abercrombie taught is no longer the centre-piece of many university departments because it is no longer the centre of so much research activity. There is still much to be learned about sounds and sound systems, but, largely due to the organisation of phonetic knowledge by Abercrombie and people like him, the bases of phonetics are quite clear. The same is not true of syntax, where ongoing research is continually leading to new ways of looking at the fundamental premises of the field. A textbook such as Abercrombie's *Elements of General Phonetics* (1967) can still stand as a valid account of much of the subject, something which is not true of any elementary textbook on syntax written nearly thirty years ago.

The study of other phonetic topics, such as the role of speech in conveying socio-linguistic and personal information, have not diminished in importance, but they have also changed in many ways. Nowadays we are less concerned with the acquisition of certain accents, such as a native French pronunciation, and more concerned with straightforward description of different accents so that our speech recognition machines can handle them. This kind of work is very much in the spirit of Abercrombie's teaching, and his contributions in this area are still important. He described many aspects of Scottish English and other dialects that had not been previously observed. His thinking on the idiosyncratic aspects of speech is also significant. His publications include valuable discussions of voice quality and the contribution of the other strands of speech that contribute to the individual characteristics of a person's voice.

The fact remains, however, that nowadays there are fewer departments teaching anything like the Ordinary Course in Phonetics. It is interesting to consider what Abercrombie might have done now, if he were once again a young person asked to start a Department of Phonetics. He would probably place the same emphasis on distinguishing between language and medium. He would also require phoneticians to be skilled performers in the tradition of Bell, Sweet and Jones, which he followed. He would have looked askance at events at a recent scientific meeting (the XIVth International Congress of Phonetic Sciences), where it transpired that several leading participants were unable to produce clicks and ejectives in words. We can speculate on what he would have thought about the new emphasis on Communication Engineering. He was always eager to keep up with the latest technical advances, acquiring in 1950 one of the first Kay sound spectrographs outside the United States for his department. When, in 1953, he heard about speech synthesized by Walter Lawrence on the Parametric Artificial Talker (PAT), he enthusiastically endorsed the idea of research in this field at Edinburgh. Nobody else in the Faculty of Arts at that time had government funding. Abercrombie led the way in securing for his department a contract for basic scientific research. In his later years he felt that the subject of phonetics in the form in which he had helped to establish it was somewhat threatened by the rapid technical advances and government research funds that led to the establishment of a very large Centre for Speech Technology Research at Edinburgh, which he viewed as swallowing up his former department. But if he had been a young person in charge, starting again, he might well have realised that that was the way of the future.

What is also certain is that he would have created a department in which there was a great deal of *esprit de corps*. Abercrombie was a remarkable leader, inspiring others to do their best. He was always willing to discuss current research or teaching problems, and to offer shrewd advice, making his department a happy place for staff and students alike. He enjoyed company, and, along with his wife Mary, welcomed visitors. At their ever-open house he would gently express concern with all aspects of the lives of his associates, while Mary merrily offered her own wisdom, and softly kept him in check. Their sherry parties, on the first Sunday of every month, were known world-wide.

Finally, on a personal note, I must acknowledge my great indebtedness to him. I always felt honoured when people referred to me as his pupil, but it was not until after I had finished writing my own textbook (Ladefoged 1975, 1993) that I fully realised how much I owed to him. As I wrote in the Preface, 'My greatest debt is to David Abercrombie, from whom I first learned what I took to be the commonly accepted dogma of phonetics; only later did I discover that many of the ideas were his own contribution to the field.' But my debts go far beyond the merely intellectual knowledge he bestowed on me. I was very lucky to have him as a teacher and a friend.

Abercrombie was a teacher who never made one feel as stupid as one often was. Only a year before his death I went to visit him and found him sitting surrounded by his books. 'Have you read this?' he asked, 'Or this, you really must.' 'No, David,' I replied, feeling about forty years younger and realising how ignorant I was. But, as in those earlier days, I got the books he recommended, and went on learning from him. I still think over things he told me, and realise that I will always be his student. He organised the subject for his time, and earned his own place in the history of phonetics.

PETER LADEFOGED
Fellow of the Academy

Note.   I am indebted for much helpful information to Mary Abercrombie, Mary Brown, John Laver and Elizabeth Uldall.

References

A complete bibliography of Professor Abercrombie's publications up to 1980 was published by Elizabeth Uldall in *Towards a History of Phonetics*, R. Asher and E. Henderson eds., (Edinburgh University Press (1981). Most of his later work is in Abercrombie (1991).
Abercrombie, D. (1964) *English Phonetic Texts* (London).
Abercrombie, D. (1965) *Studies in Phonetics and Linguistics* (Oxford).
Abercrombie, D. (1967) *Elements of General Phonetics* (Edinburgh).
Abercrombie, D. (1991) *Fifty Years in Phonetics* (Edinburgh).
Ladefoged, P. (1975, 3rd ed., 1993) *A Course in Phonetics* (London).

NORMAN ANDERSON

Proceedings of the British Academy, **90**, 251–263

James Norman Dalrymple Anderson
1908–1994

A LAWYER AMONG THE THEOLOGIANS. That is not only the title of one of his many books, but goes some way towards providing a description of Norman Anderson, Christian missionary, Islamic lawyer, academic administrator, and churchman.

James Norman Dalrymple Anderson was born at Aldeburgh on 29 September 1908. His father whom he described as 'quiet, gentle, slow, thrifty and distinctly obstinate' had been a fellow-pupil at Liverpool College of F. E. Smith, the future Lord Chancellor as Earl of Birkenhead. Anderson's mother, 'talkative, dominant, impatient, and somewhat extravagant' with 'a positive passion for moving house and visiting ironmongers, in which she would buy countless pots and pans' had Jewish blood in her veins. Her grandfather was a rabbi, but her father had converted to Christianity. Anderson spent a rather lonely childhood; his sisters were much older, and his only brother died in infancy. He describes himself as having been 'quite exceptionally slow at learning to read'. Despite his later mastery of Arabic and the remarkable breadth of his reading, he was convinced throughout his life that he was a slow reader and a poor linguist.

The family environment was marked, as was Anderson's whole life, by Evangelical Christianity. He was sent to attend St Lawrence College, Ramsgate, a small public school with an Evangelical foundation. The school had a notably strong and active Christian Union. Anderson was once moved to attempt to pray all night, fortified by ginger beer: the attempt was unsuccessful. In the school's Classical Sixth, although he already judged himself 'a shockingly bad linguist', he proved an excellent debater, and this may have prompted the advice he was given to read Law.

He had a brilliant academic record at Trinity College, Cambridge. His papers in the Law Qualifying examination were the best of the year. He took a Double First in the Tripos, became a Senior Scholar of his college, and took another First in what was then the LLB in International Law. Modest individuals, and Norman Anderson was certainly that, are never very clear how they should explain such an outstanding academic record. Is it better to hint at days and nights of ceaseless toil, or to admit to the gift of a brilliant mind which needs no such expenditure of energy? The evidence of a lifelong friend, Lord Coggan, provides some evidence of the truth of the matter;

> One of the most interesting [inhabitants of] Trinity was a young man, tall and slim, often to be seen with a bag of golf clubs over his shoulders, and the initials were J.N.D.A. In the College next to him [St. John's] there was a very undistinguished chap who lay in bed in the morning and listened to the organ of Trinity College floating through his bedroom . . .
>
> These two young men saw quite a lot of one another, and that was very pleasant, except at one part of the year when the exams were drawing near. Then it was that the young man in St John's college would hear weary steps ascending to his room in First Court, a knock on the door — and not always that — and in came a languid and worn-looking young man carrying an enormous load of legal books, who then sank into one of my chairs and groaning, with groans that continued for the space of an hour, underlined (it seemed to me totally unnecessarily, because I could not think what it would do to him) the main points in the tomes in his hand. But at about 10 o'clock the demand went forth from him to the owner of the rooms, 'Make tea'.
>
> That little incident illustrates, I think, the unfairness of life, that a man who for eleven months apparently did not do a stroke of work then proceeded to carry off three Firsts in Law. Well, what you make about justice at the centre of the universe I do not know in the face of that.

However, life between examinations was not all sport. Norman Anderson became over his four years in Cambridge a leading member and ultimately President of the Cambridge Inter-Collegiate Christian Union. Through the CICCU 'missionary breakfasts' he was much attracted by the call to the 'mission field'. He had been destined for a career at the Bar, but became increasingly uncertain whether that was right for him. At one stage he actually switched to reading Theology, but reverted to

Law after three or four days. He had considered seeking ordination, but was not wholly at ease with some aspects of Church of England practice, notably what he regarded as the almost indiscriminate baptism of infants. He had not much enjoyed the Cambridge Union, finding undergraduate attempts at wit distinctly boring. He may have wondered whether his public speaking matched the robust and forceful style of advocacy then fashionable at the Bar.

His eventual decision to serve as a missionary in Egypt was clearly prompted by a sense of vocation. Anderson often recalled, perhaps wistfully, that he could point to no moment of 'conversion'. His Christian faith was a matter of dawning realisation rather than any sudden crisis. So it was with his decision to offer himself for missionary service. He did not attribute that decision to any instance of direct divine guidance; it was 'a question of much thought, hesitation and prayer leading to a growing conviction'. He had spent a long vacation in Egypt visiting his father and working with the Nile Mission Press. He visited the Givan family, now based in Alexandria, whom he had first met through beach missions in Criccieth, and soon became engaged to their daughter Patricia.

Anderson was accepted by the Egypt General Mission, as was his fiancée. She was initially sent to Ismailia, he to Cairo to study Arabic at the School of Oriental Studies, a branch of the American University in Cairo. He found the language very difficult, and became ill. The mission had the good sense to make an exception to the rule forbidding trainee missionaries from marrying. Norman Anderson and Pat Givan were married in 1933 in Alexandria. It was to prove a remarkable marriage. Each at different stages supported the other selflessly in their work, in ill-health, and in their shared experience of grief at the early deaths of all their three children.

Egypt had its indigenous Coptic Christians and an expatriate Christian community, but the focus of the missionary endeavour was on the Muslim inhabitants. It was in a sense unpromising work: essentially the missionary was 'there for the Lord to use', seeking whatever opportunities might present themselves for serious conversation on religious matters. With this in mind, Anderson became what might now be called 'an occasional student' at the University of Cairo, attending two sets of lectures. One set was on Arabic literature, the other on the Islamic law of personal status and family relations, lectures delivered to a mixed audience including Copts and other Christians. In his autobiography, Anderson recalled one especially interesting lecture on 'the evil effects of polygamy'. Many years later, he was to choose the reform of the law of polygamy as the subject of his presidential address to the Society of Public Teachers of Law.

Already Anderson felt the urge to write, and did so in Arabic. His first book, published in 1939, *Al-'Aql w'al-Iman* ('Faith and Reason') was designed to strengthen the faith of Christian students living in a non-Christian environment. It was shortly afterwards that he first lectured on 'The Evidence for the Resurrection', published as a booklet which remained in print for over forty years. It was the first of many pieces in which Anderson spoke or wrote as a lawyer, claiming to apply the lawyer's approach to the historical evidence as to the life, death and resurrection of Jesus Christ.

As the fortunes of war moved against the Allies, Anderson sent his family to safety in Kenya and volunteered for service with the British Army. Because of his knowledge of Arabic he was asked to serve with a group of Arab guerrilla fighters, refugees from Libya, and was commissioned as a captain in the Intelligence Corps. For the next six years his work was largely concerned with the future of the territories of Cyrenaica and Tripolitania which were eventually to be incorporated in the new kingdom of Libya. While serving as Secretary for Sanusi Affairs at GHQ Middle East Forces he worked closely with the future King Idris, whose claims the British were at that stage reluctant to recognise. As the Allies advanced he became Political Secretary in Tripolitania, rose to lieutenant-colonel and full colonel, and received first the MBE and then the OBE, both in the Military Division of the Order.

After the end of the War, he visited Jeddah with Field Marshal Lord Alanbrooke, Chief of Imperial General Staff, and met both King Ibn Sa'ud and his future successor Prince Sa'ud. He continued to prepare influential papers on the future of the Libyan territories and accompanied the Foreign Secretary, Ernest Bevin, to the Conference in Paris at which these matters were discussed. Much later, in 1960, he visited King Idris in Tripoli and received the Libyan Order of *Istiqlal* (independence).

When he left the Army in 1946, Anderson was thirty eight and, like many ex-servicemen, had to consider his future. He received an appointment that was to lay the foundations for much of his future work. This was a three-year post as Warden of Tyndale House, Cambridge, a new venture sponsored by the evangelical Inter-Varsity Fellowship to provide a residential library for advanced biblical research. The Andersons were provided with a house, and Norman with a place in which he could reflect and write; he retained a study there for the rest of his life. Collecting the library was a task in which he worked with such scholars as Henry Chadwick, and it was an experience which foreshadowed Anderson's responsibilities in the Institute of Advanced Legal Studies.

He became a student again, attending lectures in Arabic and in Hebrew. He soon found himself also giving lectures, first on Islam (principally to Colonial Office trainees) and then a full course on Islamic Law in the Cambridge Law Faculty. Islamic Law affects one seventh of the world's population, and he was one of the very few in England with both a legal background and a working knowledge of Arabic. Before the end of his wardenship at Tyndale House, he was offered and accepted a lectureship in Islamic Law at the School of Oriental and African Studies in the University of London.

So began Anderson's scholarly career in Islamic Law. It also marked the start of a heavy programme of foreign travel. He was anxious to shift the emphasis in Western studies of Islamic law from the principles worked out in the Indian sub-continent to the law of the countries of the Middle East and North Africa, of which he had some personal knowledge. Newly independent governments in many of those countries were intent on codification and, where possible, modernisation of their laws, and Anderson was fascinated to observe the interaction of Islamic principles and what were perceived to be the needs of a modern society. So he spent six months in 1949 and 1950 studying in Cairo, and later two periods of three months in each of West and East Africa. He also visited Sudan, becoming external examiner for the students of Islamic Law taking the London LL B there; he described, with some pain, the difficulty of reading scripts written in Arabic script under the stress of examination conditions.

This research led to articles on Islamic law reform in journals such as the *Muslim World* and to his first major work *Islamic Law in Africa*, a study published by HMSO in 1954. It made his reputation as a leading scholar in the field, and he was awarded the Cambridge LLD and appointed to a Chair at SOAS (having already been made a Reader in 1951, and Head of the Department of Law in 1953). In September 1955 he argued in *The Times* for a more thorough study of the way in which the principles of English law were being developed in the British colonies in Africa alongside customary law and in some places Islamic law. As he observed, 'Some of these territories are progressing so rapidly along the road to independence that it is scarcely possible that multiple law, and multiple courts, can long be tolerated, except, perhaps, in regard to family law.'

He was a natural choice to serve in 1956–7 on an international panel of jurists to advise, in just such a context, on the future form of the criminal law of Northern Nigeria, that part of Nigeria most influenced by Islam. The panel recommended the adoption of a code based on the Sudanese Criminal Code, and this recommendation was accepted. Anderson wrote articles in the *International and Comparative Law Quarterly* in 1959 and 1963 on successive phases of the work.

In 1958, Anderson travelled to North America in his dual role as Islamic and legal scholar. He lectured in Princeton on aspects of Islam and in the New York University's School of Law on Islamic law in the modern world. The text of the latter lectures was published in 1959. His achievement, through that and other publications, was to rescue Islamic law for jurists; he demonstrated its vital importance, too great for it to be the sole preserve of orientalists.

In the years that followed, the time Anderson could devote to scholarship was always limited by the many other burdens he so willingly accepted. His finest scholarly work was undoubtedly his study of *Law Reform in the Muslim World* published in 1976, a development of ideas and insights earlier expounded in his 1959 book. It was at once a survey of the history of Islamic law over the previous century and a profound reflection on the task of law reform, though limited to the countries of which the author had some first-hand experience. Lawyers will always seek to protect their own body of learning, the tradition of their profession and their discipline; the urge becomes a holy duty when the law has a divine source. The task for the judge and the law reformer, faced with changes in the social and economic context in which the legal rules are set, is to seek to respond creatively while preserving the essentials. As Anderson well understood, a similar task faces the moral theologian: to take account of the new possibilities offered by scientific advance and changes in the structure of society, while neither being locked into a fundamentalist ghetto nor surrendering principle to passing fashion. Anderson could not have expected the revival, or re-emergence, of Islamic fundamentalism; the story of Islamic law reform in recent years would make very different reading.

In 1959, Anderson's career took a new turn as he was appointed Director of the Institute of Advanced Legal Studies in the University of London in succession to Sir David Hughes Parry. He served with enormous distinction for the next fifteen years, leaving the Institute with splendid new premises, one of the finest law libraries in the country, and a growing reputation as a centre of creative legal thought.

Under his leadership, Howard Drake and Willi Steiner built up the library, and began to publish the *Index to Foreign Legal Periodicals*. Anderson himself began a whole series of initiatives which reflected the breadth of his own interests in crossing the boundaries of nations and disciplines. There were collaborative ventures with Harvard (where he was offered but declined a Chair), Yale and other American Law Schools. There was the series of annual workshops, one of a number of projects supported by the Ford Foundation. Most notable were the inter-disciplinary discussion groups: lawyers joining economists, sociologists, penologists, or theologians. It was the work of the last-named group which led to a study for the Archbishop of Canterbury, published under the title *Putting Asunder*, which in turn made possible the reform of divorce law in England by the Divorce Law Reform Act of 1969. Anderson himself became chairman of the Hamlyn Trust, responsible for one of the best-known series of lectures on legal topics; two years after his retirement as a trustee he gave the 1978 lectures under the title 'Liberty, Law and Justice'.

But the greatest task was to rehouse the Institute. A handsome building, largely financed by a gift from Sir Charles Clore (and bearing his name), was eventually to rise on the north side of Russell Square. It gave several floors of library space, with working areas for visiting scholars, and also housed the British Institute of International and Comparative Law. For academic lawyers from all over Great Britain and from many overseas countries, Charles Clore House is their London base. It houses many specialist seminars, many of the postgraduate classes for the University of London LLM, and many conferences. The University of London extended Anderson's tenure of directorship by one year so that he could not only complete the move into the new building but be in office at the time of its official opening by the Queen Mother as Chancellor of the University. It is entirely appropriate that in the handsome Council chamber hangs a portrait of Norman Anderson in his Cambridge LLD robes.

A reproduction of that same portrait hangs in the Church House in Dean's Yard. It marks another major sphere of Anderson's life: his service in the central councils of the Church of England.

Until 1970, the Church's central government was divided between the clerical Convocations of Canterbury and York and the National Assembly of the Church of England (more usually known as the Church Assembly) in which the laity joined the bishops and the elected proctors for the clergy. Anderson was elected a lay representative in the Assembly, initially for Rochester diocese and from 1965 for the diocese of London. He became recognised as a leader of the Evangelical group, but as someone who was always willing to seek a full understanding of others' positions.

So, he played an important part in working, with Anglo-Catholics, on controversial issues such as prayers for the dead. Within the Evangelical constituency, he made a powerful contribution to the National Evangelical Assembly at Keele in 1967. His address, subsequently printed under the title *Into the World*, was a call to his fellow Evangelicals to take a much keener interest in social issues than had been the case in recent decades.

In 1970, the year in which Anderson was elected a Fellow of the British Academy, the Church acquired a new system of 'synodical government', with the General Synod taking over most of the functions of the Convocations and the Church Assembly. Anderson was elected Chairman of the House of Laity, to his surprise since Oswald Clark, a leading High Churchman and Anderson's eventual successor in office, was widely regarded as the front-runner. The office carried with it *ex officio* membership of all the major central committees of the Church, and Anderson's skills were greatly used and admired. He was a natural choice to be one of the English representatives on another new body, the Anglican Consultative Council, which draws together leaders from all the member churches of the Anglican Communion.

His most notable achievement in the General Synod was in the matter of the appointment of bishops. Since the time of the Reformation, bishops of the Church of England have been appointed by the Crown exercising a power of nominating the sole candidate for formal election by the Greater Chapter of the cathedral church of the relevant diocese. A process of consultation had developed, Downing Street consulting the archbishops and many others, but there were insistent calls that the Church alone should have the decisive voice in the choice of its leaders. It was a matter which, badly handled, could have put an intolerable strain on the constitutional Establishment of the Church.

Anderson played a leading part in securing a satisfactory outcome. He negotiated with Prime Ministers Wilson and Callaghan and with the leaders of the other main parties, and secured agreement, with the State and in the General Synod, to the establishment of a Crown Appointments Commission. The choice of future archbishops and bishops was limited to the names submitted by this (Church) body; so the Church gained, if not *the* decisive voice, at least *a* decisive voice. The new system came into operation in 1977, two years before Anderson retired from Church office.

Throughout his years in the General Synod he was to be seen sitting bolt upright in his front-bench seat to the left of the Chair. His office gave him an almost automatic right to speak in debate whenever he wished but he resisted the temptation to speak too often. When he did speak it was in a direct style, unfussy and often drawing directly on his personal experience or professional expertise. Despite his deep knowledge of Islam, he always opposed the handing over of redundant Christian buildings for use by other faiths, and he was anxious lest respect for the cultural and religious traditions of immigrant groups should lead to too easy an acceptance of institutions such as polygamy. He prided himself on never having made a 'party' speech. He was, oddly, not always a great success as a chairman of meetings, where he could be uneasy in large gatherings and over-forceful in smaller groups, but the genuine warmth of the tributes when he relinquished office was clear evidence of the affection in which he was held.

No memoir of Norman Anderson would be complete which did not refer to the pain he and his wife had to bear in the death of all three of their children.

Hugh, their only son, read History at Trinity College, Cambridge. Unlike his father, he greatly enjoyed Union debates and at the end of his first year was elected Secretary. The cancer which was to prove fatal prevented his then serving in that office, but in 1968 he was to fill three of the Union's offices, emerging as President in Michaelmas Term of that year. His abilities pointed to a brilliant public career, but he died in August 1970. A memorial appeal was launched by a group of remarkable distinction, including the Archbishop of Canterbury, the Prime Minister, and Lord Butler. Norman Anderson had been booked to give a five-minute religious radio talk in the week following that of his son's death. He gave a moving account of his feelings, delivered with that directness which characterised much of his Christian testimony.

There was worse to come. In 1975, Anderson was perhaps close to the peak of his career. He had received many honours: an honorary Doctorate of Divinity from the University of St Andrews on the installation in 1974 of Lord Ballantrae as Chancellor; the award of 'silk'; and in the New Year Honours List for 1975 a knighthood for his services to the Church (though it could equally have been for his work for legal education). In July of that year, within three weeks of one another, the Andersons' daughters, Hazel and Janet, died suddenly and without warning. Anderson was able to draw deeply on his reserves of faith, and the support of his friends; but it was a cruel time.

Increasingly, Anderson's writing was on religious rather than purely legal topics. He had been much in demand as a speaker to Christian groups, but was scrupulous in keeping a distinction between that activity and his professional work.

It was something of a relief to him when he began to receive invitations from universities to deliver theological lectures; he did not have to treat them as 'extra-curricular activities'. One of the first such came from Trent University, Ontario. The resulting lectures were published in 1969 as *Christianity: The Witness of History — A Lawyer's Approach*. Anderson returned to the theme he had addressed repeatedly, the proper assessment of the evidence about Jesus Christ. It may be doubted whether a lawyer, despite his familiarity with some concepts of 'evidence', has any particular skills in dealing with historical material, and this book had a mixed reception. Its approach was much influenced by that of C. F. D. Moule's *The Phenomenon of the New Testament* which had appeared a couple of years earlier, but, as a Jesuit reviewer observed, 'Anderson reads the New Testament literally, . . . from the dogmatic view point of a believer' (Quesnell in the *Catholic Biblical Quarterly*).

In 1972 Anderson travelled to Saskatchewan to give the Bishop John McLean lectures, an extended version of which was published in the following year under the title *A Lawyer among the Theologians* (London, 1973). It covers some familiar ground, for example as to the historicity of the Resurrection, but there is a strong theme of criticism of Bultmann in arguing that what we have evidence for is *belief* in the Resurrection rather than the event itself and of Bishop John Robinson's view that to be a Christian is neither more nor less than to be authentically human.

Anderson's interest in social issues, plain from his work at the Institute of Advanced Legal Studies and his role at the Keele Assembly, was to become prominent in the 1970s. He was, for example, a member of Lord Longford's group on pornography, and at the end of the decade was one of a group which helped prepare a Church response to a Law Commission paper on blasphemy.

In 1971, Anderson gave the Forwood Lectures on the Philosophy and History of Religion at Liverpool University. He chose the subject *Morality, Law and Grace* (London, 1972). Much of the text is taken up with a criticism of the 'permissive society', with 'situational ethics' contrasted with 'principled ethics'. The supremacy of biblical morality is stressed, with some commentary on the Hart–Devlin debate and a short passage on morality and law in other faiths, a subject Anderson was to return to in a more scholarly fashion some eight years later.

He reviewed some of the current social issues in the 1975 London Lectures in Contemporary Christianity, published in 1977 as *Issues of Life and Death* (London). His stance was that in considering issues such as genetic engineering, abortion and euthanasia, the biblical revelation must be wholeheartedly accepted as authoritative, with Christian tradition accorded a notably lower standing. It was an approach which might be thought to overstate the clarity of the biblical material as applied to such issues, and to undervalue centuries of Christian thought; and indeed Anderson himself avoids too literal an interpretation of the scriptural texts and devotes a good deal of space to the developing teaching of, for example, successive Lambeth Conferences.

The 1978 Bishop John Prideaux lectures at Exeter University saw Anderson addressing *The Mystery of the Incarnation* (Exeter, 1978). Much of the resulting book is taken up with a critical discussion of writings, such as some of the essays published as *The Myth of God Incarnate*, which took a radical position in the Christological debate. While his book was welcomed as a clear account of the history of that debate, and for stressing the links between christology and soteriology, professional theologians were unimpressed by Anderson's defence of the traditional position. He failed to deal adequately with modern sociological and psychological understandings of the human condition, and so produced no answer to the difficulties of what seemed to remain a docetist position (see in particular Frances Young in *Theology*, 82, 302–4). As a writer in *The Expository Times* (vol. 90, p. 129) concluded, 'In the end devotion has triumphed over reason and [Anderson] has produced a Christ who is less than fully human'.

His last major theological work was *God's Law and God's Love* (London, 1980). Based on the Henry Drummond lectures in Stirling, this drew more fully than any other of his books on Anderson's knowledge of Islam, and indeed of other faiths. It looks at understandings of law in Judaism, Islam, and in the Hindu and Buddhist scriptures, and at the problems of suffering and evil. Thereafter he published a study of *The Teaching of Jesus* (1983), largely an updated treatment of themes familiar in his early books, and some theological interludes which sit rather awkwardly in his autobiography, *An Adopted Son: The Story of my Life* (Leicester, 1985). The title of that, his last book, is a reference to Romans 8:15, not to his own personal origins.

Like many of his books, *God's Law and God's Love* demonstrates the breadth of his reading, with over 110 authors cited or quoted. In *A Lawyer among the Theologians*, Anderson apologises for the superabundance of quotations from the writings of theologians and biblical scholars which make up so many of his pages:

> These quotations may, admittedly, be regarded as highly selective, and are not nearly so wide-ranging as I should wish. [Over 110 authors are cited.] But I have never, unhappily, learnt to read at more than a snail's pace; so the demands of a busy life inevitably preclude me from reading very widely in a discipline which is not my own. I only wish I had time to deal with the subject more adequately.

The modesty was surely unaffected, but it did remain true that the greater part of Anderson's written output was outwith his academic discipline. He had a sure touch in presenting the heart of an argument, and his writing, like his speaking, has a directness which can be very moving. He never claimed to be an academic theologian, rather to be a faithful defender of the Gospel; he remained in that sense a missionary throughout his life.

Anderson was always at home in Cambridge, and it was natural that he should return there in retirement. His wife's health deteriorated sharply, and he cared for her with simple devotion. They returned to the congregation of the Round Church, which latterly used the larger premises of the Cambridge Union next door before moving again to St Andrew the Great. As those who attended Anderson's funeral realised, the style of worship, which had been classical Low Church, came to have only tenuous connections with the Anglican liturgical tradition.

Owen Chadwick, a near neighbour, and from a rather different strand in Anglicanism, records that he never saw Norman Anderson 'other than wise, sane, solid, balanced, in a way that was rather extraordinary in someone who professed an emotional and in some ways extreme form of Christian faith'. That faith, and a lively sense of assurance in the risen life, sustained him to the end.

DAVID McCLEAN
University of Sheffield

LLOYD AUSTIN   *James Austin*

Proceedings of the British Academy, **90**, 267–279

Lloyd James Austin
1915–1994

Born in Melbourne, Australia, in 1915 [November 4], he remembers the
father who first stimulated a small boy's delight in the written word, two
elder brothers and a younger, each later to become an expert in his own field
(History or Classics) and, especially, those teachers who, at different stages
of schooling, conveyed an individual or idiosyncratic sense of how words
work—in English, French, German or Latin.

THIS PARAGRAPH, from a Festschrift published in 1982, was elaborated
upon by Austin himself in 1987; his father, J. W. A. Austin, is fondly
recalled: 'Amongst my earliest memories are readings by my father to
his four sons [Ken, Mervyn, Lloyd and Noel]; he brought alive Dickens
and other English writers by his gift of empathy and his delight in
felicitous expression'; he refers to Gresham Robinson, his headmaster
at St Thomas Grammar School, Essenden, who taught his pupils to
recite verse 'in such a way as to let the words speak for themselves'; to
'Edie' Dunn, his French master at Melbourne Grammar School, who
gave him a rigorous grounding in French and kindled his life-long love
of music; and to Karl Koeppel, his Latin master, whose 'feeling for
rhythm and insistence on the poetic value of scansion, together with his
sense of the finest shades of meaning, lit an inextinguishable light'. But
the Festschrift paragraph also gives intimations of those character-traits
which were to inform all Austin's scholarly life: his strong sense of
family, both the blood-bonded and the spirit-blended, and his insatiable
appetite for a learning which his own perspicacity transformed into a
heady pleasure both for himself and others.

Intellectual brilliance took little time to make itself known: Austin graduated from the University of Melbourne in 1935 with a First, and, in 1937, he made his way to Paris, armed with a French Government Scholarship, to establish himself in the field of late nineteenth-century studies, not among the poets who were to become his life's work, but with Paul Bourget. His thesis, completed in 1939, was published the following year under the title *Paul Bourget: Sa vie et son œuvre jusqu'en 1889.*

These Paris years saw the forging of deeply beneficial and lasting friendships, notably with Paul Étard, the Librarian of the École Normale Supérieure and, through him, with Jean Pommier, Professeur de l'Histoire des Créations Littéraires at the Collège de France from 1946, in fitting succession to Paul Valéry. Austin was to have many opportunities to refer to his debt to Pommier in the course of his academic career; but his sense of gratitude to Étard was no less heartfelt:

> . . . until his death in 1962, he read all my work in manuscript with close attention, and provided thorough and detailed corrections and suggestions. Few could rival the breadth and depth of his knowledge; many distinguished scholars owe him a debt that was rarely adequately acknowledged.

In 1940, he returned to Australia, to a lecturing post in French at his Alma Mater, the University of Melbourne, a post he held until 1947, though his tenure was interrupted by the war, and three years in the Special Branch of the Royal Australian Navy Volunteer Reserve. From there, he proceeded to a Lectureship in French at the University of St Andrew's (1947–51), after which he spent a further four years in Paris. It was with the volume published as a result of this period of research— *L'Univers poétique de Baudelaire: Symbolisme et symbolique* (1956)— that his life's work can be said to have begun in earnest, although one should not overlook the edition of Valéry's 'Le Cimetière marin' published with Henri Mondor in 1954, an edition accompanied by critical essays and facsimiles of the poem's three versions.

The Baudelaire volume was designed as the first panel of a triptych, whose two other panels were to have been *Le Mystère poétique de Mallarmé* and *La Composition poétique de Valéry*. In the event, this *grand oeuvre* took other shapes, as Austin's scholarly life yielded to diverse and urgent pressures, opportunities, impulses. The 'Introduction générale' has, therefore, a particular significance, since it sketches out a founding vision which was to underpin much of Austin's later work. All three poets are at the heart of Symbolism, and not just as a precursor (Baudelaire), or as a survivor (Valéry); they have that *esprit de famille* which creates a *famille d'esprits*, a family to which other Symbolists, such as Ghil, or Merrill, or Moréas, could only dimly belong. French Symbolism is, in some respects, France's version of Anglo-German Romanticism—French Romanticism was too distracted and inhibited by its classical heritage to respond to symbolist and organicist currents elsewhere. But French Symbolism is in no sense out of its time, for it is a much more intense form of European Romanticism, seeking after quintessences rather than essences, and bringing to the creative enterprise an unusual discipline and lucidity; Modernism's subsequent, anguished equivocations about the powers, and modes of operation, of language are unthinkable without the tenacious investigations of these Symbolists into their medium. And Austin was of the persuasion that, however far language might retreat from its referential function, in order to recover some of its surrendered autonomy, in order to repotentiate itself as signifier, such a retreat has a regenerative *choc en retour* which infinitely enriches our inner experience, and our perception of the world about us. As Mallarmé, the member of the triumvirate towards whom Austin's affections most naturally gravitated, puts it: while Symbolist language might have a large portion of the never-before-heard in it, it still retained 'la réminiscence de l'objet nommé', which now, however, 'baigne dans une neuve atmosphère'.

After this second, extended Parisian stay, Austin's life was to be centred in Britain, and specifically in Cambridge. But he remained profoundly committed to his Australian origins, not only in the generous declarations of his indebtedness to Alan Chisholm, but also in his championing of the poetry of Christopher Brennan—a role pioneered by Chisholm—in his contributions to a variety of Australian journals, and in his love of cricket. It should be said that Alan Chisholm, who died, with a poignant fittingness perhaps, during the preparation of the 1982 Festschrift in honour of his pupil, gladly returned the debt of gratitude:

> In conclusion, I feel that I must, like many other Mallarmé enthusiasts, express my gratitude for the Austin publication [Mallarmé's *Correspondance*] in honour of which the present volume is issued. Without this superb piece of scholarship, it would not have been possible to follow the many tracks leading to, and through, the consciousness of a great and epoch-making poet.

Before Austin finally settled in Cambridge as a University Lecturer in 1961, and after an initial post as Fellow and College Lecturer at Jesus College (1955), he enjoyed a five-year tenure of the Chair of Modern

French Literature at the University of Manchester, as the successor to P. Mansell Jones, another path-finding scholar of late nineteenth-century literature. But once re-established in Cambridge, his career there gathered momentum, became irresistible: he was elected to a Readership in 1966, and in 1967 to the Drapers Chair of French. It was from this base that Austin all but bestrode the world of Baudelaire/Mallarmé/Valéry scholarship, in Britain and elsewhere. His assumption of the Drapers Chair coincided with his appointment to the General Editorship of *French Studies*, a post he held until 1980. During these thirteen years, he was showered with many further accolades.

Of Austin's honours it is difficult to speak, other than to recite them as the palpable evidence of the consistency with which his work attracted the respect of colleagues and institutions. The distinction of his research and writing naturally drew distinction to itself: he was elected to the council of the Association Internationale des Études Françaises in 1964, and became its president in 1969; he was elected a Fellow of the British Academy in 1968; created Chevalier de l'Ordre des Arts et des Lettres, 1972; Docteur *honoris causa* de l'Université de Paris-Sorbonne (Paris IV), 1973; Officier de l'Ordre National du Mérite, 1976; elected Membre de l'Académie Royale de Langue et de Littérature Françaises de Belgique, 1980; awarded the Prix Henri Mondor, 1981. But these honours also tell a story of an international animator of French literary study, for whom Cambridge was a point of radiation, as much as of gravitation. If Cambridge French managed to throw off a certain academic parochialism during the 1970s, if *French Studies*, in reflecting scholarly trends in Britain, seemed more in tune with critical trends abroad, then these things were in no small part due to the range of Austin's affiliations and the far-flungness of the Austinian diaspora.

1982 saw the publication of *Baudelaire, Mallarmé, Valéry: New Essays in Honour of Lloyd Austin*, a celebratory volume whose list of contributors reads like a roll-call of all that has been best over the past fifty years in the criticism of Austin's chosen period. And all of these contributors are direct forebears, colleagues, friends and pupils: Barrère and Bowie, Fairlie and Finch, Hackett and Hytier, Pichois and Poulet, Richard and Robinson, Seznec and Starobinski, to name but a few. The chief purpose of the Festschrift was to honour Austin's completion of the eleven volumes of Mallarmé's *Correspondance* (the later volumes still in manuscript at the time), a task he first became involved with in 1959, when Henri Mondor, who had just edited the first volume with

Jean-Pierre Richard, invited him to coedit the remaining volumes. After Mondor's death in 1962, Austin continued to work on the project single-handedly. The final volume was published in 1985.

> Those who know him more closely will realise the care and stimulus he has always given to undergraduates, research students and colleagues; . . . Here, he combines rare qualities: unfailingly encouraging over a long period when he believes in the worth of a project; able to present that worth freshly to the researcher; forthright and friendly in pointing out flaws.

These words from the preface of the Festschrift are borne out by other testimony. One former pupil recalls this piquant combination of the caring and the exacting. Another mentions the readiness with which he would commit all his energies to assessing work so that the best and most detailed advice could be given. And another speaks of the irrepressible enthusiasm which was itself the source of the demanding standards. To know how to blend the inspiriting with the properly critical, to instil in the student the right mixture of self-assurance and self-doubt, these remain the pedagogic ideals of the academic teacher so thoroughly embodied in Austin.

Austin's collected papers in English on the three poets were published by Cambridge University Press in 1987 (*Poetic Principles and Practice: Occasional Papers on Baudelaire, Mallarmé and Valéry*). The Prefatory Note provides us with a profession of faith:

> We live in an age when discussion of the theory of literature tends to become an end in itself. For me it is the poetry which matters above all; but the exceptional level of poetic expression attained by these poets can be largely ascribed to their penetrating insight into the nature of language and its potentialities. . . . But, by the very nature of language, the most distinctive of human creations, these poems . . . are not enclosed in an isolated realm of self-reflectivity, but illuminate the heart and mind of man.

Austin had no difficulty in reconciling the Symbolists' absorption in their own medium with his own desire to see literature reaching out into, giving shape to, informing, the lives and memories of all its readers. We are exhilarated, exalted, by these literary works, and these feelings owe as much to the poets' care for their own craft as to our care for the craft of reading.

By this time, Baudelaire was playing a relatively small part in Austin's output. *Poetic Principles and Practice* contains only one item devoted entirely to his work, dating from 1956 and specially revised in 1985 for inclusion in the volume. But it is an item which admirably exemplifies Austin's implicit insistence that large ques-

tions—'Baudelaire: Poet or Prophet?'—can only be addressed, and
perhaps answered, after an intimate inhabiting of the text in all its
self-renewing eventfulness. The lion's share of the volume goes to
Mallarmé. 'Presence and Poetry of Stéphane Mallarmé' is still quite
the best available short introduction to the poet, a wonderfully penetrating and fluent account, which, in the space of thirty pages, manages not
only to visit the majority of Mallarmé's *œuvre* and assess his *rayonne-
ment*, but to do so in a way which gives no hint of constraint, or
unseemly hurriedness; what is odd is *t*hat in such a confined space
such expansive justice is done to the subject. When this essay is put
alongside 'Mallarmé on Music and Letters' and 'Mallarmé and the
Visual Arts', then we truly have in place the critical keystones of
Mallarmé's poetic edifice. Accompanying these essays in synthesis
are articles devoted to the analysis of individual poems: 'Toast funè-
bre', 'Prose pour des Esseintes', 'Le vierge, le vivace et le bel
aujourd'hui', 'A la nue accablante tu', 'Quand l'ombre menaça de la
fatale loi', 'Le Tombeau de Charles Baudelaire'. All these are classic
interpretations, established items in the critical canon, none more so
perhaps than the study of 'Le Pitre châtié' in its two versions (1864,
1887), a study whose closing lines give some idea of how far Austin
communicated his vivid experience of text to his own writing:

> Then the summit of the poem is attained *before* the end: 'Ne s*a*chant p*a*s,
> ingr*a*t! que c'était tout mon s*a*cre' (with all its physical and symbolic
> associations of coronation and anointing with oil), in order to allow for the
> deliberate, subtle and lovely diminuendo of a last line which, after the final
> summary of sense and echo of sound in 'Ce f*a*rd', tails off into distant space
> and past time, evoking once again in its own movement and in a dying and
> whispering fall the royal consecration now washed away to nothingness,
> 'noyé dans l'eau perfide des glaciers'.

A sentence like this expresses the cumulative delight of personal
discovery, and communicates the transformation of *connaissance* into
volupté, by postponing the end of its own critical savouring. And the
reader can only relish the play between progressive amplifications and
suspensive symmetries, between ever-renewed departures and interrup-
tions equally renewed. Special mention should also be made of 'New
Light on Brennan and Mallarmé', an article which originally appeared
in an issue of the *Australian Journal of French Studies* (1969) honouring Professor Chisholm. As already mentioned, in championing
Brennan, Austin was following in Chisholm's footsteps, for Chisholm
had not only been a lifelong friend of Brennan, but had published

Brennan's *Verse* (1960) and *Prose* (1962), and biographical and critical studies of him. Austin had no illusions about Brennan's stylistic originality — 'Brennan's own poetic idiom was predominantly that of Victorian aestheticism' — but he had a justifiable pride in the achievement of Australia's only Mallarméan disciple, a disciple who unerringly understood the importance of Mallarmé's work, from the moment he encountered it in 1893. Austin took great pleasure and satisfaction in the discovery, by his research student, John Foulkes, of a missing portion of Brennan's papers in the Moran Collection in St John's College, Cambridge, and in the publication, by Axel Clark, both of a critical biography (in 1980), and also of Brennan's two earliest pastiches of *Un coup de dés* (in 1981).

That Austin responded to Mallarmé with a special empathy is borne out by the articles on Valéry gathered here: sharply intelligent, individualistic, authoritative as ever, they are not suffused with quite the same excited warmth. Perhaps some of the fault lies with Valéry. Both 'The Genius of Paul Valéry' (first given as a public lecture in 1963, as Austin's year as Herbert F. Johnson Visiting Professor to the Institute for Research in the Humanities at the University of Wisconsin, Madison, was drawing to an end) and 'Valéry's Views on Literature' enable readers to find their bearings in a work as multiform as it is extensive; 'The Negative Plane Tree' and 'Modulation and Movement in Valéry's Verse' examine more closely Valéry's poetic method. But throughout these papers, Austin's purpose remains unswervingly single: to help readers to a richer relationship with the poet, by retracing his own exploratory steps and by enacting, in his writing, the regenerative power of insight. Reading and criticism are not to be surpassed as the real sources of an individual's spiritual autobiography. To be an informed reader, and at the same time a reader available to all the promptings of *émerveillement*, this is the target that Austin sets for us.

In reading Austin's obituary notice on Jean Pommier, one might believe that he had found embodied in that past master all the qualities he himself valued and so admirably emulated: 'a rare ability to combine . . . intellectual rigour with sensitive response, an extreme *finesse* with imaginative insight, prodigious learning with verve and vitality of expression'. And one has only to look into his reviews to see, too, that Austin relished polemic to a similar degree, that his intellect was just as combative. Straight thinking of extreme acuity made it difficult for Austin to swallow inflated expression, or the exotic flavours of excessively metaphorical formulation. He hesitated to accept, even from the pens of admired colleagues, those kinds of scholarship which toyed with the decorative or ludic, when, given the depth of his feeling for literature, so much was at stake. Austin was not averse to withering observations: 'If the word "thought" can be applied to what may seem to some readers the product of a mind whose predilection for philosophical terminology is not matched by any conspicuous skill in its manipulation . . . '; 'But they [three argumentative reasons] are developed into a book only by being laboured beyond reason, in a repetitive indictment of both Poe and Baudelaire that defeats its own ends'. But when not driven to exasperation, when, on the contrary, challenged, or moved, or impressed, he was an extremely appreciative and encouraging reviewer, who none the less liked to use reviews to sort through issues still outstanding, or to recall nagging questions: 'Inevitably, some points call for discussion. . . . What did Mallarmé mean when he said . . . '; 'Inevitably, there are details which others may see differently. . . . In "Tout Orgueil", is *console* an "occasional table" . . . ?'; 'Inevitably, not all students of Mallarmé will agree with some of the judgements made here: do *Les Noces d'Hérodiade* really offer "the substance of effective theatre" . . . ?'; 'Not all readers will accept without question some of the editor's statements'. 'Inevitably, not all students/readers will agree': in this persistent reactive stance lies a further key to Austin's view of the reading community: it is peculiarly resistant to convenient consensus; it is restive, as though afflicted with an incurable intellectual questing and questioning; it is impossible to please it entirely, since it is a law of nature that its members should disagree, that great works should invite them to disagree; its disagreements are its life force, are what keeps it healthy, committed, and its members interdependent; its disagreements are what makes every member indispensable, unsupersedable.

In this 1987 volume of collected papers, Austin announced that a draft of the Mallarmé book had been prepared in 1964 (in two versions, one in French, the other in English) and that materials for the Valéry project were accumulating. But he was compelled to acknowledge: 'Work will continue on the triptych, although, at the age of seventy, it is perhaps presumptuous to count on completion'. If he did not have the opportunity to put the finishing touches to this vast enterprise, we can at least, gratefully, piece them together from all that he had already published. The same would not be true of the eleven volumes of Mallarmé's correspondence. Without the twenty-six years of energetic and tenacious scholarship which Austin devoted to the task, this priceless document would either be still unavailable, or available only in a form which left much of the work still to be done. Austin's is a tremendous achievement, and one can but return to it. Not only was the task of collection and detection immense—Mondor's own collection of Mallarmé's correspondence (comprising some 1,200 letters), initially believed to be fairly complete and publishable in some four volumes, turned out to include less than half of the extant letters (3,380 to date)—but the process of annotation, given the diversity of aspects which required commentary, tested the whole range of Austin's formidable scholarship:

> His annotation contains a wealth of precise information on the personalities with whom Mallarmé corresponded, on the aesthetic issues of his age and on the multifarious literary circles and *cénacles* within which those issues were debated. In addition, his notes contain much penetratingly expressed critical thought and remind the reader tactfully and firmly, page by page, that Mallarmé's world will make its fullest sense only to those who are prepared to accept the many difficult challenges it still presents and to bring their own powers of independent literary judgement to bear upon the documents which that world has bequeathed to us.

Fittingly, the 1982 Festschrift from which this editorial tribute is extracted, has among its contributions an article by Alison Fairlie entitled '"Entre les lignes": Mallarmé's Art of Allusion in his Thank-You Letters', an article designed both to set in motion and anticipate the rich harvest of research which the *Correspondance* could not but attract.

The pleasures to be had from these volumes of letters are manifold; not least, their resistance to completion leaves open countless opportunities for readerly speculation and tantalisation. In each introduction, Austin provides a fascinating inductive biography for the period concerned, catching the hints and glimpses of a pattern reflected in the letters; but, as Austin reminds his readers, 'il y en a d'autres que nous n'avons pas mentionnés, et que le lecteur découvrira lui-même'. As we eavesdrop on these exchanges, trying to reconstruct the *lettres-fantômes* (the letters whose existence is attested but which remain undiscovered) and to piece together relationships, private events, we are often left empty-handed: where Mallarmé remarks to Méry Laurent, 'Qui veux-tu dire, après " . . . Madame Grogos" que tu as été froissée? Je ne comprends pas, du tout', Austin can only add, unabashed, 'Nous non plus, évidemment'. But frequently our editor can suggest how a mystery might be unravelled: Mallarmé notes, in a postscript to a letter addressed to Catulle and Judith Mendès, '—Je pars à Chislehurst, pour souhaiter la fête de mon souverain'; Austin takes up the challenge with relish:

> C'est à Chislehurst, petite ville dans le comté de Kent, à quinze kilomètres au sud-est de Londres, que se réfugia Napoléon III après 1871. Il y mourut le 9 janvier 1873. Mallarmé plaisante, sans doute. Quelle était la fête de Napoléon III, né le 20 avril 1808? Peut-être le 15 août, anniversaire de Napoléon Ier, ce qui permettrait de dater cette lettre du 15 août 1871: c'était bien un mardi.

Our fullest insight into Austin's editing of Mallarmé's *Correspondance* is provided by two articles (one dating from 1968, the other from 1985) collected in his posthumous *Essais sur Mallarmé*, edited by Malcolm Bowie and recently published by Manchester University Press. This edition was a project that had played no part in his plans; if it had not been for his other collaborative work with Henri Mondor, and the honour of working closely with the critic who had done so much to establish and gather the documentary corpus on which all subsequent Mallarmé scholarship was more or less to rely, Austin would have left well alone. But he increasingly understood that, far from acting as Mondor's assistant, he would have to take the whole project upon himself; for all his learning and critical acumen, Mondor lacked training in scholarly method, and the first volume of the correspondence showed evidence of that lack: incorrect copies, doubtful dating, superfluous annotation. But if Austin could bring more rigorous scholarly procedures to bear on the edition, he could not reverse the decision already taken, to publish the letters over an extended period of time, volume by volume, rather than to wait until all possible collection and research had been completed, and then produce a single, multi-volume publication. As a result, Austin found the need to publish supplements to earlier volumes, and to catch up on errata and addenda, inevitable. In fact, however regrettable to Austin these untidy processes may have seemed, however offensive to his own formidable standards of scholarship, they are in no way a blemish on the *Correspondance*; quite the contrary. Intriguingly, they make available to us the very processes of scholarship, they put before us the researching mind which is never done with its subject, which worries away at the unsolved, long after less tenacious minds would have quietly let it slide from consciousness. The revisions and addenda corporealise the scholarly conscience, the intellectual vigilance which is impelled by the awareness that only further error can be begotten by error. And these revisions also help to maintain the critical openness, the challenge of the unfinished, that Austin wanted to generate from this work. But as Austin looks back, in the 1985 article, over the long and wearying and frequently frustrating road he has travelled, he cannot resist some wry smiles at his own expense. Among the gifts that Austin reckons indispensable to the aspiring editor of a French writer's correspondence are: ubiquity, the art of pleasing (librarians, curators, custodians, collectors), an insatiable appetite for insignificant details and infinite patience in their discovery, and the ability to prevent strikes at the Bibliothèque nationale, or documents being away at the binder's, etc., on one's research visits. And then there are the Chaplinesque vicissitudes of the pioneer 'pilots' of early microfilm readers:

> On connaissait des moments d'exaltation euphorique lorsque, à la moindre pression sur la manivelle (comme le manche à balai d'un avion), le film parcourait à une vitesse vertigineuse les jours, les mois et les années. En ralentissant, vous constatiez que vous aviez dépassé de beaucoup le but. Vous renversiez la vapeur, et vous dépassiez dans l'autre sens. Quand, par une combinaison de tact, d'adresse, de ruse et d'enjôlement, vous approchiez finalement du but, le film se calait, et refusait obstinément de bouger— jusqu'au moment où il démarrait subitement de nouveau et filait irrésistiblement en avant et où vous étiez obligé de tout recommencer.

Essais sur Mallarmé comprises eighteen articles on Mallarmé (covering the period 1951–91) and a substantial obituary notice on Henri Mondor. This is the totality of Austin's short pieces in elegant French on Mallarmé, but leaves uncollected other articles in French, nine on Baudelaire and six on Valéry. These Mallarmé articles are frequently companion pieces to English ones, and concern themselves with texts and issues already mentioned: 'Prose pour des Esseintes', 'Le Pitre châtié', 'Mallarmé critique d'art'. But there is also material on the early Mallarmé, an engrossing study of Mallarmé, Hugo and Wagner, culminating in an intrepid analysis of 'Hommage' (to Wagner), an analysis of the 'Cantique de Saint-Jean', and a pair of capital pieces on 'L'Après-midi d'un faune' (comparison of the poem's lexicon in its three versions, and an *essai d'explication*). It is gratifyingly apt that Austin's final published piece, 'Verlaine et Mallarmé' (1991), should be a reconsideration of, and supplement to, Mondor's *L'Amitié de Verlaine et Mallarmé* of 1940, filling out Mondor's picture with more recently acquired documentary evidence, drawn particularly from the *Correspondance*.

We have spoken much of debts of gratitude fully paid in Austin's life. But two vital ones have hitherto been omitted. Many of Austin's articles carry, as their first footnote, an acknowledgement of the help provided by Alison Fairlie, reading drafts, making suggestions, establishing references and so on, not to mention the assistance she provided in the classification of Mallarmé's papers (she was particularly engaged in an inventory of his library). Austin declared that his written work had been constantly improved by her sensitive and constructive criticisms, and enriched by detailed and stimulating suggestions. But there were others, too, who were piecing Mallarmé together at Valvins, cataloguing, taking copies, making calculations: his son James, a professional photographer, his daughter Suzie, and his wife Jeanne. Throughout his fruitful career, and from the first, Austin enjoyed the indefatigable support and succour of his wife Jeanne-Françoise (Jeannot) Guérin, a graduate in English from the Sorbonne, whom he met and married during his first research visit to Paris (1937–40). Her contribution to his work is clearly not to be measured by the number of acknowledgements or citations; it exceeds all measure. But in these acknowledgements, one feels the huge pleasure Austin took in being able, publicly, to celebrate a partnership in scholarship and mutual devotion.

Austin died peacefully on 30 December 1994, after sustaining a series of strokes. Their incapacitating effect was borne with the fortitude and dignity with which he had lived the whole of his challenging life, and in no way diminished his unquenchable appetite for vivid, animating experience, and for the arts which he had so unswervingly loved. At his funeral on 12 January 1995, Malcolm Bowie referred to this love in these words:

> Lloyd believed in art, not as an aesthete or a dilettante, but as one who, in a post-theological age, looked to the work of art as a model of coherence in the world, and to the rapture that artistic experience could bring as an exemplary engagement of heart and mind and senses in the fabric of the real world.

It would be foolish to suppose that one could do justice in a brief summary to Austin's truly remarkable accomplishments, to a bibliography which contains something over 160 items, to years of inspiriting and inspiring leadership and supervision, to the range of his committed interests, to his indefatigable energy. But one might be excused for suggesting that there *are* words which apply very appropriately to him, words he used of his triumvirate of poets: 'But the influence which a master most wants to exert is precisely that by which his disciples may become themselves, and masters in their turn. It was Baudelaire who revealed Mallarmé to himself, just as Mallarmé was later to render the same service to Valéry.'

Austin's writing and teaching belong to that all but lost, and certainly lamented, tradition whereby the master wants nothing better than to acknowledge his own masters, and, in his turn, to confer mastery, inexhaustibly.

CLIVE SCOTT
Fellow of the Academy

MATTHEW BLACK   *Moffat*

Proceedings of the British Academy, **90**, 283–294

Matthew Black
1908–1994

MATTHEW BLACK was born at Kilmarnock on 3 September 1908 and died at St Andrews on 2 October 1994. He was educated at Kilmarnock Academy and at the University of Glasgow, where he obtained a First in Classics and a Second in Mental Philosophy and was awarded a Distinction in his BD. He went on to the University of Bonn in the 1930s, was a pupil of Paul Kahle and collected his first doctorate in 1937. He was the parish minister at Dunbarney from 1942–7, but otherwise his life was spent as a University teacher at Glasgow (where he was Assistant to his teacher W. B. Stevenson), Manchester, Aberdeen, Leeds, Edinburgh and St Andrews. He was elected to the Chair of Biblical Criticism and Biblical Antiquities at Edinburgh in 1952 and he came to St Andrews in 1954 as Professor of Divinity and Biblical Criticism and Principal of St Mary's College. He had a long and influential tenure and became Emeritus in 1978. His scholarly output was not impaired by his new responsibilities, but he was a reforming Principal and was tenacious in the pursuit of ends on which he had determined. He amply fulfilled the expectations which had moved the Principal and Vice-Chancellor of the University, Professor T. M. Knox (later Sir Malcolm Knox), to bring him to St Andrews in 1954.

He was exceptionally industrious in his pursuit of scholarship and developed his own ideas tirelessly. He set the College a good example and his students noticed that the light was on in his study and that he was at his desk when they were retiring for the night. He had an infectious enthusiasm for his subject which he passed on to research students with whom he was particularly effective and who came from many parts of the world to St Andrews. He leaves behind him, especially in North America, a band of university teachers whose research he supervised and whose vocation he shaped.

At St Andrews the reform of the Bachelor of Divinity degree was seen as a matter of urgency and to this he had to apply himself immediately. The degree was regulated by a single Ordinance and the four Scottish Universities with Faculties of Divinity (St Andrews, Glasgow, Aberdeen and Edinburgh) marched in step. The BD was a second degree and was preceded normally by a first degree in arts, sometimes in science. At a dinner in Edinburgh on the occasion of a joint meeting of the Divinity Faculties, Sir Edward Appleton, who was then Principal and Vice-Chancellor of the University of Edinburgh, urged that the four Universities should maintain the single Ordinance for the BD, that any reform of the degree should proceed by agreement and that they should not go their several ways and allow the old unity to fall apart. The efforts to secure such agreement were protracted and fruitless. St Andrews advocated strenuously that the BD should become an undergraduate degree and the Faculty at Edinburgh favoured the same move, but there was opposition in Glasgow and Aberdeen. Matthew Black played a prominent part in all this and eventually St Andrews moved unilaterally. He had throughout pressed hard for the change, because he regarded it as necessary for the survival of the Faculty of Divinity at St Andrews. The BD as a first degree was subsequently introduced by the other three universities, one by one, but in Glasgow there were those who were convinced that the pass had been sold and there were lingering doubts about the wisdom of the reform.

Matthew Black was the recipient of many honours: he had honorary degrees from Glasgow, Münster, Cambridge, Queen's Ontario and St Andrews. He was elected a Fellow of the British Academy in 1955 and of the Royal Society of Edinburgh in 1977. He won the Burkitt Medal of the British Academy in 1962. He was made a Corresponding Member of the Göttingen Academy in 1957 and a Member of the Uppsala Royal Society of Sciences in 1979. His most original book, *An Aramaic Approach to the Gospels and Acts* had been accepted as a thesis for the degree of D.Litt. by the University of Glasgow in 1944 and was published by the Clarendon Press in 1946. There was a second edition (1954) and a further enlarged third edition (1967). The second and third editions contained an appendix on the unpublished work of Professor A.

J. Wensinck and the third edition an appendix on 'The Use of "Son of Man" in Jewish Aramaic' by Professor Geza Vermes.

Black reviews the work of those scholars who had earlier investigated evidences of Aramaic behind the Greek of the New Testament, among them Wellhausen, Nestlé, Dalman, Torrey and Burney. The similarity of his interest to that of Gustaf Dalman's *Die Worte Jesu* (1898) is noticeable, a book which was translated into English by David M. Kay, a St Mary's College professor, as *The Words of Jesus* (1902). The 'Words of Jesus' does not exhaust the scope of Black's investigation, but the topic describes an influential orientation of his book (cf. his 'Recovery of the Language of Jesus' (1957)) and the third edition of *An Aramaic Approach* is translated into German as *Die Muttersprache Jesu* (1982): the vernacular of Jesus was not Greek nor Hebrew but a dialect of Aramaic. Black's most fundamental quarrel with Dalman (also with Torrey and Burney) was that he had been undiscriminating in his use of Aramaic and had not identified the Palestinian Aramaic dialect which would have elucidated correctly the Aramaic background to the Gospels.

Black's approach was both linguistic and textual. The latter betrayed his abiding interest in the Greek manuscripts on which a critical edition of the New Testament is founded and in the science of textual criticism. In 1974 he lectured in the University of Glasgow on the occasion of the acquisition of a Tischendorf archive. The lecture was entitled 'After 100 Years: The Text of the Greek New Testament', and it was published in 1981 as part of a book, *Constantin von Tischendorf and the Greek New Testament*. He devoted attention especially to Codex Bezae whose text he compared with that of Westcott and Hort and that of Tischendorf and to which, following Wensinck, he attached special importance as a tool for the Aramaic approach to the Gospels. On the linguistic side he undertook to identify Aramaic grammar, syntax, vocabulary and idiom in the Greek of the New Testament. This involved attempts to recover original Aramaic constructions behind the Greek or to detect mistranslations in the Greek which were best accounted for as misunderstandings of an Aramaic original. His book exercised considerable influence on the course of subsequent New Testament studies and is an illustration of the advantages enjoyed by a New Testament scholar who has both classical learning and a knowledge of the Semitic languages.

The criticism of the third edition of the *Aramaic Approach* is less favourable than the verdict which was passed on the first edition. The latter was received as a book which broke new ground, while the third edition is seen as a book which, despite revision and expansion, has not taken account of the advance of Aramaic studies between 1946 and 1967 and whose thesis is still essentially the same as that of the 1946 book. It is still a critique of Aramaisms in the Gospels and Acts which were identified by those who were first in the field. New finds of first-century Aramaic at Qumran, the Genesis Apocryphon and the fragments from the caves, have not been used and account has not been taken of the progress in the study of the Palestinian Targums. It is accepted that the point which Black made against his predecessors, that the Aramaic of the Palestinian Targums is a better tool for investigating Aramaisms in the New Testament than the Aramaic of the Babylonian Targums, is valid, but the first-century AD date which he assigns to these Palestinian Targums is replaced by a third-century date. The key to further progress in the study of Aramaisms in the Gospels and Acts is the use of contemporary Aramaic sources. This criticism is, however, tempered by the acknowledgement that characteristics of first-century Palestinian Aramaic persist in the third century: the history of the language is one of continuity as well as change. The verdict is that Black's use of third-century Aramaic may have produced correct results, though the scholarly method is to use Aramaic sources contemporary with the New Testament.

Matthew Black made a journey to Jerusalem in connection with the Dead Sea Scrolls in 1959. He was given hospitality at the American School of Oriental Research and, with the help of Père de Vaux, inspected the scrolls and visited the excavations at Qumran. He was early in the new field and his book *The Scrolls and Christian Origins* (1961) arose from the Morse Lectures which he had given at Union Theological Seminary, New York, in 1956. Single lectures which he delivered on the Scrolls are published. One with the title *The Scrolls and Christian Doctrine* (1966) was the Ethel M. Wood lecture of the University of London, and another, *The Essene Problem* (1961), was given to the Friends of Dr Williams' Library. He was an editor of a book entitled *The Scrolls and Christianity: Historical and Theological Significance* (1969) to which he contributed a chapter with almost the same title as his book ('The Dead Sea Scrolls and Christian Origins').

This and the title of the Ethel M. Wood lecture show that the interest which he had in the Scrolls was that of a New Testament scholar and this is to be expected. Consequently it was the literature of the Qumran sect and not the biblical finds in the caves to which he devoted most of his attention. He did not, for the most part, compare Hebrew fragments with the Masoretic text or Greek fragments with the text of the Septuagint. He has an appendix in his book (*The Scrolls and Christian Origins*) on 'Aramaic Texts from Qumran' and he is especially interested in the scroll which has been named 'The Genesis Apocryphon', because he discerns that it has a bearing on his *Aramaic Approach*. He describes it as an 'old Aramaic Targum, almost certainly our oldest written Palestinian Pentateuch Targum probably dating to the first century BC'. He holds that it is an invaluable witness to Aramaic language and literature in the time of Jesus.

He identified the Qumran community as Essenes, set it in the context of Jewish sectarianism and discussed the extent of its connections with Christian origins. There were two principal aspects to this undertaking: Are there direct historical contacts between the Qumran community and the Primitive Church? Are any of the ritual practices of the community or any of its forms of religious belief reflected in the rituals and doctrines of the Primitive Church? He discusses the community's baptismal rites, its Messianic doctrines and its sacred meal. He offers the opinion that the Teacher of Righteousness may have been identified by the Qumran sectarians with 'the prophet like Moses' and that 'redemptive functions' may have been attributed to him. He notices that baptismal rites were common among Jewish sects in the New Testament period, but suggests that the 'Hebraists' or 'Hebrews' of Acts may provide a connection between the movement and tradition of non-conformist baptising Judaism and the Primitive Church. He judges it to be more probable that the Qumran sacred meal lies behind the daily 'breaking of bread' in the Primitive Christian community in Acts than that its model is the Passover: the Qumran material has 'added a fresh possibility to the solution of the age-old problem of the origins of the Eucharist'.

In *The Scrolls and Christianity* he states that 'there is quite strong evidence at times for some kind of link between Qumran . . . and emerging Christianity', but he then continues 'direct dependence, however, has nowhere been conclusively demonstrated'. He emphasises the decisive contributions to Primitive Christianity made by John the Baptist and Jesus who transformed 'the practices of a sect into a universal religion' and were 'towering figures'. He finally agrees with Renan that Christianity was an Essenism that succeeded and the implication of this conclusion would appear to be that Jesus emerged from Jewish sectarianism and not from the mainstream of Judaism.

The bibliography printed in the Festschrift presented to Matthew Black in 1969 (*Neo-Testamentica et Semitica*) contains books and articles which he published up to 1967. According to this list the first article (1954) which he wrote on the Scrolls ('Theological Conceptions in the Dead Sea Scrolls') was derived from two lectures which he had given in Uppsala in 1953. The second article, entitled 'Messianic Doctrine in the Qumran Scrolls' (1957) was a paper which he had read at the Second International Conference of Patristic Studies in 1955. The 'Gospel and the Scrolls', which appeared in 1959, was a paper which he had read at the International Conference on the Four Gospels in 1957. 'The Dead Sea Scrolls and Christian Doctrine' followed in 1966, the same title as the Ethel M. Wood lecture which was published in that year. He had, during this period, published three articles on the wider Jewish sectarian background, one in 1956 on 'The Account of the Essenes in Hippolytus and Josephus', a second on 'The Patristic Accounts of Jewish Sectarianism' (1959) and a third in 1965 on 'The Tradition of Hasidaean-Essene Asceticism: Its Origins and Influence'.

In the bibliography contained in the second Festschrift which he received (1979) the only item on the Scrolls which is noticed is 'The Dead Sea Scrolls and Christian Origins', the section contributed to the book which he had edited (*The Scrolls and Christianity*) in 1969. Apart from the reproduction of his 1961 book (*The Scrolls and Christian Origins*) in 1982 this seems to have been his last word on the Scrolls.

His earliest article on the Dead Sea Scrolls shows that he was in the field before September 1953 and that he was able to offer two lectures at Uppsala on that date. The plates of *The Manual of Discipline* were published in 1951 and it is likely that he had them as soon as they were available. Otherwise his articles on the Scrolls do not add significantly to what has been gathered from his book.

The 'Son of Man' topic appears in Matthew Black's published articles as early as 1948 ('The "Son of Man" in the Old Biblical Literature' and 'The "Son of Man" in the Teaching of Jesus'). The emphasis which prevails throughout his work is already present. He focuses attention on 'The Similitudes of Enoch' (1 Enoch 37–71) which he describes as a reputedly pre-Christian and Jewish Apocalypse found only in the Ethiopic version of 1 Enoch and for which he claims a Hebrew or Aramaic original. He holds that there is 'a core of apocalyptic' in the New Testament portrayal of the Son of Man and that the background of Matt. 25 is the Similitudes of Enoch. It should not be thought that this has been 'foisted on' the teaching of Jesus. 'The Eschatology of the Similitudes of Enoch' (1952) represents that the Messianism of the Similitudes, which is more developed than that of the book of Daniel, was the model of the eschatological 'Son of Man' figure in the Gospels and so passed into Christianity.

The same approach is continued in 'The Servant of the Lord and the Son of Man', his inaugural lecture given in the University of Edinburgh (1952). The portrait of the Son of Man in the Gospels owes more to the Similitudes of Enoch than it does to the book of Daniel, but the element of redemptive suffering is derived from Isaiah 53 and the Suffering Servant in the New Testament is a Messianic figure, not just a prophetic one. 'The Son of Man Problem in Recent Research and Debate' (1963) continues along the same lines, and the principal topic is that the model of the Similitudes of Enoch furnishes the background of Jewish eschatological belief in the portrayal of the Son of Man in the Gospels.

A similar combination of the characteristics of Son of Man and Suffering Servant is set out in 'The "Son of Man" Passion Sayings in the Gospel Tradition' (1969). This article combines the concern of the *Aramaic Approach* with that of 'Son of Man'. Black holds that Luke 24: 7 is derived from an Aramaic-speaking milieu and discerns further evidence of an Aramaic original in John 3: 14, where an Aramaic verb with two meanings, 'to be exalted' and 'to be crucified' lies behind the Greek verb 'to be exalted'. The main direction of his argument is that there is a non-Markan tradition of passion sayings which have an Aramaic original and that these are dominical. In a Festschrift for Anton Vogtle he wrote on 'Die Apotheose Israels: eine neue Interpretation des danielischen Menschensohns' and in the Festschrift presented to W. D. Davies he contributed an essay on 'The Throne-Theophany Prophetic Commission and the "Son of Man": A Study in Tradition History' (1976).

In the same year he collaborated, as a minor partner, with J. T. Milik in the publication of *The Books of Enoch: Aramaic Fragments of Qumran Cave 4*. He had earlier published a Greek text of Enoch, *Apocalypsis Henochi Graece* (1970). His Greek text (1–32: 6; 97: 6–104; 106; 117: 1–3) was principally founded on the two extant manuscripts, the Gizeh Manuscript and the Chester Beatty Papyrus. The larger part of the book consists of Greek fragments of the Pseudepigrapha collected by A. M. Denis (pp. 45–238). The circumstances that no Aramaic fragments of the Similitudes of Enoch were recovered from Cave 4 at Qumran, and that Milik had dated the Ethiopic text of the

Similitudes in the medieval period, presented a challenge to Black's view that the Similitudes of Enoch had supplied the eschatological features of the New Testament Son of Man and he endeavoured to offer a preliminary answer to Milik in 'The Parables of Enoch (1 Enoch 37–71) and the "Son of Man" ' (1976). He notices that there is no trace of the Similitudes in the Aramaic fragments from Cave 4 at Qumran and that the manuscripts of the Ethiopic text of the Similitudes are dated in the sixteenth or seventeenth century. He accepts Milik's conclusion that the Ethiopic version of the Similitudes was composed in the medieval period, but he assumes a continuity of tradition with 'the earlier Enoch cycle'. He argues that the New Testament Son of Man derives from the Similitudes rather than from Daniel 7 and that 'the Parables are not an alien body of doctrine within the Enoch tradition'. There are evidences of an Aramaic original behind the Ethiopic: he cites 1 Enoch 65:10, where he discerns a misreading of an Aramaic original.

The last chapter in this 'Son of Man' record is supplied by the publication of *The Book of Enoch or 1 Enoch* in 1985. This was given an impetus by the year which he spent as a member of the Institute of Advanced Studies at Princeton in 1977–8. The book contains a translation of 1 Enoch, a commentary, textual notes and three appendices. He consulted James C. Vanderkam on matters Ethiopic and the astronomical chapters (72–82) are the work of Otto Neugebauer (Appendix A). The translation is a revised version of the one done by R. H. Charles in 1912. Black does not quarrel, for the most part, with the Ethiopic text which Charles used, but he has textual variants which he prefers. He holds that 1 Enoch, except for the Similitudes, was originally written in Aramaic, but he allows for the existence of a complete book of Enoch in Hebrew. He notices that it is a matter of debate which language was the *Grundschrift* of the Similitudes, whether Aramaic or Hebrew, and he now, following Halevy and Charles, expresses his preference for Hebrew. He favours the hypothesis that the Hebrew original was first translated into Greek (so Halevy and Charles) which was then the *Vorlage* of the Ethiopic version of the Similitudes. The conclusion that the Ethiopic version of Enoch had a Greek *Vorlage* has the disadvantage of placing it at two removes from its *Grundschrift*, whether Aramaic or Hebrew.

On the Son of Man question his position does not alter and he continues to hold that the Son of Man of the Similitudes is the foundation of Son of Man christology in the Gospels. He repeats what he had said earlier that they are not an alien body within the Enoch tradition.

He dates the Similitudes in the early Roman period, probably pre-70 AD, and rejects Milik's view that their historical background is around 250 AD and that their author was a Jew or a Jewish-Christian.

The book has not been well received and Black's fundamental mistake is that he tries to accomplish too much in what ought to have been an attempt to establish a critical Ethiopic text, to translate it into English and to comment on it. The circumstance that parts of 1 Enoch are extant in Greek and that Aramaic fragments have been recovered from Cave 4 at Qumran, together with the assumption that Greek is the *Vorlage* of the Ethiopic text and Aramaic the *Grundlage* (except for the Similitudes), ought not to have been allowed to overwhelm his primary task. The outcome of this complication is that he gives the impression of being more concerned with the Greek *Vorlage*, extant or putative, than with the Ethiopic variants in establishing the text of the Ethiopic version of Enoch and his presentation and handling of the Ethiopic and Aramaic evidence have provoked criticism.

Black began in the field of Christian-Palestinian Syriac and the first book which he published was his Bonn thesis *Rituale Melchitarum: A Christian-Palestinian Euchologion* (1938), the text of a Melkite liturgical document (British Museum MS Or. 4951) with a translation into English. He read a paper to the Glasgow University Oriental Society with the title 'The Syriac Inscription of the Nestorian Monument' and this was published in 1938. There followed 'The Palestinian Syriac Gospels and the Diatessaron' and 'A Palestinian Syriac Palimpsest Leaf of Acts xxi (14–26)' in 1939. 'A Christian Palestinian Syriac Horologion' (1945) describes the contents and assesses the value of MS Or. Oct. 1019 of Berlin State Library and points ahead to his edition of that manuscript, *A Christian Palestinian Syriac Horologion* (1954). This book contains critical notes on the manuscript, comments on its vocabulary, the text of a Melkite Horologion and its translation into English. He writes on 'The New Testament Peshitta and its Predecessors' (1950), 'The Gospel Text of Jacob of Serug' (1951), 'Rabbula of Edessa and the Peshitta' (1951), 'Zur Geschichte des syrischen Evangelientextes' (1952) and 'The Text of the Peshitta Tetraeuangelium' (1953). He contributed sections on Palestinian Syriac to Franz Rosenthal's *Aramaic Handbook* (1967). 'The Syriac New Testament in early Patristic Tradition' was published in 1971 and 'The Syriac Versional Tradition' in 1972. From 1968–78 he was Chairman of the Peshitta Project which was undertaken under the aegis of the International Organization for the Study of the Old Testament. In fact this was a light task. The project was the brain-child of Professor P. A. H. De Boer and was centred in the Peshitta Institute at Leiden. The aim was to produce a critical edition of the Old Testament Peshitta and individual books, which were allocated to an international group of scholars, were prepared for publication at the Peshitta Institute.

In 1958 Matthew Black reported on 'The Greek New Testament Project of the American and Associated Bible Societies'. This was an international venture which was initiated by the American Bible Society, associated with the Württemberg Bible Society and the National Bible Society of Scotland, later with the British and Foreign Bible Society and the Netherlands Bible Society. *The Greek New Testament* was published in 1966 and its editors were Kurt Aland, Matthew Black, Bruce Metzger and Allen Wikgren. The book was designed principally for the use of Bible translators. It was an eclectic text, based on Westcott and Hort, and otherwise resting on decisions of the editorial committee. Black appraised the version in 'The U.B.S. Greek New Testament Evaluated: A Reply' (1977). The editors were each assigned special tasks and Black was entrusted with the supervision of the collation of Syriac data, so that his earlier Syriac studies were focused on this new enterprise.

There was an editorial discussion at Bangor, North Wales, in 1955 on the occasion of a meeting of *Studiorum Novi Testamenti Societas* and from then on the editors conferred and pushed ahead with their tasks at meetings which were held during the summer in America, Europe and once in St Andrews. Matthew Black's natural habitat was his study, but he enjoyed travel when it was linked with scholarship and he was stimulated by the company of his fellow editors in different settings during these years. He attended the meetings of learned societies at home and abroad and accepted invitations to deliver lectures, sometimes courses of lectures, which took him to Europe, America, Australia, New Zealand, South Africa and Japan. He was President of the Society for Old Testament Study in 1968 and of *Studiorum Novi Testamenti Societas* in 1970–1.

He devoted much time to editorial tasks and was drawn to this side of scholarly activity. The revision of A. S. Peake's *Commentary on the Bible* (1919), published in 1962 enlisted many contributors and was a large editorial task. Black was the New Testament editor and also had a general responsibility for the whole volume, while H. H. Rowley was the Old Testament editor. Black was editor of *New Testament Studies* from its inception (1955) for a period of twenty-three years and his name appears for the last time in vol.23 (1977). He was also editor of the Monograph Series of *New Testament Studies. The Scrolls and Christianity* has already been noticed. Other books of which he was both joint editor and a contributor are *In Memoriam Paul Kahle* (1968) and *On Language, Culture and Religion* (1974) which was presented to Eugene Nida on his sixtieth birthday. To the first of these he contributed 'The Development of Aramaic Studies since the Work of Kahle' and to the second 'Notes on the Longer and Shorter Texts of Acts'.

Nida had written extensively on linguistics and was a Secretary of the Translations Department of the American Bible Society. From 1956 he was closely involved as an administrator and general policy adviser in the work of the editorial committee which was producing *The Greek Bible* and was present at its meetings. Matthew Black had been made an Honorary Member of the American Bible Society in 1968. The Festschrift is divided into two parts, 'Biblical Studies' (pp. 3–183) and 'Studies in Language and Culture' (pp. 187–380).

In the obituary notice which Matthew Black wrote in the *Proceedings of the British Academy* (1965) he describes Paul Kahle as 'the doyen of European Orientalists', a superlative ascription of praise which will not command universal agreement. He praises Kahle not only for his feats of scholarship but also for the discernment which enabled him to detect the far-reaching significance of his researches and for the generosity with which he disbursed his intellectual treasures to others. It is evident that Kahle exercised a decisive influence on the young Matthew Black and inspired him at an early stage of his development, as he acknowledges in the preface of *Rituale* (1938), his Bonn thesis. It is not an exaggeration to say that he experienced an intellectual awakening and acquired a kind of scholarly curiosity in Bonn which was discernible in his subsequent work. Kahle's seminar in Bonn, he writes in the *Proceedings*, 'was a centre of learning which attracted students from all over the world'. Nor does he forget in the preface to his *Rituale* his debt to Professor W. B. Stevenson who had taught him Hebrew and Aramaic at Glasgow and had encouraged and helped his former pupil when he was taking his first steps as an academic. It is said that Stevenson taught Hebrew in the University of Glasgow as a dominie would have taught his pupils in a Scottish country school. His *Grammar of Palestinian-Jewish Aramaic* (1924) is a reminder that Matthew Black laid the foundations of his scholarship in Glasgow.

Another name which should be mentioned is that of Professor T. W.

Manson, whose obituary notice in the *Proceedings* was contributed by Matthew Black. Manson was appointed to the Rylands Chair of Biblical Exegesis in the University of Manchester in 1936 and Black was an Assistant Lecturer there from 1937–9. Black observes that in *The Sayings of Jesus*, part of a larger book, Manson had noted that behind the sayings of Jesus in Mark and Luke there was an original Aramaic document or source. In the 1937 book Manson had asserted that the bulk of the teaching of Jesus was in Aramaic which he described as 'the vernacular language of Palestine and the only language in which the majority of the people were at home'. He had further stated that the differences between Matthew and Luke in reporting the words of Jesus were to be accounted for by the translation — sometimes mistranslation — of Greek from Aramaic. These were ideas which guided Black's detailed researches.

When Matthew Black became Emeritus in 1978, he left behind a very large study which had housed his books comfortably, where they were well ordered and easy of access. He had become accustomed to this state of affairs, was attached to the room in which he had passed so many hours and found the transition to retirement in a new setting difficult. He continued to work and published a book in 1985. His new home was delightful, but it did not have a room which compensated for the loss of his study. He had brought his books with him, but he could not accommodate them in the way he had once done and they were not easy of access. In the last period the contrast between the then and the now weighed heavily on him and amounted to a feeling of exile.

He was deeply attached to his son and daughter; the progress of his grandchildren awakened his keen interest and brought him to life: he had great pride in their accomplishments. The devotion of his wife, Ethel Hall, whom he married in 1938, cannot be praised too highly.

WILLIAM McKANE
Fellow of the Academy

Note. I acknowledge help received from Fellows of the Academy, from Professor Robin Wilson, Professor Edward Ullendorff and Professor Michael Knibb. Miss Margaret Blackwood, who was Professor Black's secretary, has been a mine of information.

MURIEL BRADBROOK

Proceedings of the British Academy, **90**, 297–316

Muriel Clara Bradbrook
1909–1993

MURIEL CLARA BRADBROOK has been the most creatively influential Shakespeare scholar of our time. She was busily occupied as a college and university teacher and administrator from her appointment as a teaching Fellow of Girton in 1936, with an interlude of wartime service at the Board of Trade, on to her appointment as vice-mistress of her college in 1962, as the first woman Professor of English at Cambridge in 1965 and as Mistress of Girton from 1968 until her retirement in 1976; and for many years she travelled and lectured across the world. At the same time she was exceptionally productive in scholarship. Beginning with the two books from her twenties that can fairly be called seminal—*Elizabethan Stage Conditions* (1932) and *Themes and Conventions of Elizabethan Tragedy* (1935)—she brought out a dozen books on Shakespeare and the Elizabethan theatre, supplemented by many lectures and articles, some of which are assembled in three of the four volumes of her *Collected Papers* (1981–89); and besides these, a centenary history of Girton (*That Infidel Place*, 1969) and a wide variety of literary studies in books and articles ranging in subject from Marvell to Beckett and from Malory to Lowry, and spanning her long career, with undiminished energy in her years of nominal retirement, from her pungent essay on Virginia Woolf in the first number of *Scrutiny* (1932) to her freshly-researched lecture saluting Vaclav Havel in 1991. A friend and former research pupil, Marie Axton, has described her (in conversation) as 'the most omnivorous reader I have ever known'—and she was also an indefatigable playgoer, coupling her enthusiasm for books and plays with a piercing attention to detail and with exceptional mobility in her powers of association and recall. Perhaps the outstanding qualities of her critical writing were her intuitive insights, enriched (or, at times, encrusted) with associative cross-references, and her unfailing grasp of practical realities, reinforced by a controlled but insuppressible dry sense of humour.

She was born in Wallasey, the eldest child of her father's third marriage, with two adult half-sisters surviving from his previous marriages and then four younger brothers, one of whom died in infancy. She came, as she was proud to say, from seafaring people on both sides. Her father, Samuel Bradbrook (1856–1928), was the son of a Brightlingsea shipbuilder and had been at sea before joining the Waterguard; her maternal grandmother, Mary Elizabeth Harvey, was the daughter of a pilot and the wife of a captain and daughter-in-law of a master mariner and shipowner, all three from Falmouth. The Falmouth connection was important to her. In a late autobiographical note she called her grandmother there her 'first love', who gave her the name, 'Muriel, the bright sea, a Celtic name'; while Falmouth, familiar from holiday visits, had always been 'my spiritual home', where 'my grandmother's little house, full of curiosities from all over the seven seas' (which included a model of the elder Harvey's ship), together with 'my father's collection of poets and novels, shaped my childhood'. No doubt the fascination of the sea was to count for a great deal in her subsequent eagerness to travel, her interest in writers such as Conrad and Lowry, and her sensitivity to the local surroundings of Ibsen and of Strindberg.

Her childhood was enclosed within the family, with her father's books. John, the oldest of her brothers, recalls that she 'was very much in her own world and had quite a sharp and sarcastic tongue on occasions'. But she had delicate health, suffering from asthma until she was eighteen. Her first school was Hutcheson's School in Glasgow, where her father had moved as Superintendent of HM Waterguard in 1917, returning to Wallasey in 1919, upon his retirement. But she was not able to attend school regularly until she was thirteen, when she was admitted to a free place at the new grammar school, the Oldershaw Girls' School, in Wallasey—the headmistress, as she puts it, taking a risk on her. Oldershaw launched her, thanks to the headmistress, Violet Blyth, who was an old Girtonian, and her English mistress, Molly Kane, an Irishwoman who not only gave her a grounding in Donne as well as Shakespeare and the Romantics but fostered her lifelong admiration for Yeats and her love of the theatre. At seventeen she won an Exhibition to

Girton, to be supplemented by a State Scholarship, in those days a rare and, for those without ample means, an indispensable prize.

The tight but cosmopolitan community of Girton prepared Muriel Bradbrook for wider social horizons. And Girton meant or came to mean for her a quiet but deep identification with women's advancing struggle for equal opportunities. The older Girtonians she was to remember with respect were formidable women from the suffragette generation, women who had found the confirmed purpose and strength of will necessary to affirm themselves. The fight for the vote had partly been won a few years before she came to Girton in 1927, but not equality with men's right to vote at 21, until 1929. And educational equality was still far from perfect at Cambridge, in spite of the achievements of the women's colleges. While she was an undergraduate reading English the Professor, Quiller-Couch, still refused to admit women to his evening classes on Aristotle's *Poetics*. In 1930, after a starred First and a double First in the Tripos, she obtained nothing better than a college certificate stating that she would have been entitled to a BA if she had been a man, and a university degree certificate 'in which the word "titular" had been inserted by hand'. She did not gain her first temporary teaching post from the university until 1945, by which time she had five books to her credit, equality of opportunity in academic appointments being even further off then than now. And not until 1948 did Cambridge grant women full membership of the university, including voting rights for MAs. For Muriel Bradbrook, equality of educational opportunity, the opportunity to develop intellectual parity with men, was always to be the central plank in the feminist cause. However, this was far from a restrictive commitment. Speaking of Barbara Bodichon, the friend of George Eliot, painter, propagandist for women's rights and co-founder of Girton, she said that 'The lack of a single commitment seems to me . . . to be her rare and peculiar strength'; and (in the Foreword to Muriel Bradbrook's *Collected Papers on Women and Literature 1779–1982*) Inga-Stina Ewbank has picked out these words to characterise the multiple scholarship and outgoing human interests of the speaker herself.

She came to Cambridge at a fortunate moment, effervescent with new ideas and as yet unperplexed by fears about mass unemployment, fascism and war. Among her student contemporaries were William Empson and Jacob Bronowski, Michael Redgrave, Alistair Cooke and Malcolm Lowry, Kathleen Raine and—her next-door neighbour in Girton—her aloof senior, Queenie Roth, the future Queenie Leavis.

Her principal supervisor at Girton was the lexicographer's daughter, Hilda Murray, an exacting and evidently bracing medievalist who 'conferred on her pupils the benefit of an Oxford point of view quite opposed to that of Cambridge'. But the main drive of the new and innovative English Tripos, just established in 1926, led away from philology to literary criticism, with Aristotle's *Poetics* as one of the set books—a Tripos with no chronological cut-off, but with an emphasis on modern literature, with some requirements in reading foreign literatures, and with openings on philosophy, psychology and social history. There was no critical orthodoxy, but a prevailing tone of cool yet intensive analysis. The outstanding lecturer and formative mind was I. A. Richards, who was soon, in 1929, to publish his epoch-making *Practical Criticism*. And, besides Richards, there was the influence of his friend, T. S. Eliot; the great good fortune of Muriel Bradbrook's student generation was that new academic ideas coincided and partly interlocked with the progress of new major developments in creative literature. Miss Murray invited F. R. Leavis to Girton to take classes in practical criticism, and Leavis laid stress on modern poets, including Empson; (in her contribution to Ronald Hayman's *My Cambridge* (1977) Muriel Bradbrook asks 'how many people have been taught poetry written by a contemporary undergraduate?'). Moreover, in addition to the university, her Cambridge encompassed Terence Gray's Festival, which proclaimed itself the best avant-garde theatre west of Moscow. Something of the exhilaration of those years can be guessed from a post-obituary letter to the *Guardian* (19 June 1993), where a younger Oldershaw pupil, Sylvia Hall, recounts how Muriel, still a student, returned to her old school ('wearing a wonderful straw hat decorated with daisies and a strange, long cotton dress') to deliver a fascinating and memorable talk about Cambridge University.

At the same time, her undergraduate and post-graduate years were full of personal strain. Her father died in 1928, leaving the family badly off. Her mother died in 1934. She had to provide for her two younger brothers and their education, shepherding them both eventually into Downing College. Meanwhile, in what was now a climate of depression, she lived through a love affair which ended unhappily (she never married). 'The years 1930–6', she writes in *My Cambridge*, 'gave me a taste of extremities which have ever since enabled me to put other difficulties in proportion'. Nevertheless, these were also the years of her first books and articles, energetic and resourceful.

Elizabethan Stage Conditions, awarded the university's Harness

Prize for 1931, cleared the way for a new phase in Shakespeare interpretation. The critical assumptions of Victorian realism, implicit in Bradley's prestigious studies and polemically sharpened by William Archer against the Elizabethans, were already coming under challenge. The mass of documentation assembled by E. K. Chambers and others had thrown new light on the historical conditions, material and institutional, under which Elizabethan plays had been performed, and on the transmission of Shakespeare's texts. Stoll and Schucking had directly challenged the presumed realism of Shakespeare's characters, emphasising their conventional, even 'primitive', aspects. In his *Prefaces to Shakespeare*, Harley Granville-Barker had begun to combine historical scholarship with his practical and creative experience on the stage. Above all, T. S. Eliot was shifting the grounds of criticism from realistic psychology to the language of poetry in action, towards an ideal of drama as the projection of a poetic vision close to ritual. And, as against realism, Wilson Knight was expounding his brilliant if wilful interpretation of Shakespeare's plays in terms of a network of symbolic images. In effect, Bradbrook provided a synthesis between the new criticism and the new scholarship. She showed that, without conducing to realism (and without being 'primitive'), an Elizabethan stage gave an adaptable framework for movement and pageantry, while concentrating attention on the actors themselves and the actors' speech; the prime vehicle for dramatic action was the poetry. It was not poetry by itself that counted, however, but poetry for delivery on the stage.

One feature of her critical writing is her vigorous common sense, tempering her sensitivity and avoiding abstractions or extremes. Another is her gleeful capacity for pertinent irreverence. In her first book, for example, she adduces Eugene O'Neill to mark a contrast between modern, non-poetic techniques and Elizabethan dramaturgy: '*The Emperor Jones* produces a powerful abdominal response, as much akin to literature as the feeling of going up in a lift'. In the 1962 reissue she confesses that, knowing that Granville-Barker was to be one of the adjudicators of her prize essay, she 'was determined not to curry favour. So I slapped the examiner'. And, as she was well aware, she stung Virginia Woolf by her *Scrutiny* essay of 1932, accusing the novelist of a lack of intellectual fibre. Elsewhere, she made amends to Granville-Barker and Virginia Woolf and—within limits—to O'Neill. But she continued to produce deflating asides and terse, summarising comments, often with a dismissive edge, verging on epigram. In *English Dramatic Form* (1965), for example, she observes that although

Marlowe's *Tamburlaine* is 'iconoclastic' in relation to religious street pageantry, it 'derives its energies from the tradition it abjures'. Again, there is a similar neat placing of Pirandello's *Henry IV*: 'Pirandello suffered from the disabling weight of Italian professional theatre— probably the most powerful tradition in Europe of its kind. His cerebral drama gives an exaggerated display of intellectual agility, that does not disguise emotional poverty'. As these examples together illustrate, she was concerned for both emotional and intellectual strength in literature. Equally, from *Elizabethan Stage Conditions* onward, she was concerned to balance evaluative judgment with appreciation of the historical environment of a writer's work.

Themes and Conventions of Elizabethan Tragedy (1935) treated Shakespeare only incidentally, but surveyed in detail his predecessors and successors in tragedy, major and minor, from Marlowe to Shirley, in the light of what she brings out as their common working artistic assumptions, as distinct from those of neo-classical drama or the novel. It made a landmark in dramatic criticism. Bradbrook demoted the criteria of psychological realism on the stage, showing how the Elizabethans achieved a heightened and variegated but (at their best) coherent poetic effect. She points out how (and, to some extent, why) characters emerge as accentuated types; how action is often mixed, embracing side by side allegory and local naturalism, hornpipes and funerals, and often crowded and complicated, with the sequential links between one intensified episode and another schematised emphatically or passed over in favour of developing an interplay between different aspects of the dominant moral theme; and how Elizabethan stage speech, with its freedom in soliloquies and asides, is not an imitation of the meanders, fumblings and understatements of natural dialogue but essentially an application of rhetoric, keyed to the dramatic theme as much as the speaker, and designed for explicitness with an overlay of suggestion, conspicuous patterning and theatrical impact. In the face of critics of the school of William Archer, she points out that in drama, unlike the novel, such deviation from ordinary speech can be a positive advantage, if not a necessity, because in drama 'the dialogue has to define as well as to present the feelings' of the characters—whereas a novelist is free to explain or qualify them in his own words; drama 'must be more selective' than the novel, 'and selection is only possible through a convention'.

A convention has been defined at the outset as 'an agreement between writers and readers (or spectators), whereby the artist is allowed to distort and simplify his material through a control of the distribution of emphasis'. This definition implies that a convention is an artistic device or method departing from a (notional) unselective, photographic reproduction of actuality; and secondly, that such a device is not peculiar to a single work but is shared by a number of writers in the same genre or the same period and is presumably accepted or even encouraged by their public. One may object to Muriel Bradbrook's definition on the one hand, that it makes the compact between, say, dramatists and spectators seem too conscious and deliberate; and on the other hand, that it does not go far enough, since what may be called the writer's choice or summoning of material involves some kind of accord with his potential public over interests and values, even prior to his simplification or manipulation of it. His material may be affected by convention, as much as his method. A list of technical conventions to be found in Elizabethan plays would be of no more than descriptive use without further examination. And there is the danger, as Christopher Ricks has insisted, of treating Elizabethan stage conventions as self-justifying, self-explanatory. As a rule Muriel Bradbrook is quick to point out that what counts about a convention is how it is used, the dramatic context. But occasionally she brings forward a convention as a sufficient critical argument by itself; as when she writes that 'Credibility of slander was a most useful convention for complicating the action' — so that criticism of, for instance, Claudio in *Much Ado About Nothing* would be simply beside the point. This is one of the few places where she seems to be carried away by her thesis.

More generally, however, her idea of convention empowers a critical break-through, conjoining literary insight with awareness of the demands and opportunities of the Elizabethan stage. There is a finely-tuned chapter on Marlowe, for example ('Marlowe's sensuousness has the maximum of concreteness and the minimum of particularity'); and her chapter on *The Revenger's Tragedy* gives a highly original demonstration of her sense of poetic drama, of the interplay between stage action, allegory, topical reference and verbal imagery: 'All the betrayed women [in the play]', she writes, with reference to the central episode, 'are in a sense represented by the poisoned skull of Vindice's mistress'; and she goes on to analyse Vindice's address to the skull (the tirade already singled out by T. S. Eliot) so as to show the dramatic relevance of its charged verbal ambiguities. With Webster, her touch is not quite so sure, as when she says with regard to the ambivalence of Vittoria in *The White Devil* that the repetition of the epithet, 'devil', 'would have great force' to 'a literal-minded Jacobean audience'—though not enough to make them 'ready to take an oath, if cross-examined, that Vittoria was possessed; but then they were not accustomed to judge their impressions separately or even to analyse them out fully, and the absence of any soliloquy or choric aside from Vittoria deprives them of any direct lead for their judgment'; and there are further, similar comments on the indistinct suggestiveness of Webster's allusions to the supernatural. Here straightforward observation of the text edges over into presumptions about an audience's state of mind. However, there is at least indirect evidence to support such presumptions; and they do not interfere with sharp comments on Webster's dramatic technique—'The difficulty of *The White Devil* is that the feelings are frequently naturalistic, but the characters are not. The impression of the parts conflicts with the impression of the whole'. This is critical comment in the main line reaching back to Arnold and Johnson.

Muriel Bradbrook's attachment to a central tradition of criticism, with its concern for wholeness and balance in a writer's work and for comparative evaluation, an attachment no doubt fostered by Leavis, is prominent in her early articles, notably in her critique of William Empson (in *Scrutiny*, II, (1933)), which advanced an unusually coolly measured appraisal of *Seven Types of Ambiguity*, in spite of her high admiration of her contemporary's acclaimed brilliance: 'Mr. Empson's intellectual analysis and his emotional stimulation are each apt to get dissociated and out of focus. . . . Something more than the working of a properly qualified mind and the expression of a lively sensibility goes to the making of a great critic'. She extended her literary approach through a post-graduate year at Oxford (1935–6), where she studied under C. S. Lewis. Meanwhile, she had devised, for her work on drama, a method of her own, that she describes in the preface to the third volume of her *Collected Papers* (1983): 'I had devised a technique of reading and re-reading an Elizabethan text till the shape of its themes and conventions emerged. Sometimes I would read a great play twenty or thirty times, along with all the minor plays that have survived. I know no substitute for laminating the text into one's mind in a variety of moods and settings, the equivalent of an actor's study and rehearsal'. The effect of this intensive absorption with her subject, together with her darting intuition and remarkably retentive memory, can be seen again and again in her writings. A survey of 'Bogeymen, Machiavels and Stoics' (in *Collected Papers* III) touches on, quotes or discusses some fifty plays by Chapman and a score of other Elizabethan or Stuart playwrights (including the glancing aside, apropos of *The Virgin Martyr*, that 'Martyrdom was the one profession open equally to both sexes') in the space of sixteen pages. Sometimes what she once called (if I remember correctly) her own 'dot-and-carry manner of writing' can bewilder her reader with unexpected cross-references; as, for example, where, in *Shakespeare the Craftsman* (1969), she sets out to clarify the style of *Timon of Athens* with the help of successive allusions to Joyce's *Ulysses*, Corneille and Japanese Noh plays. In general, she remained indifferent to aesthetic theorising, although in her later work she made occasional raids on psychology. She could write concise and impressive surveys of aspects of dramatic history, but her attempt to expound a theory of development, in *English Dramatic Form* (1965), was left unsustained. And, especially in her later books, she could be accused of neglecting the clear exposition of an argument in favour of vivid and varied particulars. As Mary Ann Radzinowicz has written, in her obituary article in the *Girton College Newsletter, 1993*: 'Her books scarcely announced their theses; she had a rooted preference for the presentation of richly detailed evidence accompanied by the continuous light pressure of what Andrew Gurr has called "significant inferences"'. In a way, this shows a continuation from her apprenticeship in *Scrutiny*.

On the other hand, as she noted herself, she differed from Leavis and L. C. Knights in her fascination with theatrical performance. It is noticeable that she compares her own method of research with that of an actor studying a part—though with her slight physique and her thin, reedy voice she was quite untheatrical and undemonstrative in her personal bearing (which, however, is far from saying either constrained or ineffective). Her love of theatre and her focus on concrete details correspond to her keen appreciation of other personalities. A thumbnail sketch from her contribution to Reuben Brower's volume of essays in honour of I. A. Richards (1973) is typical of this responsiveness to personality, especially since she concentrates here on the way Richards could project himself, on Richards the performer rather than the philosopher: 'Ivor Richards cannot be met adequately through his books alone. To hear him read aloud is the best education in poetry; his voice, melancholy, slow-cadenced, sinks with an emphatic fall to clinch his argument. His impish humour, his personal courtesy and his surprising union of the authoritative and the mischievous are more fully shewn in talk, lectures, or possibly—and if he has not made any, he should do so—in film'. To anyone who knew Richards and attended his lectures this is a convincing vignette.

Apart from an over-ingenious foray into topical allusions in *The School of Night* (1936), her first book dwelling on Shakespeare, *Shakespeare and Elizabethan Poetry* (1951), was a literary study, as the title announces; and *The Growth and Structure of Elizabethan Comedy* (1955) was also mainly a survey of literary forms and conventions. But *The Rise of the Common Player* (1962), dedicated to Edith Evans, marked a decisive shift of perspective, in a pioneering study of the social conditions governing performance in the sixteenth and early seventeenth centuries and of the emergence of acting as a profession. As against the tendency to assume that a play must be a self-contained literary statement, she brought out the coexistence, during Elizabeth's reign, of performances as parts of a mixed popular entertainment, in conditions resembling a fun-fair; of acting in noble households or college halls; and of shows devised for a special occasion, addressed as 'offerings' to the principal spectator, notably the Queen. She discussed the status of the commercial player under moralistic attack and sketched the composition and progress of the first well-known companies, with a clinching demonstration that Laneham's often-cited public Letter from Leicester's famous entertainment for the Queen at Kenilworth in 1575 should be read as an elaborate puff for the newly advancing professional company of Leicester's Men; and she outlined the careers of the early actor-playwright, Robert Wilson, and the first stars of the English theatre, Richard Tarlton, the clown, and the great and prosperous tragic actor, Edward Alleyn, theatrical entrepreneur, joint patentee of the Mastership of the Royal Game and ultimately founder of Dulwich College. Much of the documentation for all this could be found in E. K. Chambers' great work; but it was Muriel Bradbrook who brought the Elizabethan actors to life as practitioners of a developing craft within a complex society. There is a similar slant towards socio-economic considerations in her articles of 1960 and 1962 on 'Spenser's pursuit of Fame' and on 'Beasts and Gods: Greene's *Groats-worth of Witte* and the social purpose of *Venus and Adonis*' (in *Shakespeare Survey* XV), where she interprets the poem in the light of a riposte to Greene's slur on Shakespeare as a thievish, unlettered player. The new outlook conveyed in *The Rise of the Common Player* did not mean the abandonment of the critic's original views, however, but a fresh development. As she does not fail to point out, Alleyn, who was Marlowe's and Shakespeare's junior by a couple of years, made his name in leading parts for Marlowe, Greene and Kyd; and she emphasises that it was the poets who in the 1580s fused together the Elizabethan public and crowned the development of a new art form—in effect, the self-sustaining dramatic poem. In the Preface she writes, extending the argument from *Elizabethan Stage Conditions*, that 'The greatest triumphs [of the Elizabethans] were in dramatic poetry, involving the special use of language as part of a larger social context, including also the "languages" of music, gesture, spectacle, the "traffic of the stage"'. The traffic of the stage in various forms, but crucially as poetry in performance, was to remain the principal object of her later studies.

A guiding thread here was her subtle and suggestive investigation of Shakespeare's relation to his actors—though it is characteristic of Bradbrook's many-sided approach that she did not isolate the subject. For example, in a late article (in *Collected Papers* IV) she interpreted *Two Gentlemen of Verona* as a piece intended for boy actors—not professionals—performing before a noble household during the plague year of 1593, when the men's companies had broken up and Shakespeare was presumably away from London; in justification she pointed to the limited demands made on the players, who have soliloquies and duets, but are not required to operate as a group (and pointed also to the play's courtly ethos of love-service, deriving from Lyly and Castiglione). By way of contrast, in *Shakespeare the Craftsman* she had described *The Merry Wives of Windsor* as a 'completely professional accomplishment', a unique portrayal of 'small town society', designed to give everyone in the company 'a good fat part'. Shakespeare's evolving relationship with his fellow-actors is precisely the main theme of that book, based on her Clark lectures of 1968. An important, well documented topic is Shakespeare's engagement with the distinctive personality of Robert Armin, his clown player from *As You Like It* to *King Lear*. Above all, Bradbrook dwells here on Shakespeare's interaction with the Burbage family, as a family belonging to what was virtually a craft guild, but a guild at work under novel, post-medieval conditions, entrepreneurial and technical. Richard Burbage's adaptability in expressing varied moods and roles within a single part and his power to dominate the audience stand out as key factors in the decisive achievement of *Hamlet*, which the critic sees as a production triumphantly self-aware. The Players within the play are supposed to be 'trudging away' from their base in the capital, but their arrival at Elsinore 'Could not really be staged at the Globe except as part of a dazzling public success. No one really advertises his own failure'; and Bradbrook suggests that the First Player was made up to look like Burbage himself, confronting the actual Burbage as the Prince; (this would not have been the only play in which Burbage came on, or was supposed to come on, in person). The tragedy draws and depends upon the audience's knowledge of older revenge plays, but it also draws upon their knowledge of more recent Burbage parts, as in *Julius Caesar*. *Hamlet*, she writes, 'is not so much a play as a geological deposit of accumulated dramatic experience. It *is* the embodied history of the English stage. . . . Because it is most traditional in theme, it is most revolutionary in terms of relationships, their precision, their definition by gestures married to words'. Rather than proposing a psychological reading of the tragedy, she emphasises its capacity to stand as an enduring, self-explanatory dramatic fiction, thanks especially to its incorporation of theatrical experience, of the play within the play. In *Hamlet* 'drama [has] come of age, arriving at a new configuration of actors and audience, in their relation to the play and the world beyond', precisely because the actors have come to be 'fully recognised as a body separate from the audience, guardians of their own craft mystery', with an identity of their own, embodying a kind of '"second world" of art', more vivid than everyday existence.

It was the Burbage family that marked out crucial moments in this development. When in 1576 the father, James Burbage, set up London's first purpose-built playhouse, the Theatre, 'what [he] really invented was the Box Office'—an indispensable preliminary to the future triumph of *Hamlet*. Much later, 'the modern theatre effectively began' in the autumn of 1608, when the son, Richard Burbage, took over the Blackfriars for the King's Men, with its requirement of new scenic and acting techniques for an intimate playhouse with an indoor stage. Bradbrook adds the important qualifying observation that Shakespeare does not simply adapt himself to a new fashion in his last plays, after 1608, but 'paradoxically recalls and transforms the romances of his youth, as the links with the old craft stage disappeared'—in effect, that is, a reassertion of professional identity and continuity. But she also suggests that it may have been Richard Burbage's death three years after Shakespeare, at the age of forty-five, that prompted their two fellow-actors to bring out the plays they had largely shared together in the nearly unprecedented grand format of a Folio.

In one respect Bradbrook's interest in 'the dynamics of performance' led her to a change of critical emphasis. In a late discussion of *Hamlet* ('Production and Performance in Blackfriars' drama' (1984); in *Collected Papers* IV) she argues for the constructive potential of 'non-verbal aspects' of a 'rich'—but, as the early printing history shows, a changeable—text, owing to the repeated interplay between Burbage and the other members of the company, including Shakespeare himself: 'Performance itself had shown that the apparent inconsistencies, contradictions, unexplained changes could add depth and integrity to the actor's role. . . . The gaps allow the actor to "breathe" inside his part'. Elsewhere, on the other hand (in *The Living Monument: Shakespeare and the Theatre of his Time* (1976)), she had noted that 'Edith Evans has always refused the part [of Lady Macbeth] because she thinks it lacks the third quarter—the development between the banquet scene and the sleep-walking scene'. But meanwhile, in her book on Webster (1980), she had dwelt on the performative value of his "poetry of the gaps", considerably modifying her criticism of his plays in *Themes and Conventions*: 'the thickly laminated dramatic poetry, built with alternating views, shifting perspectives, allows the audience to insert any variations they wish; the actor can "breathe" inside his part'. In *The Duchess of Malfi* 'the legendary, the contemporary, the dramatically ritualistic are laminated', in a manner she compares with the multiple allusions in the poetry of T. S. Eliot and Allen Tate. 'Lamination', again, is the metaphor she uses to define her own method of study in building up successive, overlapping impressions of a play. This view of an Elizabethan play in performance was not a concession to drama by way of sub-literary shocks (such as she had criticised in Eugene O'Neill). But it altered and supplemented, if it did not contradict, her original view of the hegemony of poetry; as in her article on 'Thomas Heywood, Shakespeare's Shadow' (1982; in *Collected Papers* III), where she argues that for Heywood, an actor-playwright who, like Shakespeare, neglected the printing of his own plays, what counted was not the poetry but the performance: 'Words alone represented a scenario, an operatic score for a collaborative cultural event, when actors and audience bestowed the final shaping'. Noting the burden of the new wave of textual scholarship, she adds that 'To reconstitute a dramatic text is an act of cultural archaeology'.

This view of performance involves the audience as well as actors and playwright; and reconstruction of an audience's share in a 'cultural event' implies an awareness of place, perhaps sponsorship, historical period, and occasion. In her first books Muriel Bradbrook had tried to analyse the mentality of Elizabethan playgoers in terms of their reading and their education in rhetoric. Her later comments within this area are more specific and pragmatic. She had an acute sense of topography; several of her books are furnished with maps of Elizabethan London. In *Shakespeare the Craftsman* she brought out the modernity (or actuality) of *Julius Caesar* by showing how Shakespeare's Rome resembles London in its social structure, and how Shakespeare reveals his actors' awareness of their audience, and power to manipulate it, through the speeches of Caesar, Brutus and Antony. In *The Living Monument* she brought out the significance for *Macbeth* of the public moment when it appeared—the moment of Gunpowder Plot, following hard upon the resplendent procession (in which Shakespeare, as one of the King's Men, must have taken part) welcoming James I to London and his coronation. However, with regard to *King Lear,* which she would date after *Macbeth*, she considered that the topical significance was to be found less in any oblique reference to Stuart politics than in 'the rejection of Court rites', with a deep-lying 'decision to stay with the popular stage'; adding, in her next book (*Shakespeare: The Poet in his World* (1978)), that a major source of the power in the tormented middle scenes of the play must have been Shakespeare's resentment over Harsnett's pamphlet against *Popish Impostures*, with the persistent, malicious association it makes between acting and devilry. She provides a further range of significant topical references in *The Poet in his World*: for example, with reference to *Romeo and Juliet*, she touches on the background of public fears of the plague, and she brings out the novelty of Shakespeare's treatment of the story in condemning the parents, not the young lovers; or, again, she notes that in the production of *Henry IV* by the Lord Chamberlain's Men the presentation of the historical defeat of the Northern Earls at Shrewsbury parallels and tacitly celebrates the other, nearly contemporary defeat of Northern Earls in 1569 by the first Lord Hunsdon, the original patron of Shakespeare's company and the father of their current patron. Her books are rich in suggestive links between Shakespeare and the lives or the common knowledge of his company and their audience. In her book on Webster, similarly, she provides a fuller account of the man and his milieu than had been available before, with the help of details about the London neighbourhood he lived in and with the support of two other biographical chapters, concerning Sidney's Stella, Penelope Rich, and the Spanish spy and political exile, Antonio Pérez. These two life-stories are not presented as likely source material or objects of allusion in the plays, but as 'London Legends', as Bradbrook calls them, or as parallel lives, one might say, to set beside the lives of Webster's characters; they help to bring home some of the resonance of the tragedies for a modern reader, configurations of passion and political intrigue that, by repute, at least, Webster's first audiences would have found familiar.

As a rule, her books on Shakespeare do not offer a thoroughgoing analysis, a comprehensive study in depth, of any of his plays. Instead, they provide fresh, darting perceptions into major aspects of the plays, with sidelights from scholarly digressions. But those digressions bring to bear an unrivalled command of the environing factors in Elizabethan stage conditions, literature and general history, as well as of modern, international interpretations of Shakespeare on the stage. And probably no other scholar has given us such lively, many-sided impressions of an Elizabethan play as 'a collaborative cultural event', in all the complexity of the traffic between the dramatist and his fellow-writers, the actors and the public.

Muriel Bradbrook's work on the Elizabethans accounts for something like two-thirds of her considerable output. But altogether her active range as a scholar and critic was very much wider. She drew freely on poets as far apart as Chaucer and Edwin Muir and produced studies of Marvell, T. S. Eliot and Kathleen Raine, as well as of novelists as unlike one another as Jane Austen and Conrad and Lowry. And she wrote with insight and an easy command of her material about the modern theatre over the past century: about the Paris of Sarah Bernhardt; Yeats and the Irish revival; and the progression of avant-garde drama from Strindberg and Jarry to Beckett and Pinter. She should be remembered for this work on modern drama and for her studies of some departments of twentieth-century literature in general as much as for her work on the Elizabethans. A genuinely cosmopolitan range of sympathies counts for a good deal in this achievement, backed up by her alert-minded world-wide travels. Two of her best books are *Ibsen the Norwegian* (1946) and *Literature in Action: Studies in Continental and Commonwealth Society* (1972), a highly original but somewhat neglected book where she considers modern European drama in company with the writings of New Zealand, Australia and Canada.

During the war years she learned Norwegian from Norwegian naval officers in exile in London, and she used her knowledge of Ibsen's language decisively. She transformed the already dated English view of the dramatist championed by William Archer and Bernard Shaw as Ibsen the social challenger and pamphleteer. She concentrated instead on Ibsen the poet. Not that she ignored the problematic aspects of the plays—pointing out, for example, that modern playgoers are liable to underrate the social risks Nora confronts at the end of *A Doll's House*. But she dwells on the presence in the plays of Norway, its geography and history, and of Ibsen's love-hate relationship with his country; on the continuity of themes from his lyrical poems to his plays; and on the style of his stage dialogue, 'in grain' (as she contends) with the tendency of Ibsen's language towards pithy and ironic statement or 'inference and riddle'. She brings out the poetic resonance of Ibsen's style not only in *Brand* and *Peer Gynt* but in his prose masterpieces as well. She describes *A Doll's House*, for example, as the 'first Modern Tragedy', consummating and surpassing the tradition of the well-made play, not because of its contribution to the cause of feminism, but because of its poetic concentration, in gestures and visual images and above all (using her favourite metaphor) in its 'spare and laminated speech'. 'It was no accident' (she observes) 'that it fell to a Norwegian to take that most finely tooled art, the drama, and bring it to a point and precision so nice that literally not a phrase is without its direct contribution to the structure'; and, in a telling summary, she adds, 'Ibsen will not allow the smallest action to escape from the psychopathology of everyday life'. As a critic, she was not impressed by drama with a message or by realism for its own sake, but she responded keenly to the intensity of overlapping implications in *A Doll's House*, which she even compares, in that respect, to *Oedipus the King*—though that does not prevent her from noting that the play is even overcharged with irony, and contrasting it with Ibsen's later, finer and more restrained achievement in *Hedda Gabler*.

Another side of Ibsen, his treatment of the past in relation to the present, comes to the fore in *Literature in Action*. There, Bradbrook brings out how Ibsen moved from a public to a private domain of myths, from the direct recounting of national history, legend or folklore in his early plays to a different form of composition where (as in *Rosmersholm*, for instance) the past, of an individual, a family, a society, lives on in the inhibitions and fantasies of the characters and where simultaneously the characters' present reconditions their past. This chapter in turn forms part of a broader study of drama and its value for modern society. Drama is still the most potent of the arts in making for psychological stability, she argues, because it offers a collective experience wherein divergent, possibly conflicting, impulses can meet and balance one another, an experience focused on the living voice of the actor, reinforced by gesture and by scenic effect. In modern culture, however, the imaginative binding force once exercised by tradition and by history has gone; although a modern dramatist like Eliot or Giraudoux may readapt a Greek myth for a modern application, he can no longer build on the direct authority of a traditional narrative, as Ibsen's example illustrates. Private dreams or obsessions have come to speak more powerfully to an audience than unmediated public myths; hence the emergence of the Theatre of the Absurd. The first production of *En Attendant Godot* in Paris in 1953 was as much 'a turning-point' in the theatre as the first production of *A Doll's House* in 1879. As Bradbrook expertly shows, *En Attendant Godot* stems largely from Beckett's experience of secrecy, uncertainty, tension and danger as a volunteer for the Resistance during the occupation of France. But the heroism of that traumatic period is not merely masked in the play but seemingly nullified, reduced to the language and gesture of clowns—because 'direct recording' is not possible for such 'experience of extremity', and only by transmutation can the writer 'recover it for himself, as an involuntary memory' and share it with others. Paradoxically, the communication here comes through a medium of apparent non-communication, incoherence. But it is a disciplined incoherence, Bradbrook insists (another form of that poetry of the gaps to be found in Webster—or in Chekhov). And it has proved expressive for audiences and for other playwrights precisely through its denial or caricature of explicit communication, through its commitment to blocked impulses and to memories inwardly relived, without apparent coherence, without explanation or rationalisation.

In the second half of *Literature in Action* Bradbrook turns to New Zealand, Australia and Canada. Through a series of incisive sketches she provides an English reader with what in effect is an introduction to the distinctive problems and qualities of each of these new literatures. The indirect link with the first half of the book lies in the general twentieth-century 'crisis of communication' (since 'easy communication at a superficial level' has made 'communication in depth more precarious') and in the need of the writers in each of the new countries to find a voice of their own: 'The maturity of a literature depends on the discovery of a characteristic form—not a theme or a vocabulary, but an approach'. As Bradbrook shows, each of the three literatures has been affected by distance from the mother-country, or, additionally, by a chosen self-distancing; by the social composition of the dominant settlers, their history and their contact with others (the natives, or competing European language groups); and by the configuration of the country and its geopolitical position. She brings out the corresponding traditions in each country—in surviving balladry, for instance, in the reception of modern metropolitan poetry, in variant attitudes towards England, of nostalgia or derision. And she shows how the conditions of each country have favoured a particular literary genre or a dominant image—as with the short stories of Katherine Mansfield, portrayals of small insulated groups; the long symbolic novels of Patrick White; or Malcolm Lowry's extended images of a journey. Her sharp sense of the active presence of varied component literary strands comes out, for example, in a comment on a passage of French-Canadian writing ('It was a Breton who wrote the words, perhaps forged from his own ancient tradition, little regarded'), or in her summary description of White's *The Solid Mandala*: 'The tension between the visionary and the cool, between the open myth and the satiric observer . . . corresponds to the mingling of grandiose lyric freedom and sardonic deflationary jest in the Australian tradition, the Irish and the Cockney strains, very thoroughly transmuted'. In more general terms, she observes that Patrick White's contribution has been to show 'the interaction of the life that is imposed by the nature of the country with the life that develops in the country of the mind'. This type of literary insight is strengthened by her sense of place; for instance, in a panoramic view of Sydney, or in her observation that in *Kangaroo* 'Lawrence records the healing power of the Australian landscape, the aerial fragility of the gum-trees, the defencelessness of the animals— and the violence of a tornado'. And her quick, sensitive response to personality is present as well: 'To meet Patrick White is to meet some- one who conveys at once the sense of an extremely active but a purely internal life; it is like listening to the purring of a dynamo in a power house to which there is no direct access'. *Literature in Action* is a critical achievement, all the more impressive because lightly carried.

In a recent book, dedicated to Muriel Bradbrook's memory, Giorgio Melchiori has saluted her as one of the greatest Shakespearean critics of this century. She has been widely influential through her university teaching and her firm and patient fostering of students' research, as well as through her published work. And in a very real sense she was a citizen of the world. She travelled and lectured untiringly in North America and Europe, Africa, Asia, Australasia and the Far East; and she corresponded with widely scattered friends and enquirers. She maintained that 'the fellowship of scholars, the happiest international society that really adheres, is held together by Shakespeare'; but in her case it was also held together by generosity. She was a woman of warm family feeling, but her generosity went far beyond her own family. She helped women students from abroad to adapt themselves to the strange environment of Cambridge; she went to great lengths to find ways and means to enable *émigrés* from Czechoslovakia to settle in England; she befriended South African liberals in the bitter climate of apartheid. Besides her academic honours at home—she was elected a Fellow of the Royal Society of Literature in 1947 and a Fellow of the British Academy in 1990—she received a number of academic distinctions from America, Foreign Membership of the Norwegian Academy of Arts and Sciences, and the Freedom of the City of Hiroshima.

She was a shrewdly unobtrusive academic administrator; and her contribution to the Cambridge English Faculty was greater than anything required of her. It was generally understood within the faculty, for example, that the important Judith E. Wilson bequest for the study of drama was allocated to Cambridge because of Muriel Bradbrook's friendship with Judith Wilson and with Edith Evans. And many years after her retirement from professional duties she played an active and constructive part in a faculty committee planning for a Cambridge Chair in Commonwealth and International Literature in English, a new departure in the academic programme that her own writing had no doubt helped to originate.

During her term of office as Mistress of Girton from 1968 to 1976 she launched the construction of Wolfson Court in 1969, to mark the centenary of the College and provide it with a permanent extension near to the centre of the university. But once some of the men's colleges had begun to admit women undergraduates in 1968 the question whether Girton also should go mixed became a troubling preoccupation. By a wise precaution, in 1971 the College obtained an Enabling Act which would allow the change to be accomplished smoothly if and when it was decided on. But meanwhile discussion continued among the Fellows throughout Muriel Bradbrook's Mistress-ship. Her private feelings were 'alarm' at first and probably regret at the prospect of eroding the great bastion of feminine education she had always been devoted to. But she was realist enough to face the arguments for change and stoical enough to repress her own feelings and to preside 'impartially and poker faced' (as she said later) over the discussion of alternatives. Once it was clear that a two-thirds majority among the Fellows favoured the move, the decision was reached 'cordially' to embark on what she was to call 'a gamble which paid off very handsomely'; and in

1976 Girton admitted its first male Fellows, as a preliminary to the admission of male undergraduates.

Muriel Bradbrook said she was 'very exhausted' by the time age had brought her period of office to an end. But an outsider might not have thought so. She continued to lead a very busy life. She often preached at the university church, Great St Mary's. In the first fine careless rapture of retirement she listed among the things that gave her enduring pleasure at Cambridge 'the lecture that sends me rushing to the University Library, and then writing furiously into the small hours'. She attended lectures and research seminars—retaining her capacity for disconcertingly sharp or enliveningly detailed interventions,— Shakespeare conferences at Stratford and meetings about the reconstruction of Shakespeare's Globe. And she continued to travel, and to write books and articles into her eighties. As late as February 1991 she was giving a painstakingly prepared and stimulating new lecture to the Royal Society of Literature about the life and work of Vaclav Havel, dwelling on the playwright-President's undemonstrative but unbending moral integrity. On the two last complete days of her life, in June 1993, she took part in the ceremony of welcome to the Queen Mother at Girton, and then in the university ceremony for the conferring of honorary degrees.

LEO SALINGAR
Trinity College, Cambridge

Note. There is a bibliography of M. C. Bradbrook's writings in the book of essays in her honour, *English Drama: Forms and Development*, ed. Marie Axton and Raymond Williams (Cambridge 1977), and a supplementary bibliography in her *Collected Papers* IV, *Shakespeare in his Context: The Constellated Globe*, ed. Andrew Gurr (1989).

I am extremely grateful for information and help in preparing this paper to Muriel Bradbrook's brother, Mr S. J. Bradbrook; her sister-in-law, Mrs Bohunka Bradbrook; and the archivist of Girton College, Mrs Kate Perry; also to Dr Marie Axton, Professor Anne Barton, Professor Gillian Beer, Mrs Patricia Berry (Rignold), Mr Tim Cribb, Dr Juliet Dusinberre, Dr Peter Holland, Dr Nita Mandel and Professor Alice Teichova. I am responsible if there are any mistakes.

HENRY PHELPS BROWN

Proceedings of the British Academy, **90**, 319–344

Ernest Henry Phelps Brown
1906–1994

Husband and wife held in common a faith that was strangely incongruous with their warm hearts: they were Strict Baptists, members of a sect dedicated to the worship of an unrelenting Calvinist deity. 'Whom He did foreknow, He also did predestinate': an eternity of torture awaited all those, from the foundation of the world and through ages that might yet be, who were excluded from the number of the elect. Yet the inference, that in that case it didn't matter what you did, was never taken. On the contrary, the experience of conversion, basic to evangelists of all kinds, was sought by the Strict Baptists as an earnest of their election: conversion, and the self-control that enabled them to live a sober and godly life. As a boy, he sought on his knees the assurance of escape from the wrath to come: but it was denied him, and a gulf separated him from his elders.

THESE WORDS WERE WRITTEN with understanding and with feeling. They could have been written about Henry Phelps Brown: in fact, they were written by Henry himself, in the *Proceedings of the British Academy*, about Lionel Robbins, his predecessor as a Fellow of New College, Oxford, and his colleague at the London School of Economics. The parallel is uncanny, though it is not exact. Henry's parents were Baptists, but not Strict Baptists, and for them, it must be supposed, conversion mattered even more. But the young Henry was horrified by the ceremony of baptism by complete immersion, and, try as he might, he was unable to achieve conversion, gradually distancing himself from the chapel. Even so, he said that quite late in life, he still experienced a sense of oppression and a headache on Sunday morning.

Henry[1] was born in 1906, his father being an ironmonger in Calne, Wiltshire. His mother died when he was two years of age, and his father married her elder sister. It was thought right that Henry should be kept apart from other children, and he spent much of his time alone. He learned to read, and the first book he remembered was *The Pilgrim's Progress*, which he read aloud to his stepmother. From his earliest days, he read widely in English literature, and he acquired the habit of reading the newspaper. He saw little of children of his own age. As for his father and stepmother, it was part of the Puritan ethic to withhold any overt expression of affection, and to expect a child to talk and behave in an adult fashion. Eventually, at the age of seven and a half, he was allowed to go to school, starting in the lowest form of the local secondary school. But he found it hard to get on with other children: he was precocious, well-read, and talked like an adult. After a year, he was promoted. He continued at the top of the form, but now the other boys, including the free place scholars, were mostly three or four years older, and he found himself unable to establish close friendships. At the age of twelve, he won a scholarship to Taunton School. The school had been founded to give opportunities to the sons of dissenters, though it never imposed religious tests, and by Henry's time was attracting Anglicans as well as Nonconformists. He was plunged into boarding at a school of some 700 boys, which was recovering from the impact of loss of staff during the First World War. Initially, he was miserable. At the end of his first year, when he was fourteen, he took School Certificate, and thereafter he was in the sixth form. By this time, he knew he wanted to be a writer, by which he meant a journalist. He was aware of the sacrifices that his father and stepmother were making to keep him at school, and he also knew that his father was having a struggle to keep his business going. Henry wrote offering to come back home to help in the business, but his father urged him to continue to study. The head-master advised that, if he wished to become a journalist, he should go to Oxford to read History, and henceforward he was aiming at a history scholarship. While the school atmosphere remained generally unsympathetic, there were a few positive features. His appetite for reading remained as strong as ever, and he developed a capacity for sustained work, together with an ability to get up a subject quickly, which he was

---

[1] During his boyhood, he was called by his first name, Ernest, and it was his friend, Evan Durbin, whom he met at Taunton School, and again later in Oxford, who persuaded him to use his second name. I shall refer to him as Henry throughout.

to retain throughout his life. No great shakes at conventional games, he discovered that he was a good long distance runner. He also came across Evan Durbin, who, until his tragic death in 1948, was to remain his closest friend. A growing interest in the wider world was brought into sharp focus by a visit to Bristol in the early 1920s where he witnessed a demonstration of unemployed. He became something of a socialist and thought that, when he got to Oxford, he would like to study PPE, especially economics. He duly won a history scholarship to Wadham College. After the examination, R. V. Lennard, the economic historian, wrote to him to suggest that he should not start to read PPE at once, since the school was only just beginning and was not yet well organised, and he would be wise to read History to start with.

Henry threw himself into undergraduate life with considerable zest. He renewed his friendship with Evan Durbin, and met, among others, Oliver Franks, who remained a friend throughout his life. He was active in college play-reading and debating societies: he joined the Labour Club, replaced as his ideas changed, by the Liberal Club, and the Union Society, of which he became Secretary, and contested, unsuccessfully, the Presidency in 1928. He continued his cross-country running for the college, and also the university. He was equally active academically. He won the Gibbs history scholarship; the Chancellor's Essay Prize, with an essay on *The Country Gentleman*, of which excerpts were duly read at Encaenia; and the George Webb Medley scholarship. This last was, perhaps, the most remarkable. It was awarded on a special examination in economic subjects, at that time taken in September, and open to all undergraduates. When he sat the examination, Henry had had no formal tuition in economics at all, and his knowledge was based largely on the reading he had been able to do in the long vacation following his history Finals.

Henry achieved a First in History. He took his second Finals, this time in PPE, in 1929, and he was to achieve the best First of his year. Even before the results were announced, New College offered him a Lectureship in Economics, which was later followed by a Fellowship. He was immediately plunged into the work of a college tutor. He felt that his training in economics had been insufficient, and the College granted him leave to take up a Rockefeller Travelling Fellowship in the United States for the year from September 1930 to August 1931. During this time, he was able to visit principal university economics departments and to meet prominent American economists, such as Irving

Fisher, Arthur Burns and Wesley Mitchell, J. M. Clark and many others. He had set off with the idea that economics was a literary and deductive activity, and he envisaged spending his year in extensive reading, especially in the history of economic doctrines. This approach was to be significantly modified by his experience. He was immediately struck by the eagerness of young American students to embark on empirical investigations, without being heavily burdened with any theoretical presuppositions. He saw at once his need for training in statistical method, but it was not until the final stage of his visit, which he spent in Chicago, that he had the opportunity to attend the lectures in mathematical economics and statistics being given by Henry Schultz. On his return to Oxford, he was determined to continue his study of mathematics and statistics. In the spring of 1932, he married Evelyn Bowlby, sister of Anthony Bowlby, an Oxford friend who was to become an industrialist, and of John Bowlby, who became a psychiatrist. His widow remembers him working on mathematics in the first year of their marriage.

Meanwhile, he had resumed his duties as a college tutor. Warren Young and Frederic Lee, those indefatigable, if sometimes idiosyncratic, chroniclers of *Oxford Economics and Oxford Economists* (1993), reported some evaluations by contemporary students of the performance of tutors and lecturers. The top group of nine 'good' tutors included such names as Harrod and Meade, but Henry got only into the next six — 'fair to good'. Individual comments rated him more harshly, as poor, or austere. Such evidence needs always to be taken with a good deal of salt, but it does appear to be in line with his own assessment. 'As a tutor, I was conscientious, but not stimulating. I tried to teach the subject, instead of the pupil — that is, I gave a talk that was the best account I myself would give, of the matter under discussion, instead of finding out how it looked to a pupil and getting him to talk about it from his own starting point.' He added that one reason for this approach was his fear of forming personal relations. While he found tutorials difficult and tiring, lecturing he enjoyed. His lectures were well planned and clearly presented. His wartime experience in training soldiers led him to provide a typed résumé with each lecture, and, after the war, he was regarded as one of the best lecturers at LSE.

Besides getting going as a teacher, Henry also embarked on a career of research and writing which was to continue through his life. His presidential address to the Royal Economic Society is well remembered for the sharp things he had to say about economic theory and econometrics. What is, perhaps, less well known is that his name appears in the first published list of members of the Econometric Society, which was founded in 1930. Not only was he a member, he was an active member. Volume 1, No. 1 of the Society's journal *Econometrica* was published in January, 1933, and it contained the programme of the meeting of the Econometric Society which had been held in Paris the previous October. At the first session, there was a communication from E. H. Phelps Brown on 'The statistical derivation of demand schedules: a criticism'. At that meeting, also, Henry was appointed chairman of a committee set up on source materials for quantitative production studies. This committee duly produced three reports which appeared in successive numbers of *Econometrica* in 1936. This was not the only work which Henry did for the Econometric Society. A meeting of the Society was held in Oxford in September 1936. The venue was New College, and Henry was responsible for the conference arrangements. This was the famous meeting at which some of the first interpretations of the *General Theory* were presented, notably by Hicks and Harrod.

The economics in the reports he prepared for the Econometric Society are as empirical as anyone could wish. But, at the same time, Henry was working in abstract theory, writing *The Framework of the Pricing System*, which was published in 1936. His purpose was to expound the essentials of the general equilibrium (Walrasian) model for the prices and quantities of consumer goods produced, the rewards of the factors of production engaged in producing them, and the amounts employed. The book was aimed at students with little training in mathematics or the physical sciences. Essentially, two branches of mathematics are involved: the solution of simultaneous equations and elementary differential calculus. Remarkably, Henry contrived to avoid drawing on either by making extensive use of simple arithemetical examples. The intention to avoid standard bits of mathematics was stretched at times: at one point algebraic geometry is smuggled in *en passant*, and there were some verbal contortions in introducing the idea of a function. In the final chapter, it was indicated how this austere framework could be linked to broader, as well as more familiar, themes. The book fell flat in Britain, though it was taken up, here and there, in the United States, where it enjoyed a vogue in the University of Kansas for a number of years. Hayek put his finger on the central question in a perceptive review for the *Economic Journal*, when he asked whether the whole exercise was worth while, of trying to teach the non-mathematical student the basis of the pricing system in this way. There were, he thought, ' . . . two main types of student, one with a gift for mathematics who will on the whole do better to acquire the mathematical technique first, and a second who will find an essentially mathematical reasoning, even in this disguise, of little help.' There may have been another reason why the book attracted little attention in Britain, namely the publication in the same year of Keynes's *General Theory*.

The Oxford University Institute of Statistics was founded in 1935, with a grant of £5,000 from the Rockefeller Foundation, to secure the 'orderly development of Social Studies in Oxford'. The Institute was originally conceived as a facility to serve faculty members. There was to be a Director, among whose roles was to be the promotion of the teaching of statistics, and a Secretary-librarian, but it was not intended at the beginning that there should be full-time research staff. In the early days, research was done by advanced students preparing B.Litt. and D.Phil. theses, under the supervision of the Director, or associated faculty members. The Institute also accommodated the Secretary of the Oxford Economists' Research Group. The first Director was Jacob Marschak, who had left Germany in 1933 — a refugee for a second time, having already escaped from the Russian Revolution. Henry was one of the group of dons pressing for the establishment of the Institute, and he worked closely with Marschak, when it was started. He participated in statistical seminars, and supervised graduate students. He took an active part in the work of the Economists' Research Group. He was also able to secure a grant from the Rockefeller Foundation to develop work of his own.

Throughout his life Henry displayed an uncanny gift in choosing talented young men and women as assistants, several of whom went on to distinguished careers of their own. The first of the sequence was George Shackle, with whom he produced three papers. 'Statistics of Monetary Circulation in England and Wales', Special Memorandum No. 46 of the *London and Cambridge Economic Service* (1938), established that, with certain reservations, the total of metropolitan, county and provincial clearings (MCP) could be regarded as a measure of the flow of cheque payments in the non-financial circulation of the United Kingdom. In the next paper, published in the first issue of *Oxford Economic Papers* (October 1938), they first outlined what the reservations were, including why the MCP index, and the index of MC, excluding provincial clearings, might diverge from estimates of gross national income which were being provided by Colin Clark. They then constructed a price index to deflate the figures of the MCP amounts to provide an index of real turnover. The real turnover figures bring out the apparent mildness of the recession of 1929–32. Despite the many reservations which the authors had about their real turnover index, they had sufficient faith in it as one measure of real economic activity to go on in a paper in the next number of *Oxford Economic Papers* (May 1939) to compare it with the total insured employment in four particular groups of trades in the period January 1924 to October 1938, on a monthly basis. It is hard for contemporary economists, provided with a plethora of statistical publications, not to mention data sets on tape and disk, to grasp how few series were available to applied economists before World War II. When this is taken into account, these papers are seen to have constituted a remarkable feat of statistical ingenuity. This is particularly true of the first paper on monetary circulation, which was a pioneering anatomy of the whole monetary circulation of the economy. This was not always appreciated at the time: Lionel Robbins remarked to Henry that he thought he was 'meant for better things'. In fact, work of this kind was an essential complement to the world-shaking ideas coming out of Cambridge at that time. It was a misfortune that both the basic analysis of the monetary circulation, showing the different components of money to have widely different velocities of circulation, and the hard-headed charting of trends and fluctuations in the British economy were submerged by the war, and had to be re-discovered many years later.

If the rise of Hitler were to lead to war, Henry felt that he could not remain as a teacher, a fellow of his college, and an economist engaged in research. He was aware that during World War I some economists had been drawn into public service, and he thought that there might be use for a qualified economic statistician. Accordingly, after Munich, he arranged an interview with the Chief Statistician of the Board of Trade, Hector Leak. Leak assured him 'courteously but firmly that so far from this being possible, if war came, his Department would be cut down'. Not long after, Henry called one evening at the Territorial Army barracks, with the intention of joining the Territorial Battalion of the Oxford and Bucks Light Infantry. The man in denims at the door, 'sensing that I was not their type, suggested that I might try the anti-aircraft battery that was forming in the infant school down the road'. Henry noted his good fortune inasmuch as the battalion he was stopped from joining was destined to be cut up at Mount Kemmel in May 1940, and most of the survivors spent five years as prisoners of war. But he did not mention that later he put at risk the greater survival chances of a gunner by volunteering to join a regular regiment in France in November 1939, whence he returned via the beaches of Dunkirk in the following year. This experience was to provide the background of *The Balloon* (1953), a novel he wrote some years after the war. Back in England, he participated in the defences in East Anglia, and in London during the blitz. Then he took command of a mobile battery in Algeria, going on to Tunis, and thence to Italy, where his unit was used as field artillery in the line. He was posted on promotion to be second in command of another regiment in the same role, after which he served from Cassino to the final crossing of the Po. When discharged Henry had the rank of lieutenant-colonel, which would have become full colonel had he stayed a week longer. He was awarded the MBE. This last meant a good deal to him, as was shown many years later, in 1965, when the Prime Minister's Private Secretary wrote to say that it was proposed to offer him a CBE: he replied that he had 'long been honoured to be a Member of the Military Division of that order and would wish so to remain'.

In 1942 the War Office told him that he might be released from military service to take up work with the newly formed Ministry of Production, but, after careful consideration, he decided to stay with his men. Charles Dreyfus, who served under him in Italy spoke of Henry's battery being a happy one, and of his honesty, and, above all, fairness, which earned him respect. In the light of his future concern with industrial relations, his decision did not entail such a complete loss to economics as might have appeared at the time. The Army taught him a good deal about human nature, especially in the group. He published his reflections on these matters in a paper on morale, which appeared in the *Economic Journal* in 1949.

During the war, Henry's thoughts had been concentrated on the job in hand. For the future, as did so many others, he wished only for the war to end, and that he could rejoin his family and resume his work at New College. There was much to do. The shape of economics had changed since he left it in 1939. Under the impact of the *General Theory* the division of the subject into macro- and micro- had emerged, and there was ground to be made up. Like most tutors, he found the ex-service undergraduates the most rewarding of pupils. Nevertheless, he still found tutorials uncongenial and tiring. When, in 1947, Lionel Robbins came to extend the offer of a Chair in the Economics of Labour at the London School of Economics, the relief from tutorial work was an important consideration to add to the attraction of the subject, which he saw less as a specific discipline than as a field in which he could examine economic questions in their historical setting. In addition, he could bring to bear sociological factors, as well as following up the interest in psychology prompted by his undergraduate contemporary, John Bowlby. Thus, in the autumn of 1947, he took up the post which he was to hold for the next twenty-one years. But, it would be equally true to say that he embarked on a programme of research and writing which was to last for the next forty years and more. During that time, he was to publish many papers in journals, memoranda and series of lectures, as well as eight books, of which three of the most important were written after he had retired from the LSE and returned to live in Oxford.

Soon after he had taken up his new post, there appeared in the *Economic Journal* a note of his questioning a statement by Pigou that, whereas in World War I real wages had just held their own, in World War II they had risen by 45 per cent, a figure rightly adjudged by Henry to be far too high. This note proved to be the first of a stream which appeared in the *Economic Journal, Economica, Oxford Economic Papers*, and other journals in which Henry marked out the Economics of Labour. As often as not, he was accompanied in his research by an assistant, whom he preferred to regard as a collaborator, and whose salary was paid out of an LSE research fund, on which he was able to draw with the minimum of formality.[2] In the main the papers deal with different aspects of money wages, prices, real wages, productivity and national income. Nearly all have historical depth, and many bring in several countries: an early example is a paper on 'The Course of Wage Rates in Five Countries, 1860–1939'. Some of the papers were mainly concerned with the facts over a period of time, with economic theory being implicit, or kept in the background. In other cases some issue of contemporary theory was put in the centre of the stage, an example being the study of the share of wages in the national income. Much of the work consists of the construction of time-series, very often over periods for which good data exist for some years, and scanty data for others. Henry was scrupulous in explaining exactly how

[2] In all, there were seven such collaborators, to be added to the two before the war. In writing about his research, I shall, as a rule, refer to Henry as though he was the sole author, although it is plain, as Henry was always the first to acknowledge, that the collaborators made full contributions to all aspects of the work.

he had constructed a particular series. He made as little use as possible of technical language and notation, preferring plain English. The ground covered by these research papers is very wide, but one can get a flavour of them from two examples. The first is the group of papers on 'wages down the ages' which he wrote with Sheila Hopkins between 1955 and 1961, and the second is *A Century of Pay*, written with Margaret Browne and published in 1968, which includes the results of much research previously undertaken.

The first of the 'wages down the ages' papers provides a fairly continuous record of the money wage rates of building craftsmen and labourers in Southern England, typically in Oxford, from 1264 to 1954. Over the entire period the rate for craftsmen rose from 3d. a day to 445d.: averaged over seven centuries this amounts to less than three-quarters of 1 per cent per annum. There were hardly any absolute falls, and the periods of rise were interspersed with long spells of no change in the rate, in all amounting to 500 of the 690 years covered. Equally remarkable was the stability of the differential between the rates for craftsmen and labourers. This differential declined in the hundred years to about 1410, but then remained virtually unchanged until World War I. Only since then has the differential significantly narrowed. These long periods of stability in the absolute rates and the persistence of the differential for five centuries, raise questions about the influence of convention in overriding movements which might have been expected from fluctuations in supply and demand. The second paper compares changes in money wage rates with changes in the prices of consumables. Bearing in mind that the monetary figures are for daily, and not annual, wages, dividing by the index of the price of consumables does not give us the 'real wage', as ordinarily understood, but the physical equivalent of the daily wage rate, which is still of great interest. When set out in chart form, the overall impression is of a level much the same throughout seven centuries, broken only by a period of relatively high prosperity from 1380 to 1510, and a rise that sets in from 1820 onwards, and carries us to new regions altogether. The paper ends with a question about a Malthusian explanation of the large movements prior to 1820, a theme taken up in the next paper, which shows that the remarkable fall in what the builder's wage could buy was matched by similar falls in France and Alsace, and goes on to discuss different possible influences of population pressures. By this time the attention of many historians had been drawn by earlier papers. The fourth one provided evidence from Munster, Augsburg, Verona, and Valencia, showing how, in all four places, the basketful of consumables which a day's pay would buy shrank disastrously in the sixteenth century. In the last paper, the findings were compared with those of earlier investigators, to whom, it appeared, the most striking features of the record were known, leaving a puzzle why they had been so little discussed and assimilated.

The project had come about by chance, when Henry came across a graph of the daily wages of a carpenter and an agricultural labourer from the 1270s to the 1880s, together with a graph showing the amounts of wheat the wages would buy, which had been prepared by a Swedish scholar, Gustaf Steffen. Henry thought that wheat was too narrow for the denominator, and that it should be possible to construct a more representative index of the price of consumables. But, if there was an element of chance in the launching of the project, it grew into a major contribution to economic history, not only for its subject, but also for the elegant rigour with which the work was carried out. In his Auto-biographical Note, Henry wondered whether he ought not to have made the effort to found a school, gather a team, launch a periodical, and attract graduate students. On the evidence of 'wages down the ages' it would seem he had no need to! Towards the end of the series, in 1960, Henry was elected a Fellow of the British Academy.

The second example of the scope of his research is *A Century of Pay* (London, 1968), which he wrote with Margaret Browne. This book rose out of an endeavour to revise 'The Course of Wage Rates in Five Countries, 1860–1939', which he had written in 1950 with Sheila Hopkins. In the end, the book managed to incorporate much of the research which had appeared in the journals in the intervening years. The five countries were the United States of America, the United Kingdom, Germany, France and Sweden, and the time span was extended to 1860–1960. The book contains the familiar mix of economic theory and history, with a heavy emphasis on statistical data: Henry called it 'reasoned history'. Over the whole period, there was rapid population growth in all the countries, except France. Employment also grew in line with population, but the conclusion was reached that population was not a dominant influence on industrial development. The residual question, to which Henry provided some plausible answers, was how, over the long period, the extra jobs were created. Besides population and employment, there was, over the long period, in all countries a growth of productivity. This was not steady: there were faster and slower spells, and, in particular, the check to productivity growth in Britain at the turn of the century, which clearly fascinated Henry, and which he wrote about on more than one occasion. How were the fruits of employment and productivity growth, notably pay and profits, divided among the broad classes of recipient? The analysis is conducted in terms of certain critical ratios — of wages to income, the rate of profit and the capital/output ratio. The behaviour of these ratios was by no means the same in the different countries: the most striking contrast, perhaps, was that in the period 1880–1900, during which the rate of profit fell in Germany, but rose in the United Kingdom, while the capital/output ratio rose steeply in Germany and fell in the United Kingdom. From 1860 to 1960 a comparable index of real wages rose four-fold in Germany, France and Britain, over five-fold in the United States, and seven and a half times in Sweden. Once again, there were spells of faster and slower growth. The rise in real wages in the long period was made possible almost entirely by the rise in productivity. In terms of levels, Britain was ahead until 1900, but has been behind for most of the present century.

A Century of Pay summarises and extends a great volume of research undertaken over nearly two decades, and is one of the most substantial contributions to applied economics since 1945. But it is not easy of access. It was only after 1945 that official statistics became extensively available, and prior to that much space had to be given to describing how different estimates were constructed. The authors were also anxious, as far as possible, to make the estimates for the five countries comparable. The book was not confined to statistical facts: they were moulded by economic theory into comprehensible forms which are, at the end of the day, the most challenging parts of the book. The tables and charts cry out for larger pages which would have made them easier to follow. Unfortunately, the publishers decided to cram everything into pages of the normal size, which must have deterred, and must continue to deter, all but the most persistent specialist. By good fortune, Henry himself was able very quickly to provide an excellent map of part of the terrain covered by *A Century of Pay*. He delivered a series of special lectures in Manchester University in 1968, and chose for his subject '*Pay and Profits*: The Theory of Distribution Reviewed in the Light of the Behaviour of Some Western Economies Over the Last Hundred Years' (published, Manchester, 1968). The author weighed the explanatory power of four basic types of distribution theory: bargaining theory; monopolistic pricing theory; the widow's cruse theory; and factor pricing theory. These four types are not mutually exclusive. In his exposition of the very different types of theory, and in 'testing' each one against the facts, the author was in complete control. He wrote in plain English. The result was a small masterpiece.

A Course in Applied Economics (London, 1951), the first book which Henry brought out after the war, was not part of his Economics of Labour research programme, but arose out of a course of lectures he undertook to fill a gap soon after his arrival at the LSE. He wanted to show the student how the main branches of economic analysis could be brought to bear on a selection of the problems of the day. In the first part of the book, we have the analysis of resource allocation, the pricing system and collectivism, competition and monopoly and the pricing policy of public enterprises. The second part deals with growth and stability, with a final section on the international dimension. The use of controls in parts of a predominantly market economy is not contentious; the theory of income determination, linked to national accounts, appears as main-stream economics, without need for 'Keynesian' labelling; and there is room for discussion of monetary policy without getting excited. By contrast with the *Framework of the Pricing System*, this book established itself and was frequently reprinted; a second edition, with Jack Wiseman as collaborator, came out in 1964. *The Economics of Labour* (New Haven, 1962), was the first of a planned series of Studies in Comparative Economics, being launched at Yale, which aimed to 'rethink particular branches of economics' in a world context going beyond the confines of conventional Western economics. This book displays Henry's mastery of a large canvas: it also shows him grappling with the tension between what marginal productivity analysis told him to expect to find, and what he actually observed.

The Growth of British Industrial Relations (London, 1959), was the first of two major historical studies which Henry was to write about the development of trade unions. The second, *The Origins of Trade Union Power* (Oxford, 1983), came nearly a quarter of a century later. Together, these two books provide a vivid account of the unsteady rise of British trade unions to economic power and political influence, which reached a peak in the 1970s, since when their story has been one of retreat and retrenchment. *The Growth of British Industrial Relations* was written 'from the standpoint of 1906–14', years which saw an outbreak of turbulence in industrial relations surpassing anything previously experienced in Britain, and which, some believed, brought the country to the brink of social revolution. Why did that happen, and why, in the event, did no revolt follow? The book begins with an extended account of the condition of the people and conditions of work towards the end of the nineteenth century. Subject to variations imposed by world conditions and the trade cycle, employment grew steadily, in line with population: so also did productivity and real wages. But, at the end of the century, there was a distinct slowdown, even a halt, in the rise of productivity and real wages, and unemployment was felt to be a growing evil. On the industrial relations front, the older unions were craft unions, linked to apprenticeship, and designed to keep the price of labour high, by keeping it scarce. They were themselves not interested in organising unskilled workers, but, towards the end of the century, New Unionism burst on the scene, when match-girls, gasworkers and dockers revealed an unsuspected capacity for organisation and action themselves.

Throughout their development, British trade unions had steered clear of the law. Their growing success was severely set back by the Taff Vale judgment of 1901, which rendered unions liable for any actionable wrong by one of their members. The Trades Disputes Act of 1906 restored the *status quo ante* for the craft unions, but it also opened the door for the wave of strikes by the industrial unions, notably the railwaymen and the miners, which inevitably drew the government in to settle the strikes and to avert a more general disruption of the economy. Besides its main purpose, of explaining the turbulence of 1906–14, the book had subsidiary themes. One was to explain why British trade unions, unlike those in most countries, developed as far as possible outside the law. This question is hinted at from time to time, but never fully developed. Another objective was to see how far events in 1906–14 could account for industrial relations in 1959. There is the faintest hint of complacency in the assessment of things in that year, in which output grew exceptionally fast, and unemployment fell, while retail prices barely increased at all. Both deficiencies were to be made good when Henry returned to the theme of trade union power nearly a quarter of a century later. *The Origins of Trade Union Power* (Oxford, 1983) addresses the question of the behaviour of the unions in the 1970s. Between 1968 and 1979 three successive Prime Ministers were prevented by the industrial and political power of the unions from pursuing policies they regarded as in the national interest, and all three lost the general elections which followed the defeat of their policies. Once more, the approach is historical, but there is now greater emphasis on the political and legal factors: in addition, there are three comparative studies of trade union development in the United States, Canada and Australia. In all these countries, legislation has played a major role in industrial relations, bringing into sharp contrast the way in which British trade unions had, from the earliest days, tried to keep the law at arms' length, leading eventually to the conflicts with government, both Labour and Conservative, when they attempted to legislate to check unofficial strikes, to create a framework for distinguishing between fair and unfair industrial practices, and to bring about a control of incomes. In his historical account, Henry gives explanations for the successive moves which had kept the law at a distance, but, at the same time, he stresses that these moves were not inevitable, but choices which could have been made differently. A separate chapter is devoted to 'cost-push' as a key element in the process of inflation after 1945, and it contains an account of the apparently spontaneous acceleration in the rate of wage inflation which occurred in many industrial countries towards the end of the 1960s, which Henry called the 'Hinge', and which was followed by years of stagflation. He explained the acceleration as 'the outcome of a continuous drift in the attitude of wage earners'. Older workers, remembering the Great Depression of the 1930s, tended to rate job security above militancy, but younger workers, who had experienced only full employment and rising living standards, had higher expectations and believed they knew how to fulfil them. Year by year, the balance tilted from the older workers to the younger, until the attitudes of the latter predominated. Cost-push puts in question the compatibility of full employment with free collective bargaining, and points towards incomes policy. Whereas the tone of the conclusion of *Growth* may have been tinged with complacency, the prognosis at the end of *Origins* is uncertain: ' . . . incomes policy is inescapable, but it has proved impracticable.'

For centuries, to be rich was to be a man of property, the poor had none. The landlord stood against the landless labourer. In modern times the share in national income of income from property began to fall, and increasing attention has been given to differences in the earnings of different kinds of labour as a major source of the inequality of incomes. *The Inequality of Pay* (Oxford, 1977), begins with a statistical survey of pay in many countries, with different economic and social structures, in historical depth. When classified by occupation, the structure of pay is generally similar in Western countries, although there are differences in the range between the highest and the lowest paid. Apart from the treatment of white-collar workers, it turns out that the pay structure of Soviet-type economies was similar to that of the Western countries. The study of contemporary pay structures is followed by a study of their

change through time. These surveys bring out the connection between
the pay of different occupations and the social rank or status which
those occupations hold. But, is it pay which determines status, or the
other way round? The author argues that evidence from anthropology
and ancient history suggests that in societies without differentiation of
occupation, there are no differences of status. Differences in status
begin to emerge at the same time as differences in occupation and
wealth. Once, for whatever reason, the rank orders of pay and status
have been brought into conformity, custom can be invoked in support of
anyone wishing to raise his pay, on the grounds that it is not currently
commensurate with the status of the job. But that does not resolve the
question of the direction of the link between pay and status. The
ultimate driving force, in Henry's view, is economic. In the first
instance pay is determined by supply and demand, and it is status which
eventually follows. But the market does not work with precision. It may
adjust only slowly to change, and there may be especially powerful
resistance to cuts in pay, so that at any one time there may exist quite a
wide band of indeterminacy about what the economic rate should be.
Within that band, there is scope for the independent influence of status.
One reviewer described this analysis as 'perhaps the most interesting
and original part of the book.' The book proceeds to explore the forces
which can operate within the zones of indeterminacy which are left by
the imperfection of the market. Later chapters study the various forms
of discrimination, for example against women and ethnic minorities; the
link between the occupations which young persons choose and the
social class of their parents; the association between occupation, mental
ability and education; and the influence of trade unions. The final
chapters turn to the distribution of earnings within occupations, and
the book concludes with some reflections on the possibility of reducing
the inequality of pay. 'We have found that the main cause of the
inequality of pay is the inequality of abilities to work. . . . The best
way to reduce the inequality of the effect is to reduce that of the cause.'

The writing of *Inequality of Pay* overlapped with Henry's service on
the Royal Commission on the Distribution of Income and Wealth. The
book dealt only with pay, and excluded income from property, while the
Commission covered all forms of income and wealth. Henry returned to
this broader theme in his last major work, *Egalitarianism and the
Generation of Inequality* (Oxford, 1988). The first part of this book is
a survey of the rise of egalitarian ideas since the time of the ancient
Greeks. To Plato and Aristotle, differences between people were so

fundamental, and innate, as to divide mankind into sub-species. They were prepared to discuss at length the relation between citizens, including the desirable extent of the ratio of the wealth of the richest to that of the poorest — but none of this applied to slaves. In Henry's view, the start of the long journey away from inequality was to be found in the Greeks' view of the law of nature, which was taken up by the mediaeval schoolmen. With the Renaissance and the Reformation came the rise of individualism, which fostered the political principle of equality. The French and American Revolutions proclaimed the equality of men, but again only in political terms. Although, at different times there had been arguments which extended egalitarianism to the economic sphere, the rights of property remained sacred. The move towards contemporary egalitarianism came in the nineteenth century with the creation of administrations to cope with the health, housing and education of a growing population. These changes brought about the possibility of a Welfare State, which for some had a strong component of the redistribution of income and wealth. As Henry pointed out, this movement was stronger in Europe than in the United States.

Where data exist to make tables of the number of incomes which fall within successive size intervals which are not too great, it is possible to draw charts illustrating distributions of income. The most familiar of these is the Lorenz curve, from which can be derived the Gini coefficient, as a summary measure of inequality. This approach has its ambiguities, and Henry preferred to present income distributions by means of 'Pen parades', named after the Dutch economist Jan Pen, which marshal incomes in order of size. Besides data for the United Kingdom, estimates are given for a number of other countries, for incomes both before and after tax. There is a parallel presentation of data on the distribution of wealth. These surveys are followed by a study of the processes of formation of income and wealth, with an account of the mathematical representation of some processes. Such surveys date very quickly. In this particular case, we do not get beyond the end of the 1970s. In the ordinary way, this might not have mattered too much. Henry quotes, with apparent approval, Kuznet's generalisation in 1955 that, as activity grows from a low initial level, inequality increases, but, as growth continues, it is reduced. However, in both the United Kingdom and the United States the equalising trend appears to have been reversed since the end of the 1970s. Whether this is just a blip, or represents a definite reversal of trend, remains to be seen. To a certain extent, the assumption of an equalising tendency underlies the final section of the book also. Had Henry been writing this part of the book in 1995, he might have given a different slant to his argument. Even so, these two parts of the book remain excellent expositions of how to look at the statistics of income and wealth, and how to seek a firm philosophical basis for the egalitarian aspirations still to be found in many quarters. Meanwhile, the first half of the book remains a magisterial survey of the development of ideas about equality and inequality since the ancient Greeks. This book, wrote one reviewer, '. . . is written with superb style and wit. I can think of few economic and social historians who could write a book of comparable range and quality, and none who would not profit greatly from reading it.'

Research and writing were the dominant interest in Henry's life, but he had other duties at the LSE on which he worked hard. Besides his courses in labour economics, he also took part in teaching students for the (graduate) Diploma in Business Studies, a contribution to the course which he took very seriously. And he supervised graduates writing theses, which he enjoyed, but which became more arduous as numbers increased. He was a meticulous attender at the relevant School and departmental meetings, and was always carefully listened to. He was held in high regard by his colleagues, but he was happy to leave the running of the Economics Department to Lionel Robbins, and he did not become involved in LSE affairs generally. He quite often arrived at the School on his large motor-cycle — sometimes wearing a bowler — his arrival being of much interest to foreign students especially. He received invitations to lecture abroad, but nearly all he refused. He gave three lectures on 'Economic Growth and Human Welfare' at the Delhi School of Economics in 1953, but he did not lecture abroad again until he spent a year, soon after his retirement from the LSE, teaching in a number of Australian universities.

As his reputation in the economics of labour grew, he found himself called upon for a variety of forms of public service. He sat on three Courts of Enquiry, set up by the Minister of Labour, into the remuneration of clerical workers in the steel industry, labour-only sub-contracting in the building industry (the 'lump'), and one, in which he took the chair, into a claim of London busmen. He also went overseas to serve on a committee appointed to adjudicate on a wage dispute in the copper mining industry in what was then Northern Rhodesia.

The appointment which made the fullest use of his expertise was to the Council on Prices, Productivity and Incomes in 1959. The original 'three wise men' (Lord Cohen, Sir Harold Howitt and Sir Dennis

Robertson) were appointed in 1957 to 'keep under review changes in prices, productivity and the level of incomes' and to 'report thereon from time to time'. The Council had no powers, but, presumably it was hoped that it would come up with a convincing theoretical basis for government policy on wages and prices. The First Report, of February 1958, came out with a bang. The inflation being experienced in the 1950s was a 'demand inflation'. There was a brief reference to a 'school of thought which takes a different view as to the main cause of the rise in prices', but such ideas were brushed aside. Consistently with its own analysis, the Report endorsed the government's 'crisis' measures of the previous September, which had included the raising of Bank Rate to a sensational level of 7 per cent, and it viewed the implied increase in unemployment with some complacency. Among economists, the analysis of the Report was considered one-sided. The TUC virtually boycotted the Council from then on. Sir Dennis Robertson resigned, and the economist's seat was taken by Henry, who used the Third and Fourth Reports to review a number of different proposals which were put forward from the school of thought summarily despatched in the First Report. However, the Fourth Report, issued in July 1961, was to prove the last. The Council was overtaken by events. In 1962 the government set up a new National Economic Development Council (NEDDY) in which ministers, representatives of trade unions and employers' organisations, in equal numbers, were included. There were, in addition, two independent members, of whom Henry was one. The new Council was intended to discuss economic policy and to influence opinion, rather than to lead to immediate executive action. Henry clearly hoped that he would be able to continue his advocacy of incomes policy on this larger stage, but initially he came up against the reluctance of the TUC to get involved. He understood the reasons to be that the TUC was not prepared to listen to the 'Treasury view', was not prepared to collaborate with a Tory government, and would be unwilling to accept any commitment on behalf of trade union members up and down the country, for whom it spoke, but had no means of controlling. Later on, discussions took place within the NEDDY framework, which enabled the Labour government elected in 1964 to get the general principle of incomes policy accepted by 1965.

In 1974, the Labour government set up a Royal Commission on the Distribution of Income and Wealth. Its Standing Reference was to undertake an analysis of the current distribution of personal income and wealth and of available information on past trends in that distribu-

tion. It should take into account taxation, and it could undertake studies
of particular questions. In its short life, it got through an immense
amount of work; five reports on the standing reference, and three
reports on higher incomes from employment, lower incomes and
income from companies and its distribution. It published the evidence
it had taken in writing and orally, as well as a number of specially
commissioned papers. The chairman was Lord Diamond, and on the
original Commission there were eight members, of whom Henry was
clearly the economist. There was a small staff, and the power to
commission work outside. It was natural that Henry, who became the
de facto vice-chairman, should take a major interest in the direction of
the research programme, and he threw himself into the work with great
enthusiasm. The recognition of his role must have been a factor in his
award of a knighthood in 1976. He left the Commission in 1978, at the
end of the term of his original appointment.

On two occasions Henry commented publicly on the developments
in economics during his working life. In his 1971 presidential address to
the Royal Economic Society (*Economic Journal*, March, 1972), he
expressed disquiet about the increasing divergence between the economics to be found in the academic journals and the practical problems of the
world, about which the economist might be called on to give advice. He
returned to this theme in 'The Radical Reflections of an Applied Economist', a contribution to a series of recollections of distinguished economists being published in the *Quarterly Review* of the Banca Nazionale
del Lavoro in 1980. When he began studying in the 1920s, political
economy was a field of literary and philosophical discourse which any
serious-minded and educated person could enter. However, the enormous growth in the amount of statistical information was just beginning,
and the two World Wars, especially the second, increased the demand
from both public and private sectors for people capable of handling the
materials of economic administration. The universities responded by
adding economics to their curricula, and, by the late 1950s economics
had become established as a profession, academically and occupation-
ally. As it grew, academic economics became increasingly specialised,
developing, in particular, distinct branches of economic theory and
econometric methods. To some extent, the academic and occupational
developments were linked. The assembly of quantitative data, and
sophisticated methods of analysis provided essential training for economists working in administration. However, looking back, Henry was
more struck by the divergence of theory and econometrics from the

needs of the practical economist. Economic theory might produce work of high intellectual distinction, but it appeared to be further and further removed from practical policy: nor was there any way in which such theory could be tested against reality. Senior economic advisers had told him how recruits to government economic service had found they had to unlearn their advanced theory. Ideally, any theory ought to arise from a prior acquaintance with the facts which the theory was called upon to explain. In practice, these facts might be a tangle of conflicting indicators, by no means all of them economic. The temptation for the economist to be selective, to make models based on optimising by rational agents, for example, which lead to clear cut recommendations, is great. When, for twenty years and more after World War II, most Western economies enjoyed a high and stable level of employment, many came to believe that this was because a simple Keynesian model had shown how unemployment could be avoided by manipulating fiscal and monetary levers. But, since the 1970s, that story no longer held good. Similarly with monetarism. It passed over the detailed processes with which prices, costs and incomes are fixed and changed, and relied on simple relationships between aggregates. But experience had shown that these simple models did not hold either.

Henry acknowledged that, in principle, well specified econometric models, making use of the mass of available statistical information, ought to help close the gap between models and the world as it is. But he had his doubts. In particular, he was suspicious of the running of regressions between time series. 'I do not see how any statistical procedures can enable us to ''explain'' or ''account for'' the variable taken as dependent. I do not see how the probability table can be applied to assess the significance of the relation between historical events.' As an example of the dangers of relying on a high R^2 as an assurance of having traced a causal relation between time-series, he cited the experience of the Phillips curve. The famous Phillips article had appeared in 1958, and it purported to show, using data for Britain from 1861 to 1913 for the rate of unemployment and the annual rate of increase in money wages, that the rate of wage inflation was determined by the level of unemployment. The wage history of the inter-war years, given the levels of unemployment which actually occurred, ' . . . could have been predicted fairly accurately from a study of the pre-war data', and Phillips went on to suggest that, on the assumption that productivity rose at an annual rate of 2 per cent, a level of unemployment of 2.5 per cent (which was rather higher than the prevailing rate), would secure zero price inflation. This idea swept through economics like a forest fire. Many academics and many economic advisers bought it. But, by 1972, when Henry delivered his lecture, Phillips-type relationships of a great many varieties had begun to 'break down': we were witnessing accelerating wage inflation at the same time as the level of unemployment was rising. When he reviewed the situation in 1980, Henry had not changed his mind. He chided those who thought of labour as a commodity, without seeing the point of view of the workman, and without dwelling upon the allowances which need to be made for his human passions, his instincts and habits, his sympathies and antipathies, and so on. Henry concluded his reflections by observing that what underlay his disquiet was the question: What is the object of economics? If the object of the economist was simply to study economics as it then stood, and he was to follow his personal inclination in terms of the objects of interest and the methods of studying them — well and good. But if we were to ask a more embarrassing — yet, for an economist, surely an inescapable question — what is the *use* of economics, the answer would be different. It is not a proper procedure to concentrate on the economic 'aspect' of a question, and to leave the influence of all other aspects to others. What actually happens in the economy appears as a process of history. It depends on human attitudes and expectations, cultural inheritance, waves of feeling, and the impact of particular events, and an economist needs an understanding that the quantitative relations established within the framework of economic analysis should be combined with empathy and imaginative insight. This line of argument led him to conclude that in training to become an economist concerned with policy, few of the great intellectual advances in economic theory are helpful. 'My contention is that the economist who is best equipped to understand the working of the economy around him and to advise on policy needs in point of analysis the equipment that is needed by the economic historian, and no more.' The entrant would need thorough training in statistical method, and, for the rest, his course should consist mainly of economic, social and political history. This was a conception of what constitutes a professional economist which is very different from that which prevailed in universities. Not everyone would go all the way with Henry in his strictures on economic theory and econometrics, and his suggestions for the training of future economists, but it is impossible for any working economist who lived through the Phillips episode not to go some of the way.

A tall man, Henry was fond of walking, and retained the gait of a soldier into his eighties. He had a presence on public occasions. In meetings, though he spoke rarely, he was listened to with respect; he was manifestly sincere. In private he was courteous, a warm and welcoming host, and his conversation could be enlivened with a sharp wit. From his earliest days, he had read widely, and he acquired a rich vocabulary. He appeared to write with the greatest facility, but behind everything he wrote, from a holiday postcard to a journal article there was careful thought. Just occasionally, the impact of the *mot juste* was a little diminished by the reader's need to resort to the dictionary. In most of his professional writing he used a clear, strong prose, which carried the argument steadily forward. As a rule, he kept his feelings under tight control, but on suitable occasions the simple prose moved quietly into eloquence. This can be seen in the great survey of the development of ideas which forms the first part of *Egalitarianism*, in the Memoir of Lionel Robbins which he wrote for the British Academy (1987), and from which we quoted at the outset of this Memoir, and, even more, in the Note on Roy Harrod which he wrote for the *Economic Journal* (1980).

Brought up as a Baptist, Henry gradually lost his faith, but, when he was an undergraduate he enjoyed the setting, the language and the music of chapel services. It was unemployment which prompted his early socialist leanings. The General Strike occurred in his second year in Oxford, but, while it famously brought Hugh Gaitskell into the Labour Party, it caused Henry to switch his allegiance from Labour to Liberal. He entertained some idea of going into politics, but became more and more absorbed in his academic work. Many years later, he joined the SDP, and, when that broke up, stayed as a member of the Liberal Democrats. The return of unemployment in the 1980s was a cause of great concern, to add to his lifelong preoccupation with fairness and the origins of inequality, the themes of his last two books. As a young man it was apparent that Henry was exceptionally gifted. He could have chosen to follow many careers. The one he chose suited his talents well. It gave scope for writing, which he had enjoyed from his earliest youth, and in which he excelled; he wrote verse and was to write a novel which was published, and another which was not. It gave scope for the study of history, which always gave great pleasure, and of economics, which he saw as the key for the improvement of welfare. In his work as an economist, he practised what he had preached in his presidential address to the Royal Economic Society and in his 1980 'Reflections of a Radical Economist'. Some have called him an economic historian, but the term is ambiguous. In some faculties 'economic history' is an option, an 'add-on' element in curricula. But, for Henry, history was not an option, but an essential medium in which, whenever possible, economic questions of immediate application should be set.

If then, we regard him as an applied economist, what was his achievement? Taking first his academic contribution, in many journal articles, and in *A Century of Pay*, he provided a remarkably thorough quantification of the main variables related to labour economics over long periods, and comparatively for several countries, following for labour economics the road opened up by Bowley and Colin Clark. Of his books, three were not intended to break new ground, but to teach economic theory, applied economics and labour economics in novel ways. Two books charted the development of trade unions and indus- trial relations, and two increased our understanding of inequality and the changing ideas about it. Besides his predominantly academic work, one should also mention his insistence, over many years, in articles and reports, on the importance of the cost-push element in inflation, and the complementary development of ideas for a practical incomes policy, which he believed was necessary if full employment was to be main- tained without risk of inflation. All this represents a formidable volume of research and writing, of the highest quality, as great as, or greater than that of any other applied economist of his generation, and must place him in the top rank of British economists. It is possible that his stature has not been universally perceived, partly because what lies behind the compilation of statistics is appreciated only by insiders, and partly because cost-push and the associated incomes policy are contentious. Perhaps he suffered from writing books rather than articles, so did not achieve the short-term Phillips kind of fame with a single article, offering a magic key. But he did write articles, and some of them became famous and are likely to have longer staying power. One might be content to leave it at that, had not Henry been so self-critical. A word must be said about this.

All through his adult life, Henry had felt at his best when he had an objective, and could put his head down and get on with the work. It was routine, therefore, that when *Egalitarianism* was off his hands, he should cast around to find his next subject. He started a note book in which to put down thoughts about possible subjects. Among those he considered were: Quality of life — how might it be measured, and how has it changed? Causality: is it the same in economics as in history? Then, he comes back to incomes policy, and by the summer of 1989, he had written a twenty-page draft on the 'Control of Cost-push'. In the event, the draft was carried no further. However, what concern us here are not his reflections on possible new subjects, but the comments on his own past performance which are interspersed between them. When reviews of *Egalitarianism* began to appear in academic journals a year and more later, they were welcoming. However, at the time of publication, the *Times Literary Supplement* carried an ill-informed and irresponsible review which upset him. His friends assured Henry that such a review was hardly worthy of notice, but it seems to have touched a raw nerve. The passages of self-criticism in the note book reinforce those already seen in his Autobiographical Note, and they amount to variations on the theme: 'Why have I failed to fulfil the promise of my youth?' Such thoughts may pass through the minds of many men towards the end of their lives. In Henry's case, one source of low self-esteem can be traced back to his childhood. His upbringing at home was austere. From the evangelical preaching of the Baptist chapel he learned of sin and worthlessness, but he was unable to find the relief of conversion. This can explain the origin of his self-criticism. But there seems to be less and less basis for its continuation as the years passed. At Oxford, he was highly successful in his studies, and he was active in the athletic and social life of his college, as well as in the Union Society. As a don, the one possible cause for concern was his difficulty with tutorial teaching, and this was removed when he went to the LSE, which gave him an ideal base for the development of his talents. By the criterion which economists themselves are accustomed to use, Henry's career, as an economist, was extraordinarily efficient, making the best use of the abundant intellectual resources at his disposal. So, we are left with the puzzle, why was he so critical of his own achievement? Some may be content to ignore the issue altogether. But others, who knew the man and his work, and came to have the greatest respect for his judgement in so many fields, may feel that they are obliged to take a view. Perhaps they will reflect that although his judgement was so good on so many things, it was not infallible. If it is not easy to recollect occasions on which he was wrong, there is no difficulty whatever in concluding that in this particular matter, he was just wrong. He was a good man, and a great scholar, and he did earn the highest of places among applied economists of his time.

In the summer of 1990, Henry suffered a stroke, which paralysed his left side. He made valiant efforts to recover the capacity to walk unaided, but, after a few months of painful progress, he was obliged to conclude that that was as far as he was going to get. His mental faculties were unimpaired, but he tired easily and, gradually, further writing dropped out of the picture. He retained a lively interest in current economic affairs. Once he had resolved that he would not embark on a new project, which would have the first call on his energies, he was able to return, with a clear conscience to the English literature he loved.

He was elected a Fellow of the British Academy in 1960.

DAVID WORSWICK
Fellow of the Academy

Note. In writing this memoir, I have made much use of the Autobiographical Note which Henry wrote in 1987 at the request of the British Academy. I have also drawn on the transcripts of two conversations he had with Brian Harrison, Fellow of Corpus Christi College, Oxford, in the summer of 1987. I am grateful to Evelyn Phelps Brown for allowing me access to a file of personal papers and letters relating to his professional life and to her and Juliet Hopkins for information about Henry's life. I have also received helpful comments and advice from: Arthur Brown, William Brown, Alec Cairncross, Jack Diamond, Charles Dreyfus, William Getz, Peter Hart, Sheila Hopkins, Douglas Jay, Donald MacDougall, James Meade, Kenneth Morgan, Barry Sutton, Sylvia Worswick and Basil Yamey. I thank them all for their assistance, but must add that the responsibility for what is written here is my own. The April 1996 issue of the *Review of Political Economy* (Volume 8, No. 2, published by Carfax, Oxford) is a memorial volume in honour of Henry, and includes his Autobiographical Note.

SAMUEL FINER

Proceedings of the British Academy, **90**, 347–364

Samuel Edward Finer
1915–1993

SAMUEL EDWARD FINER was one of the pioneers of post-war British political science. Until the 1950s, only a handful of universities in Britain could boast an undergraduate degree in Politics — Oxford, LSE and Manchester, for example — though a number of university colleges catered for the London External B.Sc. (Econ.) degree. In many universities, one or two academics, located in departments of History, Economics, or Philosophy, taught particular papers. The scope of the subject was similarly narrow. Political thought, of course; public administration (with special emphasis on local government), and some teaching of the government of major foreign countries — the United States, France, the Soviet Union — these were the ingredients of the subject as understood in the early post-war era. International relations, which logically seems to belong to the same family as political science, was carving out its own largely independent status.

In 1950, Finer, then a research fellow of Balliol, was appointed to a Chair at the new University College of North Staffordshire at Keele. The College, pioneered by Lord Lindsay, the former Master of Balliol, was intended to be a centre of innovation in British universities. Keele's most distinctive feature was the Foundation Year, the first-year course which all students had to take and pass before proceeding to their two principal subjects. The Foundation Year sought to correct excessive specialisation, by offering to students a course which introduced them to an overview of human knowledge. From Plato to NATO, was how it became popularly known.

Perhaps the most novel feature of Keele, however, in the early years of the College, was Finer himself, universally known as Sammy. He was prodigiously erudite; he could draw effortlessly on a vast fund of knowledge (not all of which was accurate). His knowledge was matched by his capacity for talk. There was nothing like an audience to turn him on. He was the ultimate anti-solipsist. The worst sentence that could ever have been imposed on Finer would have been solitary confinement. He was a social animal.

Finer's parents came to Britain from Romania in 1900, two representatives of the Jewish diaspora of that decade, and settled as market traders in London's East End.[1] Tragically, they both died by enemy action early in 1945. His brother Herman, 18 years older, became a noted political scientist, and provided him with a role model; Sammy's declared ambition was 'to be like my brother'. Herman's *Theory and Practice of Modern Government*,[2] first published in 1932, anticipated his younger brother's greatest contributions to the subject, for it broke with the dominant country-by-country approach, an approach that had prevailed more through inertia than for any better cause. Sammy went to Holloway School in London. His parents had hopes of his going into medicine but Herman persuaded his parents to let him follow Arts subjects in the sixth form.

Sammy won an Open Scholarship to Trinity College, Oxford, and got a First in PPE in 1937. He then read for the degree in Modern History and in 1938 obtained another First. He then spent two years as Senior George Webb Medley scholar, before joining the Royal Corps of Signals, in which he became a captain. He was stationed for a while at Catterick (an experience which perversely left him with a lasting dislike of the Yorkshire Dales), and served much of his time in the Middle East.

Demobilised in 1946, he returned to Oxford, spending four years

---

[1] For the biographic detail, especially of Professor Finer's early life, I have drawn heavily on Dennis Kavanagh's chapter *The Fusion of History and Politics: The Case of S. E. Finer* in H. Daalder, *The Autobiography of Comparative European Politics* (London, 1996) and on his chapter in the Festschrift of which he and Gillian Peele were joint editors, D. Kavanagh and G. Peele (eds.), *Comparative Government and Politics: Essays in Honour of S. E. Finer* (London and Boulder, Colo., 1984).

[2] H. Finer, *Theory and Practice of Modern Government* (New York, 1932).

there first as Lecturer in Politics at Balliol, and for his last year serving as Junior Research Fellow. In 1950, Lord Lindsay took up his appointment as first Principal of the new University College of North Staffordshire at Keele. Finer, who had already published his *Primer of Public Administration*[3] was appointed to the Chair of Local Government and Administration. Soon after the appointment Lindsay suggested that the title of the Chair be changed to Political Institutions (there was a separate Chair of Moral and Political Philosophy). And so it was: the world, after all, was Finer's parish.

Finer spent sixteen years at Keele, building up, before the great university expansion of the 1960s, what, apart from the triad of Oxford, Manchester and LSE, was one of the strongest Politics departments in the country, and establishing a reputation as one of the country's leading political scientists. By 1966, he had completed his work at Keele, and he moved to Manchester as Professor of Government, where his most notable book was *Comparative Government*.[4] In 1974, Max Beloff left Oxford, to take up an appointment as Principal of the new University College at Buckingham, leaving vacant the Gladstone Chair of Government and Public Administration. Finer was appointed to this Chair, and spent the last eight years of his formal working life in that post. His thoughts began to turn to his magisterial *History of Government from the Earliest Times*;[5] this, a book imaginative in conception and monumental in scope, was to be the chief labour of his retirement. His last years were marred by illness but he had almost completed the manuscript when he died in June 1993.

Finer was twice married: first to Ann McFadyean, and secondly to Catherine Jones. There were three children of the first marriage — Jeremy, Jessica, and Joshua.

Sammy's overpowering need to communicate was satisfied by his three roles: as teacher, as scholar, as intellectual entrepreneur. He was a charismatic lecturer for whom exposition was a two-way process. He both excited and entertained his listeners; in turn, the obvious appreciation of his hearers stimulated him. The bigger the crowd, the better. Nor

---

[3] S. E. Finer, *A Primer of Public Administration* (London, 1950).

[4] S. E. Finer, *Comparative Government* (Harmondsworth, 1970).

[5] S. E. Finer, *History of Government from the Earliest Times* (Oxford, forthcoming).

was he selective about his audience; a man without side, he seemed wholly free of any hint of academic snobbery. After a day of formal teaching, he would address his sometimes bemused hearers at the bar of the 'Sneyd Arms' in Keele village. Politics, given its subject-matter, might dispute with Economics the title of 'the dismal science', but not with Finer around. He taught undergraduates that learning could be fun; his lectures were informed by immense knowledge, enlivened by epigram (mostly, perhaps wholly, original) and enriched by paradox.

Finer, however, was much more than a brilliant teacher. His research output was large; but, more important, much of it was innovatory. It was varied in content and often imaginative in approach. He brought pace and novelty to what, in the 1950s, was the staid world of British political science. He opened up what, for the British profession, were virgin territories.

Finer's research divides naturally into four areas, to which all but a scatter of his publications belong. His three earliest books were his *Primer of Public Administration*[3] ('my little primer' as he was wont to call it), *Local Government in England and Wales*[6] and his *Life and Times of Sir Edwin Chadwick*.[7] These form a natural grouping, however anomalous it might seem to include his major biography of *Chadwick* with an introduction such as the *Primer*. The justification of bracketing them together lies in an undoubted commonalty of matter. Both the *Primer* and *Local Government in England and Wales* are concerned with the principles of administrative structure, with such issues as the relationship between areas and functions in the administration of public services, with the role of officials and the central departments. The affinity of these two books with *Chadwick* is discussed below.

In the *Primer* Finer displays two gifts which are a feature of nearly all his work: the capacity to simplify without sacrificing scholarly integrity and the ability to enliven what might seem prosaic detail. Public administration had a reputation amongst students, partly deserved, for dullness and formalism. Indeed, the character of the literature, and the teaching of the subject, may partly have reflected the vocational needs of some of its clientele. What stands out about the

---

[6] J. Maud and S. E. Finer, *Local Government in England and Wales*, 2nd ed. (Oxford, 1953).
[7] S. E. Finer, *The Life and Times of Sir Edwin Chadwick* (London, 1952).

Primer, his first book and intended as a simple introductory text, is the intellectual context in which he explains the mundane chores of public administration, and the vivid way in which he brings the subject to life. 'Over the whole report,' he writes referring to the findings of a Committee of Enquiry into the Anti-Tuberculosis Service in Wales, 'broods the stench of the sickbed, squalor, dirt, dungheaps and lingering death. The problem of areas,' he went on 'is an exercise in human miseries.'[8]

Local Government in England and Wales, published under the joint names of Finer and Sir John Maud, is a revision and updating of a book written by Maud twenty years before. It seems that the revised book was largely Finer's work.[9] *Sir Edwin Chadwick* was his earliest monograph; it is a major work of scholarship. It properly belongs with the *Primer*, and the book on local government, because of the profound way in which Chadwick helped to shape the later pattern of local government, the tensions between the centralisers and the advocates of local autonomy portrayed in the book, and the way in which perennial questions of public administration are brought into relief throughout Chadwick's career. Over and above these concerns it is an outstanding biography, and a significant contribution to English social history. It bears the stamp of years of archival research and through the life of a nineteenth-century figure, illuminates many of the problems of twentieth-century administration.

Finer had a restless mind and was soon seeking new realms. Interest in pressure groups was just beginning in British political science, stimulated partly by the American political scientist, Samuel Beer, who published two ground-breaking articles in 1956 and 1957.[10] Finer, envisaging a major research monograph, had already started work on the transport lobby in Britain. In 1956, he gave a characteristically provocative talk on BBC radio, 'In Defence of Pressure Groups',[11] a talk which might best be described as an academic manifesto. For some reason, the transport book was never completed but in 1958, he pub-

---

[8] Finer, *Primer*, p. 95.

[9] Maud and Finer, *Local Government*, p. v.

[10] S. Beer, 'Pressure Groups and Parties in Britain', *American Political Science Review*, March 1956, and 'The Representation of Interests in British Government', *American Political Science Review*, September 1957.

[11] S. E. Finer, 'In Defence of Pressure Groups', *Listener*, 7 June 1956.

lished *Anonymous Empire*;[12] this was not a book resting on detailed
study but rather sought to construct a framework for understanding
pressure groups, or 'the lobby' to use Finer's term. The book sought
to tell us in propositional form 'What is the Lobby', 'Who are the Lobby'
'What the Lobby does' and concluded with an appraisal of the significance of the lobby for democratic government. As in his BBC talk, he
emphasised the positive features of the lobby as a link between citizens
and government but voiced anxiety about the secrecy which often veiled
relations between interest groups and the state. 'Light! *more* light!', was
his call.[13]

Anonymous Empire illustrates one of Finer's most prominent
strengths. The empirical content of the book was slight, and he freely
acknowledged that newspapers, as well as *Hansard*, the reports of
organisations, and official publications were a major source.[14] Its
research claims did not lie in the empirical material the book presented;
the book was important because it was a trail-blazer. It offered to an
inward-looking, traditional and parochial national profession a new
approach and new intellectual territory. We so take for granted the study
of pressure groups today, that we have lost sight of the challenge which
such a book presented. It set out an agenda for the study of the topic.

Finer's articles in this field include 'The Federation of British
Industries'[15] (the predecessor of the CBI) and, published the year
before, 'The Political Power of Private Capital'.[16] Much of his best
work reflected his enthusiasm; but there was also a strong sceptical
streak to which he gave full scope. 'The Political Power of Private
Capital' was essentially a debunking work, calling into question some
of the most hallowed intellectual shibboleths of the Left. He did not
deny that capital could use a variety of tactics and deploy an assortment
of sanctions; the mistake of the Left was to argue that private capital
would use all of these, at virtually the same time, and in the same
country. 'What may or can conceivably happen is not the same as
something likely to happen.'[17]

Finer's work on central institutions in Britain partly overlapped with

[12] S. E. Finer, *Anonymous Empire* (London, 1958).
[13] Ibid. p. 133.
[14] Ibid. p. viii.
[15] S. E. Finer, 'The Federation of British Industries', *Political Studies*, March 1956.
[16] S. E. Finer, 'The Political Power of Private Capital', *Sociological Review*, September
1955.
[17] Ibid. p. 287.

his pressure groups phase. Like 'The Political Power of Private Capital', 'The Individual Responsibility of Ministers'[18] was a debunking exercise, this time directed not at the illusions of the Left but at the mythologies of the British Establishment. Every student of British government at the time knew that ministers were individually responsible to the House of Commons for the actions of their departments. The same students were assured that, by convention, the sanction of loss of office ensured that ministers kept firm control of their Civil Servants. Ministers whose departments blundered, or abused their powers, were expected to resign. The doctrine had already been dented, and in large measure redefined, in the wake of the Crichel Down scandal, revealed in 1954. Finer's article, published in 1956, examined all the grosser examples of departmental mismanagement, error and abuse in the past hundred years and looked at the fate of the Ministers 'responsible', concluding that relatively few Ministers in this position had actually resigned and that the operation of the sanction depended essentially on party political factors. 'It is on some sixteen or at most nineteen penitents and on one anomaly that the generalisation has been based.'[19]

Finer's next project proved to be much more controversial. Whilst transport was still unfinished his unquenchable exuberance led him into new paths. Finer had observed the way in which American scholars had exploited the greater freedom of voting in Congress to relate the ideologies of Senators and Representatives to such variables as region, the degree of agricultural employment, the percentage of foreign-born, as well as to identify the different blocs in Congress. In Britain, the rigidity of party discipline, then even stronger than it is today, concealed divisions of opinion amongst Members of the same party. One day it occurred to him that back-bench motions, put down by private Members, and often signed by considerable numbers of back-benchers, gave a simple way of identifying the attitudes of MPs. Thus was born *Backbench Opinion in the House of Commons 1955–59*,[20] published in 1961. It evoked furious and sometimes derisive strictures from politicians, journalists, and some academics. The present writer was a co-author of the book and sole author of the next volume and might therefore be regarded as a biased observer; some readers might

---

[18] S. E. Finer, 'The Individual Responsibility of Ministers', *Public Administration*, Winter 1956.

[19] Ibid. p. 394.

[20] S. E. Finer, H. B. Berrington and D. J. Bartholomew, *Backbench Opinion in the House of Commons 1955–1959* (Oxford, 1961).

therefore wish to discount his comments. What the reaction seemed to show was the unadventurous parochialism of British political science, and the primitive methodology of the non-academic critics. They had failed to absorb the injunction of Graham Wallas, made over half a century before, that, in addressing political problems, we must learn to think quantitatively.[21]

Although Finer's attention broadened in the early 1960s to embrace the political role of the military, and to comparative government, he sustained his interest in British politics and government. Like many British political scientists, he saw in the British polity a model of how governments could combine strength with democratic responsiveness. The enactment of the Labour Party's manifesto commitments in 1945 seemed to many to provide a graphic example of the way the British system could translate the popular will into a programme of far-reaching economic and social reforms. The 1960s and early 1970s saw gradual disillusionment. In February 1974 Harold Wilson became Prime Minister once again, this time as head of a minority government. Indeed, the result in that election was striking in that no two parties in combination (except Labour and the Conservatives) could muster a majority in the new House. To those who regarded the British parliamentary system with uncritical admiration, such a condition seemed a recipe for at best stalemate, at worst, disaster. Not so Finer: before the next election, called to give the government a majority, had been held, he had recanted a lifetime's belief with an article in *New Society*, 'In Defence of Deadlock',[22] a strident attack on what he dubbed 'adversary politics'.

A year later, Finer edited a new volume, *Adversary Politics and Electoral Reform*.[23] The book presented a series of chapters looking at the costs of the adversary regime, the working of the electoral system, and the experience continental countries had had with proportional representation and coalition government. The traditional defence of the British system had been that it provided strong government. The increasingly visible signs that British governments, despite their vast formal powers, were strong only in the division-lobbies at Westminster, but in the real world, cabined, cribbed and confined by pressure groups on the one hand and the electorate on the other, provoked some scholars

[21] G. Wallas, *Human Nature in Politics* (London, 1908).
[22] S. E. Finer, 'The Present Discontents: In Defence of Deadlock', *New Society*, 5 September 1974.
[23] S. E. Finer (ed.), *Adversary Politics and Electoral Reform* (London, 1975).

to make a fundamental reassessment. Finer returned to these themes during the next few years. *The British Party System 1945–79*[24] suffered in that, being one of a series of studies of national party systems, it had to conform to a strait-jacket imposed by the series' editors. Nevertheless, the book mounts a robust attack on the party system, and the 'first past the post' electoral formula which sustains it. His conclusion recalls the 'Light! *more* light!' plea with which he ended *Anonymous Empire*. 'The practitioners of politics,' he declared, 'have become professionals, and to all intents and purposes they are operating a closed shop. It is time to break it open.'[25]

Finer now entered on the most productive part of his career, that was to culminate in the massive though unfinished *History of Government*.[5] The study of military intervention in politics led naturally to his major text, *Comparative Government*.[4] It was one of his features to be thinking of the next area of research whilst still completing a current project. His interest in the Third World was already there in the late 1950s, and was reflected in his wish to reshape the syllabus for the Comparative Government course at Keele. Indeed, his initial focus was more on Latin America, whose states had been independent for over a hundred years, than Africa, most of which was still under colonial tutelage. To most British political scientists at the time, Britain was a model; it offered standards against which other polities could be assessed, and was for most the essential ingredient of introductory first-year courses in the subject. Increasingly, he came to question this view. 'Storm in Channel! Continent isolated' is a not unfair way of characterising the parochialism of the political science profession in Britain. He led the way (as he so often did) in helping British political scientists, in numbers even fewer than Gideon's army, to divert their Anglocentric gaze to the world beyond the shores of Britain, especially to the newly emerging post-colonial states of the Third World. Britain was the odd man out, not Burma or the Cameroons. It was the very virtues of the British political system, the acceptance of tacit rules, the give-and-take of political life, the way in which old forms responded to new realities, which made it politically so idiosyncratic. Britain was not therefore the

[24] S. E. Finer, *The Changing British Party System 1945–1979* (Washington DC, 1980).
[25] Ibid. p. 231.

best pattern to present to first-year undergraduates. If we sought to understand the practice of politics as it was over most of the globe, we needed to look across the water, especially at the new states.

The Man On Horseback[26] a study of military intervention in politics, grew out of a paper Finer presented to the Political Studies Association. Since no one else seemed to have examined the subject, he, in his own words, felt compelled to do so himself. He modestly averred that it had been written for the general reader, rather than his professional colleagues. He imposed his intellectual yoke lightly on his readers. He had the gift of making the most sophisticated argument seem simple, even obvious, to his public. 'The purpose of art,' declared Oscar Wilde, 'is to reveal art and conceal the artist.' As, with *Anonymous Empire*, contemporary events wrote much of the material for him. Like that book, *Horseback* displayed once again his formidable power to simplify complex phenomena, without compromising scholarly integrity. Once again, his framework for analysis was deceptively lucid. After assessing the strengths and weaknesses of the military, who seized power in so many post-colonial countries after the Second World War, he went on to examine military intervention in terms of such factors as the *disposition* to intervene, and the *opportunity* to intervene.

Horseback did more than set out the conditions of military interference. He talks of the levels of intervention, that is the form which intervention takes; in ascending order, these were influence, blackmail, displacement and supplantment. The level depended very largely on the political culture of the society. Thus, military intervention was not unknown in mature Western societies, or in the next category, countries of developed political culture; here, when it occurred, it took the form of influence, or sometimes blackmail. In countries of low political culture, and even more so in those of minimal political culture, military intervention took the form of displacement, often violent — the ejection from office of a Cabinet or President of whom the armed forces disapproved — or supplantment, the dismissal of the civilian government and the installation of direct military rule.

* * *

---

[26] S. E. Finer, *The Man On Horseback: The Role of the Military in Politics* (London, 1962 and rev. ed., 1976 and 2nd rev. ed., Westview Press, Boulder Colo. and London, 1988).

In 1966, Finer left Keele for Manchester, the biggest and most prestigious department of Politics in Britain outside Oxford and London. The six-hundred-page *Comparative Government*,[4] published in 1970, was the outgrowth of his lectures in Government 1, the first-year introductory course in Government. It reflected his interests in government as a phenomenon outside the mature democracies of Western Europe and North America. It was, however, more than a simple development of the themes of *Horseback*. It fused together several long-standing concerns. Finer, at least from the early Keele years, had sought to sketch out the scope and definition of Politics. *Comparative Government* reflected a yearning to move forward from the simple curriculum of Oxford PPE, or the London B.Sc.Econ., with their selection of the governments of four or five major powers, chosen for the not very good reason that they had always been studied.

Finer loved typologies and imposed his own so as to make sense of the diversity of political life across the world. How do you distinguish one system of government from another? He proposed four dimensions. The first was persuasion–coercion. In some states people tend to obey their rulers because they recognise the legitimacy (or if not, the utility) of government. In others they comply because of fear. At one extreme governments characteristically use persuasion and bargaining; at the other direct physical coercion. In between, however, lies a range of ways of ensuring popular acceptance of government. In some states, traditional oligarchies maintain their rule by manipulation — by exploiting feelings of deference that the population has for its traditional élites; other, more modern states invoke what he calls regimentation. Such states often have a single monopolistic party and seek the loyalty of their peoples by a kind of controlled involvement, often through the single party, without, however, yielding genuine influence to its citizenry.

All states, of course, use some coercion — even the most liberal — and many, which are for the most part highly coercive, may on occasion use techniques of persuasion, and even more, bargaining. What is important is the mix of means employed.

The other three dimensions may be mentioned more briefly. Some allow sub-groups (which might be territorial, or religious, or economic) a lot of autonomy, whilst other states tightly circumscribe the freedom of such sub-groups. Finer calls this the sub-group autonomy–sub-group dependence dimension. His third dimension, order-representativeness, differentiates between those states which put a high value on order and

stability, and those which emphasise representativeness. Lastly, present
goals-future goals, distinguishes between states which emphasise future
goods (for example, economic independence or the classless society)
and those which lay stress on present goods, for example, immediate
prosperity.

These dimensions yield a potential sixteen distinct types of state,
though in the event, Finer collapsed these into five. Liberal-democra-
cies, such as the United States and Britain, are characterised by persuasion much more than by coercion, reflect sub-group autonomy rather
than sub-group dependence, put more value on representativeness than
order, and look to the achievement of present, rather than, future goals.
The Soviet Union, in contrast, relied little on persuasion and bargaining,
and a lot on what Finer calls regimentation, plus a readiness to resort to
outright physical coercion. The regime heavily circumscribed the activities of sub-groups, and put great emphasis on the pursuit of future
goals — the classless Communist society.

The advantage of such a schema, however, lies less in the way it
classifies states such as the UK and the USSR than in the insight it gives
us into the nature of the political systems of what were then the other
120 independent states. Liberal-democratic, and totalitarian states, are
easy to recognise, but the real interest lies in Finer's three other
categories — façade-democracies, quasi-democracies and military
regimes — into which most of the 120 fall. Façade-democracies, which
are common in Latin America, are marked by the control, behind the
façade, of traditional oligarchies; the new quasi-democracies rest, like
the totalitarian states, on a mass but heavily controlled and (usually)
single party; Tunisia, Mexico and, until the deposition of Nkrumah in
1966, Ghana are examples of this class.

Military regimes were widespread amongst 'the poorer, the newer,
and extra-European states.' Military regimes are distinguished by
direct, or thinly concealed indirect, military government. Like the
façade-democracies, they are common in Latin America, and also in
Africa and the Islamic world.

The typology of *Comparative Government* was a remarkable
achievement. It was expounded with clarity, with vigour and with
authority; it reduced the kaleidoscopic diversity of government to a
few broad types, distinguished from each other by simple criteria. The
book, focusing as it did on geographic variation, was the forerunner of
his most ambitious, and most imaginative, work.

Finer modestly claimed that he wrote his book for the general reader (like *Horseback*) and his students. Of course, its value went far beyond that of an undergraduate guide. He showed that learning could not merely be fun; a highly sophisticated advancement of the subject could be made intelligible to undergraduates, and needed to employ little in the way of complex vocabulary. Polysyllabic terminologies were tedious and superogatory.

Finer's long essay on the role of the military in European state-building[27] was a link (though intellectual and not chronological) between the more specific concerns of *Horseback* and the broader tasks of *Comparative Government*. More than that, it gave him a new perspective, opening to him the prospect of his last major study, which would be at once analytical and historical. The essay, which illuminates the growth of the State in France, England and Prussia, gave full scope to his imaginative eclecticism. He seemed equally at ease in the England of Edgar the Peaceful, and the modern twentieth-century European polity. His *History of Government From the Earliest Times*[5] shows the debt which he owed, and we owe, to his work for this essay.

Finer saw his *History of Government* as the culmination of his intellectual pilgrimage. He began work on this vast enterprise on retiring from the Gladstone Chair at Oxford. He spent virtually all his eleven years of retirement on this book. By the time of his death in June 1993, he had completed all but two of the thirty-six chapters. Since his death, his widow, Kate Finer, and Jack Hayward, a former colleague at Keele and now Professor of Politics at Oxford, have taken over the manuscript, completed the two unfinished chapters, edited the book and presented it for publication. It is likely to be published in early 1997.

Finer recognised that, for all the light it shed, his *Comparative Government* was time-bound. It was an essentially static analysis. The new venture, the most exciting of his life, would cross both space and time. Until the book is published we have to rely for an understanding of its content on Professor Hayward's brilliantly lucid Finer Memorial Lecture at the University of Keele, given in May 1995, and on Finer's Public Lecture of 1982, 'Perspectives in the World History of Government', later published in *Government and Opposition*.[28] He made the development of the State the central theme of his *History*.

---

[27] S. E. Finer 'State- and Nation-Building in Europe: The Role of the Military', in C. Tilly (ed.), *The Formation Of National States In Western Europe* (Princeton, 1975).
[28] J. E. S. Hayward, 'Finer's Comparative History of Government', *Keele Papers in Politics*, 1995, and S. E. Finer, 'Perspectives in the World History of Government — A Prolegomenon', *Government and Opposition*, March 1983.

Finer identified four pure types of polity. The Palace type is exemplified, *inter alia*, by Ancient Egypt, and the Roman, Byzantine, and Chinese Empires. The second, and in a sense antithetical type, he calls the Forum. Here, the 'principle of legitimacy resides in the ruled and not the rulers'. Persuading rather than commanding is required in this polity and thus rhetoric becomes a vital political skill. Both the Church polity, and the Nobility polity, are rarely found in their pure form. The first is exemplified by Tibet, from the fifteenth century until the Chinese Communist invasion, and the second by Poland in the seventeenth and eighteenth centuries. In Poland, the monarch was chosen by the nobles and any one of these could veto legislation.

Six further types are generated by hybrids of the four pure types. Two of these are extremely rare leaving four sub-types: Church–Palace, Forum–Nobility, Palace–Nobility, and the paradoxical Palace–Forum type. The Church–Palace type has three variants of which Caesaropapism is the most well-known. The Roman Republic and Venice provide examples of the Forum–Nobility type. The Palace–Nobility type has four sub-types of which the most well-known — the King governing with his council of noblemen — was characteristic of medieval Europe. The Palace–Forum polity is distinguished by autocratic rule, legitimated by popular election or plebiscite. The modern totalitarian state is an important sub-type of this class.

The schema therefore is both imaginative and economical, reducing enormous variation to, in effect eight types, and a number of sub-types. Sammy saw no pre-ordained development, no inevitable broadening out of freedom from precedent to precedent. Some types of polity survived, others passed into the limbo of history. He would not have shared Laski's optimism of the mid-1920s: 'Democratic government is doubtless a final form of political organisation in that men who have once tasted power will not, without conflict, surrender it.'[29] On the contrary; ancient Athens, the earliest of the Forum type, had few imitators: ' . . . until the nineteenth century,' says Finer, 'it was Sparta, not Athens, that was the model for the European avant-garde. The harsh fact is that the Greek democratic *poleis* form but a tiny spot, both spatially and temporally, on the five millennia of the world's forms of government.' Just as the Darwinian doctrine of 'survival of the fittest' tells us nothing about the moral status of those species that do survive, or their contribution to the world's ecosystem, so the survival of one type of polity,

---

[29] H. J. Laski, *A Grammar of Politics* (London, 1925), p. 17.

and the extinction of another, tell us nothing about the ethical claims of each. Writing of the long march of history, Finer observed that 'progressive evolution would be a wholly misguided way of conceiving this long and tortuous process.' If we learn nothing else from Finer's *History*, we will at least learn to curb our expectations.

Finer was more than a great teacher and an innovative scholar. He also built up, what for its time, was one of the biggest departments in the United Kingdom. It is necessary to emphasise again the fragmented character of the subject in British universities for most of the 1950s. Politics, however old its lineage, had little presence in Britain. In the mid-1950s the Political Studies Association had barely a hundred members, and some of these were historians or area specialists who took little part in the Association's work. Typically, the Politics teaching complement at a provincial university consisted of two or three members, often located in an Economics or History department, and boasting no independent undergraduate degree. In terms of size as well as prestige, Oxford, LSE and Manchester dominated the profession.

Finer, the student of empires, was foremost among the empire-builders. He discerned the unique opportunities which Keele offered to the ambitious entrepreneur. Few university applicants at this stage opted to read Politics. In some schools, pupils could take British Constitution at O level or A level, but the subject was dominated by the constitutional lawyers. For nearly all departments, of whatever subject, a substantial student population was, and remains, a pre-condition of growth. What Keele did was to offer him the opportunity to attract students, in large numbers, to read Politics at either principal or subsidiary level. The Foundation Year, one of Keele's novel features, gave him his chance. The centre-piece of the Foundation Year was a lecture course to which all departments contributed, and attendance at which was compulsory for all first-year students. He ensured that he himself filled each slot allotted to the Political Institutions department. Such a large audience saw Finer, never backward as a performer, at his best. Lecturing to the Foundation Year gave him his 'fix', and students an experience. His enthusiasm, his encyclopaedic knowledge, his inexhaustible humour, guaranteed a receptive audience. So, every June, when students came to make their choices for principal and subsidiary subjects, forty or so students would enrol for Principal 1 Politics the following October, and a similar number would opt for the Subsidiary course.

Keele early adopted a formula which related the teaching staff entitlement, above a certain threshold, to student enrolments. The more students a department could attract, the more staff it could appoint. Finer seems to have been successful in his choice of colleagues. Of the six Politics specialists he recruited between 1954 and 1963, four went on to hold chairs of Politics in Britain and one became Fellow of an Oxford research college. By 1962, Keele was the fourth biggest department of Politics in the country. Finer was elected a Fellow of the British Academy in 1982.

It would have been unfair of providence to distribute so many gifts to Finer without at least a few gaps or weaknesses. Finer was enormously learned, but his grasp of detail, sometimes including important detail, could be defective. He sometimes chafed at the restraints of precision. He was a broad-brush man. He was rather like a tank general, breaking through the enemy lines, racing ahead to the next objective, and leaving pockets of resistance far in his rear, to be mopped up at leisure. 'Go to his lectures, but don't take any notes', was the advice some Oxford tutors gave their students, during his first spell at Oxford.

Moreover, there were certain developments in the subject with which Finer was never at ease. He can be pardoned for his dislike of the grosser manifestations of American behaviouralism. More surprisingly, he never seems to have been at home with the studies of electoral behaviour which burgeoned in the last twenty-five years of his life. He certainly cited their findings but his mind never really accommodated itself to the new genre. In spite of his familiarity with American political science he seemed, paradoxically for the biographer of Chadwick, untouched by the growing interest there in personality and politics; thus, the second edition of *Horseback* discusses the socialisation and recruitment of the military, but never mentions Norman Dixon's seminal work *On The Psychology of Military Incompetence*.[30]

In Finer, the iconoclast and the enthusiast sometimes strove for mastery. He began as a man of the Left and apparently voted Labour up to, and including, the election of 1955. Just as he changed his mind

---

[30] N. Dixon, *On The Psychology of Military Incompetence* (London, 1976).

on intellectual issues, so he altered his political opinions. He would relate that change to some moment of truth (not always the same moment), when the limitations of his past political creed became apparent to him. Sometimes Suez in 1956 was presented as being that moment, for he identified passionately with the new state of Israel. There was a story that he openly burned the *Manchester Guardian* at the time but this was probably one of those legends that Finer recounted against himself. As with most great communicators, Sammy was not a man to forego the pleasures of a good story. His conversion to Conservatism, however, at its furthest, was never wholly secure. During the 1970s, when he embraced proportional representation, he was even-handed in his strictures against the two main parties. As we have seen, he became highly critical of the working of British government. He stayed an iconoclast throughout his career, never wholly turning his back on his early radicalism.

In some, the ordinary human qualities seem to be exalted to a higher level. Sammy never did anything by halves. He was sometimes provocative, but always provocatively exciting; in style both of dress and speech, often flamboyant, but flamboyantly engaging; in voicing opinion, sometimes outrageous, but outrageously stimulating. He was passionate in his beliefs, but never closed-mindedly so; he was vehement in his enmities, but generous in reconciliation. He was scornful in opposition, but ardent in loyalty; gargantuan in his industry, and intense in his enthusiasms.

HUGH BERRINGTON
University of Newcastle-upon-Tyne

Note. I am grateful to Rod Hague and Rod Rhodes for their helpful comments about aspects of Professor Finer's work. I also owe special thanks to Dennis Kavanagh for sending me his chapter *The Fusion of History and Politics: The Case of S. E. Finer* in Hans Daalder's edited volume *The Autobiography of Comparative European Politics* (London, 1996). I have also profited from his address at the commemoration of Sammy Finer's life and work held at All Souls College, Oxford, on 7 May 1994. Similarly, I must thank Jack Hayward for sending me the written version of the Finer Memorial Lecture that he gave at the University of Keele on 10 May 1995 which gives a graphic account of Professor Finer's *History of Government from the Earliest Times*. Not least, I must thank him for his constant prodding of me to write this memoir.

Bibliographic Note

A Bibliography of S. E. Finer's principal publications appeared in 1984 in *Comparative Government and Politics, Essays in Honour of S. E. Finer*, ed. Dennis Kavanagh and Gillian Peele (Boulder, Colo.), pp. 16–19. One entry should be corrected, *Adversary Politics and Electoral Reform* was edited by Finer, not jointly authored.

To this list should be added:

'The Federation of British Industries', *Political Studies*, March 1956.

S. E. Finer and H. B. Berrington, 'The Parliamentary Profession in Britain', *International Social Science Journal*, 1961; rev. and repr. in *Decisions and Decision-Makers in the Modern State* (Paris, Unesco).

S. E. Finer, V. Bogdanor and B. Rudden, *Comparing Constitutions* (Oxford, 1995).

S. E. Finer, *History of Government from the Earliest Times* (Oxford, forthcoming).

JOHN GERE   *The British Museum*

Proceedings of the British Academy, **90**, 367–388

John Arthur Giles Gere
1921–1995

THE BASIC CURRICULUM VITAE of John Arthur Giles Gere — Winchester, Balliol, Oxford and the British Museum — correctly conjures up an image of a distinguished education and professional life, but gives little hint of the rich diversity and originality of character. In the course of his life Gere became a great connoisseur of Italian sixteenth-century drawings, a pioneering collector of landscape oil-sketches and a man of wit and extraordinarily wide learning, whose unusual personality made an indelible impression on all who met him.

The history of the Gere family can be traced back to the mid-seventeenth-century, when in 1644 two small boys, aged twelve and fourteen and heirs to a family estate in Devon, were for nefarious purposes sent off to the New World by a wicked uncle. The latter paid a ship's captain to accept them and then virtually abandon them on the coast of Massachusetts, where remarkably they survived on their own.

The succeeding generations of the family remained in North America until about 1867, when Gere's paternal grandfather, Edward, a manufacturer of castings for water systems, sold out to his partner after the death of his first wife. He came to England after the death of his second wife, an Englishwoman, who had died shortly after the birth of their son, Charles. Visiting her family, he met and married his wife's second cousin, in the first instance to find a mother for his child. But their union developed into a great love match, which produced five children including John Gere's father, Edward Arnold, who was born in 1873.

Gere's father was employed by the Patents Office as an examiner of patents. He took an imaginative interest in his work and in retirement during the Second World War he became obsessed with proving that the distillation of sugar beet could provide sufficient food for survival. As a result he used to follow lorries on his bicycle, picking up any of the crop which by chance fell onto the road. In a hut in the garden he set about reducing it in an old sardine tin, consuming the resulting bitter molasses, which he believed to be a very healthy diet.

Although something of his father's character was undoubtedly inherited by Gere, who was born on 7 October 1921, perhaps more important for the development of his later interests were his artistic forbears on both sides of his family, in all of whom he took great pride, hanging examples of their work as part of his collection. His father's half-brother, Charles March Gere, and two of his father's sisters, Margaret Gere and Edith Payne (the latter was married to H. A. Payne, who painted one of the Tudor scenes in the House of Lords), were all artists of the Birmingham school. In marked contrast Gere's mother's sister, Catherina Giles, was initially associated with the Vorticists in the circle of Wyndham Lewis. (Gere's mother was a formidable personality, who in more recent times would have found fulfilment by running a large organisation.)

From an early age Gere stood out from his contemporaries. At kindergarten he 'was so clever that we would defer to him even as children. I remember very vividly making and dressing match-stick figures of the characters in *The Midnight Folk*. He was mad about the book and we had a complete assembly of all the characters'.[1]

A contemporary, Sir Patrick Nairne, met Gere 'at the preparatory school, Hordle House, in the early 1930s. It was not a bad school, as schools of that period went; but it was a concentration camp for John. He was then, at the age of ten, a paid-up member of culture and civilisation — art, books, intellectual views: not at all the stuff of prep. school society. He was a rebel (though clever enough to keep out of trouble); I was a wimpish collaborateur. But we were friends, who found the same things funny. On the dreary Sunday afternoon school walks we walked together fantasising about the possibilities of

---

[1] Letter from Daffodil Andrewes to Charlotte Gere, 29 January 1995.

more agreeable Sunday afternoons devoted to China tea and crunchy bars'.[2] And 'while the rest of us in the dormitory would be playing dab cricket or reading P. F. Westerman, John would be reading Ronald Firbank. I can hear his laugh as I write'.[3]

Winchester followed, where he was happy largely due to the support and encouragement of his housemaster, Jack Parr. This was given despite Gere's incurable insubordination, which was less intentional than the result of his failure to understand the apparently irrational requirements of those in authority, a characteristic which to some degree remained with him throughout life. The attitude of other masters towards him was not improved by his success in winning numerous prizes. (In later years he suffered from a nightmare that he was to be beaten without knowing the cause.) Although many of his close contemporaries have predeceased him, something of his views of the school can be gained from what apparently he told Lord Alfred Douglas, with whom, on coming down from Oxford, he was in correspondence in connection with his projected biography of the poet, Lionel Johnson, who had also been a Wykhamist. In reply Lord Alfred wrote: 'what you tell me about Winchester & its present headmaster fills me with consternation. I had no idea of it & do not even know the headmaster's name. I am however not surprised, as it looks as if the gadarene swine rush to the ''left'' has spread all over the country'.[4]

Gere's attitude to school life must, perhaps not entirely fortuitously, have echoed that of his chosen subject, who was likewise a prize winner. Johnson 'always kept himself aloof and with a certain atmosphere of disdain: assumed, I think — consciously? or unconsciously? — as a kind of defensive armour by one, who felt that his frail physique set him at a disadvantage in the rough and tumble of life at school. . . . He was, almost ostentatiously, indifferent to all the games and athletic side of a public school — no doubt it was good for us to have in him a standing protest against the over-valuation of such things: but you will readily understand that this didn't increase his popularity'.[5] In Gere's case, there was the long painful struggle, which continued up to the age of seventeen, of trying to learn to swim. Being forced into the water, the inordinately thin boy used to cry out to those

[2] Letter from the Rt Hon. Sir Patrick Nairne GCB to Charlotte Gere, 21 January 1995.
[3] Letter from the same to the present writer, 15 February 1995.
[4] Lord Alfred Douglas to John Gere, 7 August 1942.
[5] William Busby to John Gere, 16 August 1942.

whom he saw as his tormentors: 'Do you want to see my lifeless corpse lying at the bottom of the pool?'

On leaving school in 1939, he joined the King's Royal Rifle Corps, but was immediately invalided out on the discovery of intestinal tuberculosis, which must have had an unrecognised effect on his school years. When he was cured, he went up to Oxford in 1940, reading English at Balliol. His tutor was John Bryson, who not only reconciled Gere to Oxford life, but encouraged his scholarly interests in the Pre-Raphaelites and, by example, the collecting of English and continental drawings. A contemporary, Richard Wollheim, recalls that Gere 'lived in rooms which the sun seemed never to reach, and he believed he was very shy, and he spent much of his time doing very small ink drawings of great complexity of the human figure. He had Piranesi prints, & two sang-de-boeuf pots & other things, all of which he found in the original Oxfam shop opposite Balliol — or perhaps some other junk shop, I am now uncertain. But for all his shyness, what John loved most were the foibles of his friends, which he deftly turned into myths, so that it became enough to hear their names for him to collapse in laughter. Gradually the stories accumulated, and I felt that John kept inside himself a mythology as rich as Homer or Ovid'.[6] 'John was really very private in those days, &, somewhat in keeping with the deliberately anachronistic character of wartime Oxford, he evolved a very rigid system of etiquette. Punctuality, & small rituals designed to show whether you were or were not acceptable, were very much part of it. Here I think that John might have been influenced by 'Colonel' Kolkhorst,[7] whom he admired for his eccentricity. Once I kept John waiting

---

[6] Letter from Professor Richard Wollheim to Charlotte Gere, 19 February 1995.

[7] George Alfred Magee Kolkhorst, who has been described as follows (Letter from Russell Burlingham to the present writer, 9 December 1995): 'A much-loved and eccentric figure whose heyday was the Oxford of the 20s, where the University's equivalent of the Bright Young Things disported themselves: rainbow-hued butterflies briefly fluttering against the grey stone backdrop of college and quad.

'Kolkhorst's Colonelcy was attributed by some to service in the Portuguese Medical Corps; another school of opinion holding . . . that the rank had been attained during employment with the Buenos Aires Tramway Company. In truth the cognomen was altogether mythical: he was called Colonel because he was so unlike a Colonel.

'He conducted a salon at 38, Beaumont Street. Bowra presided over a rival one at Wadham, they did not like each other and there was a certain amount of competitive manoeuvring. K. spread his nets to draw in only accredited aesthetes: Bowra was not averse to extending a welcome to hearties and the more robust as well. K.'s Sunday mornings drew a wide spectrum of ''arty'' Oxford. His intimates, dons and undergraduates alike (he was

for about 5 minutes — I am sure no more — at Balliol Lodge. John cut me dead for about a month. He kept some of this up for a few years.'[8]

On coming down from Oxford in 1943, Gere undertook a period of voluntary service at the Tate Gallery, which rapidly ended when he quarrelled, as a number of other people did, with the then director.

University Lecturer in Spanish) called him G'ug — the apostrophe, indicated by a little yawn, was supposed to imply deference. I forget if it was Colin Gill or Gerard Irvine who perpetrated the doggerel lines:

G'uggery G'uggery Nunc,
Your room is all cluttered with junk:
Candles, bamboonery,
Plush and saloonery —
Oh pack it all up in a trunk!

'Kolkhorst wore a lump of sugar round his neck on a piece of string, "to sweeten conversation". A quip by one of the circumambient wits ran:

He's the wise G'ug, who says each thing twice over,
Lest you should think he never can recapture
That first fine *careful* rapture.

'Betj. always prefaced his letters "Darling Colonel" — anticipating correspondence by an entirely different kind of author to an entirely different kind of Colonel — one memorably opened "you dear horizontal-eyed, cube-headed, wool-dressing-gowned old thing". I seem to remember reading his quarters smelt of mice and chicken soup. A large photogravure portrait of Walter Pater was prominently positioned on the chimney-piece, at some stage Osbert Lancaster, in a boldly flowing hand, had scrawled Alma Pater over the placid, heavily-moustached features of the great Oxford teacher and evangelist of the Gospel of Beauty.

'They must have been jolly affairs, those Sunday mornings. A favourite diversion was the propelling of moistened postage stamps, using coins, towards the ceiling, to which, over the years, a multitude of these had adhered. At a fairly late stage in the proceedings everyone joined hands and chanted in a circle as they revolved round Kolkhorst:

D'ye ken Kolkhorst in his art-full parlour,
Handing out the drinks at his Sunday morning gala?
   Some get sherry and some Marsala —
With his arts and his crafts in the morning! (Tune: John Peel)

This was always received by K. with "suave equanimity". . . .

"K. in later years, until his death in the mid-fifties, inhabited Yarnton Manor, a large rambling Jacobean/Victorian place a few miles west of Oxford. All windows were heavily curtained, day and night. Lunching there was like being in a nightclub, especially when — a frequent occurrence — the Colonel wound up the gramophone and put on "Just the Way You Look Tonight".

'It must have been, I think, through John's old Balliol tutor John Bryson, or perhaps more likely through Eddie (E. H. W.) Meyerstein, that he would have crossed the path of this unique and extraordinary character, as strange as any to be found in Aubrey or Hearne.' See also *To Keep the Ball Rolling. The Memoirs of Anthony Powell* (rev. ed., Harmondsworth, 1983), pp. 90–1.)

[8] Professor Richard Wollheim to the present writer, 15 September 1995.

Advised that he should acquire professional qualifications, Gere enrolled to study the history of art at the Courtauld Institute of Art, which although founded in 1932 was still a small highly specialised institution. But after one term he decided that it did not offer him what he was looking for. Despite the dire warnings of his contemporaries that he was committing professional suicide, he was soon able to demonstrate that his rapid departure from that centre of art–historical studies did not impair his future career in the museum world. In later years, anyone foolish or bold enough to describe him as an art historian was treated to an indignant denial.

On 25 March 1946 he was appointed an Assistant Keeper in the Department of Prints and Drawings in the British Museum and was immediately employed on preparing for publication the catalogue of the early Italian drawings in the British Museum by Popham and Philip Pouncey.[9] (This was a task, later referred to 'as perhaps the most valuable part of his entire education', for which he showed great aptitude. His natural editorial skills were subsequently employed on Wilde's catalogue of Michelangelo's drawings[10] and Popham's catalogue of the Parmese drawings.[11] Although an admirer of Popham, he found an immediate spiritual affinity with Pouncey, who became a lifelong friend and initially gave him precisely the training which he felt he needed. As he later recalled: 'Quite apart from the close scrutiny and discussion of the drawings themselves, he [i.e. Gere] learnt whatever he knows of clarity, accuracy, concision and exactness of expression, attention to shades of meaning, the distinction between hypothesis and fact and the relevant and irrelevant, and the ''expression of assent and dissent in graduated terms'' '.[12] Those who regularly overheard their often lengthy pursuit of a nuance will readily attest to the accuracy of this testimony.

After serving twenty years as an Assistant Keeper, he was appointed Deputy Keeper in 1966, and, on the retirement of Edward Croft-Murray, Keeper in 1973. In the latter role, he developed into a character, perhaps one of the last of a dying breed in the British Museum.

---

[9] A. E. Popham and Philip Pouncey, *Italian Drawings in the Department of Prints and Drawings in the British Museum: The Fourteenth and Fifteenth Centuries*, 2 vols (1950).

[10] Johannes Wilde, *Italian Drawings in the Department of Prints and Drawings in the British Museum: Michelangelo and his Studio* (1953).

[11] A. E. Popham, *Italian Drawings in the Department of Prints and Drawings in the British Museum: Artists Working in Parma in the Sixteenth Century*, 2 vols (1967).

[12] *The Achievement of a Connoisseur: Philip Pouncey* (Cambridge, 1985), n.p.

His staff may have been in awe of him, but they greatly admired him. He set very high standards in the care of the collections. In the best traditions of the Civil Service, he was, whatever he may have thought privately of the public, very punctilious in carrying out his public duties, often taking considerable trouble to answer a difficult or tiresome question with the fullest information. He was an excellent teacher in the skills of writing catalogue entries and exhibition labels (the ultimate exercise in concision) and in the practice of connoisseurship. He achieved this as much by example as by criticism, the latter developed benevolently but directly, a characteristic he adapted, at least where directness was concerned, to whomever he was speaking. His junior colleagues were also deeply grateful to him when he invariably defended them against what were seen as overbearing directives emanating from the central administration. In one instance his championing of their cause involved a powerful trustee, who was recommending that a senior outside scholar should be appointed to advise the Print Room about its modern acquisitions, leaving the recently appointed assistant keeper with a specialism in that field to perform in a purely subordinate role. This proposal was firmly and successfully aborted by Gere.

Another dispute, which involved Gere even more directly, raised the temperature a little higher. An equally forceful trustee was urging, against the former's objections, and thus undermining the position of the Keeper, the acquisition of an expensive and ugly drawing supposedly by Van Gogh. Gere, who saw the purchase as both undesirable for a great collection and a waste of public money, used what he regarded as a once-only option and threatened resignation. It was, however, a tribute to his standing that both the trustees, Lord Clark and Sir Lawrence Gowing respectively, continued to regard him in a friendly and admiring light. In fact the former, after a visit from Gere to his flat in Albany, went so far as to say that 'John Gere has a better eye and deeper knowledge than anyone else alive today'.[13]

But despite his widely recognised distinction Gere could never escape a lingering feeling that he was not a totally successful Keeper. This was perhaps started by the dilatoriness of the trustees in appointing him and aggravated by his increasing lack of patience with the burgeoning bureaucracy, which now affects everyone in an administrative position. In addition he suffered from a certain innate diffidence, distinctly detectable on occasions in his voice. For someone so essentially privileged this might have seemed an affectation, but was in fact

---

[13] Letter from Catherine Porteous to Charlotte Gere, 17 January 1995.

induced by an element of genuine ambivalence in his character. ('It's
not so much that I want to be Keeper; it's more that I don't want *not* to
be.'[14]). At his death the long-time Secretary of the Museum, Bentley
Bridgewater, went out of his way to say that 'I must put right any
suggestion which John may have made that his performance as Keeper
left anything to be desired. He was generally recognized as a first rate
Keeper and held in high estimation both inside and outside the
Department. . . . Both Trustees and Directors thought of him as a
very good Keeper — so, too, did his staff'.[15]

But there was, of course, his incorrigible irreverence which he
couldn't resist, although he knew it caused puzzlement if not irritation,
such as on the occasion, when, faced with Gere's resolute opposition to
a new museum initiative, the chairman of the trustees, puffing his pipe,
came up to him and, taking his arm, said in a cajoling manner: 'You
know, Gere, symposia are *a good thing*'. Responding to this rather too
obvious attempt at gentle persuasion, Gere feigned to believe that he
was being encouraged to set up homosexual drinking parties in the
Department. (Introduced to the Dean of Christ Church, Oxford, after
a barely audible memorial address, 'I told him that the Cathedral ought
to be pulled down and replaced by a properly planned auditorium with
all the advantages of modern acoustic research'.[16])

During his years at the Museum he was responsible for a number of
important purchases of drawings, such as Andrea Mantegna's *St James
led to Execution*, Sebastiano del Piombo's *Virgin and Child*, as well as
others by Bronzino and, as one might expect, Taddeo Zuccaro. He was
no less concerned with building up the representation of lesser artists,
such as Polidoro da Caravaggio, Baldassare Franceschini and Lazzaro
Baldi, in the Department's collection. He was in addition a generous
donor to the Museum and over the years gave works (landscapes, a
portrait of Mrs William Morris on vellum and a group of sketchbooks)
by his half-uncle, Charles March Gere, a drapery study by Wilkie for
The First Earring, watercolours by William Bell Scott and George
Howard, a drawing by Alexander Monro for his most celebrated sculpture, *Paolo and Francesca*, after a design by Rossetti, and a drawing by
Belisario Corenzio.

There was a nice symmetry about the pattern of his scholarly progress, which, as the attached bibliography demonstrates, was remarkably
wide-ranging. He started by working on the Pre-Raphaelites, who at

---

[14] Letter from John Gere to the present writer, 23 April 1972.
[15] Letter from Bentley Bridgewater to Charlotte Gere, 19 February 1995.
[16] Letter from John Gere to the present writer, 27 May 1992.

that time were underrated and in need of reassessment, by publishing, *inter alia*, a book, written with Robin Ironside, on the *Pre-Raphaelite Painters* (1948). He subsequently went back in time to the study of Raphael and his contemporaries, and only in the last year of his life returned to his first love by arranging an exhibition of the Pre-Raphaelite drawings in the British Museum, which was accompanied by an excellent catalogue. It represented a period to which in all aspects of its culture he felt strongly attracted.

His most significant research was done in the field of sixteenth-century Italian drawings, notably his monograph on the drawings of Taddeo Zuccaro and the two British Museum catalogues written with his friend and colleague, Philip Pouncey, *Raphael and his Circle* (1962) and *Artists Working in Rome c. 1550 to c. 1640* (1983). Both of the catalogues set new standards in the connoisseurship of those particular fields and in their scholarly exegesis, offering original judgements and characterisations in beautifully concise, highly wrought entries, which in their preparation had been subject to infinite refinement. The exemplary detailed biographies of the artists whose drawings were included provided a wider and much used work of reference. In the first volume Pouncey and Gere can be seen as pioneers in sorting out one of the most difficult problems of connoisseurship, the drawings produced by artists working around Raphael, as well as for their clear and well-argued definition of the work of the master himself. (As part of this search for convincing answers, Gere, a rare performer, gave six lectures on the decoration of the *stanze* in the Vatican by Raphael and his school, for the newly created History of Art Department at Cambridge.)

Following the establishment of art history in this country, connoisseurship has increasingly come to be looked down upon as a simplistic activity of merely determining the authorship of a work of art. In evaluating the achievements of Pouncey, Gere composed an eloquent defence of connoisseurship, which he argued added up to something very much subtler and more essential for further research than was normally conceded by art historians: 'the essence of the subject lies in the complex interaction of a host of widely differing individual artistic personalities which it is the primary duty of the historian to define and distinguish; and that no critical generalisation can be accepted as valid unless based on a foundation of secure attribution.'[17]

---

[17] 'Philip Pouncey, 1910–1990', *Proceedings of the British Academy*, 76 (Oxford, 1991), p. 535.

And both British Museum catalogues are notable for putting precept into practice. Gere's definition of the value of connoisseurship is relevant to his own achievements. But occasionally he felt challenged, albeit in a small way, to produce the synthesis that current art history seemed to demand and when writing an extended review of a book on High Renaissance painting, he tortured himself, to some purpose, to offer a personal definition in a dozen finely honed paragraphs of the meaning of the Renaissance.

Preliminary work on the second British Museum catalogue inspired the theme of his most original research, the drawings of Taddeo Zuccaro, in which he convincingly proved the pre-eminence of this Roman artist over his previously better known, longer lived and more prolific brother, Federico. A number of articles and exhibition catalogues devoted to the two brothers culminated in his masterly monograph *Taddeo Zuccaro, his Development Studied in his Drawings* (1969), which, since Taddeo's art touched so many other artists of the period, succeeded in providing a study of Roman painting at the mid-century. And in its understanding of the artist's use of drawing in the creation of a painting, it went far further than separating one hand from another, even if that, given the changing nature of Taddeo's art, was no mean feat in itself. Although Gere had convincingly established a generally accepted canon of the artist's drawings, it was characteristic of his constantly questioning mind that at the time of his death he had virtually completed an extensive revision, published in *Master Drawings*. The eighty-eight new attributions to Taddeo, increasing his *œuvre* by well over a quarter, are partly due to the reappearance of lost works and partly to Gere's conviction that he had originally adopted too narrow a view of the artist, who on reconsideration should be seen as being more various in his manner of drawing.

In addition to these volumes he wrote a number of exhibition catalogues for foreign print rooms, such as the Uffizi in Florence, the Louvre in Paris and the Pierpont Morgan Library in New York. But his most memorable exhibitions were held at the British Museum, where, for example, he assembled, in collaboration with his colleague, Nicholas Turner, almost all the drawings in English collections by Michelangelo (1979) and by Raphael (1983). These provided remarkable and very popular displays, which no other country could match and to which justice was done by the quality of the scholarship. The Michelangelo exhibition was repeated in a reduced version in New York later the same year, when Gere, ever a self-critic, took the opportunity to rework substantially some of his catalogue entries.

Following his retirement in 1981 he continued to be widely consulted by museums and collectors, contributing, for example, to exhibition catalogues of Italian drawings from the collections in Rennes and Turin, and for a number of years he served as an adviser to Christie's on old master drawings. His last assignment was as the first Lehman Visiting Scholar to the Metropolitan Museum of Art in New York in 1993.

Gere was a passionate collector, following in the tradition of the great collector-connoisseurs of the past, to whom, he was fond of emphasising, so much of our present knowledge is due. He had a particular admiration for Sir J. C. Robinson, 'who in 1870 broke new ground by being the first to publish a scientific and methodical study of an artist's drawings considered as essential elements in the reconstruction and assessment of his work as a whole'.[18] Undoubtedly this consciously chosen inheritance influenced his taste as a collector in which he showed himself to be anything but narrow. He had a keen eye for any drawing of beauty, quality or of unusual character. As a result he had a very personal and varied collection by English, Dutch, Flemish and French artists as well as naturally by Italian artists, which was very different from that made by Pouncey, who was a specialist *par excellence*. The latter was sometimes playfully disdainful of his younger colleague's purchases, as on the occasion when the latter proudly returned one afternoon with a finely executed study by Abraham Bloemart, provoking Pouncey to announce at large that it was sad to see Gere wasting his time and his money on buying a drawing of a cabbage. But as he himself was inclined to say he regarded the collecting of drawings as an extension of his work in the Museum. His more creative instincts were directed towards a new and more original field of collecting, namely small landscape oil-sketches, for the most part done *en plein air*, by artists from the seventeenth to the nineteenth centuries, predominantly French of Italian subjects. Over forty-five years he built up a remarkable private collection. Increasingly it developed into his principal passion — a pursuit fully shared by his wife — as they searched for new acquisitions in auction rooms and galleries throughout the world. Often anonymous or wrongly attributed, they were a challenge to the eye and knowledge in much the same way as are old master

---

[18] *The Achievement of a Connoisseur* ... , n. 12, above.

drawings, although it was the work's intrinsic quality which was the prime motivation in acquisition. His wife was responsible for hanging them on the walls of their house in such a way that the collection became more than the sum of its parts.

In a wider sense Gere was formidably well-informed. He had an encyclopaedic mind which could almost invariably be relied upon. If he didn't know the answer to a question, you were likely to have considerable trouble in finding out. And he wrote with such style; chiselled, polished, precise and elegant. A perfectionist to the core, he was a demon for rewriting. Over and over his MS he would go, seeking some subtle nuance which still eluded him in often complex arguments. As a letter writer he was more relaxed and many friends have choice specimens carefully preserved. In the field of literature he had a most remarkable knowledge, allied with a memory for what he had read, so that he could freely quote large sections of prose or poetry. (He urged his children to do likewise.) A passionate admirer of the Sherlock Holmes stories, he could still recall all the plots by heart. He was as well versed in, say, the poetry of Shelley and Keats as he was in the novels of Horace Vachell and Desmond Coke. He read voraciously, in practice anything he could lay his hands on, often picked up on the seat of a bus or plucked from a waste-paper basket. But above all his source of literary knowledge was related to his very extensive library. He described himself as an accumulator of books rather than a collector, caring little about condition or whether he was purchasing a first edition. He took particular pleasure in discovering books with incongruous and recondite associations, such as his copy of Meredith's poems which had belonged to E. Phillips Oppenheim. He had a particular penchant for works illustrating the backwaters of the 1890s and the biographies of ecclesiastics and lawyers, as well as collections of epigrams, table-talk and epitaphs.

It was his encyclopaedic knowledge of English literature which led to his appointment as a member of the team of revisers of the third edition of the *Oxford Dictionary of Quotations*.

> He was not only an original and wide-ranging proposer of new quotations for inclusion, but a judicious and strict critic of others' suggestions. It was entirely because John quite often gave 'G. Madan's notebooks' as the source for some of his proposals for the new *ODQ*, on the roneoed forms we distributed, that I was led to ask, 'Who is this Madan?' And so, after a very long — even by Oxford Press standards — period of discussion, gestation, and preparation, Gere and Sparrow (eds.): *The Notebooks of Geoffrey*

Madan [a miscellaneous assembly of unusual quotations, aphorisms and scraps of table-talk] was eventually published.[19]

His friendship with John Sparrow was close and long-lasting. Although reticent about being acknowledged, Gere was a substantial contributor to the latter's anthologies of Latin inscriptions, published under the title, *Lapidaria.* . . .

As is often the case, writing obituary notices of one's friends becomes one of the main preoccupations of retirement, and in this exercise Gere was a superb exponent, deftly conveying the character and appearance as well as the intellectual achievements of the deceased. Apart from his extended obituary of his friend and colleague, Philip Pouncey, for the British Academy,[20] one can particularly admire his tact and sympathy in recalling the ultimately tragic life of John Woodward, former Keeper of Art at Birmingham City Art Gallery,[21] his ability to pinpoint the mercurial and elusive character of the German art historian, Walter Vitzthum,[22] and his affectionate but pointed assessment of his predecessor, Edward Croft-Murray.[23]

Gere was a complex and fascinating man, whose character was perhaps ultimately only fathomed by his wife, as he himself acknowledged. Making a copy of the classic *New Yorker* cartoon showing a business man with his secretary on his knee, he changed the legend to 'My wife understands me'. (He had married Charlotte Douie in 1958 and they had a son and a daughter. He was extremely fortunate in his marriage since his wife not only fully shared his interests but was assiduous in attending to his wishes, which sometimes were unusually demanding in the *va-et-vient* of daily life.) Initially he was not easy to get to know, although many to the enrichment of their lives succeeded. Although we worked in the same department we did not speak for the first eighteen months of my employment, which in view of our proximity to one another was some sort of achievement. He seemed to require the right introductory note, usually in a field different from that one might suppose to have in common with him. (A colleague from another institution, on an official journey by car in Germany, only succeeded in breaking the uncomfortable silence by the chance mention

---

[19] Letter from Richard Brain, editor of the third edition of the *ODQ*, to Charlotte Gere, 19 January 1995.

[20] Op. cit. above, n.17, pp. 529–44.

[21] *Burlington Magazine*, cxx (1988), 434.

[22] *Burlington Magazine*, cxiv (1972), 721–2.

[23] *The Times*, 24 September 1980.

of a detective novel.) But once the rapport had been established he became the easiest and most communicative of friends. He was a man of contrasts. In many ways old-fashioned and conventional, he had a deeply unconventional side to his character, indeed one can say that the more one studied him the more he emerged as a true eccentric.

He had a highly rational and precise mind, which was sharp as a razor. This informed his scholarship and attitude to work. At the same time there was a strong element of fantasy and imagination which so delighted his friends. His natural wit invariably surfaced whatever the occasion. It was devilishly accurate at hitting its target. It was rarely malicious but was beautifully pointed and usually extremely funny. His humour was extended to his habit of gentle teasing of those he liked. To a younger colleague, who had just announced his engagement, Gere 'was full of congratulations, and then went on to express polite surprise at the fact that I had styled myself 'Doctor' . . . ''I was under the impression that only medical practitioners, bishops', [pause] 'and cathedral organists actually used the title . . . .'' '.[24]

With wit so much depends on circumstance and tone of voice, and Gere never lost an opportunity to take advantage of either, but as a formal example one can cite his demolition of some hugely infelicitous art history: 'Of an art critic of an earlier day it was said that in his prose the English language lay in state; in Professor [. . .]'s prose the language lies, as it were, extended on a slab in a mortuary, having been unrecognizably battered to death in the course of the author's passionate struggle to force the ultimate shades of meaning from what is clearly a hopelessly intractable medium. His efforts evoke the image of someone trying to thread a needle while wearing a pair of boxing gloves'.[25]

As far as he was political, he was to the right. He loved to play the role of Colonel Blimp or act as an old fogey, and the pose was not without some reflection of his true nature. If he so much as touched a copy of the *Guardian* newspaper, eagerly promoting a caring society, it was only to do the crossword. He extravagantly castigated Mrs Thatcher's views as being leftist and he was even heard to claim in an extreme moment that the *Daily Telegraph* was written by a group of crypto-Communists.

As a result of his grandfather being an American, Gere had parti-

---

[24] Letter from David Ekserdjian to Charlotte Gere, 17 January 1995.
[25] *Times Literary Supplement*, 11 January 1963.

cular empathy for the United States, both the country, especially New York, and the people among whom he had a body of friends and admirers. When in New York he usually stayed at the Union Club. Seated in a large, curved-back, leather-upholstered chair in the vast entrance hall, with a club-sized Scotch beside him, he looked like one of the longest standing and most genial of the members. In fact he appeared more at home there than he ever did during his membership of the Athenaeum.

An important annual family event consisted in what may be called *les vacances de Monsieur Gere*, when he became another person and delightfully, for the benefit of his friends fortunate enough to be around, revealed his capacity for clowning. ('As I get older, I seem to live from one summer holiday to another, regarding the intervening $11\frac{1}{2}$ months as a tedious distraction'.[26]) Ensconced in the unchanging Suffolk town of Southwold, the Gere family for a number of years was forced to rent an unattractive modern house near the pier, for some unexplained reason called 'Hoopers'. The level of the road was higher than the ground floor so that the house was approached by a bridge leading into the upper floor, where on your arrival you were as likely as not to be greeted by Gere playing the part of a wildly gesticulating lunatic, an act which quickly attracted an audience of gawping holiday-makers, whose increasing bewilderment only served to prolong the performance. Inside the furniture was shoddy and totally inadequate for Gere's ample frame. But the house's deficiencies were grist to the conversational mill, and there could be no greater incongruity between the house and its current occupant than the sight of Gere posing on a low stool before the cheap dressing-table with its triptych mirror. And there were gastronomic compensations. After his early morning bathe, showing that his suffering at school was not in vain, Gere had a regular diet of kippers for breakfast and dressed crab for lunch, which he himself would go and buy daily from the local fishmonger.

Unlike the casual holiday-wear adopted by most of the population, Gere always dressed like an English gentleman at the seaside; a light-weight brown jacket with a thin black stripe, waistcoat, invariably a tie, grey flannel trousers and a pair of smart canvas yachting shoes. Had he worn a boater, it would not have seemed out of place. He also carried a walking stick, which, however, had a dual purpose. He was an avid and serendipitous beachcomber, riffling through the bordering undergrowth

---

[26] John Gere to the present writer, 17 October 1972.

and along the beach, in the same way as he rummaged through dustbins in the search of copies of *The Times* or the *Daily Telegraph* for their crosswords. The treasure that was found on the shore was either kept, read or burnt. With his unerring eye for an old piece of wood in a skip, Gere was never short of firewood. On the last day of the holidays, all inflammable rubbish within a certain remote area would be gathered together and a great fire would be lit on the beach, both symbolic of the return to London and an act of cleansing the environment.

But it was at home in London that Gere was happiest. A childhood friend of Gere's son retains an image of 'him at the sitting room table reading Pope-Hennessy's *Gothic Sculpture* whilst simultaneously dipping into an obscure clerical biography and *The Loom of Youth*, and asking us to make less noise because he couldn't hear the Marx brothers on the telly'.[27] A warm and very convivial friend, Gere took great pleasure in entertaining his close friends to a delicious meal prepared by his wife and often accompanied by one of his best bottles of claret — he was a generous host who took trouble not only to choose the wine but to select the pre-dinner drinks which would particularly appeal to his guests. And it was on such occasions that reminiscences would flow. It was as if there was a different trunk of memories stored in the house awaiting the return of each of his varied range of friends, the contents of which would be taken out, polished and augmented. (Gere was a sharp observer of human follies, clipping out items from newspapers which would either be sent to friends, often embellished with witty comments, or kept for future delectation. Two albums preserved the deeds and sayings of two of his favourite subjects, trendy museum directors and liberal bishops.) Entertained by Gere's humorous observation of all aspects of life, a person from outside his profession could be forgiven for not being aware that he or she was conversing with a distinguished Renaissance scholar. Usually cleverer and better informed, he never induced any feeling of inferiority in his conversant. But towards those who had no excuse for not being *au fait*, he adopted a more stringent approach. 'Verbally when one was with him one had to be absolutely on one's mettle — he could after all pounce as mercilessly on a slovenly expression as on an absurd and/or pretentious museum director — but his own breadth of knowledge and coruscating conversation had the effect of raising the game of those around him'.[28]

---

[27] Undated letter (1995) from Paul Martin to Charlotte Gere.
[28] Letter from Noël Annesley to Charlotte Gere, 23 January 1995.

But Gere's generosity towards his friends went further than picking out choice bottles from his cellar. A number of friends in trouble or in ill-health, or in need of moral or financial support were unobtrusively helped. In his retirement, he was an assiduous visitor to sick and elderly friends to whom he would read and cheer with the gaiety of his conversation. His very sudden end on 11 January 1995, sitting in an armchair in his library in the early hours of the morning, which as an insomniac he regularly did, denied those fortunate recipients of his friendship the opportunity of offering something in exchange as he himself slipped into old age.

He was elected a Fellow of the British Academy in 1979; he was also elected a Fellow of the Society of Antiquaries in 1986.

CHRISTOPHER WHITE
Fellow of the Academy

Note. First and foremost I must thank Charlotte Gere for her continuous help and for providing information about the family history. She also kindly showed me many of the letters received from friends after her husband's death, which have been a fruitful source of quotation. I am grateful to the writers thereof for permission to reproduce. I am indebted to George Ramsden for his comments on the contents of the library. Nicholas Turner has very kindly prepared a complete bibliography, which is published here.

I would also like to acknowledge the obituaries, which were published in the *Daily Telegraph* (13 January 1995), *The Times* (25 January 1995), the *Guardian* (27 January 1995; Christopher White) and the *Independent* (6 February 1995; Terence Mullaly), the *Art Newspaper* (No. 45, February 1995, 6; Antony Griffiths), the *Burlington Magazine* (cxxxvii (1995), 319–21; Nicholas Penny), the *Art Quarterly of the National Art Collections Fund* (No.22, Summer 1995, 48–9; John Christian) and *Master Drawings* (xxxiii (1995)), 219–22; Nicholas Turner).

Bibliography

Books

Taddeo Zuccaro: His Development Studied in his Drawings. (London, 1969).
Il manierismo a Roma (Disegni dei maestri. Edizioni della Casa Fabbri) (Milan, 1971).
With Robin Ironside, *Pre-Raphaelite Painters. With a Descriptive Catalogue* (London, 1948).
Edited with John Sparrow and with a Foreword by The Rt Hon. Harold Macmillan

OM, *Geoffrey Madan's Notebooks: A Selection* (Oxford, New York, Toronto, Melbourne, 1981).

British Museum Collection Catalogues

With Philip Pouncey, *Italian Drawings in the Department of Prints and Drawings of the British Museum: Raphael and his Circle*, 2 vols (London, 1962).
With Philip Pouncey and the assistance of Rosalind Wood, *Italian Drawings in the Department of Prints and Drawings in the British Museum: Artists Working in Rome c.1550 to c.1640*, 2 vols (London, 1983).

Exhibition catalogues

The Pre-Raphaelites: A Loan Exhibition of their Paintings and Drawings Held in the Centenary Year of the Foundation of their Brotherhood (Whitechapel Art ' Gallery, London, 8 April to 12 May 1948).
Pre-Raphaelite Drawings and Watercolours (The Arts Council, London, 1953).
Mostra di disegni degli Zuccari (Taddeo e Federico Zuccari, e Raffaellino da Reggio (Gabinetto dei Disegni, Galleria degli Uffizi, Florence, 1966).
Dessins de Taddeo et Federico Zuccaro, XLIIe Exposition du Cabinet des Dessins, (Musée du Louvre, Paris, 1969).
Portrait Drawings, XV–XX Centuries (Department of Prints and Drawings, the British Museum, London, 2 August to 31 December 1974).
The Etruscan School, Centenary 1876–1976, (The Fine Art Society Ltd, London, 16 November to 10 December 1976).
Drawings by Raphael and his Circle, from British and North American Collections, (Pierpont Morgan Library, New York, 1987).
Taddeo Zuccari nel Gabinetto delle Stampe e dei Disegni della Galleria degli Uffizi (Fondazione Salimbeni per le Arti Figurative, San Severino Marche, 28 June to 20 August 1992).
Pre-Raphaelite Drawings in the British Museum, (Department of Prints and Drawings, The British Museum, London, 23 September 1994 to 8 January 1995).
With Paul Hulton, translated by Lise Duclaux, *Claude Lorrain: Dessins du British Museum*, LXVIIe Exposition du Cabinet des Dessins (Musée du Louvre, Paris, 19 October 1978 to 15 January 1979).
With Nicholas Turner, *Drawings by Michelangelo in the Collection of Her Majesty the Queen at Windsor Castle, the Ashmolean Museum, the British Museum and other English Collections* (Department of Prints and Drawings, the British Museum, London, 6 February to 27 April 1975).
With Nicholas Turner, *Drawings by Michelangelo from the British Museum* (Pierpont Morgan Library, New York, 24 April to 28 July 1979).
With Nicholas Turner, *Drawings by Raphael from the Royal Library, the Ashmolean, the British Museum, Chatsworth and other English Collections* (Department of Prints and Drawings, the British Museum, London, 13 October 1983 to 15 January 1984).

Introductions and essays

Introduction to *Dante Gabriel Rossetti, Painter and Poet*, catalogue compiled by
Virginia Surtees (Royal Academy of Arts, London, 13 January to 11 March
1973, and City Museum and Art Gallery, Birmingham, 29 March to 6 May
1973).

Preface to *French Landscape: Drawings and Sketches of the Eighteenth Century*,
Catalogue of a Loan Exhibition from the Louvre and other French Museums,
(Department of Prints and Drawings, the British Museum, London, 25 Novem-
ber 1977 to 12 March 1978).

Introduction to *The Achievement of a Connoisseur, Philip Pouncey: Italian Old
Master Drawings*, catalogue compiled by Julien Stock and David Scrase
(Fitzwilliam Museum, Cambridge, 15 October to 15 December, 1985). (The
essay was reprinted in *Philip Pouncey per gli Uffizi*, catalogue compiled by M.
Chiarini, G. Dillon and A. Petrioli Tofani (Galleria degli Uffizi, Florence,
1993).)

'I disegni di Federico Zuccari sulla vita giovanile di suo fratello Taddeo' in *Per
Taddeo e Federico Zuccari nelle Marche* catalogue compiled by Bonita Cleri,
with an introduction by Paolo Dal Poggetto (Palazzo Fagnani, Sant'Angelo in
Vado, 18 September to 7 November 1993, pp. 49–55).

Introduction to *The Study of Italian Drawings: The Contribution of Philip Pouncey*,
catalogue compiled by Nicholas Turner (Department of Prints and Drawings,
the British Museum, London, 28 January to 24 April 1994).

Catalogue entries

Entries 28, 31, 34, 35, 38, 45, 52, 80, 81, 83, 84, 85, 86 and 87 in *Da Leonardo a
Rembrandt: Disegni della Biblioteca Reale di Torino*, edited by Gianni Carlo
Sciolla (Palazzo Reale, Turin, 1989).

Entries 19, 24, 34, 50–5, 81–2 and 88 in *Disegno: Les dessins italiens du Musée de
Rennes* (Galleria Estense, Modena, 27 May to 29 July 1990, and Musée des
Beaux-Arts, Rennes, November to December 1990).

Entries 14, 20, 25, 38, 41, 59 and 69 in *Disegno: Zeichnungen von Leonardo,
Botticelli, Donatello und anderen Meistern Italiens aus dem Musée des Beaux-
Arts in Rennes und aus eigenem Bestand* (Graphische Sammlung, Wallraf-
Richartz-Museum, Cologne, 6 October–5 December 1993).

Articles

'Pre-Raphaelite Drawings', *Alphabet and Image*, 6 January (1948), 18–32.

'A Drawing by Ingres', *British Museum Quarterly*, xvi, 2 (1951) 40–1.

'William Young Ottley as a Collector of Drawings', *British Museum Quarterly*,
xviii, 2 (1953), 44–53.

'An Oil-sketch by Thomas Jones', *British Museum Quarterly*, xxi, 4 (1959) 93–4.

'Two Late Fresco Cycles by Perino del Vaga: The Massimi Chapel and the Sala
Paolina', *Burlington Magazine*, cii, 682 (January 1960), 9–19.

'Some Drawings by Pellegrino Tibaldi', *British Museum Quarterly*, xxvi, 1–2
(1962–3), 40–3.

'Taddeo Zuccaro as a Designer for Maiolica', *Burlington Magazine*, cv, 724 (July 1963), 306–15.

'Two Panel-pictures by Taddeo Zuccaro, and some Related Compositions — 1: The *Adoration of the Magi* in the Fitzwilliam Museum', *Burlington Magazine*, cv, 725 (August 1963), 363–7.

'Alexander Munro's *Paolo and Francesca*', *Burlington Magazine*, cv, 728 (November 1963), 509–10.

'A Landscape Drawing by Polidoro da Caravaggio', *Master Drawings*, i, 1 (1963), 43–5.

'Drawings by Niccolò Martinelli, Il Trometta', *Master Drawings*, i, 4 (1963), 3–18.

'The Decoration of the Villa Giulia', *Burlington Magazine*, cvii, 745 (April 1965), 199–206.

'Two of Taddeo Zuccaro's Last Commissions, Completed by Federico Zuccaro. I: The Pucci Chapel in S. Trinità dei Monti', *Burlington Magazine*, cviii, 759 (June 1966), 286–93.

'Two of Taddeo Zuccaro's Last Commissions, Completed by Federico Zuccaro. II: The High Altar-piece in S. Lorenzo in Damaso', *Burlington Magazine*, cviii, 760 (July 1966), 341–5.

'Girolamo Muziano and Taddeo Zuccaro: A Note on an Early Work by Muziano', *Burlington Magazine*, cviii, 761 (August 1966), 417–18.

'Two Copies after Polidoro da Caravaggio', *Master Drawings*, vi, 3 (1968), 249–51.

'Thomas Jones: An Eighteenth-Century Conundrum', *Apollo*, 91 (June 1970), 469–70.

'The Lawrence-Phillips-Rosenbach "Zuccaro Album" ', *Master Drawings*, viii, 2 (1970), 123–40.

'Some Early Drawings by Pirro Ligorio', *Master Drawings*, ix, 3 (1971), 239–50.

'A Drawing by Matteo Perez da Leccio', *Master Drawings*, xi, 2 (1973), 150–4.

'Drawings by Sebastiano del Piombo and Agnolo Bronzino', *British Museum Yearbook, I. The Classical Tradition* (London, 1976), 270–5.

'An Unrecorded Drawing by Dante Gabriel Rossetti', *British Museum Yearbook, I. The Classical Tradition* (London, 1976), 277–9.

'A New Attribution to Correggio', *Master Drawings*, xv, 3 (1977), 256–7.

'Philipp Otto Runge's *Raphael and his Mistress*', *Jahrbuch der Hamburger Kunstsammlungen*, 23 (1978), 73–4.

'A British Seventeenth-century Collection of Drawings', *Master Drawings*, xxxi, 4 (1993), 339–49.

'Methuen, Paul Ayshford, fourth BARON METHUEN (1886–1974)', *The Dictionary of National Biography. Missing Persons*, C. S. Nicholls ed, (Oxford and New York, 1993).

Article on Philip Pouncey, *Dictionary of National Biography 1986–1990*, ed. C. S. Nicholls (Oxford, 1996), 359–60.

Book reviews

'*Picturesque Illustrations of Buenos Ayres and Monte Video* . . . By E. E. Vidal (R. Ackerman, 1820). Replica published by Viau, Buenos Ayres, 1943', *Burlington Magazine*, lxxxv, 497 (1944), 207.

'Drawings in the Ashmolean Museum' (Review of K. T. Parker, *Catalogue of the Collection of Drawings in the Ashmolean Museum, II, Italian Schools*, 1956), *Burlington Magazine*, xcix, 650 (May 1957), 159–63.

'Classical to Mannerist' (Review of S. J. Freedberg, *Painting of the High Renaissance in Rome and Florence*, 2 vols), *Times Literary Supplement*, 11 January 1963.

'Norman W. Canedy, *The Roman Sketchbook of Girolamo da Carpi*', *Master Drawings*, xvi, 2 (1978) 180–5.

'Lanfranco Ravelli, *Polidoro Caldara da Caravaggio: i Disegni di Polidoro; Copie da Polidoro*', *Master Drawings,* xxiii–iv, 1 (1985–6), 61–74.

'*Impressionism all' Italiana*' (Review of Norma Broude, '*The Macchiaioli: Italian Painters of the Nineteenth Century* (New Haven and London, 1987)), *Spectator*, 10 September 1988, 32–3.

Exhibition Reviews

'Pre-Raphaelites at the Tate', *Burlington Magazine*, xc, 548 (November 1948), 325–6.

'Some Italian Drawings in the Chatsworth Exhibition', *Burlington Magazine*, xci, 555 (June 1949), 169–73.

'Edinburgh. The Macchiaioli', *Burlington Magazine*, cxxiv, 955 (October 1982), 647–8.

Obituaries

'Mr A. E. Popham: Authority on Old Master Drawings', *The Times*, 9 December 1970.

'A. E. Popham, Keeper of Prints and Drawings in the British Museum', *Master Drawings*, ix, 2 (1971), 173.

'Walter Vitzthum', *Burlington Magazine*, cxiv, 835 (October 1972), 721–2.

'Mr Edward Croft-Murray, Former Keeper of Prints at the British Museum', *The Times*, 24 September 1980.

'John Woodward', *Burlington Magazine*, cxxx, 1023 (June 1988), 434.

'Philip Pouncey', *Burlington Magazine*, cxxxiii, 1058 (May 1991), 312–14.

'Philip Pouncey, 1910–1990', *Proceedings of the British Academy*, 76, (Oxford, 1991), 529–44. Italian translation of the above, in *Accademia Clementina. Atti e Memorie*, xxx–i, nuova serie (1992), 39–52.

'James Byam Shaw', *The Times*, 21 March 1992.

'Sir Karl Parker: "Old Master of the Museum" ', *Guardian*, 6 August 1992.

'Jacob Bean', *Independent*, 15 October 1992.

'James Byam Shaw (1903–1992)', *Master Drawings*, xxxi, 1 (1993), 70–1.
'Sir Karl Parker (1895–1992)', *Master Drawings*, xxxi, 1 (1993), 71–3.

Published lectures

'Some Thoughts on Raphael and Michelangelo' (lecture in the Tapestry Room, Fenway Court, 30 May 1985), *Fenway Court: Isabella Stewart Gardner Museum, 1985* (Boston, 1986), pp. 7–21.
'Some Observations on the Practical Utility of Connoisseurship' (lecture at the Woodner Symposium, Boston), *Drawings Defined*, ed. Walter Strauss and Tracie Felker (New York, 1987), pp. 291–305.

Sale catalogues

Old Master Drawings from Chatsworth (Christie's, London), 3 July 1984.
The Life of Taddeo Zuccaro: From the Collection of the British Rail Pension Fund (Sotheby's, New York), 11 January 1990.
Drawings by Taddeo and Federico Zuccaro and Other Artists: From the Collection of the British Rail Pension Fund (Sotheby's, New York), 11 January 1990.

Letters

(Concerning a drawing by Palma Giovane in the British Museum, with a decorative border by Giovanni Baglione), *Master Drawings*, viii, 2 (1970), 172.
'A Taddeo Zuccaro Drawing formerly belonging to Dr Rosenbach', *Burlington Magazine*, cv, 720 (March 1963), 127.
With Keith Andrews, Hugh Macandrew and Graham Reynolds, 'Keepership of Prints and Drawings', *Burlington Magazine*, cxv, 844 (July 1973), 469.

DENYS HAY

Proceedings of the British Academy, **90**, 391–410

Denys Hay
1915–1994

DENYS HAY was an historian who made important contributions to the study of the Renaissance period and a brilliant teacher who inspired many generations of students. He was born at Newcastle-upon-Tyne on 29 August 1915. His father, a graduate in history from St John's College, Cambridge, had entered holy orders and — a combination not uncommon in that era — was employed as a schoolmaster at Newcastle's Royal Grammar School. But he died still young, and as a result of the difficulties then facing the family, Hay, an only child, at the time just one year old, was to grow up under the care of his maternal grandparents. The grandfather, Thomas Waugh, hailed originally from the other side of the border and was a staunch Presbyterian. It was he whose nightly readings from the Bible, sometimes attended with boyish impatience, introduced Hay to Christian culture. In those years the companionship of his uncle, Herbert Waugh, some thirty years older but in spirit almost an elder brother, brought much happiness; memories of his gifts as a story-teller and of their walks together in the Northumbrian countryside were long treasured. Throughout his life Hay would remember the hills and dales around Corbridge, the *Corstopitum* of the Romans, behind Hadrian's Wall. He would claim this land of the frontier as part of his inheritance, and would link it metaphorically to those intellectual frontiers with which his studies were concerned.

From his ninth year, assisted by a scholarship, Hay had, as he put it, 'the great good fortune' to attend the school at which his father had taught, the Tudor foundation of the Newcastle Royal Grammar School.

Here was still preserved something of the old humanist education. In particular Hay was to recall the high quality of the teaching of history. (A future Chichele Professor of History, Sir Richard Southern, three years his senior, also received his early education there.) One teacher of note was Sydney ('Sammy') Middlebrooke, Head of History, a name still well-remembered in the North-East, who would on occasions reprove his best pupils with the words: 'You are being merely clever'. Another, keenly remembered, was 'a remarkable teacher called R. F. I. Bunn'. Mr Bunn would, in a technique frequently to be employed by Hay in his teaching career, seize the attention of his pupils with dramatic gestures. A class would open with his writing on the black-board the words: 'AD 410. Foundation of the Newcastle Society of Antiquaries', a formula introducing the Roman withdrawal from Britain, the decay of the Wall, and the work of those who were attempting to recreate its past. It was Mr Bunn who first advised him, aged sixteen at the time, to read Burckhardt's *Civilisation of the Renaissance in Italy*, that mid-nineteenth-century classic which, if not inventing the idea of the Renaissance, has proved the starting-point for most interest in it. In his last year at school Hay received a copy, the finely-illustrated, 1929 edition of Middlemore's translation, as a prize. He retained it all his life and, whatever the different feelings the book was later to provoke, he was never to forget the sense of excitement which it roused in him at that time.

In 1934, with the aid of a Horsley scholarship, awarded by the governors of the Royal Grammar School, Hay went on to Balliol College, Oxford, there to read for the degree in Modern History. There was at that time an Italian Renaissance 'Special Subject' in the curriculum, but when Hay suggested to his tutor, V. H. Galbraith, that he might take it, he was strongly discouraged ('only for girls') and instructed to enrol instead in the course of the Regius Professor, F. M. Powicke, on 'Church and State under Edward I'. Hay knuckled under, bent his mind to manly matters, and was rewarded with a First. He might well have gone on to have become an English historian. In July 1937, a month after taking his Finals, he read a paper to the local historical society at Hexham on the Dissolution of the Monasteries in the Diocese of Durham (a diocese which included Newcastle), a work which gives evidence of researches, undertaken while still an under-graduate, in the Public Record Office and in Bishop Cosin's Library in Durham.

Yet it was at this point that Galbraith was to suggest a wider theme for postgraduate study. Presumably offered in response to his pupil's interest in Burckhardt, it could at the same time be seen as appropriate for a British historian. This was the *Anglica Historia*, a history of England by the Italian cleric, Polydore Vergil, written in England and in Urbino at the beginning of the sixteenth century. What Galbraith probably hoped for from this was something close to what his own edition of the *Anonimalle Chronicle* had provided, a work which would throw light on various incidents in English history. Hay was granted a War Memorial Studentship by Balliol and then won a Senior Demyship (a research fellowship, at that time awarded by examination) at Magdalen College, Oxford. In default of Galbraith, who at this point moved to a Chair at Edinburgh, C. A. J. Armstrong of Hertford College was assigned to be his supervisor. It must have seemed an appropriate choice in that, although without any overwhelming interest in Italy, he had, some years before, edited the chronicle of Domenico Mancini, another fifteenth-century Italian who had written in Latin about English history.

Other, informal, advisers at this time were the self-exiled Italian scholar, Roberto Weiss, who was then working on his book on humanism in fifteenth-century England, and the American Professor W. E. Lunt, who had, what was comparatively rare in the Oxford of the day, worked extensively in the Vatican archives. Maurice Powicke, who in later life would on occasions lament that he had devoted his scholarly life to the thirteenth rather than the sixteenth century, looked with particular favour on Hay's project, securing, for example, the financing of 'rotographs' (today's 'photostats') of the Vatican manuscript of Polydore's history for his use. The confidence bred of this academic support was at the same time, and above all else, reinforced by Hay's marriage to Gwyneth Morley, whom he had met at Newcastle, to whom he had become engaged in his final year as an undergraduate, and who was to be throughout his life his constant and indispensable inspiration, companion, and helpmate. The newly-wed couple, defying the comparative poverty of the research student's life, bought first one car, replaced it with another (each for under £10), and settled to domestic life and the search for a permanent job.

Despite the powerful patronage links over which Powicke presided at that time, this was not as easy as might have been anticipated. The difficulty lay in the character of Hay's research-subject, a chronicler whose life spanned the late fifteenth and early sixteenth centuries. 'I recall', Hay wrote, 'applying successively for posts in two universities in 1938 and being told by each that I could not be considered—in the one case because I was a medievalist, in the other case because I was a modernist.' In June of that year he was appointed (at a salary of £300) to a temporary lectureship at Glasgow University, where the redoubtable Professor Andrew Browning, a great friend of Galbraith, required a substitute for a member of staff on leave of absence. That ended in May 1939, and despite Browning's testimonial ('in particular,' Hay was to reminisce, 'I recall the phrase "class discipline good"'), and despite some five articles published or in the press, it seemed that no post was available. For the moment a Bryce Studentship sustained him at Oxford; eventually, in the same year, he was appointed to a first permanent job as an assistant lecturer at the University College of Southampton.

The College did not, at that time, possess anything like the range of buildings and the numerous and distinguished staff that the University of Southampton boasts today. Hay was the kindest of men but was always amused by all forms of anything which might be interpreted as pretension. Later he would tell of his being greeted on arrival by some dignitary with an offer of sherry. 'We like to think,' this worthy announced, as they gazed together through an office window at a waste of Nissan huts in muddy fields, 'that we preserve here something of the spirit of Oxford'. As it happened, an all too imminent future was to offer him very many more such landscapes, without any such ambitious claims. In the tumultuous days of July 1940, he was deemed to be no longer in a 'reserved occupation', was called up for military service, and inducted—the result, it may be assumed, of those second-hand cars—into the Royal Army Service Corps. A married man, already a father, Hay, however anxious to do his duty, may be supposed to have found it difficult to adapt wholeheartedly to the role of 'the happy warrior'. He himself was to write of relieving the 'lengthy boredoms' of army life by reading history, while in periods of leave he is on record as turning eagerly to those rotographs with which he had been provided in earlier days. Only after two years of lorry-convoys and the like was more stimulating work to be found for him.

In 1941 Professor W. Keith Hancock had been appointed to be the 'Supervisor' of a series of official 'civil histories' of the war commissioned by the War Cabinet. At that time A. D. Lindsay, Master of Balliol, a friend of Hancock, was aware of the underemployment of Hay's abilities, while his patron and friend, Maurice Powicke, had become a member of the enterprise's advisory committee. No doubt on their recommendation Hay was appointed in the summer of 1942 to the team of some twenty-four historians serving in London as 'first narrators' of the non-military aspects of the war. The three years which followed gave a most valuable experience in his craft. In his article on the civil history, Hay has described how, together with J. D. Scott, he was commissioned, under the general supervision of the eminent economic historian, M. M. Postan, to study the design and development of weaponry. This gave, he explained, 'an insight into government at the highest policy-making points of power which would have been hard to acquire in any other way', and it showed the frequent unreliability of records and memories. Above all, he continues, with that openness which was typical of him, it offered:

> training of a very high order in honest history and sensible techniques of research. . . . I owe much to the critical and imaginative commentaries on my own work by Professor Postan, to whom I would like to express my thanks. At the time I found it hard to be told, as Postan slapped the table sharply with the back of his hand, that my first effort (on the design and development of the 25 pdr gun) was "Hamlet without the prince of Denmark". But I suppose that the *dramatis personae* were more evident in later work and have perhaps survived into other and remoter fields than those I associate with the blacked-out London of the last years of the war and the first years of teaching at Edinburgh, where a large filing-cabinet full of my War History notes used to glare reproachfully at me as I kept a couple of lectures ahead of my class.

Days of work on history were punctuated by frequent nights as part of the famous St Paul's Cathedral fire-watching squad. On this duty he formed a lifelong friendship with another member of the civil history's team, Richard Titmuss, in his time an influential writer on social policy, and one who, like Hay's own Polydore Vergil, was to find his writings frowned on by some government officials. Before the war ended Hay was to write an article for the *Economic History Review* on the official history of the Ministry of Munitions which had been compiled during the First World War, and here he emphasised the political risks, 'the gauntlet of high-level scrutiny in the Cabinet-Office', to which many of the volumes produced by academics at that time had been exposed.

Twenty years later the book, 'ground out', as Hay put it, by himself, Scott, and Postan, eventually reached print. Meanwhile, with the end of hostilities, the post at Southampton remained open to him. He was called from there however through the good offices of B. Humphrey Sumner. Sumner had taught Hay in his undergraduate years, and had just relinquished a briefly-held position as Professor of History at

Edinburgh in order to become Warden of All Souls. In the interest of Richard Pares, his successor in the Edinburgh chair, Sumner wrote to Hay, successfully urging the advantages of the Scottish capital and its university. Denys Hay arrived in January 1946, to be joined by Gwyneth, with their children, Sara, aged eight, and Richard, aged four. Four years later another daughter, Jenny. was to be born to them. After some early changes of residence, they became established in the pleasant area of Fountainhall Road, where Hay was amused to learn (all land-tenure under Scots law being feudal) that his feudal superior ('a Scottish gentlewoman who never, I am glad to say, called on me for knight-service') lived in Florence.

In Edinburgh Hay was committed to teaching of a great range and variety. In his first two terms he gave sixteen lectures on German history between 800 and 1806, and lectured three times a week on European history between 476 and 1500 and between 1715 and 1920 respectively. Subsequently he was to fill in the sixteenth- and seventeenth-century interval. In later days, when undergraduate teaching became increasingly specialised, Hay's remark to incredulous junior members of staff that he had lectured and held seminars on a time-span 'from the Merovingians to Bismarck' was, in fact, understated. Shortly after, he went on to deliver lectures on the whole history of medieval Britain, to offer an optional European honours course, and Special Subjects on Anglo–French history in the later Middle Ages. (Because very few students at that time were willing to tackle Italian, Hay was some twenty years at Edinburgh before offering an undergraduate course on the Renaissance.)

However daunting the extent of this teaching may have appeared to others, it was clear from the beginning that the then slim young man, bounding through the door to address the class, had found his *métier*. To students who were accustomed to a distant and formal relationship with their teachers, Hay brought deflation of pomposity, enthusiasm, and immense stimulation. This was in no way associated with any dropping of standards but the reverse. In the Scottish four-year honours system the classes of the first two years, which were shared with students reading for a general degree, were often considered at that period as occasions of undemanding and passive learning. Hay's first shock to undergraduates was to announce that they should not hope to pass exams on their lecture-notes alone, for they would not do so. In the place of exam-fodder they were offered incentives to read and think and a vast widening of horizons in historical study. Frequent were the dramatic openings, reminiscent of the classes of his old schoolmaster, Mr Bunn. Hay would stride to the lectern with an enormous Bible clutched in his hands, bang it down with a great dusty crash, and then hold forth on the central role of the scriptures in the understanding of medieval culture. Or the class might open with a map pinned upside down on the blackboard so that his audience could consider how Europe looked from Byzantium or then again how Dante conceived of Italy. And in place of the wearying cruces of constitutional history which had hitherto so often formed their staple pabulum, he would talk to his classes about Marc Bloch and *mentalités*, not in terms of uncritical acceptance, for, as we will see, he was often cool towards them, but in an attempt to broaden the meaning of what historical study might mean.

By general consent the best teaching of his early years at Edinburgh was in his European Honours course covering the years 1324 to 1449. Here again, much was expected of his pupils. They were confronted with extracts from Platina's *Lives of the Popes* and with the difficult Latin of Marsiglio of Padua's *Defensor Pacis*. At that time, Hay thought of this immersion in Latin as an essential part of the undergraduate's experience of medieval history. When an English translation of the *Defensor Pacis* came to be published he changed the prescription to the untranslated *Defensor Minor*. Later, like everyone else, he had to come to terms with the modern world, though students were still called upon to tackle foreign books not available in translation. He himself remained as stimulating as ever. 'His lectures,' wrote one pupil, 'reminded me of a Catherine Wheel, shooting off sparks in different directions, and above all, they were trying to make the students think for themselves. . . . I have the feeling that his teaching involved a continuous sacrifice of sacred cows, often with an irreverent (but completely commonsense) manner, in order to provoke the class into seeing a subject with fresh eyes.' At a time when many universities were marked by a notable stuffiness, the irreverence stood out. In one story Hay is found asking one of his pupils, the staidest product of Edinburgh's genteel Morningside, to write a paper on: 'To what extent was Boccacio a humanist in *The Decameron*?' The student asked whether this should be read in an expurgated or unexpurgated edition. 'Good God, man, unexpurgated!'. When the student returned with a predictably stern denunciation of the work's immorality, Hay, assuming a fine Jean Brodie accent, commented gravely, that in comparison with the fabliaux the tales of the *Decameron* should provoke 'nothing more than a *refained* titter'.

At the same time that Hay was first developing those teaching skills that were to mark out his academic life, he was embarking, with the remarkable energy which characterised these early years, on many projects. He gave classes for the Workers' Educational Association, taking the bus to the mining village of Ormiston. Again, at the time of his arrival the University of Edinburgh provided no common-room for members of its academic staff. Hay persuaded the Lecturers' Association to back a campaign to secure one. As a result this amenity was finally if grudgingly conceded, a move which could be seen as a first step towards the provision of that commodious Staff Club which now stands in Chambers Street. Above all, it was at this time that he brought to completion those studies on Polydore Vergil which had been interrupted by the war and which were now to establish him securely as an authority of the Renaissance. In 1950 the Camden Society published his text of Books XXIV–XXVII of Vergil's chronicle covering the years 1485–1537. Based upon the collation of a surviving autograph manuscript with the first three sixteenth-century printed editions, it was accompanied by an English translation of the Latin original. This was followed two years later by a definitive study of its author, *Polydore Vergil: Renaissance Historian and Man of Letters*. Hay considered here the career of one of the last foreigners of the Middle Ages who, as Papal Collector and Archdeacon of Wells, made a life in England. He examined those humanist literary writings produced by Vergil in Italy before his arrival in England (writings which constituted his main claim to fame throughout Europe in the sixteenth century); and he set out the importance of Vergil's *Anglica Historia* (much of whose substance passed on through Hall's *Chronicle* to Shakespeare) in creating a long-enduring image of the English past. Hay was not blind to the prosaic character of his author's mind; what appeared in his works, he recognised, was an unoriginal but industrious application of humanist scholarship. Yet in one sense it was this that constituted Polydore Vergil's principal interest: he provided a 'clear mirror of the age', marking the meeting of Italian and Northern traditions of learning and intellectual life. This study provides the foundations for almost all Hay's major historical interests henceforth: the Italian Renaissance, its spread to the Northern world, historiography, and the personnel and character of the Renaissance Church.

In these years, however, Hay was still experimenting with a variety of historical interests. Willing to turn his hand to any task, he saw through the press and supplied index and bibliography for an edition, published in 1951, of *The Letters of James V*, a book which, already for the most part in galley proof, had been left uncompleted at the death of Robert Kerr Hannay in 1940. The lectures which he delivered to his students formed the basis for his short textbook, *From Roman Empire to Renaissance Europe* (1953; reissued under the title, *The Medieval Centuries*, 1964). Again, he published two articles, based in part on searches in the Public Record Office and the manuscripts of the British Museum Library, on the divisions of the spoils of war in Anglo–French conflicts, and on the Scottish Borders. The theme of the borders in itself was congenial to him and one to which in general terms he would occasionally return in later life. Yet he was to admit to a certain weariness with the detailed archival researches into documentary sources which that type of enquiry demanded and he made a conscious decision to abandon them. More congenially for one who liked to paint, on a wide canvas, he gave notice of a new preoccupation with his lecture to the 10th International Historical Congress, held at Rome, in September 1955. This was dedicated to a subject on which he had been gathering materials for some years and which was to form the theme of his *Europe: The Emergence of an Idea* (1957; revised edition 1968). This brief but most original and brilliant of his books, an exercise in what Marc Bloch had called 'historical semantics', sought to chart the growth in the later Middle Ages of 'a gradual consciousness of Europe as more than a geographical term'. It detailed that process by which, eventually, in the seventeenth and eighteenth centuries, the term 'Christendom' decayed and that of 'Europe' took its place. It was written, he was to explain, in response to that mood of the 1950s which welcomed the birth of 'the European idea'. In Britain, of course that sentiment, was, as it still is, muted and confined to limited circles. But in harmony with it, he offered a cautious prophecy: 'the reluctant patriotism of the Briton, compared with the warmer loyalties of the Englishman, the Scot, and the Welshman, may perhaps offer a model for continental development within a United States of Europe'.

By that time the progressive muscular atrophy, which had already begun to afflict Richard Pares during the war, had tragically reached a stage where he was compelled to resign his appointment. It was precisely then, in 1954, that the University had decided to create two Chairs of History in place of the existing one. That of modern history went to the diplomatic historian, David Horn; that of medieval history to Hay. Under the Pares regime the Honours degree had already been restructured. As Hay was to put it: 'The next fifteen years were to see

even more radical changes in the department: more staff, more speci-
alities, more subdivisions and greater variety of all kinds'. These were
the heady years of the Robbins Report and university expansion, with
all the advantages and disadvantages that these brought. For the History
Department both might seem to be symbolised by the move in 1967
from a corner of Robert Adam's late-eighteenth-century 'Toun's
College' to a new, very 1960s, building in George Square.

In those and subsequent years Hay's ability to attract the finest
medievalists to his staff, in particular those specialising in European
subjects, and the constant sympathy, support, and inspiration he offered
them, were to play an important part in securing the reputation of the
Edinburgh History Department as one of those pre-eminent in Britain.
His sincerity and innate sense of justice made him the ideal head of
department, senior colleague, and mentor of students. With this went
always fun and conviviality. At Fountainhall Road the Hays offered an
hospitality in which the eminent visitor and junior lecturer met and
were firmly persuaded to socialise. At the same time the novice was
guided to attaining the standards of the department, largely by being
encouraged to recognise his own virtues and defects. One such, now
very senior, tells of how Hay attended one of his own prentice classes:
'maintaining a fixed expression through what, even by my indifferent
standards, was a wretched lecture, an attempt to catch up with my
programme. Afterwards he asked me to see him later in his room. I
believed my lecturing career would be brief. He made one comment:
"When you are lecturing, remember to pause between sentences." '

In the meanwhile, Hay was being drawn deeper and more widely
into European cultural history. He was to write the introduction, and to
complete the editorial revision of the first volume, *The Renaissance
1493–1520*, of the *New Cambridge Modern History* (1957), and to write
chapters on 'Literature: the printed book' and 'Schools and Universities' for the second volume (1958). Invited to give the British Academy's Italian Lecture in 1959, he returned to the theme of Renaissance
historiography with a discussion of Flavio Biondo's *Decades*. It was
against the background of these studies that Hay was preparing what is
still the most influential of his works, *The Italian Renaissance in its
Historical Background* (1961). In 1957 Cambridge University Press had
invited Hay to write a volume on the Italian Renaissance. It was, as Hay
believed, 'a desideratum of our day', something designed to meet a
clear need both in the academic world and among general readers. With
typical tolerance Hay described John Addington Symonds's diffuse and

highly coloured *Renaissance in Italy* (in seven volumes, 1875–86) as 'a remarkable and neglected work'. That excluded, however, there was, before Hay's book, no other study in English, from the time of the translation of Burckhardt, in which an historian considered together the political history and the history of Renaissance art and ideas: 'I cannot think of any place where the questions are treated in a general way, where the whole question is reviewed'. By this time there were several claims that the Renaissance had never taken place, arguments concerning its relation to other earlier Renaissances — the Carolingian, Ottonian, Twelfth-Century Renaissances — and often among many cultured laymen a confused and generalised hostility to the whole theme, the contention of C. S. Lewis, for example (repeated in an essay by W. H. Auden), first that the Renaissance had never existed and secondly, that it was, at the same time — the influence of Ruskin lingered here — a deplorable and evil development. It was essentially as a well-written explanatory filling of a gap that Hay's book, despite, perhaps because of, its brevity, acquired importance.

Given that the one thing all seemed agreed on was that Burckhardt was no longer adequate, Hay might, like his friend, Roberto Weiss, have abandoned any definition of the Renaissance as a period and returned to the eighteenth-century notion of a purely cultural phenomenon, of a 'rebirth of polite letters [i.e. the classics]', combined with various changes, as interpreted by Vasari, in the development of the fine arts. This was not possible for him, partly because, as he would proclaim, not just occasionally and in unbuttoned mood but seriously and consistently, there were whole areas of that classical literature which the humanists so revered which he himself regarded with distaste. ('I would readily concede that most Latin prose writers are ineffably boring, being pompous to please their pompous readers'.) But also, and much more than this, because one of his strongest convictions was that there was an intermediate period between modern and medieval history which it was convenient to call the Renaissance. One writes here 'Renaissance' rather than 'Italian Renaissance', in that, despite the book's title, it is made clear from the start that what is to be dealt with is 'a phase in Italian and European history . . . the Renaissance in Europe as a whole'.

The introductory pages, in fact, consist of a reiteration of what Hay had advanced for many years, and which was to remain central to his historical periodisation: namely that the years 1300–1700 in European history had their own particular unity and inner coherence. Already, in an address to the Anglo–American Conference of Historians in 1951, in arguments honed, we are told, in discussions with Richard Pares, he had sought to justify this concept. This was a period of 'enormous innovations'. It was 'an age of kings', in which an overwhelming community of political and economic interest united these kings to 'the town', this at a time when town and country were almost evenly matched in economic importance. In intellectual life it was 'essentially lay and yet essentially Christian'. Lay domination of Christianity produced an epoch 'marked by a series of heresies and schisms', matched by 'a remarkable growth of patriotic sentiment which at times verges on nationalism'. These broad generalisations, whose formulation was perhaps facilitated through the writing of the wide-ranging lecture courses demanded by the Edinburgh system, could be seen as gaining momentum from personal experience. In view of the way he had been rejected, back in 1938, when applying for posts both as a medievalist and a modernist (occasions frequently to be reinvoked), it is not surprising to find that among the claims made for the advantages of the schema which he proposed is the consideration that it would 'protect the student of the no-man's land around 1500, enabling young historians to expand their interests on both sides of this date; the present division unfortunately almost compels them to gravitate to a recognisable and marketable "medievalism" or "modernism" '. This periodisation occurred again in the preface to his textbook of European history of 1953, where Hay wrote of 'three epochs [AD300–800; 800–1300; and 1300–1700] each of which seems to possess a coherence of its own'. With some blurring at the margins, this time-span remains in his *Italian Renaissance*, where it is explained that nearly all that was to be unique in this European period 'was first and most purely expressed in Italy'.

In fact, the work soon makes plain that very little of what is comprised by the Renaissance, now defined or redefined as 'a new educational programme and a new attitude to literature and morality . . . a new art and a new place for art in the life of the individual and the community', was to be found within the peninsula before the 1380s. 'Italy was not ready for the novelties hinted at by some of her sons.' At this point Hay unveils the principal influence behind his thought, the 'masterly, indeed epoch-making' writings of the German-American historian, Hans Baron, whose principal work, *The Crisis of the Early Italian Renaissance*, had been published in 1955. Hay, who always particularly appreciated the wide overview and daring synthesis, followed Baron in seeing the birth of true Renaissance values as springing from a group of men writing between 1380 and 1440 in defence of Florentine republican 'liberty' against threats from the aggressive princely powers of the Duchy of Milan and the Kingdom of Naples. Learning, directed at that time to immediate and pressing political problems, lost its 'medieval', its 'unworldly' character; a new morality was born which praised civic pride and the 'active' life, embraced rather than rejected wealth, developed a secularised view of wisdom. As a result political thought, literature, art, history, and attitudes to education were all challenged.

From Florence these values were then, Hay argues, carried to the rest of Italy, where, if the Republicanism that produced them did not generally exist, they at least made an appeal to similar civic environments. Here he seeks to distinguish the different forms of the Renaissance as expressed in the principates, Venice, and the Papacy. In Florence itself — here resting largely upon the interpretation of the Florentine intellectual historian, Eugenio Garin — the rise of the Medici, who sapped the republican ideal 'led to airy abstraction and to art for art's sake', to, at least, a dilution of true Renaissance ideals. Hay then goes on to consider the transfer of the Renaissance from Italy to the Northern world, a northern Europe seen as 'ripe for the adoption of the new attitudes and the new manners', and where therefore the principal problem is to explain why their arrival was delayed until the sixteenth century. Finally he reaffirms the periodisation he started out with by indicating a terminus for the movement or period with that *Crise de la Conscience Européenne* which Paul Hazard had detected at the beginning of the eighteenth century.

Since the writing of the book, thirty-five years ago, there has, of course been a great deal of thought and a great deal of research devoted to this subject; and even at the time of writing this was a very large theme to be elaborated within a small frame (some 80,000 words). A particular difficulty, not perhaps resolved, might lie in reconciling the two parallel periodisations found within it: 'the European Renaissance' (1300–1700) and 'the Italian Renaissance'; the one, to take just one example, 'an age of kings', the other supposedly triggered by a republican response to a monarchical threat. Again, by 1966, Baron's thesis, on which Hay had drawn very deeply, was the subject of strong controversy. In that year Hay passed a sabbatical at the Newberry Library in Chicago, where Baron was Distinguished Research Fellow, and, it is said, was to some extent distracted from his own studies by the need in these circumstances to offer moral support to Baron. None the less, anyone who believes with Hay that 'periodisation as such is admittedly artificial and arbitrary but it is necessary for practical purposes' will find merit in a work which will continue to provide a concise and skilfully written point of view, a focus for discussion on what has established itself as a perennial historical problem.

Certainly on publication it was received with enthusiasm by the learned world. As a result, in the years to follow, Hay — who took his role as a teacher, in the widest sense of the word, with great seriousness — wrote or edited a large number of works on the theme with an educational or popularising purpose (*The Renaissance Debate*, *The Age of the Renaissance*, etc.). In the same spirit he took on the general editorship of Longman's very successful *A General History of Europe*, a series which has been of use to many generations of undergraduate students, he himself writing the volume *Europe in the Fourteenth and Fifteenth Centuries*. Later too he was to edit the *Longman History of Italy*, for which series, together with John Law, he wrote *Italy in the Age of the Renaissance 1380–1530*. In addition to these textbooks he published several articles on aspects of, above all, the interaction of Italian and European culture (one may single out here in particular the studies on the reception of the Renaissance in England and in Scotland). At the same time as an antidote to what he may have felt to be the high level of generality in these writings, he also published an edition and translation (1967), prepared in cooperation with W. K. Smith, of the *De gestis Concilii Basiliensis commentariorum libri ii*, written by the humanist and future pope, Aeneas Sylvius Piccolominus.

In the ten years which followed that work Hay's scholarly interests were principally directed to a consideration of the Italian Church in the Renaissance period. At that time, surprisingly enough, this had not yet been the subject of any general study. Much had been written on the papacy and the Papal Curia and much on particular aspects of it, such as, for example, Franciscanism. But the humdrum world of parish and diocese, the lived everyday world of the Church, had passed very largely ignored. It was this lacuna which Hay's *The Church in Italy in the Fifteenth Century* (1977, a book based upon the 'Birkbeck Lectures' which he had delivered in Cambridge in 1971) sought to fill out. It considered such themes as diocesan and parochial organisation, the state of clergy and laity, and (a subject on which he could write, of course, with particular authority) 'The Italian Renaissance and the Clergy'. Here, once again, Hay ambitiously tackled a very large theme, and elected to write of it in quite short compass. As a pioneering work it has an immense usefulness, and, until, and perhaps beyond, such time as a series of local diocesan investigations have come to provide a closer look at the ground, its generalisations are likely to offer a stimulating introduction. No one was more convinced than Hay himself of the need for others to continue the task he had begun. Writing in the Festschrift for Eugenio Garin, published two years later, on 'Historians and the Renaissance during the last Twenty-Five Years', Hay was to state his belief that 'intensive research' still remained to be done on three themes (the three which had always most fascinated him in his studies in this area): education; the effects of the Renaissance on Italian archaeology and historiography; and the 'cultural and spiritual history of the Church in Italy during the fourteenth and fifteenth centuries'.

On historiography in fact, though not simply within the compass of the Renaissance, he published, in the same year as *The Church in Italy*, a concise, and entertaining overview, *Annalists and Historians: Western Historiography from the Eighth to the Eighteenth Centuries*. Based upon his teaching over a long period in Edinburgh, the first general survey of the subject since Fueter's book of 1911, it is a work which enshrines those historical values in whose defence he had long argued. These were conservative, perhaps even, in some respects, old-fashioned. For Hay — and in this he felt himself at times fighting against the tide — history was a branch of literature. Writing in 1962 as editor of the *English Historical Review*, he observes:

> The greater the technical complexity of the problem discussed in Article or Note the greater the need for clarity in exposition. It is tiresome to read a contribution — dealing with new ideas or based on new material — which is confused or ill-written, or both. There is no virtue in being difficult to understand and a hard question is no more significant for being investigated obscurely. . . . The advice I have been bold enough to give in this paragraph is addressed, it may be felt, only to beginners; it is not.

Hay's enthusiasm for lucidity and order in historical writing was reinforced by his recognition that his own apprenticeship in the art had not been effortless or unaided. Over forty years later, with a generosity which made him willing to acknowledge what many would be all too anxious to forget, he recalled the experience of submitting an article to the *English Historical Review* in 1938, describing how the then editor, Sir George Clark, 'rewrote it, to my anger and mortification, and in doing so must have spent the best part of three days, turning my turgid incoherence into something more or less reasonable'. During his own time as editor, Hay was, in that tradition, to assist many young historians in the same way.

The insistence on intelligibility formed a part of his resistance to the idea of history as an arcane science. It is a theme he touched on in the course of a presidential address to the Historical Association in 1969:

> Articles are of interest to those who write them and to those who read them. I think sometimes that they are almost the same people, so technical are the subjects discussed, so rebarbative the style, so absent the general inferences. Snooks writes an article which only Snooks can appreciate. It was not always so. Members of the generation which saw the birth of the *English Historical Review* had been brought up to regard history as one of the several 'literary' genres, and they read it in the pages of the general magazines of the day.

Turning from style, Hay's attitude to the substance of history was traditional. If he acknowledged the inspiration of Marc Bloch, he was generally indifferent to the preoccupations of most of Bloch's post-war followers:

> And what (I hear you say) about *Past and Present*? I believe we should all take our hats off to *Past and Present*. And then put them on again. It is our British *Annales* — though, thank God, it is only a tenth the size of that monstrous publication. In *Past and Present* we do have broad surveys, brilliant reappraisals of big topics, and kites flying briskly in the breeze. . . . Yet I suspect that in twenty years time scholars young and old will still be turning up the dreary old *EHR* rather oftener than they refer to the files of *Past and Present*. The solid, highly particularised and annotated articles in the *EHR* are the hard, gritty bricks from which the Great Wall of history is steadily if slowly built.

He was, as those words might suggest, and as appears clearly in *Annalists and Historians*, essentially a positivist, one who believed that historical understanding developed through a process of accretion. And in other ways too he recalled the Oxford of the 1930s. He spoke often of 'the primacy of politics'. 'Politics are, so it seems to me, infinitely more significant than *conjuncture*.' Contemporary developments in historical study often provoked scepticism. 'Demography is guess-work before the nineteenth century and even then it is not very clear how far population variables were (or are?) a significant index of public priorities or pressures.' Economic theory was to be approached with extreme scepticism: 'a "model", meaning, I take it, "a fiction" '. Family history was (he seems here to be thinking of such aspects as infanticide and birth control) 'a rebarbative subject', and (inserted, it may be suspected, as a proud boast) 'I have never been trained in the techniques and terminology of modern sociological concepts regarding the family'. Confronted with a discussion about the inventor of that 1960s theory that 'the medium is the message' (something which might have been expected to interest one versed in the history of printing), he merely commented: 'I had always thought that Marshall McLuhan was one of Napoleon's generals'.

Beyond his teaching and publications, Hay's urbanity and energy gave him an easy entrée and smooth passage through many offices in academic life. He was a president of the Edinburgh branch of the Association of University Teachers, Dean of the Faculty of Arts in Edinburgh from 1961–2, and trustee of the National Library of Scotland from 1966. From 1958, together with Goronwy Edwards, then from 1959–65 alone, he was editor of the *English Historical Review*. 'One reason', he was to observe, 'why the learned quarterlies are such good value is that they are directed and managed by a group of fanatics who are prepared to ruin their careers and imperil their marriages by acting as editors'. He calculated the time involved in the editorship as sixteen hours a week including the entirety of every fourth weekend, and gives an autobiographical vision of wife and children involved in 'cutting up the lengths of articles, reviews and short notices required to fill up the predetermined number of pages'. Again, he served in many offices in the Royal Historical Society (of which he was Literary Director 1955–8; a Vice-President 1961–5 and 1971–5; and from 1981 an Honorary Vice-President). He was unfailingly active in the Historical Association from 1967–70, in which period he was responsible for the act which united it with the Scottish Historical Association. Everyone asked: 'How can he possibly find the time?' It seemed a punishing schedule. Whether or not as a result, his health began to suffer and in 1969 he had a first heart attack.

The doctors successfully urged him to banish his pipe, but were less successful in persuading him to slow down. From 1971 to 1975 he served as Vice-Principal. These were still the days before the party had ended, when the university limousine waited upon its senior officers to bear them to receptions and banquets. Hay enjoyed this aspect of his role, but much more than that the sense of continuity which came from sitting in the Old Senate Room under Raeburn's portrait of the great

Enlightenment historian, Principal William Robertson (pictured with Muratori's *Annali* on his desk), like him, and like the Florentine Scholar-Chancellors of the Renaissance, Salutati and Bruni and Poggio, uniting the contemplative and active life. Thereafter, he did indeed begin to take things more easily, though still taking on new tasks: from 1978 as joint editor of the Oxford Warburg series, and in 1980–1 as President of the Ecclesiastical History Society. Meanwhile many honours came to him. He was elected a Fellow of the British Academy in 1970, a Foreign Honorary Member of the American Academy of Arts and Sciences in 1974, and Fellow of the Royal Society of Edinburgh in 1977. He received honorary doctorates from Newcastle in 1970, from Tours in 1982, and was appointed Commendatore al Ordine del Merito della Repubblica Italiana in 1980. He was the recipient of two Festschriften, and will, posthumously, be honoured with a memorial volume, the triple crown.

On his retirement from Edinburgh in 1980, after a time as Visiting Professor at the University of Virginia, which like all his American visits (Cornell in 1963, and, as we have seen, Chicago in 1966) he much enjoyed, he held from 1980–2 a temporary post as Professor of History at the European University Institute at the Badia Fiesolana outside Florence, a less happy experience. The Hays were unfortunate enough to be lodged with a landlady who embodied true Florentine *durezza* (there were great conflicts about the permissibility of putting up a card-table to work on, and so on), while his colleagues had different historical interests from those which he pursued. Return to Edinburgh was a relief. Here his studies still continued, and he still published, though less prolifically. And hospitality continued: assessments of new restaurants were to be tested at first hand; he would still turn up at 'The Denys Hay Medieval and Renaissance History Seminar' and at any other historical treats which were going. Very common was the experience of the visiting speaker who found the form before him vividly coming alive, belying all appearance of sleep, and interjecting a penetrating question opening with the deceptively modest words: 'I seem to remember having read somewhere . . .'. His death, on 14 June 1994, at the age of seventy-eight, came at the end of a life which was fruitful and active almost to the last.

In appearance Hay was of middle height, broad of countenance and, from middle age, of ample frame, with a suggestion of bagginess, wispy hair which gave him a wind-blown look, appropriate enough for one who always brought with him great gusts of fresh air. His habitual expression was vivacious and benevolent, the eyes quick to light up with amusement, the face bending forward keenly in conversation to signify enjoyment or to act out scorn on hearing of unpalatable opinions or displeasing neologisms. (These loomed large. Friends received offprints of his review of an American book on historiography signed 'From one historicist to another'.) His voice was cultured yet unaffected, loud but both sonorous and firm. His speech was frequently enlivened by faintly archaic, often alliterative, colloquialisms; he would speak of (it could be rather austere or superior) people as 'sweeties'; would observe that 'those chaps have been living high off the hog'; would describe a compliant external-examiner as 'a biddable buddy'; would hope to meet soon 'the lucky lady' whom a friend had married. His manner was bluff, patrician, salted with impishness. His wit has been described as 'conspiratorial'; it had the effect of making his listeners feel joined with him in an alliance against all the follies of life. Very common was the expression of (a quite feigned) fear of authority-figures ('Of course, Smith is scared stiff of Richard [Pares].' Pause. 'But then we're all scared of Richard.').

He had a natural kindness and many stories are told as examples of this by those who knew him. He approached the world with an optimism tempered by realism. ('Historians are relativists. By understanding the past they become understanding, or at any rate some of them do.') Though doubt always struggled with belief, each Sunday he attended mass at the Episcopalian Church of St John in Princes Street. His happiness was rooted above all in his family, in his children, and Gwyneth, his wife, 'who has counted bishops, typed chapters, corrected my English, listened to endless diatribes and encomia, and sometimes lived in the cold discomfort of Roman winters'. Outside that domestic circle, Denys Hay would have wished to be remembered as an historian, a scholar, friend, and above all, as a teacher. In one of his last essays he debated whether politics had changed as a result of Renaissance humanism, whether Burckhardt's famous 'state as a work of art' had ever really come into existence. Certainly, he concluded, the style of politics had altered, because now those who were to run the world had been educated in the humanities. At which point his mind turned to Balliol. *Floreat domus de Balliolo* — ugly Latin, but it recalled the tradition of that college in which education was seen as intimately bound up, as function or justification, with public service. 'Humanists,' he ended, 'if

I may quote myself, are all educators. I do not believe there is a nobler calling.'

JOHN LARNER
University of Glasgow

Note. I am indebted to discussion with and information from Dr David Chambers, Dr Robert Donaldson, Professor A. A. M. Duncan, Professor A. Goodman, Miss Alison E. Harvey Wood, Mrs Gwyneth Hay, Mr Richard Hay, Mr John V. Howard, Dr Maurice Keen, Mr J. F. X. Miller, and Professor J. A. F. Thomson. Miss Harvey Wood has provided a 'Bibliography of the works of Denys Hay' in *Renaissance Studies*, 2, 2 (1988), 347–55.

JAMES JOLL

Proceedings of the British Academy, **90**, 413–437

James Bysse Joll
1918–1994

JAMES JOLL died in London on 12 July, 1994, aged seventy-six. Professor Emeritus at the London School of Economics, he was one of the most eminent and productive historians of his generation. Joll held a chair of international relations, and made a lasting contribution to debate about the origins of the First World War; he also wrote widely on movements and ideas of the European left, and was the author of a sophisticated general book on modern European history that set the standard in the field. Running through all his work was a strong interest in the connections between ideas, culture and politics. This reflected the great importance that culture played in his life. James Joll was a man of wide reading, took an exceptionally well-informed interest in the visual arts, and had a lifelong love of music (he was a gifted pianist). He also possessed a very strong sense of right and wrong, yet there was absolutely nothing of the martinet about him. James Joll was, as everyone who met him quickly realised, a man of quite unusual warmth and kindness.

When eminent academics are immortalised on canvas, usually at the point of retirement, they are invariably painted in aldermanic mode. The portraiture is naturalistic and competent; the distinguished person wears a dark suit and tie. James Joll was painted wearing a green tie and no jacket, sitting next to an alarm clock with no hands. The artist was an American modernist master, R. B. Kitaj, who also happened to be a friend. The work in question (it is in private possession) was on show to the public at an exhibition that opened just weeks before Joll died; the

major Kitaj retrospective at the Tate Gallery. Work number 28 was a
large canvas called *From London (James Joll and John Golding)*.[1]
Painted in 1975–6, its central figures are two men with whom Kitaj
had recently begun a lasting friendship, Joll himself and his companion
of nearly forty years, the painter and art critic John Golding. At that
time Kitaj had become increasingly interested in the human figure, and
the painting dates from the period when he coined the term 'school of
London' to describe figurative artists such as Auerbach and Freud. A
few years later Kitaj would start to practise what he was already
championing. *From London* is a painting in a different idiom, however,
one that the artist favoured in the 1970s. His two figures are placed in
flat, carefully delineated planes of colour, surrounded by a collage of
objects representing the world his friends inhabited. And where better
to begin an appreciation of James Joll, an historian to whom the arts
meant so much, than with the busy, allegorical composition of an artist
obsessed with history?

James Joll is shown in profile seated towards the left of the canvas
and facing the same way. Behind him lies the world of cultured
domesticity; a Mondrian hangs on the wall. Immediately in front of
him, a small and enigmatic figure wearing a flat cap leans against a
tree — looks, indeed, as if he might be perched on an invisible branch
like a weightless character out of a Chagall. This poor but respectable
worker is a marvellously disturbing presence, and the historian of
socialism and anarchism is looking steadily towards him. In the foreground is a table with books, three of them carrying clearly visible
names: Léger; Wollheim, the philosopher and writer on aesthetics, a
close friend of Joll's; and Gramsci, the Italian Marxist writer on whom
he was then preparing an introductory work. The firmly cosmopolitan
title, the scholarly allusions, the icons of modernist high culture — these
point to some of the many facets of James Joll's life. Serious-minded
but never pompous, he was a man of genuinely European sensibility and
interests, who read and spoke many languages and always shunned
Little-Englandism.

James Bysse Joll was born in Bristol on 21 June 1918, the son of
Lieutenant-Colonel H. H. Joll and his wife Alice Muriel Edwards. He
was an exhibitioner at Winchester, which he disliked, then studied for a
year at the University of Bordeaux after leaving school, thereby adding
French to his already fluent German. The slightly older Richard Cobb,

---

[1] The painting is reproduced in *R. B. Kitaj*, ed. Richard Morphet (New York, 1994), p. 142.

who spent a year in France between Shrewsbury and Oxford (the first of many), was later to speak of the 'second identity' he acquired as an Englishman gone native.[2] James Joll's time in Bordeaux during the period of the Popular Front government in France and the outbreak of the Spanish Civil War was also a crucial experience. It opened his eyes to a larger world, and gave him subjects he would later pursue with great success as a professional historian.

In 1937 he took up a scholarship at New College, Oxford to read Greats, but his undergraduate career was interrupted by the outbreak of war. Joll was commissioned in the Devon Regiment in 1940 and served as intelligence officer of the 203 Infantry Brigade during 1941–2. He was then recruited into the Special Operations Executive (SOE). The 'Baker Street Irregulars' were created in July 1940 to 'set Europe ablaze' by acts of sabotage on the occupied Continent. Joll was trained as an agent, to be parachuted into Hungary. This was never a very successful theatre for the SOE, and after the Germans took over Hungary in March 1944 the SOE changed its plans for Joll. He was assigned to its Austrian, and then later to its German section. There he apparently refused on one occasion to be party to a covert operation he considered completely unscrupulous — an example of his strong moral sense that will surprise no one who knew him at any stage of his life. He worked in Germany on counter-intelligence duties from April to October 1945. About all of these experiences, James Joll remained very reticent. He shared the same background as many other young SOE operatives, but was not the swashbuckling type who would readily have imagined himself (as others in the SOE did) to be emulating a character from John Buchan or Dornford Yates.

Joll returned to Oxford in 1945 to complete his degree. Before the war he had read Greats; now he read PPE, in which his philosophy tutors included Isaiah Berlin and Herbert Hart. From 1946 he taught Politics at New College, of which he became a Fellow two years later. At the same time, he was tapped by the Foreign Office to join the team working under the direction of Sir John Wheeler-Bennett to classify and edit captured German foreign policy documents from 1918–45. For a six-month period in 1948 Joll acted as editor-in-chief. His dual-track activities in these years prefigured the two areas in which he was to make his greatest contribution as a scholar: the history of political ideas, and the history of international relations, in both cases broadly

[2] Richard Cobb, *A Second Identity: Essays on France and French History* (Oxford, 1969).

defined. This combination of interests was apparent in his first book, published in 1950 as part of the series on the British Political Tradition edited by Alan Bullock and William Deakin. The aim of the series was, as the editors put it in their general preface, 'to present from sources of the most varied kind, books, pamphlets, speeches, letters, newspapers, a selection of original material illustrating the different facets of Englishmen's discussion of politics'. (Even after 1945, it was clearly assumed that Englishwomen did not go in for that sort of thing.) Joll's volume, the third in the series, was a selection on the theme *Britain and Europe: From Pitt to Churchill 1793–1940.*[3] It was characteristic of Joll that he not only rounded up the usual suspects, in the shape of Castlereagh, Palmerston, Gladstone and other parliamentary notables, but found the space to include some lines from Tennyson's *Maud* ('We have proved we have hearts in a cause, we are noble still,/And myself have awaked, as it seems, to the better mind.') It is equally in character that, looking for a way to pin down the Foreign Office mind in his introduction, it was a passage from Proust's *Within a Budding Grove* to which he turned.

In 1951 Joll served as William Deakin's principal assistant in setting up St Antony's College, Oxford. This was a new graduate college, made possible by a large bequest from the Aden businessman Antonin Besse, and it became an important centre for the teaching of modern history and politics — especially of Europe and the Middle East. In the field of German history, to take a prominent example, St Antony's has been one of the most important academic bases in Britain for visiting scholars, comparable to Princeton's Institute for Advanced Study as a favoured destination of German historians on sabbatical. Klaus Bade, Erich Matthias, Thomas Nipperdey, Gregor Schöllgen, Michael Stürmer, Peter-Christian Witt — these and dozens of others (with highly diverse views) have spent time at St Antony's, held seminars, and fostered the exchange of ideas between British and German historians. Often, figures who were to make major reputations came to the Woodstock Road some years before those reputations were established. James Joll had a major part in laying the foundations of all this. He was one of the college's founding fellows and served as its Sub-Warden from 1951–67, contributing much to the establishment of St Antony's as an institution whose graduate students and visiting fellows gave it a truly international atmosphere. This achievement was time-consuming, for Joll

[3] London, 1950.

took his teaching obligations and heavy administrative duties very seriously. Perhaps it prevented him from writing a major monograph in his thirties and forties.

He was, nevertheless, very productive in his Oxford years. Between 1955 and 1964 he wrote three books and edited a fourth. They share certain common characteristics. Joll is concerned with political ideas in a broad European setting, putting a wide range of printed sources to telling use. He constructs his narratives with unobtrusive literary skill, has a sharp eye for the unfamiliar quotation, and writes with a distinctively dry, ironic voice. A common thread in the subject-matter of these books is Joll's sympathetic interest in the political left — not the dogmatic left that was sure it had history on its side, but the radicals, socialists and anarchists who grafted a concern for social justice on to the emancipatory promise of the Enlightenment, and stood against a narrow chauvinism as Joll himself always did.

The first of these books was *The Second International*.[4] It is a subtly crafted work that draws on sources in English, French, German, Italian and Dutch. The great themes of the international (in fact, largely European) socialist movement in the decades before the First World War are all there — the rapid growth of its member-parties, the disputes between disciples of anarchism and Marxism, the problems caused by nationalism (especially in the multi-national Habsburg monarchy), the debates over 'reformism', 'revisionism', and whether socialists should, if the opportunity arose, participate in 'bourgeois governments'. Not least, Joll considers the discussions that marked the efforts of the Second International to come to terms with the threat of war — efforts that were to yield so little in the summer of 1914. The book is built around the German and French socialists — the large, disciplined mass party of German Social Democracy, the weaker, more fissiparous French movement — and the fraternal bickering that so often marked their relations. But Joll's pages also contain a large cast of minor characters (concern with individual historical actors runs through all his books), and present a persuasive account of the International as a whole.

While the book distributes its emotional sympathies widely, Joll clearly finds himself more drawn to the French than the German socialists. Running implicitly through his account is the contrast between a Gallic left that consorted in cafés with writers and painters,

---

[4] London, 1955, rev. ed. 1974.

and a German party that sought 'blind insistence on doctrinal uniformity'.[5] That nimble dialectician Karl Kautsky is described, rather unfairly, as a 'fanatic'; the dourly unimaginative Marxist Jules Guesde is at least credited with composing sub-Baudelairean verse. This is not the only occasion when Joll treats a commitment to the arts as, in effect, a redeeming feature, a sign of human generosity. He quotes an opponent who called Rosa Luxemburg 'that pedantic and quarrelsome person with her mechanistic interpretation of marxism'. His next sentence begins with a 'but', and a revealing one: 'But her political rigour and intellectual achievements were accompanied by a warmth, charm and sensibility, (she even used to sing songs by Hugo Wolf), rare in the socialist world . . .' . [6] The book strikes the urbane tone that would inform all Joll's work. Of the July 1914 meeting between the French trade union leader Léon Jouhaux and his German counterpart Karl Legien we are told: 'As neither spoke the other's language, it is not surprising that little was said — nor that it is uncertain what that little was'.[7] This is deft — and a shade donnish. *The Second International* is less substantial than many of Joll's later books, but it still holds up remarkably well as an accessible and perceptive synthesis of the subject. Joll's account bristles with *aperçus*. He discusses the German Social Democrats as a 'state within the state' ten years before Peter Nettl and Gunther Roth wrote classic analyses of this phenomenon, and he talks about the co-operation of liberals and socialists against the anti-'immorality' clauses of the *Lex Heinze* almost twenty years before Robin Lenman (one of Joll's own students) brought that obscure measure to the full attention of scholars. Joll reveals a similar mastery of the Allemanists, Broussists, Guesdists and other French socialist groupings, at a time when the Anglo-Saxon Ph.D. mills had not yet ground them into more easily digestible form.

Four years later, Joll edited a collection of St Antony's Papers on *The Decline of the Third Republic*.[8] He wrote an introduction to the volume, and contributed an essay on the making of the Popular Front. The leader of the Popular Front government, the socialist Léon Blum, was one of the three figures who featured in the book Joll published the following year: *Intellectuals in Politics*.[9] It is the most original work of

---

[5] *Second International*, p. 105.
[6] Ibid., p. 100.
[7] Ibid., pp. 161–2.
[8] London, 1959.
[9] London, 1960.

his Oxford period. The book contains three self-standing but connected essays: on Blum, who became leader of the French Socialist party after it had been weakened by the split with the Communists in 1921; on Walter Rathenau, the German industrialist and would-be philosopher first propelled into public life when he became head of the newly-created War Raw Materials Department in 1914; and on Filippo Tommaso Marinetti, the Futurist artist who provided some of the ideological underpinnings for Italian Fascism. The three men were born within ten years of each other, and all had made careers in other fields before they took part in political life — with less than happy consequences. As the author laconically notes: 'Entry into politics led to Rathenau's death; it endangered Blum's life and made nonsense of Marinetti's.'[10] The book offers a subtle examination of the contradictions, frustrations and compromises of intellectuals in politics, although most readers will probably feel that Joll is at his best dealing with the pre-political periods of his characters' lives. His exegesis of their writings is often superb, showing how easily Joll moved in the larger intellectual history of France, Germany and Italy (and, indeed, Britain, for the Marinetti essay has a good account of the artist's impact on figures such as Wyndham Lewis and C. R. W. Nevinson). The book has some wonderfully crisp characterisations: Rathenau's 'dehydrated mysticism' would be hard to beat.[11] And the author is, as one would expect, very good when it comes to the striking detail: Blum's enormous admiration for *Mansfield Park*, Rathenau's fondness for discussing metaphysics over smoked salmon and Rhine wine. He even — another gastronomic note — mentions Marinetti's advocacy of Futurist cookery, with its fierce attack on pasta — although it was left to a rather different sort of writer, Elizabeth David, to popularise this particular debate in *Italian Food*, which quotes Marinetti's ringing proclamation that 'spaghetti is no food for fighters'.[12]

Joll wants to explore the various kinds of interplay between career and calling, politics and culture. Re-reading the book, one is struck by some of the parallels with Peter Gay's 1974 Cooper Union lectures, later published as *Art and Act: On Causes in History*. Gay also considers three prominent figures — Manet, Gropius and Mondrian — and

[10] *Intellectuals in Politics*, p. ix.
[11] Ibid., p. 87.
[12] E. David, *Italian Food* (Harmondsworth, 1977), pp. 93–4. See also N. O'Sullivan, *Fascism* (London, 1983), p. 143.

tries to weigh the different parts played in their respective achievements by the private inner world, the craftsman's imperative, and the broader public culture. Joll, like Gay, places individuals at centre-stage; but both are also concerned with larger social, cultural and political currents during the decades on either side of 1900, the period that historians (following art historians and literary critics) are beginning to call the era of 'classical modernity'.

Joll's great feeling for this period was also apparent in his next book, *The Anarchists*.[13] It is a less original work than *Intellectuals in Politics*, and — curiously, perhaps — there was already a much more extensive and distinguished English-language literature on the subject than there was on the Second International when Joll wrote his first book. One thinks of H. N. Brailsford on Shelley, Godwin and their circle, E. H. Carr on Bakunin, Gerald Brenan on the Spanish anarchists, Franco Venturi on the Russian Populists, George Woodcock on almost everyone. Eric Hobsbawm had published his pioneering study on *Primitive Rebels* in 1959; and for the earlier parts of his book Joll could also draw on another classic, Norman Cohn's *Pursuit of the Millennium* (1957). To contextualise in this way does not diminish Joll's achievement. His account, based on printed sources in many European languages, is rich, sure in judgement and unfailingly intelligent. It exhibits a generous sympathy for history's losers, yet addresses the contradictions within anarchism, including the obvious fact that the same generic term covers both kindly, ruminative philosophical anarchists, and those who perpetrated acts of individual terror. Not least, the book is extraordinarily wide in its range of reference, from the Albigensian heretics of the thirteenth century to the post-Gandhian Indian social reformers, Jayaprakash Narayan and Vinobha Bhave.

The vice of this virtue is that the book has a certain unruliness, no doubt appropriate to the subject. Part One is devoted to the roots of anarchist thinking in religious Utopianism, Enlightenment ideas of perfectibility, and the mystique of revolution (and devoted revolutionary) spawned by 1789. Part Two, covering the middle years of the nineteenth century, is built around two dominant figures: Proudhon and Bakunin. The third part, easily the longest and arguably the most original, begins with the anarchist 'outrages' of the 1870s and 1880s and ends with the Civil War in Spain. It is here, and particularly when he deals with the years around the turn of the century depicted in

[13] London, 1964.

Conrad's *The Secret Agent* and Henry James's *The Princess Casamassima*, that Joll's account seems to slip into a higher gear. That is notably true of a short but very stimulating chapter on the cultural revolt of the 1890s called 'Saints and Rebels', which deals among other subjects with Prince Peter Kropotkin and his disciples, the rediscovery of Max Stirner's work in Germany, and the appeal of anarchism for French artists and writers of the *fin de siècle*. As Joll notes, when the Paris police raided Jean Grave's paper, *La Révolte*, in 1894, the subscription list included Alphonse Daudet, Anatole France and Stéphane Mallarmé, as well as others more actively engaged in the anarchist movement such as Signac and Pissarro. *The Anarchists* is an uneven book, but it is also more multi-faceted than *The Second International*. At its best it cuts deeper.

By the second half of the 1960s, Joll's association with Oxford was approaching thirty years' duration. He was a popular and greatly respected figure in the university. His circle of friends included not only colleagues in modern history such as Alan Bullock, William Deakin, Agnes Headlam-Morley and A. J. P. Taylor, but an extremely wide range of others: Isaiah Berlin, Maurice Bowra, Patrick Gardiner, John Sparrow, Robin Zaehner. Joll enjoyed the stimulation of Oxford; he also felt its stifling qualities. In *The Second International* there is a wonderful anecdote that he must have enjoyed recording. Jules Guesde, anxious to alter the thinking of the German Social Democrats on a particular doctrinal point, tried to enlist Engels' support through an intermediary, a Frenchman who taught modern languages at Oxford. Engels' irritated response was entirely in character: 'The idea of leading the European working-class movement from Oxford — the last bit of the real middle ages that still exists in Europe — is incredible . . .'.[14] It is not a view of Oxford Joll would have shared. But his personal life, his wide cultural interests, and the challenge of teaching in a great metropolitan university all made London attractive. In 1967, therefore — at about the same age when the lives of Léon Blum and Walter Rathenau were fundamentally changed — he accepted the offer of the Stevenson Chair of International History at the London School of Economics.

James Joll already moved comfortably between the intellectual worlds of Oxford and London. Professionally, however, the decision to go to London placed him in a new setting. The LSE was, of course, a very peculiar institution: stimulating and querulous, an important

---

[14] *Second International*, p. 52.

source of new thinking on both left and right, intensely English yet strongly touched by Continental thought through powerful figures such as the sociologist Karl Mannheim, or (in Joll's time) Ernest Gellner and Ralf Dahrendorf. Joll certainly found some aspects of the School more congenial than others. He was a man of great institutional loyalty, however, and became an important, much-liked member of its senior professorial ranks.

The 'School' was the institution to which James Joll now owed his immediate allegiance; but his move to the capital also made him part of the larger London School of History. In substance and style, this marked a sharp break from Oxford. The London school owed much more to the nineteenth-century German model of what a school of history should be. The emphasis was squarely on professionalism rather than donnish inspiration: students were to be trained, not encouraged simply to graze in the great libraries. Research students had long been expected to serve their apprenticeships by writing a Ph.D., something that was still regarded as a bizarre Teutonic notion in many Oxford circles at the time when Joll left. The Institute of Historical Research, as the sternly Rankean name suggests, conveyed the message that good writing was all very well, but the footnotes had to come first. In these and other ways, James Joll was entering a different world — although the fact that his Oxford years had been spent at St Antony's probably made the contrast less stark than it would otherwise have been. During the fourteen years he spent at London University, before taking early retirement in 1981, Joll succeeded in combining the best from both systems. Thoroughly professional in his own habits and a very conscientious supervisor of dissertations, he happily never adopted the view that irony or elegant prose were suspect attributes.

One of the strongly German aspects of the London School of History was the power of the professor. Its hold was weakening in the 1960s, although there were still instances of junior lecturers who mowed the professor's lawn at the weekend. This was not James Joll's style: his instincts were strongly collegial, not hierarchical. Altogether more congenial were three other aspects of London: the importance attached to the history of ideas, a tradition of strength in international relations, and the high profile enjoyed by modern European history, represented by professors such as Douglas Johnson (France), R. F. Leslie (Poland) and Christopher Seton-Watson (Italy). Above all, Joll struck up a productive professional relationship with the German *émigré* historian, Francis Carsten, who had taught in London since the late 1940s and became Masaryk Professor of Central European History in 1961. For many years the two men taught a paper called 'Autocracy, Democracy, and Dictatorship', dealing with Germany from 1860 to 1945. It consistently proved to be one of the most popular 'optional papers' among history undergraduates. Joll and Carsten also ran an important research seminar on modern German history, which met in the School of Slavonic and East European Studies in Russell Square.

German history had always been important to Joll, from his post-war editorial work alongside Wheeler-Bennett to the pioneering essay on Walter Rathenau. In the 1960s he played a central role in introducing English-speaking readers to one of the most explosive debates in modern German history: the 'Fischer controversy' over the origins of the First World War. In 1961 the Hamburg historian Fritz Fischer published a book called *Griff nach der Weltmacht*. Most of the text documented the consistent expansion of German aims in 1914–18; but the opening chapters dealt with the background to the outbreak of war, a subject the author returned to in a second book on the years 1911–14, *Krieg der Illusionen*. Fischer argued that the German role during the July Crisis of 1914 had been more aggressive and intransigent than generally assumed, and he questioned the distinction between 'good Germans' such as Chancellor Bethmann-Hollweg, and 'bad Germans' in the High Command and on the Pan-German radical right. These claims alone would have guaranteed the book a stormy reception within the conservative German historical profession of the early 1960s. What ensured controversy, and made the Fischer debate a symbolic landmark in post-war German historiography, were two further arguments in his book. First, he explicitly suggested lines of continuity between German aims in the two world wars, thus antagonising the majority of his fellow German historians, who preferred to see Hitler as an aberration. Secondly, he pointed to the role played by economic interests in pre-1914 Germany, emphasising the contribution he believed German domestic social and political instability had made to the outbreak of war. The hostility that Fischer and his mainly younger supporters faced in the Federal Republic was immense, and it came in political as well as scholarly form. Not until the 1980s, when the *Historikerstreit* broke out, was there to be an historical controversy of comparable dimensions.

For many English observers at the time, it might not have been automatically apparent why Fischer's arguments aroused such a heated response. After all, A. J. P. Taylor's almost contemporaneous book on the origins of the Second World War also drew lines of continuity between German foreign policy in the 1930s and earlier.[15] Taylor, moreover, had long been arguing that the 'good Germans', however well-meaning, had never amounted to very much. James Joll's great service was to show the significance of Fischer's work within the German context, and to place it more generally within the twists and turns of First World War historiography. In 1966 he wrote an article on Fritz Fischer and his critics for *Past and Present*; the following year he contributed a sympathetic but not uncritical introduction to the English edition of Fischer's book.[16]

In April of the following year, Joll made a direct and very important contribution to debate over the origins of the war in his inaugural lecture at the LSE: *1914: The Unspoken Assumptions*.[17] It is a little masterpiece of subtle, wide-ranging reflection. Joll suggests that a key reason for continued interest in the events of July 1914 was 'the discrepancy between the importance of the events themselves and of their consequences and the ordinariness of most of the politicians and generals making the key decisions'.[18] These were men caught up in a grave crisis: uncertain and fatalistic, they fell back on instinctive reactions, traditions and modes of thought. To understand their motives, it was necessary to uncover their unspoken assumptions, the things that 'went without saying'.[19] W. N. Medlicott, the previous incumbent of the Stevenson Chair, had remarked in his own inaugural lecture of 1955 on the limitations of the purely diplomatic documentary record. Joll went further. Not only were there actors who did not appear in that record: the words of those who did appear were neither transparent nor self-evident. What tone did they use? Did they express regret, relief, surprise?

This warning against a literal-minded reading of the diplomatic record no doubt carried more authority coming from a historian who had demonstrated his own expertise at sorting out documentary evidence. Certainly it was salutary. In 1961, for example, Ronald Robinson and John Gallagher had enjoyed great success with a book that claimed to

[15] A. J. P. Taylor, *The Origins of the Second World War* (London, 1961).
[16] 'The 1914 Debate Continues: Fritz Fischer and his Critics', *Past and Present*, 34 (1966), reprinted in H. W. Koch (ed.), *The Origins of the First World War* (London, 1972); F. Fischer, *Germany's Aims in the First World War* (London, 1967).
[17] London, 1968.
[18] *The Unspoken Assumptions*, p. 5.
[19] Ibid. p. 6.

have located 'the official mind of imperialism'. Whatever revisionist
virtues *Africa and the Victorians* might have possessed, however, it
rested methodologically on the shaky assumption that decision-makers
said what they meant and meant what they said.[20] Joll, a man of good
sense, did not subscribe to this kind of common sense. In the inaugural
lecture he illustrates his concern about documentary fetishism with
some remarks on that other *succès d'estime* of 1961, Fritz Fischer's
Griff nach der Weltmacht. He points out that our view of the notorious
'September Programme', a prime exhibit in Fischer's case, cannot rest
on the contents of the memorandum alone, but on 'our general view of
the mentality, the *Weltanschauung*, of the German leaders'.[21] While
many of Fischer's German critics reacted (or over-reacted) unhelpfully
to his arguments, Joll's point is one that would now be widely accepted
by historians at different points on the historiographical spectrum.
Fischer's first book was a great landmark work; but his claims are
potentially undermined — ironically, given the politics of the controversy — by a conservative literal-mindedness in reading evidence that
plays down context, overlooks nuance and sometimes comes close to
presenting a 600-page shopping list of German 'war aims'.

Historians should aim to reconstruct the presuppositions, the 'ideological furniture', of those charged with making decisions in 1914, says
Joll. But how? He has thoughtful, if ultimately agnostic observations
about incorporating psychology and 'economic factors' into our
accounts. In some of the most original passages of the lecture, he
then turns to the values and moral codes that politicians had absorbed
in their youth. So, for example, we shall better understand Sir Edward
Grey's schoolboy sense of honour if we understand that he always
remained a 'high-principled, slightly priggish Wykehamist' (a gentle
side-swipe at his old school).[22] The second half of the lecture expands
deftly on this theme. Educational systems, the influence of vulgar–
Darwinist and distorted Nietzschean ideas, the varieties of anxiety
and hope with which Europeans of the *belle époque* contemplated the
prospect of war — all feature in an elegantly constructed case for the
study of mentalities. The wide range of reference is characteristic of
Joll: Hegel and Bergson rub shoulders with British diplomatic histor-

[20] Ronald Robinson and John Gallagher with Alice Denny, *Africa and the Victorians: The
Official Mind of Imperialism* (London, 1961).
[21] *The Unspoken Assumptions*, p. 8.
[22] Ibid., p. 12.

ians, Sir Joshua Reynolds and Alban Berg are as integral to the argument as political memoirs. Joll's title, 'The Unspoken Assumptions',
has become a part of the historical vocabulary, like 'the enormous
condescension' of posterity (E. P. Thompson), 'the invention of tradition' (Eric Hobsbawm and Terence Ranger), or 'imagined communities' (Benedict Anderson). Like those other happy phrases, it has
been worn smooth by repetition; but it first gained currency by pinning
down an important omission, or limitation, in prevailing ways of looking at its subject. Joll believed passionately that the study of international relations should not be wilfully self-limiting. 'What we call
International History must in fact embrace all kinds of history', he
argued, for 'any attempt to insist on a too rigid departmental division
of historical studies into economic history, diplomatic history, military
history, art history, and so on, must lead to an impoverishment of our
historical understanding.'[23] Outstanding international historians of a
later generation, including Akira Iriye and Paul Kennedy, have shown
what can be gained from broadening the scope of the subject in some of
the directions so eloquently mapped out by James Joll.

Joll's inaugural lecture ranged over the whole of Europe for its
examples, but the focus was on one particular crisis. A year later, he
offered a larger, synoptic view of European history in the 1969 Mon-
tague Burton Lecture on International Relations at the University of
Leeds.[24] Joll was already working on his next book, which was to be a
general history of modern Europe, and in the lecture we can see him
trying out some of his ideas. He approaches the subject at three levels.
The first is the very long-term. Joll gives us a striking broad-brush
account of how 'Europe' might be defined, beginning with a discussion
of its porous borders (the Atlantic, the Urals, the Mediterranean), then
turning from geography to common history: the legacy of the Roman
Empire, Christianity, the scientific revolution and the Enlightenment.
This sets the stage for the second level, which concerns Europe from
roughly the mid-nineteenth century to the mid-twentieth century. Joll
sets out the forces that offered potential for co-operation and integration
(common ideas and institutions, industrial technology and free trade,
organisations like the International Red Cross), and shows how they

---

[23] Ibid., p. 24.
[24] *Europe: A Historian's View* (Leeds, 1969). From the same period, see also 'Europe
Supreme', in J. M. Roberts (ed.), *Europe in the Twentieth Century*, vol. 1 (London, 1970),
and 'The Decline of Europe', *International Affairs* (Special Anniversary Issue, 1970).

were outweighed by the nationalist and imperialist rivalries that culminated in the world wars of the twentieth century, leading in turn to the post-1945 division of Europe. Over the same period, as he notes, Europe's place in the world also shrank as the material and ideological weapons of imperialists were appropriated by non-European peoples seeking their independence. The third and final level of the lecture, with which Joll begins and ends, addresses the issues facing Europe at the end of the 1960s: the crushing of the hopes carried by the 'Prague spring', the prospects for unification within (Western) Europe, the emergence of renewed nationalist sentiment among small European nations such as the Basques, Bretons and Scots.

The Burton Lecture suggests the depth of Joll's erudition, as well as his deft handling of potentially overwhelming material. He belonged to a generation that thought and wrote in ambitiously large terms. Many of the themes sounded in his 1969 lecture were also the themes of prominent contemporaries or near-contemporaries such as Geoffrey Barraclough, E. H. Carr and Eric Hobsbawm. But there is, one feels, a difference in tone. Joll seems more pessimistic, not just in the rather sombre, edgy remarks with which the lecture ends, but in the larger lament for a lost liberal Europe.

In 1973, James Joll produced a full-scale interpretation of modern European history. *Europe since 1870: An International History* shows him at his best.[25] Perhaps only those who have written a general history will fully appreciate the skill that has been deployed in selecting and organising material. Joll opted for thematic chapters (only two out of fifteen carry dates), but these are not narrow 'subject chapters' that divide the world into politics, economics, society, the arts, and so on. Instead, wherever possible, these strands have been interwoven, so that we gain a stronger understanding than we do from most general histories of the connections between, say, industrialisation and culture, or politics and ideas. In several respects Joll has made his own task even harder by eschewing some of the techniques that can spread the weight of a long text: grouping chapters into overarching sections, or lining up the arguments in the manner favoured by some historians ('seventhly . . . '). The formal structure of the book is very light. Its success as a continuous narrative incorporating analytical themes therefore rests on two things: the wonderfully skilled handling of juxtapositions from one subject to the next, and the sheer quality of the writing. The second of

[25] London, 1973; reprinted in Pelican Books, 1976.

these virtues comes as no surprise, although perhaps in one sense it
should: this is the work of a highly accomplished essayist sustained
over almost five hundred pages. To give just one example of many, this
is Joll's comment on Armistice Day 1918: 'The victorious powers did
not yet count the cost of their victory and the defeated did not yet
believe the extent of their defeat'.[26] As for the handling of material,
consider the opening chapter. Joll begins vividly with the Franco–
Prussian War, then tracks through the great powers in turn to illustrate
not only 'The New Balance of Power', but the main elements of the
domestic order in Europe; a brief consideration of two smaller countries — Belgium and Spain — then allows him to point up contrasting
paths of social and political development in the later nineteenth century.
Just twenty-five pages, and he has set the scene, conveyed basic
information, introduced leading figures, and established central lines
of argument. Only once does Joll's touch seemingly desert him. The
chapter on Europe after 1945 is surprisingly boneless, a reminder of the
dangers that stalk any general account — and of the unobtrusive mastery that otherwise gives *Europe since 1870* its great coherence. The
word unobtrusive should be emphasised. There are some general works
of history that, as it were, leave their pipes and ducts exposed — the
literary equivalents of the Beaubourg. That was decidedly not James
Joll's style. Modernism, for which he had such a great and informed
enthusiasm in the arts, was not something he permitted to invade his
writing of history.

The pivot of the book is the First World War. Dealing with the pre-
1914 years, Joll's starting point is the free-trade liberalism that reached
its high point in the 1860s. He shows how it was variously challenged
by State intervention, socialism and imperialism. Two outstanding
chapters ('Liberalism and its Enemies', 'The Industrial Society and
its Critics') then consider the widespread cultural revolt of the late
nineteenth century, something treated by many historians of the
1960s and 1970s as a straightforward 'anti-modern' spasm, but permitted its full complexity by Joll. He brings these threads together in his
treatment of the war ('The European Crisis') and its aftermath; and this
sets up a discussion of cultural ferment, international instability and the
struggle betwen democracy, Communism and Fascism that structure his
account of the 1920s and 1930s.

Two points stand out, I think, when it comes to the architecture of

---

[26] *Europe since 1870*, p. 239.

the book. The first is that, while Joll clearly (and with good reason) sees the First World War as a genuine caesura in European history (and in Europe's relations with the non-European world), the moral centre of his book is the period that straddles the conflict — roughly, the years from the 1880s to the late 1920s, the era of electrification and the cinema, vastly expanded bureaucracies and unprecedented political mobilisation, new kinds of urban living and revolutionary experimentation in the arts. *This*, the period of classic modernity, is what Joll writes about with incomparable insight. Secondly, the real culmination of the book is (again, with good reason) Hitler's War and his defeat. What the author has to say about the years after 1945 is well-informed and often shrewd, but one feels that he is less engaged than in the earlier parts of the book. Joll the citizen was clearly not at all indifferent to the events he lived through as a mature man; but we sense that Joll the historian has lost some of the intellectual energy apparent earlier in the work. He is respectful towards the Marshall Plan; the Coal and Steel Community is duly noted; but it comes as no surprise that Apollinaire figures more often in the text than Adenauer.

As it happens, Dada also receives more mentions than the Dawes Plan. But the book does not skimp on industrialisation, nor on the links between the economy and changes in both political and cultural spheres, on which Joll is very good. More obviously neglected are subjects that had, by the 1970s, become typical of a still optimistic, expanding social history — population, the family, social mobility, diet, crime. The book has seven maps, but no tables. Joll himself, writing in the introduction about the space he gives to individuals rather than 'vast global movements', notes drily: 'If this seems old-fashioned, then this is old-fashioned history.'[27] Except, of course, that it isn't. In one respect it is a very new-fashioned history. Joll is much more concerned with the city than the country, with workers than peasants, with bourgeois sophisticates than aristocratic primitives. It is striking that rural society hardly ever appears directly in these pages. Instead it keeps coming into view as a political or cultural construct: Tolstoy's idealised peasants, the blood-and-soil fantasy of German racialists, Robert Blatchford's *Merrie England*. Rural Europe, aristocratic Europe, pious and clerical Europe — these, too, have a smaller place in Joll's account than one might expect. It is notable that very little time is wasted on 'clerico-Fascism' or the authoritarian inter-war regimes in many of the small

[27] Ibid., p. xii.

(and some not so small) European countries. Salazar is not mentioned; even the domestic origins of the Spanish Civil War receive little attention compared with the impact of the struggle on international politics and the European imagination, so that John Cornford, Julian Bell and George Orwell appear in the text, but Gil Robles does not.

James Joll warms much more to the shock of the new than the persistence of the old. At one point he quotes one of his favourites, the Russian poet Vladimir Mayakovsky: 'After seeing electricity, I lost interest in nature. Not up to date enough.'[28] Joll himself certainly did not 'lose interest' in nature. Nor was he a vulgar progress-monger: one of the virtues of his 'old-fashioned' approach is that it side-steps the more tiresome aspects of the 'modernisation theory' fashionable when he was writing. He respects the quirks of his characters and the ironies of history. As the pessimistic note sounded in his 'Epilogue' suggests, he is no uncritical admirer of the streamlined, modern materialist world. What unlocks his enthusiasm is not the future in 1973, but yesterday's future. He was an intellectual wedded to Europe in the age of classical modernity from 1880 to 1930. And, for all its impressive fair-mindedness and balance, *Europe since 1870* is a book that—like all major books—tells us more about its author than he perhaps knew, or intended.

James Joll continued to revisit subjects on which he had written earlier in his career. In the 1960s he wrote on Walter Rathenau's relationship with the maverick journalist, Maximilian Harden, and contributed an introduction to the German edition of Rathenau's diaries.[29] Together with David Apter he edited *Anarchism Today* in 1970; the following year he wrote for an Einaudi Foundation volume on contemporary anarchism.[30] Italian political thought remained a subject of abiding interest: an important by-product of this was Joll's crisply perceptive book on another 'intellectual in politics', the Italian Marxist Antonio Gramsci, for the Fontana Modern Masters series.[31]

---

[28] Ibid., p. 305.

[29] 'Rathenau and Harden: A Footnote to the History of Wilhelmine Germany', in M. Gilbert (ed.), *A Century of Conflict 1850–1950: Essays for A. J. P. Taylor* (London, 1966); W. Rathenau, *Tagebuch 1907–1922*. Hrsg. und kommentiert von H. Pogge von Strandmann. Mit einem Beitrag von James Joll und einem Geleitwort von Fritz Fischer (Düsseldorf, 1967).

[30] Apter and Joll, *Anarchism Today* (London, 1970), which includes Joll's own article, 'Anarchism—A Living Tradition', also published in *Government and Opposition*, v, 4 (1970); 'Anarchism between Communism and Anarchism', in *Anarchici e Anarchia nel Mondo Contemporaneo* (Turin, 1971).

[31] *Gramsci* (Glasgow, 1977).

It was, however, the origins of the First World War that he returned to most often during these years, a subject on which Joll was also helping to shape the direction of new research through the graduate students he supervised. When Imanuel Geiss and Bernd-Jürgen Wendt put together a Festschrift for Fritz Fischer in 1973, he contributed an article on 'The English, Friedrich Nietzsche and the First World War'.[32] (Nietzsche, like Croce, was a recurring point of reference throughout Joll's writings.) Then, in 1978, he took stock of the debate — and more — in a lecture at the newly-opened German Historical Institute, London.[33] 'War Guilt 1914: A Continuing Controversy' surveys the vicissitudes of the debate from the 1920s to the 1960s, before coming to the crux of the lecture: the growing importance since the 1960s of interpretations that emphasised the 'primacy of domestic policy' in the coming of war. Joll, always generous in acknowledging the work of others, points to the arguments of post-Fischer historians such as Volker Berghahn, Wolfgang J. Mommsen, Hartmut Pogge von Strandmann, and Peter-Christian Witt. They had made a fairly convincing case for the *Primat der Innenpolitik* in the German case, suggests Joll; but what about the domestic circumstances of the other powers on the eve of war? He then offers a perceptive, sure-footed discussion of the problems facing two of them in 1914: Britain and France. The following year saw the publication of a further article on the decision-makers in 1914 and their 'freedom to choose', in a Festschrift for his mentor and friend, Isaiah Berlin.[34]

Fittingly, James Joll's last book dealt with the causes of the conflict. *The Origins of the First World War* was commissioned for the Longman 'Origins of Modern Wars' series.[35] Published in 1984, it was already being reprinted for the fourth time the following year. To employ a viticultural term that its author might have appreciated, this was a sweet, late harvest — a *Trockenbeerenauslese*. The book is, as Charles Maier has rightly called it, a 'masterly synthesis'.[36] Twelve years on, it remains the first work that one would recommend to undergraduates

[32] I. Geiss and B.-J. Wendt (eds), *Deutschland in der Weltpolitik des 19. und 20. Jahrhunderts* (Düsseldorf, 1973).
[33] P. Kluke and P. Alter (eds), *Aspekte der deutsch–britischen Beziehungen im Laufe der Jahrhunderte* (Stuttgart, 1978).
[34] 'Politicians and the Freedom to Choose: The Case of 1914', in Alan Ryan (ed.), *The Idea of Freedom: Essays in Honour of Isaiah Berlin* (Oxford, 1979).
[35] London, 1984.
[36] *New York Times*, 17 July 1994.

fresh to the subject, while resembling the routine textbook only in its 200-page length. It is hard to think of another historian who could have explicated better the unstable brew of European politics on the eve of war: German ambitions, Austrian fears, French grievances, Russian expansionism, British anxieties. Joll begins with the July Crisis, before showing, in a series of superbly judged chapters, how the decision-makers of 1914 were constrained by their own previous decisions and the larger forces within which they operated — the alliance system, strategic plans and armament programmes, domestic pressures, conflicting economic interests and imperial rivalries. A final chapter on the 'mood of 1914' returns to a favourite theme, surveying the assumptions of politicians and military men, but looking also at popular attitudes as they revealed themselves in invasion-scare novels and school-books, youth movements and navy leagues.

And the conclusion? On the debate about the German responsibility for the war, Joll adopts what might be called a modified version of the Fischer view. Germany is shown as a prime mover, but the strong version of a pre-emptive strike argument is rejected, and Joll notes the importance of Austrian 'pull' as well as German 'push' in the final crisis. On the larger question of how we should combine the different levels of long-term analysis with the immediate causes of the war, Joll suggests that we probably have to resign ourselves 'to a kind of two-tier history'.[37] What we should *not* do is signalled clearly enough. No very satisfying explanation is likely to come, argues Joll, from attempts to quantify the causes of the war — or wars — by the *devotees* of conflict resolution and crisis management. (He is, however, predictably more civil towards such efforts than the more hard-faced exponents of International Relations, or 'IR', often are towards the work of hopelessly wishy-washy, humanistic historians.) On the other hand, Joll rejects those — especially English historians — who believe that only the immediate actions of politicians and the short-term reasons for them can be discovered. Between the neo-positivism of the computer-programmers and the blinkered empiricists, Joll makes a plea for something that is more historical than the former, more ambitious than the latter. And that prompts a fine rhetorical trope at the end of the book. In his introduction, noting the problem of combining so many different kinds of explanation, Joll had allowed himself the ironic observation that 'ideally, no doubt, an account of the causes of the First World War

---

[37] *Origins of the First World War*, p. 205.

would lead to a moment of profound Hegelian insight in which everything in the world would be related to everything else and all the connections and patterns would become clear'. Two hundred pages later, he returns to Hegel from a rather different angle. After mildly scolding those who see history as simply one damn decision after another, he continues: 'But many of us are sufficiently Hegelian, if not Marxist, to want to try to bring into our explanations the moral values of a society, the *Zeitgeist*, as well as the economic interests of the participants both as individuals and as members of a class'.[38] This is a final grace-note in a book containing many. It closes the circle opened by the earlier reference to Hegel, and offers us a credo that is no less firm for being gently expressed.

In the same year that *The Origins of the First World War* appeared, James Joll delivered the Annual Lecture of the German Historical Institute London.[39] The lecture discussed historians and national views of the past in Britain and Germany, a subject with contemporary resonance at a time when a core curriculum and the national 'heritage' were being debated in Britain, and 'identity' was becoming a central theme in West Germany. There was also appropriateness in the fact that Joll was invited to give the lecture. He had been one of the British historians who participated in the Anglo–German group of historians established in 1968, the initiative that paved the way for the German Historical Institute. He was subsequently one of the two British scholars (Eleanora Carus-Wilson was the other) who gave lectures at the Institute's formal opening in November 1976.[40] Joll's high standing in the scholarly world was honoured in other ways. In 1977 he was elected a Fellow of the British Academy. Joll twice spent a year at the Princeton Institute for Advanced Study, and was also visiting professor at Stanford, Iowa and Sydney. Not least, he accepted many invitations to deliver distinguished named lectures, including the Stevenson Memorial Lecture, the Martin Wight Memorial Lecture, and the first Richard Storry Memorial Lecture.[41]

---

[38] Ibid., pp. 5, 205.

[39] *National Histories and National Historians: Some German and English Views of the Past*, 1984 Annual Lecture of the German Historical Institute (London, 1985).

[40] See *Aspekte der deutsch–britischen Beziehungen*.

[41] 'The Ideal and the Real: Changing Concepts of the International System 1815–1982', The 30th Stevenson Memorial Lecture, *International Affairs*, 58 (Spring 1982); 'Two prophets of the twentieth century: Spengler and Toynbee', 1984 Martin Wight Memorial Lecture, *Review of International Studies*, 11 (1985); 'Interpreting Japan', 1st Richard Storry Memorial Lecture, St Antony's College, Oxford (1987).

Over the years, James Joll contributed to a variety of Festschriften. In addition to those already mentioned, for Fritz Fischer and Isaiah Berlin, he wrote essays for volumes honouring (or, in one case, commemorating) Leonard Montefiore, Hans Rothfels, A. J. P. Taylor, Francis Carsten and Federico Chabod — a strikingly diverse company.[42] In 1984, Joll was himself the recipient of a Festschrift bearing the apt title *Ideas into Politics*.[43] The volume gives some indication of the range of subjects pursued by Joll's pupils. There are articles on German workers, the French Right, the British Foreign Office and Italian Fascism; the links between economics and politics are well represented; but so are political ideas, international relations and cultural modernism. What is also striking about this collection is the distinction of its contributors, men and women of five different nationalities who taught in universities throughout the world.

Nothing could have been more misleading (or more characteristically modest) than James Joll's remark in the introduction to *Europe since 1870* that he had observed four decades of European history 'from the comparative safety and detachment of an English middle-class life'.[44] Joll prized a cultivated domesticity very highly, but he was the least insular of men. Even before the war, which moulded his life as it did the lives of so many contemporaries, his natural instincts were strongly anti-insular. He moved easily in European scholarly and intellectual circles, and lectured also in Australia, the Americas and the Far East. Travel, notoriously, can narrow the mind; but not in Joll's case. His generous, internationalist cast of mind is in evidence throughout his work, especially perhaps the lectures and essays at which he excelled. It shows in the subjects he wrote about, and in the way he wrote about them. When Joll commemorated his former colleague Richard Storry in 1987 with a lecture on 'Interpreting Japan', he was returning to a subject he had first broached nearly a quarter of a century earlier.[45]

---

[42] 'Germany and the Spanish Civil War', in M. Beloff (ed.), *On the Track of Tyranny: Essays presented to Leonard G. Montefiore* (London, 1960); 'The Historian and the Contemporary World', *Geschichte und Gegenwartsbewusstsein: Festschrift für Hans Rothfels zum 70. Geburtstag* (Göttingen, 1963); 'Rathenau and Harden', in Gilbert (ed.), *A Century of Conflict 1850–1950: Essays for A. J. P. Taylor* (see n. 29 above); 'Walter Rathenau — Intellectual or Industrialist?', in V. R. Berghahn and M. Kitchen (eds), *Germany in the Age of Total War: Essays in Honour of Francis Carsten* (London, 1981); 'Socialism between Peace, War and Revolution', in S. Bertelli (ed.), *Per Federico Chabod (1901–1960): II. Equilibrio Europea e Espansione Coloniale* (Perugia, 1980–1).

[43] *Ideas into Politics: Aspects of European History 1880–1950*, ed. R. J. Bullen, H. Pogge von Strandmann and A. B. Polonsky (London, 1984).

[44] *Europe since 1870*, p. xii.

[45] 'Japan — Asian State or Western Society', *Listener*, 31 December 1964.

Indeed, this wide interest in extra-European as well as European societies and cultures was already apparent in his essays during the 1950s,
where, alongside articles on Georges Sorel and Heinrich von
Treitschke, we find occasional pieces on the Middle East and Mexico.[46]

If Joll's formal subject-matter was broad, so too was his understanding of what constituted a historical source. His inaugural lecture
had urged historians not just to read behind the documentary record, but
to take music, literature and painting seriously. It was something he
himself did supremely well. Joll was also aware that the range of
possible historical sources is much wider still. As he observed in his
1984 lecture at the German Historical Institute:

> For most ordinary people their view of the past is a random and fragmentary
> one, made up of family recollections, war memorials, television pro-
> grammes, holiday visits to castles and palaces, the associations of objects
> in their homes — a shell case from the First World War, or — especially for
> the British — a brass tray from India, a wooden African tool brought home
> by an uncle who had served in the colonies — a whole range of disconnected
> and often trivial experiences out of which it is very hard to construct any
> sense of a continuous history.[47]

Joll welcomed the study of popular attitudes by professional historians.
Like the French historian of the First World War, Marc Ferro, he was
especially interested in film as a source for modern history, and served
as chairman of the Inter-University History Film Consortium. This cut
two ways, for film — like radio talks and popular writing — was also a
means of communicating history to a broader audience. Joll directed
and narrated the Film Consortium's film *Fascism*, just as he broadcast
on BBC radio and wrote for non-specialist publications such as *History
Today*. It was important, he believed, that historians 'not treat history
just as a private kaleidoscope' or 'try to escape the responsibility of
forming the historical awareness of a wider public'.[48]

In American universities the term 'good citizen' is used to denote
the person who takes teaching, administration and the small, thankless
tasks of academic life seriously. James Joll was an exemplary citizen in
this sense. He was also a well-informed and engaged citizen in the more
conventional sense. His sympathies were always broadly on the left

---

[46] 'Georges Sorel: The Unorthodox Marxist', *Listener*, 3 January 1952; 'Treitschke and the
Prussian Legend', *History Today*, March 1952; 'Arabs and Jews: the Onlooker's Dilemma',
Listener, 5 June 1952; 'A Historian in Mexico', *Listener*, 9 April 1959.
[47] 'National Histories and National Historians', p. 3.
[48] Ibid., p. 23.

(although he disliked the dogmatic or trendy), and he was saddened by what he perceived as the mean-spirited mentality in Britain during the last years of his life. Joll's beliefs were firmly held, but by temperament he was not someone to posture or wear his heart on his sleeve. On two occasions, however, his strong sense of moral duty led him to take a course of action that cut against the grain of his natural reserve. In 1956, his deeply held feelings over Suez caused him to lead a public protest by Oxford colleagues against the invasion. Then, in 1979, he gave shelter to his old friend and John Golding's colleague at the Courtauld Institute, Anthony Blunt, after Blunt had been named in the Commons as a former Soviet spy. This exposed him to widespread vilification in the press. I can remember telephoning him shortly after the story broke, to say how much I admired his personal act of courage and loyalty. In retrospect it is remarkable that he was answering calls; but, characteristically, he was. And it was equally in character that, after thanking me, he managed to find dry humour in the situation by remarking that not all of his callers had expressed the same feelings.

I first met James Joll in the spring of 1976. He responded graciously to the offprint of an article I had sent him, and invited me to give a paper to his research seminar with Francis Carsten. There, and over dinner in Bertorellis, I first experienced his great warmth and interest in others. Later that year I moved to a post in London, and we became colleagues. We examined together, and met at seminars and academic occasions hosted by the German Historical Institute and the newly-founded German History Society (of which he was a loyal supporter). We also became personal friends. James encouraged and helped me in countless small ways; he was a mentor and a model of academic integrity. I have never met a kinder man in university life. Short in stature, he had a distinctive way of rocking slightly on his feet as he talked; and his talk managed to be, at once, enthusiastic and diffident. James was patient and tolerant, always looking for the virtues in the most unlikely person or the most unpromising piece of work. It required practice at reading between the lines to discern when a review of his was, in fact, expressing disapprobation. I can recall seeing him angry on only one occasion, when we happened to be sitting next to each other while David Irving presented his 'revisionist' views on Hitler during a panel discussion at the German Historical Institute. It was, I think, not just the arguments that James found disagreeable, but the self-dramatising, game-playing way in which they were presented. Although the least pompous of men, James took academic and intellectual life seriously, and had his own gentle way of intimating what he felt about self-regard or academic bullying. He was a warm, generous, very modest man, good-humoured and often funny, with a gift for friendship. 'History, like art, offers us an opportunity to enlarge our experience,' he wrote on one occasion.[49] He enlarged ours, not just through his work, but through his largeness of mind and goodness as a person.

DAVID BLACKBOURN
Harvard University

---

[49] *Europe since 1870*, p. xii.

GEORGE SAYLES   *Painting by M. G. A. Sayles*

Proceedings of the British Academy, **90**, 441–463

George Osborne Sayles
1901–1994

GEORGE OSBORNE SAYLES was born on 20 April 1901 at Unstone in Derbyshire. His father, Larret Pearson Sayles, who had been born in 1867 at Rawmarsh in Yorkshire, had moved to Glasgow and become a dissenting minister by the time of his marriage in 1890. He had then studied theology at the Free Church College in Glasgow between 1890 and 1894. By the time of George's birth he was working as a commercial traveller, though later that same year he was ordained a deacon in the Church of England and became a curate at Whittington in Derbyshire, close to Unstone. In 1902 he was ordained a priest and he went on to hold a second Derbyshire curacy at Heanor (from 1906 onwards), before getting his own parish of Awsworth in Nottinghamshire in 1910. George's mother Margaret, the daughter of Robert Brown, was five years older than his father. She came from Lanark and had been a schoolteacher prior to their marriage. George was the sixth of seven children, though only four survived infancy. His elder brother Clifford and George were the only boys. George was effectively the youngest child of the family as his younger sister was one of those who died. He probably attended a local primary school before transferring to Ilkeston County Secondary School in 1914. He was fortunate to have been just young enough not to be called up for service in the First World War. He did, however, join the Officer Cadet Training Unit of the local Sherwood Foresters during the last year of the war and, had it continued, would probably have found himself at the front.

In 1920 he became a student at the University of Glasgow, having been awarded an open bursary to study there. This provided him with financial support for three out of the four years which an Arts degree takes to complete in Scottish universities. Initially, he seems to have intended to read French. During his first year, however, he was required to study two other subjects as well and chose Latin and Constitutional Law and History. It is quite possible that he chose the latter for no better reason than that classes in it lasted for only two terms. He seems, however, to have discovered in consequence that he enjoyed history and performed well in it and in his second year it was Honours History rather than French for which he opted. He completed his undergraduate career in only three years, effectively doing two years work in his final year. This was probably for financial reasons. His father's stipend was not large and there was probably no question of his supporting George for a fourth year at university. It did not prevent him gaining First Class Honours in History in 1923.

As an undergraduate, Sayles had been taught by Professor Dudley Julius Medley (1861–1953), who had been a lecturer and then a tutor at Keble College, Oxford before being appointed to the relatively new Chair in History and Law at Glasgow in 1899. Medley was the author of a successful single volume undergraduate textbook on English constitutional history.[1] It was apparently intended as a replacement for the three volume *Constitutional History* of Bishop Stubbs, both for Oxford students and for students at those other universities where English Constitutional History was studied. However, it differed significantly from the older work not only in its length but also in its chronological range. It was only a single volume rather than three, and it brought the story of the British Constitution much closer to the present than did the work of Bishop Stubbs, which went no further than the end of the Middle Ages. Medley also produced a replacement for Stubbs's *Select Charters*.[2] Again, Medley's volume covered a much longer period and in the second edition (of 1926) he even included the 1920 Government of Ireland Act and extracts from the Irish Free State Constitution of 1922. He also made far greater concessions to the frailty of the twentieth-century undergraduate by translating documents in Latin as well as those in French. Medley was a formative influence on the young

---

[1] D. J. Medley, *A Student's Manual of English Constitutional History*. The first edition appeared in 1894 and the final (sixth) edition in 1925.

[2] D. J. Medley, *Original Illustrations of English Constitutional History*. The first edition appeared in 1910 and a second edition in 1926.

Sayles. By the time Sayles studied with him, a major illness had turned Medley into an indifferent lecturer but it was probably nonetheless from his lectures as well as from his books that Sayles learned of Maitland and his work on the English medieval parliament and it was thus Medley who inspired him with two of his lasting enthusiasms. Medley was also probably responsible for setting the subject of the Ewing prize essay in 1922. Sayles was awarded the essay medal in 1923 for his paper on 'The King's Council in English History'. Forty years later he was himself to acknowledge that it had been his work on this essay that had 'ultimately determined the course of my future historical research':[3] here again, then, it was Medley who played a crucial part in determining the future direction of Sayles's historical work.

Even before taking his Finals, Sayles had decided that he wanted to do research in English medieval history and had successfully applied for a Carnegie Research Fellowship to enable him to travel to London for this purpose. His plan was to pursue his interest in the king's council in medieval England and he already knew that what he wanted to investigate was the role of the council in parliament. He had probably already read A. F. Pollard's *The Evolution of Parliament*, which had been published in 1920. In it Pollard had written of the unpublished King's Bench plea rolls of the reign of Edward I in terms that suggested they merited detailed investigation for the light they were likely to shed on the role of the king's council in the administration of justice in Edwardian parliaments.[4] Sayles came to London in the autumn of 1923 to follow up this suggestion. Pollard, who had become Director of the newly established Institute of Historical Research in 1921, was not himself a medievalist but was willing to supervise Sayles's research and delighted to have his first research pupil from a Scottish university at the new Institute. Sayles received a basic grounding in the techniques necessary for conducting research in medieval records from Hubert Hall, attending the classes he held in King's College London on Palaeography, Diplomatic and Historical Sources. He also received an introduction to the King's Bench rolls themselves from Ernest Jacob, who was then working on plea rolls of a slightly earlier period in connection with his first book, *Studies in the Period of Baronial Reform and Rebellion*, which was to be published in 1925.

---

[3] Quotation from a typescript 'Statement' dated October 1962, compiled for the Institute of Advanced Legal Studies, London among his papers.
[4] A. F. Pollard, *The Evolution of Parliament* (London, 1920), p. 35.

Sayles spent only a single year in full-time research. In the autumn of 1924 he was offered a junior appointment back at Glasgow as an Assistant in the History Department, evidently an opportunity too good to miss and probably another turning-point in his early career which can be ascribed to Medley. He was promoted to a Lectureship in 1925 and to a Senior Lectureship in 1932. Despite his research interests, Sayles was not required, indeed not allowed, to teach any of the main courses in medieval history. These were taught by D. C. Douglas. His main teaching responsibilities lay instead in the field of Modern European History. He was, however, also permitted to teach one short course on medieval charters for the small number of Honours students and was sometimes given a chance to lecture Honours students on early British history. When he applied for a Chair at Aberystwyth in 1930 the Principal of Glasgow, R. S. Rait, described him as 'an effective and valued teacher', whose teaching had been 'greatly appreciated by his pupils'. It was shortly afterwards that he was approached to apply for a Chair in Medieval History at the University of Cairo. The salary and the status must have been tempting but Sayles declined the offer. Cairo was too far both from his family and from Chancery Lane.

Once he had begun teaching it was only during vacations that Sayles was able to continue research for his thesis. On his return to Glasgow, he had transferred to working on a Glasgow Ph.D. under the nominal supervision of his old undergraduate teacher and head of department, Medley. He was evidently still sanguine at this stage that the King's Bench rolls would contain the information he was seeking, for the title given to the projected thesis when it was approved by the Faculty of Arts in December 1924 was 'Parliamentary Institutions in the Reign of Edward I: A Preliminary Investigation based on the 'Coram Rege' Plea Rolls'. Sayles worked away steadily over the next eight years and he seems to have spent the greater part of each vacation in London, mainly at Chancery Lane. He did not find what Pollard had led him to expect. What he did, however, discover was much to shed light on the history and workings of the court of King's Bench in the reign of Edward I and more generally on the legal history of the period. He therefore decided to utilise this material for a thesis centred on the court of King's Bench instead. In April 1932 Sayles submitted his application for a doctorate (though by now it was for the grander D. Litt., rather than the Ph.D. for which he had originally registered) for a thesis on 'The Court of King's Bench under Edward I, with a selection of cases from the unprinted Plea Rolls' plus other (printed) papers. In June of that same year he was awarded his doctorate. It was this thesis that Sayles subsequently turned into the first three volumes of *Select Cases in the Court of King's Bench* which were published by the Selden Society in 1936, 1938 and 1939.[5] Any selection of enrolments from a series of rolls is personal. There are inevitably some enrolments which Sayles omits which another legal historian might have printed and enrolments which he prints which others might have omitted. In general, however, there is little to fault in selection, transcription or translation. Even more valuable are the introductions and appendices to these volumes. The introduction to volume I dealt mainly with the personnel of the court (its justices and officials and the professional lawyers who practised there) and in the appendices to the volume Sayles published the first accurate scholarly lists of the justices not just of the King's Bench but also of the Common Bench and for the reign of Edward II as well as that of Edward I. He also printed a wide range of supporting documentation from a variety of sources dealing with the topics discussed in the introduction. In the introduction to volume II Sayles looked in detail at the way the court worked: the jurisdiction it exercised, the way its processes worked and how cases were pleaded there as well as at the compilation of the plea rolls of the court which recorded all this. This remains the best general introduction to the way royal courts worked during the second half of the thirteenth century. The introduction to volume III was more diffuse, dealing with topics such as the application and interpretation of statutes and the position of the Crown when acting as a litigant, but it picks up much of wider legal interest in the cases printed in all three volumes. The skill with which the editing of these volumes was done is all the more impressive when one remembers that Sayles had become an expert on the court of King's Bench more by accident than by deliberate choice: indeed, he himself described the work which went into these volumes as 'begun largely in ignorance . . . continued in obstinacy and completed with relief'.[6]

His first interest was, and remained, the history of the English parliament during the Middle Ages. While working on King's Bench he was also working through other materials in the Public Record Office which might shed light on the history of parliament and of the king's council during the thirteenth and fourteenth centuries: indeed, his first two short articles in the *English Historical Review* and in the

---

[5] *Select Cases in the Court of King's Bench Under Edward I*, vols. I–III (Selden Society vols. lv, lvii, lviii).

[6] *Select Cases in the Court of King's Bench*, vol. I, p. vii.

Bulletin of the Institute of Historical Research, published in 1925 and
1926, printed parliamentary and conciliar material recently recovered
from unsorted Miscellanea at the Public Record Office.[7] Public Record
Office Miscellanea also supplied the material for another short article
he contributed to the *Scottish Historical Review* in 1927.[8] By then
Sayles had met the older scholar with whom his name is, and will
always be, inseparably linked, H. G. Richardson. The meeting took
place in the summer of 1927 in the Round Room of the Public Record
Office. Richardson shared Sayles's interest in the English medieval
parliament and was himself then preparing his classic paper for the
Royal Historical Society on the origins of parliament which was published in 1928. When their discussions indicated the closeness of their
views about parliamentary origins and the early history of parliament
they decided to pool their scholarly efforts in the field. Thus began a
partnership which was to last some forty years. Not long after Richardson's death, Sayles wrote a memoir of Richardson for the *Proceedings
of the British Academy*.[9] This is an invaluable, though inevitably one-
sided, source of information about their relationship. It seems clear
from this that Sayles had always found Richardson somewhat aloof
and distant, lacking small talk and without much personal charm.
Initially, however, Sayles had clearly been impressed by Richardson's
enthusiasm and energy, and believed that they would be able to achieve
great things together. In retrospect, Sayles also noted the obverse of this
same trait, Richardson's inability to stick at any one thing for long, 'the
constant danger that a new interest, a new path of investigation, would
divert his attention'. Sayles was also (in retrospect at least) embarrassed
by his collaborator's persistent willingness to enter into formal commitments for the production of scholarly volumes, rendered damaging only
by his equally recurrent failure to meet those commitments. The
memoir indicates that by then Sayles had discovered this to have
been a long-standing character flaw and applied not just to the volumes
which they had jointly undertaken but also to several other books which
Richardson had promised to produce long before they had met. He

---

[7] 'Representation of Cities and Boroughs in 1268', *English Historical Review*, xl (1925),
580–585; 'Parliamentary Representation in 1294, 1295 and 1307', *Bulletin of the Institute of
Historical Research*, iii (1926), 110–15.
[8] 'The Guardian of Scotland and a Parliament at Rutherglen in 1300', *Scottish Historical
Review*, xxiv (1927), 245–50.
[9] 'Henry Gerald Richardson, 1884–1974', *Proceedings of the British Academy*, 61 (1975),
pp. 497–521.

cannot have known this when they began their collaboration. In hindsight, Sayles also judged that one reason for this had been that Richardson had been too much of a perfectionist. Sayles remembered with evident exasperation that 'so often I urged him not to get it right but to get it written'. It is a reasonable guess (though it can be no more than this) that for this very reason much of what appeared under their joint names may in fact have been written, at least in rough draft, by Sayles but was then subjected to Richardson's detailed criticism. This was also evidently true of what appeared under Sayles's name alone for the prefaces to his volumes invariably thank Richardson for his invaluable criticism.

In the early years of their collaboration Richardson and Sayles were very productive. They published their first joint article in the *Bulletin of the Institute of Historical Research* in 1928.[10] In it they established the first list of meetings of parliament during the reign of Edward I to be based solely on what they considered to be the only kind of solid contemporary evidence, that of official records. From this they were able to demonstrate the probability that during the first half of the reign there had been a plan to hold regular twice-yearly sessions of parliament and this in turn supported their contention that already by the beginning of the reign parliament had taken recognisable institutional form. They also sounded for the first time one of the major themes which were constantly to recur in their joint work on the English parliament. This was the claim that the essence of parliament was a functional one, 'the dispensing of justice by the king or by someone who in a very special sense represents the king'.[11] Parliament might also legislate and consent to taxation and under Edward II it was to deal with an increasing admixture of political and diplomatic business. However, all these matters could be (and sometimes were) dealt with elsewhere and thus were never essential ingredients of its work. Although this article was originally envisaged as a single collaborative venture, by the time it was published it had become the first of three related joint articles published in the *Bulletin* during 1928 and 1929. The second provides a similar list of parliaments for the reign of Edward II.[12] It is only in the third article that they finally reached

---

[10] 'The Early Records of the English Parliaments: The English Parliaments of Edward I', *Bulletin of the Institute of Historical Research*, v (1928), 129–54.
[11] Ibid., 133.
[12] 'The Early Records of the English Parliaments: The English Parliaments of Edward II', *Bulletin of the Institute of Historical Research*, vi (1929), 71–88.

what was ostensibly the subject of all three articles, the records of parliament and more specifically the nature and origins of the so-called 'Exchequer series' of Parliament Rolls of the reigns of Edward I and Edward II.[13] In it they corrected Stubbs's erroneous assertion that these were journals of parliament and correctly characterised them as no more than a haphazard and incomplete series of files connected with proceedings before both council and parliament. They also insisted, more controversially, that the real history of parliament in this period was the history of parliamentary procedure and its development and of 'the expedition of matters of justice and administration' at parliament: how business came before parliament, how it was classified and by whom, the stages through which it passed, the groups which considered it. Even before this history had been written, however, they confidently predicted that 'the contributions of judges, ministers and clerks to the development of parliament' would be found to be 'out of all proportion greater than the contribution of any other body of men there represented regularly or intermittently' such as 'barons, knights or burgesses'.[14] In two further articles (published in the *Bulletin* in 1930 and 1931) they took the story of parliament as they saw it down to 1377: establishing a reliable list of parliaments for the reign of Edward III based on the official record of proceedings and on writs of summons and insisting, despite their own evidence to the contrary, that justice remained the primary function of parliament even in an era where petitions to the king's council or chancery outside parliament had largely replaced private petitions to parliament.[15] By the time these articles were published they had also taken up their own challenge of investigating not only the personnel involved in parliament but also how the later thirteenth- and fourteenth-century parliament functioned. The results were published in three articles in the *English Historical Review* in 1931 and 1932.[16] During this first period of collaboration they also published a number of other more specialised articles drawing attention

---

[13] 'The Early Records of the English Parliaments: The Exchequer Parliament Rolls and Other Documents', *Bulletin of the Institute of Historical Research*, vi (1929), 129–53.
[14] Ibid., 145.
[15] 'The Parliaments of Edward III', Parts I and II, *Bulletin of the Institute of Historical Research*, viii (1930), 65–77 and ix (1931), 1–18.
[16] 'The King's Ministers in Parliament, 1272–1307', *English Historical Review*, xlvi (1931), 529–550; 'The King's Ministers in Parliament, 1307–1327', *English Historical Review*, xlvii (1932), 194–203; 'The King's Ministers in Parliament, 1327–1377', *English Historical Review*, xlvii (1932), 377–397.

to materials relating to the parliamentary history of this period which one or other of them had come across in their researches.[17]

From early in their collaboration Sayles had seen that partnership as leading to the production not just of articles but also of a full-length book or books on the English medieval parliament. His original suggestion, made late in 1927, was for a book of documents relating to the working of the English parliament on the model of the *Textes relatifs à l'histoire du parlement* which Charles Langlois had produced to illustrate the workings of the *parlement* of Paris. Richardson cannot have been enthusiastic, for the idea was taken no further. In 1928 their joint plan was apparently for a book on parliament under Edward I and Edward II which was to incorporate material from the articles they were then publishing in the *Bulletin*. It may also have been intended from the first to incorporate the material which later went into the articles published in the *English Historical Review* on the royal officials involved in the running of parliament and on the evolution of the procedures of parliament. During 1928–9 Sayles obtained financial support for this volume from the Glasgow University Publication Fund and from the Carnegie Trust (the latter also promising support for a possible second volume) and by December 1929 he had also interested the Clarendon Press in publishing it. Shortly after this, however, these initial publishing plans were blown badly off course when the two collaborators became involved in Colonel Wedgwood's semi-official project for a 'History of Parliament'. Discussions with Wedgwood led to Richardson and Sayles signing a formal agreement to write the first volume of Wedgwood's *History of Parliament* in August 1933. This was to cover the period down to 1377, and with money from the Pilgrim Trust Richardson and Sayles established an office near Parliament Square in which their team of research assistants could work. It is, however, difficult to know why or how things ever got quite this far. It must quickly have become evident that Wedgwood and Richardson and Sayles had very different ideas about what such a volume should cover. Wedgwood knew that what he wanted were biographies of members of the House of Commons; Richardson and

---

[17] 'The Parliament of Carlisle, 1307 — Some New Documents', *English Historical Review*, xliii (1928), 425–37; 'The Provisions of Oxford: A Forgotten Document and Some Comments', *Bulletin of the John Rylands Library*, xvii (1933), 3–33; 'Parliamentary Documents from Formularies', *Bulletin of the Institute of Historical Research*, xi (1934), 147–62; 'The Parliament of Lincoln, 1316', *Bulletin of the Institute of Historical Research*, xii (1935), 105–107.

Sayles were equally clear that this was a woefully inadequate approach to the subject. They may have hoped to convince Wedgwood that any History of Parliament worthy of that name needed to be much more than a prosopography of members of one of its houses. If so, they failed. In February 1935 they cancelled their agreement. By then, however, the original impetus for producing their own volume on the history of parliament in the thirteenth and fourteenth centuries had apparently been dissipated. All that did appear (in 1935) was an edition of a number of hitherto unprinted parliament rolls and subsidiary documents.[18] This continued the work of Cole and Maitland in printing rolls omitted from the eighteenth-century edition of the *Rotuli Parliamentorum* but it was no more than a useful preliminary to producing a comprehensive history of parliament, not a substitute for it.

It was perhaps inevitable that the collaborators would be drawn by their work on the sources for the history of the English parliament in the fourteenth century into a detailed re-examination and reassessment of the *Modus tenendi parliamentum*. They first began working on the *Modus* in the early 1930s and initially planned a paper on its dating and origins for the *English Historical Review*. The thesis of the paper was to be that the *Modus* belonged to the reign of Richard II and not, as was generally believed, to the reign of Edward II, and also that the English version of the *Modus* was derived from the Irish and not, as previous scholars had believed, the reverse. Discussions with the editor of the *English Historical Review*, Previté-Orton, led to a more ambitious project agreed with the Cambridge University Press in 1935 for a new edition of the *Modus* and of three associated treatises (on the Steward, the Marshal and Trial by Combat) with an extensive introduction. But, although Richardson did some textual work for the volume in 1937, the project seems thereafter to have dropped out of sight. It was not to be revived for some twenty years. Another offshoot of their work on the early history of parliament was a lengthy paper concerned with medieval legislation which appeared in the *Law Quarterly Review* in 1934.[19] This provided a masterly overview of the nature of statute, of the knowledge of statutes by litigants, of the process of drafting and publication of statutes and of the status and development of the official and unofficial collections of statutes made in the thirteenth and four-

---

[18] *Rotuli parliamentorum Anglie hactenus inediti, MCCLXXIX–MCCCLXXIII* (Royal Historical Society, Camden 3rd ser., 1 (1935)).

[19] 'The Early Statutes', *Law Quarterly Review*, 1 (1934), 201–23, 540–71.

teenth centuries. Although it is possible to make detailed criticisms of parts of this work it is, and is likely to remain, the classic article on the subject.

Richardson and Sayles were also drawn into the investigation of other medieval parliaments. Richardson had from the first emphasised the importance of viewing the English parliament from a comparative perspective and particularly in the light of the apparently very different development of the *parlement* of Paris. The collaborators did not publish any joint work on that institution but among the earliest fruits of their partnership were articles on two other parliaments which showed close resemblances to that of England and which they also thought might be helpful in providing clues to its development. In 1928 they published a paper on the Scottish parliaments of the reign of Edward I.[20] Unsurprisingly, they found that the Scottish parliament also had the king's council at its core and that its primary purpose too was the dispensing of justice. This remained their only foray into Scottish parliamentary history, although Sayles was later to serve on the Committee on the History of the Scottish Parliament from shortly after its formation in 1937 until it finally produced two volumes, ironically of a purely prosopographical nature, in 1992. In 1929 they published their first work on the Irish parliament.[21] This was an institutional study of the Irish parliament in the reign of Edward I with much the same focus as their work on the English parliament: concerned with establishing when parliament met, who was present at its meetings and how it did business. Their most significant work on the Irish parliament was only to be published after the Second World War.

After 1934, when David Douglas left Glasgow for a Chair at Exeter, Sayles began teaching medieval history at Glasgow on a regular basis. It was probably at this time that he produced a first version of his lectures on the history of medieval England from the Anglo-Saxon invasions down to the late thirteenth century which was later to form the basis of his successful undergraduate textbook, *The Medieval Foundations of England*. The mid-1930s were also a time of significant change in his personal life. In 1935 he met his future wife, Agnes, while on a cruise round the Western Isles. She was the daughter of George Sutherland, a partner in a family firm of yarn merchants in

---

[20] 'The Scottish Parliaments of Edward I', *Scottish Historical Review*, xxv (1928), 300–17.
[21] 'The Irish Parliaments of Edward I', *Proceedings of the Royal Irish Academy*, xxxviii (1929), section C, 128–41.

Glasgow (M'Lennan, Blair and Munsie). They were married in 1936. Their first child, Michael, was born in 1937; their daughter, Hilary, in 1940.

Sayles was too old for military service in the Second World War and the Principal of Glasgow University rescued him from being drafted into war-time service as a Civil Servant in the Board of Trade. He was therefore able to go on lecturing and examining at Glasgow throughout the war. His contribution to the war effort took the form of membership of the local Home Guard and service as an Intelligence Officer to the District Commissioner for Civil Defence in the West of Scotland, whose headquarters were in Glasgow. His duties as Intelligence Officer included the supervision of the responses by the local emergency services and others to air raids. When his brother-in-law, Alec Sutherland, was called up for war service in 1941 he also took over the management of the family firm of M'Lennan, Blair and Munsie.

The first Selden Society volume jointly edited by Richardson and Sayles by coincidence also appeared in 1941.[22] The volume seems to have been an almost accidental by-product of their joint work on the early history of parliament. One of the topics they saw as requiring investigation was the origins of petitioning in parliament. This naturally led them to look for the forerunners of this practice in the initiation of litigation by plaint and by bill (rather than by writ, the normal method) in royal courts during the first half of the thirteenth century. Most of the work of selecting the relevant enrolments (which are mainly, but not exclusively, from sessions of the General Eyre) seems to have been done by Sayles alone. The volume also contains an important introduction which places the use of plaints in a wider context and makes a significant contribution to our understanding of the origins of the action of trespass. It was also apparently during the war that Sayles did the main work needed to turn his lectures on early medieval England into *The Medieval Foundations of England*, although this was not published until 1948.

Even before the war was over Sayles had begun to apply for professorial posts away from Glasgow. In 1944 he applied unsuccessfully for a Chair at Liverpool. In 1945 he succeeded in an application for the Chair at the Queen's University, Belfast. He remained in Belfast for the next eight years. At Queen's he taught the main second-year lecture course on the history of medieval Britain, which looked in detail

---

[22] *Select Cases of Procedure without Writ Under Henry III* (Selden Society, vol. lx (1941)).

at a number of topics in British history: for a general textbook survey there was (from 1948 onwards) his own *Medieval Foundations of England*. Sayles's interests had, as we have seen, already taken him into Irish history and while at Queen's he took various steps to encourage its teaching and study. He was also instrumental in gaining support from the Northern Ireland government for a project for the publication under his own general editorship of the surviving fifteenth-century registers of the archbishops of Armagh, one of the major sources for Irish medieval ecclesiastical and social history. Sayles planned to use a typed version of the nineteenth-century transcript of the registers in the Armagh Public Library (which he managed to have temporarily transferred to Belfast and then filmed) as the starting-point for work on the texts. He must have hoped that once these had been collated with the originals progress would be rapid. It turned out, however, that there were major textual problems with the registers which needed to be resolved before any of them could be published since it appeared likely that some, if not all, of them had material that properly belonged to others in the series. In the end only one of the registers (that of Archbishop Mey) was edited in that rarest of objects, a joint thesis, by W. G. H. Quigley and E. F. D. Roberts. This was only completed after Sayles had left Belfast in 1955. The thesis formed the basis of a printed edition published in 1972.[23] Sayles had hoped to retain the general editorship of the series even after he had left Belfast but was replaced by his former colleague J. W. Gray and the whole project seems then to have languished. Fortunately, the Irish MSS Commission has now revived the plan and it seems likely that the remaining registers will at last find their way into print.

While Sayles was in Belfast he also played a wider role in the historical and cultural world of the province and of Ireland: as president of the Ulster Historical Society (between 1946 and 1949); as a member (from 1946) and subsequently as Chairman (from 1949) of the Advisory Committee on the Official War History of Northern Ireland, helping to supervise the writing of a single volume history of *Northern Ireland in the Second World War* published in 1956;[24] as a Governor of the Northern Ireland Council for the Encouragement of Music and the Arts (from 1947); as a member of the Irish MSS Commission (from

---

[23] *Registrum Iohannis Mey: The Register of John Mey Archbishop of Armagh, 1443–1456*, ed, W. G. H. Quigley and E. F. D. Roberts (Belfast, 1972).

[24] J. W. Blake, *Northern Ireland in the Second World War* (Belfast, 1956).

1949), only the second member to be appointed from north of the border and a position he retained till his death; and as Fellow of the Royal Irish Academy (from 1952). Shortly before he left Belfast he spent a short period (in 1952) as a Visiting Professor in Louvain and in the winter of 1952–3 made his first visit to North America as a Fulbright fellow. While in North America he visited all the great medievalists of the day and spoke at most of their universities. North America was clearly impressed by George Sayles. His lecture on Edward I at Johns Hopkins was printed *in extenso* (with a photograph of the lecturer) in the *Baltimore Sun*; S. E. Thorne, subsequently a good friend, judged his lectures at Yale (where he gave the Woodward lectures) to have been 'excellent, well prepared, perfectly delivered and suited precisely to their audience(s)'. Sayles was to return to the United States in 1960–1, just in time to see the Kennedy–Nixon presidential debate on television, and was invited back to New York to be the first Kenan Visiting Professor at New York University for the fall semester of 1967. For this he made his first transatlantic crossing by air. His last visit to North America was in 1969 when he was a Visiting Member of the Institute for Advanced Study in Princeton.

As we have seen, Richardson and Sayles had first published on the Irish parliaments of Edward I in 1929. Although they seem to have continued working on the Irish parliament and more generally on Irish medieval administration during the 1930s it was not until 1943 that Richardson published an article on the so-called Irish 'Statute Rolls' of the fifteenth century[25] and not until 1947 that they jointly produced a collection of documents relating to the Irish parliament and great council, mainly of a fourteenth-century date, for the Irish MSS Commission.[26] The history of the Irish medieval parliament was also the subject of the first joint book (other than books of edited documents) published by the collaborators. This appeared in 1952, more than twenty years after the start of their collaboration.[27] The book was written from an unrivalled knowledge and mastery of the primary

---

[25] H. G. Richardson, 'The Irish Parliament Rolls of the fifteenth century', *English Historical Review*, lviii (1943), 448–61.

[26] *Parliaments and Councils of Medieval Ireland*, vol. I (Irish MSS Commission, 1947).

[27] *The Irish Parliament in the Middle Ages* (Philadelphia and London, 1952). The volume was published as no. 10 in the series of Studies presented to the International Commission for the History of Representative and Parliamentary Institutions (*Commission Internationale pour l'Histoire des Assemblées d'États*). Sayles was not, however, invited to become a member of the Commission until 1956. A second edition appeared in 1964 but this was no more than a reprint with minor corrections.

sources on both sides of the Irish Sea and it is unlikely that it will ever be superseded as the standard monograph on the subject. A similarly close acquaintance with the wide range of relevant primary sources is also evident in their indispensable reference work, *The Administration of Ireland*.[28] This provided the first reliable lists of royal officials and justices active in the lordship of Ireland for the period down to 1377. Although it did not appear until 1964 most of the work for it had been completed while Sayles was still in Ireland.

Despite his continuing interest in Irish history, by 1953 Sayles had decided that he did not wish to remain in Belfast until retirement. He chafed at the difficulties encountered in travelling to the mainland, especially in summer, and the obstacles that this posed to working in English archives and libraries. He seems also to have been apprehensive about the possible resurgence of political and military activity in Northern Ireland. Thus, when the Burnett-Fletcher Chair of History and Archaeology at the University of Aberdeen fell vacant, he made a successful application for it. Since there were already two established medievalists teaching at Aberdeen (Kathleen Edwards and Leslie Macfarlane) Sayles did not lecture in medieval history while he was there. Instead he returned to lecturing on the subject he had taught during his earlier years at Glasgow, modern European history. His only contact with the teaching of medieval history was through tutorials.

In 1956 the University of Glasgow decided to create several new Chairs, one specifically in Medieval History. This post was not advertised but Sayles was approached to discover if he wanted it and he indicated his interest. Sayles was indeed an obvious candidate. He was a distinguished medievalist who was a graduate of the university and had spent more than half of his teaching career there. The appointment committee, however, was also faced by the claims of an internal candidate, E. L. G. Stones. Stones was much younger than Sayles and had published much less. He was, however, seen by the committee as 'good professorial timber'. Had they been certain that Stones would have succeeded Sayles in his General History Chair at Aberdeen, there is little doubt that the committee would have recommended the appointment of Sayles. They judged, however, probably correctly, that the chances of Stones being appointed to the Aberdeen Chair were small. They therefore left it up to the University Court to make the choice

---

[28] *The Administration of Ireland, 1172–1377* (Irish MSS Commission, 1963).

between the two men. After both had been interviewed it was Stones who got the Glasgow professorship. This was clearly a major professional disappointment for Sayles. He must have relished the possibility of crowning his career by a triumphant return to his undergraduate university, and the blow was all the greater when his successful rival had not achieved as much distinction as himself.

It is not wholly clear when or why Sayles resumed work on the court of King's Bench. In 1957 he wrote as though he had always intended, from the very beginning of his work on King's Bench, to continue on past the end of Edward I's reign and through to 1340. In 1307, he noted, the court had yet to assume two of the more important areas of its classic jurisdiction (proceedings initiated by indictment and by bill) and by taking his enterprise down to 1340 he would reach the period by which the court had reached its classic medieval form.[29] There is, however, little evidence of this having been the original scheme in the three volumes which were published prior to the Second World War and, as we have seen, his thesis had dealt only with the functioning of the court during the reign of Edward I. It also seems clear from what he says in 1957 that he had not done any substantial work on the post-1307 period prior to the war and had been kept from doing so by 'the intervention of war and of post-war committments'.[30] The implication seems to be that he had not resumed work on the court until the early 1950s, and perhaps only after his move to Aberdeen. The Aberdeen years produced not only volume IV of *Select Cases in the Court of King's Bench*, which appeared in 1957 and printed selected enrolments from the reign of Edward II, but also volume V of *Select Cases in the Court of King's Bench*, which appeared in 1958 and printed selected enrolments from the period 1327–1340.[31] Like the pre-war volumes both came with substantial introductions and appendices. These covered many of the same topics as the earlier volumes but also some new ones, such as the identity and functions of the king's legal representatives from the reign of Henry III onwards and the place of equity in King's Bench. The two introductions also in part corrected or amplified things that had been said in the earlier volumes, so that even the legal historian

---

[29] *Select Cases in the Court of King's Bench Under Edward II*, vol. IV (Selden Society, vol. lxxiv (1957)), p. v.
[30] Ibid.
[31] *Select Cases in the Court of King's Bench Under Edward II*, vol. IV (Selden Society, vol. lxxiv (1957)); *Select Cases in the Court of King's Bench Under Edward III*, vol. V (Selden Society, vol. lxxvi (1958)).

whose main interest is in the earlier period finds it necessary to consult these volumes as well as the three earlier volumes when looking for Sayles's latest thoughts on the topics which interested him or for relevant documentation.

It was also while Sayles was still at Aberdeen that he and Richardson wrote most, if not all, of their second joint book, *The Governance of Medieval England*, although it was not published until 1963 and just after Sayles's early retirement from Aberdeen. This is a lively but quirky book, written in a polemical and argumentative style and with many interesting things to say. It is less clear that it benefits from being cast in the form of a polemic against the views of Bishop Stubbs, a feature for which Sayles, rather than Richardson, probably bears the responsibility. It certainly gives the volume a dated feeling for few medievalists of the current generation will have read the *Constitutional History* or will readily understand why Richardson and Sayles thought Stubbs such an important target. Nor is it clear that the authors' methodology in rewriting the constitutional history of the period from the Conquest to Magna Carta solely from primary sources and with almost no reference to the work of other scholars (except where they are attacked for their errors in interpretation) is one that adequately expresses their debt to others within their scholarly tradition. What it does capture quite well is their sense of being outsiders and men whose work had not received its proper due. The volume was a *succès de scandale*, selling even better than Edinburgh University Press had expected. The collaborators also projected a second volume which would have covered the period from Magna Carta to the beginning of the Reformation Parliament. Parts of it were certainly written but ultimately the second part of the project was abandoned.

Sayles took early retirement in 1962 when offered generous financial support by the Rockefeller Foundation of New York, allowing him to research and write in London without administrative and teaching responsibilities but with an institutional affiliation with the Institute of Advanced Legal Studies.[32] The grants gave him the equivalent of the professorial salary he was foregoing for a five-year period, and were made on the strong prompting of his American friend and colleague, S. E. Thorne. Sayles was persuaded (largely, it seems, by American

---

[32] Papers relating to the two grants he received are to be found in folder 614, box 70, series 401, R.G. 1.2, Rockefeller Foundation Archives, Rockefeller Archive Center, North Tarrytown, New York.

enthusiasm, though also in part by American money) to resume work on the court of King's Bench, the work for which the Harvard Law Faculty had awarded him the James Barr Ames Medal (and Prize) in 1958. Thorne had presented Sayles with the award at the Selden Society annual meeting of 1959 where Sayles gave the talk later published as 'The Court of King's Bench in Law and History'. The award of the medal gave Sayles immense satisfaction, for the same medal had been awarded over half a century earlier to the historian for whose work Sayles had the greatest respect and with whom he was most pleased to be compared, F. W. Maitland. But he did not in the end produce the four further volumes which he had originally projected. What did appear were a sixth volume of *Select Cases in the Court of King's Bench* covering the period from 1340 to 1377 (in 1965) and a seventh volume covering the period from 1377 to 1422 (in 1971).[33] The introductions to these volumes focused mainly on the personnel of the court, though there was also a discussion of the court's movements and of the history of the court of the *aula regis*.

Sayles also continued working on a number of joint projects with Richardson. One was for a single-volume survey of law and legislation in medieval England covering the period from the earliest surviving Anglo-Saxon law-code (that of Aethelberht of Kent) down to the early Tudors. This was planned as a companion work to what was still seen as a two-volume project on the governance of medieval England but also as a revision and expansion of their work of the 1930s on the early statutes. In the end, however, all that appeared (in 1966) was a fragment of the larger work: their slim book, *Law and Legislation from Aethelberht to Magna Carta*, whose main focus was on the law-books and legislation of the eleventh and twelfth century. Much of what they wrote in this book was challenging and controversial: the more controversial of their theses (particularly their arguments challenging the genuineness of part of the legislation of Henry II) has not found general acceptance among specialists but has led to a useful re-examination of the relevant material. Other joint projects made much less progress. In his application to the Rockefeller Foundation Sayles mentioned a volume on *Procedure by Bill in the Later Middle Ages*. This was intended to be a continuation of *Select Cases of Procedure Without*

---

[33] *Select Cases in the court of King's Bench Under Edward III*, vol. VI (Selden Society, vol. lxxxii (1965)); *Select Cases in the Court of King's Bench Under Richard II, Henry IV and Henry V*, vol. VII (Selden Society, vol. lxxxviii (1971)).

Writ Under Henry III. It would have utilised transcripts of material from the plea rolls which Sayles had procured as early as 1938 and also printed a number of treatises on procedure by bill from this period. Nothing appeared. His applications also talked of working on the history of parliament and finally producing *The Medieval Parliament in England.* Sayles had already attempted to revive the original projected history on a number of previous occasions. It may have been Richardson's work on a paper on 'The Commons and Medieval Politics' for the Royal Historical Society in 1945 which led to renewed negotiations between Sayles and the Clarendon Press and a renewed attempt by Sayles to interest his collaborator in resuming work on their joint volume. In June 1947 Sayles had their joint articles specially mounted on 300 large sheets and noted in the margins his own corrections and additions. He then sent the corrected sheets to Richardson for his amendments and comments. Richardson certainly received the corrected sheets but he did nothing further with them. In 1954 Sayles again wrote to Richardson about their joint enterprise, sketching out some of the main chapters of the proposed book ('Beginning', 'Hero King', 'Edward II' and 'Commons and Peers'). The subject was again mentioned in correspondence between the two collaborators in 1963. By now the proposed volume was also to contain a bibliographical survey of the subject, probably a reworking of parts of their extended, albeit querulous, 1961 essay on 'Parliaments and Great Councils in Medieval England'.[34] A new publisher had also been found for the volume. This time it was to be Edinburgh University Press and the book was scheduled to appear in the autumn of 1964. Again the deadline came and went without any text being submitted for it proved impossible to motivate Richardson to return to work on their joint project and Sayles evidently felt he could not proceed without that co-operation. There was a different story in the case of the volume of text and introduction to the *Modus tenendi parliamentum* which had been awaited almost as long. Sayles resumed work on the project in 1959 and by 1963 had produced a text and an introduction incorporating Richardson's work and sent it to his collaborator for comment. Publication of the volume was then scheduled for 1965. The publication date came and went without Richardson returning the draft text. When Sayles looked over Richardson's papers after his death (as his literary

---

[34] 'Parliaments and Great Councils in Medieval England', *Law Quarterly Review*, lxxvii (1961), 213–36, 401–26.

executor) it became plain that Richardson had failed to return the draft
not because he had lost interest in the project but because he had gone
on working on it. A further project which apparently originated with
Richardson and went back to the early 1950s was for a joint volume
called *Clio's Web* concerned with the writing of history. By 1962 a
major part of this had apparently been written and the joint authors had
secured a contract for its publication. In 1964 they considered changing
publishers to Penguin (who would have paid more) but Richardson
demurred at the 'straight-jacket' of a contractual obligation to deliver
the text by September 1965. All that has ever appeared was the short
fragment entitled 'Clio's Web' which appeared in a collection of
miscellaneous pieces by Sayles published in 1982.[35]

It was only after the death of Richardson in 1974 and after he had
himself retired that Sayles finally managed to bring a number of these
projects to at least partial completion. The longest-running was their
work on the English medieval parliament. *The King's Parliament of
England* (published the year after Richardson's death) was a much
shorter book than the one they had planned and with many fewer
footnotes, but it was a distillation of the essence of the larger work
and in consequence more readable than the planned book would ever
have been. Sayles did not go on to write the bigger book, but he did
agree to the republication with corrections and additions of the papers
which he and Richardson had written over the years on the medieval
parliament.[36] It contained much of what the bigger book would have
contained minus the connecting passages. In his final years Sayles
published a third book on the English medieval parliament.[37] This
was a volume of selected materials in translation, drawn mainly but
not exclusively from the Public Record Office, which were intended to
illustrate the functions of the English parliament during the period
1258–1350. It resembles the book first suggested by Sayles to Richardson over sixty years earlier. The material is arranged chronologically,
parliament by parliament, rather than thematically and it makes no
attempt to be exhaustive or to place the material in any wider social
or even political context. Its real merit and purpose lies in providing
pièces justificatives for the view of the functions of the English parlia-

[35] G. O. Sayles, *Scripta Diversa* (London, 1982), pp. 1–16.
[36] H. G. Richardson and G. O. Sayles, *The English Parliament in the Middle Ages* (London, 1981).
[37] G. O. Sayles, *The Functions of the Medieval Parliament of England* (London, 1988).

ment during this period which Richardson and Sayles had so long been propounding. A modern edition of the *Modus tenendi parliamentum* was eventually provided by others, not by Sayles,[38] but in 1981 he did finally publish a paper containing the main arguments for a later date and an Irish origin for the *Modus* first formulated half a century earlier.[39] Historians have found the arguments interesting but few have been convinced by them. A third joint project was the publication of a new edition and translation of the late thirteenth-century treatise *Fleta*. Richardson had begun work on this during the Second World War. The task was not a particularly difficult one since there was only a single MS of most of the treatise and the main job of the editor was to identify the sources (mainly passages in *Bracton* plus statutes, a register of writs, and passages from *Walter of Henley*) from which the author had compiled his text. Soon after beginning work Richardson had called in his long-term collaborator to assist him. Sayles had a seventeenth-century edition of *Fleta* retyped during the Second World War by typists working for M'Lennan, Blair and Munsie and the two collaborators seem then to have set to work comparing this text with photostats of the original. It was envisaged that the work would be published by the Selden Society in four volumes: the first volume to be an introduction, commentary and index to the whole; the other three to contain text and translation. Volume I, which could only be completed once the other volumes had been finished, will never now appear. Volume II, although already in proof in 1944–5, only appeared in 1955, apparently because of differences between Richardson and the Literary Director of the Selden Society (T. F. T. Plucknett) over the translation of technical terms.[40] Volume III was in typescript by 1965 but did not appear until 1972.[41] Volume IV, the work of Sayles alone, finally appeared in 1984.[42] In this final volume there is at least a brief introduction considering, among other things, the date of the treatise, the relationship between *Fleta* and *Bracton* and the authorship of the treatise. In it Sayles stubbornly (albeit loyally) maintained, despite the weight of contrary evidence, Richardson's view that the treatise had no connection with

[38] N. Pronay and J. Taylor, *Parliamentary Texts of the Later Middle Ages* (Oxford, 1980).
[39] 'Modus tenendi parliamentum' in *Anglo-Irish Relations in the Later Middle Ages*, ed. J. F. Lydon (Dublin, 1981), pp. 123–52 (and reprinted in his own *Scripta Diversa* at pp. 331–60).
[40] *Fleta*, vol. II, ed. H. G. Richardson and G. O. Sayles (Selden Society, vol. lxxii (1955)).
[41] *Fleta*, vol. III, ed. H. G. Richardson and G. O. Sayles (Selden Society, vol. lxxxix (1972)).
[42] *Fleta*, vol. IV, ed. G. O. Sayles (Selden Society, vol. xcix (1984)).

Matthew of the Exchequer and did not derive its name from having been written in the Fleet prison.[43] It seems doubtful whether it was really worth producing a new edition of a text of which there was already an adequate, if not perfect, seventeenth-century edition available, particularly when there were other contemporary texts (like Gilbert of Thornton's *Summa*) still awaiting publication. The translation and annotations are, however, certainly useful. A fourth and less substantial joint project was an edition of material mainly from the Public Record Office and principally from Ancient Petitions and Ancient Correspondence relating to Ireland and the treatment of Irish affairs by the king's council in England. This had first been accepted for publication by the Irish MSS Commission in 1936 but was finally completed by Sayles alone and appeared over forty years later, in 1979.[44]

Retirement also brought Sayles a number of scholarly honours: a fellowship of the British Academy (in 1962); an honorary doctorate from Trinity College, Dublin (in 1965); an honorary doctorate from his *Alma Mater* Glasgow in 1979 (a second D.Litt. to match the one he had earned for his thesis in 1932); election as a Corresponding Fellow of the Medieval Academy of America (in 1980). Sayles had been a Council Member of the Selden Society since 1941 and a Vice-President between 1953 and 1956. In 1985 he was elected one of its Honorary Members.

George and Agnes Sayles had moved from Aberdeen down to Crowborough in East Sussex, some thirteen miles from Goudhurst (the retirement home of his collaborator, Richardson) in 1962. George's retirement was a productive one until his eyesight began to fail in the mid-1980s. He remained cheerful even then and even in the face of adversities in his family life: the premature death in 1989 of his son Michael, who had become a career officer in the RAF, and the onset of a debilitating disease in his daughter Hilary, which forced her into early retirement from her appointment in the Kunsthistorisch Institut of the University of Utrecht but also brought her home to live close to her parents in Crowborough. George Sayles died in hospital on 28 February 1994 after a fall at home. His widow Agnes survived him for less than two years, dying in December 1995. Their ashes now lie together in the Necropolis in Glasgow.

---

[43] See Richardson's review of Denholm-Young's *Collected Papers on Medieval Subjects* in *Law Quarterly Review*, lxiii (1947) at 377.

[44] *Documents on the Affairs of Ireland before the King's Council*, ed. G. O. Sayles (Irish MSS Commission, 1979).

George Sayles did not reach the very peak of his chosen profession and was denied even the Medieval History Chair at Glasgow for which he was so eminently qualified, but the quantity and quality of his scholarly work were recognised in the honours he received in the later years of his career and after his retirement. During his long career as a publishing scholar he produced work of enduring value by himself on the medieval court of King's Bench and in co-operation with H. G. Richardson on the English and Irish medieval parliaments and English medieval legislation. George Sayles is one of the few legal and constitutional historians who have written since Maitland whom it is not wholly inappropriate to compare with him. The quality of Maitland's writing and the sheer breadth and liveliness of his intellectual interests make him much the greater historian but it is no small compliment to Sayles that such a comparison is even thinkable.

PAUL BRAND
Institute of Historical Research, London

Note. I gratefully acknowledge the assistance I have received in compiling this memoir from the late Mrs Agnes Sayles (George Sayles's widow) and from Miss Hilary Sayles (his daughter), both in giving me access to his papers and in their personal memories; from Professor A. A. H. Duncan, who not only contributed his memories of George Sayles but also conducted research in the archives of the University of Glasgow on my behalf; to the Rockefeller Foundation Archives in the Rockefeller Archive Center, North Tarrytown, New York for sending me copies of the papers relating to grants made to George Sayles; to the Carnegie Trust for the Universities of Scotland for material relating to their grants to George Sayles; to David Sellar for doing research on my behalf in the New Register House in Edinburgh on the Sayles family; to Professor Bruce Lenman for sending me a memoir of George Sayles's time at Aberdeen; and to Professor J. H. Baker and Martin Sheppard for access to their correspondence with George Sayles.

JOHN SUMMERSON *Walter Bird*

Proceedings of the British Academy, **90**, 467–495

John Newenham Summerson
1904–1992

JOHN NEWENHAM SUMMERSON was born in Darlington on 25 November 1904. His father, Samuel James Summerson, was the manager of a family firm which manufactured rail track. It had been established in the 1840s by Samuel's father Thomas, a working man who had risen to be Inspector of Permanent Way on the Stockton and Darlington Railway. Samuel was in his mid-forties when he married Dorothea Newenham, whose father was a poorly-paid clergyman, but whose forebears were Anglo-Irish gentry from Coolmore in County Cork (as a young man John Summerson was sometimes to use 'Coolmore' as a *nom de plume*). Samuel died in 1907, leaving his widow with an independent income and the responsibility of bringing up their only child. Physically weak, John was sent first to a small preparatory school at Weymouth and then to the more 'bracing' environment of Riber Castle near Matlock, where he rapidly developed both physically and intellectually. The four years he spent as a pupil in this strange, ugly, but not entirely 'unromantic' house on its Derbyshire hilltop were remembered by him as 'among the most luminous and liberating of my life and [those] in which architecture first intruded itself into my adolescent brain'.[1] From Riber he went on to Harrow, which proved less congenial, though the teaching was 'mostly excellent', and it was here that he learned to write what John Betjeman called his 'cool, Harrovian prose'. Here, too, a talent for playing the organ was fostered

[1] It was in Woore's bookstall in the market at Derby that Summerson bought his first architectural books. The present writer was to do the same in the 1930s.

by the music master, Dr (later Sir) Percy Buck. It was through organ-playing that the boy began to develop a latent interest in architecture. Organs led to organ-cases and organ-cases to the churches that housed them. In the Vaughan Library at Harrow he 'browsed through architectural and topographical literature as an alluring side-issue from my organ studies' and in the holidays he was 'always in and out of cathedrals and churches, playing organs whenever I had the chance'. Buck told Mrs Summerson that if her son took up the organ as a profession, he 'could choose, in effect, between Westminster Abbey and St Paul's', but he was somewhat dismissive of organ-playing as a career and by 1922 it had become clear that architecture, rather than music, was to be the dominant interest of John's life. As architecture could not be studied at Oxford or Cambridge, the offer of a place at Pembroke College in the latter university was given up, and in his eighteenth year he was admitted to the Bartlett School of Architecture at University College London, with the intention of gaining a degree in architecture and in due course practising it as a profession.

Under Albert Richardson and Hector Corfiato the Bartlett School offered a strictly traditional training, sustained by Richardson's enthusiasm for eighteenth- and nineteenth-century classicism and by Corfiato's *Beaux-Arts* expertise. Promising students were encouraged to try for a Rome Scholarship at the British School, but Summerson 'did not much like this way of designing and never got anywhere in the competition'.[2] He did, however, spend a good deal of his time with a fellow student called Denis Mirams sketching and making measured drawings of old buildings in Norfolk, Oxford, Paris and elsewhere. Another student friendship, that was to last for a lifetime, was with Peter Fleetwood-Hesketh, a member of a wealthy Lancashire family, who later wrote a notable guide to the architecture of that county.

In 1926–7 Summerson spent an obligatory six months in an architect's office, that of W. D. Caröe, a specialist in churches who worked for the Ecclesiastical Commissioners in Millbank. Here the work was dreary and badly paid and he left with relief in May 1927. Thanks, however, to an allowance from his mother, he was not dependent on his meagre earnings from Caröe's office, and in the summer he joined Fleetwood-Hesketh in a tour of Northern Europe that included

---

[2] A 'Design for a College Chapel by Mr J. Summerson (Third Year)', illustrated in the *Builder*, 28 August 1925, 319–20, appears to be the only relic of his architectural pupilage. It is a Gothic design much influenced by Liverpool Cathedral.

Hamburg, Copenhagen, Stockholm, Berlin and Holland. Back in England, he first joined the office of an obscure architect called Low ('the nearest thing to Scrooge I have ever met') and then that of a famous one in the person of Sir Giles Gilbert Scott R.A. But neither the mediocrity of the former nor the distinction of the latter did anything to make a young man of naturally intellectual tastes into an effective architectural practitioner. His commitment to a conventional career as an architect was in fact wavering. 'I had scraped through my course at the Bartlett with little credit and taken a second-class degree. I had done time in three architects' offices but learnt very little from the experience. . . . I was ambitious to make some sort of mark in architecture but the possibility of practice was not only remote but distasteful. Writing appealed to me but I had no obvious talent for it'.

In this predicament Summerson applied for, and obtained, a junior teaching post at the Edinburgh College of Art. For this his abilities as a draughtsman and designer were, in his own words, 'utterly insufficient'. He was, in fact, much less able than some of his pupils, among whom were Basil Spence and Robert Matthew, young men of his own generation of whose superior ability he was painfully conscious. The appointment was, however, part-time, and Summerson occupied himself by writing,first for the *Architect and Building News* and then for the *Builder*, by learning German, and (in the vacations) by foreign travel. In 1930 the librarianship of the Royal Institute of British Architects fell vacant, and Summerson applied for a post for which he was in many ways well equipped (if not formally qualified). He was short-listed and interviewed, but the job went to another architect, E. O. ('Bobby') Carter. Humiliated by his inadequacy as a teacher, Summerson now resigned the Edinburgh post and returned to London, where his continued dependence on his mother (and hers on him, for she had few friends of her own) was an added source of discontent.

Residence in London did, however, give Summerson the entrée to a more intellectual society than that afforded by architectural schools and offices. Finally emancipating himself from the constraints of his mother's flat in Hampstead, he moved early in 1932 to Bloomsbury, where he met, among others, Geoffrey Grigson, C. E. M. Joad, Hugh Ross Williamson and other journalists and writers. Grigson introduced him to a wider circle which included the novelist Antonia White, the sculptor Barbara Hepworth, her artist husband Ben Nicholson, and her sister Elizabeth, a ballet-dancer, whom he was later to marry. He was now writing fairly regularly for such periodicals as the *Builder*, the

Architect and Building News, *Country Life* and the *Bookman*, and had sporadic employment in architects' offices, including that of Clough Williams-Ellis. He continued to travel, notably in 1931 to Russia, where he was briefly arrested for inadvertently photographing the police headquarters in Moscow.

Then in 1932 the lucky find in a Bloomsbury print-shop of a collection of drawings by John Nash and the Reptons turned Summerson's attention in the direction of architectural history. There ensued an article in the *RIBA Journal* and, more importantly, the idea of a biography of John Nash, the centenary of whose birth would fall in 1935. Writing *John Nash* initiated him into the documentary sources of English architectural history in the British Museum, the Public Record Office and elsewhere. Both readable and scholarly, Summerson's biography of George IV's architect was something new in English literature and at once established its author's reputation as an architectural historian. A full-time job as assistant editor of a weekly periodical, the *Architect and Building News*, precluded any further historical writing for the time being, but Summerson now had an established place in the literary and intellectual society of the 1930s. He was, moreover, a member of the MARS (Modern Architectural Research) Group which pioneered the 'Modern Movement' in England. In 1937 he found time to submit for a RIBA Prize (which he duly won) an essay entitled 'The Tyranny of Intellect: The Mind of Sir Christopher Wren'. Himself an intellectual who had found his *métier* in writing rather than in design, Summerson saw in Wren another intellectual, one in whom freedom of invention was inhibited by an academic and scientific background, and who only gradually responded to the freedom of the baroque and never exploited its possibilities as fully as his pupil Hawksmoor was to do. This was followed in 1939 by 'The Great Landowner's Contribution to Architecture', in which, perhaps not uninfluenced by Marxist insistence on the economic basis of society, he explored the pattern of landownership and patronage which had so largely determined the growth of London outside the City. This preliminary investigation of London's architectural history was to develop later into *Georgian London*, but already in 1939 it showed that Summerson had a grasp of the historical processes which underlie architecture that was unique among historically-minded architects in Britain (in the 1930s there were, of course, scarcely any architecturally-minded historians).

When the Second World War supervened Summerson realised that recording the fabric of the past before it was destroyed had suddenly become more urgent than investigating its history. It was largely his initiative that led (with the encouragement of Sir Kenneth Clark) to the establishment of the National Buildings Record, with Walter Godfrey as Director and Summerson as his deputy. Broadly speaking Godfrey was responsible for the overall administration, Summerson for the recording of threatened or bomb-damaged buildings, not only in London, but in cities and towns all over England. Many of these dated from the eighteenth and nineteenth centuries, periods whose architecture had then been little studied, and in selecting buildings for record Summerson had to search periodicals such as the *Builder* and the *Building News* as well as moving round the country in the wake of German bombers. From early in 1941 to the summer of 1945 his life was devoted to the commissioning of drawings and photographs for the Record. A selection of these, with an introduction by J. M. Richards and well-informed notes by Summerson, was published by the Architectural Press in 1942 as *The Bombed Buildings of Britain*

Then in 1945 the death of A. T. Bolton made vacant the curatorship of Sir John Soane's Museum in Lincoln's Inn Fields — apart from the Royal Commission on Historical Monuments, whose remit excluded buildings later than 1714, almost the only post for an architectural historian in the country. Summerson's appointment, already envisaged by the Trustees before Bolton's death at the age of eighty, was effected without delay. Nominally part-time and initially poorly paid, the post gave Summerson a base from which to pursue his career as an architectural historian without unduly restricting his freedom of action. The Soane Museum was to remain the centre of his life for thirty-nine years. In 1945 the immediate problem was the repair of the fabric damaged in the blitz (which he achieved with a grant from the Pilgrim Trust, making the drawings for much of the work himself), and the reinstatement of its contents, evacuated for safety in 1942. Under Bolton the Museum still had the character of a private house to which the public and the scholar had only limited access. The new Curator was determined to open the Museum on a regular basis and to make its contents freely available to students. This the funds at the Trustees' disposal would not permit, and in 1947 Summerson was instrumental in negotiating a Treasury grant which led eventually to a Statutory Order (1969) giving the Museum a status similar to that of the British Museum, entirely dependent on the State financially, but under the control of its own Trustees. In 1968 he persuaded the Trustees and the Treasury to take over the adjoining house, No. 12 Lincoln's Inn

Fields, designed by Soane himself and leased to tenants since 1813, as a much-needed extension that was essential to the proper functioning of the Museum. Meanwhile he and Dorothy Stroud, the Assistant Curator, had initiated weekly lectures for the benefit of visitors and made the great collection of drawings accessible to students, while catalogues of the classical and Egyptian antiquities were commissioned from appropriate experts. When Summerson retired in 1984 there was scope for further cataloguing of drawings, archives and printed books, but his curatorship had seen the transformation of a 'near bankrupt private charity' into a cherished and much-visited museum of international repute.

From 1944 onwards Summerson was to write, lecture[3] and broadcast about architecture and architectural history without intermission for some forty years. Although he claimed to 'have no fluency as a writer', he did in fact have an enviable facility for writing what appeared to be effortlessly elegant and lucid prose. But the driving force behind his output was intellectual rather than literary: the incentive was (in his own words) 'always *curiosity* — curiosity about architecture, its roots and branches, its practitioners and expositors and, in the broadest and most elusive sense, its meaning'. Linked with curiosity was 'the desire to crystallise my findings in words which . . . make those findings comprehensible and, if possible, eloquent'. Eloquence in exposition came easily to him, and behind it was a rigorous and penetrating mind that rarely failed to get to the heart of an architectural problem, whether it was the source of a motif or the evolution of a style. But to satisfy curiosity in a manner that was intellectually valid meant research, and one of Summerson's achievements was the way in which, without any historical training, he identified and exploited those documentary sources that were relevant to his current inquiry, whether they were the records of the Crown Estate Commissioners, the Declared Accounts of the Office of Works, or the wills and inventories of a family of Jacobean artisans. With a few honourable exceptions (notably Willis and Clark's *Architectural History of the University of Cambridge*, published in 1886), such sources had been generally neglected by earlier writers on English architecture, making Summerson's achievement as a self-taught historian the more remarkable. So far as nineteenth-century architecture was concerned, he had as an example

---

[3] He lectured regularly on the History of Architecture at the Architectural Association from 1949 to 1962, and at Birkbeck College from 1950 to 1967.

the work of H. S. Goodhart-Rendel, by whose brilliance as a lecturer and writer he was much impressed, and whose celebrated card-index of Victorian churches was firmly based on contemporary periodical litera- ture and the records of the Incorporated Church Building Society. At the same time he was absorbing the established principles and techni- ques of art-historical scholarship as they were understood on the Continent. Here the arrival in 1933 of the Warburg Institute was crucial. Summerson regularly attended its seminars at Thames House, Millbank, and sat at the feet of Saxl, Wind, Kurz and above all Wittkower, whose lectures on Palladianism were (he wrote later) 'a turning-point for many of us'. Faced with Wittkower's 'wonderful intuition for discerning the problems behind a building's physiognomy and devising . . . a strategy for solving them', the 'magnetic enthusiasm of a Richardson or even the epigrammatic brilliance of a Goodhart-Rendel seemed to belong to a different and departing world'. When to professionalism in research and unfailing felicity in exposition, whether oral or written, there were added an unusually perceptive eye and a retentive visual memory, Summerson's exceptional equipment as an architectural historian becomes clear.

After *John Nash* came *Georgian London* (1945), perhaps the first study of a European capital that attempted not only to establish the characteristics of its architecture, but also to show how these had been shaped by the ambitions of its landowners, the capabilities of its building trades, and the regulatory restraints of its municipal authori- ties. Elegantly printed (despite wartime restrictions) by the Cresset Press, its success was immediate, and it remains a classic of British architectural history. A sequel to be entitled *Victorian London* was long on Summerson's agenda, but in the end the investigations needed to make historical sense of so vast a subject proved to be too great for its fulfilment. Articles on 'The London Suburban Villa' (1948), 'The Victorian Rebuilding of the City of London' (1974), 'Charting the Victorian Building World' (1990), a chapter in *The Victorian City* (ed. Dyos and Wolff, 1973), and a lecture on 'The London Building World of the Eighteen-Sixties' (1973) were, however, valuable by- products of this unfulfilled project.

In 1946 Summerson was invited by Nikolaus Pevsner to write the volume on *Architecture in Britain 1530–1830* for the Pelican History of Art. It took six years to write and generated several subordinate studies that are of permanent value in themselves, notably one on the Elizabethan surveyor John Thorpe, whose drawings (in the Soane

Museum) are a key source for the understanding of Elizabethan architecture, and another on the typology of the English country house in the eighteenth century. The volume eventually published in 1953 proved to be a magisterial survey that has provided the framework within which British architectural history from the Renaissance to the Gothic Revival has been studied ever since.

The interest — starting with John Thorpe — that Summerson had shown in Elizabethan and Jacobean architecture led to the invitation to contribute substantially to the third volume of *The History of the King's Works*, edited by the present writer. This involved an investigation both of the organisation and personnel of the royal works from the mid-sixteenth century to the time of Inigo Jones, and of the architectural history of the royal palaces during the same period. The extensive documentation made this a somewhat formidable task which he conscientiously discharged, remarking wryly that it was 'both a penalty and a compensation for never having done a Ph.D. thesis in my youth'. Though 'nothing spectacularly new' emerged from Summerson's involvement in the *King's Works*, it provided the incentive for his lecture on Inigo Jones, delivered in the British Academy's 'Master Mind' series in 1964 and printed in its *Proceedings* for the following year. Much of this paper was absorbed into a Pelican paperback on *Inigo Jones* which was published in 1966.

It was, however, Wren rather than Jones whose architecture was to be for Summerson a lifelong preoccupation. The brilliant prize essay of 1937 was followed in 1953 by a deceptively simple but sophisticated biography in the 'Brief Lives' series, in which proper attention was paid to Wren's scientific work as well as to his architectural achievement; in 1960 by an essay on Wren as President of the Royal Society; in 1961 by an important investigation into the evolution of the design of the dome of St Paul's Cathedral; in 1963 by 'The Sheldonian in its Time' (a lecture given in that building when receiving an Honorary Degree from the University of Oxford); in 1970 by a catalogue of drawings for the London City Churches that (largely as a result of his own intervention) had been acquired by the National Art Collections Fund when they were sold at auction in 1951; and in 1990 by a further paper on the dome of St Paul's. In his work on St Paul's Summerson showed that he could tackle a strictly architectural problem of considerable complexity with the authority that he had doubtless admired in Wittkower's studies of St Peter's, Rome.

Among Summerson's other writings as an architectural historian, the most notable were his study of the architecture of Sir John Soane, his investigation of the origins of the square and the crescent as characteristic elements in English town planning, and his *Classical Language of Architecture* (1964), a masterly introduction, characteristically free from pedantry or jargon, that has been translated into several foreign languages, including Japanese.

Although it was as an architectural historian that Summerson would eventually achieve celebrity, in his early years as a writer he was as much concerned with contemporary architecture as with that of the past. What is more, he was committed to the 'Modern Movement'. As early as 1930, in an article in the *Scotsman*, he shocked his superiors at the Edinburgh College of Art by evoking a vision of the Princes Street of the future as 'a glittering spectacle of steel, glass, and concrete'. In London his membership of the MARS Group brought him into contact with the leading Modern Movement architects in England, such as Maxwell Fry, Serge Chermayeff and Amyas Connell. It was he who wrote the captions for the Group's famous propagandist exhibition of 1938, attended by Le Corbusier as guest of honour. In 1941 he published an article entitled 'The New Groundwork of Architecture' which was something of a Modernist manifesto. In it he called for the abandonment of tradition as 'architectural Toryism', and with it 'the traditional idea of the architect's place in society — the genteel lackey of the wealthy, the man who turns surplus profits into picturesque country houses and imposing city façades. . . . The architecture of today must be the architecture not of a class but of the community itself.' The 'need for parade' would vanish and new architectural beauties would be rediscovered, 'deeper and subtler than any which the fourteenth or eighteenth centuries knew', though not perhaps the Greeks.

What drew Summerson to the Modern Movement was above all its strongly intellectual character. This was a time when (as he wrote later) 'a good many young men bought themselves black hats and discovered that architects were, or should be, intellectuals' rather than 'gentlemen or scholars'. 'Here', he wrote approvingly of Tecton's High Point flats in Highgate, 'is architecture which sets the standard of intellectual modernity firmly on English soil'. In the 1930s and early 1940s as a broadcaster and architectural journalist he took the Modern Movement very seriously, but as early as December 1940 he privately admitted (in a letter to Ben Nicholson) that the MARS Group had failed in its mission and that the kind of architecture it had preached would never win general acceptance in Britain. As time went on his own approach became more that of a commentator than of a protagonist, and when in 1957 he attempted to establish a 'Theory of Modern Architecture', the result was an academic essay that was (as he himself subsequently admitted) both 'philosophically unsound' and of doubtful relevance for the British architects of the day. By this time his interests had shifted away from the contemporary towards the historical. Already in 1948 he thought of himself as 'in practice' as much 'an antiquary' as 'an architect', and in 1955 he confessed to having 'scarcely looked at modern stuff' for so long that 'the description and criticism of modern buildings [for an Arts Council exhibition] comes as a quite new problem'. It was, however, perfectly in keeping with his former loyalties that in 1984 he should rather quixotically have championed Peter Palumbo's ill-advised scheme to plant a tower designed by Mies van der Rohe in the heart of the City of London, and on lecturing tours in the United States he continued eagerly to visit the works of Mies, Frank Lloyd Wright and other masters of modern architecture in that country. Back in England he found the 'post-modern' fascinating but regrettably lacking in principle and integrity. However, in his last critical article, on James Stirling's extension to the Tate Gallery, entitled 'Vitruvius Ridens' (*Architectural Review*, June 1987), he conceded that British architecture could not forever have sustained the high seriousness of the Modern Movement and that what Stirling had designed was acceptable as a sophisticated architectural joke that was at the same time 'lucidly and functionally planned'.

It was characteristic of Summerson that although committed to the Modern Movement he did not reject the past (as so many of its adherents did), and that at the same time he viewed the past with a degree of detachment that absolved him (unlike Pevsner) from any suggestion that he saw it through modernist eyes. His paper on 'Butterfield and the Glory of Ugliness' (1945) was written too early to have been, consciously or unconsciously, prompted by the 'New Brutalism', and only in his analysis of the 'personal style' of Sir John Soane can a mind attuned to the studied simplicities of the Modern Movement perhaps be seen searching for similar qualities in the work of a neo-classical architect.

Detachment (though not indifference) characterised Summerson's long involvement in the cause of architectural preservation. In 1937 he was one of the first members of the Georgian Group, and he was an original member both of the Committee for Listed Buildings that advised the Minister for Housing and Local Government under the Town and Country Planning Act of 1944 and of the Historic Buildings Council (1953). In both these capacities he played an important part in establishing the criteria for State intervention and State aid that are still in force, and from time to time he intervened decisively in favour of some important building that was at risk, such as Arbury Hall when threatened by coal-mining in 1953. Always highly discriminating in his assessment of buildings worth preserving, he enjoyed playing the part of *advocatus diaboli* when some marginally 'outstanding' building came up for consideration. Cool in the face of conservationist enthusiasm, he was particularly mistrustful of an attitude towards the past in which sentiment was not controlled by critical judgement. So, in addressing the Thirties Society in 1983, he gently ridiculed their devotion to a decade so 'lacking in vigour of invention or refinement of style'. More notoriously, his failure, in 1961, to support opposition to the demolition of some houses in one of Dublin's 'longest, dreariest and most monotonous Georgian streets' was never forgiven. Nor did he subscribe to the Ruskinian dictum that 'restoration is destruction', preferring in the last resort to preserve authenticity of design rather than the last vestiges of original craftmanship. In 1963 he wrote enthusiastically about the way in which historic buildings in Oxford had recovered their architectural identities as a result of refacing. 'Architecture,' he wrote, now 'springs from the past into the present in a way which few can have foreseen.'

Summerson received many honours and awards. He was appointed CBE in 1952. A knighthood followed in 1958 and in 1987 he was appointed Companion of Honour. He was elected a Fellow of the British Academy in 1954. In 1976 he was awarded the Royal Gold Medal of the Royal Institute of British Architects, a recognition not only of his eminence as a critic and historian of architecture, but also of his persistent attempt 'to bridge the gap between the architectural profession and the world of Art History'. He was a Fellow of University College London, an Honorary Fellow of Trinity Hall, Cambridge, and received Honorary Degrees from the Universities of Leicester (1959), Oxford (1963), Edinburgh (1968), Hull (1971) and Newcastle (1973). He was Slade Professor of Fine Art at both Oxford (1958–9) and Cambridge (1966–7) and Ferens Professor of Fine Art at Hull (1960–1). A Festschrift in his honour entitled *The Country Seat* was published by Penguin Books in 1970.

Summerson was a member of nearly all the public bodies connected with architecture and its history: the Listed Buildings Committee of the Ministry of Housing and Local Government (1944–66), of which he was Chairman from 1960 to 1962; the Royal Fine Art Commission (1947–54), whose 'long and often excessively boring meetings' he enlivened by an independence of judgement that was sometimes almost perverse ('Summerson', declared it Secretary, Godfrey Samuel, 'just hates being in a majority'); the Royal Commission on Historical Monuments for England (1953–74), where his expert guidance in the description of classical buildings was particularly valuable; and the Historic Buildings Council (1953–78). He was also a member of the Historical Manuscripts Commission (1959–83) and of the Advisory Council on Public Records (1968–74), and a Trustee of the National Portrait Gallery (1966–73). In 1961 he was appointed Chairman of the National Council for Diplomas in Art and Design, a body set up to ensure that there was a uniform standard in art education throughout the country. Its decisions were controversial, and although it was an assignment which Summerson fulfilled with credit, it was with relief that he withdrew from it in 1970.

From 1949 to 1965 Summerson was a member (and for much of the time Chairman) of 'The Critics', a popular and very successful radio feature in which a panel of critics discussed in turn a book, a play, an art exhibition, a film and a radio programme. His felicitous broadcasting manner was equally evident in the many talks which he gave on various BBC services, the texts of which were often published subsequently in the *Listener*.

In 1938 Summerson married Elizabeth, daughter of H. R. Hepworth and sister of the sculptor Barbara Hepworth. The birth of triplet boys in 1946 was an event which complicated the Summersons' domestic life for some years thereafter. It necessitated the purchase of the house (No. 1, Eton Villas, on the Chalk Farm estate) in which Summerson was to live for the rest of his life. Lady Summerson died in 1991.

Summerson was a tall, elegant man whose well-groomed appearance and urbane manner gave him an air of patrician assurance. By the 1960s the Bloomsbury intellectual had become part of the English 'Establishment': a member of the Athenaeum and the Beefsteak Club, a Fellow of the British Academy and of the Society of Antiquaries. Though generally reserved and undemonstrative, he was not in the least pompous: students found him unexpectedly approachable and he could be an agreeable companion and an amusing correspondent. In his later years he was disabled by deafness, emphysema and Parkinson's Disease, but continued to write with undiminished authority as long as he could hold a pen. He died on 25 November 1992, aged 87.

HOWARD COLVIN
Fellow of the Academy

Note. The earlier part of this memoir is based largely on an unfinished autobiography by Summerson, a copy of which he sent to the Academy expressly for the use of his obituarist. The remainder is derived from personal knowledge, from Summerson's own papers, bequeathed by him to the British Architectural Library, and from his letters to Ben Nicholson in the Tate Gallery Archive. One letter of 1948 to Ernest de Beer (Bodleian Library, MS Eng. c. 3118, f. 145) is referred to. The text has benefited from perusal by Sir Alan Bowness, Professor J. Mordaunt Crook, Dr Mark Girouard, Mr John Harris, Mrs Margaret Richardson and Dr David Watkin.

Select Bibliography

This is an expanded version of the bibliography provided by Summerson himself for the Festschrift of 1970. Not only did that not cover the last twenty-four years of his life, but it omitted several publications of an earlier date that deserved inclusion. Use has been made of a copy of the 1970 bibliography in Sir John Soane's Museum to which Summerson made additions up to 1990. Like the 1970 bibliography this one is 'select' in the sense that it excludes ephemeral journalism and some minor reviews of books, buildings and exhibitions. Books, articles and reviews are listed under each year in that order.

1927

Measured drawing of the London, County and Westminster Bank, Lothbury (by C. R. Cockerell), *Builder*, 17 July 1927, 979; redrawn for inset plate in *Architect and Building News*, 1 March 1935.

1928

'A Small Country House in Sussex planned by Women Architects', *The Queen*, 7 March 1928, 30–1.

1929

'An Early Modernist: James Wild and his Work', *Architects' Journal*, 9 January 1929, 57–62.

1930

'The Tweed Bridges from Peebles to the Sea', *Quarterly of the Royal Incorporation of Architects in Scotland*, 34 (1930), 44–52.

'Modernity in Architecture', *Scotsman*, 21 February 1930, followed by correspondence in 'Points of View' at various dates in February and early March.

'Architecture and the Byzantine Genius', *Builder*, 20 June 1930, 1185–6, with sketches by J. S.

'A Cubist Architect: Some Recent Schools at Hilversum by W. M. Dudok', *Builder*, 19 December 1930, 1038.

1931

'Notes on Architecture in Two Russias', *Master Builder*, January 1931, 16–21.

'The Art of the Victorians', *Country Life*, 20 June 1931, 791–2.

'The Terrace Houses of Edinburgh', *Builder*, 14 August 1931, 264–5, and 21 August 1931, 302–3.

'Primitive Architecture in Ireland', *Quarterly Illustrated* of the Royal Incorporation of Architects in Scotland, 1930–1, 6–17 (the 'Quarterly' prize essay for 1930–1).

1932

'The Romantic Element in Architecture', *Architectural Design and Construction*, ii, 5, March 1932, 225–9.

'Shakespeare Memorial' (the Stratford-on-Avon Theatre), *Scotsman*, 22 April 1932.

'Gothic Treasure Island' (Gotland), *Builder*, 1 July 1932, 8–9, with sketches by J. S.

'This Age in Architecture', *Bookman*, October 1932, 13–14.

1933

S. O. Addy, *The Evolution of the English House*, revised and enlarged from the author's notes by J. S. (London, 1933).

'A Repton Portfolio', *RIBA Journal*, 25 February 1933, 313–24.

1934

Architecture Here and Now, with Clough Williams-Ellis (London, 1934).

'The Crown Commissioners' Inheritance', *Architect and Building News*, 12 January 1934, 41–4.

'The Work of H. S. Goodhart-Rendel, FRIBA', *Brick Builder*, March 1934, 13–17.

'Recent Work of Mr. E. Vincent Harris', *Country Life*, 28 April 1934, 423–6.

'Ersham House, Canterbury' (obituary) with measured drawings by J. S., *Architect and Building News*, 1 June 1934 (supplement), unsigned.

'Northumberland Tragedy' (obituary of Swarland Hall, with measured drawing by J. S.), *Architect and Building News*, 15 June 1934, 304, unsigned.

'Harrow School', *Country Life*, 14 July 1934, 36–42 and 21 July 1934, 64–9.
'John Nash' (paper read before the RIBA, 3 December 1934, with discussion), *RIBA Journal*, 22 December 1934, 225–36.

1935

John Nash: Architect to King George IV (London, 1935; rev. ed., 1949).
'Architecture' in *The Arts Today*, ed. G. Grigson (London 1935), 253–88.
'An Idealist's Achievement: New College, Finchley Road' (obituary), *Architect and Building News*, 20 September 1935, 338–9, unsigned.
'General Wade's House: An Obituary', *Architect and Building News*, 11 October 1935, 42, unsigned.

1936

'The Strange Case of J. M. Gandy', *Architect and Building News*, 10 January 1936, 38–44.
'Building a House', *Country Life*, 16 May 1936.
'Southampton: The Town and the Port', *Architect and Building News*, 19 June 1936, 327–32, unsigned.
'Theatre Royal, Bristol', *Architectural Review*, November 1936, 167–8.

1937

'James Wyatt', in *From Anne to Victoria*, ed. B. Dobrée (London, 1937).
'Forty Years of British Architecture' (Royal Academy winter exhibition), *Listener*, 13 January 1937, 60–2.
'A Speculative Builder in the Time of Wren' (Nicholas Barbon), *Architect and Building News*, 15 January 1937, 86–9.
'Sir John Soane', *The Times*, 20 January 1937.
'The Tryanny of Intellect: A Study of the Mind of Sir Christopher Wren in relation to the Thought of his Time' (RIBA Silver Medal essay), *RIBA Journal*, 20 February 1937, 373–90; reprinted in *Heavenly Mansions*, 1949.
'Premises Coming Down', *Listener*, 3 March 1937, 390–3.
'Leeds Pre-View', *Architect and Building News*, 18 June 1937, 334–42, unsigned.
'Creative Housing', *Listener*, 4 August 1937, 223–5.
'Architect Laureate' (Sir Edwin Lutyens), *Night and Day*, 28 October 1937, unsigned.
'Building Boom', *Listener*, 29 December 1937, 1418–20 and 5 January 1938, 20–2.

1938

'Architecture at the Empire Exhibition' (Glasgow), *Listener*, 18 May 1938, 1064–6.
'Norwich City Hall', *Listener*, 3 November 1938, 934–5.

1939

'The Great Landowner's Contribution to Architecture' (paper read before the RIBA, 20 February 1939), *RIBA Journal*, 6 March 1939, 432–49.

'Abstract Painters' (Ben Nicholson), *Listener*, 16 March 1939, 573–4.

'Architecture, a Changing Profession', *Listener*, 20 April 1939, 830–2.

'The Building of Bloomsbury', *The Times*, 10 June 1939, 13–14.

'The Villa Vernacular', *Listener*, 27 July 1939, 188–90.

Doodle of anthropomorphic order, unsigned, *Architects' Journal*, 3 August 1939, 164 and 11 April 1940, 379.

1940

English Castles (Peacock Colour Book, London, 1940).

'The "Poetry" of Le Corbusier' (lecture delivered at the Warburg Institute), *Architect and Building News*, 5 April 1940, 4–6; reprinted in *Heavenly Mansions*, 1949.

'The Fate of Modern Architecture', *Listener*, 23 May 1940, 1002–3.

'Pugin Effigy: A Christmas Reminiscence', *Architect and Building News*, 27 December 1940, 181–2.

'The Unromantic Castle' (Riber Castle, Matlock), *Architectural Review*, February 1940, 55–60, signed 'John Coolmore'; reprinted in *The Unromantic Castle*, 1990.

1941

'Norman Shaw', *Listener*, 3 April 1941, 493.

'Ruins and the Future' (BBC Home Service broadcast), *Listener*, 17 April 1941, 563–4.

'Gandy and the Tomb of Merlin', *Architectural Review*, April 1941, 89–90.

'St George's-in-the-East: An Obituary Note', *Architectural Review*, November 1941, 135–40.

'The Monuments in the Church of St Nicholas, Deptford', *Mariner's Mirror*, xxviii (1941), 277–89.

'The New Groundwork of Architecture', *World Review*, 1941; reprinted in *Modern Essays 1939–41* ed. A. F. Scott, London 1942, and in *This Changing World*, ed. J. R. M. Brumwell (London 1944).

'The Place of Preservation in a Reconstruction Programme' (paper read before the Architectural Association, 28 October 1941), *RIBA Journal*, December 1941, 24–8.

1942

The Bombed Buildings of Britain, with introduction by J. M. Richards and notes by J. S. (London, 1942; 2nd enlarged ed., 1947).

'Bread & Butter and Architecture', *Horizon*, vi, No. 34, October 1942, 233–43: reprinted in *Architect and Building News*, 25 December 1942; *English Digest*,

January 1943; and *Plan* (organ of the Architectural Students' Association), 2, (1944).

'London Hereafter', *Listener*, 22 October 1942, 532–3.

Review of S. Giedion, *Space, Time and Architecture* (1941), *Architectural Review*, May 1942, 126–7.

1943

The Microcosm of London by T. Rowlandson and A. C. Pugin (16 plates from Ackermann's London, 1808–10), text by J. S. (King Penguin, London, 1943).

'Sir Reginald Blomfield' (unsigned leading article), *Architects' Journal*, 7 January 1943, 3.

'Cotton-King Architecture' (poem), *Architects' Journal*, 3 June 1943, 361, signed 'John Coolmore'.

'London Regrouped', *Listener*, 1 July 1943, 16.

'Theatre Royal, Bristol', *Architectural Review*, December 1943, 167–8.

1944

'Edwin Landseer Lutyens (1869–1944)' (unsigned leading article), *Architects' Journal*, 6 January 1944, 3.

'Sir Edwin Lutyens (1869–1944)' (unsigned leading article), *Architect and Building News*, 7 January 1944, 3.

'Sir Edwin Lutyens: 1869–1944' (BBC Forces Programme broadcast), *Listener*, 13 January 1944, 46; reprinted in *The Spoken Word*, ed. R. Church (London, 1955), 136–7.

'Plan for Plymouth' (BBC Home Services broadcast), *Listener*, 4 May 1944, 491–2.

'Rebuilding the City', *Listener*, 14 August 1944, 1216.

1945

Georgian London (London, 1945; reprinted 1947; New York, 1946; rev ed., Harmondsworth, 1962; 2nd ed., 1969; 3rd ed., 1978; new ed. London, 1988).

'Architecture on the Door-step' (paper read before the Architectural Association, 24 April 1945), *Architectural Association Journal*, May 1945, 149–55.

Statement, in dialogue form, on the re-planning of the area near St Paul's Cathedral, *Architectural Review*, June 1945, 198, signed 'John Coolmore'.

'Russian Architecture: The Historic Background', *Architect and Building News*, 23 November 1945, 128–30.

'William Butterfield', *Architectural Review*, December 1945 (Gothic Number), 166–75; reprinted in *Heavenly Mansions*, 1949.

'Dulwich Art Gallery: An Obituary', *Architects' Journal*, 20 December 1945, 447–51.

1946

Architecture in England (The Arts in Britain, No. 10), published for the British Council, 1946.

'Architecture and Music' (BBC Home Service broadcast), *Listener*, 7 March 1946, 301–2.

'Town Gazing' (BBC Home Service broadcast), *Listener*, 13 June 1946, 769–71.

'Regency Brighton', *Spectator*, 26 July 1946, 85.

Review of W. H. Godfrey, *The Church of St Bride, Fleet Street* (Survey of London, 1944), *Listener*, 26 December 1946, 923–4.

1947

The Architectural Association, 1847–1947 (London, 1947) (published for the Architectural Association).

'Heavenly Mansions: An Interpretation of Gothic' (paper read before the RIBA, 10 December 1946), *RIBA Journal*, 29 January 1947; reprinted in expanded form in *Heavenly Mansions*, 1949.

'Regent's Park', *Spectator*, 25 April 1947, 457–8.

'How We Began – The Early History of the A.A.' (paper read before the A.A., 16 April 1947), *Architectural Association Journal*, May 1947, 129–40.

'An Elizabethan Treasure House' (Knole) (BBC Third Programme broadcast), *Listener*, 8 May 1947, 700–1.

'St Stephen, Walbrook: A Revaluation' (BBC Third Programme broadcast with H. S. Goodhart-Rendel), *Listener*, 21 August 1947, 299–301.

'The Subtle Magic of Sir John Soane' (the Soane Museum, on the occasion of re-opening to the public: BBC Home Service broadcast), *Listener*, 11 September 1947, 427–8.

1948

Ben Nicholson (Harmondsworth, 1948).

'1851 — A New Age, a New Style' (BBC Third Programme broadcast in 'Ideas and Beliefs of the Victorians'), *Listener*, 19 February 1948, 295–8; reprinted in *Ideas and Beliefs of the Victorians* (London, 1949; New York, 1966).

'Pugin at Ramsgate', *Architectural Review*, April 1948, 163–6.

'The London Suburban Villa', *Architectural Review*, August 1948, 63–72, reprinted in *The Unromantic Castle*, 1990.

'Brighton Pavilion and the Regency Festival' (BBC Third Programme broadcast), *Listener*, 5 August 1948, 193–4.

'Bristol and its Architecture' (BBC Third Programme broadcast in 'Buildings and Places' series), *Listener*, 2 September 1948, 837–8.

'A Place of Inspiration' (Chiswick House: BBC Third Programme broadcast), *Listener*, 16 September 1948, 409–10.

1949

Heavenly Mansions and Other Essays on Architecture (London, 1949).

'Architecture and Modern Painting', *London Calling*, 19 March 1949, 12, 18.

'On Knowing Britain' (five broadcast talks on the BBC Regional Programme for North America), *London Calling*: 1. 'London in Space and Time', 12 May

1949, 6–7; 2. 'Two Famous University Cities', 2 June 1949, 9–10; 3. 'The North Country', 16 June 1949, 6–7; 4. 'Elizabethan England', 30 June 1949, 6–7; 5. 'Heritage of Victorian Age', 25 August 1949, 9–10.

'What Makes a Good Room?', *Listener*, 21 July 1949, 94.

'Change, Decay and the Soane Museum', *Architectural Association Journal*, October 1949, 50–3.

'J. M. Gandy: Architectural Draughtsman', *Image*, 1, Summer 1949, 40–50.

'John Thorpe and the Thorpes of Kingscliffe', *Architectural Review*, November 1949, 291–310; reprinted in *The Unromantic Castle*, 1990.

Review of J. H. Harvey, *An Introduction to Tudor Architecture* (1949), *RIBA Journal*, December 1949, 69–70.

1950

Chambers' Encyclopaedia, 'Architecture' and other articles as advisory editor for architecture.

'Sir John Soane's Museum' in *The Nation's Pictures*, ed. A. Blunt and M. Whinney (London, 1950).

Review of R. Turnor, *James Wyatt: A Biography* (1950), *New Statesman*, 29 July 1950, 128.

Review of *Recollections of Thomas Graham Jackson*, ed. B. H. Jackson (1950), *New Statesman*, 30 September 1950, 329.

Review of K. Clark, *The Gothic Revival* (2nd ed., 1950), *Spectator*, 29 September 1950, 348.

1951

The Iveagh Bequest, Kenwood: A Short Account of its History and Architecture, (London County Council, revised ed., 1956; reprinted 1988).

The Old Church Garden, St Marylebone London. The Story of its Foundation with an Appreciation of the Old Parish Church (St Marylebone Society, 1951).

'Soane: The Case-History of a Personal Style' (paper read before the RIBA 12 December 1950), *RIBA Journal*, January 1951.

'New Patterns in Art and Society' (BBC Home Service broadcast in 'Framework of the Future' series), *Listener*, 15 March 1951, 417–18.

'South Bank Architecture' (The Festival of Britain), *New Statesman*, 12 May 1951, 529–30.

'Lansbury' (The Festival of Britain), *New Statesman*, 16 June 1951, 679.

'Coventry Cathedral', *New Statesman*, 8 September 1951, 253–4.

'South Bank Postscript', *New Statesman*, 6 October 1951, 363–4.

'Christopher Wren at Work' (drawings of St Paul's in the Bute Sale at Sotheby's, 23 May 1951), *The Times*, 11 October 1951.

'New Architecture in Whitehall', *New Statesman*, 3 November 1951, 489.

'A Piece of New London' (Churchill Gardens), *New Statesman*, 29 December 1951, 755.

Reviews of C. Hussey, *The Life of Sir Edwin Lutyens* (1950) and A. S. G. Butler,

The Architecture of Sir Edwin Lutyens (1950) as 'Books in General', *New Statesman*, 17 March 1951, 321–2; and *RIBA Journal*, August 1951, 390–1.

Review of N. Pevsner, *Cornwall* and *Nottinghamshire* ('Buildings of England; Nos. 1 and 2, 1951) as 'Books in General', *New Statesman*, 15 September 1951, 285–6.

1952

Sir John Soane (London, 1952).

'Bristol' in *Portraits of Towns*, ed. E. Molony (London, 1952), 27–36.

'A Question of Taste' (BBC Home Service broadcast in 'A Letter to Posterity' series), *Listener*, 31 January 1952, 175–6.

'Drawings for the London City Churches' (acquired by the RIBA Library from the Bute sale), *RIBA Journal*, February 1952, 126–9.

'Corbusier's Modulor', *New Statesman*, 23 February 1952, 213–14.

'Architecture and Painting', *Marg* (Bombay), 2 (1952), 2–5.

Review of D. Green, *Blenheim Palace* (1951) as 'Books in General', *New Statesman*, 12 April 1952, 438–9.

Review of W. Ison, *The Georgian Buildings of Bristol* (1952), *New Statesman*, 5 July 1952, 20–1.

Review of J. Betjeman, *First and Last Loves* (1952), *New Statesman*, 4 October 1952, 382.

Review of T. Howarth, *Charles Rennie Mackintosh and the Modern Movement* (1952) as 'Books in General', *New Statesman*, 27 December 1952, 784–5.

1953

Sir Christopher Wren, 'Brief Lives', No. 9 (London, 1953; reissued in Collins' 'Makers of History' series, 1965, and in 'Anchor Books' Hamden, Conn., 1965).

Architecture in Britain 1530–1830 (Harmondsworth, 1953; rev. eds 1955, 1958, 1963, 1969, 1970, 1977, 1983, 1991).

'The Adam Style' (BBC Home Service broadcast on an Adam exhibition at Kenwood), *Listener*, 27 August 1953, 335–6.

Review of H. S. Goodhart-Rendel, *English Architecture since the Regency* (1953), *New Statesman*, 9 May 1953, 556.

Review of O. Hill, *Scottish Castles of the Sixteenth and Seventeenth Centuries* (1953), *New Statesman*, 17 October 1953, 458–60.

Review of R. Macaulay, *Pleasure of Ruins* (1953), as 'Books in General', *New Statesman*, 12 December 1953, 764.

1954

'The Society's House: An Architectural Study', *Journal of the Royal Society of Arts*, cii, 4936, 15 October 1954.

Review of L. Whistler, *The Imagination of Vanbrugh and his Fellow Artists* (1954), *New Statesman*, 17 July 1954, 79–80.

1955

A New Description of Sir John Soane's Museum (London, 1955; rev. ed., 1966; 3rd ed., 1969).

'Music and Architecture', *Quarterly of the Royal Incorporation of Architects in Scotland*, May 1955, 46–50.

'Museums as Architecture', *Museums Journal*, December 1955, 31–8.

'Theobalds: A lost Elizabethan Palace', *Listener*, 31 March 1955.

Review of John Harvey, *English Mediaeval Architects* (1954), *New Statesman*, 29 January 1955, 152–3.

Review of C. Hussey, *English Country Houses open to the Public* (1953) and H. Gordon, *A Key to Old Houses* (1955), *New Statesman*, 18 June 1955, 847–8.

1956

'Ten Years of British Architecture, 1945–55', Introduction to *Arts Council Exhibition Catalogue*, 5–15.

'The Coventry Glass', *New Statesman*, 14 July 1956, 41.

Review of E. Kaufmann, *Architecture in the Age of Reason* (1955), *Times Literary Supplement*, 1 June 1956, 324.

Review of V. Furst, *The Architecture of Sir Christopher Wren* (1956) and E. Sekler, *Wren and his Place in European Architecture* (1956), *New Statesman*, 16 June 1956, 705–6.

Review of W. Gropius, *The Scope of Total Architecture* (1956), *New Statesman*, 29 September 1956, 381.

Review of O. von Simson, *The Gothic Cathedral* (1956), *New Statesman*, 8 December 1956, 759–60.

1957

'The Case for a Theory of Modern Architecture' (paper read before the RIBA, 21 May 1957), *RIBA Journal*, June 1957, 307–13; reprinted in *The Unromantic Castle* (1990).

'Downing Street' (No. 10), *The Times*, 28 August 1957, 9.

'Three Elizabethan Architects', *Bulletin of the John Rylands Library, Manchester*, 40 (September 1957), 202–28.

1958

'The Preservation of Georgian and Victorian Architecture' (paper read before the Royal Institute of Chartered Surveyors, 31 March 1958), *Chartered Surveyor*, May 1958, 605–10; discussion, ibid., June 1958, 657–9.

'Henrietta Place, Marylebone and its Association with James Gibbs', *London Topographical Record*, xxi (1958), 26–36.

1959

T. Dannatt, *Modern Architecture in Britain* (London, 1959) with introduction by J. S., 11–28.

'The Building of Theobalds, 1564–1585' (paper read before the Society of Antiquaries, 2 December 1954), *Archaeologia*, xcvii, (1959), 107–26.

'The Classical Country House in Eighteenth-century England' (Cantor Lectures, delivered in March 1959), *Journal of the Royal Society of Arts*, xvii (July 1959), 539–87, reprinted in *The Unromantic Castle*, 1990.

'Oxford University Architecture 1950–65', *Oxford Magazine*, 5 March 1959.

Review of K. Downes, *Hawksmoor* (1959), *New Statesman*, 19 December 1959, 885–6.

1960

'Sir Christopher Wren, P.R.S.', in *The Royal Society: Its Origin and Founders*, ed. H. Hartley (London, 1960), 99–105.

The Architectural History of Euston Station, British Transport Commission, 1959 (1960). (Printed but not published, the author being informed that it 'might create undue interest' in the demolition of the hall and portico.)

T. Davis, *The Architecture of John Nash* (London, 1960), with introduction by J. S., 9–18.

'A Great Museum Piece Doomed' (Euston Station portico), *The Times*, 11 June 1960, 9.

1961

What is a Professor of Fine Art? (Inaugural Lecture as Ferens Professor in the University of Hull), (Hull, 1961).

H. J. Dyos, *Victorian Suburb* (Leicester, 1961), with foreword by J. S., 7–10.

'The Penultimate Design for St Paul's Cathedral', *Burlington Magazine*, ciii, March 1961, 83–9, reprinted in *The Unromantic Castle*, 1990.

'Hogarth's "Entertainment"'' (BBC 'Painting of the Month' series), *Listener*, 16 November 1961, 822–3. (Illustrated folder with historical notes issued separately. Article and notes reprinted together in *Enjoying Paintings*, ed. D. Piper, Harmondsworth, 1964.)

'Pevsner's Progress', review of N. Pevsner, *Outline of European Architecture* (6th jubilee edn., 1960), as 'Books in General', *New Statesman*, 20 January 1961, 100.

1962

'The Labours of Your Ancestors', *Punch*, 19 September 1962, 400–2.

1963

The Classical Language of Architecture (text and illustrations to accompany six BBC talks delivered in May–July 1963). (Text of six talks and illustrations published London: Methuen and MIT Press, U.S.A., 1964; rev. ed., 1980.

Translations have been published in Swedish (1968), Italian (1970), Spanish (1978), French (1981), Portuguese (1982), German (1983), and Japanese (1989).

'Urban Forms' in *The Historian and the City*, ed. O. Handlin and J. Burchard (MIT Press and Harvard University Press, 1963), 165–76.

'The British Contemporaries of F. Lloyd Wright', in *Studies in Western Art*, iv (Princeton University Press, 1963), 78–87.

'The Changing Face of Oxford', *The Times*, 15 May 1963, 13.

'The Sheldonian in its Time', *Oxford University Gazette*, 6 December 1963; also issued separately as a pamphlet (Oxford, 1964).

1965

'Inigo Jones' (British Academy 'Master Mind' Lecture), *Proceedings of the British Academy*, l (1965), 169–92, reprinted in *The Unromantic Castle*, 1990.

'Walter Hindes Godfrey' (biographical notice), *London Topographical Record*, xxii (1965), 127–34.

'Kirby Hall, Northamptonshire', 'Hardwick Hall, Derbyshire' and 'Hatfield House' in BBC 'Painting of the Month' series, *Listener*, 21 January, 25 February and 25 March 1965, each with illustrated folder issued separately.

1966

Inigo Jones (Harmondsworth, 1965).

The Book of Architecture of John Thorpe, edited with biographical and analytical studies by J. S., *Walpole Society*, xl (1966).

C. J. P. Beatty (ed.), *The Architectural Notebook of Thomas Hardy* (Dorchester, 1966), with foreword by J. S.

'Ruskin, Morris and the ''Anti-Scrape'' Philosophy', *Historical Preservation Today* (Williamsburg, Va., 1966), 23–32.

1967

'Morals and Mime: The Essential Hogarth'. Introduction to *Hogarth Exhibition Catalogue* (Richmond, Va., 1967).

'Carlton House Terrace', *Notes and Records of the Royal Society*, xxii (1967) 20–2.

Review of M. Girouard, *Robert Smithson and the Architecture of the Elizabethan Era* (1966), *Architectural Review*, April 1967, 250–1.

1968

Review of H. E. Stutchbury, *The Architecture of Colen Campbell* (1967), *Architectural Review*, August 1968, 150.

1969

'Royalty, Religion and the Urban Background', in *The Eighteenth Century*, ed. A. Cobban (London, 1969).

1970

Victorian Architecture: Four Studies in Evaluation (Bampton Lectures delivered at Columbia University, New York, 1968), (New York and London, 1970; paperback, New York, 1971).

'English Townscape', in *The Shell Guide to England*, ed. J. Hadfield (1970).

'The Law Courts Competition of 1866–7' (extracts from a paper read at the RIBA), *RIBA Journal*, January 1970, 11–18.

'Drawings of London Churches in the Bute Collection: A Catalogue', *Architectural History* xiii (1970), 30–42.

Review of *Le Corbusier: Last Works*, ed. W. Boesiger (1970); H. Geretsegger and M. Peintner, *Otto Wagner* (1970); and L. K. Eaton, *Two Chicago Architects* (1969), *Encounter*, September 1970, 65–8.

1971

A Description of Maps and Architectural Drawings in the Collection made by William Cecil, First Baron Burghley, now at Hatfield House, Roxburghe Club 1971, with R. A. Skelton.

'H. S. Goodhart-Rendel' in *Dictionary of National Biography 1951–60*.

'Kirby Hall', *Sunday Times Magazine*, 23 May 1971, 39–43.

Review of R. Paulson, *Hogarth: His Life, Art and Times* (1971), *Observer*, 14 November, 1971.

Review of P. Thompson, *William Butterfield* (1971), and P. Stanton, *Pugin* (1971), *Sunday Times*, 7 November 1971.

1972

Review of M. Whinney, *Wren* (1971), and K. Downes, *Sir Christopher Wren* (1971), *Architectural Review*, March 1972, 196.

Review of H. Hobhouse, *Thomas Cubitt* (1971), *Architectural Review*, April 1972, 259–60.

'Pugin and Butterfield' (review of P. Thompson, *William Butterfield* (1971), and P. Stanton, *Pugin* (1971)) *Architectural Review*, August 1972, 97–99.

'Architecture, Royal Academy' (review of architecture in the Exhibition of Neo-Classical Art, Burlington House), *The Times*, 8 September 1972.

1973

The London Building World of the Eighteen-Sixties (Walter Neurath Memorial Lecture), (London, 1973), reprinted in *The Unromantic Castle*, 1990.

'London, the Artifact', in *The Victorian City, Images and Realities*, ed. H. J. Dyos and M. Wolff, i (London and Boston, 1973), 311–332.

'Belsize 1780–1870' in *Belsize Park*, ed. Leonie Cohn (1973), 19–27.

Review of D. Linstrum, *Sir Jeffry Wyatville* (1972), *Books and Bookmen*, June 1973, 14–15.

1974

'Jones, Inigo' and 'Wren, Sir Christopher', in *Encyclopaedia Britannica* (15th ed., 1974).

'Heritage is a Sadder Word Now', *The Times*, 12 July 1974, 13.

'Going, Going, Gone' (review of 'The Destruction of the Country House' exhibition at the Victoria & Albert Museum and book of same title, ed. R. Strong), *New Statesman*, 25 October 1974, 578.

Review of S. Orgel and R. Strong, *Inigo Jones, The Theatre of the Stuart Court* (1973), *Books and Bookmen*, January 1974, 9–10.

Review of J. M. Crook and M. H. Port, *The History of the King's Works*, ed. H. M. Colvin, vi (1973), *Books and Bookmen*, November 1974, 20–21.

1975

The History of the King's Works, ed. H. M. Colvin, iii (1975): 'The Works from 1547 to 1660' in Part I, and Part III. 'The Royal Castles', by H. M. Colvin and J.S.

'Margaret Whinney' (obituary notice), *Burlington Magazine*, cxvii, November 1975, 731–2.

'Landscape with Buildings' (amplified version of TV broadcast), in *Spirit of the Age*, ed. J. Drummond (Book Club Associates, 1975).

Review of D. Watkin, *The Life and Work of C. R. Cockerell* (1974), *Architectural Review*, March 1975, 183–4.

Review of B. Fletcher, *History of Architecture on the Comparative Method* (18th ed., 1975), *Books and Bookmen*, August 1975, 30–1.

1976

The Victorian Rebuilding of the City of London (Russell Van Nest Black Memorial Lecture, Cornell University, College of Architecture, Art, and Planning, 3 May 1974), (Cornell, 1976; reprinted in the *London Journal*, iii (1977), 163–85 and *The Unromantic Castle*, 1990.

The Architecture of Victorian London (Page-Barbour Lecture for 1972, University of Virginia), (Charlottesville, Va., 1976).

'The Building of Bloomsbury', *Camden History Review* 4 (1976), 17–18.

'The Master Builders: Adam', *Observer Colour Supplement*, 27 August 1976.

Review of H. F. Hutchison, *Sir Christopher Wren* (1976) and B. Little, *Sir Christopher Wren: A Historical Biography* (1975), *Books and Bookmen*, April 1976, 32–3.

Review of R. Wittkower, *Palladio and English Palladianism* (1974), *Journal of the Society of Architectural Historians* (USA), xxxv (1976), 146–7.

Review of W. Feaver, *The Art of John Martin* (1975), *Architectural Review*, June 1976, 352.

Review of J. Hook, *The Baroque Age in England* (1976), *Books and Bookmen*, September 1976, 32.

'Kensington: The Museum Area' (review of *The Survey of London*, xxxviii (1975), *Books and Bookmen*, August 1976, 20–1.

Review of N. Pevsner, *A History of Building Types* (1976), *Architectural Review*, December 1975, 381.

1977

'The Beginnings of Regents Park', *Architectural History*, 20 (1977), 56–62.

Review of W. B. O'Neal, *Jefferson's Fine Arts Library* (Charlottesville, Va., 1976), *Times Literary Supplement*, 24 June 1977, 760.

Review of J. R. Martin, *Baroque* (1977), *Books and Bookmen*, July 1977, 34.

Review of L. Puppi, *Andrea Palladio* (1975) and D. Guinness & J. T. Sadler, *The Palladian Style in England, Ireland and America* (1976), *Books and Bookmen*, June 1977, 22–3.

Review of M. H. Port, *The Houses of Parliament* (1976), *Journal of the Society of Architectural Historians* (USA), xxxvi (1977), 264–5.

Review of A. Saint, *Richard Norman Shaw* (1976), *London Journal*, iii (1977), 125–30.

'What is Ornament and what is not', *Via III* (Philadelphia, 1977).

Review of David Bryce Exhibition, *The Times*, 19 February 1977.

Review of N. Penny, *Church Monuments in Romantic England* (1977), *Times Literary Supplement*, 9 December 1977, 1445.

1978

'Sir John Soane and the Furniture of Death', *Architectural Review*, March 1978, reprinted in *The Unromantic Castle*, 1990.

Review of D. J. Olsen, *The Growth of Victorian London* (1976), *Journal of the Society of Architectural Historians* (USA), xxxvii (1978), 62–3.

1980

The Life and Work of John Nash, Architect (London, 1980).

'Viollet-le-Duc et le Point de Vue Rationnel' (translation of essay in *Heavenly Mansions*) in *A la recherche de Viollet-le-Duc*, ed. G. Bekaert (Brussels, 1980).

Review of J. M. Robinson, *The Wyatts* (1979), *Times Literary Supplement*, 25 January 1980, 791.

Review of W. Ison, *The Georgian Buildings of Bath* (1980), *Bookmen* (USA), July 1980, 27–8.

Review of S. Lyall, *The State of British Architecture* (1980), *Building Design*, 4 July 1980.

Review of A. Braham, *The Architecture of the French Enlightenment* (1980), *Burlington Magazine*, cxxii (1980), 442–3.

Review of M. Lutyens, *Edwin Lutyens* (1980), *Times Literary Supplement*, 17 October 1980, 1160.

Review of D. Watkin, *The Rise of Architectural History* (1980), *Architectural Review*, August 1980, 70.

1981

'Arches of Triumph: The Design for Liverpool Cathedral' in *Lutyens* (Arts Council Exhibition Catalogue, 1981), 45–53, reprinted in *The Unromantic Castle*, 1990.

'W. H. Godfrey' and 'A. E. Richardson' in *Dictionary of National Biography, 1961–70*.

Review of J. Rykwert, *The First Moderns* (1980), *Architectural Review*, January 1981, 63–4.

Review of D. Cole, 'The Work of Sir Gilbert Scott' (1980), *Burlington Magazine*, February 1981, 108–9.

1982

The History of the King's Works, ed. H. M. Colvin, iv, (1982): Part I, 'The King's Houses', by H. M. Colvin and J. S.; Part II(ii), 'The Defence of the Realm under Elizabeth I', by J. S.; (iii), 'The Defences in Detail', by M. Biddle, H. M. Colvin and J. S.; (iv), 'The Scottish Border', section on Berwick-upon-Tweed by M. Merriman and J. S.; Part III, 'Bridge and Harbour Works', Dover Harbour by M. Biddle and J. S., Berwick-upon-Tweed Bridge, by J. S.

Review of *The A to Z of Georgian London*, with Notes by Ralph Hyde (1981), *Daily Telegraph*, 20 February 1982.

'Obituary for E. J. Carter', *Architects' Journal*, 16 June 1982.

Review of H. R. Hitchcock, *German Renaissance Architecture* (1981), *Architectural Review*, June 1982.

1983

'Margaret Dickens Whinney', memoir in *Proceedings of the British Academy*, lxviii (1982), 637–42.

'Soane: The Man and the Style' in *John Soane* (London, 1983), 9–24.

'L'unione delle arti; La Casa di Sir John Soane' (with English translation), *Lotus International*, 35 (Milan, 1983).

'Vitruvius Ludens' (James Stirling), *Architectural Review*, March 1983, 19–21.

'Demolishing the Thirties Myth', *The Times*, 17 December 1983.

Review of C. Jencks and W. Chaitkin, *Current Architecture* (1983), *Architectural Review*, May 1983, 75.

Review of P. de la R. du Prey, *John Soane: The Making of an Architect* (1982), *London Review of Books*, 17–31 March 1983, 17.

1984

'The Old Hall of Lincoln's Inn' (anniversary address to the Ancient Monuments Society), *Transactions of the Ancient Monuments Society*, NS, 28 (1984), 8–22.

'The Evolution of Soane's Bank Stock Office in the Bank of England', *Architectural History* xxvii (1984), 135–149, reprinted in *The Unromantic Castle*, 1990.

Review of D. Stroud, *Sir John Soane, Architect* (1984), *Books and Bookmen*, July 1984, 11.

Review of T. Friedman, *James Gibbs* (1984), *Times Literary Supplement*, 30

November 1984, 1363–4. See also letter from J. B. Bury about 'dosserets' in ibid. 1501, and reply by J. S., 4 January 1985, 13.

1985

'What is the History of Construction?', *Construction History*, i (1985), 1–2.

'John Wood e la tradizione inglese del progetto urbano' (translation of the essay in *Heavenly Mansions*, with some revised passages), *Casabella* (Milan), May 1985.

Foreword to *Adolf Loos* (Arts Council Exhibition Catalogue, 1985).

'The Architecture of British Museums and Art Galleries', Introduction to *The Fine and Decorative Art Galleries of Britain and Ireland* (National Art Collections Fund, 1985).

Review of E. McParland, *James Gandon, Vitruvius Hibernicus* (1985), *Times Literary Supplement*, 5 July 1985, 741.

Review of J. Orrell, *The Theatres of Inigo Jones and John Webb* (1985), *Burlington Magazine*, cxxvii, July 1985, 463.

Review of A. Stuart Gray, *Edwardian Architecture* (1985), *Listener*, 5 December 1985, 34–5.

1986

The Architecture of the Eighteenth Century (incorporating 'Royalty, Religion and the Urban Background', in *The Eighteenth Century*, ed. Cobban (1969)) (London, 1986).

'Raymond Charles Erith' in *Dictionary of National Biography, 1971–80*.

Review of G. Rubens, *W. R. Lethaby, His Life and Works 1857–1931* (1986), *Listener*, 1 May 1986, 26–7.

Review of J. Dixon Hunt, *Garden and Grove* (1986), and four other books on garden history, *Times Literary Supplement*, 28 November 1986, 1353.

1987

'Vitruvius Ridens or Laughter at the Clore' (on James Stirling's extension to the Tate Gallery), *Architectural Review*, June 1987, 45–6.

1988

'Arcos de Triunfo: El Proyecto para la Catedral de Liverpool', *Composición Arquitectonica*, i, October 1988 (Bilbao) (translation of essay in *Lutyens*, 1981, with large colour plates).

1989

'Architecture 1850–1900' in *The Cambridge Guide to the Arts in Britain*, ed. Boris Ford, vol. 7 (1989); 'Architecture 1900–1945' in vol. 8 (1989).

Review of J. Onians, *Bearers of Meaning* (1988), *Times Literary Supplement*, 2–8 June 1989, 615.

Review of J. Harris and G. Higgott, *Inigo Jones, Complete Architectural Drawings*, (1989), *Society of Architectural Historians of Great Britain Newsletter*, 41, Winter 1989, 10–11.

1990

'Sir Nikolaus Pevsner' in *Dictionary of National Biography 1981–5*.

'Classical Architecture' in *New Classicism*, ed. A. Papadakis and H. Watson, (1990).

'J. H. Mansart, Sir Christopher Wren and the Dome of St Paul's Cathedral', *Burlington Magazine*, cxxxii, January 1990, 32–6 (an extended review of K. Downes, *Sir Christopher Wren: The Designs of St Paul's Cathedral* (1989).

Review of J. S. Ackerman, *The Villa: Form and Ideology of Country Houses* (1990), *Times Literary Supplement*, 6–12 July 1990, 730.

Review of A. Byrne, *Bedford Square* (1990), *Architects' Journal*, 8 August 1990, 59–60.

Review of D. Cruickshank and Neil Burton, *Life in the Georgian City* (1990), *Architectural Review*, June 1990, 12.

1991

'John Nash's Statement, 1829', *Architectural History*, 34 (1991), 196–205.

Introduction to *50 Years of the National Buildings Record* (Royal Commission on the Historical Monuments of England, 1991).

Review of R. Harbison, *The Built, the Unbuilt and the Unbuildable* (1991), *Architects' Journal*, 3 July 1991, 56.

Review of R. Tavernor, *Palladio and Palladianism* (1991), *Architecture Today*, March 1991.

1992

'Ruskin, Morris and the ''Anti-Scrape'' Philosophy', in *Decantations: A Tribute to Maurice Craig*, ed. A. Bernelle (Dublin 1992), 224–50.

1994

'On Discovering ''Greek'' Thompson', in *Greek Thompson*, ed. G. Stamp & S. Mckinstry (Edinburgh, 1994), 3–4.

1995

'The Beginnings of an Early Victorian Suburb' (the text of two lectures on the Chalk Farm Estate given in 1958), *London Topographical Record*, xxvii (1995), 1–46.

BRINLEY THOMAS

Proceedings of the British Academy, **90**, 499–517

Brinley Thomas
1906–1994

WELL KNOWN AS A MONETARY ECONOMIST, a champion of the Swedish school of economics, and a student of labour mobility, Brinley Thomas was appointed to the Chair of Economics and Social Science at the University College of South Wales and Monmouthshire, Cardiff, in 1946. While presiding over the growth of a major complex department and participating actively in public life, he established a reputation as the world authority on the economics of migration. Exposing a major weakness in classical international trade theory, he described how migration of labour and capital had linked the nineteenth-century American and European economies, and he developed the concept of the Atlantic Economy. A series of books and articles secured his position as the leading analyst of nineteenth-century economic growth.

After his retirement in 1973 he built on already strong links with American universities, and was still teaching and researching while in his mid-eighties. In these later years he extended his interests back into the eighteenth and seventeenth centuries and developed an important interpretation of economic growth in terms of energy crises. His last book, published shortly before his death, ended with a plea that economic theorists should pay more attention to the irreversibility of time, and return to Marshall's concern for a biological approach to economic change.

His first book was published when he was thirty; his last when he was eighty-seven. Including articles, his publications spanned sixty-four years.

Brinley Thomas was born into the small mining community of Pontrhydyfen on 6 January 1906. His father had worked his way up to the position of deputy mine manager. A chapel deacon, Welsh-speaking and with Welsh values, he and his wife sacrificed to ensure that Brinley, his brother and three sisters were well educated. After passing the public examination young Thomas went to the local grammar school, which he left at the age of seventeen with a scholarship that took him to the University College of Wales at Aberystwyth. Torn between history and law as subjects of study, he chose the former. Required to take a related subsidiary subject, he also began to study economics.

The department of history was not to his liking, and he secured permission to switch his main allegiance to economics. At the age of twenty he graduated with First Class Honours, and two years later, in 1928, was awarded his MA with distinction. While working for it he was active in the Fabian Society and became President of the United Kingdom Students Section of the League of Nations Union.

High unemployment in coal-mining deprived his father of a job. Convinced that his studies had but begun, Brinley felt that he had to contribute to the family purse. His brother had yet to complete his medical studies, and his three sisters had to be considered. He left the university to teach evening classes in Pembrokeshire. Fortunately his father obtained a post as deputy manager in Porth, in the Rhondda Valley. His family migrated across the mountains and he resumed his studies. Helped by a Fellowship from the University of Wales, he went to the London School of Economics to work for a Ph.D., which he received in 1931. While there he wrote his first short paper, 'The Organisation of Religion in Wales', which appeared in the *Welsh Outlook* in 1929.

By-products of his Ph.D. were three papers. The *Welsh Outlook* published 'Men, Machines and Maintenance' in 1930. In the same year *Economica* printed 'The Migration of Labour into the Glamorganshire Coalfield (1861–1911)', and in 1931 the *Economic Journal* printed 'Labour Mobility in the South Wales and Monmouthshire Coal-mining industry, 1920–30.' His family experience and his love of history had already begun to carve his personal niche in economics.

In the *Economic Journal* paper he based his statistical analysis on information from the annual exchanges of unemployment books in forty-six Ministry of Labour offices in South Wales, using as his model an investigation undertaken in Lancashire by Jewkes and Campion. He concluded that the South Wales coal-miners were not as immobile 'as some people tend to think'. They were more mobile than the Lancashire cotton workers. He gave three main reasons for such stickiness as there was: the high proportion of the unemployed who were married with children; shortage of houses in the new area and the burden of house-ownership in the old area; and the physical effects of being unemployed for a long time, including the 'sinister' tendency of the unemployed to adapt their life-style to their new circumstances. He was relying not only on statistics but also on the insight provided by his own experience and wide reading of government and other reports — an approach that never left him. He was also making points that were always to colour his thinking about migration.

After a spell as research assistant at the LSE he was awarded the Acland Travelling Scholarship that allowed him to spend nine months in Berlin studying German financial and economic crises, and to con-tribute a section on Germany to Hugh Dalton's *Unbalanced Budgets: A Study of the Financial Crisis in Fifteen Countries*. It also gave him first-hand knowledge of the rise of Nazi Germany, and an opportunity to practice an impishness that never left him. He smuggled out an old German flag, which he cherished to the end of his life. Encouraged by Dalton, he disregarded the rules of behaviour on the German railways and teased and tormented Nazi soldiers who were travelling in the same compartment. Once Dalton had to dash from London to save him from prison.

His adventures in Germany were followed by six months in Sweden, where he returned many times, adding Swedish to his other foreign languages of English and German. While there he familiarised himself with the work of David Davidson, who had held the Chair of Economics at Uppsala from 1890 to 1919, and had played a significant role as an adviser to his government on the economic policy that a neutral country should adopt. Thomas considered that this neglected economist had widened the scope of monetary theory, so that it was no longer concerned so narrowly with the value of money. In celebration of Davidson's eightieth birthday he wrote his next paper, 'The Monetary Doctrines of Professor Davidson', published in the *Economic Journal* in 1935. In it was a passage that could have been about himself:

> The barrier of language tends to make the flow of ideas as between large and small countries a one-sided affair. Economists in a small country must necessarily be linguists: and before they embark on original work they have usually mastered the recognised classics. But, unfortunately, it is often

> only after a long time-lag that their important contributions receive due
> recognition in the outside world

This article was quickly followed by his first book, *Monetary Policy
and Crisis: A Study of Swedish Experience* (London, 1936) in which he
emphasised the importance and quality of Swedish economic analysis
and its application to government policy. There was 'a northern shrine
where the English-speaking pilgrim may . . . derive inspiration, if he is
prepared to take upon himself the burden of a difficult language'.

He discussed the impact of the First World War on inflation in
Sweden, and the part played by economists in minimising it. Then he
reviewed the monetary and trade cycle theories of Wicksell and later
Swedish economists, and contrasted them with the doctrines of the
Austrian School, then so influential in England. This led to a consideration of the application of these ideas in the management of the Swedish
economy from 1924 to 1935. His conclusion contained a truth that was
more novel then, but even now is sometimes unheeded: 'The example
of Sweden indicates that a slump can be shortened and a recovery
accelerated when the Government and the Central Bank co-operate to
diminish uncertainty and to furnish the conditions necessary for a
revival of investment.'

He returned from Sweden to the LSE where his lectures used
Myrdal's terms *ex ante* and *ex post*, until then unheard in England.
(They seem to have first appeared in print in England in an influential
article by Ohlin in the *Economic Journal* in 1937.) One of his students
was the young G. L. S. Shackle, who wrote that he was 'of all the
teachers of economics of my time the one most charged with celestial
fire, the one who swept the brain of at least one hearer with a rustling
wind inspiration'.

But monetary economics and public finance, in which he had begun
to establish a reputation, were a diversion from the path that this
'English-speaking pilgrim' had chosen. Later he told me how he viewed
his study of migration as his *pererindod*, his pilgrimage on which he
progressed towards his goal only through immense dedication and
effort. During the remainder of the 1930s his publications were all
concerned with labour mobility and showed an increasing interest in
international migration.

A Leverhulme Scholarship enabled him to spend the year 1938–9
surveying migration trends in the British Commonwealth. When war
broke out in September 1939 he was in Canada. He reported to the

British Embassy and became attached to the War Trade Department of the British Embassy in neutral Washington, where he put his knowledge of German to good use. While working in New York he met Cynthia Loram, an artist and art historian, whom he married in 1943, and by whom he had a daughter, Patricia.

When America entered the war he became Director of the Northern Section of the Political Intelligence Department of the Foreign Office, where his flair for languages helped him in his contact with undercover agents in northern Europe. When Denmark was finally liberated he had to visit the country with whose resistance movement he had become so involved. Required by protocol to be in uniform, he was amused and thrilled to be made a temporary full colonel. After meeting and thanking many whom he had known only by their code-names he was presented with a beautiful Danish tea-set by its designer, who had been one of his contacts.

At the end of the war he returned to the LSE, but the chair of Economics and Political Science in the University College of South Wales and Monmouthshire, in Cardiff, was vacant. He was appointed to it in 1946, and changed the title to Economics and Social Science. Fortunately for economics his attempt to secure adoption as a parliamentary candidate a few years later failed. (It was probably prompted by a desire to influence economic policy in line with his knowledge of the role of academics in the management of the Swedish economy.) He remained in his Chair at Cardiff until his retirement in 1973, actively participating in university affairs and Welsh public life as well as pursuing his research, in which there was now an important change of emphasis. He had noted that until 1900 the significant migration from Britain had been to the United States — a fact that had been ignored by most ninteenth-century British literature on the subject. His attention to the British Commonwealth gave way to a detailed study of 'the Atlantic community of nations' and so to his discovery of 'the Atlantic Economy.'

As he had already shown in his study of Swedish monetary theory, Thomas relied heavily on a critical reading of early works. His Honours students were expected to sit a paper on the History of Economic Thought, and as he dissected the views of classical economists he displayed a rare blend of scholarship, clarity of presentation and infectious enthusiasm. Close to his desk in his study at home he had filing-card cases crammed with notes he had taken while reading the classics, both famous and obscure, some going back to his student days. He put them to good use in his study of international migration, which was to occupy most of the rest of his life.

His *magnum opus*, entitled *Migration and Economic Growth* (Cambridge), was sponsored by the NIESR and published in 1954. It was eagerly awaited. His main ideas and the preliminary fruits of his statistical and historical investigations had already appeared in 'Migration and the Rhythm of Economic Growth, 1830–1913', published in *The Manchester School* in 1951. They clearly indicated a completely new interpretation of nineteenth-century growth. The dust-jacket to the book he fondly called 'MEG' carried his own summary of his major findings:

> . . . between the 1840's and World War I, when the United States was absorbing labour and capital from Europe, the long cycles in home construction in the United Kingdom and the United States were inverse to one another. In the era during which Great Britain was the leading creditor nation, there was never a chronic sterling shortage: the main reason for this was the alternation of phases of intensive domestic investment on either side of the Atlantic. In periods of active trans-Atlantic migration and capital exports, investment and income per head rose rapidly in the United States and slowly in the United Kingdom; in periods of dwindling migration and capital exports, it was Great Britain's turn to experience a relatively vigorous upswing in home construction and real income per head. In the former periods Great Britain was supplying sterling through foreign lending and in the latter periods through a growing import surplus. The inverse relation between British and American cycles of home construction ceased when the United States checked immigration and emerged as the leading creditor nation responsible for nearly half of the world's manufacturing output.

To appreciate the significance of this study we need to look at the critical account of the classical view with which Part I began. He argued that the classical economists 'theorized on two different planes'. In discussing international trade they 'had nothing to say about migration between countries; their doctrine was usually illustrated by exchanges of British goods for the produce of other sovereign countries . . . where, if only for reasons of language, it was perfectly reasonable to assume that international mobility of labour would be negligible.' He held this assumption to be a source of much wrong thinking in the development and application of the theory of international trade. Even greater error arose from the other aspect of the dualism in classical thinking.

While trade theory virtually ignored migration, discussion of Mill's 'larger community' of countries had a great deal to say about emigration.

On the one hand, there was the static theory of international trade, based on the law of comparative costs, which gave scientific justification for the policy of free trade. On the other hand there was the dynamic theory of colonization, based on the law of diminishing returns and the tendency of profits to fall to a minimum. The art of colonization was listed as one of the few exceptions to the general rule that there must be no State interference with private enterprise: it was held to be not only desirable but indispensable that the Government should spend money on promoting the emigration of labour and capital from the mother country to overseas territories.

What was important to Wakefield and J. S. Mill was that the social structure of 'non-competing groups' — labourers and proprietors — that existed at home should be created and maintained in the colonies. Sending surplus labour to the surplus land of the colonies would bring benefits to the proprietor class at home only as long as the emigrant labourers were prevented by 'the sufficient price' of land from becoming peasant proprietors.

This theory provided Marx 'with a most congenial text'. But Marx's greatest contribution to economic thought was his attempt to formulate a theory of economic development. The later Victorian theorists had not continued the classical questioning of the nature of economic evolution. 'The territory of economic dynamics was abandoned and the vacuum was filled by the Marxists, who have been highly skilled in extracting the maximum of surplus value from their intellectual monopoly.'

Social structure and economic dynamics became key concepts in the development of Thomas's theory. He rejected Vincr's assertion that the classical economists had assumed place immobility and occupational mobility, and that the latter had played no significant part in their theory. The vital phenomenon omitted was class mobility. After reviewing the contributions of Sidgwick and the debate between Edgeworth and Bastable (between 1897 and 1903) he pointed out that a few years earlier the Swedish economist, Wicksell, had been 'at pains to hammer home . . . that free trade theory rests on the fundamental assumption that the population of a country is a kind of property-owning democracy with capital and land fairly uniformly distributed among the members.'

After illustrating his assertion that 'the whole discussion' of the mobility postulates of classical theory afforded 'a good example of the limitations of static models', Thomas wrote one of his key statements:

> The surprising thing about the [Edgeworth–Bastable] controversy . . . was the apparent failure of both sides to appreciate the real significance of emigration of labour from an old country. . . . The course of economic development since the eighteen-forties should have made it perfectly clear

that an innovation such as free trade implied by its very nature a movement of labour and capital from England to the undeveloped countries. The United Kingdom was a member of a wider community of nations which was undergoing a dynamic transformation under the impact of technical progress, and this entailed an interregional distribution of factors of production. The process called for a theory of economic development embracing the mutual relationship between national specialization, internal mobility, international migration and the course of trade. An analysis of the process of emigration is not complete unless the assumptions about internal migration are made clear.

He summarised his conclusions. The static pure theory of international trade rested on the assumption of perfect internal mobility between classes as well as occupations. When class immobility was postulated the analysis was closer to the facts of the free trade period: but then 'the interaction between the degree of internal immobility and the rate of external migration' required us to drop the assumption of international factor immobility. There was need of a theory of development that explored the dynamic inter-relationships just described.

While his study of economic thought showed him the lack of such a theory, it was his pursuit of history that showed him the need. As he was to show increasingly in his later years, he was an avid reader of British and American economic and social history, and loved few things more than old newspapers and other contemporary accounts. Economic theory that ignored 'how people tick' was doomed, and evidence about how people ticked long ago was essential to his exploration. Some of this evidence had to be statistical.

In using statistics to study migration he relied most on three techniques. He used age-distribution tables and life expectancy data to estimate numbers of net immigrants over a period. He followed the American economist Kuznets in examining growth and major fluctuations with the aid of data for overlapping decades. He devoted a great deal of effort to fitting trends (usually second degree parabolæ) to lengthy time series, and to examining annual deviations from these trends.

He had reservations about all three techniques, especially trend-fitting. I was his research assistant at this time. We had long discussions about the validity of fitting mathematical trends by methods well suited to physical investigations in which time did not appear as variable. When used with time series these methods attached as much importance to data for every single year, and so the trend value in any year was determined as much by actual values for future years as by actual values for past years: yet how could economic behaviour be so symmetrically dependent on past and future?

We tried to devise a trend that in every year reflected only past data. Eventually he decided that this was not his area of expertise. It would be better to be criticised for using standard if unsatisfactory techniques than have interest in his analysis of migration take second place to discussion of what would inevitably be a controversial and unsatisfactory attempt to devise a new way of fitting trends to historical data. But he had to keep in mind that statistical analysis alone would not be enough to support his conclusions.

Whenever statistical evidence pointed to an important conclusion he would devote whatever time and effort might be necessary to checking whether other evidence supported it. Evidence of all kinds had to be considered and interpreted. 'Statistical "facts" do not speak for themselves: their story has to coaxed out of them. In approaching the subject' he had 'certain hunches as to the best way of wheedling out the truth'.

Having noted that 'emigration from the United Kingdom as well as from the continent of Europe showed marked peaks and troughs with a span almost double that of the business cycle', he set out to examine these fluctuations 'in relation to changes in the rate of economic growth in the United Kingdom and the major receiving country, the United States.' This implied 'a study of capital exports, international trade, domestic investment and national income'. His study of international migration was part of a study of the process of economic growth — not of a single country but of a vast economic region that straddled the Atlantic.

Schumpeter's work on innovations as agents of dynamic change, and his emphasis on the risk of vital elements of causation becoming concealed by over-aggregation, became part of Thomas's own thinking. But he criticised Schumpeter and Akerman for tending 'to overlook those variables which bring about changes in the balance of economic power within the international community'. Instead he would view 'movements of population and capital from one country to another as an expression of growth in the international economy' which would be 'looked upon as a whole. By approaching the time-series of each country with this hypothesis in mind, we shall not expect them all to tell the same story and we may come across structural turning-points' that had not previously been identified.

There was need of:

> a concept of economic development which stresses the widening of markets, the dynamic of increasing returns, and the international mobility of labour and capital as a medium through which an international economy grows and changes its character. . . . Migration not only induces but is itself partly determined by changes in the structure of the international community.

In examining these changes there would be special attention to the 'minor secular swings, showing an average interval of about eighteen years from peak to peak' that so many of the statistical series revealed. A Malthusian cycle of extreme population pressure, leading to similar cycles in emigration, which would influence methods of production in the receiving country, was part of the explanation. Another was the sensitivity of building activity to changes in population. All this led to changes in relative attractivenesses of old and new countries as places for investment by the old countries, and so to cycles in capital flows.

This was the area to be studied in the main part of the book with every tool on which he could lay his hands, statistical and historical, refined and crude. In the end everything had to gel, and make sense to a very critical, well-informed and honest mind. If it did not, he was dissatisifed; and dissatisfaction had to be turned into understanding.

He began with a careful account of the sources and limitations of migration statistics, and a detailed analysis of migration from the United Kingdom 1840–1940 and of Irish emigration over a similar period, finding clues about how the emigrant communities had ticked. Occupying three chapters and supported by several pages of statistics, Part II is a model of how the evaluation and analysis of historical statistical data should be approached.

Part III began with a reprint of his *Manchester School* article. Empirical studies of international migration had already asked questions about links between its cyclical movements and the short business cycles of the countries concerned. Thomas noted that graphs of immigration into the United States from Great Britain and Germany in the period 1831–1913 displayed not only short cycles but also 'minor secular fluctuations' with a span of about eighteen to twenty years. Asserting that 'two short words are better than three long ones', he called these 'long swings'. The British series showed major troughs in 1840, 1860, 1878, and 1897; the German series in 1843, 1862, 1878 and 1898. Similar patterns were revealed for immigration from Ireland and Scandinavia. Simon Kuznets had already drawn attention to the existence of 'secondary secular movements' in the American economy. It was time to extend the area of analysis. Arguing that a study that confined itself to business cycles was 'bound to leave out important features of economic developments', Thomas explored 'the long upswings and downswings in international migration and the rhythm of economic growth of the United States and Great Britain respectively in the period 1830–1913'.

Later chapters showed him at his best in obtaining statistics and extracting meaning and inspiration from them. Insisting that 'you can't make bricks without straw', he revealed an ability to maximise the output–input ratio, always carefully checking his conclusions against other historical testimony, and his own powerful reasoning.

Internal migration often entailed change of occupation. Thomas persuaded the Bureau of the Census to release unpublished data which he used to examine the social classes attained by immigrants from England, Wales, Scotland and Ireland. He went on to comment on the links between immigration and social mobility, and how this was changing over time.

With Schumpeter's waves of innovation in mind, he was delighted to find that statistics of patents granted for inventions in the United States showed sharp rises at the same time as the big upswings in immigration. As the 'widening' of capital structure (defined as a declining or constant ratio of capital stock to GNP), testified, these were periods of increased productivity. Booms in immigration stimulated invention. No wonder America found fame as the home of mass production.

In a chapter on internal and international migration he produced evidence that when migration within an 'old' country (such as Britain or Sweden) was low there was also low home investment; at the same time capital exports and emigration were high. In the 'new' country statistics of internal migration were less obtainable. He used data about Negro migration as a proxy for total internal migration, and argued that swings in external migration were also inverse to those of internal migration in the countries that received the international migrants — a proxy and argument that he later rejected, as we mention below.

Other chapters traced the origin and impact of American restrictions on immigration, which he considered to be against the interests of an expanding international economy, and the changing pattern of migration to the Dominions. In concluding he wrote of his awareness 'that the analysis has done little more than touch the fringes of a complex subject'. There was need of more empirical work, but perhaps he had done something to 'indicate in what directions further work might bear fruit'.

One passage from the last chapter is particularly pertinent to a current argument:

> The fact that the United States is a country of internal free migration and free trade makes it easier for it to solve problems of interregional balance of payments than if the various States had immigration quotas, exchange restrictions and tariff barriers. Equilibrium is not re-established without some decline in the standard of living of the weak region; the two conditions, however, ensure that the decline is kept within bounds and that a breathing space is allowed so that the region's productive capacity can be restored.

His earlier emphasis on language differences as a barrier to migration reminds us that the comparison of a contemplated United Europe with the United States of America is seriously weakened by the absence of one of these conditions.

The book contained 138 statistical tables, 80 of them full-page, and 43 statistical diagrams or charts. It was well received, especially in America. Economic historians and sociologists paid it most attention. It sparked off a lively debate about long swings and the Atlantic Economy to which he contributed several more papers, contributions to books and lectures on both side of the ocean.

With 'MEG' out of the way, he set about honouring a long-standing promise to direct a study of the Welsh economy. This led to *The Welsh Economy: Studies in Expansion* (Cardiff, 1962) which he edited and partly wrote. It was an opportunity to return to his theme. He used historical statistics, particularly of the coal and steel industries and house-building, to show that the growth of South Wales was more in tune with that of the United States than of England. Steam coal made South Wales part of the export sector. When English capital formation was in decline, South Wales was prospering. High overseas demand drove up Welsh coal prices, leading to rising incomes and rising marriage and birth rates.

This finding quickly rekindled his interest in regional disparities, and initiated a laborious statistical enquiry, based largely on Inhabited House Duty statistics, that eventually produced enough straw for a few more bricks, which he used to great effect in 'Demographic Determinants of British and American Building Cycles 1870–1913', which appeared in Donald McCloskey (ed.), *Essays on a Mature Economy* (London, 1971). The paper reappeared the next year as Chapter 2 of

MAUD — *Migration and Urban Development: A Reappraisal of British and American Long Cycles* (London, 1972).

Except for Chapter 3, on the role of international capital movements, a few minor passages and some statistical tables, the whole of 'MAUD' appeared as the lengthy 'Part IV: Reappraisal' of 'MEG II' in 1973, a full long swing after the first edition. Parts I–III differed very little from the first three parts of 'MEG I' but used better statistics where these existed. I recall the glee with which he waved aloft a copy that he had somehow acquired of Feinstein's newly completed but unpublished thesis, full of new historical statistics of capital formation. Here was something new against which to test his theories. What could be better?

The 'lively debate about long swings and the Atlantic Economy' had been 'facilitated by superior quantitative methods and a marked improvement in the range and quality of historical statistics.' Spectral analysis had confirmed his assertion that long swings were no statistical mirage; and nobody had been able to refute the existence of the long term inverse relationship to which he had drawn attention, 'at least in the period 1870–1913'.

He considered the criticism that the inverse nature of the long swings was fortuitous: 'that the operative forces were in the domestic sphere and not in any interacting process'. After producing other counter-arguments he insisted that holders of this view had not paid enough attention to demographic factors. One-sided and American-centred arguments were rejected.

Even Schumpeter had failed to consider the whole as more than the addition of its parts, but 'secular growth entails internal shifts within the aggregate via international factor movements; the expansion of the whole may well express itself through disharmonious rates of growth in the parts. This is what happened in the Atlantic economy . . .'. There was

> . . . an interregional competition for factors of production within the Atlantic Economy, with the Old World and the New World alternating in their intensive build-up of resources. This is the essential characteristic which distinguishes these long swings from short business cycles. Long swings are fluctuations in the rate at which resources are developed, whereas the short business cycles are fluctuations in investment in producer durables and inventories.

This alternation led to the inverse relationship, and

> . . . it seems to be a condition of this inverse investment cycle that (a) a substantial part of the capital formation is sensitive to the rate of population growth, and (b) the rate of population growth is mainly determined by the net

migration balance. The mechanism also entails an inverse relation between internal and external migration.

He produced a carefully thought out formal statement of a model, with nineteen equations and two identities, which was too imprecisely specified to be of immediate econometric value but is a useful summary of his thinking.

In 'MEG I' his explanation of the inverse relationship had not ignored monetary influences but these had not formed an important part of the mechanism. In 'MEG II' this had to be remedied with the help of statistics that had been produced by Friedman and Schwarz and other recent work. The controversy about the long swing could not 'be settled by models . . . which ignore international interaction and which take no account of the transmission mechanism linking money with other economic variables.'

> From 1879 . . . to 1913 the leading countries of the Atlantic economy were on the gold standard. The financial dominance of London and the international repercussions of the Bank of England's policy were major factors. In each country there was an interaction between the 'real' economic magnitudes and the changes in the supply of money entailed by the discipline of the gold standard.

This was part of the explanation of the 'inverse rhythm of growth in United Kingdom, the leading lender, . . . and the United States and other countries of new settlement. . . '.

In the pre-1913 Atlantic Economy, 'the inverse cycle was propelled by real determinants but . . . in the crucial phases when expansion gave way to contraction, changes in the stock of money played a significant part in influencing the course of the economy.'

The analysis was extended to Canada, Australia and Argentina. Another chapter looked at the dynamics of the 'brain drain', one of the more significant features of migration in the years between his two editions. It was concerned both with the flow from Europe to America (encouraged by high United States government spending on research and development) and with the outflow of graduates from developing countries who trained more than they could use. Negro migration and the American urban dilemma occupied the penultimate chapter. A brief look at more recent American and European experience ended with an inquiry into 'the solemn question whether we should say farewell to the Kuznets cycle' (or the long swing). Despite the 'moving epitaph' written by Abramovitz, his own view was that it was still alive. The ending of Bretton Woods in 1971 was possibly 'the beginning of a new process of interaction which could entail systematic long swing divergencies between growth rates in the United States and an enlarged European community of comparable magnitude.' It is too early to dismiss the suggestion.

His second edition appeared in 1973, the year of his retirement from the Chair he had held for twenty-seven years. His department had grown to provide courses in social science, personnel management, law and accountancy. Brinley had towered over it, a stranger to democracy. When he arranged an appointment or set a deadline he expected it to be observed. His colleagues appreciated that in applying the same rule to himself he was allowed considerable latitude. Impatient with inefficiency, he could be generous over mistakes made and admitted in honest effort. Sloppy thinking earned either light-hearted ridicule or scorn. A very private man who seldom saw the need to explain himself, he appeared hard at times; but he was capable of great kindness and helped many. What he would not tolerate was anything that seemed to interfere with his work or his department. A slightly built man, usually neatly dressed with a dominating shining balding head, and a small inquisitive nose, he had blue eyes that could twinkle with mirth or glare with a searing intensity that none could ignore. Appreciative of good food, rugby, beer and honest company he could be the life and soul of a party. His nimble command of words and sense of the incongruous frequently led to loud shoulder-shaking laughter that infected all around. At times it took control and rendered him incapable of serious discussion. His penetrating staring scowl was a warning to keep out of his way but within his reach. Even then, occasionally some colleague who knew him well would light upon a happy thought or verbal quip and turn his wrath into mirth.

When I was his research assistant I attended some of his honours courses. One of these was scheduled for 10.00, but he always arrived promptly at 10.20, having been at work on his book until only six or seven hours earlier. One morning I was working in his room when he suddenly arrived at 10.00. It was fifteen minutes before his class started to drift in, and as each student arrived his glare darkened. A memorable explosion of frightening anger was imminent. But a brave student ventured that abundant experience of *ex post* actual arrival times had caused him to alter his *ex ante* ideas. Brinley's eyes cleared, his shoulders shook and the lecture had to be abandoned.

He had served on the National Assistance Board (which led to his appointment as OBE in 1953) and as Chairman of the Welsh Council (which led to his advancement to CBE in 1973). He had spent considerable periods abroad, especially in the United States where he was a visiting professor at Johns Hopkins for a term in 1968 and a National Science Foundation Fellow at Brown University in 1971. The importance of his work on the Atlantic Economy was recognised by his peers when he was elected a Fellow of the British Academy in 1973. One of his proudest moments was when the National Eisteddfod honoured him by accepting him into its bardic circle in recognition of his services to his beloved country.

On retirement from his Chair he became director of his college's Manpower Research Unit and quickly developed further research and teaching links with American and Canadian universities. These provided him with the opportunity to continue his studies in a congenial atmosphere where he spent half of every year. His summers were spent mainly in his home in Cardiff, with his extensive library.

In 1993, fifty-seven years after the publication of his first book and a full long swing after his retirement, his final volume appeared. *The Industrial Revolution and the Atlantic Economy: Selected Essays* (London), contained ten essays, most of them updated and revised versions of papers published elsewhere. Two had pre-dated his retirement, but most of the rest were first published between 1980 and 1991. Two chapters came more or less untouched from 'MEG II'. Two others were portraits of Robert Owen and a challenging analysis of the beneficial impact of the industrial revolution on the Welsh language. The remaining six chapters showed how three main questions had fired his interest in the last quarter of his life. They were pulled together in an impressive Introduction, written when he was eighty-six, that summarised a new interpretation of economic growth and its prospects.

One question was whether his model that identified and so well described the Atlantic Economy in the nineteenth century could be applied to the eighteenth century, in which a few writers had identified the possibility of long swings. He detected a 'striking similarity', with three long upswings between 1703 and 1776 and an inverse relationship. But after 1760 the effects of a shortage of timber, charcoal and iron were increasingly evident, and the marginal cost of supplying iron-intensive goods to the colonies was rising. This prompted his second question: 'was this energy crisis different in kind from previous shortages?'

He took a new look at the energy shortage in the seventeenth century, invoking fourteen contemporary writers and an array of Swedish (and other) statistics to inspire his thinking. It led to a rejection of Nef's argument that there was a first industrial revolution between 1540 and 1640, when the use of coal led to no fundamental change in the nature of the economy. But between 1640 and 1680 there was a severe crisis within the timber economy. This produced incentives to adopt coal-centred techniques which led to the development of engineering skills and expertise that gave Britain the edge over other countries. We learned how to smelt metals, including iron, from ores with coal or coke, and how to use steam to pump water from mines. For several decades low population growth was accompanied by an abundance of energy: but then came 'a population explosion and an acute energy shortage intensified by Britain's excessive defence commitments after the Seven Years War' (1756–63). A few years later, 'the loss of the American War was the last nail in the coffin of the charcoal iron age'. Attemps to solve the energy crisis by massive increases in imports of timber and charcoal iron failed.

> The organic economy was caught in a Malthusian trap. How could an unprecedented swarming of people on a small island be made consistent with a rising standard of living? This was impossible if the economy remained basically organic: it was necessary to change the energy base from the flow of solar energy to the stock of fossil fuels.

What eventually enabled this to be achieved was the discovery in 1784 by Henry Cort (to whom he devoted a chapter) of how to use coke instead of charcoal in the refining of pig-iron. 'Thanks to the Cromwellian energy crisis British inventors had evolved the expertise which enabled them to solve the post-1760 crisis.'

Thomas concluded his Introduction with the suggestion that now another energy crisis has to be solved. There has to be a switch from the stock of solar energy embodied in fossil fuels back to the flow of solar energy. One way of achieving this is indicated in a prediction by the Nobel Laureate N. F. R. Calvin, one of his colleagues at Berkeley, that by the end of the century commercially adequate efficiency of the photochemical cell will enable us to store renewable solar energy for use by people everywhere.

While working on 'MEG II' he had become 'increasingly aware that the evolving Atlantic economy should be treated as an ecological system'. His first paper on this topic was published in 1975. His work on energy crises confirmed his view. Following his habit of a lifetime, he went back to earlier writings and in 1991 published 'Alfred Marshall on Economic Biology' in the *Review of Political Economy*. The final chapter of his last book built on these. Entitled 'A Plea for an Organic Approach to Economic Growth', it examined Marshall's case for economic biology. Economic change is an irreversible evolution, and biological models and analogies should be used instead of mechanical ones, in which time is treated as reversible. Marshall was at pains to stress this, and promised to write about it in a second volume of his *Principles*, but he failed to do so, giving weak health and pressure of other work as his reasons. Thomas argued that his papers revealed another reason — an intellectual dissatisfaction with his own ideas about how to treat time.

> Marshall's basic insight was that the study of economic growth must mean the abandonment of mechanical equilibrium models based on the reversibility of time. This message was not heeded by his successors.
>
> When Marshall recognized the full implications of irreversibility he rejected his mechanical model of growth and called for a biological approach. Yet . . . when the study of economic growth became a major preoccupation in the 1950's and 1960's, Marshall's conclusions were ignored and mechanical models similar to the one which he had discarded became a prominent element in economics curricula everywhere.

In stressing the need for 'theories of growth which will be "in time" not "out of time" ', Thomas was voicing the same dissatisfaction with the treatment of time as he had expressed when fitting trends to time series forty years earlier.

In 1976, three years after his retirement and to mark his seventieth birthday, his Festschrift was published by the University of Wales Press. *Population, Factor Movements and Economic Development: Studies Presented to Brinley Thomas*, edited by Hamish Richards contained essays by several distinguished international scholars and others, like Richards and myself, who began academic life as his research assistant. A few months before his death in 1994 I visited him in his home where he lived with his books. He talked of his love for Sibelius and for fine paintings, and of books he was reading. Then he picked up his Festschrift and read out a sentence I had used to end a personal note about him, 'There's a whole long swing of life and output yet to come,' he read in a voice that had lost none of its slightly nasal resonance. 'You were right,' he said. 'There was, and I've done it. Now it's time to have a rest.' He told me of how he was relaxing — reading and thinking about the economics of New Testament times.

After his death his daughter found, on a table next to his favourite chair, chapter headings for a new book looking back over his life and times. Scholarship, reading, researching and writing were this Welshman's life to the very last.

J. PARRY LEWIS
University of Manchester

EDWARD THOMPSON   *Berrows Newspapers*

Proceedings of the British Academy, **90**, 521–539

Edward Palmer Thompson
1924–1993

EDWARD PALMER THOMPSON was born on 3 February 1924 near Oxford, the younger of two sons of Edward John Thompson and Theodosia Jessup Thompson. The household was high-minded and liberal. The father, son of Methodist missionaries in India, followed the family tradition, although he left the ministry in 1923, after twelve years in India and (during the Great War as chaplain) in the Middle East, where he met his wife, herself a Methodist missionary from a New England family rich in jurists and public servants, with its own missionary connection with the Levant. Edward sen., himself a writer, poet and historian, left India shortly before Edward jun.'s birth for a Fellowship at Oriel College, Oxford and, eventually, a University Lectureship in Bengali. India had been the main field of his missionary activity, India's national struggles were to be the main concern of his secular public activities, and India was also to be the major subject of his historical writings. The young Thompsons were to grow up breathing the atmosphere of Indian freedom, and probably better acquainted with the famous figures of the Indian independence movement than with those of British politics. Edward claimed that Jawaharlal Nehru, between spells in jail, showed him how to keep a straight bat.

That the younger Thompsons should, in the atmosphere of the 1930s, have extended the family liberalism leftwards to Communism, is not surprising. They were not the only children of progressive-minded parents, even in Oxford, to do so. Both Edward and his brother Frank, his senior by three years, grew up in that town, where they went to the Dragon School before Frank was sent to Winchester, from which he naturally passed to New College. For financial reasons the younger Edward was sent to his father's old school Kingswood, a Methodist establishment, which may or may not have a bearing on the fact, obvious from the references to Methodism in his later historical writings, notably in *The Making of the English Working Class*, that the tradition of John Wesley was not a part of the family heritage which he was anxious to make his own.

Frank's career at Oxford, where he joined the Communist Party, showed every sign of scholarly, literary and social brilliance. He volunteered for military service in 1939 and was captured and executed at the age of twenty-four by the Bulgarian government during the war while leading an SOE mission in support of the Bulgarian partisans. Edward co-edited the story of this mission and some of Frank's wartime diaries and lectures for publication in 1946 (*There Is A Spirit In Europe* (London)). Some of his poems were published in later anthologies of World War II poetry and one was used as a text for the official celebrations of the fiftieth anniversary of the end of the war.

Frank was important to his younger brother's life, not only because Edward was deeply loyal to family tradition, and indeed in later years integrated it into his historical research. He was to publish his father's letters to Rabindranath Tagore, investigated Frank's tragic wartime mission both in Britain and Bulgaria, and had made some progress towards a critical account of this still unclarified episode. It was also because Edward's relation to Frank was central to his development. It was, I think, a complex relation of admiration for and competition against a brother who, in life, had appeared as the more favoured and brilliant, and who by his death acquired the status of a hero and martyr of the war of anti-Fascist resistance. While Frank fought, Edward left Kingswood for Cambridge, where he stayed for a year at the then stolid and Tory Corpus Christi College before being called up in 1942. (The college, some of whose senior members showed minimal enthusiasm for the youthful Thompson, was eventually to make him an Honorary Fellow.) He served as a subaltern in the 17/21st Lancers in the North African and Italian campaigns, leading a tank squadron in the battle of Cassino. Like Frank, he had joined the Communist Party.

In 1945 he returned to Cambridge, where he met his comrade, colleague and lifetime partner, Dorothy Towers—also a youthful Communist—whom he married in 1948.

Although he did not know it, the pattern of his work as a historian, writer and public activist was set in these immediate post-war years. For, though he completed part I of his Cambridge History Tripos, he chose not to continue his formal studies, but took an immediate degree, as was then possible for ex-service undergraduates. He spent his remaining year at Cambridge reading independently, mainly in the history and literature of the Elizabethan period. As the most cursory glance at Thompson's work shows, he was at least as interested in literature as in history. The two interests were all the more inseparably merged, because he saw himself primarily as a writer. His first publications, in a left-wing cultural review, were a short story and poems, and towards the end of his life he returned to publishing both poetry and fiction. Indeed, when the Communist Party established or formalised a number of 'cultural groups', he chose to be active in the Writers' Group rather than the Historians' Group, which flourished from 1946 to 1956. Although both Thompsons were members, he played no important part in the very active intellectual debates of that group. Nor was he associated until the late 1960s with the historical journal *Past & Present*, founded under the Group's auspices, only joining its Board, of which he remained a cherished member until his death, in 1969. Unlike his wife, he never undertook dissertation research. On the contrary, he deliberately rejected the option of a purely academic career as a university teacher, as he also spurned the metropolitan life. Like several left-wing ex-service graduates of historical or historico-literary bent at the time, he opted for the provincial world of extra-mural 'workers' education, but not before the Thompsons had done their revolutionary duty in the summer and autumn of 1947 by helping to build the so-called 'Youth Railway' from Samac to Sarajevo in Tito's Yugoslavia. Edward commanded the British Brigade of a few hundred volunteers in this international enterprise, assisted by Dorothy as Brigade Secretary and Martin Eve, later Edward's publisher, as 'cultural officer'. His deputy, a left-wing Christian Fabian, recommended the West Riding as the place to go for the aspiring adult educator. That is where the Thompsons went.

The West Riding offered a more practical advantage, the support of an old family friend, Guy Chapman, then Professor of Modern History at the University of Leeds who, with Norman Gash, also provided research supervision for Dorothy. Though Chapman's support got Edward short-listed for a post as staff tutor in history and literature in the University's Department of Extra-mural Studies, it would probably have been insufficient to get him appointed. 1948 was the first of several years when it was to become virtually impossible for a known and active member of the Communist Party to get a teaching job in or around British universities, although no attempt was made to remove those already in place in what Americans now call 'tenure-track' posts. Fortunately the formidable Sidney Raybould, then head of the department, was a strong believer in intellectual pluralism, and deliberately sought to find representatives of various points of view, however heterodox. Thompson may therefore have been actually appointed *because* he was a Communist, probably a unique case at that time. Still, those who recall the radiant charisma, both personal and intellectual, of the young (as of the older) Thompson, will not doubt that he interviewed wonderfully well. Politics apart, at the age of twenty-four he must have been a hard man not to appoint.

The West Riding was the Thompsons' base from then on. All their children were born there—Ben (1948), Mark (1951), and Kate (1956). For seventeen years Edward led the life of the adult education tutor, not all that dissimilar from that of the political campaigner which filled his spare time. He knew the 'unsocial hours' of the itinerant speaker, the endless journeys to and from evening classes in Hemsley, Otley, Dewsbury and as far afield as Middlesbrough, but also the hospitality, tea and comradeship of people engaged in self-education and good causes. His students, in turn, recognised that there was something special about what a future member of his Batley class described as 'a tall, rangy sort of fellow' whose 'nervous energy'—another contemporary impression—'was so abundant that he would pull constantly at his sweater till, before his students' mesmerized gaze, it was seen to unravel.' A surviving BBC film of Thompson passionately explicating a poem by Blake to an adult class, vividly recalls this phase of his career.

There is no measuring what his writings owe to his experience of life in what was still an old and barely reconstructed region of the first Industrial Revolution, not so far removed from the memory of the handloom weavers whose large-windowed cottages were still visible in the old textile villages. (To understand their history, he bought himself a loom and learned to weave.) It is characteristic that *The Making of the English Working Class* is dedicated to two of his working-class adult students, Dorothy and Joseph Greenald. Without the Yorkshire years the book might not, in fact, almost certainly could not, have been written.

Had it been published some years earlier, it might well have also been dedicated to the West Riding members of the Communist Party, a strongly working-class organisation in a classic district of the old industrialism, who kept Thompson's liking and respect even after he ceased to share their loyalties. For eight years he was, to all appearances, a devoted and unquestioning Communist activist, a brilliant, handsome, passionate and oratorically gifted young man, plainly regarded by the party leadership as an obvious asset. During this period he wrote the first of his books for the party's publishing house, *William Morris, Romantic to Revolutionary* (1955, revised 1977). In the summer of 1956 he suddenly emerged as one of its most prominent critics. Within a few months he was no longer in the party. For the rest of his life, though always campaigning on the left, he was to keep aloof from complete identification with any political party—even the Labour Party which the Thompsons joined in the early 1960s, over the resistance of party authorities suspicious of firebrands who had very likely not put their Marxism behind them, but refused to answer questions on the subject.

What drove Thompson into rebellion, together with other Communist intellectuals, was the failure of the British Communist Party to face the issues raised by Khrushchev in his denunciation of Stalin at the 20th Congress of the Soviet Communist Party in February 1956. There is little doubt that he, like some others had felt uneasy about some aspects of the Soviet Union before then, and about the *modus operandi* of the British Communist Party. Nevertheless, it is almost certainly wrong to suppose that many of them, and certainly not Edward Thompson, were potential dissidents waiting for an opportunity to secede. Indeed, the usual course for intellectuals who changed their minds about Marxism, Communist policy or the Soviet Union, had been simply to leave the party, as a succession of the student recruits to the party of the 1930s and 1940s had done since 1939. This course Thompson and his fellow rebels specifically disclaimed. The rebellion of 1956 was that of men and women whose immediate object was not to secede from the party but to reform it.

It seemed evident to many, perhaps most, members of the party's 'cultural groups'—certainly to the historians, who became the major centre of politico-intellectual dissidence—that Khrushchev's revelations about Stalinism, required a major and self-critical rethinking, both of the history of the Soviet and the British Communist Parties. Khrushchev had at least confronted the past, though spectacularly failing to make a satisfactory, let alone a 'Marxist', analysis of it. He had merely put the blame entirely on Stalin ('the cult of personality'). The

British Communist Party leadership refused even to admit the seriousness of the revelations, and insofar as it did so by implication, it
resisted, and did its best to avoid and to stifle, discussion of them within
the party. It was this refusal that drove hitherto loyal intellectuals into
rebellion and was to convince Edward Thompson that a party structured
on the centralist, orthodox and disciplined Marxist-Leninist lines of the
Communist Party was politically and intellectually unacceptable.
Together with John Saville, economic and social historian (and later
Professor) at the University of Hull, he set up a small duplicated
discussion journal within the party under the title, borrowed from an
early nineteenth century publication designed 'to renew and reinvigo-
rate a flagging Jacobin radicalism',[1] and patently chosen by Thompson,
The New Reasoner.

After a few months the party suspended those connected with the
New Reasoner from membership. However, by this time the invasion of
Hungary by Soviet troops appeared to confirm the worst suspicions of
the critics. The *New Reasoner* group resigned from the Communist
Party, headed by Thompson, who increasingly emerged as its most
eloquent and stylish spokesman, and—for the first time—a widely-
known personage on the national intellectual Left. The *New Reasoner*
re-emerged as a printed quarterly in 1957. Two years later it combined
with another product of the ferment of 1956, the *Universities and Left
Review* (animated by another ex-Communist-Party historian, the youthful Raphael Samuel, later father of the *History Workshop Journal*) to
form the *New Left Review*, which is still in existence. However,
Thompson's close association with the journal came to an end in
1962, when the *Review* was taken over by Perry Anderson and a group
of younger Oxford Marxists, whose intellectual and political style was
not his.

For some time after 1956 he made, or joined in, various attempts to
establish a socialist position to the left of the Labour Party which failed,
like the *May Day Manifesto* which he launched with Raymond Williams
and Stuart Hall (1966). Neither were the various Trotskyist and
Trotsky-derived groups and parties of the period to his taste. The British
New Left after 1956 never managed to become a political force, as
distinct from an intellectual one, nor did Thompson. Eventually, after a
period of relative political quiescence in the 1970s, he was to discover a
new political vocation in the revived movement for nuclear disarma-

[1] B. D. Palmer, *E. P. Thompson, Objections and Oppositions* (London, 1994), p. 74.

ment of the early 1980s. In this movement he was to occupy a position of extraordinary prominence, somewhat analogous to that occupied by Bertrand Russell in the early stages of the Campaign for Nuclear Disarmament (CND) after 1958. The Thompsons had naturally been associated with the CND since its foundation, but only as local activists.

It is thus evident that Thompson's history and his politics are inseparable. He was and remained essentially 'The Historian as Activist'—to quote the title of a study of his work in the *American Historical Review*.[2] Nothing illustrates this better than the massive volume published in 1963 which—justifiably—made him famous almost overnight. *The Making of the English Working Class* is the exact opposite of a work written *sine ira et studio*. Indeed, few historical works have been written with so avowed, passionate and partisan a purpose, namely—in the phrase that instantly identifies itself as his— 'to rescue the poor stockinger, the Luddite cropper, the "obsolete" handloom weaver, the "utopian" artisan, and even the deluded follower of Joanna Southcott, from the enormous condescension of posterity.'

Like almost all of Thompson's works, it had outgrown its origins. Just as the 900 pages of *William Morris, Romantic to Revolutionary* had started as a review of a long-forgotten book by an American author who had aroused his anger, so the 848 pages of *The Making* had begun as the first chapter of a textbook of British working-class history from 1790 to 1945. (The publishing house of Gollancz understandably decided to stick with what they got.) Similarly *Whigs and Hunters* was to start as a contribution to a volume of essays on eighteenth-century crime which he was editing with some of his former students. On this occasion the very bulk of the book added to its force.

A book written with such polemical verve and passion—'a long, sprawling, closely documented book which nevertheless has something of the point and vigor of a pamphlet', noted a (literary) reviewer[3]— might have been expected to meet a polemical reception, as indeed the Communist Thompson's book on William Morris had done. Yet, so far as can be discovered, only one serious reviewer (Gertrude Himmelfarb) dismissed it, at considerable length, as 'a tract that has all the appurtenances of conventional history'.[4] Though the specialists' reception was

---

[2] M. Bess, 'E. P. Thompson: The Historian as Activist' *American Historical Review*, 98, 1, February 1993, 19–38.

[3] J. Gross, 'Hard Times. "The Making of the English Working Class"', *New York Review of Books*, 16 April 1964, 8–10.

[4] G. Himmelfarb, 'A Tract of Secret History', *New Republic*, 11 April 1964, 24–6.

far from uniformly favourable,[5] few reviewers denied its sheer power and extraordinary impact. 'With the publication of this new book' the *New York Times'* reviewer—an established American social historian—held that the man who had been 'one of Britain's angry young socialist historians . . . showed every sign of becoming not just an angry middle-aged historian, but one of the leaders of the British historical profession'.[6] Superlatives—'a work of commanding authority and permanent importance',[7] 'a magnificent book, a book that will be read for many generations to come',[8] came not only from the expected quarters, but from those who disagreed strongly with his views. One of the most hostile judges thought that what he regarded as Thompson's 'obsession may have helped him to write a great book.'[9]

Whatever the peer assessment, there could be no doubt of the book's impact on the less expert public. 'Mr Thompson has unquestionably arrived', wrote the same hostile reviewer. 'Students are not only reading his book—they are sometimes buying it—at three and a half guineas a time; the danger is that they may read nothing else.' The readership of *The Making* expanded with the growth of the (increasingly radicalised) student population of the decade. By 1968 Penguin Books chose to celebrate the publication of its thousandth volume by issuing it in paperback. It has never been out of print since.

The Making of the English Working Class changed Thompson's life. It turned him for some years into an official academic. In 1965 he was appointed to the new University of Warwick as Reader, where he founded and directed the Centre for the Study of Social History. The move to the Midlands—first to Leamington Spa, eventually to Worcester—also allowed Dorothy Thompson a more permanent academic career at Birmingham University and to continue her studies on Chartism, which her husband did not wish to duplicate. This is a major reason why *The Making of the English Working Class* was not pursued further into the nineteenth century, as one might have expected. Instead he extended his enquiries backwards into the eighteenth century, which

---

[5] For contemporary negative criticisms, cf. R. Bendix in *American Sociological Review*, 30(4) August 1965, 605–6; R. K. Webb in the *Massachusetts Review*, 6(1) Autumn–Winter 1964–5, 202–8; 'The Making of the English Working Class?' (1965) in R. M. Hartwell, *The Industrial Revolution and Economic Growth* (London 1971) pp. 361–76.

[6] H. Ausubel, 'The Common Man as Hero', *New York Times Book Review*, 26 April 1964, 44.

[7] J. Gross, 'Hard Times', loc. cit., 10.

[8] S. Thernstrom, 'A Major Work of Radical History', *Dissent*, XII, 1, Winter 1965, 90–2.

[9] J. D. Chambers, 'The Making of the English Working Class', *History*, LI (1966), 183–8.

was henceforth to be at the core of his research interests. He did not totally abandon the nineteenth century, but his publications in this area are not central to his work.[10]

From a scholarly point of view Thompson's years at Warwick were remarkably fruitful. Starting with the influential studies on 'Time, Work-Discipline and Industrial Capitalism' and 'The Moral Economy of the English Crowd in the Eighteenth Century', (1967 and 1971 respectively) he began to lay the foundations for a far-reaching reconsideration both of pre-industrial society and, in effect, of his own historical perspectives, which were to be brought together in a work to be called *Customs in Common*, to which he looked forward from the early 1970s. Equally important, certainly from Thompson's point of view, Warwick gave him the opportunity of teaching and working with a group of research students, which was to produce both his own third book, *Whigs and Hunters: The Origins of the Black Act* (London 1975) and the volume of his and his students' studies on eighteenth-century crime, for which it had originally been intended, *Albion's Fatal Tree* (London 1975).

A number of papers in this general field were published during the early and mid-1970s, notably 'Patrician Society, Plebian [sic] Culture' (*Journal of Social History* 7, Summer 1974), 'The Web of Inheritance', an introduction to the volume *Family and Inheritance* (Cambridge, 1976), edited by Thompson, Jack Goody and Joan Thirsk, the report of an earlier *Past & Present* conference, 'Folklore, Anthropology and Social History' (*Indian Historical Review*, III (2), 1977), originally given to the Indian Historical Congress in 1976[11] and 'Eighteenth-Century Society, Class Struggle Without Class?' (*Social History*, 2/2, May 1978, 33–65.) Other studies remained at the seminar stage, or were not published in English.[12] The discovery of folklore and folklore studies, neglected in *The Making*, soon becomes evident, as does the stimulus of social anthropology, which fertilised so much British historiography in the 1950s and 1960s, but also his reservations about the directions of some practitioners of that discipline.[13]

---

[10] e.g. E. P. Thompson, 'The Political Education of Henry Mayhew', *Victorian Studies*, 11 (1967); E. P. Thompson and Eileen Yeo (eds.), *The Unknown Mayhew: Selections from the Morning Chronicle 1849–50* (London, 1971).

[11] Both are reprinted in E. P. Thompson, *Persons and Polemics* (London, 1994), the latter under the title 'History and Anthropology'.

[12] 'Rough Music: *le charivari anglais*', *Annales, Economies, Sociétés, Civilisations* 27, 1972.

[13] Cf. 'Anthropology and the Discipline of Historical Context', a review of works by Alan Macfarlane and Keith Thomas, in *Midland History*, 1 (3), Spring 1972, 41–55.

It was also during these years that he entered the mainstream of professional history, as a member of the editorial board of *Past & Present* and as a pillar of the international Round Tables on Social History, organised by the Paris *Maison des Sciences de l'Homme (MSH)*, which met irregularly in Paris and in other European academic centres, bringing together established and often prestigious scholars from the United States of America and three or four European countries with rising talent. That brilliant impresario of the intellect, Clemens Heller, who (under the supportive leadership of Fernand Braudel) had turned the *MSH* into a major centre of international scholarly exchanges, recognised both the moment for internationalising the field of 'social history', and that Thompson was central to it. He was not easily convinced to enter the milieu of international academic colloquia and conferences which was far from his usual habitat, nor was he a natural cosmopolitan, still less at ease with some styles of discourse popular on the continent. I recall the luncheon at which Heller (who had come to London specially for the purpose) successfully persuaded him to join the enterprise. By 1976 the Round Tables had exhausted their initial field of discussion—the history of the working classes in the more general context of class relations—and shifted into the region where history, social anthropology and *Volkskunde* meet, before fading away. In this they paralleled Thompson's own development during the 1970s. These were also the years when, thanks to a perceptive and understanding editor, Thompson acquired, for the first time, a wider platform than that of the inward-looking socialist Left for his views on public affairs. To the weekly journal *New Society* he was, for several years after 1967, to send—usually to be collected from the last possible train arriving in London before, or sometimes after, the deadline— some of his most eloquent denunciations, several of which were repub- lished as *Writing by Candlelight* (London, 1980). On the basis of these one might safely regard him as one of the very finest writers of English polemical prose, 'the best political essayist today in the tradition of Swift, Hazlitt, Cobbett and Orwell.'[14]

His spell at Warwick came to an end in 1972, with a public flourish. He resigned after a conflict between students and the university admin- istration, whose offices were occupied. The documentation found there appeared to show that university officials were monitoring the political activities of students and staff, as well as other more serious interfer-

[14] B. Crick, 'Thompson and Liberty!', *Manchester Guardian Weekly*, 11 May 1980.

ences with civil liberties, not least those of American visitors to the Centre for Social History. Though Thompson's view of the contemporary student ferment was far from uncritical, he plunged into action, using the material discovered to edit an instant denunciatory Penguin book with a self-explanatory title: *Warwick University Ltd: Industry, Management and the Universities* (Harmondsworth, 1970). The episode sharpened Thompson's sense of civil freedoms under threat from encroaching authority, to which he was to give frequent and powerful expression in his writings on public matters in this decade. He increasingly devoted his pen to the defence of Common Law and Constitution.

However, even before the crisis at Warwick, Thompson had decided to resign from the university. He was never at ease with organisations, structures and timetables: his preference was for friendships, informality and the surge of movements, although for his juniors even the friendship and informality of this large man with 'wild, prematurely greying hair' who 'looked like he had just strolled in from the moors' could be formidable. There is a Blakean air to the description by one of them: 'He was intense and energetic and had piercing eyes.'[15] At all events he turned, with relief, 'to pursue the career which he had always wanted, of freelance writer',[16] varied by occasional spells of teaching in universities, mainly in North America.

Two things now made this easier: Dorothy's full-time appointment at the University of Birmingham, and his mother's death, which provided the means for buying the splendidly named Wick Episcopi, a tree-flanked eighteenth-century country house with a vista over Worcestershire pastures across a ha-ha. Furnished for comfortable living in unaffected taste, it was to become the Thompsons' lasting home. Some time earlier he had also come to rent a spectacularly inaccessible and primitive ancient Welsh farmhouse on a mountainside of equally spectacular beauty overlooking Cardigan Bay, from the architect and environmentalist Clough Williams-Ellis, who loved to collect intellectuals as part-time tenants. To Hafotty the Thompsons retreated from the tensions of English life by means of a hard-wearing Land Rover. These are the settings in which his friends like to recall him: angular, craggily handsome, already, like many other large men in middle age, slightly bent forward, gardening in Wick—as he did to the last, when health permitted—or pottering about the forecourt of Hafotty, reporting on his

---

[15] Cited in Palmer, *E. P. Thompson* p. 104.
[16] From a memorandum by Dorothy Thompson.

latest sighting of the local hen harrier. In both places the Thompsons welcomed friends from far places—and for most of their friends both Wick, and, notoriously, Hafotty, were far and not easy to reach—with easy hospitality. Both were working homes, though only Wick held Edward's very substantial primary and secondary libraries. He visited other archives and libraries as animals on the veldt go to water-holes: intermittently, out of necessity though with profound enjoyment. They were not his regular habitat. Big cities, even those with Public Record Offices and British Libraries, were places to visit, not for living.

It is not easy to say how and why these extraordinarily fruitful years in Thompson's intellectual life came to an end sometime in the later 1970s. What is clear is that, some time before 1979, when he was to plunge full-time into the anti-nuclear agitations, the eighteenth-century studies, into which he had entered with such zest, began to mark time. For a time much of his energy was pre-empted by a lengthy settling of accounts with the writings of Louis Althusser, then surprisingly influential on the young intellectual Left. The results were published, together with important earlier intra-Left controversies—notably Thompson's historically powerful critique of Perry Anderson and Tom Nairn, 'The Peculiarities of the English'[17]—as *The Poverty of Theory and Other Essays* (London, 1978). The reasons why Thompson turned aside from his researches to fight a major ideological battle against this antagonist, are not clear. They are probably to be sought in his acute sense of isolation from the intellectual young of the 1960s New Left, to which he gave expression in a moving interview in 1976.[18] There can be no question of Thompson's passionate outrage at the fashions then capturing the radical young. Still, even if *The Poverty* contains some of Thompson's most interesting reflections on the nature of the historical project, it is a pity that he did not let himself be diverted by those who tried to convince him that his work on the eighteenth century was more important than the demolition of a philosopher who would in any case soon drop out of ideological sight. When he returned to the eighteenth century at the end of his life, he had a decade of scholarship to catch up, other topics—Blake and the days of the young Wordsworth—competed for his interest, and much of the original *élan* of his plunge into pre-industrial society had been lost. He

[17] Originally published in the *Socialist Register*, 1965, 311–63.

[18] Interview with E. P. Thompson in *Radical History Review*, 3, Fall 1976. It is reprinted in *Visions of History. Interviews with E. P. Thompson et al.* (New York, 1984).

was too ill to recover the lost impetus of the 1970s. In the form finally published, *Customs in Common*, in spite of all its many brilliancies, could be described as 'a mélange of four previously published works (and a very long . . . reply to critics of the "moral economy") as well as two unpublished "road papers" pulled out of his academic hat . . . a somewhat awkward sum of its parts, overdeveloped here, underdeveloped there.'[19] It remained a torso, a master's 'work in progress', but not a new masterpiece.

However, from the end of 1979 both history and socialist ideological argument of the old type dropped into the background, as the cause of nuclear disarmament took over Thompson's life for the next five years. During this period he wrote extensively but almost exclusively on the dangers of nuclear war,[20] which, through the European Nuclear Disarmament Appeal (END) he did his best to detach from the debates between East and West. The proposal to station a large number of missiles of a new type on European soil had revived the flagging anti-nuclear movement. How far the great peace-movements of the early 1980s contributed to ending the Cold War remains a matter of debate. However, this is perhaps to read history backwards. The issue that mobilised so many at the time, was not, in the first instance, ending the Cold War, but the sudden mutual escalation of nuclear armament which appeared to bring the globe once again to the edge, and perhaps over the edge, of nuclear extermination.

This was certainly Edward's view. Nothing, he felt, could now be more urgent than the fight against what he called 'the doomsday consensus'. In the course of these years he became, as never before, a public figure: the most powerful voice and pen of the anti-nuclear movement in his own, and in some other countries. From 1980 to 1985 he drove a powerful physique to the limit, endlessly criss-crossing the frontiers of 'nineteen or twenty different countries',[21] speaking, writing, arguing, being seen. Hundreds of thousands grew familiar, in the giant demonstrations of the early 1980s, with his dramatically rock-ribbed look, the flying hair (now white), the passion exploding in voice

---

[19] 'Proto-nothing', review article by D. Levine, *Social History*, 18(3), October 1993, 382.

[20] E. P. Thompson, 'Notes on Exterminism, the Last Stage of Civilization', *New Left Review*, 181 (1980). Several of his writings were reprinted in *Zero Option* (London, 1980), *Double Exposure* (London, 1985), *The Heavy Dancers* (London, 1985), EPT (ed.), *Star Wars* (Harmondsworth, 1985), EPT and Dan Smith (eds.) *Protest and Survive*, (Harmondsworth, 1981), EPT *et al. Exterminism and Cold War* (London, 1982).

[21] E. P. Thompson, *Persons and Polemics* (London, 1994) p. 360.

and gesture, in short, the sheer star quality of his public presence, of which he was not unaware. Millions more learned to recognise them through the cameras of the mass media. Those were the years when public opinion polls placed him among the Britons most admired by their contemporaries, and perhaps for a time, among the men, the most admired. (The Queen, the Queen Mother and Mrs Thatcher continued to run ahead of him.)

By the middle of the 1980s the danger of immediate nuclear crisis seemed to have receded. In any case the missiles against which the movement had mobilised, were now installed. By 1985 Thompson's 'total immersion in the peace movement was easing' and he was struggling, doubtfully ('if, or as, I return to my trade' he wrote late in that year[22]) to find his way back to history. But by this time his health had begun to give way.

He himself put down its initial deterioration to 'some bug' he had picked up at a conference in New Delhi. But, in any case, his constitution had probably been pushed beyond its limits during the years of campaigning. He was in hospital for much of the winter of 1987. The collapse of his health became obvious in the next years, during the lecturing visits abroad which the Thompsons' financial situation increasingly made necessary. (After Warwick they could rely only on Dorothy's academic salary supplemented by Edward's literary earnings, mainly the continuing, but hardly life-supporting, royalties from *The Making*.) Illness in Canada in 1988, and a further spell in a New Jersey hospital in 1989–90 revealed, or added to, the extent of his physical breakdown. From then on, increasingly immobile in England, in and out of hospital, the flame of his mind and passion playing round the prematurely aged ruins of his body, he lived at death's door, but refused to die.

His physician, he reported, thought that 'I evidently must have some mission in the world still, since I have narrowly escaped death twice'.[23] He had. He was surrounded by fragments of uncompleted projects, lectures intended to turn into books, or plans postponed: *Customs in Common*; his book on William Blake (with Marx, William Morris and Vico the inspiration of a lifetime); the period of the early Romantic poets (subject of a brilliant set of Northcliffe Lectures in 1982); the enquiry into his brother's death. He even branched out into new projects: India, his father's relations with Rabindranath Tagore, which

---

[22] Palmer, *E. P. Thompson*, p. 141; EPT, *Persons and Polemics*, p. 361.
[23] Palmer, *E. P. Thompson*, pp. 143–4.

produced an 'unbidden and unplanned book' published shortly before his death,[24] even the case of Sampson Occum, an American Indian whose struggles to reclaim customary native lands in the American revolutionary era, he had chosen in 1988 as the subject of the Herbert G. Gutman memorial lecture in New York. One must agree with the friend who writes 'his last years were a self-imposed and, one suspects, pressured commitment to finish up a series of writing projects.'[25]

By the time he died, he had published *Customs in Common* (London, 1991) and the Tagore Book; the Blake book, *Witness Against the Beast* was about to come out (London, 1993) (shadows of what they might have been, but still). He had collected together such of his papers as he wished to preserve, *Persons and Polemics* (London, 1994), and had made what arrangements were possible, for the remaining projects. Before his health broke down finally, he had also managed to publish his only novel, *The Sykaos Papers* (London, 1988), a Swiftian satire on a dark world. He knew he had no time for more. Fortunately he had time to demonstrate the victory of spirit over physical ruin in a moving television film of the two Thompsons at Wick, made by a friend, *A Life of Dissent*. He died, a few days after returning from hospital for the last time, peacefully in his garden at Wick on 27 August 1993.

How can we assess Thompson's achievement? He was many things, but he will be remembered longest, as he probably would have wished to be, as a historian.

First, the quite extraordinary impact of his writings must be noted. The *Arts and Humanities Citations Index* recorded him (for the period 1976–1983) as among the 100 most-cited twentieth-century authors in any field covered by the Index, and the most cited of the four names in the list described as 'historians'. The early 1980s almost certainly saw him at the peak of his fame, but, to judge by the *Social Sciences Citations Index*, in which he also figures very prominently, his then published historical writings maintained virtually the same rate of citation for the rest of the decade, and probably fell no more than five per cent below it in the first half of the 1990s.[26] Moreover, in his

---

[24] *Alien Homage: Edward Thompson and Rabindranath Tagore* (New Delhi, 1993).

[25] Palmer, *E. P. Thompson* p. 150.

[26] I am obliged to Ms Lise Grande for these calculations. The figures for 1995 are estimates based on the citations through April 1995, the last available at the time of writing. The works counted are: *The Making of the English Working Class*, *William Morris* (reprinted 1977), *Whigs and Hunters* (1975) and Thompson's articles in *Past & Present* (1967 and 1971), the *Journal of Social History* (1974) and *Social History* (1978).

lifetime a substantial number of studies took his work and thinking as their subject: an unusual situation for historians not yet in their grave.[27]

Much of this is due unquestionably to his exceptionally enthusiastic reception in the United States, where even the official academy welcomed him with fewer hesitations than in his own country, as is indicated by his election to the American Academy of Arts and Sciences in 1979, before the British Academy in 1992. Nevertheless, his influence was greatest and most immediate among the radical young scholars then flocking into the explosively growing field of 'social history'. The initial reading of *The Making* 'resonated perfectly with the hopes of a generation of radical scholars that common people could make their own history, and that sympathetic historians could write it using such imaginative tools as reading upper-class sources "upside down", pursuing oral history of the living, and "decoding" behaviour of the dead.' Even for those in the social sciences outside the narrowly historical field, 'he sent a quenching shower of spring rain across a parched landscape.'[28]

His considerable impact on historians, political scientists and notably on sociologists, was by no means confined to the United States and Britain, where he was described as 'the historian of the sociologists'.[29] (A 1988 survey of the field of sociology cited him in five out of its twenty-two sections, though, oddly enough, not in that on 'Social Movements'.[30]) In spite of its purely English subject and the enormous costs of translation, *The Making*—described by a Spanish historian as

[27] Among others: A. Dawley, 'E. P. Thompson and the Peculiarities of the Americans', *Radical History Review*, 19, Winter 1978–9, 33–59; B. Palmer, *The Making of E. P. Thompson: Marxism, Humanism and History* (Toronto, 1981); C. Calhoun, *The Question of Class Struggle* (Chicago, 1982); also 'E. P. Thompson and the Discipline of Historical Context', *Social Research*, 61(2), Summer 1994, 223–4; E. K. Trimberger, 'E. P. Thompson: Understanding the Process of History', in T. Skocpol (ed.), *Vision and Method in Historical Sociology* (Cambridge, 1984), pp. 211–43; S. Desan, 'Crowds, Community and Ritual in the Work of E. P. Thompson and Natalie Davis', in L. Hunt (ed.), *The New Cultural History* (Berkeley, 1989), pp. 47–71; H. J. Kaye and K. McLelland (eds), *E. P. Thompson. Critical Perspectives* (Philadelphia, 1990); M. Bess, 'E. P. Thompson: The Historian as Activist', *American Historical Review*, 98(1), February 1993, 19–38. H. J. Kaye, *The British Marxist Historians: An Introductory Analysis* (Oxford, 1984) deals at length with EPT.

[28] A. Dawley, 'E. P. Thompson and the Peculiarities of the Americans', *Radical History Review*, 19, Winter 1978–9, 39.

[29] A. Giddens, 'Out of the Orrery: E. P. Thompson on Consciousness and History', in *Social Theory and Modern Sociology* (Stanford, 1987), p. 203.

[30] N. Smelser (ed.), *Handbook of Sociology* (Newbury Park; Beverly Hills; London; New Delhi, 1988).

'possibly the most imaginative work produced by European social history' made its way across the Channel. In France Pierre Bourdieu made himself Thompson's champion, as did *Le Mouvement Social*; in Germany his influence on the new field of '*Alltagsgeschichte*' came through Hans Medick and his colleagues at the Max Planck Institute for History in Göttingen; while Spain (where university radicalisation in the last years of Franco had stimulated interest in all historians associated with the Left) published him as soon as the dictator was in his grave. In India his writings helped to inspire the subsequently influential 'subaltern school'. Indeed, interest in his work was such that local enthusiasts collected together and published his smaller historical studies long before he himself came to do so in *Customs in Common*: in 1979 in Spain, in 1981 in Italy, in 1980 in Germany.[31]

For Thompson's scholarly influence was (and remains) far from confined to *The Making*, though his reputation among the wider public is virtually identified with this book, which, indeed, towers over the rest of his work. From 1975 the citations of his other historical writings, notably of the influential 1967 and 1971 *Past & Present* papers, always outnumbered the references to the major work, and by a widening margin.

Secondly, intellectually Thompson remained a controversial figure throughout, though few who knew him as a person, however exasperated, resisted his warmth, his charm, his humour, or even a detectable element of puzzled vulnerability. His death was probably received with more personal grief than that of any other British historian of his time.

He made enemies on political grounds, though, oddly enough, not in the proverbially acrimonious universe of discourse of the ideological Left, where he found the targets for some of the heaviest salvos of his intellectual artillery, without ever losing the admiration of his adversaries and victims. Some (and it should be said, only *some*) of those who stood to the right of Thompson politically, found it difficult to admit, or at least publicly to recognise, the stature of a man with whom they disagreed so strongly. For Thompson did not do much to discourage his image as the radical outsider. His relation both to the everyday

---

[31] E. P. Thompson, *Tradición, revuelta y conciencia de clase: Estudios sobre la crisis de la sociedad preindustrial* (Barcelona, 1979); *Plebeische Kultur und moralische Ökonomie. Aufsätze zur englischen Sozialgeschichte des 18. und 19. Jahrhunderts* von Edward P. Thompson, ausgewählt und eingeleitet von Dieter Groh (Frankfurt, 1980); E. P. Thompson, *Società patrizia, cultura plebea: Otto saggi di antropologia storica sull'Inghilterra del Settecento* (Turin, 1981).

world of university and politics was spiny. For some his life as a free scholar might even look like 'self-imposed exile in Worcester'.[32] He was a non-conformer by instinct, who refused to let his name go into *Who's Who*. Such men tend to attract controversy and do nothing to repel it.

A third observation arises from the nature of Thompson's intellectual production: a unique, and uniquely impressive, but never wholly controlled, amalgam of poetic intuition and empathy, a high-powered intellect, passion, and words. He was both an analytical and a romantic historian, a sort of English Michelet on a more modest scale. Though he had the true scholar's hunger for script and print ('As I passed the New York Public Library this morning', he told an audience in 1985, 'I felt a knife inside me—the sense of how long it was since I had been able to work . . . there'[33]), as a researcher he was more like a pioneer explorer or a tracker pursuing sometimes convoluted trails, than a cartographer. His voyages of discovery were neither planned from the outset nor— except in a stylistic sense—finished. Not by chance his most powerful arguments, like his books, began as *pièces d'occasion*.

That is why an assessment of his historical work is unusually difficult. Thompson's influence was pervasive, but he formed no 'school', and such 'schools' as tried to narrow his work for their own purposes, as by turning him into a 'culturalist', oversimplified the complexities of his thought. He had no 'disciples', although some important American scholars such as the late Herbert Gutman, transformer of United States labour history, derived their ideas directly from him, and some of his concepts, for example, that of the 'Moral Economy', inspired important work elsewhere.[34]

He was essentially an opener, not a closer, of horizons and arguments. Not a single proposition of *The Making* has gone unchallenged, and few scholars today would simply subscribe to its argument, even supposing that we can formulate it precisely. Even some of his earliest admirers thought his account debatable or incomplete. And yet it was immediately seen as 'a landmark in historiography' in which he 'has

---

[32] P. Flather in the *Times Higher Education Supplement*, 20 February 1981.

[33] E. P. Thompson, *Persons and Polemics*, p. 360.

[34] H. G. Gutman, *Power and Culture: Essays on the American Working Class*, edited by Ira Berlin (New York, 1987), esp. pp. 18–22; J. C. Scott, *The Moral Economy of the Peasant: Rebellion and Subsistence in Southeast Asia* (New Haven, 1976). For a more general survey, Dawley, op. cit. (see n. 27, above) and R. Wells, 'E. P. Thompson, *Customs in Common* and Moral Economy', *Journal of Peasant Studies*, 21(2), January 1994, 263–307.

rearranged history'.[35] And this must also remain the consensus of judgement today.

His major contribution is as the historian of the world as seen and experienced by the poor and the obscure, a task which required both imagination, empathy, the scholar's erudition and capacity to recognise the otherness of his subjects and their times: in short, Thompson's peculiar gift of marrying the methods of old-style literary history and literary criticism with those of historical research. But, though he shared the passion of antiquarians and recoverers of past feeling, he transcended this by the analytical ability to situate the experience of the poor in a changing pattern of relationships between wider social forces and—as became increasingly evident in his later writings—the webs of community, law and the State that held all together. Last, but far from least, he knew how to find the words for both his passion and his intellectual analysis.

The research contributions of even the finest historians have a restricted shelf-life. Their work has obsolescence built into it. Lucky those with the gift of words which can outlast their footnote references. In any century there are few of these. It is safe to say that Thompson is one of them. As an obituarist wrote: 'Thompson's work combined passion and intellect, the gifts of the poet, the narrator and the analyst. He was the only historian I knew who had not just talent, brilliance, erudition and the gift of writing, but the capacity to produce something qualitatively different from the rest of us, not to be measured on the same scale. Let us simply call it genius in the traditional sense of the word.'[36] On reflection the obituarist maintains his judgement.

E. J. HOBSBAWM
Fellow of the Academy

Note. I am greatly indebted to Mrs Dorothy Thompson. Other friends and students of Edward Thompson have been consulted, notably John Saville, as have my own memories and the obituaries (for a list of which see note 4 to the introduction of B. D. Palmer's *E. P. Thompson: Objections and Oppositions* (London/New York, 1994)). To this biography I am also indebted.

---

[35] Cf. S. Thernstrom in *Dissent*, XII(1), Winter 1965, 90–2; A. Briggs in *Scientific American*, January 1965, 125, 128.
[36] *Independent*, 30 August 1993, 14.

RALPH TURNER   *Walter Stoneman*

Proceedings of the British Academy, **90**, 543–553

Ralph Lilley Turner
1888–1983

Sɪʀ Rᴀʟᴘʜ Tᴜʀɴᴇʀ ʜᴀᴅ ᴛʜʀᴇᴇ ᴄᴀʀᴇᴇʀs, and was equally renowned in each of the three. His first career was that of an Indian Army officer in the First World War, whose service commanding Gurkhas lay in India and Palestine and was rewarded with the Military Cross at the end of the war; the second career was that of an Indo-Aryan scholar, one of the most distinguished of his time, whose work still inspires today; finally, he was the Director of what became the School of Oriental and African Studies, first during a period of uncertainty and then during a period of post-war expansion and success.

Ralph Lilley Turner was born on 5 October 1888. He was educated at the Perse School in Cambridge, and was introduced to Sanskrit by his headmaster, W. H. D. Rouse, who habitually introduced the best of his sixth-form Classics pupils to that subject, but rarely with such success. Turner then gained First Class Honours in both Classics and Oriental Languages at Cambridge, and was elected in 1912 to a fellowship at Christ's College, the fellowship being awarded for his pioneering work on the survival in Nepal of a Buddhist Sanskrit manuscript tradition.

Deservedly, he dedicated his *Collected Papers 1912–1973* to the memory of Rouse. These papers are selected so as to constitute a corpus of phonological criteria fundamental to his major contributions to the comparative linguistics of Indo-Aryan. Significantly, however, the first paper is a discussion of the phonetics of the word accent in classical Latin. He brought the disciplines of classical philology to Indian linguistic study, and later he was to bring his experience of Indo-Aryan phenomena fruitfully to bear on the problems of accent in both Greek and Latin (in 1912, 1915 and 1930).[1]

Turner subsequently joined the Indian Education Service, and was appointed Lecturer in Sanskrit at Queen's College, later to become the Hindu University of Benares. His attention then turned to Gujarati and, inspired by Jules Bloch's historical-descriptive study of Marathi, then nearing completion, Turner went on to devote his researches in India specifically to the evolution of the modern Indo-Aryan languages from Sanskrit (1915, 1921).

Having been a cadet in the Cambridge Officers Training Corps, he was attached to a battalion of the Gurkha Rifles in 1916, and had reached the rank of captain by the end of the war. His admiration for his troops was aptly demonstrated by the dedication in the Preface to his *Comparative and Etymological Dictionary of the Nepali Language*: 'My thoughts return to you who were my comrades, the stubborn and indomitable peasants of Nepal. Once more I hear the laughter with which you greeted every hardship . . . . Uncomplaining you endure hunger and thirst and wounds; and at the last your unwavering lines disappear into the smoke and wrath of battle. Bravest of the brave, most generous of the generous, never had country more faithful friends than you.' He transcribed some of the epic songs and prose narratives in which his men recalled the exploits of their battalion, the 2/3 QAO Gurkha Rifles, in both France and Palestine. By this stage, Turner had mastered the Nepali language, although, as he regretted in the same Preface, he had never been able to enter Nepal. After the Second World War, however, he visited Nepal twice, the second time representing the Queen at the coronation of King Mahendra.

Having married Dorothy Rivers Goulty, he returned to India after the war to inaugurate a Chair of Indian Linguistics at the Hindu University of Benares. In 1922 he was appointed to the Chair of Sanskrit in the University of London and thus started his close attachment to the School of Oriental Studies.

In the period up to 1937 Turner had published around forty articles on Indo-Aryan linguistic themes, mainly in the field of historical phonology, of which those on Gujarati, Sindhi, and Romani have

---

[1] Publications referred to in the text under date of appearance are to be found in their full form in 'Writings of Sir Ralph Turner (Books and Articles)', *Bulletin of the School of Oriental and African Studies*, xx (1957) xiii–xvi.

been particularly valued by other scholars. The long 1921 paper on Gujarati phonology remains the starting-point for any historical study of that language; of particular value was the establishment of the conditions for the development of the two varieties of *e* and *o* vowels (to which a further article was devoted in 1925). The three papers on Sindhi were concerned with the conditions giving rise in that language to a series of retroflex implosive consonants, a type almost unique in the sub-continent. The 1926 paper on Romani, later republished as a monograph, firmly established the position of these dialects in relation to other Indo-Aryan languages. Two of his papers on mutually-related subjects, 'The Phonetic Weakness of Terminational Elements in Indo-Aryan' (1927) and 'Anticipation of Normal Sound-changes in Indo-Aryan' (1937) have proved to be highly relevant to comparable phenomena in a wider range of languages.

The *Comparative and Etymological Dictionary of the Nepali Language* is in fact much more than the plain title might convey. For each entry contains not only the Sanskrit or other origin of the word, but also, where attested, all the cognate forms in the other Middle and Modern Indo-Aryan languages. Each of these cognates is then listed in a language-by-language index (compiled by his wife, herself a Cambridge classicist) alongside the Nepali form under which it is cited. It was thus possible in effect to use the work as a general etymological dictionary of the Indo-Aryan languages; and was uniquely valuable to scholars in this role until the completion of the great definitive work, *The Comparative Dictionary of the Indo-Aryan Languages*. It is quite remarkable that, as Turner notes in the Preface to the Nepali Dictionary, none of the university presses would venture to undertake the publication of the work – this duty being shouldered by the Government of Nepal, the Royal Asiatic Society, and the eventual publishers, Kegan Paul.

In 1937 Turner succeeded Sir Denison Ross as Director of the School of Oriental Studies, while continuing to occupy the Chair of Sanskrit. On appointment, he was quickly involved first with the building of what is now part of the present School and its move from its original site in Finsbury Circus, and then in the hurried evacuation of the School to Cambridge at the outbreak of war in 1939.

Of Turner's time as Director of the London School a former member of staff has written:

> Many must have wondered at the time and many more wondered thereafter how so dedicated a scholar of so retiring a disposition brought himself to

accept appointment to an office, some of the responsibilities of which were not likely to be congenial to him. He was certainly not driven by personal ambition or love of power. He did have a good head for business and a grasp of the financial aspects not always found in the holders of high academic office. But what really moved him to accept the Directorship seems to have been his strong sense of duty, a vision of the role awaiting the School if adequate financial resources were made available to it, and a steadfast determination to do all that in him lay to make that vision into a reality.

As Director, he was a living illustration of the distinction which is often made between the attributes of the politician and those of the statesman. He had few of the qualities and aptitudes of the former; he shrank from publicity and had no taste for public occasions and speech making; he was not an agile academic tactician, nor was he a conspicuously gifted chairman of committees, being too tolerant and courteous to deal effectively with irrelevance and prolixity; he relied more on the inherent strength of the case he was advocating than on forcefulness and artifice in its presentation. On the other hand, he had many of the virtues of the true statesman: a clear vision of his long-term strategic objectives, patience, persistence and determination in seeking to attain them, and the indispensable gift of sensing when the time had come for decisive action.

He became Director when the School had been in existence for twenty years. Though its achievements in that period had been highly creditable and its staff included a number of scholars of distinction, it had to struggle against the most severe penury and, despite the firm and enlightened backing of the Court and Senate of the University, its future must still have looked precarious. One of the immediate objectives was to improve the financial position and to extract the maximum advantage from the School's membership of the federal University of London.

The last of these objectives was the first to be realised, when in 1938, with financial help from the Rockefeller Foundation, the Department of the Languages and Cultures of Africa was inaugurated, with Professor Ida Ward as its Head. This was the first such department in a British university and led to the change in the School's name to 'The School of Oriental and African Studies'.

The second objective was of a different nature, more a continuing process, the momentum of which had to be maintained. It did not begin with Turner's tenure of the Directorship, nor did it end with his retirement, but its importance to the School was one of his articles of faith. He saw that specialist institutions standing on their own not only were especially vulnerable but also were in danger of becoming unduly introverted. Membership of a strong federation was therefore greatly to their advantage. That advantage was enhanced for the School when it was enabled to leave its old building in Finsbury Circus and transfer its activities to a new site in the central University precinct in Bloomsbury, a long and complicated exercise finally accomplished though not initiated during Turner's Directorship. In his valedictory address in 1957 he noted with satisfaction that, whereas in the School's early years the only real academic link with other colleges was the tenuous one of membership of the Board of Studies in Oriental Languages and Literatures, by the time of his retirement members of the staff were participating in the work of no fewer than eleven Boards of Studies and providing the chairmen of four of them.

The most important task of all, was to improve the financial position. On Turner's initiative, the Foreign Office, the India Office, the Colonial Office and the War Office were persuaded to set up an Inter-departmental Committee to consider the School's case for increased financial assistance. A detailed exposition prepared under his direction convinced the Committee, which recommended to the Treasury that the School's income should be nearly doubled. The Treasury, however, turned a deaf ear; expansion on the scale envisaged would, said the Chancellor of the Exchequer, have to wait for 'happier times', the Treasury version of the Greek Kalends. A few months later, the country was at war.

Even before that, when it had become probable that the outbreak of war would not be long delayed, Turner had begun to urge upon the service departments that they were seriously under-provided with personnel trained in Asian languages, particularly Japanese and Chinese. After hostilities began, he redoubled his efforts. When full allowance has been made for other preoccupations, the complacency and unimaginative short-sightedness of the responses he received almost beggar belief. As late as August 1941 he was told by the War Office that 'we are at present reasonably insured in the matter of officers knowing Oriental languages'. He must at times have felt like Mirabeau: 'J'aurai probablement le sort de Cassandre; je prédirai toujours vrai et ne serai jamais cru.' When Japan attacked and a series of disasters rapidly followed, his warnings were at last seen to have been justified; and the School was called upon at short notice and with limited resources to train many hundreds of young servicemen in Chinese and Japanese for intelligence duties in Eastern theatres of war. By the time the requirement came to an end nearly 1,700 such students had been trained at the School.

Meanwhile, with his usual foresight, Turner was already looking ahead to the post-war period. The ever-growing importance of the countries of Asia and Africa (and the USSR) in world affairs, and the consequent need to build up in Britain an adequate fund of expertise in the languages and cultures of their peoples provided what he perceived to be a unique opportunity to try and secure the future of Asian and African (and Slavonic and East European) studies in British universities. As early as autumn 1943 he began to prepare the ground. Largely as a result of his patient and unflagging advocacy, strongly backed by Lord Hailey, the Secretary of State for Foreign Affairs appointed in 1944 the Scarbrough Commission of Enquiry into means of improving the study in post-war Britain of Oriental, Slavonic, East European and African languages and cultures. Turner took the lead in supplying and marshalling evidence for presentation to the Commission, which worked with exceptional speed to produce by 1946 a report effectively endorsing all his arguments in favour of a major expansion in the provision for these studies in British universities and the building up of the School and its sister institution, the School of Slavonic and East European Studies, as the main centres. His great satisfaction with this result of his protracted labour was exceeded only by that which he felt when the first post-war government decided to implement the recommendations in full and made substantial ear-marked grants available for the purpose.

None knew better than Turner that expansion on the scale envisaged should ideally have been spread over a period of ten to fifteen years to minimize any danger to the maintenance of academic standards. Neverthe-less, recognising that the financial climate might quickly deteriorate and wishing to take advantage of the pool of promising young scholars who were being released from the armed forces after having their interest awa-kened during service in Asia or Africa, he decided on a bold course of rapid recruitment and training while the funds were available and before other national needs emerged to claim priority. In the event his judgement in this also was vindicated. The quality of the staff appointed in the period of maximum expansion from 1947 to 1952 was almost uniformly high and the mistakes remarkably few. The result was that when the chill wind of financial retrenchment began to blow in the closing years of his Directorship, the School had ample strength to withstand it. By any standards, he had been an outstanding Director and left the School permanently indebted to him.

Many honours were conferred on Turner, notably his knighthood in 1950. This must be regarded as a recognition of his service during the war and his period of office as Director during the critical years in the life of the School. The honour which he prized the most, however, was his Honorary Fellowship of Christ's College, Cambridge. He was elected a Fellow of the British Academy in 1942, and was an honorary member of academies and learned societies in India, Sri Lanka, France, Germany, Czechoslovakia, Norway and the United States of America. He was President of the Philological Society, 1939–43, President of the Royal Asiatic Society, 1952–55, and was awarded their Triennial Gold Medal in 1953. Whilst President of the Philological Society, he was also its Treasurer, 1931–62, again a phenomenal achievement. Although this was at a time when the School's expansion, and therefore his respon-sibilities, were at their height, he did not push even the most mundane tasks on to other officers of the Society or onto his own office at the School. Such vital, but mundane, tasks as the reclamation of income tax through charitable covenants, and defaulting subscribers, were all dealt with by him.

Turner never permitted his administrative duties to inhibit his scholarship. In the period 1937–57, he published five major articles and numerous printed versions of official speeches, ceremonial addresses, and similar matters. He also continued the work on the massive task he had set himself many years earlier: the production of *The Comparative Dictionary of the Indo-Aryan Languages* (1966–85). Wounded in the assault upon Jerusalem during the First World War, in hospital he briefly had the leisure to consider how best to approach the work which became his crowning scholastic achievement: how a pioneering etymological analysis of Nepali was to be made the basis of a comparative study of the modern Indo-Aryan languages, similar to that which had already been undertaken for the Romance languages. This work is, in itself, a massive undertaking for the life of any one scholar, particularly as it was achieved without the use of research assistants, let alone when considered in conjunction with his other works, administrative responsibilities and substantial efforts for the School. This work was not mentioned in the obituary published in *The Times*, presumably because it had been prepared at the time of his retirement, and it probably seemed inconceivable to the Editor that such a vast undertaking could possibly be produced after retirement. The omission was remedied by a communication from three of his colleagues, who clarified the issue.

Like its provisional predecessor, *The Comparative and Etymological Dictionary of the Nepal Language* of 1931, the completed *Comparative Dictionary* was immediately accepted as the basic reference work for all diachronic study of the languages of India, being generously utilised and fully cross-referenced in the new editions of the Dravidian etymological dictionary and *Etymologisches Wörterbuch des Altindoarischen*, and making a contribution to Anglo-Indian etymology in the latest revisions of the Oxford English dictionaries.

When Turner first went to India, his interests lay in the languages of Gujarat and Nepal. Summers spent with his wife in Almora and Naini Tal had permitted him to develop an interest in the archaic dialects of the Himalayan region. In London he had the opportunity to work with researchers from India and Ceylon but also with linguists such as Grierson, Lorimer, and Morgenstierne who were exploring hitherto unknown languages of the north-west frontier. Turner considered the problems of the phonology of both Sindhi and the Gypsy languages, and his solutions to basic problems have yet to be superseded (1924, 1926). After the groundwork had been laid in the Nepali dictionary, it fell to him to evaluate newly discovered Asokan Prakrit inscriptions from South India, and this proceeded to the solution of some major outstanding problems of Middle Indian phonology (1931, 1936).

The *Comparative Dictionary* began appearing in fascicules in 1962.

This was added to in 1971 by an Index of 140,000 lexical items and a computer-based listing of each occurrence of every individual sound-sequence attested in the parent language, based on his wife's work as a collaborator over the fifty years of the dictionary's evolution. Further articles appeared over the next ten years, evaluating the data which had been collected; and a volume of Addenda on which he worked periodically was published posthumously. Although known as an Indo-Aryanist, he was a philologist and especially an Indo-European philologist.

In 1957 the School of Oriental and African Studies published a special volume of its *Bulletin* in honour of Turner, with contributions from fifty-seven scholars; it also listed over seventy of his publications, dating back to 1912.

In speech Turner was a man of few, but wise, words. In one oral report at the end of a summer term on the School's work over the past academic year he publicly disclaimed the power of a Homer to weave poetry from something as dry as a 'Catalogue of ships'; but a glance at his writing at once reveals his combination of scholarly precision and an attractive and enlightening English style. He was a great pipe-smoker (he grew his own tobacco, and for a year or two cured it himself, later sending it for curing to the British Tobacco Growers Association), and one felt that this put other pipe-smokers at their ease when, in accordance with the etiquette of the times, newly appointed staff paid a formal call on him as Director during their first year of service. A mutual exchange of tobacco puffs lessened the need to keep up a continuous conversation. Those who have known him, however distantly, and worked with him, however fleetingly, retain an enduring memory of an officer and gentleman and a most distinguished scholar.

One of his daughters recalls his family life:

> When he came back to England in 1922 he settled with Dorothy and their first daughter, who had been born in India, in Bishop's Stortford in a rambling Victorian house with extensive gardens. 'Haverbrack' was their home for fifty years, where two more daughters and a son were born, where friends and graduate students were entertained and where he found his happiest relaxation. Bishop's Stortford was chosen as half-way between London and Cambridge for in those early years his ambition was to go back to Cambridge (and he might well have followed in Rapson's chair). But he never regretted the turn of events that led him to stay in the London School.
>
> The garden was his delight. He spent many happy hours redesigning, planting hedges (the great yew hedge round the tennis court he continued to cut on a ladder until his 80s), constructing steps and paths, tending his

cuttings bed. He was a great constructor in concrete: water tanks in the greenhouse, a dipping pool in the garden, and special pits for his MS slips for the Dictionary as a wartime precaution (later converted into excellent compost pits with return of peace). The garden with its various areas, different levels and secret corners was a children's paradise for hiding games.

He had an affinity with small children and was very fond of them and they were glad when they could entice him out of his study to play in the garden. He was also a very good storyteller. His own family gave him great happiness and he was proud of their achievements and various careers. It was a special pleasure that both his son and a grandson followed him to Christ's.

Just before the war he and Dorothy opened their home to a young German Jewish boy from Berlin who lived with them all through the war. The house in wartime was also home for a succession of London evacuees. Both he and his wife were air-raid wardens and took their turns on night duty at the local post.

Family ties were close and important to him: the network of relatives was almost tribal. The close bond with his two brothers' families was cemented by long joint holidays in August in Wales and Christmas at their mother's house in Cambridge.

Not given to social life outside the home he and Dorothy preferred to work in the study in the evenings. Relaxation was talking to friends on the south-facing verandah under the wisteria (and there were often friends from early years at school, and university and army service). Dorothy was the anchor in the neighbourhood and its doings and made the local contacts.

He was a capable handyman, though disclaiming any real carpenter's expertise, and took DIY to extremes. He mended slippers with pieces from rubber hot water bottles, constructed bunks in the cellar for safe sleeping at the start of the war, and always preferred to service his car. Undoubtedly this urge to mend and adapt, as well as his abstemious nature, was an inborn thrift from his nonconformist background. I think he always felt an affinity with Bunyan, having been brought up in Bunyan's Chapel in Bedford in child-hood. He also preferred old clothes (and sometimes these needed to be diplomatically 'lost'!). His only dressing gown was a survivor from his teens.

An old friend has written:

The impression which Ralph Turner made on most people who met him was that of a man at peace with himself and his fellow beings. This was, no doubt, mainly due to the inherent benevolence and serenity of his person-ality, but it was enhanced by the happiness of his marriage and the domestic contentment and stability within which he lived. A quiet man, sparing of speech, he listened with care to the opinions of others and was grateful for the help he derived from them. There was nothing ostentatious or over-bearing in his dispostion. He shunned the limelight and was content to lead by example. Because his example was so good and the affection he inspired in his staff was so great, he was served well; and, in turn, he was always careful to acknowledge the contribution others had made to the achievement of his objectives.

His devotion to his scholarly interests was absolute and unwavering. He was still at work only a week before his death at the age of 94 and a visitor could walk along the path immediately outside the window of his study without disturbing his concentration. . . . Though he did not look very robust, he was endowed with a hardy constitution. In the coldest weather he wore neither overcoat nor hat and was pleased when the temperature fell to a level which enabled him to skate on the fens. In his later years, when he rarely left his home at Bishop's Stortford, nothing pleased him more than to be visited by former colleagues, with whom he would sit and talk. To the last his memory was clear and accurate and the conversation often returned to the Great War and his friends and comrades, the Gurkha soldiers. As he did not forget them, so will he never be forgotten by those who had the privilege of serving him and enjoying his friendship.

He died peacefully in his own home, on 22 April 1983.

R. H. ROBINS
Fellow of the Academy

Bibliography

A list of the 'Writings of Sir Ralph Turner (Books and Articles)', compiled by D. M. Johnson was published in *Bulletin of the School of Oriental and African Studies*, xx (1957), xiii–xvi. The following are additional items:

'Transference of Aspiration in European Gypsy', *BSOAS*, xxii, 3 (1959), 491–8.
Some Problems of Sound-change in Indo-Aryan (P. D. Gune Memorial Lectures, 1), (Poona, 1960), x, 60pp.
'Indo-Arica IV. Sanskrit *śvāśura-*', *BSOAS*, xxiii, 1 (1960), 106–8.
'Past Tense of the Verb ''to give'' in Palestinian Gypsy', *Journal of the Gypsy Lore Society*, 3rd ser, xxxix, 1–2 (1960), 28–30.
'Sanskrit *venú-* and Pali *velu-*', *Bulletin of the Deccan College Research Institute*, 20 (1962), 345–6.
'√sañj in Middle and New Indo-Aryan', *Indian Linguistics*, 25 (1964), 56–7.
'Sanskrit *buddhi-*' in *Indo-Iranica. Mélanges présentés à Georg Morgenstierne* (Wiesbaden, 1964), 174–6.
A Comparative Dictionary of the Indo-Aryan Languages (London, 1966), xx, 841pp.
'Geminates after Long Vowel in Indo-Aryan', *BSOAS*, xxx, 1 (1967), 73–82.
'Kashmiri *sagun* ''to irrigate'' ' in *Mélanges d'indianisme à la mémoire de Louis Renou* (Paris, 1968), 725–6.
A Comparative Dictionary of the Indo-Aryan Languages: Indexes, Compiled by D. R. Turner (London, 1969), ix, 366pp.

'Type *aśvatara* in New Indo-Aryan' in *Pratidānam. Indian, Iranian, and Indo-European studies presented to F. B. J. Kuiper* (The Hague, 1969), 319–20.

Lawrence Roger Lumley, 11th Earl of Scarbrough (Obituary), *BSOAS*, xxxii, 3 (1969), 686–9.

'Early Shortening of Geminates with Compensatory Lengthening in Indo-Aryan', *BSOAS*, xxxiii, 1 (1970), 171–8.

A Comparative Dictionary of the Indo-Aryan Languages. Phonetic Analysis, by R. L. Turner and D. R. Turner (London, 1971), viii, 235pp.

'Pali *phāsu-* and *dātta-*', *BSOAS*, xxxvi, 2 (1973), 424–8.

Collected papers 1912–73 (London, 1975), xvi, 435pp.

'*dī-* and *uḍḍī* "to fly" in Indo-Aryan', *BSOAS*, xlii, 2 (1979), 358–60.

'Preservation of Original Aryan Vocabulary in the Modern Languages', *BSOAS*, xlii, 3 (1979), 545–7.

'Implosive *d-* + *y-* or *r-* or *h-* in Indo-Aryan', *BSOAS*, xlv, 1 (1982), 84–7.

A Comparative Dictionary of the Indo-Aryan Languages: Addenda and Corrigenda, edited by J. C. Wright (London, 1985), xi, 168pp.

RUDOLF WITTKOWER

Proceedings of the British Academy, **90**, 557–571

Rudolf Wittkower
1901–1971

WHEN RUDOLF WITTKOWER DIED, at the age of seventy, on 11 October
1971 he was the Avalon Foundation Professor Emeritus in the
Humanities at Columbia University. Columbia was the setting for the
final chapter of his distinguished and energetic career as an art historian; in the course of that career he transformed our understanding of
Renaissance and Baroque art and architecture. A full appreciation of
Wittkower's achievement, however, must acknowledge, along with his
formidable record of pioneering scholarship, his special talents as
educator. A most generous man, large of person physically and socially,
he was an ideal teacher, one who inspired confidence in his students
through his own demonstrated faith in their ability. With an enormous
capacity and zest for work, he was able to conduct his own research and
write even as he meticulously organised his lectures and seminars,
supervised the research of graduate students and guided their careers,
and, as Chairman, led the Department of Art History and Archaeology
at Columbia to its position of pre-eminence among international centres
of art historical teaching and research.

Born on 22 June 1901 in Berlin, he was the second of four children
of Henry and Gertrude Ansbach Wittkower; his family lineage could be
traced back to the distinguished Jewish community of eighteenth-
century Berlin. Wittkower studied first at the University of Munich
and then at Berlin, where he received his Ph.D. in 1923 under Adolf
Goldschmidt. His thesis was on painting in quattrocento Verona, then
very much art-historical *terra incognita*, and his first publications were

devoted to Domenico Morone and his followers (*Jahrbuch für Kunst-wissenschaft*, 1924–5, 1927). Although he was to re-engage the art of the Veneto later in his career, Wittkower's scholarly attention was turned to Rome in 1923 with his appointment as Research Assistant at the Bibliotheca Hertziana. This was to be the site of his early development as an independent scholar; promoted to Research Fellow in 1928, he remained there until 1932. It was at the Hertziana that the major concerns of Wittkower's scholarship took shape — above all, the art of Michelangelo and Gianlorenzo Bernini.

Wittkower's first important project at the Hertziana was the orga-nisation and completion of the monumental Michelangelo bibliography that had been initiated by the institute's director, Ernst Steinmann, some twenty years earlier. Under their joint authorship, *Michelangelo-Bib-liographie, 1510–1926* appeared in 1927 as the first volume in the series 'Römische Forschungen der Bibliotheca Hertziana.' It was the younger collaborator's energy and organising intelligence that proved catalytic in bringing this great project to fruition. These were the qualities that Wittkower also brought to the ordering of the Hertziana itself, creating the bibliographies that make it such a hospitable research facility. During these years began Wittkower's engagement with lesser-known Italian sculptors, as he began to write the entries for Thieme-Becker, *Allgemeines Lexikon der bildenden Künstler* (1925–34), and to publish fundamental studies on Camillo Rusconi (1926–7), Alessandro Algardi (1928), Stefano Maderno (1928–9), Melchiorre Caffà (1928–9), Lor-enzo Ottoni (1929), and Francesco Mochi (1930–1). Like their subjects, these articles radiated from the creative master at the core of Wittko-wer's interests, Gianlorenzo Bernini — the artist with whom the scholar was to become most closely identified.

As a necessary foundation for a full monograph on Bernini, Witt-kower set out to study the drawings and the working methods of this central figure of Baroque art. His collaborator on the project was Heinrich Brauer, who had written his dissertation on the rich collection of Bernini drawings at Leipzig. Their two-volume *Die Zeichnungen des Gianlorenzo Bernini*, published in 1931, did indeed provide that foun-dation. Once again, Wittkower found himself pioneering in a field that had been neglected by contemporary art history, or, worse, rejected as unworthy of serious study. (In his preface to the reprinted edition of 1970, Wittkower recalls that Bernard Berenson, upon being shown photographs of drawings by Bernini, confessed to feeling physically ill.) 'Rubens, Caravaggio, Rembrandt, Velasquez and Poussin have found their interpreters and a larg appreciative public,' Wittkower wrote in the preface to *Gianlorenzo Bernini, The Sculptor of the Roman Baroque* (1955). 'Only Bernini, once the brightest star amongst the great artists of the seventeenth century, still suffers from comparative neglect.' This book summarised only a part of Wittkower's own extensive research on Bernini, which had begun with work on *Die Zeichnungen*. He had already written major entries on Bernini's architectural and planning projects — the Baldachin of St Peter's, the Palazzo Barberini, the Piazza of St Peter's, and the fountains.

Wittkower's commitment to Bernini came to be founded on more than the obligations of historical scholarship, for the very magnitude of the artist's enterprise, the variety of his projects and the energy with which they were undertaken, found a special resonance in the ambition and personality of the scholar. Between the scholar and his subject there seemed a perfect fit (Wittkower's students often noted the physiognomic resemblance of their teacher to the portrait bust of Scipione Borghese carved by Bernini); admiration for the creativity and originality of the artist clearly inspired the art historian.

The triumphal monument of Wittkower's own scholarship, the culmination of his work on the Baroque, was his contribution to the Pelican History of Art series, the volume on *Art and Architecture in Italy 1600–1750* (1958). Here the scholar's creative response to a daunting challenge demonstrates an ambitious reach and precise control worthy of his favourite artist. In this magisterial and beautifully written study (which was awarded the Banister Fletcher Prize) Wittkower organised for the first time an incredible range of art-historical material — painting, sculpture, and architecture. Shaping his complex subject with critical intelligence and methodological awareness, he effectively returned the Italian Baroque to the history of art. Declaring the organisational structure of the book, the table of contents itself is a model of art historical clarity. Establishing the guiding parameters of style, setting the co-ordinates of chronology and geography, balancing centre and periphery, adjusting focus on individual artists and local schools and on the several media and genres, it testifies to the historical imagination and skill of the author himself. (Wittkower's talent for clear historical synthesis informs his chapter on 'The Arts in Europe: Italy' for the first volume of *The New Cambridge Modern History* (1957), a twenty-five page introduction to the High Renaissance in the visual arts remarkable for the intelligence of its vision, its perspective and sense of proportion, and for its precision of expression.)

In meeting the challenge of the Pelican volume, setting forth the rationale for his choices, and acknowledging the implications of the results, Wittkower articulated the principles that guided him as a scholar. These same principles accounted for his success as a teacher, for they reveal the particularly personal dimension of his historical criticism. Within the constraints of format and space, he explained in the Foreword,

> It was necessary to prune the garden of history not only of dead but, alas, also of much living wood. In doing this, I availed myself of the historian's right and duty to submit to his readers his own vision of the past. I tried to give a bird's-eye view, and no more, of the whole panorama and reserved a detailed discussion for those works of art and architecture which, owing to their intrinsic merit and historical importance, appear to be in a special class. Intrinsic merit and historical importance — these notions may be regarded as dangerous measuring rods, and not every reader may subscribe to my opinions: yet history degenerates into chronicle if the author shuns the dangers of implicit and explicit judgements of quality and value.

He went on to make explicit his own judgement of the relative importance of the media in the history he was writing: 'Excepting the beginning and end of the period under review, i.e. Caravaggio, the Carracci, and Tiepolo, the history of painting would seem less important than that of the other arts and often indeed has no more than strictly limited interest — an ideal hunting-ground for specialists and "attributionists".' Wittkower recognised that the great achievements of the Italian Baroque, the truly original work, were in architecture and in sculpture, that Italian painting made its real contribution 'in conjunction with, and as an integral part of, architecture, sculpture, and decoration.' 'The works without peer,' he concluded, 'are Bernini's statuary, Cortona's architecture and decoration, and Borromini's buildings as well as those by Guarini, Juvarra, and Vittone. But it was Bernini, the greatest artist of the period, who with his poetical and visionary masterpieces created perhaps the most sublime realisation of the longings of his age.'

Wittkower's first project at the Hertziana, the Michelangelo bibliography, provided another foundation for his subsequent scholarship. In particular, he began to address the problem of Michelangelo as architect, and two articles of fundamental importance followed quickly upon the publication of the bibliography: one on the dome of St Peter's (*Zeitschrift für Kunstgeschichte* (1933)), the other on the Laurentian Library (*Art Bulletin* (1934)). Confronting the problem of Mannerism in architecture, and countering the Wölfflinian notion of Michelangelo as a Baroque architect, his approach to the Library vestibule combined close measured analysis and interpretive response to the 'ambiguous, conflicting energies' of Michelangelo's creation. 'The Laurenziana,' he concluded, 'stands at the beginning of a completely new approach to architecture. The ideas conceived and carried out here went far beyond anything that other architects dared imagine. Here is the key to a wide area of unexplored or misinterpreted architectural history, and the explanation of much that was to happen in the next two centuries and beyond.' Typically, a bifocal critical vision informed Wittkower's approach, as he looked beyond the object of his immediate investigation to discern the larger field of its situation and to plot the dimensions of further inquiry.

Wittkower left the Hertziana in 1932 to assume a temporary position as lecturer at the University of Cologne. The following year he, his wife, the former Margot Holzmann (whom he had married in 1923), and their son Mario (born in 1925) left Germany for England. His father having been born there, Wittkower could claim British citizenship. The move was, of course, part of that larger wave of intellectual migration inspired by the rise of National Socialism. With the transfer of the Warburg Library from Hamburg to London in 1934, Wittkower found a new centre for his scholarship; he was appointed by the director, Fritz Saxl, to an unsalaried position at what was to be known as the Warburg Institute, with which he was to remain affiliated, as research member and lecturer, throughout his career in London. The new situation offered Wittkower a new set of challenges and opportunities as he turned to the kinds of broad iconographic problems that had inspired Aby Warburg and informed the organisation of his library. The first volume of the *Journal of the Warburg and Courtauld Institutes* (1937–8) carried four articles by him that mark this new direction in his work and attest to his expanding range: 'Patience and Chance: The Story of a Political Emblem'; 'Physiognomical Experiments by Michelangelo and his Pupils'; 'Miraculous Birds, 1. "Physiologus" in Beatus Manuscripts; 2. "Roc": An Eastern Prodigy in a Dutch Engraving,' and 'A Symbol of Platonic Love in a Portrait Bust of Donatello.' Indeed, the early volumes of the journal are filled with articles by him on an impressive array of subjects, from the 'Marvels of the East' through symbolic motifs in the classical iconography of the West to problems in the history, style, and iconography of architecture.

The Warburg library led Wittkower's curiosity beyond the traditional borders of European art history and iconography, especially to Egypt and the Near East, as he studied the migration and interpretation of symbols. As at the Hertziana, so here too did he lay the foundations for future research, much of which would be presented in lectures and in his teaching — and only published posthumously in a volume of selected lectures, *The Impact of Non-European Civilizations on the Art of the West* (1989).

Still, at the core of Wittkower's interests remained the problems generated by his early projects on Michelangelo and Bernini and his engagement of the figures and monuments of the Italian Baroque. In 'Carlo Rainaldi and the Roman Architecture of the Full Baroque' (*Art Bulletin* (1937)), perceiving a revival of certain Mannerist tensions, he, explored 'the problem of orientation in centrally planned buildings' and extended the inquiry to include buildings by Bernini, Cortona, and Borromini. Then, as he traced it back to its earlier articulation in Renaissance architectural practice and theory, the theme provided the first part of what was to become perhaps Wittkower's most broadly influential book, *Architectural Principles in the Age of Humanism* (1949; rev. ed., 1962). In the Warburg journal he had already published 'Alberti's Approach to Antiquity in Architecture' (1940–1) and 'Principles of Palladio's Architecture' (1944, 1945), which would comprise the two core parts of the book. The final part was the most ambitious, 'The Problem of Harmonic Proportion in Architecture.'

'When this book first came out,' Wittkower wrote in the introduction to the American edition (1971), 'it was unexpectedly given a very friendly reception. To my surprise it caused more than a polite stir'. Sir Kenneth Clark wrote in the *Architectural Review* that the first result of this book was "to dispose, once and for all, of the hedonist, or purely aesthetic, theory of Renaissance architecture," and this defines my intention in a nutshell.' *Architectural Principles in the Age of Humanism* did indeed establish an entirely new foundation for our understanding of Renaissance architecture. Wittkower had set out to dispel the notion that this art, inspired by the pagan forms of classical antiquity, was essentially profane and unfit for a truly Christian culture. He cited Ruskin's moralising criticism of an architecture 'pagan in origin . . . in which intellect is idle, invention impossible, but in which all luxury is gratified and all insolence fortified' (*Stones of Venice*) and Geoffrey Scott's hedonistic defence of it as 'an architecture of taste, seeking no logic, consistency, or justification beyond that of giving pleasure' (*The Architecture of Humanism*). Wittkower demonstrated instead that Renaissance architecture, like every great style of the past, was based on a hierarchy of values culminating in the absolute values of sacred architecture.' He insisted that 'the forms of the Renaissance church have symbolical value or, at least, that they are charged with a particular meaning which the pure forms as such do not contain. Both the theory and the practice of Renaissance architects are unambiguous in this respect.' Through Wittkower's probing studies, then, the sacred purpose of this architecture was redeemed and the probity of its designers reaffirmed.

Wittkower's recourse to the theoretical writings of the Renaissance, his search for the articulation of values and the justification of practice, came with his own distance from the monuments themselves. Closer to library resources than to the buildings during these years, he himself found new rhetorical purpose in his research: to define and defend the architectural culture of the Renaissance, to establish the principles and aspirations of its architects. In so doing he effectively returned the art to its culture. Renaissance architecture could be seen in its highest ambition as a grand imaginative effort to reconcile the nobility and commensurability of classical form with the purity of Christian purpose — the equivalent in stone of a *theologia platonica*.

However much Wittkower developed his thesis on the basis of Renaissance theory, his critical vision remained focused on the kinds of practical problems faced by designing architects, above all in their effort to understand ancient Roman architecture and adapt its forms to new ends. By focusing on problems like the adaptation of the freestanding classical column to a wall architecture or of the classical temple front to the façade of a Christian basilica, he reformulated both the precise professional issues and the larger cultural dynamic. The creative response was what interested him, the effort of the Renaissance architect to understand the past in light of the present and its immediate needs. Wittkower recognised in the architecture the kind of creative dialogue with classical antiquity that lies at the very core of the Renaissance as an historical and cultural phenomenon.

Like Alberti, Palladio was a publishing architect, and Wittkower's exploration of his culture led to a remarkably wide range of relevant issues: from the social making of the architect and his professional status, architectural patronage and cultural tradition, to the geometry of planning and the phenomenology of architectural experience. Each section of 'Principles of Palladio's Architecture' opened a new path for further exploration. In the investigation of harmonic proportion in architecture, Wittkower confronted the practice and theory of architectural imagination and signification. Following the mathematical traditions of architectural theory and practice, he demonstrated their powerful hold on Renaissance thought and shaping influence on Renaissance culture. Palladio, in particular, proved responsive to developments in musical theory, and the proportions of certain of his buildings deliberately declared their consonance with the larger, Pythagorean order of the universe. Although subsequently questioned by a more materialist and less idealising generation of architectural historians — students more interested in the socio-economics of building patronage than in the architect's imagination and inventiveness — Wittkower's findings have been vindicated by recent sophisticated mathematical analysis of Palladio's designs.

Studying the 'optical and psychological concepts' underlying Palladio's church of the Redentore, and extrapolating from his own experience and analysis of its space, Wittkower discerned the operations of a 'scenographic' principle in this architecture. It is this experiential dimension that gives special force to his critical account, which articulates the viewer's own mobile encounter with architecture. From such deep understanding of Palladio, Wittkower traced the further development of this scenographic approach to the greatest Venetian monument of Baroque architecture. His analysis of Longhena's S. Maria della Salute (*Journal of the Society of Architectural Historians* (1957), and *Saggi e memorie di storia dell'arte* (1963)) alerted us to a continuing tradition in Venetial architecture, one based on the articulation of space as the controlling element in a design intended to be felt by eye and body.

Students in Wittkower's courses on English architecture recall the enthusiasm with which he narrated his explorations of architectural space; the image of this large man climbing the narrow steps into Wren steeples confirmed in the most human way this scholar's personal responsiveness to the works that he studied with such energy and delight.

Wittkower's involvement with English art was, of course, a direct consequence of his move. Cut off from direct contact with the Italian monuments that had commanded his attention, he quickly took advantage of new opportunities offered. In 1941, with the great art collections of England in safe hiding and the Warburg Institute itself transferred out of London, he and Saxl organised a travelling exhibition of photographs devoted to British art and its roots in older cultures of the Mediterranean; Wittkower prepared the sections on the post-medieval period. The images and accompanying explanatory texts were published as a book after the war, *British Art and the Mediterranean* (1948; reprint 1969). It was indeed this exploration of the Mediterranean roots of art in England that led to his first publication on the Palladian tradition, 'Pseudo-Palladian Elements in English Neo-classical Architecture' (*Journal of the Warburg and Courtauld Institutes* (1943)). Sensitive to the migration of forms, he outlined the emergence of an English style out of the transformation of Italian motifs — what we might today call creative misprision. He went on to publish studies of Inigo Jones, Lord Burlington, and William Kent.

The collections and libraries of England afforded Wittkower new fields for exploration. From his early experience working on Bernini, he expanded to make the art of drawing a special area of his expertise, especially, of course, Baroque drawings. In 1937 he collaborated with Tancred Borenius in writing the catalogue of the collection of old master drawings formed by Sir Robert Mond. He also collaborated with Anthony Blunt on the preparation of the first two volumes of Walter Friedlaender's *The Drawings of Nicolas Poussin* (1938, 1949). At Windsor Castle he sorted out the problems of the Carracci drawings, laying the foundation for our understanding of the three different hands of the two brothers and their cousin. *The Drawings of the Carracci in the Collection of Her Majesty the Queen at Windsor Castle* (1952) provides a model of modern connoisseurship, rich in both critical observation and art historical scholarship.

Connoisseurship was not an end in itself for Wittkower. His interest in drawings was an integral part of his concern with artistic production, a way of following the artist at work. One of the exhibitions he inspired at Columbia was *Masters of the Loaded Brush: Oil Sketches from Rubens to Tiepolo* (1967), for which he wrote the introduction to the catalogue. Through this exhibition a wider public was introduced to the challenges as well as the pleasures of the *bozzetto*, and the very concept of the 'loaded brush' became more clearly articulated as an aesthetic and art-historical problem in creative process. The Slade Lectures Wittkower delivered at Cambridge in 1970–1 were devoted to the sculptor's practice; his death unfortunately prevented revision of the preliminary text, which was published posthumously as *Sculpture: Processes and Principles* (1977).

A remarkable combination of intelligence, imagination, energy, and good humour made Wittkower an ideal scholarly collaborator. It seems only fitting that his last works of collaboration should have been with his wife, who had worked closely with him throughout his career and shared especially his interest in the eighteenth century. Their first book together was *Born under Saturn: The Character and Conduct of Artists — A Documentary History from Antiquity to the French Revolution* (1963), a survey that organised a wealth of documentary and anecdotal material — and that has been translated into every major European language plus Japanese. Typically, Wittkower's involvement with such powerful artistic personalities as Michelangelo and Bernini led to a wider systematic exploration of the artist as an individual in society. Together, the Wittkowers translated and edited *The Divine Michelangelo: The Florentine Academy's Homage on his Death in 1564*, published in the quadricentennial year (1964), and Wittkower himself continued to explore the problem of the creative individual in 'Francesco Borromini: personalità e destino,' published in the acts of the conference sponsored by the Accademia Nazionale di San Luca in Rome, *Studi sul Borromini* (1970), and more generally in 'Genius: Individualism in Art and Artists,' his contribution to the *Dictionary of the History of Ideas* (1972).

In London, in addition to his association with the Warburg Institute from 1934, he was appointed Durning Lawrence Professor at University College in 1949; he held that position until 1956, when he departed for New York to assume the chairmanship of the Department of Art History and Archaeology at Columbia, where he had been a visiting professor the previous year. Wittkower had already experienced the American university scene, having taught at Harvard in the summers of 1954 and 1955. Howard Hibbard was a student in those seminars, and in the warm and detailed obituary notice he published in the *Burlington Magazine* (CXIV (1972), 173–7) he recalled that experience: 'I shall never forget my first impression of that awesome figure, who immediately proved to be so gentle, so generous, and so kind. Wittkower gave seminars that drew a self-selected group of students, all of whom, like the writer, were profoundly and permanently influenced by the seriousness, range, and enthusiasm of his scholarship. But it must be said that Wittkower too was impressed with his new students — perhaps our combination of enthusiastic naïveté and admiration was a novelty.'

Wittkower recognised the potential of this American enthusiasm. His new appointment offered the kind of major challenge that brought out the best qualities in the man and inspired his best talents; he saw the opportunity to build and he welcomed it. He enjoyed recounting the story of his negotiating with the dean of the graduate faculties at

Columbia: Wittkower warned him that his appointment would cost the university dearly, for he did indeed intend to build. (The department's annual budget reportedly rose from $50,000 to over $600,000 during his tenure.) A central aspect of Columbia's attraction was the Avery Memorial Library, the best collection for architecture and archaeology in the country. The department faculty already boasted some major scholars — most notably, Otto Brendel, Julius Held and Meyer Schapiro — but it lacked leadership and direction. Seeing the potential, Wittkower began to expand the faculty by opening new fields — with the appointment of Edith Porada in ancient Near Eastern art — and inviting a younger generation of outstanding scholars to Columbia — including Robert Branner, Howard Hibbard, and Theodore Reff. He recognised that an art history department in the City of New York — with its formidable art collections, research facilities, and professional resources — had both the opportunity and the obligation to study the world history of art. At Wittkower's retirement in 1969 the programmes of the department did indeed encompass the world — from Europe and the Americas to Africa and Asia, from the ancient Near East to the contemporary scene in New York. In addition to new appointments, he invited a series of distinguished visitors — including his old professional adversary, Charles de Tolnay, who taught graduate seminars on a regular basis, and connoisseurs like Philip Pouncey, Janos Scholz, and Federico Zeri. He created seminars in co-operation with museum curators and collectors to assure that his students had the opportunity to study works of art directly. There was no aspect of the study of art that did not find its place within the generous arena of the curriculum as envisioned by Wittkower.

Beyond the curriculum itself, Wittkower created an Advisory Council, a group of friends from the New York art world dedicated to supporting the goals and programmes of the department. Typically, that support came from projects that involved students and contributed to their education: a series of loan exhibitions (including *Masters of the Loaded Brush*) prepared in graduate seminars, the catalogues written by students. The aim was to raise funds for scholarships to enable students to travel. Wittkower wanted his students *in situ*. (As a young beneficiary of such a travel grant, I recall his very clear instructions about rising early in Venice to make the most efficient use of the morning light in visiting churches; the later afternoon and evening hours were, of course, to be reserved for reading and writing. He was also very clear about what manuscripts my wife, then a graduate student in musicology, should be exploring in the Marciana.)

Wittkower was proud of his achievement in transforming the Department of Art History and Archaeology at Columbia; he was an empire-builder. Columbia's sister institution and main competitor was the Institute of Fine Arts of New York University, which had itself been built with a faculty of emigrant scholars from Europe, among them Richard Krautheimer. Wittkower recalled his vision of somehow co-ordinating the programmes of the two departments. Realisation of that vision seemed perpetually frustrated by the personal ambitions of the scholars themselves: both Wittkower and Krautheimer were scheduled to teach seminars on Rome, and neither was willing to cede to the other. 'Had we been able to agree,' I remember Wittkower reporting to his faculty in the mid-1960s, with a chuckle but also with gleam in his eye, 'then we would have created the greatest art historical machine in the world!'

Colleagues and students will remember Rudi — as obituary notice becomes reminiscence, that is the name that seems most natural — as a genial and generous giant. He had faith in the ability of students, was always encouraging and supportive. He allowed the intellectually ambitious student to reach out, testing new fields and trying new methods; he was prepared to offer the less secure student ideas and topics that he knew were realisable, projects that would be gratifying because he knew that they would yield genuinely interesting and even important results. Any measure of his contribution to art history must inevitably take into account the scholarship that he enabled, that is, the achievements of his students and younger colleagues. His effect was at once inspiring and catalytic.

The courses he offered were themselves exploratory, even though his students may have assumed that he had already written the book on the subject, for his lectures were so clearly organised, the learning so sure. It was his ability to shape material, to present it coherently, that made his lectures so accessible — whether he was setting out the typologies of Renaissance architecture, the personalities of Baroque sculptors, or the complexities of the classical tradition in the Renaissance. In seminars his students found themselves at the frontiers of art-historical knowledge — for example, probing seventeenth-century Venetian painting when it was still relatively uncharted territory. Wittkower himself was constantly pushing the limits of his own scholarship, in courses like 'The Impact of Non-European Cultures on European Art', which had its roots in his earliest involvement with the Warburg tradition but was further enriched by his subsequent engagement of eighteenth-century problems (for example, 'Piranesi e il gusto egiziano'). At the time of his death he was expanding the scope of his own studies in preparing the Matthew Lectures at Columbia; these were published posthumously as *Gothic vs. Classic: Architectural Projects in Seventeenth-Century Italy* (1974), and honored by the Society of Architectural Historians with the Alice Davis Hitchcock Award (1976).

Wittkower was not a spectacular or mesmerising lecturer; he was, rather, both formal and accessible, inviting his audience to accompany him and to follow the logic of his presentation. With full confidence in their ability to follow — but ever aware of his pedagogic responsibility to assure that they did — he taught his students the ways of art history, how it was done.

In the spring of 1968 the Columbia campus was in turmoil. Student rebellion against a university administration out of touch with changing social and political realities escalated to a provocative level, culminating in violent police intervention. Several prominent members of the faculty, distinguished scholars who remembered the university violence of their own earlier careers in Germany, could only view the current events with dismay as a rehearsal of that past. Although he had shared their pilgrimage, Rudi Wittkower maintained a clearer and more objective vision; his calm offered an important ethical example. And that example, as well as a very definite political acumen, held his department together; marshalling peers like Otto Brendel and Meyer Schapiro, he managed to bring conflicting generations together and to turn a time of crisis into a shared moment of self-reflection. The events of 1968 only confirmed Rudi's rare wisdom and benevolence as a leader.

Following his retirement from Columbia Wittkower assumed a series of honorary appointments; he was Kress Professor in Residence at the National Gallery of Art in Washington (1969–70), Slade Professor at the University of Cambridge (1970–1), and, in the year of his death, he was a member of the Institute for Advanced Study at Princeton. His institutional energies extended well beyond his own department — to programmes like that of the Centro Internazionale di Studi di Architettura Andrea Palladio in Vicenza.

He had since 1958 been a Fellow of the British Academy — which had awarded him its Serena Medal the previous year — and in 1959 was elected to the American Academy of Arts and Sciences. In Italy he was a member of the Accademia dei Lincei (1960), the Accademia di Belle Arti in Venice (1959), and the Accademia Olimpica in Vicenza (1970).

Posthumously, he was named Commendatore of the Ordine al Merito della Repubblica d'Italia (1972) and was recipient of the American Institute of Architects Award (1986). He received honorary degrees from Duke University (1969), Columbia University (1970), Cambridge University (1970), and the University of Leeds (1971).

The honours and awards, however, hardly offer adequate measure of the man who took such joy in his work, in both his scholarship and his teaching. He took similar deep satisfaction in the achievements of his students and younger colleagues. His generosity was indeed large, and he delighted in it. For myself, I can recall that satisfaction as he watched over my own development from student to colleague, continuing to nurture a fresh Ph.D. — joking that had he remained in the Veneto and not proceeded to Rome in his own youth I might not have had a field. I will never forget the image of his arrival in Venice in 1963 — I was then a graduate student working on my dissertation: a *motoscafo* (*linea* 2) slowly approached the Accademia *pontile*; there he was, standing in the open prow, a cigar in his mouth, surveying the aquatic urban spectacle before him with appropriating gaze and satisfaction — Rudi *trionfante*.

DAVID ROSAND
Columbia University, New York

Bibliographic Note

A bibliography of Wittkower's publications up to 1966 was included in the two-volume Festschrift published on the occasion of his sixty-fifth birthday: *Essays in the History of Art Presented to Rudolf Wittkower on his Sixty-Fifth Birthday* and *Essays in the History of Architecture* . . . , edited by Douglas Fraser, Howard Hibbard, and Milton J. Lewine (London, 1967). It was supplemented in the obituary notice by Howard Hibbard in the *Burlington magazine* (CXIV (1972), 173–7).

In 1989, to commemorate the twentieth anniversary of his retirement from Columbia, the Department of Art History and Archaeology sponsored a symposium; the papers were published as 'Essays in Honor of Rudolf Wittkower' in a double issue of *Source: Notes in the History of Art* (VIII–IX (1989)). On that occasion the Department and the Istituto della Enciclopedia Italiana published a full bibliography: *The Writings of Rudolf Wittkower*, edited by Donald M. Reynolds — which also reprints Hibbard's moving obituary notice.

Many of Wittkower's individual studies have been reprinted in four volumes of his collected essays: *Palladio and English Palladianism* (London, 1974), *Studies in the Italian Baroque* (London, 1975), *Allegory and the Migration of Symbols* (London, 1977), *Idea and Image: Studies in the Italian Renaissance* (London, 1978), and in *Selected Lectures of Rudolf Wittkower: The Impact of Non-European Civilizations on the Art of the West* (Cambridge, 1989).